A Baedeker of Decadence

GEORGE C. SCHOOLFIELD

A Baedeker of Decadence

CHARTING A LITERARY FASHION,
1884–1927

Yale University Press
New Haven &
London

Set in Sabon type by Keystone Typesetting, Inc.
Printed in the United States of America by Sheridan Books.

Library of Congress Cataloging-in-Publication Data
Schoolfield, George C.
A Baedeker of decadence : charting a literary fashion, 1884–1927 /
George C. Schoolfield.
p. cm.
Includes bibliographical references and index.
ISBN 0-300-04714-2 (cloth : alk. paper)
1. Decadence (Literary movement) 2. European literature — 19th century —
History and criticism. 3. European literature — 20th century — History and
criticism. I. Title.
PN56.D45S27 2003
809'.911 — dc21   2003052549

A catalogue record for this book is available from the British Library.

The paper in this book meets the guidelines for permanence and durability of the
Committee on Production Guidelines for Book Longevity of the Council on
Library Resources.

10   9   8   7   6   5   4   3   2   1

To Gloria and to Sunny:
Amor gignit amorem

Contents

Baedekers

[At a bookstore, Des Esseintes] was suddenly struck by a page of Baedeker describing the London art galleries . . . he bought a Baedeker and left the shop.

Joris-Karl Huysmans, *À rebours* (1884).

I noticed a young couple which had come from Lausanne to Lucerne with the same train as I, stayed at the same hotel, and now continued their trip with the same boat . . . on the basis of a whole series of small observations I had arrived at the conclusion that they were newlyweds and were taking a wedding trip. He stood upright with his face sunken in his Baedeker, she sat looking at the landscape.

Ola Hansson, *Sensitiva amorosa* (1887).

I resumed . . . my dream while leafing through some Baedeker guides on my pillow. Each of these titles, *Belgium, Germany in Three Parts, Italy,* suddenly stirred a corner of my being.

Maurice Barrès, *Le Culte du moi: Un Homme libre* (1889).

In his library he even had all the Baedeker guides . . . Among his bound books and periodicals, one would resemble Baedeker, wearing scarlet and gold, like someone who, on Monday morning, leaves sorrow behind and escapes and travels away from everything.

August Strindberg, *I havsbandet* (1890).

"Papa doesn't trust Baedeker," the young girl said with a quiet smile.

> Louis Couperus, *Noodlot* (1890–1891).

"Take the Baedeker, it's there on the table, and look it up."

"Look," exclaimed Ippolita, reading in the Baedeker. "At Segni there's the inn of Gaetanino."

> Gabriele D'Annunzio, *Il trionfo della morte* (1891).

Giulia Street lies, to be sure, away from that quarter which is regularly flooded by tourists equipped with red books, but on that account it was all the more pleasant for people who did not want to mix into these barbarian attacks on the eternal city.

> Julius Zeyer, *Jan Maria Plojhar* (1891).

And so she looked for a book. The first one to fall into her hands was a fat, red travel guide, oldish, perhaps from Innstetten's days as a lieutenant. "Yes, I'll read in that, there's nothing more calming than such books."

> Theodor Fontane, *Effi Briest* (1895).

When [Cornelie] was finished unpacking and sat down and looked around, she suddenly felt very lonely. She thought of the Hague, of what she had left behind. But she did not want to think; she took her Baedeker and studied the Vatican.

> Louis Couperus, *Langs lijnen van geleidelijkheid* (1900).

Mrs. Herriton did not proceed. She was not one to detect the hidden charms of Baedeker. Some of the information seemed to her unnecessary, all of it was dull.

> E. M. Forster, *Where Angels Fear to Tread* (1905).

I must really limit myself to a couple of modest 'hints' and for the rest leave you to Baedeker, no: rather to your own mood and inner dispensation, which will lead you to everything on this happy trip . . . For if Baedeker is insufficient here and there, it is completely useless for Venice; one cannot see this city according to its selection, in which everything is worth seeing or nothing.

> Rainer Maria Rilke, letter of March 24, 1908, to Gisela von der Heydt.

"I hope we shall soon emancipate you from Baedeker."

"And no, you are not, not, not to look at your Baedeker."

Their noses were as red as their Baedekers.

> E. M. Forster, *A Room with a View* (1908).

Baedeker, of course! This little red object can . . . be regarded as a scourge of Venice, this household account book of the tourist who, anxious that the debit and credit of the trip agree, drives its victims from bridge to bridge, from museum to museum, from hotel to hotel, instead of letting people grant themselves a moment of breathing space or peace of mind.

Anders Österling, "Dying Venice," *Människor och landskap* (1910).

"But you didn't get to the Lake of Taunitz?" "No, we didn't. It's not in Baedeker."

Hjalmar Söderberg, *Den allvarsamma leken* (1912).

Ten years in the Austrian capital wouldn't exhaust its charms, yet as most travelers allow themselves about a week or ten days, it is best to follow good old Br'er Baedeker. And here I leave him, for I am essentially a rambler.

James Gibbons Huneker, "Vienna," *New Cosmopolis* (1915).

Our capital city belongs to the region of the world beyond the grave. Ordinarily nothing is said of this when compiling geographical maps, guides, indices; our honored Baedeker keeps tellingly quiet about it.

Andrei Bely, *Petersburg* (1913/1916/1922).

Preface

The intention of *A Baedeker of Decadence* is to present samples of the novelistic literature that emerged from a cultural mode of the last decades of the nineteenth century, a mode or an attitude — "movement" might be too strong a word, implying a concerted effort — often called by its French name, *la décadence,* in flattering or dubious tribute to the country where it initially flourished and which produced its "breviary," Joris-Karl Huysmans's *À rebours.* In these works there is frequently a sense that a national culture, having flowered, is bound for mongrelization or annihilation; in fact, the literature of this fin de siècle may talk of an end of the world. The decadent, who regards himself as being set apart, more fragile, more learned, more perverse, and certainly more sensitive than his contemporaries, is aware that he is a Roman of the decadence, watching, despising, and fearing the "great blond barbarians" (in Verlaine's phrase), the vulgar bourgeoisie, and the teeming proletariat: the debacle of 1870–71 gave a painful reality to the decadent vision. Supremely egocentric and sometimes supremely wealthy, the decadent can form his own artificial paradise as he waits for the end, enjoying the thought of his intellectual and aesthetic superiority and his coming death, even as he fears his destruction.

The choice of narratives has been made to remind the reader that a kind of international decadent canon existed; it contained, certainly, *À rebours,* D'Annunzio's *Il piacere,* and Wilde's *Picture of Dorian Gray.* Louis Couperus's

Noodlot, admired by Wilde, and Georges Rodenbach's *Bruges-la-Morte* are examples of the basic material, as it were reduced to psychological studies of the neurotic decadent, quite incapable of life, save in a world of his own devising. In Strindberg's *I havsbandet* the decadent becomes a scientist, in Tavaststjerna's *I förbund med döden* a bank clerk — and nobleman — suffers from thanatophilia. *Trætte Mænd* by Arne Garborg, to an extent a gloss on Kierkegaard's "Diary of the Seducer, also qualified for membership in the decadent canon, and for a while was remarkably popular in the lands of the German tongue. The *Pentateuch* of Stanisław Przybyszewski, likewise widely read in German, is an erotic extravaganza growing out of the author's own pathology, while his *Satans Kinder* turns the decadent into a manipulative anarchist. Leopold von Andrian-Werburg's "Der Garten der Erkenntnis," a brief, autobiographical tale of homoeroticism and (remarkably) patriotism, not only became a cult book in Austria and Germany but won a small but admiring readership in France and Holland; Rilke's "Die Letzten" was immediately characterized by reviewers as a decadent work (dealing as it did with the long and declining family line and the problems of the aesthetic existence, to which a fillip of mother-son incest was added); yet it did not achieve any larger currency and, indeed, has remained little noticed even by Rilke specialists. Into a picture of the decadent's isolation Arthur Machen's *Hill of Dreams* inserts a reconstruction of Celtic-Roman Wales. Bram Stoker's *Dracula* demonstrates some main patterns of the decadence (e.g., the special lifestyle of the count, who is the last of his ancient clan, and the count's plan to create an artificial vampiristic world, controlled entirely by himself), employed for the making of a best-seller; Thomas Mann's three "decadent" stories are small masterpieces that have maintained themselves in the world's literary consciousness until the present. *A cidade e as serras* of Eça de Queirós, where the decadent is apparently cured, Hjalmar Söderberg's *Doktor Glas,* where he is not, although he may wish to be, and Valle-Inclán's *Sonatas,* where — an aristocratic dandy — he has no desire for salvation, have become classics in their respective literatures. Two novels from Ireland, Moore's *A Drama in Muslin* and *The Real Charlotte* by the cousins Somerville and Ross, are included as a picture of the decadence of a social group, the Anglo-Irish estate owners. Herman Bang's *De uden Fædreland,* although not one of the Dane's stronger works, is shot through with elements of decadence, particularly the strain of national decay, paralleled by the decay of the overrefined protagonist. The decadent pattern, or elements of it, held on for a long time, in the Australian H. H. Richardson's *Maurice Guest,* in the American James Gibbons Huneker's *Painted Veils,* and in the Icelander Halldór Kiljan Laxness's *Vefarinn mikli frá Kasmír.*

The temptation was present, of course, to choose other texts in which a Roman model was prominent, corresponding to the popular belief that the decadent novel is largely about paraphilia. Uncle Anton in Couperus's *Van oude mensen, de dingen die vorbijgaan* likes to sit amidst his collection of Latin pornography, imagining that he is Tiberius in the swimming pool; and Hadrian's boy Antinous often crops up as a sign of sexual perversion. Rachilde's transvestite Raoule in *Monsieur Venus* is stimulated — some twenty times in the novel's course — to take her (never quite defined) pleasure with her effeminized boyfriend by references to Antinous; in Herman Bang's *Haabløse Slægter* the sophisticate Bernhard Hoff, thinking to mislead the young actor William Høg (of ancient lineage, bad nerves, and delicate good looks), puts an Antinous bust on the mantelpiece before he begins to play his mood-music (not Wagner but Anton Rubinstein); Monsieur de Phocas, the nom de guerre of Jean Lorrain's duc de Fréneuse, is fascinated by a bust of Antinous he has seen in the Louvre, and especially by the eyes, which, he says, he would have set with emeralds. (The narrator is not taken aback by Fréneuse's green-eye fixation; he knows that Fréneuse is an atavism: "This man has already lived in past times, under Heliogabalus and Alexander VI and the last Valois kings — or, more precisely, under Henri III himself.") Of all the Roman emperors, Heliogabalus wins the decadent popularity contest hands down: his extravagance, his artistic gifts, his epicene quality, made him the antique forerunner of the Wittelsbach, Ludwig II of Bavaria. Heliogabalus exists in more or less historical literary form, in Jean Lombard's *L'Agonie* and Stefan George's *Algabal* (dedicated to Ludwig II), in Blei's *Der Dandy* and *De berg van licht* of Couperus; but he is also a signpost for the modern world, just as Antinous is.

Of the foreign-language texts chosen, about half are available in English translations, some new, some quite antiquated. Others have never appeared in English or are little known, and so the need to describe action and characters has made their respective treatments swell. Translations are by the author, save in Chapter 1, where Baldick's fluent version has been used, Chapter 3, where Georgina Harding's ancient text is cited, but with passages omitted by her turned into English by the author, Chapter 16, where the translations of Eça by Ann Steele and Roy Campbell are too good to be meddled with, and Chapter 18, where Lowe-Porter has historical value. On some occasions, elsewhere, a felicitous earlier rendering and the author's may jibe. If a work has been translated into English, the title of the translation, italicized, follows the original. Otherwise, the translation of the title is not italicized.

The thanks to be extended are many: to the reference librarians at Yale's Sterling Memorial Library, in particular Alan Solomon, Dale Askey, Emily Horning, Jeffry K. Larson, and Susanne Roberts; to the indefatigable interlibrary loan staff at Sterling, Maureen M. Jones, Elizabeth P. Johnson, Vinita Lovett, and May E. Robertson; to the ever generous personnel at Sterling's circulation desk; to Susan Eggleston Lovejoy, reference librarian, and to Karl Schrom and Kathy Manzi in the Yale Music Library; to Charles S. Fineman, librarian for collection development of the Widener Library at Harvard; to Houchang Chehabi of Boston University and Jay Lutz of Oglethorpe University, both formerly of Yale, for their aid in obtaining out-of-the-way French texts; to Eleanor Saulys, business manager of the Yale German Department, for her exhaustive botanical knowledge; to David Schafer of Hamden, Connecticut, for his expertness in the languages and religions of the Middle East; to Suzanne Fusso of Wesleyan University for enlightenment about Russian decadence, and to Vassily Rudich for his wealth of information on this and other topics; to Peter Demetz and Edward Stankiewicz of Yale for helpful observations about, respectively, Czech and Polish decadence; to Susan Brantly, Niels Ingwersen, and Richard Ringler of the University of Wisconsin, Madison, for aid with Laxness's attributions, as well as to Gísli Pálsson, director of the Institute of Anthropology at the University of Iceland; to Margaret Cormack of the College of Charleston and Stofnun Árna Magnússonar for Laxnessiana; to David H. Schimmelpennick van der Oye, of Brock University, Yale College, 1979, for his pursuit of a Couperus edition; to Mary Wideburg, Yale College, 1983, for her detailed index to *À rebours;* to John Hoberman of the University of Texas who, as an undergraduate at Haverford College, made a translation of *Trætte Mænd,* never published but long and gratefully used by the author in courses on decadence at Yale; to Carolyn Kalhorn of the orchestra at the Paris Opéra, Yale College 1992, for her abiding interest in the decadence project; to many other students in decadence courses and seminars at Yale over the decades; to Cécile Dêtré-Cohen, manager of the World Language Center at the Yale Bookstore; and to Harry Haskell and the late Edward Tripp of the Yale University Press, and the acute manuscript editor, Susan Abel. Special gratitude must go to Michael Schmelzle of Trinity College, Hartford, sine quo non, for his virtuoso computerizing of the typed and sometimes scarcely legible manuscript, to Tessa Lee of the Yale German department for her similar service, and to Martha Sherman, a savior in the nick of time, and, above all, to Gloria Schoolfield for her patient and heroic endurance, in the home, of a collector of decadence, as well as to Susan Schoolfield-Hines and Marguerite Schoolfield-Compton.

The germ cell of the author's interest in the phenomenon of literary decadence was the writing of an underinformed review of Rafael Koskimies's *Der nordische Dekadent* (1968); he was further inspired by the violent objections hurled by the quondam editor of the Yale College Programs of Study at the description of the course, "Readings in Basic Decadence," which then became a column filler in the *New Yorker.* The basis of eight chapters in the book was a series of lectures delivered to the Yale University Woman's Organization.

France

JORIS-KARL HUYSMANS

Daniel, interpreting Nebuchadnezzar's dream about the great image, his "head of gold, his breast and his arms of silver, his belly and his thighs of brass, [h]is legs of iron, his feet part of iron and part of clay," bravely prophesied to the monarch the decline and destruction of empires, his own and those to come. The Neo-Latin and vernacular lyric of the Renaissance liked to ponder the ruins of Rome and of other cities of the empire; looking at Trier, Augusta Treverorum, the German humanist Conrad Celtis beheld a "Rome reduced to shards, thick clusters of shrubs growing in the atrium."

When *À rebours* (*Against the Grain, Against Nature*) appeared, in April 1884, it summed up currents that had been in the cultural air for a long time. In 1734, Montesquieu published *Considérations sur les causes de la grandeur des Romains et leur décadence;* some thirty years later, Edward Gibbon brought out the several volumes of *The History of the Decline and Fall of the Roman Empire* (1776–88). The word *decadence* itself—meaning a falling away from a previous state of strength—had come very much into scholarly and publicistic currency by the 1830s; Désiré Nisard used it copiously in his *Études de moeurs et de critique sur les poètes latins de la décadence* of 1834; here, he tried to single out some of the elements of a "decadent style" in Roman literature of the Silver Age, in his essay on Lucan: "[Art] lies entirely in the details, in the depiction of material objects: the moral sentiment has been excluded from it . . . the soul has naught to do here . . . everything is for the pleasure of the eyes . . . Lucan casts himself into the most perilous novelties . . . he violates the language in order not to be imitative . . . the poem of Lucan [the *Pharsalia*] is a work of erudition, although surely not of critical erudition." These words could very well be from a description of *À rebours,* lying fifty years in the future.

Again in 1835, there had appeared a book evidencing a curiosity, to be associated with decadence, about sexual aberration—aberration that (as every reader of Petronius and Suetonius knew) was part and parcel of the Roman decline. Theóphile Gautier's *Mademoiselle de Maupin* has, of course, a contemporary setting, but, before the book turns to the narrative account of transvestism and lesbianism, the long preface looks to the past, to two empires that had declined and fallen. Like Sardanapalus, the last king of Assyria (whose death, amidst nude female bodies, had just been painted, in 1827, by Delacroix), Gautier would give a "large prize to anyone inventing a new pleasure"; the bill of fare, he continued, at the Café Anglais in Paris was a poor and primitive thing compared to that even of Trimalchio's feast in Petronius' *Satyricon:* the French Regency, with its culinary and erotic extravagances, was only a wretched imitation of the "great voluptuaries of Baiae, Capri, and Tibur." (The classic illustration of this Roman world of elegance and orgies was given, shortly, by Thomas Couture, in *Les Romains de la décadence* of 1847, showing Romans spread out at their banquet tables, amidst girls and boys who rather modestly offer sexual thrills.) This world of exquisite pleasure, though, was shot through with anxiety: if the Romans had had extravagantly developed appetites, on all scores, they had also become womanish and effete and had been destroyed by the barbarians. In *Sylvie* of 1854, Gérard de Nerval, looking back a decade or so to his youth, put it this way: in the midst of brilliant talk in "the ivory tower of the poets, . . . our discussions rose to such a height that the most timid of us would sometimes go to the window to see if the Huns or the Turcomans or the Cossacks had at last come to cut short the argumentations of sophists and rhetoricians." And, as morals went by the board, in the search for new thrills, and as the apprehensive looked for the barbarians to appear at the door or in the atrium, language itself fell into fascinating decay. In his introduction to the collected edition of Baudelaire's works of 1868, Gautier describes the *Word* (with a capital W) as being summoned to "express everything," "pushing it to the last extreme." This is a *locus classicus* on the decadent style in literature, and deserves to be quoted at length. "In this connection, one may recall the language, already marbled by the greening of decomposition and, as it were, gamy, of the later Roman Empire and the complex refinements of the Byzantine school, the final form of Greek art fallen into deliquescence. But such, no doubt, is the necessary and fatal idiom of these peoples and civilizations when artificial life has replaced natural life, and has developed unknown needs in mankind." Three years later, on March 1, 1871, troops of the German Empire, just proclaimed at Versailles, marched into Paris (in his journal Edmond de Goncourt notes: "I hear music — *their* music"), and the brief reign of the Commune showed a more terrifying kind of barbarism, or so it seemed, come from within French society itself.

By the 1870's, the word *décadent* cropped up everywhere; the young critic and inexhaustible novelist-to-be, Paul Bourget, wrote that "we accept this terrible word *decadence,* without pride and without humility." But pride, on the part of those who were shortly to describe themselves as decadents, was surely there; maybe Verlaine mocked their bored arrogance when, in the sonnet "Langueur" of 1883, he set down the famous lines: "I am the Empire at the end of decadence, / Watching the great blond barbarians pass, / While composing acrostics of indolence / With a stylus of gold where the sun's languor dances." Languor, the inability to act, and ennui, became signs of the decadent attitude, signs cultivated and gladly borne. Bourget put it neatly, speaking again from outside the phenomenon, in his *Essais de psychologie contemporaine* of 1883: "If the citizens of a decadence are inferior as workers for the nation's greatness, are they not much superior as artists of the interiors of their soul? If they are clumsy at private or public action, is it not precisely because they are so terribly well suited to solitary thought? If they are poor reproducers of future generations, is it not precisely because the abundance of subtle sensations and the exquisiteness of rare sentiments have made virtuosi of them, sterile but refined, virtuosi of pleasure and of pain . . . a German chieftain of the second century was more capable of invading the empire than a Roman patrician was of defending it . . . [a patrician] erudite and refined, curious and disabused . . . is it not the fatal lot of the exquisite and the rare to be wrong in brutality's presence?"

The perception of decadent self-congratulation to be sensed in these lines, or in the decadents they described, the new Romans of the late Empire, is striking, and it is to be found elsewhere, put much more eloquently by true believers — true believers who liked to think that they comprised a very small and select cult indeed. In 1893, almost a decade after the appearance of *À rebours,* at a time when decadence was in full flower (was it a plant like those monstrosities favored by Des Esseintes?), the Austrian poet and critic Hugo von Hofmannsthal, not yet nineteen, in an essay on D'Annunzio's *L'Innocente* (where a nobleman sees to it that his infant son catches a mortal cold) spoke about the sensibilities of those who truly could understand the Italian's work: "We observe our life, we empty its goblets prematurely, and yet remain infinitely thirsty. . . . We have, as it were, no roots in life and wander, clairvoyant and yet day blind shadows, amidst the children of life. We! We! I know full well that I do not speak of this whole and mighty present generation. I speak of a few thousand people, scattered throughout the great cities of Europe." How finely sad or sadly fine it was to be a *decadente superiore,* in the term of the Italian physician Cesare Lombroso, or a *Degenerierter höherer Gattung* ("a degener- ate creature of a higher species"), as the consoling Dr. Deroge calls his young friend Edmond Veraine in Gerhard Ouckama-Knoop's novel of 1898, *Die Dekadenten* (The Decadents), a member of the doomed and happy-unhappy few. The very year that Hofmannsthal wrote his apostrophe, a Dane, Johannes Jørgensen (who eventually, like Huysmans, would embrace Roman Catholi- cism), had a character in his novel, *Livets Træ* (1893, The Tree of Life), proclaim: "I am a Darwinist and a decadent. I believe that the brutal will live and the beautiful will die . . . The earth will be filled with the crudest and roughest plants, while those that are beautiful and tender grow ever rarer, and are destroyed." Taking examples from Danish dendrology, Jørgensen's Niels Graff goes on: "The ugly fir tree is crowding out the bright and gentle beech in our islands . . . everything we love, art, poetry, the exquisite, the rare, belongs to what will die." Finally, Jørgensen tells us who the fir trees are: "It is the Prussians and the Yankees who will inherit the earth, covering it with their millions as though with a huge monotonous fir forest." The Prussians, of course, had conquered and mutilated Denmark in the war of 1864, they would defeat France in 1870–71; as for the Americans, we immediately recall Des Esseintes's cry of pain in the last chapter of *À rebours,* to the effect that "the vast *bagnio* of America has been transplanted to the continent of Europe: this was the limitless, unfathomable, immeasurable scurviness of the financier and the self-made man." At the end of the passage quoted above, Jørgensen cries out: "Look at France, dying, alone and expelled from society, on the edge of Europe — the last guardian of the holy flame." In his diary for 1877, the Genevan Henri Amiel stated that French literature, personified by the poet Théodore de Banville, made him think of Pergamos and Alexandria and the "epochs of decadence, when beauty of form conceals poverty of thought and a spent heart," but added that "[t]he German is a barbarian from his cheekbones to the soles of his feet."

Not everyone, to be sure, was as enthusiastic about the antivulgarian mes- sage of *À rebours* as Jørgensen: Huysmans-bashing — and then decadent- bashing — became a popular occupation of moral-minded contemporaries. The German-Hungarian journalist Max Nordau, in the chapter "Ego-Maniacs" of his *Entartung* (1892–93, *Degeneration*), decried, for example, "the drivel about teas, liqueurs, and perfumes," put together — in imitation of the French

Parnassians — "by ransacking technical dictionaries," the "mechanical fish" in Des Esseintes's aquarium windows in his dining room are "the dream of an ironmonger, retired from business and become an idiot." The Belgian Iwan Gilkin, who decided (not altogether incorrectly) that "the best part of [*À rebours*] is its critique of furnishings and painting and letters," found that "the personage of Des Esseintes drowned in this deluge of digressions," and scored, among other things, the banquet held by Des Esseintes, to celebrate the loss of his potency, as "infantile baroqueness." He concluded that the book was like "a torch falling into a well, illuminating the growing depravity of art, the burgeoning perversion of intelligence and of the senses. For several years now, critics have compared contemporary decadence with that of the old Roman Empire. The reading of *À rebours* makes this comparison striking."

The Austrian Hermann Bahr (who borrowed from *À rebours* with both hands for his own decadent novel, *Die gute Schule* [The Good School] of 1891) spoke of the decadents, with Huysmans as their main figure, in this way: "Since they have lost nature, they have lost art as well. It is *their* nature to be inartistic, since they are unnatural." Nietzsche, excoriating Wagner with terms he had learned from Bourget, wrote, in *Der Fall Wagner* (1888, *The Wagner Case*), that "Life, equal vitality, the vibration and exuberance of life are repressed into the smallest formations, the remainder is poor in life. Everywhere paralysis, strain, or hostility and chaos . . . the whole does not live at all any more: it is composed, calculated, artificial, an artifact." (In decadence, Bourget had found "an independence of single cells," no longer serving the whole.) Lombroso called the decadents "a new variety of literary madmen . . . literary *mattoids* [those slightly mad], in all their old vanity, but with the appearance of novelty." Even Arthur Symons, who coined the phrase about *À rebours* as "the breviary of decadence," and who was in much an admirer of decadent letters, as we shall see, felt obliged to tell the readers of *Harper's Monthly Magazine* (again in 1893), with a strong undercurrent of censure, that the literature of decadence — Huysmans again named as its chieftain — was the perfect expression (and but another term for) the "*maladie fin de siècle,* certainly typical of a civilization grown over-luxurious, over-inquiring, too languid for the relief of action, too uncertain for any emphasis in opinion or in conduct . . . it has all the qualities that mark the end of great periods, the qualities that we find in the Greek, the Latin, decadence: an extreme self-consciousness, a restless curiosity in research, an over-subtilizing refinement upon refinement, a spiritual and moral perversity."

But the praise was equally strong; in the same passage, Symons called "this representative literature of today . . . a new and beautiful and interesting disease." Ola Hansson, the Swedish critic and novelist, wrote: "Let us enjoy the beauty of this literature, which seems to us to be like a woman's face, in which the veins can be perceived beneath the sickly white skin. And in whose eyes with their hectic death-shimmer and mute but tormented question we behold a reflection of this life, which is a riddle, its only sure element decay." Plainly, Symons and Hansson see an attraction in decadence quite apart from (if related to) its disgusting illumination of the malaise of the time — the slimy walls of a well — noted by Gilkin. Havelock Ellis, however, in 1897, made a tribute to the book that was direct; it was a revolt against a nature that had on its side "the blind forces of robust vulgarity." "So the more fine-strung spirits are sometimes driven to a reaction against nature like that of which Huysmans has been the consistent representative." For Symons, again, in his essay on Huysmans (1892), the book's "fantastic unreality, its exquisite artificiality" are "the logical outcome of that hatred and horror of human mediocrity, of the mediocrity of daily existence, which we have seen to be the special form of Huysmans's *névrose.*"

In the same essay, Symons also says: "To realize the full value, the real charm of *À rebours,* some initiation might be deemed necessary." A common misconception about the book is that Jean Floressas Des Esseintes is a dandy; for example, Émilien Carassus, in *Le mythe du dandy,* lists him together with Wilde's Dorian Gray (another possible misconception), and D'Annunzio's Andrea Sperelli as the prime literary representatives of the *dandy fin de siècle.* This misapprehension arises, probably, from the circumstance that the model for Des Esseintes seems to have been a living person, Count Robert de Montesquiou, a portrait of whom by Baldini is on the cover of the Penguin Classics edition: poetaster, friend of Whistler, and arbiter of elegance in late nineteenth-century Paris; Proust's Baron Charlus is also supposed to have been patterned on him. The text of Chapter 1 does make it altogether plain that Des Esseintes has been a dandy, but with his decision to retire to Fontenay-aux-Roses he is a dandy no more. His dress has been dandyistic: he is given to "wearing suits of white velvet with gold-laced waistcoats" and "sticking a bunch of Parma violets in his shirt front in lieu of a cravat"; he has delivered the "sermon on dandyism" to the tradesmen who supply him with garments and shoes conforming to his "encyclicals on matters of cut." But these matters, like the "dinners with men of letters which were greatly talked about," have now been left behind. The banquet all in black is not only a farewell to Des Esseintes's sexual life but a farewell to his dandyistic existence. A main intent of the dandy, as both Barbey d'Aurevilly and Baudelaire observed, was to astonish, while never himself being astonished: *nil admirari;* yet Des Esseintes's new home, his "thébaïde raffinée," is intended "not to astonish other people but for his own personal pleasure." Still, a perceptive observer might rejoin that if Des Esseintes had ceased to be a dandy, astonishing those who saw him, he — or his creator — continued to maintain this main dandyistic habit toward the book's readers, who are meant to be astonished on every page by the esoteric quality of Des Esseintes's new and private existence.

In another respect, too, Des Esseintes would seem to be distinct from the dandy as the latter often appears in life and letters. The dandy comes, as it were, out of nowhere, and creates his dandyistic image; the origins of Beau Brummell are obscure, and we know nothing of the family lines of such great dandies of detective-and-criminal literature as Arsène Lupin, Sherlock Holmes, E. W. Hornung's Raffles, Knut Hamsun's Johan Nilsen Nagel. The decadent, on the other hand, is keenly and consistently aware of his lineage, of coming from a long line of which he is the last representative, a final and barren scion often physically (or emotionally) feebler than his forebears, but having a sensitivity, an awareness of life's decay and imminent ending which the forebears, in their sturdiness and confidence, lacked. (Des Esseintes cannot have Rudolphe Bresdin's *Comédie de la mort* on his wall without pondering its terrible message.) The gallery scene in the Château de Lourps at the opening of *À rebours* is of enormous importance, for it provides an illustration of illustrations of the decline of the house of Floressas Des Esseintes. The frequency with which this scene, in one way or another, is repeated in the literature of decadence demonstrates its centrality for the concept of decadence itself: without the ancient family, the family line, there is nothing to fall away from, *decadere*. Dorian Gray loves to stroll through the "picture gallery of his ancestral house and look at the various portraits of those whose blood flowed in his veins" (and to wonder if "some strange poisonous germ crept from body to body until it reached his own"). Just so, Des Esseintes has received a poison from over the centuries, albeit skipping generations — he strongly resembles the *mignon* of Henri III, the homosexual Guise monarch who turns up so often as an indicator of perversion in the literature of decadence. In *A ilustre casa de Ramires (The Illustrious House of Ramires)* of the great Portuguese novelist Eça de Queirós, the pathetic but likable and putatively last of the Ramires line (which has owned its castle and played its role in Portuguese history since — again on the first page — "the middle of the tenth century") has a nightmare, after having been made acutely aware of his own physical cowardice, a nightmare in which his ancestors appear to him, "all of them magnified by the sublime habit of commanding and conquering." Even before *À rebours,* Herman Bang, in *Haabløse Slægter* (1880, Hopeless Generations), causes his protagonist William Høg (who wants — without talent — to be an actor) to go to the church where his splendid ancestors are buried (Part 2, chapter 1): "He cast everything he had suffered, all his humiliations, all his shadows, onto the shoulders of the might dead, and they could bear them." The gallery thus can turn into the church or family chapel, in which the decadent may be frightened (the case with the pusillanimous Gonçalo Ramires) or from which he can gain some sense of strength: in the novella "Mot skymningen" (1912, Toward the Dusk) by the Finland-Swede Runar Schildt, the last of the Weydel line, Birger, is prompted to take up the hopeless task of saving the family estate by just such a visit. Or the gallery may become, simply, a family tree: in Rilke's "Die Letzten," the mother of Harald Malcorn (the family has come down in the world, economically, while moving physically upward to a flat in a large apartment building) encourages her son to recite the genealogy of the Malcorns, who appear to go back into the mists of time; little Hanno, in Thomas Mann's *Buddenbrooks: Der Verfall einer Familie* (1901, *Buddenbrooks: The Decline of a Family*), horrifies his father by drawing a black line after his name in the family chronicle — he senses that he will be the last of that line, too. Or the narrator can provide an account of the lineage, speaking as though for the protagonist; for example, in D'Annunzio's *Il piacere* (1889, *The Child of Pleasure*), in which we learn, among other things, that the Sperellis were superb Latinists in the Renaissance. Andrea Sperelli himself can use his mastery of Latin to make obscene puns on the text of the Vulgate.

The ties of Des Esseintes to the past are brought home to us in any number of ways — not least in his many displays of detailed learnedness (another decadent trait). The folios of Du Cange's great dictionary, *Glossarium mediae et infimae Latinitatis*, are set out — or at least one of them is — on the old church lectern of wrought iron in Des Esseintes's study; the whole of chapter 3 is devoted to the wonderful sweep through Latin literature, in which Des Esseintes's constant attention to detail and his apparently perverse views on what is attractive in this literature are presented — and in which Des Esseintes, as well, introduces the thought of fascinating decay both of the Roman tongue (aping Gautier on Baudelaire) and of the Roman state (Claudian wrote while "the Empire was crumbling to ruin all about him"). At the same time, he presents that particularly titillating aspect of the decline, sexual aberration, in his reconstruction of Petronius and, still more important, in his juxtaposition of Heliogabalus — that rottenest of the Roman emperors, the Syrian crooner and self-styled empress, his series of "emperors" chosen for a night in his bed — with the stern Tertullian. The church's poetic past is likewise present here (see the affection for Fortunatus' hymn, *Vexilla regis*) and again at the end of chapter 6, as Des Esseintes peruses Avitus' *De laude castitatis*, in praise of chastity, a topic in which he now must needs be interested. In the musical chapter 15 he tells us how he loves Gregorian chant, and, talking of another art, in the brilliant chapter 5, he gives us the famous reproductions of Moreau's *Salomé*, emphasizing both the antiquity of the scenes and the antiquity of Herod himself, lust rising in his old loins at the sight of Herodias' nubile daughter. A special frisson comes by means of the contrast of age and youth in erotic tension. Subsequently, in the section on Moreau's *Apparition*, Des Esseintes slides over into a kind of primitive fear of woman, as "the true harlot . . . [who] subjugated the [male's] will more surely with her charms — the charms of a great venereal flower, grown in a bed of sacrilege, reared in a hothouse of impiety." Woman is the *radix malorum*.

Surprisingly, the persistent affection for the past is coupled with a remarkable affection for aspects of the present in Des Esseintes's mind. We are repeatedly told, of course, that he detests the modern world; his retreat to the thébaïde of Fontenay-aux-Roses is a flight from his century (*le siècle*); as he enters his carefully sybaritic monkish life, he condemns his century's vulgarity again and again. The *siècle* is a time when new money is king (Des Esseintes has inherited old money, and never wants for it). It would be better if the little boys fighting over the loathsome sandwich (in chapter 13) had never been born; the world has entered an age when even honest houses of prostitution have been transformed into less honest taverns, at which assignations can be vouchsafed a false air of romance. It is an age on which Des Esseintes wishes to take revenge, in small as in large; his preparation of the potential murderer, Auguste Langlois, is a case in point. All has become mediocre; "like a tide race, the waves of human mediocrity are rising to the heavens and will engulf this refuge," he says he leaves for Paris at his physician's orders, and he wonders if "the terrible God of Genesis and the pale martyr of Golgotha would not prove their existence once for all by renewing the cataclysms of old, by rekindling the rain of fire that once consumed those accursed towns, the cities of the plain." Nevertheless, he paradoxically enjoys the technical advances of the detested century, evincing an almost erotic love for the steam engines Engert and Crampton (named after prominent engineers of the time), and he has the technical gifts to lay out, down to the tiniest detail, the artificial sea cabin of his dining room. (A resemblance between Des Esseintes and Ludwig II of Bavaria can readily be noted: in his medievalism, Ludwig employed the most modern electrical and mechanical developments in order to realize his visions of an artificial, Wagnerian realm.) As a matter of fact, *À rebours* is a builder's and interior decorator's manual in a very practical sense. It lacks only blueprints.

If Des Esseintes is a realist, in his devising of the setting for his special and isolated pleasures (and he will be followed in this by D'Annunzio's Sperelli, George Moore's John Norton in *A Mere Accident,* Conan Doyle's Thaddeus Sholto in *The Sign of the Four,* and so forth), he is also a man who enjoys cozy dreaming in his lair. Yet he is not quite a "fantastic dreamer," as he has been called: he admires fantasy, within limits, and has "the fantastic tangle" of Bresdin's *Bon Samaritain* in his collection. Yet it is worth noting that the print deals with a representation of realia, albeit run wild. When he ventures to "the most fantastic of visions" of Odilon Redon, he is at first fascinated but grows terrified, reminded of "the feverish nights and frightful nightmares of his childhood." The trip to England in chapter 11, which gets no farther than Paris, is dependent not so much on Des Esseintes's power of imagination as on his choice of the right Parisian milieus (and the right bad weather). He needs quite tangible stimuli for his visions, as he did for his vices in the past; as his erotic life was flagging, he required, he thought, the fancied masculinity of the — it turns out — disappointingly feminine Miss Urania, the tricks of the ventriloquist (reciting a diaphonal passage from Flaubert's *La Tentation de Saint Antoine,* or pretending that an angry husband is at the door), to achieve fleeting erotic excitement. (Something of Huysmans's own conventional views on homosexuality may be detected in the third of the erotic experiences recalled in chapter 9: the affair with the boy in the porkpie hat, who asks for the way to the Rue de Babylone, is so unnatural, so "artificial," that it arouses Des Esseintes most effectively of all.)

It is probably unnecessary to dwell further on the urge of Des Esseintes to the artificial, or what a contemporary critic in Vienna, Rudolph Lothar, called his "fieberndes Behagen am Unnatürlichen," "his febrile pleasure in the unnatural," his desire to "slap Mother Nature in the face." The very title of the book refers to this desire; in the first English translation it is rendered as *Against the Grain,* or, in German, *Gegen den Strich.* (Lothar, explaining it in his review, asked his readers to imagine a cat that wanted to be stroked in the wrong direction.) This urge is presented to us often enough, and with grotesque examples — the unfortunate tortoise, his back set with jewels, the invention of the taste-organ, the collection of real and hideous flowers that seem particularly artificial, the sleigh ride in Des Esseintes's room during the hottest part of the year, the diet of peptone enemas. What, though, is most important about the pursuit of the artificial is its revelation, again, that Des Esseintes lives forever at second hand: he is not a creator of art or literature, but reflects on what he has seen or read (in chapter 3, in 5, in 14), and re-creates it, or suggests it, in words. He is in essence an arranger, a collector, of stones, of plants, of books, of sensations.

Des Esseintes wants to be in total and absolute control of his little world. Here, once more, our earlier strictures about the abandonment of dandyism by Des Esseintes must be adjusted a little: he remains a dandy in his desire not to be surprised, to have a milieu arranged wholly according to his wishes and pleasures. That he fails in this effort is plain: in the past, even before the retreat to Fontenay-aux-Roses, his life of hedonism was broken by the awful and comical surprise of the toothache and the visit to the dentist Gatonax in chapter 4 (in a passage, nota bene, directly following the presentation of the particular delights of the lapidary art and of the taste organ, in which latter instance the mouth was the recipient of pleasure, not of humiliating pain); at Fontenay, at the end of chapter 10, he faints when he throws the window open and, in the blast of fresh air, thinks he still perceives traces of the perfumes he has decided to avoid, because they brought up memories of a vulgar erotic association of his past. His stomach rebels, and he is driven to the ineffectual cures of the "digester" and the enemas, " 'without any of the vulgar, bothersome business of eating.' " The most shattering evidence, though, of his lack of control is the dream of the virus at the end of chapter 8, in which panic fear of female sexuality (and of the venereal disease Des Esseintes associates with it) constitutes the first symptom of his collapse: "These nightmares occurred again and again, until he was afraid to go to sleep."

Des Esseintes wants surety. He would like, it becomes more and more clear, to find it in the Roman Catholic faith, he shores himself up by surrounding himself with objects and (sometimes boringly) with books from or about the church — and we arrive, at last, at another apparent paradox in his attitudes: the lover of the artificial has a yearning for the authentic. In the last chapter, he longs for the days when the aristocracy was not decayed, when the clergy was not commercial, when holy wafers were not themselves synthetic, when "Radegonde, Queen of France, used to make the altar bread with her own hands." The breviary of decadence, the great celebration of artificiality, is simultaneously an outcry against the specious, the mass-produced, the adulterated. Des Esseintes orders books printed in a single, private edition, an extravagant undertaking which, nonetheless, has a good reason behind it: these would be the real books, made for himself alone. It could be proposed that George Gissing's *Private Papers of Henry Ryecroft* (1903), has a standpoint — for all its stodginess — not so far away from that of Huysmans's glittering book: Ryecroft, like Des Esseintes, retreats from the world, and surrounds himself — he tells us repeatedly — with his own carefully selected books, his own objects of art. Maybe Ryecroft, too, bittersweetly sentimental and comforting and wholly unshocking, is a part of *À rebours*'s extended progeny. Maybe *À rebours* is by no means as unhealthy a book as it might seem.

Yet it is unhealthy, with some of its implications, not least by its revelling in depictions of cruelty (the engravings, *Persécutions religieuses,* of Jan Luyken), and by its apparent belief that a strong sin is better by far than mediocre lukewarmness: "It seemed to Des Esseintes that a frightful glory must result from any crime committed in open church by a believer filled with dreadful merriment and sadistic joy, bent on blasphemy, resolved to desecrate and defile the objects of veneration." The suggestion is developed by Huysmans in his next book, *Là-bas*, in which the sodomizer and murderer of children, Gilles de Rais, is redeemed not just by the strength of his final repentance, but equally by the very enormity of his sin — which was real, authentic, a part of a world that was true, the late middle ages. The spirit of the decadence (with its inherent denial of humanity to all save the decadent dreamer himself, its search for the new thrill, its ability to organize complex and sterile paradises only for its own pleasure) may look forward to certain horrors of the twentieth century. Trying to explain what decadence was, in an essay of 1894, Herman Bahr paid at least subtextual attention to its hints of inhumanity as he listed what he thought were its four main characteristics. The first: it was a literary mode in which the "nerves," not the emotions, played the main role: a decadent does not seek feeling; he seeks moods — he does not fall in love; he contrives situations which will give him pleasure. Bahr's second point is that the decadent seeks the artificial before all else, as we know. In the third place, the decadent has a feverish urge toward "the mystic" — which may be the equivalent of Des Esseintes's toying with the apparatus of the church, and his very wish for the mystic experience that does not come. (Of the characteristics listed by Bahr, this is the one most difficult to find in decadent texts; rather, as will be seen later on, it may be detected in the decadent's urge — again paradoxical — to escape from the decadent life he so carefully nurtures.) Finally, Bahr says that there is "an insatiable drive to the monstrous and the boundless," to which we might join the inability of Des Esseintes, for all his carefulness, to know when to stop. In his curiously pedantic way, he is a maximalist, trying to say something about all the arts, trying to list all the bizarre and 'gangrenous' plants, all the strange stones. And, in his telling affection for Jan Luyken, he does not know when to check his shivering delight in cruelty. Fourteen years after *À rebours,* Octave Mirbeau wrote *Le Jardin des supplices (Torture Garden),* in which a young man is conducted through an Indo-Chinese garden where, amidst exquisite surroundings, the most horrible torments are carefully prepared and enacted. (His guide is an English girl, who becomes sexually aroused by these scenes.) The garden, we are told, would have pleased Des Esseintes.

Without exaggeration, we may speak of a Des Esseintes cult: there are the poems addressed to him by Mallarmé (a tribute to the exemplary "patience" with which the rooms at Fontenay are fitted out), by Jean Lorrain (who, to please Huysmans's hero, conjured up visions of late Baroque Spain, filled with cruel Infantas, enervated Infantes, brocaded surplices, and burning dogs of Jews), and of the Swede Wilhelm Ekelund (who imagines a Des Esseintes

trapped forever in the shabby interior of a third-class railway compartment).
The literary fashion spreads with wonderful rapidity, author after author
making his own version of the "epicurean mystic and apostle of decadence" (in
Ola Hansson's words) who incorporated within himself the almost superstitious unease so many cultural critics felt, now that the end of the century
was approaching—and *fin de siècle* also becomes a catchword. The sober
Swiss, Edouard Rod, launders Des Esseintes for *La Course à la mort* (The Way
unto Death) of 1885; the keeper of the journal despises Paris, and suffers from
a hypersensibility, a *faculté de la vibration*, which makes him long for death (a
longing increased when his beloved Cécile, who has coughed into her handkerchief for some time, passes away); he makes the trip to London which Des
Esseintes accomplished only in his imagination, but finds that metropolis "ten
times more active, ten times more awful than Paris" and can console himself
only by looking at the *Astarte Syriaca* and the *Demoiselle élue* and the *Venus
Verticordia* of Dante Gabriel Rossetti; he retreats to an actual monastery,
Heisterbach in Germany, and happily quotes its motto, *Solitudo janua coeli.*
Rod's diarist makes do with a very modest Latinity; in Moore's *A Mere Accident*, John Norton shows a passion for Late Latin and a knowledge of it
almost rivaling Des Esseintes's. His monkishness leads him to plan to turn his
mother's estate into an aesthetically pleasing monastery, much to Mrs. Norton's distress; she persuades him to give up his dream of holy orders, and to
become engaged, but marriage is avoided when the unlucky young lady is
raped by a tramp and commits suicide. Perhaps it is just as well; for John—
unlike Jean Floressas, who is impotent from excessive activity, and Rod's
diarist, who likes his girls either chastely moribund or in Rossetti's paintings—
is simply asexual, unless we are to put a more pointed interpretation upon his
appreciation of the choirboys of Stanton College.

Decadents begin to turn up in the oddest places, for example on the South
Swedish farm in *Fru Marianne* (again 1887) of the feminist Ernst Ahlgren,
Victoria Benedictsson, who had learned about Huysmans and company from
her fellow Scanian, Ola Hansson. Benedictsson's book is, perhaps, most readily described as *A Doll's House* with a better male partner and a happy ending;
Marianne is at first cosseted by her farmer husband, Börje, but at last is
accepted by him as an equal, and the two read *Progress and Poverty* together.
In the interior of the book, however, a childhood friend of hearty Börje's
appears, Pål Sandell—a fragile fellow who fixes up his quarters as prettily
as he can and gives a banquet reminding Börje of Thomas Couture's painting.
We are almost surprised when Pål attempts to seduce Marianne, appealing to
her by his knowledge of the latest French literature, and by blinking his
"satiny eyes" or "reptile eyes": for he obviously is more deeply attached to the

masculine Börje, to whom Sandell's suicide note — after the failed seduction and his departure — is primarily directed.

The indefatigable George Moore is less disapproving of his decadent mouthpiece in *Confessions of a Young Man* (1888) than Benedictsson has been of Sandell; and much in the confession is a tribute to *À rebours,* a book taken very seriously — "that prodigious book, that beautiful mosaic . . . In hours like these a page of Huysmans is as a dose of opium, a glass of some exquisite powerful liquor." Within his financial limitations (which force him to live mostly in rented rooms), Moore's young man tries to be like Des Esseintes, railing against "democratic art" and "the Americans that come over here" and "the plague of vulgarity that will sweep away the world," and he keeps — even as he reviews French and English literature in Huysmans's essayistic manner — a pet python named Jack, in an effort, we must assume, to emulate Des Esseintes and his tortoise. Incidentally, Moore's young man has reached the decadent's classic age of thirty, or a bit more, as has his contemporary Thaddeus Sholto in Conan Doyle's *Sign of the Four,* who has "just turned his thirtieth year." By means of Sholto's apartment, "the oasis of art in the wilderness of South London," in the tumbledown Sholto mansion, Pondicherry Lodge, the creator of Sherlock Holmes kept up with the decadent Joneses, providing a small-scale counterpart to Fontenay-aux-Roses; it has oriental furnishings and "a subtle aromatic odor." The rabbitlike Sholto finds his "hookah an invaluable sedative," and has recruited Holmes, he says, because the detective is " 'a man of retiring and I might even say refined tastes, and there is nothing more unaesthetic than a policeman.' " Sholto is not merely a decadent insert; in his brief appearance, he serves as a pale doubling of Holmes, who injects himself with cocaine on the first and last pages of the novel. But, altogether unlike Sholto, Holmes is the owner of an active intelligence (in which he resembles Des Esseintes) and a man who, when he wishes, abandons his languor for an almost preternatural physical vigor.

In 1902, Jean Lorrain (Paul Duval) presents perhaps the ultimate decadent in *Le Vice errant: Les Noronsoff* a Russian nobleman of inexhaustible wealth who has been forced to leave his homeland because of the use he made of dancing girls and handsome muzhiks in his Petersburg orgies. Though only thirty-four, Wladimir Noronsoff, now resident in Nice, is a sick man, but not so ill that he can tame his urges; a family curse, bestowed on a fourteenth-century forbear by a Bohemian gypsy, has made the family's women into nymphomaniacs; in the present generation, the wires are crossed, and Wladimir cannot control his lust for men and boys. He lives in his splendid villa with his mother, his overseer, his physician, his pet monkeys, a Polish countess (who has some handsome sons), and a retinue of muzhiks, all clad in white like the squires of the Grail in *Parsifal*. In good time, Wladimir falls into a serious decline; a planned gigantic festival of *Adonis and Venus* (starring one of the countess's sons), to be held in honor of two visiting Englishmen, does not take place; the countess persuades one of the traveling Englishman, Lord Feredith, to marry her, and his yacht, the *Edward III,* sails away. (The nymphs and fauns, hired from among the local populace for the festival, almost lynch Wladimir; Lorrain calls attention to resemblances with Jean Lombard's Heliogabalus novel.) But worse is to come: rising from his sickbed, Wladimir attempts to drink the blood of a handsome muzhik sleeping in the corner, and then kidnaps a Neapolitan fisherman, the stalwart Tito Biffi. Biffi escapes, and, when Wladimir pursues him to the fishmarket, Biffi's fiancée slaps him with a flounder, knocking him head over heels. At last, Wladimir does die, but not before predicting destruction for the European cities which have marked the stages of his decadent career—all the hordes of the East will come, he says yellow barbarians, to rape and burn and murder. To be sure, Jean Lorrain was making fun of decadent extravagance (as Huysmans may well have in *À rebours*). G. K. Chesterson certainly had such an intent when, in *The Napoleon of Notting Hill* (1904), the king of that rebellious quarter of London wears a dandyistic uniform of his own devising as the colonel of his regiment, "the 1st Decadent Greens." Green is the color of absinthe and of decay.

Yet, in popular literature, decadent figures survived for years to come, appearing—here adventurous and conniving like Dracula—in John Buchan's book for boys, *Prester John* (1910). The atavistic black missionary, John Laputa, with his knowledge of the African past and his ability to use that knowledge to his own ends, means to shake the British empire to its foundations, or perhaps to rule the world. He is so powerful and so beguiling that he almost seduces his main opponent, the canny Scots boy, David Crawford, into doing his bidding, before he dies after a final recital with *Liebestod* overtones. "We are going to die together, Crawford . . . Unarm, Eros, the long day's task is done." Laputa is both a splendid classicist and a Shakespearian.

2

Ireland

GEORGE MOORE

Decadence has an important second meaning for literary and cultural studies. Not only is it a description of works whose protagonists are the "fragile flowers of a dying century," as in *Bruges-la-Morte, Noodlot, Trætte Mænd, A cidade e as serras, Der Garten der Erkenntnis,* "Die Letzten," and so on, or the egomaniacal aesthetes of *À rebours, Il piacere, The Picture of Dorian Gray,* the *Sonatas;* it also applies to the falling away, the *de-cadere* of small cultural, social, or linguistic elites, whose long rule over submerged indigenous populations was nervously perceived to be coming to an end — as indeed it was. Some literary examples are the Baltic-German community in the works of Eduard von Keyserling (e.g., 1908, *Dumala,* 1914, *Abendliche Häuser,* Evening Houses); the Germans of northern Bohemia in Fritz Mauthner's *Der letzte Deutsche von Blatna* (1887) and *Die böhmische Handschrift* (1897); the desiccated German-speaking officialdom of Prague in Gustav Meyrink's *Walpurgisnacht* (1917); the Swedish-speaking middle or upper class of Finland in Gustav Alm's (Richard Malmberg's) *Höstdagar* (1907, Autumn Days), Schildt's story "Mot skymningen," and Ture Janson's *De ensamma svenskarna* (1916, The Lonely Swedes); and a multitude of novels from the Anglo-Irish Ascendancy. This last-named group, in the phrase inspired by Elizabeth Bowen's *Bowen's Court* (1942) and used to fine effect by Julian Moynahan in his *Anglo-Irish* (1995), experienced a first "Indian summer" more or less simultaneously with like phenomena in Estonia and Finland and in the short and intense blooming of "Prague German" literature. Pressure or threat encouraged awareness: in the Estonian case during the intense Russification policies under Alexander III and Nicholas II; in Bohemia and Moravia with Czech nationalism; in Finland with the rapid growth of Finnish language and cultural awareness; in Ireland during the decade of the Land League and Parnell's efforts to create Irish home rule — in other words, during the 1880s. (The belletristic result in Ireland, however, expanded later, when it had become abundantly clear that the decay could never be reversed, and so could be thoroughly lamented.) Obviously, there was also a fear abroad on larger stages, expressed most unforgettably in Rudyard Kipling's "Recessional" of 1896: "The tumult and the shouting dies, / The captains and the king depart" and "Lord God of Hosts, be with us yet, be with us yet." The death of monarchy was predicted in the all-too-little read Liparian novels of Couperus, from 1903 and 1905, and the corrupting forces of colonialism and its someday destruction are the theme of Kipling's *Man Who Would Be King* (1897), of Couperus's *De stille kracht* (1900, *The Hidden Force*), and of Conrad's *Heart of Darkness* (1902).

In Ireland, conveniently for literary historians, the coming collapse gets the handiest of locations in "the big house," the great building on the gentry's estate. In the aging Edith Oenone Somerville's *Big House at Inver* (1925), Inver House was "one of those large gestures of the minds of the earlier Irish architects, some of which still stand to justify Ireland's claim to be considered a civilized country." The predominance of the big house — loved or detested — in Anglo-Irish letters is attested to at a very practical level by the inclusion of a long article, called simply "Big House," in the *Oxford Companion to Irish Literature* (1996), listing specimens from Maria Edgeworth's little and unexpected masterpiece of 1800, *Castle Rackrent,* narrated by a faithful steward who is nonetheless aware of the failings of four Rackrents in successive generations, to the present, for example, in William Trevor's *Fools of Fortune* (1983) and the film based on it. In Trevor, during the Anglo-Irish War of 1921–23, the big house of Kilneagh is burned by the IRA, as were, in fact, more than two hundred big houses during the Anglo-Irish War and the subsequent Civil War of 1923–24, a series of cultural atrocities of which Somerville thought as she wrote her history of Inver. (In fact, the big house at Inver is accidentally burned after it is sold to a wealthy Englishman, set afire by the senile Captain Prendeville.) The big house, in literature, is a popular and hardy plant; a decade and a half after Trevor, Annabel Davis-Goff published the best-selling *Dower House* (1997), which takes place in the 1950s and 1960s; the house is not the big house of Dromore, but a smaller one, Fern Hill, built as a residence for the once grand family's widows and now occupied by an ineffectual second son, the father of the girl narrator — he ends a suicide. The material is such a rich one that it can be exhausted only with difficulty: the novels are peopled by eccentrics, the action usually plays out against historical events, from the Fenian uprising of 1868 to the establishment of the Irish Free State, an event which, as R. B. McDowell has shown, caused many owners of the big houses to sell out and leave for England. (Anglophile Americans are more likely to identify with the interesting inhabitants of the mansion than with the toilers in the kitchen or in the fields.) An English-born author, the late J. G. Farrell, created a wildly comic transformation of the big house in his *Troubles* (1970); the big house becomes a once grand resort hotel, the Majestic, besieged by invisible forces during the "Troubles" of the Anglo-Irish War, and slowly collapsing before it is burned by a demented Irish servant. Long before, in "Upon a House Shaken by the Land Agitation" in *The Green Helmet and Other Poems* (1910), W. B. Yeats praised the "high laughter, loveliness, and ease," "the passion and precision" such big houses bred; in his last play, *Purgatory* (1938), the big house has again been burned down, its "jokes and stories have vanished." The big house has always had its wistful or nostalgic friends. Hubert Butler, a member of a genuinely ancient Anglo-Irish family, who stayed on after the foundation of the Republic, wrote in "The Country House after the Union" (1957) that the country house of Ireland was a "place which once generated life and diffused it." (By "after the Union," Butler meant the abolition of the Irish Parliament in 1800, which marked the beginning of the Ascendancy's long slide into desuetude.)

It is scarcely sure that George Moore, the author of *A Drama in Muslin* (1886), his third novel, would have joined Yeats in his lament or have agreed with Butler. After the premature death in 1879 of his father, George Henry Moore, a Roman Catholic politician, a Fenian, and a sometime member of Parliament, George Augustus Moore, the son (1853–1932), inherited the family home, Moore Hall at Ballyglass in County Mayo; with his income, he studied painting in Paris from 1873 to 1879, when, forced by the failing profits from the estate, he returned — not to Ireland, but to England, beginning his literary career and meanwhile paying annual visits to his properties. (In time, Moore's younger brother Maurice, after a distinguished career in the Irish regiment, the Connaught Rangers, took over the running of Moore Hall until it was burned down by the IRA in 1921.) George's relations to his younger brother were bad, not least because of George's detestation of the Roman Catholic faith in which the boys had been born and reared. In 1903, the author made a public decision to turn Protestant, arguing in a letter to the *Irish Times:* "When will my unfortunate country turn its eyes from Rome —

the cause of all her woes?" Two years before, the author had moved back from London to Ireland, to play the role in the Gaelic revival (like Yeats, he did not really know Irish) he would describe in his trilogy, *Hail and Farewell* (1911–14); the same year as that of the publication of the final volume, *Vale,* he returned to London and to the house, someday to be legendary, at 121, Ebury Street, each year thereafter adding to his varied bibliography.

Moore had long since achieved international literary celebrity for *Confessions of a Young Man;* his fling at Huysmanian decadence had been followed by the realistic *Esther Waters,* while his John Norton of *A Mere Accident* reappeared in the triptych *Celibates* (1896). Then came the novel about a Wagnerian singer, *Evelyn Innes* (1898), and its sequel *Sister Teresa* (1901), the last as unflattering toward Catholicism as were the anticlerical stories of *The Untilled Field* (1903) and the novel *The Lake* (1905). His production grew increasingly more self-referential; the would-be erotica of *Memoirs of My Dead Life* (1906), and *Hail and Farewell* shade over in *Avowals* (1919) into impressionistic criticism, as the *Confessions* had done years before. *The Brook Kerith* (1916) was a skeptical but not unfriendly novel about Christ told through Joseph of Arimathea; its archaizing stylistic urge becomes stronger in *The Pastoral Love of Daphnis and Chloe* (1924) and *Aphrodite in Aulis* (1930), in which Moore depended on his reputation for elegant naughtiness to attract readers. Moore had difficulty, as will be apparent, in concentration on the perfection of a single work; he claimed to have learned to write literate and literary English only after having mastered French — but he was a notorious exaggerator and prevaricator.

At the start of his career, thanks to his long residence in Paris, Moore became a peripheral but not unimportant figure in European decadent letters: the self-concern of the *Confessions,* the attempts at preciousness in the manner of *À rebours,* his obsession with oddities of sexual behavior, his plunge into Wagnerism with *Evelyn Innes,* all bear witness to what could be called his decadentism. Further, the persona he presented in fact in Paris, and the *Confessions,* was that of a Wildean aesthete. But he never attained nor really strove after the extravagances of Huysmans, D'Annunzio, and Wilde; he had much too strong an interest in the nuances of human behavior for that: witness *Esther Waters, The Untilled Field, The Lake,* the last about a priest who fakes his drowning and leaves for America and freedom; after the *Confessions,* he demonstrated some of the same social engagement shown by Huysmans before *À rebours,* for example in *Marthe, histoire d'une fille* (1876). Wilde seems to have thought that Moore was too unfinished, too lacking in concentration to construct a perfect pose for himself, although Moore would surely accomplish that in his late years as a naughty sage on Ebury Street. The Wildean witticism on the protean Moore was: " 'Moore always conducts his education in public.' "

Moore's awareness of social issues helped him in the construction of his novel bearing on the decay of the old order in Ireland; his prime intention was not so much a political as a protofeminist one—his own time would have called it Ibsenian. As the title indicates, the book is about a dilemma of women of the age; *A Drama in Muslin* was published seven years after *A Doll's House* and three after Jonas Lie's *Familjen på Gilje (The Family at Gilje)*: in a somewhat freer Norway, the heroine refuses marriage (her suitor is a dandy, her beloved a drunk), and becomes a schoolteacher. Moore's argument is that contemporary life in Ireland (as elsewhere) allows women of station only two possibilities: to marry, however unhappily, or to spend an existence of fruitless and idle spinsterdom. (Further down the social ladder, Kate, in Moore's *A Mummer's Wife* [1885], deserts her asthmatic husband to run away with an actor, is coarsened by the theatrical life, and dies an alcoholic; Esther Waters drudges to rear her illegitimate child and bring him to manhood.) The working title of the book was simply "*The* Galway *Girls*"; the girls from County Galway's estates are caught in the strong but fine cloth of the dresses in which they, most of them, go on the search for husbands, participating in a "mummery in muslin." The girls are five in number; when they graduate from St. Leonard's School at the Convent of the Holy Cross in North Wales, they return, impractically educated, to their homes across the Irish Sea. They are the plain but brainy Alice Barton; her beautiful but frivolous sister Olive; the delicate Violet Scully, with her "almost complete lack of bosom" and her "small aristocratic head," inside which was "a sharp but narrow intelligence, . . . an intelligence that would always dominate weak natures," inherited from a mother who had worked in a Galway grocer's shop; May Gould, after Alice "the cleverest girl in the school," whose "sensuous nature was reflected in the violet fluidity of her eyes." Unlike these four, Lady Cecilia Cullen, the daughter of a lord, has no marriage prospects, since she is a hunchback; a Protestant, Cecilia is much drawn to Roman Catholicism. The other girls are all from the Roman Catholic gentry of Galway, like the Moores themselves in County Mayo. (George Moore was proud of the fact that his great-grandfather, George Moore, a successful wine merchant and a born Protestant, had married for love while at Bilbao, with the daughter of a noble Irish family, fled to Spain during the "Flight of the Earls" [1607].) Moore plays no confessional favorites: the Catholic gentry is no better than—indeed, interchangeable with—the Protestant. The Protestant representation in the cast, apart from Cecilia, includes her father, the foppish Lord Dungory, of Dungory Castle, a master of ambiguous repartee in French, and his two spinster daughters, older than Cecilia, Lady

Jane and Lady Sarah, "old and ugly" zealots who start a Protestant school, to which their brother — showing an indifference which "looks upon all religions as equally good" — objects because "it makes me hated in the neighborhood," that is, among the Catholic peasantry. He has no wish to convert them; "they are paying their rents very well now." The conversion of Cecilia to the Roman Church she has so long admired, and her taking of the veil, are of no concern to him: " 'In fact, [it] might incline the priest very much towards us.' " (This remark is made near the novel's end, after the storm of murder and outrage caused by the Land League has passed.)

At the announcement of Cecilia's joining a sisterhood, the reaction of the ladies Cullen, Jane and Sarah, is such (" 'far beyond fainting,' " is Lord Dungory's description) that he takes sanctuary in the place that has been his constant refuge for past years, Brookfield, the estate of the Bartons not far from Castle Dungory. (Dungory actually existed; its choice as the residence of the indifferent Protestant, the Lord, was Moore's private joke on his arch-Catholic, celibate friend Edward Martyn, whose family owned it.) Moore leaves the nature of the relationship between Lord Dungory and Mrs. Barton somewhat in the dark; he is her constant companion, the cicisbeo of the still beautiful woman, with the "heart-shaped Lady Hamilton face" and "Lady Hamilton eyes" (like the mother of Dorian Gray in the portrait hung in the gallery at his country house). Mrs. Barton's hair is "touched with dye sufficiently to give it a golden tinge," and she has a figure like her moral character: both are elegant, refined, supple. "There was about Mrs. Barton's whole person an air of falseness, as indescribable as it was bewitching . . . Her artificiality was her charm." Her husband is handsome and still youthful, a dabbler in the arts, a painter of small talent, "twanging his guitar" in his "gaudy smoking jacket"; he "wore a flowing beard, his hair was long, and both were the color of pale *café au lait*." He is a devotee of "historical painting with a good deal of flesh"; compelled to meet a delegation of his tenants, "he could think of nothing but the muscles of the strained back of a dying Briton, and a Roman soldier who cut the cords that bound the white [female] captive to the sacrificial oak." Later, when the unrest is at its worst, he imagines that he will head a mounted company against the troublemakers.

Arthur Barton's invaluable aide is his agent, the vulgar and vigorous Mr. Scully, Violet's father, who speaks Irish, as Mr. Barton does not. Unhappily, Mr. Scully's usually good relations with the tenants have been poisoned by the "bullying and insolent manner" of Scully's son, Fred, a ne'er-do-well of some thirty years of age, to whom "pleasure meant horses, women, eating." His sister Violet cannot endure the improprieties of his conversation. The Scullys are socially a cut below the other parents of the girls who return from St.

Leonard's, not just the Bartons and Dungory but Mrs. Gould as well. "The Goulds were of an excellent county family . . . some ancestor had come back from India with the money that had purchased the greater part of the property" of Beechgrove, "one of those box-like mansions, so many of which were built in Ireland under the Georges." Three generations of landlordism have passed, "considered sufficient repentance for shopkeeping in Gort, not to speak of Calcutta." (Gort is a market town in south Galway, not far from Castle Dungory.) "Since then the [Gould] family history had been stainless, spent in the breeding and training of horses, cub-hunting [hunting young foxes], and drinking." The earlier squires of Beechgrove had survived until seventy, but the latest had died at fifty-five, leaving the fat and good-natured Mrs. Gould behind with May. The girl had "apparently resolved to keep up the [family] traditions as far as her sex was supposed to allow her." A love of horseflesh has brought May together with Fred Scully.

The great event of Book 2 is the migration of hopeful mothers and daughters to Dublin in February 1882, for the presentation of the debutantes in the drawing room of Dublin Castle, the beginning of the great marriage mart, the mummery in muslin. There they will receive the ceremonial kiss from the lord lieutenant, a reminiscence of the droit du seigneur, as Moore slyly remarks. Lovely Olive Barton is to be the star of the evening and the season, according to her equally lovely mother's plans. These were hatched the previous summer at a rowdy ball, given by the spinsters of County Galway, at the horse-fair town of Ballinasloe. Before the ball, May Gould comfortingly reflected that "as no very unpopular landlord was going to be present, it was not thought that an attempt would be made to blow up the building." But at the ball, little Mr. Burke, the younger brother of the bachelor marquis of Kilcarney, learns that the marquis has been murdered.

Mrs. Barton directly fixes her sights on the new marquis for Olive, discouraging her daughter in her romance with Captain Hibbert, a handsome and Catholic but unmoneyed officer in the regiment stationed at Gort. Unfortunately for Mrs. Barton, the marquis, at the castle levee, is drawn not to Olive but to Violet Scully. The new marquis of Kilcarney, in whose tiny form is hidden a tempered version of a decadent aesthete, is struck not by the "plain appealing of Olive's Greek statue-like beauty," but by Violet's "exquisite atavism," showing the "hectic erythism of painters and sculptors in a period preceding the apogee of an art"; the lord lieutenant kisses Violet so warmly that his wife looks up in surprise.

The first marriage expedition to Dublin, ending in the disappointment of Mrs. Barton's hopes for Olive (who has not forgotten Hibbert), brings disaster to May Gould: she admits the lubricious Fred Scully to her room at the Shelbourne. (The debutantes have all put up at the classic Dublin hotel, save Violet with Mrs. Scully, the latter of whom felt she could better further *her* plans for her daughter and the marquis by taking a house on Fitzwilliam Place.) May becomes pregnant, Fred flees to Australia, and, thanks to the practical aid of Alice Barton, May is able to disappear from Galway to a rented room on Dublin's North Side, on Mountjoy Square, lower-middle-class, and the home neighborhood of Francie Fitzgerald, the heroine of Somerville and Ross's *Real Charlotte* (1894). (Both Moore and Somerville-Ross are keenly aware of the meaning of Dublin addresses.) May's baby dies, and she returns to Beechgrove to continue her life as an impassioned horsewoman and, as far as we know, the lover of one or several of the officers from Gort. She tells Alice that " 'some of us cannot remain spinsters,' " but she is " 'determined to be a good woman yet.' "

Alice has been able to support May during the pregnancy by income received from her writing. In this avocation, she has been encouraged by the author John Harding, a visitor from England, whom she has met at the Shelbourne. Ever mindful of sales, Moore points out in a footnote that Harding is also a character in his *A Modern Lover* and *A Mummer's Wife*—in the first instance, a novelist "whose books were vigorously denounced by the press as being both immoral and cynical," in the second, a writer for the theater. (Harding would return in the story "The Way Back," later called "The Fugitives" in *The Untilled Field*: still an author and older, Harding has now been turned into an Irishman.) The budding intellectual romance is stifled when Alice refuses to visit Harding in his Dublin apartment; but they continue to correspond after Harding's return to England. The arrival of his letters at Brookfield, though, are the catalyst for the violent declaration of lesbian love made by Cecilia to Alice. To Cecilia, men are "libidinous monsters." Daring for his time, Moore also introduced lesbianism among nuns in *Sister Teresa*.

One more sad story remains to be played out, one more result of the failed husband-hunting foray to Dublin of 1882, and of its fruitless repetition the next year. Olive's "thoughtless brain" is not distracted by this second (and barely described) assault on the Dublin marriage mart, or by a subsequent journey abroad, an "intermediate series of flirtations with foreign titles," during which Lord Dungory and Mrs. Barton enjoy themselves, "talking and laughing gracefully." Back in Ireland, Olive begins clandestine meetings with Hibbert again, and an elopement is arranged, but it too ends unhappily. Slipping away through the night to meet the captain, Olive is intercepted by a Mrs. Lawler, the owner of an adjacent estate with whom the Bartons do not associate because she is a "bad woman." Mrs. Lawler tells Olive that she has been Teddy's—Edward Hibbert's—instructress in love: " 'It isn't to you a man comes for the love he wants; your kisses are very skim-milk indeed.'" Thrown to the ground by the muscular Mrs. Lawler, Olive sprains her ankle, and spends the night in the dank woods. (The relationship between Mrs. Lawler and Hibbert is like that between Mrs. Manley and Fred Scully as he laid siege to May Gould.)

Coming down with pneumonia, Olive is nursed back to health by Alice and the district physician, Dr. Edward Reed, who spent ten years serving the peasants of remote Donegal. Love springs up between the socially conscious Reed and Alice, the admirer of intelligent men — her love for her father as a "great artist" has been diluted by her slow realization that he is only a "blond-bearded dreamer." Just as Alice has secretly rejected her family's Catholicism, so the "straight-souled girl" has been a secret supporter, like Reed, of the Nationalist cause, cognizant of the oppression of the peasantry: when her mother complains of the "sour and wicked looks" and the dirtiness of their fellow worshipers in the Catholic chapel, her daughter does not chime in. She had "already begun to see something awry in each big house being surrounded by a hundred small ones, all working to keep it in sloth and luxury." Mrs. Barton has only contempt for Reed, the son of a small shopkeeper, the product of a national school (one of the state schools for elementary education, set up in the 1830s), and a self-made man. She refuses to attend the wedding of Alice and Reed, nor will she allow Barton to do so ("his supply of paints, brushes, canvases, and guitar strings would be cut off"). The couple is married on a rainy December day in 1884 (Moore takes pains with chronology, however improvisatory he can be with events) at a pro forma Roman Catholic ceremony, presided over by Father Shannon, "large, pompous, and arrogant," and leaves for England; Reed, already the author of a successful medical book, sets up practice in London.

On the way out of Ireland, the newlyweds pass "here and there a dismantled cottage, telling to those who know the country a tale of eviction and the consequent horrors: despair, hunger, revenge, and death," and then the "great gateways and the white Martello-tower-like houses of the landlords." In fact, the big houses are not at all like the round stone towers put up along the Irish coast against the French invasion during the Napoleonic Wars, but the phrase is meant to suggest the embattled state of mind of the owners of the boxlike mansions. As a symbolic good deed for the wretched peasantry they are abandoning, the honeymooners pay the debts of a householder about to be evicted.

Two-and-a-half years later, in a cultured and cultivated suburban London home (in *Confessions of a Young Man*, Moore praised "dear, sweet Protestant England"), Olive comes unannounced to visit her sister Alice, because she 'couldn't stay at home any longer.'" Once upon a time so dissatisfied with the prospects of Captain Hibbert (now in India), Mrs. Barton now pursues a Captain Gibbon for her daughter, and "the whole county laughs." Other news of Galway follows. Riding in a "pounding match" (cross-county race), May Gould has collided with Mrs. Manley and given up horses for painting. " 'Ireland is worse than ever, we shall all be ruined, and they say Home Rule is certain,' " the vague and perpetually troubling policy by which Ireland was to take charge of its own affairs; to Olive's primitive understanding, home rule would mean the final ruin of the landlords. In the summer of 1881, as the Galway girls returned from convent school, Mr. Barton had commented on the "disturbed state of the country," and the unrest caused by Parnell and his campaign for home rule. Then, Olive's only comment had been a question: "She asked if Mr. Parnell was good-looking."

In Moore's depiction, the society of the big houses is not fit to survive. It is morally rotten, hopelessly and unimaginatively selfish, and its cultural values are represented by the exceptional ability of Lord Dungory to make quips in French and to quote "the divine Alfred de Musset," and by Mr. Barton's dabbling in the arts. The lazy and complacent Mr. Barton's best quality, apart from his good nature, is his "bewildering" air of seeming "purposely to laugh at himself." His father had been an eccentric, spending fifty years in his study "imagining himself a Gibbon and writing unpublished history and biography."

The "brace of baronets" who might have been catches for some few among the women growing old while waiting for a husband (the Miss Duffys, the Miss Brennans, the Honorable Miss Gores), are worthless prospects: Sir Richard is a notorious drunkard, even in this world of heavy drink; Sir Charles has a "dirty little crowd of illegitimate children about the stable yard" whom he would have to send abroad (America, Australia) before he could marry. The squires around them are given over to horses and drink — for example, the cousins Mr. Ryan and Mr. Lynch, whose "dirty hands fumbled at their shirt studs that constantly threatened to fall through the worn button holes," the result not of poverty but of sheer slovenliness. The brightest of the squires, Mr. Adair, who took honors at Trinity and on whom, it is rumored, Gladstone himself has cast his eye for a government post, is an impossible bore in his learnedness, forever demonstrating a knowledge of Ireland's history quite singular in the Dungory-Barton circles.

To be sure, the people off whom the landlords live are no more attractive than their masters; at the mass attended by Mrs. Barton and Alice, the peasants listen devoutly to the "appallingly trivial" ceremony. The gentry (this is Alice's perception) prayed "elegantly, with refinement. Their social position was manifest in their religion as in their homes." But the peasantry, filling the body of the chapel, grunt, cough, and spit, praying "coarsely, ignorantly, with the same brutality as they lived." Nevertheless, history has made them what they are, their "dried and yellowing faces [bespeaking] centuries of damp cabins, brutalizing toil, occasional starvation." With her clear intelligence, Alice — alone of her family — realizes this, as does Dr. Reed. But, having done their good deed at the auction, Alice and her husband will remain in orderly, peaceful England forever.

The Ireland that they abandon has in truth become a frightening place, "in a time of darkness and constant alarms," for all the dinner parties and excursions and liaisons of the gentry: "They saw that which they had taken to be eternal, vanishing from them even as a vapour." (Emphasizing the solemnity of what he says, Moore paraphrases the New Testament's warning to those who rejoice in their boastings (James, 4:14–16): "Of what is your life? It is even a vapour, that appeareth for a little time, and then vanisheth away.") If the countryside was "filled with threats, murder and rumour of many murders," the Dublin to which the mothers and daughters travel so hopefully in February 1882, is likewise frightening amidst the festivities. Dungory, who has accompanied Mrs. Barton and the daughters (while Barton is in Bruges for art studies at his wife's expense), grows nervous, spreading stories that "the city is undermined." Assassins wait to kill the lord lieutenant, "many plots are hatched for the blowing up of the Castle." Even the elegant squares have gone to rack and ruin; "like crones in borrowed bonnets some are fashionable with flowers in the rotting window frames." St. Stephen's Green, recently dolled up by a wealthy nobleman, looks like a "school treat set out for the entertainment of charity children"; Merrion Square is "infinitely pitiful." Riding to the castle on the opening evening, the Bartons — their carriage caught in the procession of carriages — see the "narrow drain-like river" by the lightning flashes (theatrically enough, an electrical storm rages), while "on the left" is "squalor multiform and terrible." The Dublin poor have turned out to watch the parade of finery.

This grim set piece, and the extended depiction of the false grandeur of the castle, are followed by a memorable nocturnal tour of Dublin. (In the Nighttown of *Ulysses,* Joyce had a not inconsiderable predecessor in Moore.) At the close of Book 2, the Dublin section, Mrs. Barton, following Mrs. Scully's lead, has moved out of the Shelbourne, taking up residence on Mount Street, the better to entertain and look for candidates. But in her desperation, she has made a social mistake: she and her daughters attend a vulgar charity costume ball and find themselves in the company of the "rag, tag and bobtail of Catholic Dublin," and so are struck from the list of those to be invited to private dances at the castle. Aware that she is losing the contest for the marquis with the Scullys, Mrs. Barton tries to snatch victory from the jaws of defeat. Worn down by repeated invitations, and by the faithful Dungory's depiction to the marquis of how his estate will be divided among the peasants, even as he lives, a miserable exile, in a Belgian boardinghouse, the marquis weakens, and Mrs. Barton dangles Olive's dowry of twenty thousand pounds before him. Not having the courage to refuse her to her face, he bolts, darting off to the Scullys' nearby residence on Fitzwilliam Place. There, overcome by [Violet's] "frail sweetness," and ignoring her "sharpness," as Moore writes with some irony, the marquis, Lord Kilcarney, proposes, and is directly accepted. The quondam Galway shopgirl, the mother-in-law *in spe,* cleverly withdraws: Kilcarney leaves the house only after midnight. The encumbrances of Castle Kilcarney will turn out to be not as bad as the new marquis had thought, and the wedding gifts are splendid. The bride will be presented at the second (and more exclusive) drawing room in Dublin Castle a year later. In a preface to the revised second edition of the novel from 1915, simply called *Muslin,* Moore tells about the dog's life the marquis leads with his domineering wife.

Kilcarney's walk could be followed in a Baedeker for Ireland of the 1880s, if such existed. He goes a short distance north from Fitzwilliam Place to Merrion Square and sees a house in which a ball is taking place, a ball to which he, the great catch, has been invited; he is reminded that if he enters, every eye will be on him. Now he is struck by the cold truth of what he has done by throwing the Bartons' twenty thousand pounds away, and "before him rose the spectre of the Land League," and the ruin it would cause him. Crossing the Liffey, he finds himself beside the statue of Daniel O'Connell on Sackville Street (from 1924, O'Connell Street), "the man who had begun the work" with the Catholic Emancipation Act, O'Connell who "had withdrawn the keystone of the edifice" of landlordism. Then he recrosses the river, and "walk[s] to and fro beneath the colonnades of the Bank of Ireland," "the silent power that protects him"; but soon "a new power would turn him a beggar upon the world." Passing by Trinity College, he thinks: "This ancient seat of learning would perish before the triumphant and avenging peasant." And: "Wealth, position, and power were slipping from him; all he possessed in the world was [Violet Scully's] thin white face—delicate and subtle as an Indian carven ivory." Going back across the Liffey, northward, he looks again at the gloom of Sackville Street, where "a taint of assassination of doom [lies] in the air." Kilcarney is in a bad way. Notably, looking up the broad street, he does *not* see the Nelson Pillar, the symbol of a protective empire; Oliver St. John Gogarty wrote that the Pillar was "the grandest thing we have in Dublin, the great Doric column that upheld the Admiral." (It was blown up in 1966, fifty years after the uprising of 1916, and some eighty years after the marquis's terrifying walk.) Out on the O'Connell Bridge once more, over the "brown, sullen Liffey, in which bodies could so easily disappear," he is again struck by remorse at what he has done by choosing the "little, thin, white face" instead of the Barton money. The shades of his ancestors crowd about him (a scene that like that in Gilbert and Sullivan's *Ruddigore,* from a year later, and like the nightmare of Gonçalo Ramires in Eça's *A ilustre casa de Ramires,* reproached for his weakness by his mighty ancestors). As so often in the age of decadence — see the opening of *À rebours,* see Bang's *Det graa Hus,* see *Buddenbrooks* — the strong men of the past have brought forth a weakling. "Yes, he was ruined, utterly ruined. But with twenty or thirty thousand pounds he would have been able to fight [that terrible Land League] and conquer it."

The endings of the chapter and the walk are scary and grandiose. Murder is over for the night, the violins have stopped playing at Merrion Square, and "the girls sleep their white sleep of celibacy." The city sleeps too, "the shameless squalor of the outlying streets is enwrapped in grey mist," but "against the sky the Castle still stretches out its arms as if for some monstrous embrace." We do not know if the little marquis takes some small comfort in the sight.

The nightmare of the agrarian troubles ends suddenly. The murders so much on Lord Dungory's and Lord Kilcarney's minds reach a climax. During a dinner party at Brookfield on May 7, 1882, after the first Dublin trip, the report comes that the new chief secretary of the government, Lord Frederick Cavendish, second only to the lord lieutenant himself, and the undersecretary Thomas Henry Burke, have been stabbed to death — with surgical knives! — outside the Vice-Regal Lodge in Dublin's Phoenix Park. The perpetrators were members of a Fenian terrorist group, the Invincibles. The coarse Mr. Ryan expresses a bitter truth: he is glad the officials have been assassinated, for now the British government will be compelled to take the strongest measures. Miraculously, the country is pacified, a complex process Moore crams into a long and complex paragraph. The agent, Mr. Scully, sums up the happy result: " 'Rents paid, cattle high, [Parnell's] Land League dead.' " He might have added: " 'and my daughter's going to marry a marquis.' " Indeed, the Land League was suppressed but Gladstone's evenhanded Land Act removed some of the grossest injustices, and Parnell's power in Parliament increased, until he was brought down, as every romantic reader of history knows, by his affair with and marriage to Mrs. Kitty O'Shea, and by the hateful opposition to the Protestant Parnell by the Roman Catholic clergy Moore so detested. The fall of Anglo-Ireland, crumbling, was put off until the next century.

3

Italy

GABRIELE D'ANNUNZIO

In the essay "The Literature of Decadence," in *Harper's Monthly Magazine* for November 1893, by which Arthur Symons introduced continental
decadent literature to the English-speaking world, he wrote: "In Italy . . . Gabriele D'Annunzio, in that marvelous, malarious *Piacere* [1889], has achieved
a triumph of exquisite perversity." Subsequently, Symons had reason to think
about *Il piacere* once more; he functioned as an adviser to Georgina Harding
as she made her translation, *The Child of Pleasure* (1898), and rendered "the
sonnets and other verse contained in the novel into English verse." He offered
two suggestions to her, he tells us in his introduction, while emphasizing that
he had not gone through the text of her work. The one was that she use an
English rendering of the title of the French translation, made by Georges
Hérelle in 1895, *L'Enfant de volupté* (which title was meant, one suspects, to
suggest in its turn a famous book about Parisian high life in the 1830s, Alfred
de Musset's *Confessions d'un enfant du siècle*); the other was that she follow
the "rearrangement" of the text prepared by D'Annunzio himself for the
French edition.

The Italian Urtext of *Il piacere* begins with what is Part 3, chapter 2, in the
English version, where Count Andrea Sperelli-Fieschi d'Ugenta waits in his
elegant rooms, his *buen retiro,* at the Casa Zuccari by the Spanish Steps to
receive Elena Muti, "after her long and mysterious absence" of almost two

years. Then, in a flashback, the Italian original returns to the passage that is Part 1, chapter 2, of the English version, with its ingressus (about the Italian nobility being engulfed in "the gray deluge of democratic mud" — "il grigio diluvio democratico odierno" — the translator omits the word *today's*), and its story of the Sperellis (in lieu of a family-gallery episode), and of Andrea Sperelli's strange upbringing by his father. To this, there is affixed (again in the original) what is the opening chapter of the English version, the regular Wednesday night dinner party at the home of Sperelli's cousin, the marchesa d'Ateleta — at which gatherings Sperelli sees Elena Muti (for the first time), ascending the stairs "with a slow and rhythmic movement."

The second part, the idyllic episode of Sperelli's recovery from his dueling wound at the estate of Schifanoja and the incipient love affair with Donna Maria Ferres y Capdevila, is "identical" in the two languages (*identical* is a word to be taken with a grain of salt, for reasons to be listed presently). The third part begins again more or less identically in both versions, but the English version then has the story of the reunion with Elena, from which Sperelli emerges so bitterly disappointed, inserted at the chronologically proper place, as chapter 2. The English chapter 3, where Sperelli reflects upon and accepts the demotion of his love for Elena to "a mere carnal lust, a piece of gross sensuality," somehow corresponds to the Italian's Part 3, chapter 2, but has a long omission at its start, including the opening sentence which contains the title of the book: "Così, d'un balzo, Andrea Sperelli si rituffò nel Piacere," "Thus, with a bound, Andrea Sperelli reentered the life of Pleasure," with a capital *P*.

The other rearrangements of the text in its latter two parts are less consequential; the long Part 3, chapter 3, of the Italian version is at the midpoint of the English version's Part 4: it ends with the visit of Sperelli and Maria to the Belvedere at the Villa Medici: there Maria Ferres sees an erotic epigram by Goethe written, in Andrea's hand, on the pillar of the little temple, and detects the date and the name, "Die ultima februarii 1885, . . . Helena Amyclaea"; to quell her suspicions, Andrea kisses her so that "his kiss flowed in her blood" even as she felt "a ruthless torture grind deep into her heart, that name — oh, that name," "quel nome, quel nome!" D'Annunzio's prose is nothing if not emotionally overcharged. The Italian Part 4's three chapters become the five concluding chapters, six to ten, of the English. Evidently, Georgina Harding, or her publishers, felt that English readers liked to have their passion served up in smaller — or shorter — doses than did Italians. Totting up: the English version has thirty chapters, as opposed to sixteen in the Italian.

However, the Italian version is longer, and now a return should be made to the word *identical,* used with such trepidation above. The English translation omits a great many passages that would have shocked a late Victorian reader's sensibilities; on the flyleaf of the copy in Yale's Sterling Library, an unknown hand has written: "Beware of translations by Victorian ladies." These omissions are mostly in Parts 1 and 3. For example, in Part 1, page 49 of Harding's text, a merciful curtain of silence is drawn over the passage in Elena's sickroom at her residence in the Palazzo Barberini, after Elena — with "a band of white linen around her face, like a nun's wimple" — has raised herself up from the pillows, taken Andrea's head between her hands, drawn him to her, and "their lips [have] met in a long and passionate kiss." Miss Harding went thus far and no farther. The passage in the Italian (as in the equally nonprudish French and German versions, the latter from 1898 and called, rather abruptly, *Lust*) goes on; only fragments from it can be quoted here. "The Crucifixion of Reni," which hung over Elena's bed, "lent the shadow of the bed curtains an appearance of sanctity"; this is followed by phrasing that needs no commentary at all: "She drew him to her, uttered her passionate wish, kissed him, fell back, surrendered herself to him." The line really does not seem shocking to modern eyes, but worse is to follow (and to be omitted), a more complex description of the stages of intercourse, to be sure so swathed in D'Annunzio's rhetoric that it has to be read a couple of times before one understands what is going on. Another omission is on page 53; it is worth noting not just for sensationalism's sake but because a German scholar, Erwin Koppen, has suggested that Wilde got his phrase and notion "to cure the soul by means of the senses and the senses by means of the soul" from it: "Questa 'spiritualizzazione' del gaudio carnale" — "This spiritualization of carnal delight, caused by the complete affinity of their bodies, was perhaps the most remarkable of all the forms their passion took." D'Annunzio hints at oral sex.

The longest omissions, among the some twenty-five major ones made by Miss Harding, occur in Part 3, Chapter 1, of the English version, the chapter in which Andrea Sperelli, catching up after he has returned to Rome from the pure air of Schifanoja, exchanges scandalous stories with his friends. (They get to know, for example, much about a physiological oddity of Giulia Moceto and the consternation it may cause even in the most virile lover.) The chapter, as well, describes the dinner of the young nobleman and their assortment of ladies from the demimonde at the Restaurant Doney: it is a verbal, but not a physical orgy. The young men are all, in the best decadent manner, very learned. The worst things they say are in Latin, which gives them a double opportunity, or even a triple one, to feel that they are of a superior caste: they can think of themselves as representatives of the Renaissance, in which Latin was still the language of cultured men; they can feel superior to, and titillate, their female companions with their remarks, at the import of which the girls have to guess (the linguistic process turns the demimondaines even more into the used creatures of these representatives of the Roman nobility); and with Latin, they may, as well, make those sallies into blasphemy that—as in the bedroom scene between Sperelli and Elena Muti—provide the extra thrill. Wittingly or unwittingly, Georgina Harding retains some remnants of the passage, with semiquotations of ecclesiastical texts, for example, in the sentence from Saint Bernard's sermon from which Sperelli extracts a "voluptous motto" for Giulia Arici, the "lower part of whose face [had] a frankly animal look. Her eye-teeth, which were too prominent, raised her upper lip a little, and she continually ran the point of her tongue along the edge to moisten it, like the thick petal of a rose running over a row of little white almonds." The motto is "Rosa linguatica, glube nos," "Tongued rose, unpeel us," for which invention Musellaro salutes Sperelli: "'What a pity that you are not at the table of a duke of the sixteenth century, between Violante and Imperia [the names of courtesans], with Pietro Aretino, Giulio Romano, and Marc' Antonio." (Pietro Aretino, the author of the obscene classic *Ragionamenti,* comes first, before the Mantuan architect and Flaminio, the poet and humanist.)

The orgiastic excitement of the scene (which we could say has the "infantile baroqueness" of which Huysmans's black banquet has been accused) is increased by its description of some of the girls (e.g., Bébé Silva resembles a "restless schoolboy, a depraved little hermaphrodite, dressed like a dandy"), and by—once more—the attachment of terms from the church to the once and present lover of Sperelli, Clara Green, an English girl whom Sperelli introduces as "ancilla Domini, Sibylla palmifera, candida puella," the "handmaiden of the Lord, the palm-bearing Sibyl, the immaculate girl," to which his friends reply, in chorus, "Ora pro nobis." (We have already been told that, back home in England, she has been a model for the poet-painter Adolphus Jeckyll—read Dante Gabriel Rossetti—and has sat for him as a *Sibylla Palmifera* and a *Madonna with the Lily.*) At bottom, the narrator adds, "She possessed no spiritual qualities whatsoever," even becoming "tiresome in the long run by reason of that sentimental romanticism so often affected by English demi-mondaines, which contrasts so strangely with the depravity of their licentiousness." It could be added that, in the Roman orgy, the polyglot quality of the conversation is increased by Clara Green's repeated entreaty to Andrea, "'Love me tonight, Andrew,'" which the other girls do not comprehend at all—their English is even weaker than their Latin. "'What's this howling about?' what's it mean?' asked Maria Fortuna: 'Does she feel ill?'" Harding omits the concluding three pages of the orgy.

In connection with this verbal reconstruction of Thomas Couture's *Les Romains de la Décadence:* Clara Green's very name (and not just her mixture of Pre-Raphaelite purity and depravity) itself had a decadent air for the reader of the fin de siècle. Green had already become the color of the decadence — not the green of blooming nature but the green of decay, in Gautier's description of later Latin language; the green color of the decadents' favorite drink, absinthe; the green of Wilde's early essay, "Pen, Pencil, and Poison, a Study in Green," about the forger and poisoner Thomas Wainwright, who "had this curious love of green, which in individuals is always the sign of a subtle artistic temperament, and in nations is said to denote a laxity, if not a decadence, of morals." There is, in addition, the green of Wilde's own green carnation and those of his followers at the premiere of *Lady's Windermere's Fan,* in 1892, which passed into Hichens' *Green Carnation.* When the villainous homosexual Karl, in Otto Julius Bierbaum's late-decadent novel from Germany, *Prinz Kuckuck* (1908–1909), goes to London, he makes a beeline for the Klub der grünen Nelke (the Club of the Green Carnation) and even Michael Arlen, in the best-seller of the 1920s about effete Londoners, *The Green Hat,* knew very well what he was doing with his title.

After this consideration of the central orgy in the book, far more shocking than Couture's painting, in its intent if not its effect, it is appropriate now to return to the remainder of the text in order to search for decadent signs, and D'Annunzio's comments upon them. The time of the narrative, as customary in novels of the decadence, is the present; the action begins in November 1884, and continues — in the straight chronology of the English, French, and German versions — to the spring of 1886, when Sperelli defeats and humiliates the nervous Rutolo, his rival for the favor of Hippolyta Albonica, in the gentleman jockey's race, only, through carelessness, to be almost mortally wounded by Rutolo in the subsequent duel. (Sperelli never enjoys his prize, nor does Hippolyta receive the gift of the death's head, with clock and inscription, "Tibi, Hippolyta," which Sperelli means to give her. She dies of typhus, thus adding one more perverse thrill to the book: she gets the embrace not of Sperelli but of death — a theme that comes back in the macabre drawings by Francis Redgrave, in the erotically obsessed Heathfield's possession.) Book 2, at Schifanoja, takes place in the late summer and beautiful autumn of 1886, "a Saint Martin's summer, a summer of the dead"; Book 3, Sperelli's return to his beloved Rome, goes late into the same autumn, and continues into the winter of 1886–87 (with the wonderful description of a snow-covered Rome and Sperelli's vain wait in his carriage for what he thinks will be a tryst with Elena, before the Palazzo Barberini. Or will it be Donna Maria? "Incedit per lilia et super nivem," "she enters through the lilies and over the snow," he thinks, with psalmic echoes, in his last outburst of idealization of the pure beloved.) Book 4 then moves into the spring of 1887 (with the peripatetic and carefully plotted carnal seduction of Donna Maria) and ends at "ten o'clock on the morning of the June 20th," with the auction of the effects of the disgraced husband of Maria, "His Excellency, the Minister Plenipotentiary for Guatamala."

Some contemporary Italian readers of *Il piacere*—which, understandably, was a succès de scandale—took umbrage not only at the book's numerous passionate scenes and quasi-obscene passages, but at a small and seemingly unimportant section which alluded to a current event. The date is "the second of February 1887," in this book of swelling verbal arias and precise details (the precise details also to be found in *À rebours* and, to an extent, in *Dorian Gray*). Maria Ferres and Sperelli attend a chamber music concert, its numbers lovingly described, as is the concert hall itself, the Palazzo dei Sabini, filled with "golden light" and with "the faded look of age," lending "a curious additional flavor to the exquisite enjoyment of the audience." On this date, too, "the Parliament was disputing over the massacre at Dogali; the neighboring streets and squares swarmed with the populace and with soldiers." The reference to the uproar comes as a brutal intrusion into the delicate musical world. Maria Ferres leaves the concert early; in her, "the pure Siennese madonna," Sperelli has, for the first time, beheld "the elegant woman of the world," one of the steps toward his identification of her with Elena Muti and his seduction of her. During the latter part of the concert, then, Sperelli forgets "his sentimental and passionate preoccupation" with Maria and comes—with "corrupt senses"—to the thought of leading her into a vulgar adulterous affair. Still, he arrives at his extraordinary plan of resolving "the two women into one," thus possessing "a third, imaginary, mistress, more complex, more perfect, more true because she would be ideal." (Sperelli's idealization of his own base scheme is indicative of his ability to lie, most of all to himself.) The trigger of his perverse notion is the resemblance between the two real women's voices, which Sperelli had noted long ago in the carriage on the way back to Schifanoja after he had first met Donna Maria: "That voice! how curiously like Elena's were some tones in Donna Maria's voice!" At this point "the mad thought" of mingling the two women flashes through Sperelli's brain, the mingling that will lead, we know, to the physical seduction of poor Maria, and Andrea's inadvertent and catastrophic mention of Elena's name during the "first full night" he and Maria will spend together.

The pendant to the concert scene is again worth attention: Elena is also present at the concert and, at its end, made perhaps a little jealous by having seen Sperelli with his *incognita,* engages—once they are in her carriage—in a typical gesture of the femme fatale; we remember its use in an English painting of the nineteenth century, John William Waterhouse's *La Belle Dame sans Merci,* in which the seductress twines her tresses around the knight's neck, and in Shaw's *Man and Superman,* where Ann Whitefield, laughing, throws her boa around John Tanner's neck, calling herself a boa constrictor. Elena takes her boa, and casts it over Andrea "like a lasso," draws him to her, and kisses him, in a repetition of the scene on the bed, two years before in the Palazzo Barberini. (Carriages are places of love in the nineteenth-century novel; on the window of his carriage, Sperelli has inscribed: "Pro amore curriculum, pro amore cubiculum," "The vehicle for love, the cubicle for love.") Now, the carriage has passed through the throngs mentioned before, near the chapter's opening: "Horror at the tragedy enacted in a far-off land made the populace howl with rage . . . Through all the clamor, the one word *Africa* rang distinctly." News had just been received in Rome of the massacre of an Italian column near Dogali in Eritrea by an Ethiopian force of twenty thousand men, on January 26. At this juncture, Sperelli makes the remark which so enraged patriotic readers against Sperelli's creator: "'And all this for four hundred brutes who had died the death of brutes,' murmured Andrea, withdrawing his head from the carriage window." Once again, Sperelli had betrayed the indifference to the fate of the common man shown elsewhere in the novel. The "sensibility of his nerves" is offended by the uproar about Dogali, as it is by the lewd songs of the workmen which he hears twice in the novel (on his way to a tryst with Elena, and at the end, in the empty apartment of the Ferres family), and even by the sight of a wretched peasant woman and her sick child during the excursion to the Campagna.

Readers outraged by Sperelli's murmur, who transferred their rage to D'Annunzio, did not realize, we suppose, that the remark was a part of D'Annunzio's effort to make a critical, indeed an unfriendly, portrait of the nobleman. Early on, the audience is told a good many unpleasant things about Sperelli. He has had his mind corrupted, "not only [by] overrefined culture, but also by actual experiments, and in him curiosity grew keener in proportion as his knowledge grew wider." The "expansion of that energy caused in him the destruction of another force, the moral one . . . he never perceived that his whole life was a steady retrogression of all his faculties." His father's upbringing of him had taught him "to love everything pertaining to art," but the same father had "not scrupled to repress the moral force in him," and had given him that cynical motto by which (the decadent creed of selfishness in still another formula) he turned the human beings around him into his marionettes, his creatures. "*Habere non haberi* is the rule from which the man of intellect should never swerve," to which are subjoined some other rules of selfish decadent conduct: "Regret is the idle pastime of an unoccupied mind," and "To avoid regret, the best method is to keep the mind continually occupied with new fancies, new sensations." Andrea Sperelli's "willpower was extremely feeble"; he turned into a sophist, he delighted in obscuring the truth, he grew insincere: "Insincerity — rather toward himself than toward others — became such a habit of Andrea's mind that finally he was incapable of being wholly sincere or of regaining dominion over himself."

However, those who objected to Sperelli's social indifference, his viciousness, and to the remark about Dogali, as if D'Annunzio were the spokesman of such attitudes, cannot be criticized for their misapprehension. After all, it is the narrator and not Sperelli who makes the observation about the "gray deluge of democratic mud." A major problem with the book is D'Annunzio's ambivalent attitude toward his protagonist, who is, to an extent, his alter ego. At the same time as D'Annunzio tells us about Sperelli's "falseness" and "moral ruin," he obviously relishes and, as it were, participates in Sperelli's many other qualities. The sentence about the gray democratic mud continues: it is "gradually engulfing that particular class of the old Italian nobility in which from generation to generation were kept alive certain family traditions of eminent culture, refinement, and art," and it is to such a family that Sperelli belongs. "He was, in truth, the ideal type of the young Italian nobleman of the nineteenth century, a true representative of a race of chivalrous gentlemen and graceful artists, the last scion of an intellectual line." The mixed message D'Annunzio sends in Part 1, chapter 2 of the English text will lead the observer of the decadent's role in literature back to a problem confronted in À rebours and The Picture of Dorian Gray. Huysmans admires Des Esseintes's detestation of the vulgar and "synthetic" nineteenth century, but, in the dentist episode and the story of the peptone enemas, he seems to be making fun of his literary character, condemning his exaggerated refinement; Wilde plainly has a condemnatory message about Dorian's vanity and pride, but the portrayal of Dorian's aesthetic existence is drawn, by and large, with great care and affection, even though Dorian, at the end, dies horribly. The ambivalence may again rise from Wilde's own admiration and envy of a would-be participation in the golden life of the ever youthful Dorian. (Both Wilde and D'Annunzio were envious outsiders in the noble world they admired, and to membership in which they pretended. Wilde had his fantasies of a descent from the "kings of Ireland," but nonetheless was the Dublin Irishman of somewhat tainted origin who, from Oxford on, like to hobnob with — and entertain and snipe at — a social stratum to which he did not really belong, and which, as has often been argued, made him a scapegoat, a scandal, and a hissing. D'Annunzio had come to Rome from the backwoods Abruzzi; his father — whose patent of nobility was shabby indeed — had specialized in small town Don Juan-ism and financial peccadilloes.)

A number of aspects of Sperelli will remind us of traits of Des Esseintes (and, to a smaller extent, of Dorian). D'Annunzio wrote his translator, Hérelle, on November 14, 1892, that *"Il piacere* is a very curious book, wholly impregnated with art, that perhaps has some relationship to *À rebours.*" Sperelli is at the end of a long line; Sperelli has his specially designed lair in the Casa Zuccari (it contains, by the way, an octagonal room, like that in Dorian Gray's town home); Sperelli is an avid collector of objets d'art, for which purpose he has unlimited funds; Sperelli has the faithful servants also vouchsafed Des Esseinted (although Terenzio is more sympathetic than the Frenchman's silent couple); Sperelli is interested in all the arts (like Des Esseintes and, in the patched-together eleventh chapter, Dorian Gray); Sperelli — as we have seen — is a hypersensible being, of great aesthetic (but not moral) refinement, filled with contempt for the masses, a seeker after ever more unusual thrills, and an experimenter with them. Further, like Des Esseintes before his removal to Fontenay-aux-Roses, Sperelli is the center of a circle of dandies; it could be imagined that the conversation at the black banquet, had Huysmans taken the trouble to compose it, would have resembled that at the Restaurant Doney. (Wilde's banquets are much primmer, but the conversation considerably wittier.)

However, Sperelli has some features which set him off, apparently, from his literary brothers in decadence. In a banal phrase: he is simply more believable than Des Esseintes and Dorian. The French decadent becomes almost unreal in the extravagance with which he sets up his thébaïde; Dorian has entered, somehow, into a pact with supernatural powers. But Sperelli could have existed, and no doubt — in one form or another — did. His interest in collecting, his amatory adventures, his dandyism do not cross the boundaries of the possible. He is not biologically degenerate, as Des Esseintes is; he is a fine swordsman, a fine horseman, a rider to hounds in the Anglophile Roman society of which he is a member. (We never see Des Esseintes taking any sort of exercise; when Dorian Gray goes riding, it is only to get from one part of his estate to another.) Sperelli has a creative ability not granted either Des Esseintes or Dorian Gray, and he is patently heterosexual, as Des Esseintes and Dorian patently are not.

On these last two points, a few comments of hesitation might be made, which again would point in the direction of Sperelli's full membership — and *Il piacere*'s — in what Hans Hinterhäuser has called the canon of decadence: *À rebours, Dorian Gray,* and the *Sonatas* of Ramón del Valle-Inclán are the other books in Hinterhäuser's exclusive club. We are richly informed on what Sperelli has written, the tragedy *La Simona,* "which possessed a singular charm," the verse play *Il re di Cipro,* the *Favola d'Ermafrodito* which contained "lines of extraordinary delicacy, power, and melody"; he knows his own poem by heart and quotes from it to himself. At their first meeting, Elena Muti tells him she has read it ("exquisite"), and after he gives it to Donna Maria, she says, with that solemnity displayed by all his characters: " 'No music has ever moved me like this poem' " — she has received, as her diary reports, the twenty-first of the twenty-five extant copies. Sperelli also can write rapidly, although he appears to have labored long over the "rare epithets" of *The Fable of the Hermaphrodite,* with "the luminous metaphors, the exquisite harmonies, the subtle refinements which distinguished his metrical style": he is ready to compose a madrigal for Donna Maria at the drop of a hat or a braid, and in the Schifanoja episode he simply pours out the four sonnets that he immediately inscribes (no blank surface seems safe from him) on the pedestal of a herm at the estate. Similarly, he is a gifted etcher, and we are told at some length about the engraving made of Elena Muti lying under the "wondrous counterpane" bearing the signs of the zodiac — an engraving reproduced in reality by the Italian artist Aristide Sartorio, in which we see both Elena and the wolfhound Famulus. (Sartorio showed Elena on top of the spread, but in a directly preceding passage — of course omitted by Miss Harding — D'Annunzio had described "la nuditá" of Sperelli's mistress. "Sometimes, while Andrea was in the other room, she got undressed with mad haste, . . . and called the beloved. And when he hastened in, she offered him a veritable picture of a goddess, tucked into a section of the firmament.") Nonetheless, this dwelling on Sperelli's marvelous creative powers may also be D'Annunzio's own self-advertisement, his contribution to his own public image: his readership was certainly intended to confuse him with his hero. (Contemporaneously, in Norwegian letters, Knut Hamsun would do much the same thing.) But, in his anomalous creativity, anomalous in the usually sterile figure of the decadent, Sperelli is also the typical decadent quoter of the works of others: Petrarch, Shakespeare, Goethe, Shelley. Just so the passionate engraver Sperelli is likewise a passionate collector; in fact, his collector's zeal is far stronger than his engraver's hand, about which we hear little once the fact has been established that Sperelli (and his maker) are men of many talents. In Sperelli, D'Annunzio has his cake and eats it too: he augments his own literary persona and keeps to the decadent formula.

The same might be said of the sexual orientation of Sperelli: he again seems anomalous by reason of the heterosexual direction of his active libido (he is surely not in the same condition as Des Esseintes). But D'Annunzio cannot resist sprinkling almost obligatory hints that Sperelli may have at least a trace of another kind of sexual interest. He is fascinated by the figure of the hermaphrodite, "that gentle monster with his ambiguous form"; Dorian Gray's fascination with Gautier's "Contralto" is another instance of this decadent concern. And, oddly enough, Sperelli sees in Donna Maria, of all people, a trait that seems, at least in passing, to remove her from the realm of the unimpeachably feminine. Describing her, D'Annunzio (or Sperelli) turns away from that great mass of hair which (like the *chevelure* of Fru Elvstad in *Hedda Gabler*) had attracted the attention and aroused the envy of her schoolmates; instead, he tells about what is on her forehead: "The shorter locks in front were thick and wavy as those that cover the head of the Farnese Antinous" — the signaling name of Hadrian's male lover. (D'Annunzio's mistress, Barbara Leoni, was informed in his love letters that he kept a large and inspiratory bust of Antinous in his study.) Furthermore, in the same section, Donna Maria's voice, like that imagined one of the statue in Gautier's "Contralto," is "ambiguous, with double chords in it, so to speak. The more virile tones, deep and slightly veiled, became feminine, as it were, by a harmonious transition." Remarkably, "it was the feminine note in the voice that recalled the other," that is, Elena Muti. We are never left in the dark about the complete femininity of *that* goddess in human form; when Sperelli first sees her, she demonstrates the undulating gait of Venus.

Finally, placed between Donna María (whose small doses of boyishness or maleness may remind us of those to be found in Sibyl Vane) and Elena Muti, Sperelli is a decadent in a sense shared, importantly, with Des Esseintes and Dorian: he wants salvation — not a religious salvation, as in Des Esseintes's case, or a moral one, as in Dorian's, but a human one. Like Dorian (who toys with the idea of a choice between a pale heterosexuality and an alluring homosexuality), Sperelli thinks, for a while, of choosing between a femme fatale (from whose erotic charms he never really wins free) and a sweet savior woman, Donna Maria. Weakening, though, he drags the latter down into the carnality from which he has sought, not very effectively, to escape.

Elena Muti continues to tempt Sperelli, even after she has passed along to another lover, Galeazzo Secinaro, Barbadoro, Golden Beard — impressed probably by the stories of Galeazzo's exploits in India. She has wept, to be sure, when she first denied herself to Sperelli during their reunion ("Addio! Addio! and when the carriage turned away she threw herself back exhausted and burst into a passion of slowly tearing the roses to pieces with her poor frenzied hands"). Yet she gets over her fit of noble renunciation quickly; before long, she lures Sperelli into her carriage, and he cannot forget "the flash of the smile with which she had thrown that sort of smooth and perfumed snake around his neck." That Sperelli associates her with snakes, the typical animal-familiar of the femme fatale, is indicated in a small verbal detail as well: the word following *Helena* in the inscription of the Belvedere at the Villa Medici is *Amyclaea,* from Amyclæ, the Latian town infested (according to Vergil) by serpents. And Amyclæa is also a sobriquet of Venus/Aphrodite. Further, that Elena plays a Venus role is shown by her strong interest in the rock-crystal vase which once belonged to Niccola Niccoli, the humanist, with the representation of the young Trojan Anchises untying the sandal of the goddess. Later the vase passes — like Elena herself — into the hands of Sir Humphrey Heathfield, and Sperelli spies it in their apartment. Does Sperelli, the Roman nobleman par excellence and devoted lover of the city, somehow see himself as an Anchises — who fathered, with Venus, Aeneas, the founder of the city of Rome?

In an altogether obvious nomenclature, Elena bears the name of the Trojan temptress, Helen, while her opponent, Maria, has the name of the supreme woman savior. Hans Hinterhäuser has classified a character in the *Sonatas* as being revirginized (rather like the Virgin Mary): although a mother, of the omnipresent Delfina to whom she is so devoted, Donna Maria Ferres is made to seem sexually unawakened. (A subsidiary remark: we shudder to think of her in the embrace of the loathsome Ferres, to whom — there is a trace of Arthur de Gobineau's thought about the degeneration of races through mixing here — D'Annunzio attributes "something disagreeably brutal and morose, that indefinable air of viciousness which belongs to the later generations of bastard races.") Tributes are made to her piety; she is given the air of the maiden in the tower — we think of "Rapunzel, Rapunzel, let down your hair" and Mélisande in Maeterlinck's drama and Debussy's opera — as, in Part 2, chapter 2, Andrea cries to her: " 'Let down a rope of your hair to me that I may climb up,' her wet hair, that clung to her like a huge mantle." Sperelli, who used liturgical phraseology to point up the depravity of Clara Green, also uses biblical texts in the case of Donna Maria. Following the suggestion of his cousin Francesca, he thinks of her as a *turris eburnea* (from the Song of Songs), or the inhabitant of such an ivory tower — a being "enclosed within the magical circle of her purity as in a tower of ivory forever incorruptible and inaccessible"; later, in his "moral degradation," "abiezion morale," Sperelli takes as a motto a verse from Psalm 51 to serve as a tool of seduction: "Purge me with hyssop and I shall be clean, wash me and I shall be whiter than the snow." This cleansing was, in fact, what Sperelli had hoped for in the days of more or less pure love at Schifanoja; now it is used to persuade Donna Maria to surrender to him.

For all her religious training, Donna Maria is a particularly pathetic and vulnerable victim of Sperelli's strategy, his carrying on "the two campaigns, the conquest of the new and the reconquest of the old love." She has revealed her great emotional sensitivity in the scene at Schifanoja during which she sings Paisiello: the force of the song overwhelms Sperelli, rendering him speechless for once. Music, the most spiritual of the arts, Donna Maria's art, almost captures and changes Sperelli; in the music she performs, though, there is also the thought of death. After singing for the company at Schifanoja, she plays eighteenth-century music, "so melancholy in its dance airs, that sound as if they were intended to be danced to in a languid afternoon of Saint Martin's summer, in a deserted park, amid silent fountains and statueless pedestals, on a carpet of dead roses by pairs of lovers on the point of ceasing to love one another." It is particularly a gavotte of Rameau, which Donna Maria has dubbed the Gavotte of the Yellow Ladies, that enchants Sperelli, as he sits in his chambers at the estate, and which he himself tries to play — a melancholy tune that has the hint of the death of their love in it. (Maria plays it again for him in Rome, before she leaves one of her gloves on the piano for him — an uncharacteristic flirtatiousness which shows the road she is taking under his tutelage.) The delicacy of the gavotte is matched, maybe, by the delicacy of the verses of Shelley, Sperelli's gift in return for the eighteenth-century music to which he is introduced by her; Donna Maria becomes so enchanted with Shelley that she calls him "our poet," and when she and Sperelli go, at her request, to Rome's English Cemetery, and to the graves of Shelley and Trelawny, she is so moved that she cries, " 'I shall die.' " (To this, the moralizing narrator adds: "But she did not die. Better a thousand times for her that she had.")

The fragile Donna Maria, the musician, the lover of Shelley, is shattered forever, through her misuse by the corrupt Sperelli (who may realize at the end what he has done); yet it can be proposed that her art, music, rules the book in a way not immediately apparent. *Il piacere* has a symphonic form, in four movements: the first part is the Allegro, in which the themes of Sperelli and Elena are introduced, the second, at Schifanoja, is the slow movement, full of deep and serious emotion, Part 3, with the jokes of the friends and the return of Sperelli "with a bound" to Pleasure, is the Scherzo, and the fourth part is the finale, allegro again, in which the main themes, of Sperelli, Elena, and Donna Maria are intertwined, all of them present at the end of the action — which is also a return, in its hopeless way, to the beginning. Talk of auctions opened the book; a sad auction closes it. This musical structure binds the novel together; we cannot quite define D'Annunzio's attitude toward his own hero, but we can define his careful construction of the work, a care improved upon by the translator Hérelle — he is, despite the verbiage, as careful a craftsman as those artists and artisans whose works Sperelli admired.

There is, as well, another linking element in the novel, the narrator's and Sperelli's devotion to Rome, the splendid background of Sperelli's decline and fall. It has been argued that Rome is a neutral or backdrop observer of the events of the book, like the impassive Buddha Sperelli buys at the final auction. Yet it could be countered that Rome in truth has a negative role to play;

only at Schifanoja, with its holy groves, its *temenoi,* does Sperelli think seriously of a new life, influenced by Donna Maria. Back in Rome, he returns to
Pleasure, and she becomes Pleasure's victim too — although she implores Sperelli, like a mother, "to be good." Rome was a popular setting for novels of the
day, for example, Bourget's *Cosmopolis* (1893), Zola's *Rome* (1896), Louis
Couperus's *Langs lijnen van geleidelijkheid* (1900), James's *Golden Bowl*
(1904); in *Il piacere,* despite the aesthetic glory with which it is surrounded,
Rome may have the role of the more obviously dangerous cities of the literature of decadence, Georges Rodenbach's *Bruges-la-Morte,* D'Annunzio's and
Thomas Mann's death-bringing Venice.

4

Sweden

AUGUST STRINDBERG

August Strindberg's *I havsbandet* (1890) became accessible to an English-reading public two decades after its publication. In the wake of Strindberg's death (1912) several of his autobiographical novels, his debut novel, *Röda rummet* (1879, *The Red Room*), the immensely popular *Hemsöborna* (1887, *The People of Hemsö*), and his stories came out more or less simultaneously, and at the same time two translations of the text here in question, one by the quasi-official translator, Ellie Schleusner, called *By the Open Sea*, in London and New York, and the other, *On the Seaboard*, by Elizabeth Clark Westergren, in Cincinnati. The Schleusner version omits a major passage from the last chapter, while Westergren retains it. Her translation, reprinted in 1974, is preferable to the Schleusner version, although less well known: its relative obscurity is witnessed to by the fact that neither a once standard English biography, by Mortensen and Downs (1949, 1965), nor the monograph of Eric O. Johannesson, *The Novels of August Strindberg* (1968), mentions it; rather they adduce only Schleusner. Fortunately, a new and mostly satisfactory translation, by Mary Sandbach, called by the Schleusner version of the title (London, 1984, and Athens, Georgia, 1985) has become the standard in English. Strindberg's novels have remained, in English, in the shadow of the main works of his dramatic production; while *The Red Room* came out in a new translation in 1967, others, its semisequel *Götiska rummen* (1904,

Gothic Rooms), and *Svarta fanor* (1907, Black Banners) remain untranslated, as does the short novel *Tschandala* (1889 in Danish, 1897 in Swedish), which in its theme, the intellectual man in a struggle with lower beings, is a predecessor of *I havsbandet:* Andreas Törner, a professor from the new Swedish university at Lund, fights against the crafty Jensen, terrifies him with a magic-lantern show, and has him eaten by his own dogs. The Sanskrit word *tschandala* means an impure being, a member of the lowest caste; Nietzsche uses it in *Götzen-Dämmerung* — "the Tshandala are the fruit of adultery, incest, and crime."

First planned in 1888, *I havsbandet* was conceived, and encouraged by Strindberg's publisher, Bonnier, as a repetition of the best-seller about life in the Stockholm skerries, the broadly comical *Hemsöborna,* and its pendant, *Skärkarlsliv* (Skerry Life), the best-known story in which is *Den romantiske klockaren på Rånö* (The Romantic Parish Clerk on Rånö), about the isolation and dreams of a failed organist in the skerries. In his introduction to this second skerry book, Strindberg wrote that having shown the bright side of skerry life in the former, its "half-shadows" in the latter, he would perhaps in future complete the picture with "the shadows" themselves. (In this formulation, he ignores the conclusion of *Hemsöborna:* the clever outsider Carlsson, never good at sea, disappears and is presumed drowned during an effort to bring the corpse of his wife — the elderly widow he has married for her money and property — to the church island for burial; he is unlamented by her son and the other fishermen.) *Hemsöborna* and *Skärkarlsliv* are exclusively Swedish in their allusions; *I havsbandet,* taking place in the same insular world, has a much broader perspective. Axel Borg is a product and representative of European culture in the fin de siècle. It has long been recognized that Strindberg got some of his inspiration from Victor Hugo's *Les Travailleurs de la mer* (1866): the enlightened fisherman Gilliatt, owner of the modern steam trawler *Durande,* sees it sabotaged by his conservative fellows; after a disappointment in love, he drowns himself — "his head vanished beneath the water. There was nothing left but the sea." But too little attention has been paid, in the extensive literature on *I havsbandet,* to the fact that Strindberg discovered Huysmans while the novel was gestating. (As early as 1898, Oskar Levertin, ever perceptive, detected resemblances between Huysmans's development and Strindberg's.)

On February 19, 1889, Strindberg wrote to Ola Hansson — who introduced so many names from recent French letters to the Swedish public — with remarkable enthusiasm: "Yes, that Huysman[s]! Was ist das! Is it the final desperate effort to make belles-lettres, or is it something new . . . Huysman[s] approaches the newspaper, the critique, the review . . . Or is it Alexander's grief that no new worlds are left to conquer, now that Zola and Poe took the last ones?" Further: "Huysman[s] is not degenerated! He is overtaxed by [reading] newspapers every day, by the chance to get over and get past Zola, by [his] unmarried condition, by women! perhaps." Then Strindberg added a postscript: "Do you have another Huysman[s]?" Evidently, Strindberg had borrowed a copy of *À rebours* from Hansson; the two were living not far apart in Denmark at the time. The initial echo of Huysmans comes in the second chapter of *I havsbandet:* Borg furnishes his bare gable-room at the home of the coastguard Vestman, whose brother, a customs officer, has brought Borg to Österskär, where it is his assignment to teach the local inhabitants rational methods of fishing. (The cottage is the official residence of the customs officer, who, however, does not live there; but, as Borg immediately notices, he is conducting an affair with the complacent Vestman's wife.) On the first night of his stay, Borg is irritated by the emptiness of his room, whose "naked walls were those of a cell in a medieval cloister," a resemblance which does not impel him, in his imagination, to fit it out with the ecclesiastical and medievalizing trappings of the study in Des Esseintes's thébaïde at Fontenay-aux-Roses. Nonetheless, Borg is an aesthete, as Sven Delblance wrote about him in 1979: he feels a desire "to paint the walls full of sunny landscapes of palms and parrots, to spread a Persian rug across the ceiling, to lay the skins of animals on the floorboards, lined like a ledger, . . . to lift a ceiling lamp over his writing table . . . to put a pianino against one short wall, to fill the long wall with bookcases," and on one of his imaginary sofas, "to put a little woman's figure, no matter whose!" The female figure will shortly acquire features and will have dire consequences for Borg. After his vision vanishes, Borg puts out the light, jumps into bed, and like a frightened child pulls the covers over his head. Before his stay on Österskär is out, Borg will be reduced to his second childhood.

After a walk beside the undemanding sea the next morning, "an open, large, blue, faithful eye," Borg returns to his chamber, and makes "a room within the room," hanging his bedclothes from a nail in the ceiling, thus cutting off his sleeping quarters from his "study" which he outfits in a demonstration of his membership among Des Esseintes's progeny. Miniaturizing Des Esseintes's effort to violate the laws of nature, he sets up a large lamp whose porcelain base is chiseled with imaginary animals and flowers, "showing the power of the human spirit to violate nature's fixed, monotonous forms," a key phrase in the Huysmanian connection. Borg is a scientist, a man of reason with an overriding belief in reason's powers, and the emphasis of the furnishings shifts from the cozily aesthetic (the specially carved inkwell, the vermilion sealing wax, the vignettes on the pencil box, and so forth, objects for "use and beauty") to the scientist's tools. He places his microscope and diopter on the table (to be sure, their varnish and brass shed a warm golden glow about them); his library, described at great length, does not, unlike Des Esseintes's, contain Du Cange's great medieval Latin dictionary or the poems of Baudelaire. Borg has no antiquarian or modern literary interests. Instead, he unpacks an entire reference library, encyclopedias, handbooks, even Baedeker's guides, bibliographies, publishers' catalogues, periodicals, serials, all bound in various colors, some, "like the *Encyclopaedia Britannica,* solemn and black-clad in a whole procession" and the *Revue des Deux Mondes* in salmon pink. Borg has, he believes, all the world's knowledge at his fingertips. Scholarship has noted, several times, the Faustian urge of Borg; the library reflects Strindberg's own strong scientific interests, which caused him, at work on *I havsbandet,* to pester Bonnier for germane references and made him consider casting literary creation overboard for the sake of the many scientific pursuits that absorbed him.

The knowledge of Borg has saved his life, as well as that of the customs officer and his crew who sail out to the island in the first chapter. It was the time of Strindberg's greatest enthusiasm for the Nietzschean concept of the Übermensch, and the newly appointed inspector of fisheries, who has never sailed before, gives instructions, based on his instant observations of wind direction and atmospheric pressure, enabling the people in the cutter, hit by a squall, to reach Österskär safely — but not without an almost fatal miscalculation on Borg's part: he is never as wholly in control as he thinks. The customs officer is astonished but also filled with contempt as he sees the "little bundle lying in the stern"; his brain-battery run down by his intellectual effort, Borg has collapsed: his fits of exhaustion occur repeatedly throughout the novel.

At the very start of the voyage, the customs officer has no reason to trust the inspector's competence for his new position. A little man, Borg is dressed in a wholly unsuitable and dandyistic get-up — a beaver-colored spring coat, broad moss-green trousers, a cream-colored foulard around his neck, boots of crocodile skin with rows of black buttons on their shafts of brown cloth, and salmon-colored kid gloves, which he does not want to damage, but they split all the same when he takes the tiller. The costume demonstrates both Borg's unawareness of the world he enters, and a desire to challenge that primitive and hostile society. Something effeminate attaches to him: he speaks in a voice "more resembling a woman's than a man's." Most striking about his garb is a bangle on his right wrist, a serpent biting its tail, which he will twice use for quasi-magical purposes, his uroboros. (Strindberg does not use the term, but scholarship has identified it as a symbol of an "eternal return.") He sports a thin little black mustache, and "black bangs evenly cut." These three features, the bangle, tiny mustache, and haircut, may have been suggested by a photograph of the young Herman Bang.

A commonplace of the literature on *I havsbandet* is that the love-and-hate intrigue of the novel is one more specimen of Strindberg's persistent concern with the relationship between men and women, and the impossibility of its happy resolution. Borg is not the only outsider on Österskär; shortly, the "girl" Maria and her mother, the widow of a minor Stockholm functionary, arrive to spend their summer vacation. Borg is immediately attracted to Maria, however much he is put off, early in their acquaintanceship, by her suggestion that they go swimming in the nude together, and her jeering laughter when he excuses himself by saying that he has no swimming clothes and does not like to swim in cold water. As she takes off her boots, he goes to another part of the little island, Svärdsholm, to which they have rowed; inventive as always, he prepares an outdoor steam bath for himself, reclines in one of the "easy chairs" of stone sculptured by the sea, and dozing, rests his mind, before pondering the stages (the scientist Borg likes to analyze developmental periods) through which Maria has passed and concluding that she "must have been bankrupted by some amorous affair." Observant as he is, Borg, thinking she is a young girl, has still misjudged Maria's age, until it turns out that she is thirty-four, only two years younger than Borg. Further, he does not notice the pictures Strindberg — or the owner, the fisher Öman — has hung in the cottage the newcomers have rented: a lithograph portraying Samson and Delilah in shameless detail, and Joseph with Potiphar's wife. (A picture of Samson and Delilah hangs on the wall in the inn where Jude Fawley and Arabella Donn take tea on their first afternoon together.) Yet in time he grows more anxious. During a reconciliation ending one of the several crises in their relationship, which has arisen when Maria, her advances again repulsed, asks: " 'Are you a man?' " with her jeering laugh, Borg puts his head in her lap but warns her not to cut his hair as he falls asleep. In good time, Borg grows still more observant; seeing her peel a chestnut with her long fingers and sharp teeth, he thinks of a mandrill. Yet this thought is mixed with compassion: he means to try to lift her from her "lower intelligence" to a state closer to his. Further, she has a prognathous jaw "all too unnecessarily developed" for someone who has stopped needing to "seize, grip, and tear apart uncooked meat." In the retrospective introduction to *Le Plaidoyer d'un fou* (1887, *The Confession of a Fool,* 1913, *A Madman's Manifesto,* 1971), Strindberg's lightly disguised account, composed in French, of his affair with and disastrous marriage to his first wife, Siri von Essen, he tells how he noticed warning signs, his thoughts of Samson, and Siri's resemblance to a she-panther. The Strindberg figure is named Axel, like Borg, and Siri is named Maria.

At the same time, Borg slowly and diffidently desires Maria, just as "Axel" in *Le Plaidoyer* describes and resists the charms of "the Baroness": watching Maria and her mother unpack, Borg sees her "supple undulations" as she bends over. Directly, putting her sexual power to work, Maria weakens his authority before the islanders — who at any rate despise him as he despises them. He confiscates their nets, as a part of his program to reform their ruinous and unscientific fishing practices; the island women take them back, and the sheriff is called, but Maria persuades Borg to drop charges. The islanders admire her for her persuasion, and Borg loses face; "he had succumbed to his own impulses, or the interest in winning something from this woman." The weakening of Borg continues: she persuades him to be playful, to dance and sing "like a Hottentot"; to impress her, he undertakes the apparently impossible task of remaking nature, of creating an artificial world out of nature's parts. After the bathing scene, boasting to Maria about his close knowledge of nature, he accepts her challenge to make "an Italian landscape with marble villas and pines out of this horrible paysage of gray stone," and will do so on her birthday, three weeks away. With exceptional effort, the little man imitates a Böcklin painting, with "a pine, a cypress, a marble palace, and a terrace with trellised oranges"; he does so on Svärdsholm which, when he first visited it, had seemed to him to be "a conglomeration of landscapes, collected from all [climatic] zones," and, in its midst, "a park, a bit of inland nature transported out here." Knowing that the hot summer air will refract against the cold water's surface, he intends to produce a mirage. The paradise of nature on the little island, where he first meets Maria and her mother, will be turned into an artificial paradise of illusion (as is true of Des Esseintes, Ludwig II, Mendès's King Frédéric in *Le Roi vierge,* Verne's Captain Nemo). He feels disgust at his abuse of nature (Hans Christian Andersen's tale of the terrible punishment of the girl who tramped on bread occurs to him), but he consoles himself with a thought that could have been borrowed from Des Esseintes: "If nature had not set to work so hastily creating the [various] species, it was not from lack of will but only from lack of ability." Nature's originality failed, Borg's succeeds, but the result is not what he had intended. Viewed from Österskär, the intended Italianate scene on Svärdsholm seems illuminated by "a colossal moon, corpse white, rising over a churchyard with black cypresses" — a terrifying rival to the actual moon, which hangs "palely" in the summer morning sky. The superstitious skerry people gain new respect for him, even regarding him as a magician, and Maria, who has treated him more and more condescendingly (having borrowed knowledge from him, as Maria does from Axel in *Le Plaidoyer*), falls down and worships him, in a scene that calls Christ, the worker of miracles, to the onlookers' minds. Simultaneously, a lay preacher appears, one of Strindberg's numerous and not altogether skillful coincidences, summoned to the island from the mission board at the request of the vacationing ladies, following Borg's suggestion, who wishes to bring some order into the islanders' disorderly lives. Borg has been impressed by the discipline a Sunday service on board a gunboat in the island's harbor has brought to the crew. The preacher is likewise impressed by Borg's mirage, and reads from Revelations 6:12–17. "The moon became as blood . . . every mountain and island was moved out of its place . . . for the great day of his wrath has come, and who shall be able to stand?"

As in the case of Borg's dangerous instructions in the cutter and the distorted mirage, Borg's suggestion has backfired. The preacher becomes a rival and an enemy to Borg; again by happenstance, Borg has known and ruinously insulted the man in their schooldays. The preacher wins the favor of the fisherman, by turning the story of the five loaves and three fishes to his advantage, as Maria sails out to bring in the catch from a herring run, the location of which she has deduced from Borg's careful statistics and, again, his boasting about them. On this expedition, she is accompanied by Blom, an assistant the government has sent out to Borg. Already having behaved as a flirt, not only toward Borg but toward the "embarrassed sailor" who brought the ladies to the island, Maria is immediately captivated by Blom, younger, physically stronger, and less inhibited than Borg, and begins an affair with him, despite her informal engagement to Borg; he spies his assistant and his fiancée together on the beach, from one of those easy chairs on which he recharges his batteries after the strain of Maria's company — her "profile of a bird of prey" leans toward Blom's "big apelike head with its enormous cheeks," "its pointed, narrow skull without a forehead" and the body's "masses of superfluous flesh, whose vulgar lines and oversized hips are reminiscent of a woman resembling the Farnese Hercules." After Maria gives the islanders momentary prosperity by means of the drift-net fishing she has borrowed from Borg's plan, Borg breaks his engagement but undertakes an odd sort of revenge on her. The last line of Axel's *Plaidoyer* runs: "I have avenged myself, we are quits."

Borg employs his bangle twice. On the first occasion, before the appearance of the assistant Blom, Borg, tired from his exertions on Svärdsholm, has refused to join the ladies when they summon him; Maria has a fit of what he classifies as a "psychological ailment which went under the still vague name of hysteria." He cures her in his capacity as a magician by showing her his bangle and giving her the grotesque cure of a dose of asafetida, a popular and bad-tasting home remedy in Strindberg's day (Booth Tarkington's Penrod is terrified of it), followed by balsam from the mellow Carrageen alga (seaweed), to quiet her stomach, and then a symphony of taste (like Des Esseintes's): "the classical rue, . . . the heavenly angelica, the homely smelling spearmint," a touch of gardebenedict, and a drop of juniper oil, massaging her with moods and an imaginary tour of the world, topping the trip off with lemon juice and

sugar, a comical display of Huysmans's *epithètes rares,* and a first revenge in
which the childishness of Maria — "a child of thirty-four!" — is not forgotten.
Recovered, she holds him back (he is exhausted by the hocus-pocus and again
needs to recharge his batteries), but he feels an emotion "something like what
he imagined a young girl would feel under the influence of a seducer's attack."
Escaping at last to one of his easy chairs, he resolves to leave the island, but,
pursued by Maria, as she kneels before him as a suppliant, he persuades
himself that he is falling in love again. Yet the warning signs are present (as
repeatedly in *Le Plaidoyer*), the second Samson allusion (" 'Don't cut my hair
as I sleep on your breast' ") and the sight of an adulterous couple, the customs
official and his brother's wife. Borg puts the blame on the woman: " 'If I were
her husband, I should drown her.' " (Strindberg employs the brutal verb
sumpa, to stuff her in a container of water, like a caught fish.)

Borg's bangle comes into service again after Maria and Assistant Blom have
been applauded for a huge herring catch, the result of Borg's work. He sends
Maria a letter by his orderly (who, in one of Strindberg's lapses, is never
mentioned elsewhere in the text); lying, Borg tells her that he is not free to
marry because of an erotic entanglement from the past. The mother and Blom
leave Österskär; Maria stays behind. Invited to a ball on board a corvette
anchored off Österskär, the inspector — dressing to impress — puts on his doc-
toral tails, his six medals (he is, of course, a scientist of international standing),
and his bracelet, "which he had not worn since the day of his engagement,"
i.e., the day of Maria's hysteria and its radical cure, and in this regalia visits
Maria, to his eyes at first "more beautiful than he had seen her for a long time,"
then hard and ugly, his "adversary." Persuading himself that she is a believer in
free love (she is reading a gift from Blom, Erna Juel-Hansen's then sensational
En ung dames historie [1888; A Young Lady's Story]), Borg brings himself to
seduce her — Strindberg omits to say that she eyes the bangle, although she is
impressed by his assortment of decorations — in order to take his final revenge,
and to free himself at last from her sexual attraction. Breaking his promise to
visit her the next day (he does not take her to the ball), he feels liberated; he receives a letter from her, which tempts him without his having read it; he puts it
in the flame of his Bunsen burner, to be consumed with "the squeak of a bat."

Borg decides to spend the winter on the island, setting up his laboratory and
library in the cottage the ladies once occupied; he begins what he thinks will be
the execution of enormous plans, for example, a study of the present ethnogra-
phy of Europe, in this effort writing nearly a hundred letters on a single day — a
sign that his brain, in his isolation, is "running wild." He does not wish to
return to Stockholm to be persecuted, he thinks, for his ambition and talent, in
his dual capacity as "a nobleman and independent thinker." (His appointment

in the skerries had been a kind of banishment.) The nobility to which Borg belongs is quite fresh; his father had won the noble escutcheon because of *his* accomplishments as an engineer and topographer, who participated in the digging of the Göta Canal and the construction of Sweden's first railroads. Father and son are members of Zarathustra's "new nobility, the like of which the world has never seen," in *Die fröhliche Wissenschaft*.

The son has been given a careful and rational upbringing by his father, who fashions him into a replica of himself, ridding him of the "megalomania of Christianity," and supplanting it with the tenets of the intellectual aristocrat, holding lower beings (children, women) in contempt; the father has warned him in particular against the "basest of all impulses, the sexual." The boy has been conceived only so that the father's superiority will be preserved; conveniently dying early, the mother in Borg's curriculum vitae of Chapter 3 receives next to no attention. (Borg's father has an equivalent of sorts in the father and mentor of Andrea Sperelli, the artistically gifted libertine.) Borg's life, as it is told, is an attempt to follow this "example and teacher," in his excessive zeal for rational classifications as in his contempt for lower beings. The growing insanity of Borg has its root in his emulation of the overwhelming father, and is enhanced by his intentional isolation — from Maria, whom he has desired, feared, and despised, and from the people of the island, also feared and despised, like his colleagues on the mainland.

The painful story of Borg's terminal destruction is told in a rush in the last two chapters, its beginning marked by the observation of the corvette's doctor that Borg is a "sick man," after Borg has advanced another of his theories, about the waste of nitrogen in the atmosphere. Des Esseintes's physical breakdown, which leads to his grotesque theory and practice of nourishment by means of peptone enemas, takes place in his haughty isolation at Fontenay-aux-Roses, Borg's — far more radical — in the dangerous world of the hostile islanders. Mari (i.e., also Maria), the faithless wife of the fisherman Vestman, dies suddenly. In his capacity as a quondam government official, Borg is summoned to write a death certificate for Mari, whom, he discovers, Vestman has killed for her infidelity by driving a nail into her head. Seeing Mari together with Vestman's brother, the customs official, on the beach, Borg had remarked to Maria that the wife deserves death, not the brother: " 'He is not married, that is the difference'. " Vestman's daughter has probably not been fathered by him but by the brother and is thus the product of a kind of incest, a baser being, a Tschandala; she is deformed, "with too large a head and fish eyes."

The stages of the decay of Borg, alone in this hostile and brutal world, a "dangerous company," are described by Strindberg in rapid detail. He thinks he must heal his soul from "the gunshot wound" it received during his attachment to Maria (in belated defiance of his father's injunctions to chastity), and he curbs his sexual drive by taking potassium bromide and cutting down his diet. His sense of persecution grows, and his sense of a comforting nature — which he had celebrated in his description, for his oarsman Vestman, of the grandeur of the sea and the development of life from it in chapter 3 — dwindles. His brain running full tilt, he develops a plan to join Sweden, "this island country," to Europe: by means — an extension of his father's actual accomplishments — of express trains running southward to the Öresund and a steam ferry to Copenhagen (a plan in fact already being realized), he will restore the use of Latin in the Lutheran church and as the language of scientific discourse, thus a practical and modern replication of the antiquarian *latinitas* cultivated by Des Esseintes and Moore's John Norton. (In this diatribe, Strindberg takes a step toward the Catholicism with which he toyed in his later writing, the Catholic course taken by Huysmans.) Borg jots these thoughts down and stuffs them in a drawer, knowing that no newspaper would print them, and so they reach the reading public as the editorial of a madman in *I havsbandet.*

As a result of the instruction in salmon fishing he has given the fisherman Vestman, whom he regards as the brightest of the islanders, the salmon catch is restored for the island, and, much as Maria got credit for the herring, so Vestman enters mainland newspapers as the salmon-saver; Borg is slandered in the press for the purposelessness of his mission (he "knew nothing but believed he could teach everything"), the resignation from his post that follows makes him the defenseless object of surreptitious warfare by his neighbors, who damage the roof of his cottage and break into the cellar; his books and instruments are soaked. He ponders suicide, a thought which fills him with an irrational yearning for his mother. He is protected from the village children who stone him by the motherly servant of the fisherman Öman (a main opponent of Borg from the start, but now the man from whom he rents his cottage); he presses his head against her broad bosom and says: " 'I want to sleep with you' " — as her lover or her child? Borg undergoes a reduction to the child's estate he has despised; comforted by the lay preacher who visits him in his decay (and who brings the news that Maria has married Blom), he asks the preacher to tell him the story of Tom Thumb: in the arms of the customs official who carried him, exhausted, onto the island, he had looked like "Tom Thumb and the giant." Now he wants to hear the comforting tale of the tiny boy who outwits the giant — as he did, on the boat underway to Österskär. He asks the preacher to recite the Lord's Prayer, to the pastor's surprise, since he knows Borg is an unbeliever. Borg retorts that he believes in a "fixed point outside, which Archimedes wished for," but — the Nietzschean speaks through the suddenly coherent Borg—not in Jesus, " 'an invention of vengeful slaves and wicked women.' " Horrified, the preacher leaves, refusing to listen to Borg's plea to hold his hand; as he goes, he says that Borg fears death, to which Borg agrees, adding that, however, he does not fear judgment, since " 'the work judges the master,' . . . 'I have not created myself.' " The rejoinder may be taken as a reference to his own father, who created and shaped him.

After the identification of Mari's killer, culminating in Borg's charges against the "vulgar mass," to which the execution method of a nail in the cranium had come down from the nobility and priesthood of the middle ages — "everything comes from above" — Borg challenges Vestman to put him in the madhouse and thus save himself from prison. Borg's knowledge of Vestman's guilt haunts the temporary detective; he fears the very madness he has suggested; he fears that Vestman will murder him to silence him. He thinks once more of suicide, but wants — like his father — to see his family line continued, and so — outdoing his father, who took the "ordinary path" the woman-hater otherwise scorned, arguing that "[b]reeding should be left to the lower classes" — Borg decides to create progeny by scientific means. The passage, faintly echoing the creation of the homunculus by the famulus Wagner in Goethe's *Faust,* Part 2, is excised by Ellie Schleusner in her translation. He places his own sperm in a couveuse with the "motionless female" (Strindberg neglects to indicate the source of the eggs), the "quickest, most agile males, the fiercest men," penetrate "the membrane," and a fetus is produced, as Borg watches through his microscope. An inadvertent turn of the screw on the spirit lamp that warms the couveuse makes the albumen curdle, and the experiment ends. Borg's father has not been outdone. Having once more tried to create artificial nature, as when he made the Italianate scene, Borg bungles and fails. Nonetheless, Borg understands his failure; lamenting his lost child, he tells the preacher: " 'If you were a woman instead, I could live again, for woman is man's roots in the earth!' "

The descent of Borg into madness, at once creative and sterile, continues. The dramatist Strindberg makes effective use of offstage sound, as he already has, from chapter 9 on, by means of the sounding buoy, tethered off Österskär, "shrieking out on the sea, like a tragedian when he recites [his lines]." Borg identifies his lot with that of the "solitary being," chained to a rock for the good of others, as he has been since he began his attempts to bring reason into the island's fishing practices. During a terrible storm on the day before Christmas Eve, the buoy cries out endlessly, "as if it were calling for help." A steamer has wrecked offshore, and Borg thinks he hears cannon shots. (Do they come from the small cannon used to fire lifelines out to the stricken vessel? There is evidently a coastguard station on Österskär; Vestman is identified as a coastguardsman.) Borg also thinks he hears the cries of human beings, another sound effect not further explained. Cut off from human concerns outside himself, Borg is interested only in the jetsam from the wreck, dolls, "resembling little children, very brightly dressed," some of which — in his desire to have a child, and in his childishness — he tries to warm in his cottage. He has no kindling; he breaks up the last remnant of his sanctum, a bookcase, lines up the dolls on his sofa, leaving their vests on as he undresses them, and sleeps on the floor. He is found the next day by Öman's maid, the customs office confiscates the dolls, Borg's offspring and playthings. The kindly servant, seen before as a mother and mistress, invites "the dear little gentleman" to eat Christmas porridge at Öman's.

Strindberg was proud of his book and its finale; submitting the manuscript to Bonnier on June 7, 1890, he called it "the promised thunderer of a book, in a great new Renaissance style . . . The last chapter is grandiose, and is built on Homunculus, the Dolls, and Hercules-Jesus, which I won't sacrifice on any account." Seeing his face in a mirror, the "half-insane man" realizes that he looks "like a savage." His mind seems to clear; he steals a boat and puts out to sea, turning and spitting at the three-branched Christmas candlestick in the window of the customs house, where the murderer Vestman "celebrates Jesus," whom the Nietzschean Borg defines as "the pardoner, the idol of all criminals and wretches." Looking at the sky, he remembers "something about the Christmas star, the guiding star to Bethlehem," whither the "three deposed kings" had gone, "as fallen celebrities to worship their own tininess in the smallest of the children of men," who later became "the declared god of all small creatures." These "Christian magicians" have paid a penalty: "not a single point of light in the firmament" has been named after them. Borg's guiding star is Beta in the constellation Hercules, "the god of strength and wisdom," who finally succumbed to the stupidity of a woman after having served Omphale in his madness for three years. (Omphale and Deianira serve as surrogates for Maria, who weakened Borg, thereby hastening his downfall.) Intending suicide, Borg sails on toward the demigod who immolated himself, "out to Herakles, who liberated Prometheus, the bringer of light, [and] himself the son of a god and a human woman." (Unhappily, in her translation Sandbach mistranslates *befriade* — *liberated* — as bred.) The change from Hercules to Herakles is intentional; Strindberg distinguished between the Roman Hercules of the preceding paragraph, the performer of the twelve labors, and the Greek Herakles. Strindberg believed that the Romans made an athlete of their Hercules, while the Greeks kept Herakles as a symbol.

Prometheus, chained to a rock in the Caucasus before his liberation by Hercules (Herakles) in eagle's form, is adduced by Strindberg not only for his quality as a benefactor of man, punished for his good works (as Borg, on the island, has been), but because he is the son of a Titan and a Titan himself. In the longest of the passages describing the chained buoy whose sound pursues Borg, the instrument's cry is called "a solo for Titan with the accompaniment of storm." Another, earlier passage bearing on the finale is in chapter 9, where Borg comes to one of his several decisions to free himself from Maria: he finds himself automatically scribbling "Pandora" and looks up the name in a handbook of mythology to find that she and her box were sent down to mankind by the gods as a scourge because Prometheus had stolen fire. The phrase following the word *Prometheus* in Strindberg's final paragraph, *ljusbringaren,* "the bringer of light," has Prometheus as its referent; the next phrase, "själv son av en gud och en kvinnomoder," "himself the son of a god and a mortal mother," here Zeus and Alcmene, refers to Herakles/Hercules. The continuation of the sentence tells more about Herakles, whom "the barbarians then falsified into a virgin's boy, whose birth was greeted by milk-drinking shepherds and braying asses." Strindberg — his daughter Karin Smirnoff remembered him as "knowing everything" — alludes to the association made in Renaissance literature and art between the suffering Hercules, *Hercules patiens,* and the suffering Christ. In the letter accompanying the manuscript, as we have seen, Strindberg ended his catalogue with "Hercules-Jesus."

In *Jenseits von Gut und Böse* (*Beyond Good and Evil*), section 243, Nietzsche says: "I hear with pleasure that our sun is underway in a swift movement toward the constellation of Hercules and I hope that the human beings on the earth will resemble the sun in this." Borg sets a course toward the "new Christmas star," Beta in Hercules, sailing across the sea, "the all-mother, in whose womb life's first spark was lit, the inexhaustible spring of fruitfulness and love, life's origin and life's foe." The book's last sentence is again filled with allusions, backwards in the text. In his death at sea, Borg will find the reunion with the mother so briefly remembered when he first contemplated suicide. And he will find the reunion with nature, from which he had broken by his distorting imitations of it. On his first expedition out to sea with Vestman, Borg, through his "sea telescope," had observed the development of life from undersea (with specimens, beginning with the lazy and inert flounder and proceeding to the "wonderful music of the long-tailed ducks"), so exhausting himself that Vestman, even then, decided that Borg was a little touched (*wurmig*). On his last expedition with Vestman (the only man on the island to whom Borg felt drawn, because of the latter's glimmer of intelligence), he told Vestman again about the wonders of nature, speaking about mirages, asking his oarsman if he and his brother had visited Svärdsholm, where, to please Maria, Borg had tampered with nature. He learned that someone (Borg) had "run wild there—nobody goes ashore there any more." The island paradise was ruined. As his madness increased, Borg himself perceived that nature, with which he had previously sought company, now had become "dead for him." The sea he had worshiped seemed small and constraining even as his ego grew. A commentator, Walter Berendsohn, notes a parallel to Werther's letter of November 3 when he was on *his* way to suicide: "Oh, when this splendid nature stands in my presence like a lacquered little picture." Before the sea, once more beloved, kills Borg (like Hugo's Gilliat), the bond with nature is restored.

The ending of *I havsbandet* suggests—and must be contrasted with—the last pages of *À rebours*. Ailing, Des Esseintes is forced by his failing health to return to Paris and the human mediocrity he despises and from which he has fled. Yet there is an imaginary sea voyage in Des Esseintes's concluding plea to God to take pity on "the Christian who doubts, the incredulous one who would believe, the convict of life who sets out alone, in the night, under a sky which no longer is lighted by the consolatory signal lights of the old hope." Borg gladly and triumphantly rejects that hope; a decade later on, with *Till Damaskus* and beyond, Strindberg tentatively followed the Christian course toyed with in Des Esseintes's plea. Famously, nature makes Des Esseintes ill, Borg can be made well only by a return to it. But Borg has never been wholly the aesthete that Des Esseintes so clearly and preciously is. At the picnic Borg lays out for Maria on Svärdsholm, and in whose course he accepts Maria's challenge to conjure up the Italianate landscape, he shows himself as a historicizing aesthete of a comically smaller caliber than the great collector Des Esseintes. He lays out butter on "a scrap of Henri II fayence," puts biscuits in a dish from the Marienberg pottery in Stockholm, the sardines on a saucer of mottled-blue Nevers, all suggesting to him an earlier age "when one revered beauty in life and handicraft itself was subordinate to learning and art." But this aesthetic Borg falls prey to Maria; when she breaks the china and consoles herself with the remark "Luckily it was just old stuff," he suppresses his "petty thought" about the loss and experiences only paltry regrets.

In 1891, Strindberg called, *I havsbandet* his most mature work, best beloved among all he had written. The critical reception in Sweden was unfriendly; the novel was antidemocratic, anti-Christian, and boring in its helter-skelter learnedness, oversexual, and parodistic in its vulgar scientific experiment, the attempt to create a child. One anonymous critic ventured into the decadent realm by detecting the resemblance between Borg's appearance and Herman Bang's. Among the few friendly voices, the most perceptive were Ola Hansson's, in *Nord und Süd* (1891, "The Sublime Fantasy of a Poet"), and that of Valdemar Vedel in Denmark, a foe of naturalism, who found it "refreshing and indeed edifying in its inspection of everything that culture has accomplished, how it can transform the conditions of life, how it can refine and develop the brain's instrument to an unbelievable extent." Outside Scandinavia it did better: a German translation appeared in 1891, reaching a third edition in 1901; in "Der Roman vom Übermenschen" (in *Menschen und Bücher,* 1893), Marie Herzfeld wrote that "the interest of the book is not exhausted in its attempt to sublimate an 'homme fin de siècle' into superman." That the book got two simultaneous translations into English is a sign, a little belated, of the fascination offered by its protagonist and his congeries of ideas — Darwinism, Nietzscheanism, aristocratism. How close Borg stands to other fictional aristocrats of the mind can be seen by glancing at Captain Nemo and, for that matter, Professor Aronax, in *Vingt Milles Lieues sous les mers* (1870), the superscientist Mr. Edison in Villiers de l'Isle-Adam's *L'Ève future* (1886), or the eponymous Raffles Haw in Arthur Conan Doyle's novel (1891), who, enormously wealthy because of an invention (like Alfred Nobel's dynamite), lives isolated on his magnificent and technologically advanced estate (an artificial paradise), and plans to move mountains, dig canals, and send rivers down into the center of the earth, all to benefit the mankind he despises. Haw falls in love with a treacherous young woman and dies of a broken heart. (In his power of mind, Haw is a relative of Holmes.) It has been asked if Verner von Heidenstam's *Hans Alienus* (1892), about the course through life of a willfully superior man, was not written in rivalry to *I havsbandet;* in Johannes V. Jensen's *Kongens Fald* (1901), the alchemist Magister Zacharias is burned at the stake as a magician, together with his homunculus Carolus, the possessor of a computerlike brain; and in Jensen's *Madame d'Ora* (1904) the Faustian scientist Edmund Hall (the discoverer of the x-ray) ends up being arrested for murder in the shambles of his laboratory.

Kafka admired *I havsbandet,* which he read, according to his diary, on the Karlsplatz in Prague in the spring of 1915, "with a sense of well-being." The elderly Przybyszewski in his autobiography, forgetting his personal aversion to Strindberg of the past, called *I havsbandet* "one of the best novels, not only of Swedish literature but of European literature taken large."

5

England

OSCAR WILDE

The Picture of Dorian Gray was first printed in *Lippincott's Monthly Magazine* for June 1890, shortly after Arthur Conan Doyle's *Sign of the Four,* which had come out in the journal in February of the same year. That the two short novels appeared there almost simultaneously has a certain importance for our argument on decadence, since *The Sign of the Four* is the most "decadent" of all the Holmes texts. As for Wilde's novel, it is our business to try to detect — the task should be an easy one, like shooting sitting ducks — its decadent elements. (A matter of some related interest in connection with *Lippincott's Monthly Magazine,* and the spirit of the times, is that Rudyard Kipling's *Light That Failed* was published there in January of 1891, another novel in which a painting plays a central role, Dick Heldar's portrait of the harlot Bessie; also, it is a book filled with misogyny — going blind, the artist is rejected by the liberated woman Maisie, his masterwork is destroyed by Bessie, and he finds his only mainstay in the male company of his war-correspondent friends.

Dorian Gray was extensively augmented and to some degree revised when it was published in book form. (See Wilfred Edener's edition of the *Urfassung.*) Six chapters were added, to bring it up to book length and to inject it with a melodramatic subplot, as well as to provide previews of Wilde's stage dialogue in the great comedies to come. The new chapters were the following: chapter 3 begins with the conversation between Lord Henry Wotton and his uncle, Lord

Fermor, who informs the nephew about the background of Dorian and the circumstances surrounding his birth; it continues with the account of the luncheon at the house of Henry's aunt, Lady Agatha, which gives Henry one more of his many opportunities to be Wildean, by means of epigrams, as he continues his verbal seduction of another guest, Dorian himself. In particular, Henry's "praise of folly" is "brilliant, fortuitous, irresponsible. He charmed his listeners out of themselves, and they followed his pipe-playing" — Lord Henry is a hedonistic Pied Piper of Hamlin. "Dorian Gray never took his eyes off him, but sat still like one under a spell, smiles chasing each other over his lips, and wonder growing grave in his darkening eyes." Chapter 5 starts the subplot: we meet the ex-actress Mrs. Vane and her son, the rough-and-tumble James, about to set out for Australia at the age of sixteen to make his fortune (his sister Sibyl is seventeen, and it is hinted that she, made of finer stuff, has had a different father); we hear James's threat — made rather operatically, a kind of equivalent to "la maledizione" uttered by Monterone in Verdi's *Rigoletto* — as in a "glimpse of golden hair and laughing lips, and in an open carriage with two ladies, Dorian drove past." (For a moment, we may be confused, but the golden hair and the laughing lips belong to Dorian, not to his female companions.) Sibyl identifies him as her Prince Charming, but James does not see him, although he wishes he had: "'for as sure as there is a God in heaven, if he ever does any wrong, I shall kill him.'" Chapter 15 contains the dinner at Lady Narborough's after Dorian has murdered Basil Hallward and compelled his sometime friend, Alan Campbell, to dispose of the body. Note, by the way, that — one of Wilde's smaller borrowings from Huysmans — Dorian coolly appears in the drawing room wearing a "large buttonhole of Parma violets"; we remember the Parma violets that Des Esseintes wore in lieu of a cravat when he was still a dandy. At this dinner, during which Lord Henry shines again ("'Isn't he incorrigible,' cried Dorian, leaning forward in his chair," still — years after their first meeting — under Lord Henry's spell), an end-of-the-world tone is introduced into the conversation and the book. Playing up to Lord Henry, Lady Narborough has uttered an aperçu of her own: "Nearly all the married men live like bachelors, and all the bachelors live like married men,'" and Lord Henry murmurs that catchword of an overtired nineteenth century, "'*fin de siècle*,'" to which Lady Narborough retorts, expanding the thought of the imminent end, "'*fin du glôbe*,'" "'I wish it were *fin du glôbe*,'" said Dorian with a sigh. "'Life is a great disappointment,'" a statement of decadent ennui following what should have been a supreme decadent moment for Dorian, the killing of another human being, something that Des Esseintes hoped to effect only at second hand. The next chapter, 16, is also new, a terrifying and sometimes terrible piece of writing: we are allowed to accompany Dorian ("a mad craving [has] just come over him") on one of his mysterious disappearances, during which he indulges the same decadent *nostalgie de la boue,* yearning for the mud, that captured Des Esseintes when he was accosted by the boy with the porkpie hat. Dorian rides through a ghastly London to the docks of the East End; in a den of vice, he meets one of his sometime victims, Adrian Singleton, and is on the brink of being slain by James Vane, returned from abroad and determined to hunt down "Prince Charming": he escapes only because of his singular retention of his youthful good looks. Chapters 17 and 18 finish off the Vane story: James peers through the window of the Selby Royal Conservatory, Dorian sees him and faints, and then believes, at last, that he is saved from retribution: Vane is killed by the shot of Sir Geoffrey Clouston, whose usually infallible aim has been thrown off by Dorian's sudden access of tenderness for a young hare. "As [Dorian] rode home, his eyes were full of tears, for he knew he was safe." (Once more, in the Selby Royal chapters, Lord Henry has the opportunity to be "Prince Paradox," in his several bouts of repartee and stichomythia with Gladys, the pretty duchess of Monmouth; he also continues his tutelage — it has lasted some eighteen years now — of his adept, telling Dorian: " 'The only horrible thing in the world is ennui, Dorian. That is the sin for which there is no forgiveness.' ")

These additions to the magazine version were accompanied by a series of small but not unimportant changes made here and there throughout the text. Wilde was plainly nervous about the candor with which he had portrayed the homosexual nature of Basil Hallward's devotion to Dorian. For example, in chapter 9, a reference to something "purely feminine" in Hallward's nature is deleted, as well as Hallward's statement — just before the visit of the friends to the theater in order to observe Sibyl Vane as Juliet — to the effect that " 'It is quite true that I have worshipped you with far more romance of feeling than a man usually gives to a friend. Somehow I had never loved a woman.' " Likewise gone is Basil's admission to Lord Henry that he and Dorian walked home together from the club " 'arm in arm.' " (In revising the text, the author also took away some physical gestures that might have implied an intimacy between Lord Henry and Basil: in the opening chapter, Lord Henry is no longer allowed to "lay his hand on Basil's shoulder" as he talks about his marriage, and Basil's reaction is likewise omitted — he shakes Lord Henry's hand off, in the Lippincott version, as he says: " 'I hate the way you talk about your married life, Harry.' ") A curious change, in Wilde's evident effort to give his text more respectability, comes in chapter 10, as Dorian begins to examine the "yellow book" that Lord Henry has sent him; it is in the description of the book's "jeweled style . . . full of argot and archaisms, of technical expressions and of elaborate paraphrases, that characterizes some of the finest work of the French school of the *Decadents*"; in the book version, the last word is changed to *Symbolistes*.

Of course, these efforts on Wilde's part were scarcely sufficient to protect the text, even in its new form, against charges of crypto-homoeroticism; in the *Scots Observer*, W. H. Henley decided that Wilde wrote "for outlawed noblemen and perverted telegraph boys" (an allusion to the Lord Arthur Somerset scandal), and the *Daily Chronicle* said, "It is a tale spawned from the leprous literature of the French decadent." Revelatory signs remain everywhere in the book text. Basil Hallward's love for Dorian is described as "such love as Michel Angelo had known, and Montaigne, and Winckelman, and Shakespeare himself"; to Lord Henry, Basil mentions the face of the favorite of the Emperor Hadrian, the Bithynian boy Antinous, in conjunction with Dorian's face, as starting points for a new epoch in art (chapter 1), and later, in chapter 9, he describes Dorian, in the beloved's presence, as Antinous, albeit unnamed: "Crowned with heavy lotus-blossoms, you had sat in the prow of Hadrian's barge, gazing across the green turbid Nile." (Here, Wilde quotes from his own poem, "The Sphinx.") As his image decays, Dorian sinks into a baser kind of homosexuality, appearing at a costume ball (chapter 11) as Anne de Joyeuse, a male Admiral of France despite the name but also a mignon of Henri III, in a "dress covered with five hundred and sixty pearls." Dorian's nature is patently bisexual; he seems to have "ruined" both young men and young women by the score, and the secret that gets the obstinate Alan Campbell to do Dorian's dirty work with Basil's corpse is probably that of Alan's "Uranism"; the whole story of Dorian's double life, as Peter Ackroyd remarks in the introduction to the Penguin edition, points in the homosexual direction.

More comically, many of the women in the novel are, to put it mildly, not very attractive; "Lady Brandon screeches out in her curiously shrill voice," Lady Victoria Wotton has "a shrill voice," the women laughing in the pit at the theater have voices "horribly discordant and shrill," Mrs. Vane has "crooked, false-jeweled fingers, and a shallow, secretive nature," Lady Narborough possesses the "remains of a very remarkable ugliness," Mrs. Vandelur is "so dreadfully dowdy," the Duchess of Harleigh has "ample architectural proportions," and so forth. (The allusion to Isabella II of Spain in chapter 3 may also have meant something to the nineteenth-century audience, which knew of the queen's countless lovers and lack of discrimination in choosing them.) The attractive women are few; two of them, of course are dead before the book begins — one of Dorian's forebears, Lady Elizabeth Devereux ("he knew her life and the strange stories that were told about her lovers"), and then his mother, Lady Margaret Devereux, "with her Lady Hamilton smile" (the reference is to

Emmy Hamilton, "that Hamilton woman," the mistress and then the wife of Horatio Nelson) and "her wine-dashed lips" and her "loose Bacchante dress." Thus a taint attaches to the Devereux beauties, as it does to the duchess of Monmouth who, in the Selby Royal episode, makes no bones about her adulterous hankering for Dorian, despite (or because of) his bad reputation. Sibyl Vane must be added to this short list; but she, we are told, is boyish, and Dorian particularly admires her in roles requiring disguise as a boy, Rosalind as Ganymede, Imogene as Fidele, the page. (When the three friends see Sibyl on the stage, at last, in a female part, Juliet's, she has lost her artistic talent; her voice has become "declamatory" and has "the painful precision of a schoolgirl who has been taught to recite by some second-rate professor of elocution." Near book's end, Dorian decides to spare the last of the attractive women in the tale, the shadowy figure of Hetty Merton; readers (like Lord Henry) may doubt that the sacrifice was a very painful one for him.

Dorian Gray himself, when first we see him, has almost the air of a girl, passing from one suitor to another, as Basil — seeing Dorian leave his protection at the end of chapter 1 — appeals to Lord Henry: " 'Don't take away from me the one person who gives to my art whatever charm it possesses . . . Mind, Harry, I trust you.' " Then, at the end of the next chapter, having begged Dorian in vain not to go with Lord Henry (as Lord Henry watched with "an amused smile"), "the painter flung himself down on a sofa, and a look of pain came into his face." *The Picture of Dorian Gray* is a novel about different kinds of homoerotic love: Basil is the highminded and platonic lover of Dorian, Dorian becomes the (slowly ruined) disciple of Lord Henry, eventually embarking upon a bisexual career far more varied and certainly more notorious than that of his teacher — about whose *vie érotique* we learn almost nothing, save that he is in a very strained marriage: Lord Henry watches, we suspect, and lets others play the game. Yet the homosexual circumstance does not, in and of itself, make *The Picture of Dorian Gray* into a "decadent" novel, any more than does Wilde's affection for the key word from the Verlaine sonnet, "Langueur." Lord Henry speaks "languidly" (chapter 1), the air is "languid" in Basil Hallward's garden (chapter 1), Lord Henry has a "low, languid voice" that fascinates Dorian (chapter 2), Dorian Gray saunters "languidly" with Lord Henry to the tea table, and so forth; Dorian even speaks "languidly" to Basil when he meets him on the night of the murder. (A variant on the omnipresent *languid* is *listless*; the rival in frequency to this word cluster is the verb *fling*.) Stormy emotion is frequently indicated by the verb, as in the description of Basil's jealous behavior, quoted above; elsewhere, on first beholding Dorian, Lord Henry "flung himself down on the divan and opened his cigarette case," and then, eyeing the ever more desirable boy, a few pages farther on, he "flung himself into a large, circular arm-chair and watched him." After having detected the initial change in the painting, Dorian "rose from the table, lit a cigarette, and flung himself down on a luxuriously cushioned couch that stood facing the screen." Other favorite words are *cruel, cruelty,* which come thick and fast after Dorian has caused the suicide of Sibyl Vane, and — to be sure — *poisonous, poison,* in connection with both books and blood lines.

One of the remarkable aspects of *The Picture of Dorian Gray* is that it can be described as belonging to many different subforms of narrative: it has aspects of the drawing-room comedy (in the luncheon and dinner scenes, and in the constant barrage of witty cynicisms from Lord Henry); it has elements of the mystery and the supernatural tale; it is a novel about inexorable fate, as Wilde claimed in *De Profundis.* (Wilde much admired a novel about a homosexual-heterosexual triangle, leading to murder and double suicide, by Louis Couperus, *Noodlot, Footsteps of Fate.*) It is like Pater's *Marius the Epicurean* in its frequent statements, again from Lord Henry and echoed by Dorian, amounting almost to a tractate, about an eccentric, aesthetic philosophy of life: "To realize one's nature perfectly — that is what each one of us is here for," rephrased in the motto, "To cure the soul by means of the senses, and the senses by means of the soul," which Lord Henry utters while gazing with his "dreamy, languorous eyes," first at Basil and then, we must assume, at Dorian. And, certainly, Wilde takes pains to give his book the air of a novel of the decadence; it is a text that directly suggests Huysmans's *À rebours,* which Wilde discovered and devoured almost as soon as it came out.

There are two occasions in *Dorian Gray* where it might seem that there is a direct reference to Huysmans's classic. The first of these occurs in chapter 2, where Lord Henry, watching the effect his words have had upon the boy, remembers a book "that he read when he was sixteen, a book which had revealed to him much that he had not known before." However, Lord Henry could not very well have been only sixteen in 1884, when *À rebours* appeared; besides, in *De Profundis* Wilde described Walter Pater's *Studies in the Renaissance* as the "book which has had such a strange influence on my life." The second occasion is the mention in chapter 10 of the "yellow book" Lord Henry sends to Dorian after Sibyl Vane's death; Dorian "flung himself into an armchair and began to turn over the leaves." "It was the strangest book that he had ever read. It seemed to him that, in exquisite raiment and to the delicate sound of flutes, the sins of the world were passing in dumb show before him . . . It was a novel without a plot, and with only one character, being, indeed, simply a psychological study of a certain young Parisian who spent his life trying to realize in the nineteenth century all the passions and modes of thought that belonged to every century except his own . . . There were in it metaphors as monstrous as orchids and as subtle in color . . . One hardly knew at times whether one was reading the spiritual ecstasies of some medieval saint or the morbid confessions of a modern sinner. It was a poisonous book . . . For years, Dorian Gray could not free himself from the influence of this book . . . or he never sought to free himself from it." Now, literal-minded scholarship can easily discover discrepancies between Huysmans's text and the account given of it in *The Picture of Dorian Gray*. Des Esseintes does not suffer from the fear of mirrors that haunts the "fantastic hero" of Wilde's "French novel," and, in the "seventh chapter" of *À rebours* Des Esseintes does not imagine that he is this or that Roman emperor, Tiberius, Caligula, Nero, Domitian, Heliogabalus, although Huysmans has taken delight in describing the last-named in the review of Latin literature in chapter 3. But these details that do not jibe are simply Wilde's half-hearted attempt to cover the trail to Huysmans; any reader of the time who had some knowledge of what had just happened in French literature would ignore them and identify the "poisonous book" as *À rebours* all the same.

As a matter of fact, in his lengthy chapter 11, Wilde tries to do what Huysmans had done in several chapters — and by the employment of Huysmans's trick of copying from technical handbooks and cultural histories: Wilde's sources, as was found out long ago, were manuals published by the South Kensington Museum, on jewels and musical instruments, William Jones's *History and Mystery of Precious Stones*, Ernest Lefebvre's *Embroidery and Lace*, Daniel Roch's *Textile Fabrics,* and, for the disquisition on the colorfully murderous Italians of the Renaissance adduced *ad finem* in the chapter, John Addington Symons's *The Renaissance in Italy*. Notably, while Wilde apes (and rivals) Huysmans in his sections on perfumes, music, lapidary art, and embroidery and fabrics (sometimes outdoing the breviary of decadence), he does not attempt to vie with Huysmans in those fields where Huysmans shows such mastery, namely, in the presentation of Latin literature, of Moreau and other graphic artists, and of French literature.

However, French literature of the nineteenth century *is* used by Wilde to create one of the more fascinating passages in *Dorian Gray*. After both cases of Dorian's committing a murder, indirectly or directly, the perusal of a book follows: in the former instance, that of Sibyl Vane's death, it is the "poisonous book" just discussed; in the case of Basil Hallward, it is Théophile Gautier's *Émaux et camées*. The morning after Hallward's murder, having slept quite peacefully, looking like "a boy who has been tired out with play or study," Dorian seeks to drive away the memory of what he has done by dressing himself "with more than his usual care" and "talking to his valet about some new liveries that he was thinking about getting made for the servants at Selby," and by being variously bored or annoyed by his mail. Still, the memory keeps coming back; like Laurent in Zola's *Thérèse Raquin*, compulsively sketching the murdered Camille, Dorian draws "first flowers and then human faces . . . every face he drew seemed to have a fantastic likeness to Basil Hallward's." Then he turns to the book of Gautier, in "Charpentier's Japanese-paper edition, with the Jacquemart etching," given to him by Adrian Singleton, in days (or nights) when their relationship was happier. The first poem his eye falls on is one of the "Études des mains" — the reader is supposed to know that Lacenaire was the mass murderer Pierre-François Lacenaire (1800–36); it is painful but appropriate for Dorian to read about the "cold yellow hand" of the dead criminal and then to contemplate "his own white tapered fingers." (In the next chapter, at the opening, the narrator tells us that it seemed "those finely-shaped fingers could never have clutched a knife for sin, nor those smiling lips have cried out on God or goodness.") Dorian passes on to other poems, to the "Variations sur le Carnaval de Venise" (he remembers that he was in Basil's company in Venice, a main city of decadence), to the "Chanson" about the swallows of Smyrna, to the "Nostalgies d'obélisques" (with the Nile passage that Wilde imitated for his own poem about the Sphinx), and finally to the poem "Contralto," a description of the *monstre charmant* that crouches in the porphyry room of the Louvre. Looking up the poem's whole text, the reader will discover that it is about a statue of a figure neither masculine nor feminine ("Est-ce un jeune homme? est-ce une femme, / Une déesse, ou bien un dieu?") and will realize that the poem — after the reading of which "a horrible fit of terror" comes over Dorian — has reference to Dorian's bisexual eros. (It may be added here that Dorian's own name, apart from sounding Greek — "in the Dorian mode" — is also bisexual, used both for men and women.)

Other decadent traits in the novel are plain enough: for example, Dorian's construction of *his* artificial world (for his everlasting youth is supremely artificial, against nature), and the decay of the painting itself as Dorian, artificially, continues to bloom. There are, as well, such standard and subsidiary decadent factors as the protagonist's enormous wealth, his circumstance of being the last of his line, and his stroll through the picture gallery of Selby Royal. But above all, it is Dorian's selfishness, his inability to think of others save in their capacity as actors on his stage, as "marionettes," that puts him most squarely into the same box as Des Esseintes. He has learned the lesson from Lord Henry, but he has been a willing and gifted pupil. At the outset of their friendship, Dorian has put himself on display, for admiration: "Dorian Gray stepped up on the dais, with the air of a young Greek martyr [we are to think of Saint Sebastian] and made a little *moue* of discontent to Lord Henry, to whom he had taken rather a fancy." He plays a role, but with the intent of moving others; Lord Henry soon teaches him how to formulate the process of watching and being watched in order to achieve ultimate pleasure. After Dorian learns of Sibyl's death, he cries (it has briefly occurred to him that Sibyl might have saved him from the decay he has perceived in the picture): " 'My God, my God! Harry, what shall I do? You don't know the danger I am in, and there is nothing to keep me straight [an interesting choice of word]. She would have done that for me. She had no right to kill herself. It was selfish of her.' " But under Lord Henry's direction the supremely selfish Dorian quickly becomes consoled and admits that he is by no means as affected by Sibyl's death as he should be: " 'It seems to me to be simply like a wonderful ending to a wonderful play. It has all the terrible beauty of a Greek tragedy, a tragedy in which I took a great part, but by which I have *not* been wounded.' " Henry — "who found an exquisite pleasure in playing on the lad's unconscious egotism" — encourages him in his conception of himself as the unconcerned actor who can also take the step across the footlights to watch the play: " 'Suddenly we find that we are no longer the actors but the spectators of the play. Or rather we are both. We watch ourselves and the mere wonder of the spectacle enthralls us.' " Arguing out the question of the death of Sibyl Vane in the next chapter with Basil Hallward (and expressing the hope that her death was not "a vulgar accident" but, more gloriously and dramatically for the purpose of this imagined play, a suicide), Dorian repeats Lord Henry's arguments, simplified: " 'To become the spectator of one's own life, as Harry says, is to escape the suffering of life.' " Actually, he does not tell Basil the whole truth about his stance toward life; at the conclusion of the talk with Lord Henry, he has decided *not* to pray that the picture would cease to change: "If the picture was to alter, it was to alter. For there would be a real pleasure in watching it." Like Brand in Ibsen's epic fragment, like the aesthete of Kierkegaard, Dorian has become a watcher of life, even his own dark spiritual life; the picture will endure decay for him. "He would be safe" he concludes; he has, he thinks, achieved the surety about life for which Des Esseintes also strove, and has found a new thrill into the bargain.

With both Lord Henry and Dorian so avid to reconstruct life as a theater for their own pleasure (in which they will, like Des Esseintes, pursue their desire "for a new sensation"), it is surprising, perhaps, that the reader learns nothing about the actual plays they see together. What they do attend, and what we are informed about, is the opera. In chapter 4, Lady Victoria says that she saw Dorian with her husband at the opera " 'the other night,' " at a performance of what Dorian recalls was *Lohengrin:* " 'Yes,' " she continues, " 'it was Lohengrin. I like Wagner's music better than anybody's. It is so loud that one can talk the whole time without other people hearing what one says.' " Dorian politely but firmly refuses to agree with her. " 'I never talk during music, at least during good music.' " *Lohengrin* may have a special meaning for Dorian: like Elsa in that opera, Sibyl Vane does not know the name of her beloved, her Prince Charming, for a long time: " 'Why, you don't even know his name,' " James Vane says to her in the park. She begins to use Dorian's first name only after their engagement, it seems, and in that awful final interview after the disastrous performance, uses it repeatedly, nine times. Later, we discover she has never found out his last name: " 'She knew only my Christian name,' " Dorian tells Basil, trusting he will not be summoned by the police. For his own part, the mentor, Lord Henry, hesitates to reveal names of his favorites to others: " 'When I like people immensely, I never tell their names to anyone. It is like surrendering a part of them.' " Dorian has applied this teaching to himself; Lohengrin, it will be remembered, forbids Elsa ever to ask his name: "Nie sollst du mich befragen" — a command she transgresses against on their wedding night. The marriage is not consummated, she dies, and Lohengrin sails away, with his swan, to return to the realm of the Holy Grail. Actually, Dorian is an admirer of Wagner, the great composer (in Nietzsche's hateful formulation) of decadence; in chapter 11 we learn how he "would sit in his box at the opera, either alone or with Lord Henry, listening in rapt pleasure to *Tannhäuser* and seeing in the prelude to that great work a presentation of the tragedy of his own soul."

Tannhäuser is a still more important opera than *Lohengrin* for Dorian; he regards himself — following the decadent's habit of interpreting himself as a figure from history or from art or from literature, the necessary surrogate for a real existence, a real self-examination — as the knight who has been in thrall to a (homosexual) Venusberg, a knight who yearns for redemption but who does not have the strength of belief to achieve it. In *The Ballad of Reading Gaol*, Wilde would write:

> For who can say by what strange way
> Christ brings his will to light,
> Since the barren staff the pilgrim bore
> Bloomed in the great pope's sight.

We recall Wilde's own bitter joke about his audience with Leo XIII, after the poet's imprisonment and exile: "My cane did not bloom." We recall, too, Aubrey Beardsley's obscene use of the Tannhäuser legend in *Under the Hill, or The Story of Venus and Tannhäuser*.

In a way, *The Picture of Dorian Gray* is an opera about failed redemption, or at least a play on that topic set to occasional music. In the penultimate

chapter, in the last conversation between Lord Henry and Dorian, the former
asks his friend to " 'play me a nocturne, and, as you play, tell me, in a low
voice, how you have kept your youth.' " (Lord Henry is growing old and tired;
he envies Dorian.) The nocturne is by Chopin; we may guess it is opus 37,
number 12, composed by Chopin on Majorca, a piece which was a favorite of
the decadents (we shall come across it again in Hjalmar Söderberg's *Doktor
Glas*); in 1888, the Chopin admirer Friedrich Niecks warned against "the
beautiful sensuousness" of the nocturne, "luscious, softly rounded, and not
without a certain degree of languor . . . let us not linger too long in the
treacherous atmosphere of this Capua — it bewitches and unmans." When
Dorian ceases, Lord Henry beseeches him to continue: " 'Why have you
stopped playing, Dorian? Go back and give me the nocturne over again.' " He
even offers Dorian the possibility of a new conquest, " 'young Lord Poole . . .
He has already copied your neckties, and has begged me to introduce him to
you.' " But Dorian refuses, even though Lord Henry tells him he has " 'never
played so well as tonight.' " The reason, Dorian retorts with childlike or childish simplicity, is " 'I am going to be good. I am a little changed already.' " Like
Des Esseintes wishing from time to time for faith, Dorian, from time to time,
has had his fits of wishing "to be good," with Sibyl, with Hetty, in the present
unspecified way — perhaps he is resisting the lure of young Lord Poole.

For all the apparent glory of his eternal youth, Dorian has not been happy. A
sign of his unhappiness has been, everywhere, his lachrymosity: he weeps on at
least seven occasions in the novel. The first outburst comes when he realizes
that he will grow old, in chapter 2: it occurs immediately before he expresses
the fateful wish " 'I would give my soul [to be always young],' " which is then
fulfilled. He weeps again as he thinks he will stab the canvas whose eternal
youth he envies. He weeps when, in the conversation with Basil which leads
to the latter's murder, Basil tries to get him to pray, quoting from Isaiah:
" 'Though your sins be as scarlet, yet I will make them white as snow.' " He
weeps at Selby Royal after James Vane has looked through the window at him,
and he thinks "of the image of his sin again," "swathed in scarlet." He weeps
when he "knows" he is "safe," after the death of Vane. He weeps when, on the
final evening of his life, he thinks of "the monstrous moment of pride and
passion [in which] he had prayed that the portrait should bear the burden of
his days," and then, one last time, he resolves "to be good." The tears of
despair of his youth have become tears of contrition, meant to wash away sins;
The Picture of Dorian Gray seems about to become the legend of someone
who has realized the true root of his sins, his pride, his *cenodoxia,* and who
intends to make that fault disappear by his resolve — again like a naughty
child — to be good. Yet, as before, the contrition does not last; Dorian stabs the

portrait so that "the hideous image" will be dead, the image of his conscience; "without its hideous warnings, he would be at peace." Like Des Esseintes, he wants immediately surety, not the painful process of change. And he does not get the peace he wants, as far as we can tell: "There was a cry heard, and a crash. The cry was so horrible in its agony that the frightened servants woke, and crept out of their rooms." The cry, in this operatic novel, can only remind us of the cry of Don Giovanni at the end of Mozart's opera as, still prideful and unrepentant, he is dragged down to hell.

Many readers have detected in *The Picture of Dorian Gray* a resemblance to *Faust,* whether Goethe's work or the operatic version by Gounod. Observers in the novel itself talk about a pact with the devil. The whore at the opium den of chapter 16 reports to James Vane: " 'They say he has sold himself to the devil for a pretty face,' " the pretty face being not a Gretchen's or Marguerite's but his own. Elsewhere, Basil has told Dorian that the portrait itself has " 'the eyes of a devil,' " and the image on the canvas then seems to whisper to him that he should hate and kill Basil Hallward. Alan Campbell asks him, " 'What devil's work are you up to' "; the women in the opium den say, " 'There goes the devil's bargain.' " His trip to the London docks is like a trip into hell: "The fog was lighter here, and he could see the strange bottle-shaped kilns with their orange fan-like tongues of flame." (A pattern of flame symbolism threads through the novel: hearing the seductive talk of Lord Henry, the very young Dorian thought that life had "suddenly become fiery-colored. It seemed to him that he had been walking on fire"; watching him, Lord Henry noticed that "his nature had developed like a flower, had borne blossoms of scarlet flame," and "he thought of his friend's young fiery-colored life, and wondered where it was going to end.") Taking Basil to the room where he is to be killed, Dorian sets the lamp on the floor and, spookily, "A cold current of air passed them, and the light shot up for a moment in a flame of murky orange." The flames of hell do not envelop Dorian's ugly body at the end, as they do that of the unrepentant Don Giovanni, but (for the imagination of the intensely superstitious Wilde) Dorian may very well have landed in them, since they have surrounded him so much during his earthly career. Yet Dorian is not the devil himself; that is Lord Henry—also called Harry, a name suggesting the Old Harry, Lord Henry with his "pointed brown beard" and his "olive-colored face and worn expression" and "his low languid voice" and his "cool, white flower-like hands," Lord Henry who says to Dorian, after he has talked him out of any remorse for the death of Sibyl Vane: " 'We are only at the beginning of our friendship, Dorian.' " The friendship may last for eternity. Lord Henry Wotton is a perfect devil of the decadence, subtle, aesthetic, sly. Something oddly primitive lies in the decadent mode: even as it somehow takes the end of the

nineteenth century as a doomsday, an end of the world, so it admits, or suggests, the possibility of the devil's existence — Huysmans intimates such a belief for his protagonist Durtal in *Là-bas,* from the same year as *The Picture of
Dorian Gray.* And in this medieval mindset, the seducer sinner may search,
like Tannhäuser, for the woman savior (even as the woman, Tannhäuser's
Venus, the femme fatale, is also the devil's agent in other decadent texts). In
The Picture of Dorian Gray, the savior role is played, briefly and in an uncon-
vincing way, by Sibyl and by Hetty, or, rather, Dorian briefly imputes the role
to them, and the reader may connect the very shadowy presence of the girls
with Wilde's homosexuality. *The Picture of Dorian Gray* is a holy legend, or
an unholy legend, of decadence, not its breviary, as *À rebours* was.

The great and continuing popularity of *The Picture of Dorian Gray* can be
attributed to its dealing with some essential questions of human existence: the
gnawing of vanity, the desire to stay young at all costs, the overriding urge of
human selfishness. Nonetheless, that the book, and Wilde himself, came in for
literary persiflage is understandable, however little that persiflage may indicate any deeper understanding of what Wilde's novel was all about. *The Green
Carnation* (1894) of Robert Hichens is an amusing book; the *répliques* of
Lord Henry and the externals of Wilde himself are melted into Esmé Amarinth, and Lord Reginald is at once a comical (and babyish) Dorian and
Wilde's vicious friend, Lord Alfred Douglas. The depiction of a week in the
country at Mrs. Windsor's "desert in the oasis" is intended to make us laugh,
as is the grand climax with the catch on "rose-white youth," to the tune of
"Three Blind Mice" and the not altogether ecclesiastical interest which the
local choirboys, in their robes and little else, seem to arouse in Esmé. All these
silly figures and happenings are set off against the solid common sense of Lady
Locke (and her son Tommy); Lady Locke has spent her life around military
men (while she finds the creatures of the green carnation not to be men at all),
and her husband has died "at his post of duty" in the Straits Settlements. *The
Green Carnation* is mostly froth, but contains the message, aimed at a respectable public, that such beings as Esmé and Reginald are not to be taken seriously, and that what Lady Locke stand for *is.* Such parodies of the decadence
were common enough: in France there was Paul Beauclair and Gabriel Vi-
caire's *Les Déliquescences d'Adoré Floupette,* in England G. S. Street's *Autobiography of a Boy,* in Portugal, the infinitely more skillful *A cidade e as serras*
of Eça de Queirós. We should not read *The Green Carnation* today if it were
not for Wilde and *The Picture of Dorian Gray.* For all the laughter Hichens'
book can still arouse, it misses the point: the decadent novel can deal in very
earnest matters.

6

Holland

LOUIS COUPERUS

In October-November 1890, the second novel of Louis Couperus (1863–1923), *Noodlot,* was published in the Amsterdam newspaper, *De Gids;* Couperus was already well known, thanks to his highly successful *Eline Vere, een Haagse Roman,* which had appeared in the newspaper in 1888 and as a book the next year. According to "A Tribute and a Memory," in *Silhouettes* (1925), by Edmund Gosse, *Noodlot* was recommended to Gosse — who knew Scandinavian languages and Dutch — by a transplanted Netherlander, Maarten Maartens, who made a career in Britain by writing about his homeland. Gosse "liked it very much," and shortly had it included in the "peacock-pink covers" of his International Library, issued by Heinemann. It was translated as *Footsteps of Fate* by Clara Bell, with an introduction by Gosse, "The Dutch Sensitivists." For *Noodlot*'s title, the still more unfortunate *Fostering a Viper in His Bosom* had been proposed by Heinemann, to which Couperus had objected. It aroused so much interest that *Eline Vere* itself was published in English in 1892, translated by J. T. Grein, lacking the final chapter (36), which brings the big book to a happy close, with two marriages; evidently the publisher, Chapman and Hall, believed that it would be more dramatic to have the Hague novel end with the suicide of the unhappy Eline.

Oscar Wilde, whose *Picture of Dorian Gray* had appeared in book form the same year (1891) as Mrs. Bell's translation, caught the intimations of homosexuality in Couperus's novel and sent Couperus a praise-filled letter, together with a copy of *The Picture of Dorian Gray.* Couperus was not impressed; he claimed to have been put off by the cascades of paradoxes. Shortly, Couperus's cousin and bride, Elisabeth Baud Couperus, translated *Dorian Gray* into Dutch, and it appeared at L. G. Veen, the house of *Noodlot.* An extended correspondence between Wilde and Couperus (and Couperus's wife) did not come to pass. The trials and imprisonment of Wilde cannot have failed to capture Couperus's uneasy attention. In his notebooks for 1896, Hofmannsthal wrote: "Dorian Gray: the actual experiences of Wilde cast a sinister light on the book, a tormented reality."

The contrast between *Eline Vere* and *Noodlot* is striking enough: the upper-class Hague world, described through its refined entertainments, social friendships, and familial connections, is replaced by a set of scenes abroad, in London (chapter 1), in Norway (chapter 2), London again (the long chapter 3), the climax at Scheveningen (chapter 4) and finally London (chapter 5). The cast of characters is as small as that of *Eline Vere* (inspired by *Anna Karenina*) is huge. In Couperus's semiautobiographical *Metamorfose* (1897), the second novel by Couperus's alter ego, Hugo Aylva, *Schaakspel (Game of Chess),* is described as follows: "It was an altogether different art from that of his first book, *Mathilde.* In *Mathilde,* to be sure, fate [*noodlot*] inevitably prevailed, but everything else had been dear and charming and familiar and conciliatory. And in *Game of Chess,* nothing was conciliatory. All was gray, sharp, irreconcilable, hard. Through the lily chamber of Emilia [Elisabeth Vaud], the revelation of the vision of life stormed like a gray Apocalypse. Dolf den Bergh [a close friend, Gerrit Jaeger] nodded his head in agreement; in mute terror, Emilia wrung her hands and listened trembling, filled with horror . . . In her horror, she saw Hugo for the first time . . . He was passive, wholly passive . . . He had not questioned his earthly existence, it was of no concern to him; it was a matter of the terrifying power of Life. Thus Aylva regarded it all; thus she learned it from him, from *Game of Chess.* A moment long she was afraid, afraid of life, afraid of the Power, afraid for herself, afraid for Aylva. But in herself she had the sweet gift of eternal hope." In his obscure rhetoric (*Metamorfose* is Couperus's only major book never translated into a foreign language), Couperus approaches the secret of his sexual ambivalence. However, the novel was dedicated not to Gerrit Jaeger but to another friend, Frans Netscher. Couperus and Netscher had read Zola together, and Netscher was brave enough to have expressed criticism of the emotional extravagance in Couperus's work. He appears as the conciliatory and vigorous Scheffer in *Metamorfose;* Couperus, hopelessly unathletic himself, admired Netscher's gift for sports, especially cricket.

The plot of *Noodlot* is readily retold and must be, since the English transla-tion has never been reprinted. As so often in the literature of decadence, it has an air of extreme melodrama, bordering on the risible — think of *Dorian Gray.* On a snowy night, a shabbily dressed stranger waits outside White Rose Cot-tage, on Adelaide Road in a new suburb of London; the stranger addresses the approaching owner of the cottage, Frank Westhove, a Dutch engineer, in the latter's own language. Almost tramplike in appearance, the stranger is Robert van Maeren, returned to Europe after hard times in America. Frank offers a refuge to Bertie, a friend from schooldays whom Frank used to protect from bullying. Frank is large and manly; Bertie is small and fragile. Immediately at home in the comfort of the Cottage, where Frank, a bachelor, lives with two servants, Bertie — ingratiating and catlike, as he is called so often in the text — stays on and on; Frank introduces him to members of his club and to the "skating-rink girls," demi-mondaines, whom Bertie treats with considerable contempt. The engineering career of Frank is neglected in the two friends' round of pleasure. But Frank is made uneasy by Bertie's periodic absences, from which he returns pale, exhausted, and tattered; yet Bertie quickly rein-states himself in Frank's favor, making fun of Frank's efforts to locate him through the aid of the police, and Frank becomes "enslaved to Bertie as if to opium or morphine." All the same, Frank has sufficient self-insight to realize that he has somehow become debased, forgetting the ideals of his childhood home; after further disappearances, Frank resolves to send Bertie away — but Bertie snares him once more in "velvet bonds," and to Frank it seems, finally, that he cannot exist without Bertie. There is no physical intimacy between the two; it does not occur to Frank that Bertie's excursions are homosexual adven-tures (nor could it have been directly stated in the fiction of the day, any more than in Dorian's case). All the same, Frank sees his dependence on Bertie as a "sickness" of the soul, which leads him — "large and sturdily built and healthy" — to construct a philosophy of "frivolity"; life is a comedy and to be played as such. Aware of Frank's gnawing discomfort, Bertie proposes that travel would do him good, and, quite by accident, mentions Norway. Fate begins to play its role. In the summer of 1889, Couperus made a trip to Norway in the company of a brother-in-law, to recover from the completion of *Eline Vere,* but he was depressed by the persistently rainy weather. Norway was a popular travel goal in those years, in part because of the growing Ibsen craze.

Bertie's suggestion turns out badly for the parasite. In Trondheim, the friends chance to meet Sir Archibald Rhodes and his daughter Eve, as they argue about the directions to the Geitfjeld they have found in their Baedeker: Eve trusts the guidebook, and Frank agrees with her. A friendship between

Frank and Eve immediately springs up, to Bertie's muffled dismay: Eve is lively and pert, and, like Sibyl Vane, boyish—she has "something of a merry little coachman" about her in her hiking costume and her blue jockey cap. But she is also feminine; the cap sits on her "thickly braided, reddish golden hair." As her father remarks in affectionate teasing, Eve is a sometime aesthete, and she readily admits that, for a while, she in fact was. (A reference to the "Rapturous Maidens" in *Patience* lies close at hand, although Couperus does not make it.) " 'We piled up our hair like turbans, dressed in loose garments of damask and brocade, with enormous puffy sleeves, and sat together uttering foolish things about art. We held a sunflower or a peacock's feather quite gracefully in our little white fingers and were utterly mad.' " From this phase, described ironically by Eve, she has gone on to the classics, Dante and, above all, Spenser's *Faerie Queen,* of which Frank knows nothing at all. Both she and Frank are enchanted by their majestic surroundings, "as if they moved in a magnetic circle of sympathy." The passage is important: Frank has been pleased by the air of superficial aestheticism Bertie has brought to his bachelor's quarters at White Rose Cottage, and this refinement comes to him full force in Eve, but he is refreshed by Eve's company: "He felt something in himself become renewed and healthy, and he would have liked to open his arms to embrace the air."

The tour continues; the travelers, now a group, sail up the coast to Christiansund (Couperus erroneously has Christiansand, which lies in the south of Norway), and there, in the sunset, the faces of Frank and Eve seem to turn red, "like two peonies, two happy masks, colored by the red of the sun, like the grimaces of clowns." The couple is caught in fate's drama, the tragic nature of which they do not understand. At Molde, leaving Bertie sulking at the Grand Hotel, Frank, Eve, and her father set out on a hike through the rain; Eve surprises Frank with a question about "what kind of man" Bertie is, to which Frank's answer is evasive, telling a little about the misfortunes Bertie has had. Eve reveals that she did not like Bertie at first but then perceived "a poet" in him, a judgment Frank hears with a mixture of "jealousy and sadness." The gray rain clouds give him a sensation of the threat of an ineluctable fate, which would destroy Eve. (The verbal repetition of *noodlot* is as telling, or monotonous, as the repetition of the fate-melody in *La forza del destino.*) Arriving at the top of the path, from which they have a vague view out over the fjord and the peaks beyond, it seems (so the narrator says) that the mountains are weeping "like thin, unmoving ghosts." The mood of the hikers darkens, as they are overcome by a "superhuman melancholy." Eve suddenly states that she has done modern reading; she understands the cry of the debilitated Oswald, "the sun, the sun," in *Ghosts,* and, having said so, falls into a fit of trembling. She has seen "the alms [*aalmoes*] of a sunset" from the heights; the narrator reports (and we are to remember it at the novel's finale) that toward the ocean in the west, "something pale gold and faint rose, scarcely a couple of lines of rose and a bit of gold," shines through.

Back in London, in December, Bertie, who has now been in Frank's care for a year, realizes he is threatened by the growing romance, which turns into an engagement. However aware he is of his own debasement (more sharply than Frank, he also has his fits of self-contempt), he is unwilling to return to his life of poverty. "Since fate had determined that he bring Frank and Eve together" through his chance mention of Norway, then he, "a base toy of fate," would see to it that they are separated. He has fantasies of taking Eve along on one of his excursions to London's slums, to be raped by men with animal-like faces; he imagines that Eve and her father burst in on one of Frank's "orgies of the past" with the skating-rink girls, and that Sir Archibald curses Frank when Eve pleads for him, "as in the fourth act of an opera"; he imagines that Eve finds Frank (now in "a modern drama") in the arms of his pretty housekeeper. (The opera reference is not a chance one; Couperus, a devoted opera fan, employed Gounod's *Le Tribut de Zamora* as a constitutive part of *Eline Vere*.)

Then Bertie's dreams turn to a plot. He has noticed that Eve detects something "Byronic" in him and entertains a sisterly affection for him. (Concomitantly, Eve has detected an indolence and indecision in Frank, for the presence of which — in "that great strong body" — she treasures Frank all the more.) Like a "spider" (twice) Bertie contrives to weave a web of suspicion around Eve, as Frank grows jealous at their long conversations, in which Bertie suggests to her that, after all, she and Frank are not made for one another, and that Frank has maintained a relationship behind her back, a suggestion backed up by fate (*noodlot*) when Frank is familiarly greeted by a woman in a cherry-red hat at the theater: helping fate, Bertie has called the woman's attention to Frank's presence in the crowd and then belabors the point with Eve. (The behavior of Bertie repeats that of Vincent Vere, Eline Vere's parasitical cousin, who encourages the break-up of Eline's engagement.) After a long conversation with Bertie, filled with compassionate hints about some unnamed secret, Eve, alone, grows aware of "a coming horror" and recalls the spectral fjord at Molde, and the sunset she saw there. At length her suspicions so wear on Frank that, in a fit of rage, he becomes physically abusive, seizing her wrists so violently that "bracelets" appear. A break ensues; Frank writes first to Eve and then to her father, asking for forgiveness; fate strikes again: Bertie, having under the name Swell, in his American hard-luck days, known Sir Archibald's butler, now bribes the man to intercept Frank's letters. For this purpose he borrows money from the unwitting Frank.

Without a reply, Frank is in despair; persuaded by Bertie, they leave the

country together, despite Frank's now depleted finances. Bertie's travel proposal is made to Frank in a scene that borders on the erotic; "with a movement
like a caress, Bertie slipped nearer, leaned his head on the arm of Frank's chair,
his hands woven round his knees, he resembled, in the half twilight, in the
glow of the fire, a lithe panther; his eyes flickered like blackly golden panther
eyes." The scene takes place after Bertie has outlined for Frank the emotional
advantages of a platonic friendship: Why cannot Frank forget his rejected love
for Eve? They, Bertie and Frank, would always be together in a "calm, chaste
blueness of brotherhood, in the golden ecstasy of their mutual sympathy,
without women." And in another erotic episode, Bertie, asking for a final loan,
to be passed along to the butler, approaches Frank in his bedroom, and falls
down beside Frank's bed, sobbing in gratitude when Frank agrees. Leaving, he
hears Frank's snores through the door and has a moment of self-contempt:
" 'Oh God, how is it possible that I am as I am?' " Throughout these scenes,
Couperus takes pains to keep Frank free of any taint of overt homosexual
affection for Bertie, all the while not letting the reader forget Frank's internal
softness, his kindness, and his genuine affection for his friend. But Frank is
likewise repeatedly portrayed (save for *his* passing moments of self-loathing
at his dependence on Bertie, and his violence toward Eve) as a man of monu-
mental lack of self-insight, or, as Bertie says at the novel's climax, " 'stupid,
stupid.' "

Frank and Bertie roam throughout the world for two years, often suffering
hardship after Frank's money runs out, but a hardship which Bertie welcomes
as a part of the "brotherliness of their being together." At last they earn
enough, in "factories, in insurance companies, on newspapers," to return to
Holland, where they grant themselves a rest on the shore at Scheveningen —
the closest Couperus comes in this novel to the refined milieus of *Eline Vere*.
Frank stays mostly indoors. Bertie's contemplation of the sea is disturbed by
the renewed intrusion of the query "Chance or fate?" The answer, of course, is
fate. He sees Sir Archibald and Eve as they stroll along the sands, "emotion-
less, marionettes" in the drama over which human beings have no control.
(The Swede Bo Bergman, in the most famous of his poems, "The Marionettes"
[1903], employs the image of human beings as "poor marionettes," controlled
by a pull on their strings; Somerville and Ross do the same in *The Silver Fox*
[1898] — itself a "fate" novel; Schnitzler has a trio of plays called, collectively,
Marionetten [1902–1904]. And in *Metamorfose*, Hugo Aylva is a reader,
during his crisis days in Paris, of Maeterlinck's marionette dramas.) Convinced that he cannot change fate's decision, Bertie makes no effort to flee, or
to persuade Frank to leave. "Perhaps it would have cost him only a word," but
the word is not spoken, as he falls under the spell of waiting for fate's next step.

Without fail, on the ever emptier beach (autumn is coming) Frank meets Eve and her father, and their old happiness is immediately restored — Eve is especially delighted to learn that Frank has not married. In a conversation with Sir Archibald, the matter of the missing letters is partly cleared up, but Bertie's role becomes clear to Eve only as Frank mentions Bertie's efforts to dissuade him from visiting the Rhodes to demand an explanation for their silence. Seized by another of her fits of trembling, Eve demands that he ask Bertie for the truth, while begging him to remain calm — she remembers the fit of rage which started their separation.

Entering their rented villa, Frank grows annoyed — for the first time since he has known him — by the "tired cat" posture of Bertie, "half lying down, languishingly charming," and does not realize that it is Bertie's way of hiding his fright. Under Frank's questions, Bertie admits the truth and, in his defense, adds that he kept the letters from the Rhodes because he wanted to stay with Frank. And then, expanding his defense, he offers an analysis of himself; he is as he is, and cannot help himself, although he would gladly be different. Belligerently or desperately, he says he is too complicated for Frank to understand him, and "a stupid beast without brains." Frank beats Bertie to death — Couperus has a weakness for the description of lethal violence, initially encouraged by his reading of Zola's *Thérèse Raquin,* and culminating in the horrors at the end of his Heliogabalus novel, *De berg van licht* (1905–1906). Eve comes too late: "One eye was a shapeless spot, half congealed, half liquid, the other burst out of its oval socket, like a great opal of sadness." (Couperus must have been aware of the effect he made with "oval" and "opal.") Frank surrenders to the police; looking at the dark clouds, Eve remembers Molde, where she felt terror for the first time.

During Frank's two-year sentence for manslaughter, served at a prison in the dunes of Scheveningen, Eve and her father remain in The Hague; upon his release she looks forward to marriage with him, over her father's objections, as the hallucinations which have tormented her briefly diminish. Frank grows ever more melancholy, for which Eve — motherly as before — loves him dearly, again drawn to the difference between his frail gentleness and his powerful physique. He is promised a place in a Glasgow engineering firm; Eve is to inherit her late mother's fortune. Nevertheless, the image of Bertie comes between them, something like the phantom of Camille in *Thérèse Raquin* coming between Thérèse and Laurent. Eve's spirit darkens in her companionship with Frank, and she dreads — without admitting it — the Sundays when Frank comes to visit. On a particularly gloomy day — they live in London now — she cried out, remembering Molde, " 'I have been ill ever since that day,' "and she wants to go to Italy and, in Oswald's words, see "the sun, the sun." Frank's unconsolatory reply is that he wants to break their engagement, for he has grown old, and she is still young. Eve retorts that she too is old, because of their experience, but that marriage will rejuvenate them — Frank is her "great child." She has no fear of Frank, placing all the blame on Bertie, but Frank defends his friend, who could not help himself, a reprise of Bertie's own arguments before the murder. Instead, Frank despises himself, and this sense of guilt toward Bertie crushes him: " 'I was fond of him once, and now I could tell him that I do understand — that I forgive him.' " All along, Eve has sensed an abnormality in Frank's devotion to Bertie, although in her Victorian innocence (her father did not want her to read *Ghosts*), she could not put a name to her fears and hesitated to do more than notice Bertie's feminine appearance and mode of behavior.

As Eve cries that she could " 'strangle, strangle' " Bertie, and as the clouds grow darker, the fear of an attack of "visionary thunder" comes over her again; in one of the novel's several *coups de théâtre,* she discovers a vial of poison in Frank's pocket, a "tiny dark blue bottle," like the silver vial marked with a death's head which Jan Maria Plojhar keeps and whose contents his bride Catarina drinks so that she can die with him, in Julius Zeyer's novel of 1891, like the bottle of cyanide Hamsun's Nagel carries with him in *Mysterier* (1892). Eve throws the bottle into a corner and believes it has broken; Frank confesses that he intended to take the poison after his farewell, suggesting that she could be happy with someone else. In a grim love duet, Eve says that they were fated for one another; it was "noodlot," at which Frank recalls Bertie's favorite word, now capitalized in the speeches of both the partners. Watching the endless rain, unwilling to let Frank leave her, Eve falls into an "ecstasy of joy," proposing that they die together: " 'It will be wondrous . . . rose and silver and gold around us, like a sunset,' " the ambiguous sunset they saw, "two happy masks," at Christiansund, and "the alms of a sunset" seen at Molde, long ago. She finds the vial, which has not smashed (" 'It is Fate which did not wish to let it be broken' "), and drinks half the contents. Passive to the end, easily influenced by those he loves, Frank — seeing that she waits for him — drinks the other half and dies. Eve hears the storm and the thunder, "a supernatural thunder on the wheels of the spheres," and sinks, twisting, onto Frank's corpse. Her father's old hand opens the door. Small wonder that Gerrit Jaeger turned *Noodlot* into a play. It had its premiere in Rotterdam in 1892, a little more than two years before Jaeger (to whom Couperus had dedicated *Eline Vere*) took his own life.

The narratives about emotional problems which come in rapid succession after *Noodlot* are less melodramatic than *Noodlot*. In *Een zieltje* (A Little Soul), in fact written during the summer before *Noodlot*, a timid boy, Kareltje, falls innocently in love with his vigorous Uncle Frank, and drowns himself when Frank tells him to be a real boy and not sentimental. The novella *Eene illusie* (written in 1890, published in 1892) is the account of the inability of Carel Armand to love the poetess Tila "as a woman," one of Couperus's many self-portraits. *Eene illusie* makes a particular point of Carel's physical triumphs over other women and ends with the double lament of Tila (who wants to see Carel "over" her, not kneeling at her feet!), and of Carel, who despairs at his failure to create an illusion of erotic love with Tila. In *Extase* (1891, *Ecstasy,* translated in 1894), the widow Cécile van Evan falls in love with Taco Quaerts, a man about town and sportsman (in whom Couperus scholars have seen another of Couperus's great friends, the army officer Johan Hendrik Ram); Quaerts destroys their delicate relationship by an access of his brutal sexuality. In *Langs lijnen van geleidelijkheid* (1900, *The Inevitable,* in the American edition, *Love Inevitable* in the British, 1930), Cornélie de Retz van Loo goes to Rome for art studies — she is a faithful reader of her red-bound Baedeker — and tries to support herself writing for the home press on the rights of women. She has divorced her husband, Baron Brox, because of his brutality, his tyranny, and his unfaithfulness. In Rome, she meets the gentle and impoverished artist Duco, a fellow Netherlander, but, in a remarkable scene, is drawn back to Brox by his animal magnetism. In all four works, the recondite theme of homosexuality, variously disguised, can be made out, in little Kareltje, in Armand, in the gentle affection of Cécile for the (suddenly impotent) Quaerts, in Cornélie's submission to the power of the loathsome Brox. In the long prose poem *Psyche* (1898, English 1900), the Satyr clips Psyche's wings so that she can engage in sexual orgies, and she lives to regret it; in the companion piece *Fidessa* (1899), the much-tried nymph of the title rejects sexuality but is joined to her beloved Sans-Joye in a mystic marriage after the knight's death. The fear of sexuality and a yearning for it, in one form or another, can be discerned throughout.

Of all the *paralipomena,* however, the most revealing is a "vision" which Hugo Aylva, in the fourth, penultimate part ("The Book of Anarchism") of *Metamorfose,* experiences during his stay in Rome. It takes place in the East Indies; in a school game, an eleven-year-old, Kareltje, "pale, blond, not strong, but a madcap," is injured by Arnold, older and strong for his years. Arnold begs Kareltje to forgive him, and the two become fast friends; Arnold "likes Kareltje more than all the girls together." The charm for Arnold was "precisely [Kareltje's] doll-soul, something womanlike, which was no girl, and spoke to *his* youthful dreamer's soul, as something he could possess and protect and simply love." The relationship is chaste but fades when Kareltje, "a little cat," goes into dark corners with other boys.

At the same time, and subsequently, Couperus built a body of narrative work in which a homosexual substratum can be detected only with difficulty: he turned to novels about the imaginary Mediterranean empire of Liparia, *Majesteit* (1893, translated in 1894 by Teixeira de Mattos and the poet Ernest Dowson), and its sequel, *Wereldvrede* (1894, World Peace): Othomar, the indecisive son of a stern-willed monarch, succeeds to the throne after the latter's assassination and must deal with such pertinent contemporary problems as the decline of the monarchy, workers' rights, and anarchism. The novella *Hoge troeven* (1896, High Trumps) is a pendant to the Liparia novels: King Wladimir of Thrace, resembling "a young Caracalla," seduces and abandons his mother's innocent lady-in-waiting, at the exiled mother's court with its "strange decadence." Couperus recalled his childhood in the Dutch East Indies — he had visited his relatives there in 1899 — in *De stille kracht* (1900, *The Hidden Force*, 1922, 1985) and approached, in a somewhat gingerly but still sensational fashion, the dangers — not least of all moral — to which the white ruling class was exposed. Then, from 1901 to 1903, he published the four parts of what is generally regarded as his masterpiece, *De boeken der kleine zielen* (1901–1903, translated separately from 1914 to 1918, and issued collectively in 1932 as *The Book of the Small Souls*), a return to the settings in The Hague and familial involvements of *Eline Vere*. As an epilogue to what could be called the Netherlandic phase of Couperus's writing, he composed the short novel *Van oude mensen, de dingen die voorbijgaan* (1906, *Old People and the Times That Pass*, 1918), about an ancient crime of passion in Java and its effect, half a century later, on families in The Hague, a tour de force in which the principal characters are nonagenarians.

Hereafter, Couperus took his themes largely from antiquity, by means of which he could return to the question of sexual identity that had so troubled him as a young man, but now with a patina of learnedness and, as it were, respectability. The turning point was the above-mentioned Heliogabalus novel, on an icon of decadence (see Stefan George's *Algabal* and Jean Lombard's *L'Agonie*), in which the emperor falls in love with the charioteer Hierodes, a relative to Quaerts and Brox. Couperus supported himself in a fairly lavish style by his pen: travel books from the sunny Mediterranean world (Eve's desire is fulfilled), *Antiek tourisme: Roman uit Oud-Egypte* (1911, *The Tour: A Story of Ancient Egypt*, 1920), *Herakles* (1913), *De Komedianten* (1917, *The Comedians*, 1926). The more sophisticated American reading public of the 1920s could now confront the lesbian aristocrats and catamites of ancient Rome with some equanimity. Then came a rendering of Apuleius' *Metamorphoses* as *De verliefde ezel* (1918, The Enamored Ass), *Xerxes of de Hoogmoed* (1919, *Arrogance, The Conquests of Xerxes*, 1930), and *Iskander: De roman van Alexander de Grote* (1920, Iskander, The Novel of Alexander the Great), like *De berg van licht, Herakles,* and *De verliefde ezel,* translated into German but never into English. The later works betray a considerable decline in inspiration, for all the continued brilliance of Couperus's language. The Italian student of decadence Mario Praz wrote: "It is to be lamented that Couperus, gifted as he was to sense the dramatic events in the existence of the bourgeoisie, let his eye fall on Heliogabalus, the catamite from antiquity." Throughout Thomas Mann's works (e.g., *Tonio Kröger, Death in Venice, Felix Krull, The Magic Mountains, Dr. Faustus*), hints or more than hints of Mann's repressed bisexuality can be detected, used far more effectively than by Couperus in his final antique period.

But in *Noodlot,* certainly, and some of the short novels or novellas surrounding it, the same topic, although more or less concealed, is essential and formative. No doubt, *Noodlot* is badly flawed. Its insistence, verbal and otherwise, on "fate" becomes tiresome — it does not have the music of Verdi's fate-opera to support it. On February 14, 1891, in response to the discussion *Noodlot* (and *Eline Vere*) caused among the Dutch public, the educator C. H. den Hertog held a lecture, subsequently published as *Noodlottig determinisme* (Fateful Determinism), in which Den Hertog at great length analyzed and warned against the removal of moral responsibility that such "determinism" entailed; his peroration brought up *Die Leiden des jungen Werthers (The Sorrows of Young Werther)* and the imitations in real life that Werther's suicide notoriously had called forth. Reading *Noodlot* with its "superficial determinism" could be detrimental for Holland's youth. *Noodlot* was a harmful book, a charge not at all far removed from that made by Edward Carson, not yet knighted, during Oscar Wilde's first trial, about *The Picture of Dorian Gray.* (Carson was far franker about the homosexual element in Wilde's novel than was Den Hertog in his admonitory lecture, which slides past the topic.)

A paradox of Couperus's novel is that Bertie, its most obvious decadent specimen, is also its toughest. He has gone it alone in America and, although he frequently complains of his lack of will, his abulia, he quickly — from the novel's start — hatches plans for his survival; only in the penultimate chapter, at Scheveningen, does he wholly succumb to "fate" or "inertia," and wait for his punishment (in which he is reduced to a spectacle of utmost physical horror, quite like that of Dorian, "loathsome of visage," after he has stabbed his portrait and died with that horrible cry on his lips). Bertie, near the end, has a moment of complete self-insight vouchsafed only partially to other protagonists of decadence, to the egomaniacal Sperelli only at the end of *Il piacere,* to Dorian in his resolution "to be good," to Rodenbach's Viane in his recognition of Jane Scott's viciousness; Bertie feels "a horrible tiredness, a tiredness so empty and desperate that it almost seemed to be a physical need of death." He proclaims his insight to himself and then to Frank, in his long curtain speech: he is what he is. Frank remembers Bertie's words: they are the cause of his forgiveness of Bertie and his own crushing sense of guilt — an apologia offered to his unaware audience by Couperus, guilt-ridden at his sexuality.

Bertie's two victims are also what fate (or their heritage) has made them, with backgrounds for which the text offers few but salient details. Frank is deeply drawn to the "normal" world of his parents, for the memory of which he sometimes resists his London life of pleasure; Eve suffers when her father — who has already made fun of her earlier aestheticism — refuses to listen to her anguished suspicions of Frank and his supposed heterosexual infidelity; she calls upon her mother, long since dead. The appearance of *Ghosts* in the Molde episode, which otherwise may seem to be an almost unnecessary bow to Ibsenism, to the persistent bad weather of the play, and Ibsen's effect on fragile nerves, is pertinent: in both instances, Frank's and Eve's, the lovers are affected by parental love or its absence, as is the case in a more complex fashion in *Ghosts;* in both instances, they are afflicted by inherent weaknesses not altogether understood: Frank by the softness or womanliness of his spirit (in that extremely virile bachelor's body), Eve by the refined sensibility leading to the hallucinations which beset her at Molde and then return with greater and greater intensity in the final chapters of the book. Frank is an earlier version of the sturdy captain in *De boeken der kleine zielen,* Gerrit van Lowe, who deeply loves his children, his wife, and his home, rejects his former mistress after a belated reunion, and then, weakened by physical illness and realizing he cannot escape his own feminine soul, which fits so ill with his body, his calling, and what he wants his life to be, kills himself. Just so Eve, the apparently reformed aesthete, the devotee of sunsets and literature, falls prey to aestheticism like her predecessor in Couperus, Eline Vere, who injects that aestheticism into all the relationships of her life and dies after trying to sing Beethoven's scena, "Ah perfido!" — life has constantly been perfidious to her. Frank and Eve, more fragile than Bertie by far, are indeed, as the German critic Hermann Menkes wrote in a major review of Couperus's work in *Die Zeit* for 1895, "hothouse plants that die from their own aroma, late-come beings of a century that is tired unto death." The readiness with which Eve imagines death as a splendid sunset, and with which, grown "old," Frank decides to share death with her, fully qualifies them as "Spätlinge eines todmüden Jahrhunderts." Hofmannsthal apostrophized the decadents, including himself, in the passage ending: "as it were, we have no roots in life, and wander, clear-sighted and yet day-blind shadows, among the children of life."

Much of the melodramatic overlay in *Noodlot* — the coincidences, the verbal repetitions, the emphasis on Bertie's feline nature and the velvet night of his eyes — has to be understood by reference to Couperus's desire to explain and yet conceal his sexual nature, to tell and not to tell about a love that dares not speak its name. The often noted blindness of Frank to the nature of his affection for Bertie, Eve's groping suspicions about Bertie's proclivities (on which Frank is so close-mouthed), are a sign of Couperus's unwillingness or inability to confront his own being, of a Couperus understandably afraid to challenge the restrictions of his time, and yet wanting quite desperately to talk about himself. One of the miracles of successful artistic repression in Couperus is the absence, after the hints in the works clustered around *Noodlot,* of his life's central problem until he returns to it in the Heliogabalus novel. Wilde bravely lived up to the truth in the (still evasive) answers to Carson after the latter's reading of the conversation between Basil Hallward and Dorian: " 'It is quite true that I have worshipped you with far more romance of feeling than a man usually gives to a friend — somehow, I have never loved a woman.' " Hallward, remember, is murdered by Dorian.

From 1900 on, Couperus, with his wife, had lived principally at Nice, owning a villa there from 1908 to 1913; he cultivated friendships on the boulevards of the city which, according to Jean Lorrain's *Le Vice errant,* was the center of well-heeled homosexual culture. A recurring figure from the Mediterranean causeries, written for *Het Vaderland,* is Orlando, perhaps imaginary, perhaps not, a handsome, wise, but faintly comical acquaintance from the beaches of Nice. The Couperuses also made extended trips to Florence and Rome, experiences given narrative form in the weak *Aan de weg der vreugde* (1908, On the Path of Joy), a retelling of *Extase,* in which an inhibited Dutch woman is fascinated by the virile Aldo Ardo. In one of the causeries, published on December 23, 1911, the author recalls his epistolary exchange with Oscar Wilde, Wilde's enthusiasm for *Noodlot,* and the Dutch translation of *The Picture of Dorian Gray* by his wife. The book was sent to him with Wilde's "long, hearty, sympathetic letter; the volume itself had an extremely artistic gray-white binding ornamented with gilded pomegranates." In continuation, the causeur tells how, on a rainy day in Florence, he encountered an old friend, a waiter he had once known in Milan, now the companion and cook of a middle-aged English gentleman, come down in the world but still possessing the remnants of youthful beauty. Meeting the gentleman, Couperus observes that: "the violet-blue eyes looked tired, like faded violets; around the mouth were tired wrinkles and furrows . . . An old ulster hung on the somewhat stooped back, there was something gentle, fine, and broken about him." Happy to find someone who speaks English, the gentleman recognizes Couperus's name and confesses that he is the "prototype of Dorian Gray . . . the shimmering Dorian Gray of the shimmering Oscar Wilde." The causeur and his new acquaintance, who states that he is a bundle of nerves, quite rheumatic, and forced to be careful with his food, go to the movies at "Dorian's" suggestion, to see a sentimental drama, a farce, and a newsreel of Italian soldiers embarking for Tripoli. (It is the beginning of the Turkish-Italian War of 1911–12.) Then they part, and the causeur goes home to his wife, beside the fire, and tells her, " in a voice broken by melancholy," that he has met the hero of the book she translated long ago. The causerie, with its repeated descriptions of "Dorian's" past glory and present decay, is open to several interpretations, including the remote but attractive one that Couperus in fact encountered Wilde's sometime friends, either Robert Ross or Alfred Lord Douglas, in Italy: Richard Ellman has argued that Ross, not "Bosie," was the model for Dorian. Wilde met the rose-white youth Douglas only after the publication of his novel. But the possibility really does not matter: what counts is the repeated pleasure Couperus takes in describing how old and shabby, with cotton stuffed in his ears, "Dorian" has become, and the evident relief with which Couperus returns to wife and hearth.

The "Dorian Gray" causerie — written eleven years after Wilde's death — is a fitting epilogue to the revealing-concealing text of *Noodlot*.

7

Norway

ARNE GARBORG

It is appropriate to begin the discussion of Arne Garborg's diary-novel, *Trætte Mænd* (1891, *Weary Men*), with a brief account of Garborg's life. He was born in 1851 at a farm called Garborg, in Jæren, a section of southwestern Norway known for its bad weather and rocky soil, for its disproportionately large contribution to the great nineteenth century migration to North America, and for the strong hold that pietism — what we might call religious fundamentalism — had upon its inhabitants. To the disappointment of Arne Garborg's father, a stern man and a stern pietist, the eldest son was not interested in taking over the farm; instead, he wished to be a teacher, and, even as a teenager, got a post as instructor in a country school (1866–68), then continuing to a pedagogical seminary. In 1869, his father sold the farm and, subsequently, killed himself; Garborg appears to have thought that he, the somehow disloyal son, was responsible for the father's death. After more training at a teacher's college, in 1873 Garborg went to Christiania (which, in 1924, would be redubbed Oslo) and there attended the same preparatory school, Heltberg's "student-factory," which had earlier readied Ibsen, the peasant-poet Vinje, Bjørnson, and Jonas Lie for the university's entrance examinations. A budding career as a journalist was interrupted by two crises, religious and linguistic, which Garborg underwent almost simultaneously. The first had to do with a loss of faith: Garborg turned radically away from Christianity, partly under the influence of the Danish critic Georg Brandes and, in 1878 published what was in essence a defence of his new position, his first novel. *Ein Fritenkjar* (A Freethinker), about a theologian whose intellectual honesty impels him to confess that he can no longer continue to preach the Christian faith. His existence becomes impossible, he is ostracized, his marriage goes to pieces, and, at his grave, he is condemned by his son, who has become a traditional Lutheran minister. The book cost Garborg, two years later on, a travel stipend for which he had applied to the Storting, the Norwegian parliament. The second crisis will be described shortly.

Garborg's literary production continued to be a thorn in the side of conservative Norwegian society. The novel *Bondestudentar* (1883, Peasant Students) is a picture of a student from the country, Daniel Braut, who abandons his ideals and swiftly becomes an opportunist; in a kind of sequel, *Mannfolk* (1886, Menfolk), Garborg confronts the sexual problems of young men who have no "legitimate" outlet for their erotic drives. Unable to marry, for economic reasons, they find a not very safe safety valve in seductions of servant girls (a practice in which some older, married men are substitutes) and with prostitutes. Then, in *Hjaa ho Mor* (1890, At Mama's), again with considerable naturalistic detail, Garborg recounted the story of Fanny Holmsen, half-heartedly pursued by the government clerk Gabriel Gram but eventually persuaded, by her mother, into a marriage with an elderly (i.e., fortyish) and worn-out man whom, not unjustly, the daughter calls Death from Lübeck, an allusion to a wood carving of a skeleton in the North German city. The next book was *Trætte Mænd*, which was destined to remain—in a number of ways—a singular item in Garborg's oeuvre. Thereafter came the novel *Fred* (1892, *Peace*), in which Garborg told the story of his father's fate, the epic-lyrical cycle *Haugtussa* (1895), almost immediately set to music by Edvard Grieg as his Opus 67, its sequel *I Helheim* (1901, In Hell), the play *Læraren* (1896, The Teacher), and the diary-novels *Den burtkomme Faderen* (1899, *The Lost Father*) and *Heimkomin Son* (1908, The Son Returned). Garborg's creative literary career was pretty well over by the turn of the century; his main energies were given to a kind of autobiography, *Knudaheibrev* (1904, Knudahei-Letters), in which—as in the cycle *Haugtussa*—he celebrated the essential vitality of Norwegian country people, a making-up for what he may have implied with the contemptible Daniel Braut of *Bondestudentar*. His diary was published by his wife after his passing in 1924.

In later life, Garborg was something of a disappointed man. A strong believer in a republican form of government, he was unhappy when a Danish prince was imported, as Haakon VII, to be the ruler of the new kingdom of Norway, after the "personal union" with Sweden was dissolved in the so-called (and, happily, bloodless) Union Crisis of 1905. (In his diary for October 15 of that year he wrote: "On November 4 we'll get our Danish king. Whom we'll take because he's got an English wife"; on November 23, Garborg continued: "He has assumed the name Haakon, and the crown prince will be named Olav. A Danish-speaking King Haakon and a Norwegian-Danish King Olav. It's comical, but a people without a nationality are comical. What can be done about it?") These complaints had their origin in his language crisis of the 1870s: Garborg's hopes for a change in the linguistic composition of Norway had not been fulfilled — certainly not in the measure he had wished. Since the sixteenth century, Norway had been the larger but less important component in the so-called twin empire of Denmark and Norway, ruled by Danish kings and, to some extent, through Danish officials, with its sole university in Copenhagen; in 1814, under the terms of the Treaty of Kiel and as a penalty for Denmark's loyalty to Napoleon, Norway had become semiautonomous, in the "personal union." Long after the dissolution of the Danish tie, the language of government, of commerce, of the cities, and of letters remained Dano-Norwegian, conforming to Danish rules of grammar and orthography, but pronounced as if it were Norwegian, and (as in Scottish English) with local coloring in vocabulary: "Even when Norwegians spoke Danish that was lexically and grammatically perfect, they were still . . . Norwegian in sound." In the 1850s, a movement arose to give Norway its own spoken and written language, based upon country dialects, particularly those of the west; this new tongue (composed of very old elements) was at first called *landsmål* ("country-language," but with the further implication of "language of the land"), as opposed to a new and flattering name for Dano-Norwegian, *riksmål* (language of the "nation"). Garborg, who had learned to write (and speak) Dano-Norwegian in school, was one of the most gifted advocates of the freshly created and — to some — more authentic Norwegian. By choosing it as his instrument, a choice he described in his *Den nynorske Sprog- og Nationalitetsbevægelse* (1877, The New Norwegian Language and Nationality Movement), which he wrote in Dano-Norwegian, he went against the common literary practice of the time. Dano-Norwegian had overwhelming merits on its side: it emphasized the common cultural heritage with Denmark (the great comedy writer Ludvig Holberg was born in Norway but had his literary career in Denmark, Søren Kierkegaard had lately become of great importance for literature as well for theology in Norway); it was a subtle and supple language, wholly formed, with an established grammar and orthography; it gave Norway's writers the populace of Denmark as an additional — and larger — reading public. (The plays of Ibsen, the plays and novels of Bjørnson, the novels of Jonas Lie and Alexander L. Kielland — to name Ibsen's major contemporaries — came out simultaneously in Copenhagen and Christiania, or were printed in Copenhagen and shipped north to the Norwegian capital.) Dano-Norwegian was also easily read by the intelligentsia in Sweden and Finland; and it had plenty of skillful translators into German, translators who provided an ancillary — and enormous — public for Norwegian authors.

By this decision Garborg seemed to have deprived himself of these advantages; his later disappointment at the lack of Norwegian enthusiasm for the "native" language was obviously exacerbated by his concern for his own literary career. (In January 1906, he told his diary that "[Christiania] — which is supposed to be the 'capital' and 'elegant' — is stripping itself more and more of everything Norwegian. Earlier we heard some Norwegian on the streets, perhaps we heard more than that. Now I listen as closely as I can, and when I come on children at play, they all speak school Dano-Norwegian.") As early as *Peer Gynt* in the 1860's, Ibsen had made fun of the landsmål or nynorsk enthusiasts; Knut Hamsun, only a few years youger than Garborg, reviled the movement and wrote all his books in Dano-Norwegian or riksmål or *bokmål,* as it came eventually to be called. (*Book language* was a mildly pejorative term, on which zealots for nynorsk insisted.) When Garborg's productivity was over, he continued to fight for the language in which he believed, making renderings of *Faust* and the *Odyssey* into nynorsk, and, oddly enough, translating the great Dano-Norwegian Holberg. Toward the end of his life, Garborg was several times seriously considered for the Nobel Prize in literature, on the strength of his work from the 1880s and 1890s; according to reports that slipped out of the Swedish Academy, his candidacy foundered on his championship of New Norwegian and on the timidity of the Nobel Committee: a prize to him, it was reasoned, might seem to favor the smaller of Norway's two languages. Indeed, all the Norwegian winners of the prize, Bjørnson in 1903, Knut Hamsun in 1920, Sigrid Undset in 1928, were writers of the riksmål or bokmål.

Now, about Garborg's language, an exception must immediately be made to the Garborgian linguistic rule. *Trætte Mænd* is not written in the nynorsk Garborg used in his other books (save for a play and a monograph on the novelist Jonas Lie); instead, it is composed in a brilliant Dano-Norwegian — after all, that is the language Gabriel Jeronimus Gram, who keeps the diary, would have written: he is a member of Norway's army of officials, a native of the old town of Bergen who has settled in Christiania. Gram's language is a sign for Garborg, too, of Gram's decadence, and of his belonging to the past or, perhaps, of his having no future. Paradoxically, this atypical book in Garborg's production has become the work by which he is best known outside Scandinavia or, at any rate, in the German-speaking world, where he found his principle foreign audience. When it appeared in German as *Müde Seelen*

(Tired Souls) in 1893, the dramatist and novelist Johannes Schlaf wrote: "No Frenchman can vie with this Germanic thoroughness and intimacy, with this courage for diving into the deepest and most dangerous depths of emotional life, a courage which sometimes borders on foolhardiness." Or, Schlaf again: "Garborg has perhaps succeeded in writing the most perfect emotional novel, stages of the soul, which our modern literature has to show." Marie Herzfeld — who translated the novel into German — stated that it "is the most gripping, most all-embracing depiction of this disease of the spirit [the hopelessness of the fin de siècle] of our time." In the rather turgid opinion of Heinrich Hart, the Berlin critic: "We have already got to know more than enough about the distorted fin de siècle masks of these homunculi, produced in test tubes, who, like the hero of Huysmans's *À rebours,* fascinate in their turn all the little test-tube writers about literature . . . Garborg for the first time gives us a real person, who has struggled until he is exhausted in the pounding surf of our time and now, with his frozen hands, clutches at the first plank that presents itself, to see whether it will carry him ashore." Tomáš Garrigue Masaryk, someday to be the first president of the Republic of Czechoslovakia, was so fascinated by the book that he entered into a correspondence with the author. (A decade before he read *Weary Men,* Masaryk had written a dissertation titled "Der Selbstmord als soziale Massenerscheinung der modernen Zivilisation" [Suicide as Social Mass-Phenomenon of Modern Civilization].)

Thus, the path that Garborg took into the European literary consciousness was the same as that earlier followed by Ibsen, Bjørnson, and Lie — German translation. Garborg, whose own stays in Germany had been relatively short, in 1889–90 and 1890–91, had the good fortune of attracting a major translator, Marie Herzfeld, to deal with the manifold difficulties of his nynorsk texts and the special subtleties of *Weary Men;* his novels came out at the house of an ambitious young publisher, Samuel Fischer of Berlin, whose journal, *Freie Bühne,* serialized *Müde Seelen* before its publication in book form. In a German literary world already well disposed toward things Scandinavian, not least because of the Ibsen fever, Garborg came to be regarded as "a true Germanic" and Marie Herzfeld, again, claimed that his "naturalism" was much more "humane, deeper, more consequential" than that of Flaubert and Zola. The publication of *Müde Seelen* had been preceded by *Aus der Männerwelt* (1888) and *Bei Mama* (1891), and followed by *Bauernstudenten* (1902); this meant that German readers of *Weary Men,* if they had followed the other books, knew something about several of the diary-novel's main characters: as said, Fanny Holmsen and Gabriel Gram are in *Bei Mama,* and in *Aus der Männerwelt* Georg Jonathan appears, the bastard son of an English sailor (who claimed to be a captain) and a Norwegian grocer's daughter. That novel also told how the adult Jonathan aided Helena, a servant girl seduced by the student Laurits Kruse and ogled by the now married theological candidate Daniel Braut (the protagonist of *Bauernstudenten* and a subsidiary figure in *Aus der Männerwelt*) when *her* illegitimate child had sickened and died. A reader who knew these facts was predisposed to like Jonathan (who also had taken the brave and almost unheard-of step of marrying his mistress), Jonathan, who told a friend that "prostitutes don't do it for pleasure's sake." In the same novel a younger Dr. Kvaale appears; he hesitates to marry his longtime fiancée because he has contracted syphilis.

Unhappily, Garborg's German fame — unlike that of Ibsen or Hamsun — did not last much past 1900. This falling off in interest may have come from several circumstances: that his production had dwindled, that he was not a man of Hamsun's ilk, able to call attention to himself, and that the "naturalism" of his earlier works, before *Weary Men*, had perhaps come to seem a little passé. As for *Weary Men*, it had proved to be a popular but difficult book for German readers (and still more difficult for Scandinavians): even Heinrich Hart had said that "it was not a novel in the true sense of the word," and Felix Poppenberg had mentioned its "interrupted, fragmentary, and aphoristic form."

Garborg never penetrated the literary consciousness of the English-speaking world; the works of his that did appear in English, during the 1920s, were two novels with a Norwegian country setting, *The Lost Father* (1920) and *Peace* (1929). No Arthur Symons (who may not have been able to read German), no Edmund Gosse (the great English champion, with William Archer, of Ibsen) took up Garborg's cause. Only one more or less contemporary account of *Weary Men* exists in English — in a survey of "Contemporary Scandinavian Belles lettres" by the historian and Scandinavian enthusiast R. Nisbet-Bain for the journal *Cosmopolis* for 1896: "Garborg's latest development has caused his radical friends no small uneasiness — *Trætte Mænd* is obviously inspired by Huysmans's [novel about conversion] *En route,* and arrives at precisely the same conclusion — the utter vanity of life divorced from religion." Like many other readers, Nisbet-Bain may have missed the book's point, and the proposal that it is influenced by *En route* is improbable since that account of a return to the Roman Catholic church came out in 1895, four years after *Trætte Mænd*. Furthermore, in her diary for 1908, Garborg's wife, Hulda, wrote that her husband did not like to read at all, although what little he read he judged quickly and with surprising accuracy: "I scarcely think that [Garborg] had read any of Huysmans or the other [French decadents] when he wrote *Weary Men*. I got hold of *Là-bas* and *En route* only later, but I scarcely think that he read them either.") Nisbet-Bain, however, more or less correctly analyzes the book as an indictment of decadence and decadents. "Garborg is most severe upon the so-called Decadents, those super-refined neurasthenics, cynical hedonists, with a languid penchant for the bizarre, the eccentric, and the unclean, who 'no longer believe in anything, or interest themselves in anything, or have the energy to hold fast to anything; but simply lie supine and try to wring a drop or two of art out of their own jaded perceptions.'"

At the end of his review of *Weary Men* in *Freie Bühne,* Heinrich Hart — who evidently had learned to read Dano-Norwegian — called attention to what he saw as the difficulties of translating the text: he was concerned about "these nervous vibrations of thought, these trembling sounds of the emotions, these lightning-swift snapshots of [the] moods of nature and the spirit," which made the book into "one great lyric poem." He remarked, "I simply fear that no translator will be able even to approximate this prose and this verse. But what does it matter? Even so, the value of the book will be perceived." Actually, the real difficulty of translating *Weary Men* lies not so much in rendering its lyrical passages into German (the German language already had a nicely equivalent style, from Romanticism), but in dealing with what the Czech comparatist Pavel Fraenkl has called "parody and pastiche." The diaries of Gabriel Gram are in fact a remarkable display of virtuosity, on Garborg's part, in recreating not just the Dano-Norwegian language but the mixed style that a Gram would have used in his diary; the entries are shot through with borrowings from the jargon of academics and prostitutes, from other languages, from authors that Gram would have read. Gram has, as it were, no language of his own. Capturing the diary's 'borrowed' quality is sometimes possible in a translation, sometimes not. Although a man of thirty-eight, the bachelor Gram retains a good deal of student slang in his speech and written style — for example, as Johs. A. Dale has pointed out, when talking of his former drinking companion, Pastor Løchen, Gram calls him his "brother in the galleys" and "fellow dipsomaniac" and "a converted brigand," while styling himself a "bandit." Gram's use of foreign words is still more important; like the coterie of friends in *Il piacere,* Gram and his male acquaintances cannot get along without them: German (*sittlich entrüstet, Einerlei, Weltschmerz, Erscheinung*), English (*if you please* and, more luridly, *self-abuse*), French (*cabinet d'aisance, prostituée, vérole*), and, of course, the Latin so often served up in D'Annunzio's novel — but not by any means as masterful a Latin. Here, the phrases are almost all tags that, once upon a time, every schoolboy knew: *jacta est alea, in optima luce, taedium generale, commune naufragium,* the Catullan *aeterna nox sine luce,* the Goliardic "edite, bibite, collegiales, post multa saecula nulla pocula," the Horatian "Naturam expellas furca" (from *Epistles,* I, x, 24) which — another schoolboy joke — is given Norwegian syntax: "Naturam pellas furca ex." (The rest of the line is omitted, since the participants in the conversation already know it:

"Tamen usque recurret" — "You can drive out nature with a pitchfork, nevertheless it will come back again and again.") French is employed, of course, for the great mottos of the decadence, as in the "Fin de siècle, fin du globe" passage at Lady Narborough's dinner in *Dorian Gray*. The opening of section 35, in Part 2, is "Fin de siècle, fin de siècle, fin de la culture européenne" (followed by a sweeping view of the destruction of the monuments, churches, and galleries of Paris by "black-fisted proletarians," no doubt a memory — here used as a prophecy for the future — of the Commune: it is one of the most often quoted passages in the novel). Georg Jonathan himself — for all his opposition to the hopelessness of the fin de siècle — thinks of "putting on a fin de siècle mask," a not unimportant passage for interpreting the end of the novel; at the novel's end, too, Jonathan says, "fin de siècle, agonie de la bourgeoisie" upon learning that Gram has decided to (re)enter the Christian church.

Beyond the many words and phrases that give the text an almost macaronic air, there are the quotations from, or allusions to, other works of literature — in contrast to Huysmans's practice, works that are quite well known. Garborg is determined not to make his Gram seem exceptionally intellectual or well informed (as Des Esseintes obviously is); Gram moves on familiar paths. Goethe's *Faust* is a major source of quotations: Gram has read it in school or at the university. Very early in the diary, Gram — already thinking about a woman savior — lets his Norwegian text slide over into the prayer of Gretchen to Virgin Mary in the "Zwinger" scene of *Faust,* Part 1, "Ach neige, du Schmerzensreiche, / dein Antlitz gnädig meiner Not" (Oh lower, thou rich in pain, / Thy countenance mercifully to my despair). The pregnant girl's prayer to the Blessed Virgin for succor also functions as Gram's first prayer for a woman savior — any woman — and at the same time points forward to his approach to the Roman Catholic faith. A part of the Goethean passage returns in Part 2, where it is the Virgin Mary, "du Schmerzensreiche," who is clearly addressed, after Gram has thought — like the protagonist in Edmond Rod's *La Course à la mort* — that he will be converted and enter a monastery: "To enter the sacred Catholic Church and [to go] from there to the monastery." Later still, the Goethe text is wholly transformed into the liturgical formula "Thou blessed among women." (The possibility of a Roman Catholic salvation seems to be furthered still more by the quotation of five strophes from Heinrich Heine's "Die Wallfahrt nach Kevlaar," furthered, that is, until we read the poem completely: the sick boy is visited by the Virgin Mary but, when the sun comes up, he is dead. Garborg omits the poem's thrice-repeated praise of the Virgin. Gram likes to talk a great deal about the pleasant prospect of his own death but can grow frightened at the realization of its finality.) The *Faust* quotations continue with a section from Faust's despairing monologue, near the opening

of the play, where the scholar, still old, talks about the fragility of hope, to
which Gram adds: "Would the same Dr. Faustus have done better by enjoying
the cup of poison [as Faust almost does at the end of the scene in Goethe] than
by listening to the Easter morning hymn?" (Ringing out, the hymn keeps Faust
from taking the poison.) Almost at the end of the diary, the Easter hymn from
Faust does sound for Gram, too, or at any rate is quoted by him, plucked from
his interior treasure chest of familiar quotations. "Once again, the Easter bells
are ringing out over the world, once again the morning song is heard, "Christ
ist erstanden, / Freude dem Sterblichen, / den die verderblichen, / schleich-
enden, *erblichen* / Mängel umwanden.' " (Christ is risen, / joy to the mortal /
whom ruinous, / creeping, *hereditary* / flaws encircled.") The passage, apart
from signifying Gram's perception that the church will save him, has a special
meaning for him as a decadent; very early, he had told his diary about his
"hereditary deficiencies." They came from the fact that his father, an old man
"with tired, thin blood," "a decrepit playboy," and an "old wretch," "fell into
the arms of his little housekeeper," and Gram was the product of the union.
According to Gram, his father had "the good taste" never to marry the socially
inferior mother, who appears to have been excluded from the rearing of her
son. Readers of *Aus der Männerwelt* may have seen a contrastive parallel here
to the case of Georg Jonathan: both the energetic Jonathan's parents are presumed to have been young and vital, and Jonathan has been brought up by his
doting mother. The tired Gram, not yet forty, persists in calling himself "an old
man," and remarks — sexually apprehensive of women as he is — that "in the
presence of Venus every man is an impecunious oldster."

Gram relies heavily on quotations — poems or snippets of poems by the
Norwegian poets Wergeland and Welhaven, lines from Wagner's *Ring* (the
words of the dragon Fafnir, used to characterize a certain kind of husband,
inactive but possessive: "Ich liege und besitze. / Laß mich schlafen"), a line
from the traditional Danish hymn of Ingemann, "Lovely is the earth, / Splendid God's heaven" — this, appropriately, is employed when Gram considers
marriage with the prim and proper Elise Berner. There are even a number of
poems which may be from Gram's own hand, an exceptional display of creativity on Gram's part.

Sometimes, names are mentioned, as signs of the decadent's reading: Schopenhauer, Huysmans, Bourget. But if Gram is made out to be somewhat familiar with the new decadence and its philosophical forebears, he is also made out
to have had a thorough grounding in Holy Scripture (which he may, however,
change to suit his own convenience). The biblical quotations are several, and
become more frequent as the mood of the diarist becomes more religious. The
jumble of quotations from Genesis which "pleasant old Sven Brun" serves up

at the marriage ceremony of Bjølsvik is the beginning of the series: " 'In the sweat of thy face shalt thou eat thy bread . . . thorns also and thistles shall it bring forth for thee . . . till thou returnest into the ground, for out of it wast thou taken; for dust to dust, and unto dust thou shalt return. In sorrow shalt thou bring forth children, and thou shalt be true to thy husband, and he shall rule over thee.' " Gram takes pleasure in these brutally old-fashioned instructions which put woman in her place, but thinks that they may go over the head of the bride; he also takes pleasure in the fact that Brun, inappropriately enough, has used phrases commonly employed in the burial service—Gram likes to toy with thoughts of death, even at weddings. Other quotations from the Good Book are even more comforting for him; dreaming outside the stave church on his trip to Hitterdal, he thinks: "Even a hardened old rationalist like me is properly touched: 'Come unto me and I will give you rest,' the old, tarred farmer's church says to me, and I come and find rest." But he does not go inside; the church has been restored—i.e., it is not authentic any more but synthetic, like those nineteenth-century holy wafers against which Des Esseintes rails—and it smells of "tourism and the present." (For Gram, religion should have an air of antiquity about it, like the twilit mystique of the village church Barbey d'Aurevilly describes in "À un dîner d'athées" in his proto-decadent collection, *Les Diaboliques*.)

Elsewhere Holy Scripture can also be used by Gram for less consoling purposes, and his choices are often inadvertently revelatory about him. The message of "a German optimist," is, for him, like the person without charity in 1 Corinthians 13, "a sounding brass and a clanging cymbal"; of course, Gram himself is quite without the charity (or love) which is the central word of the famous passage. More directly, in Part 2, chapter 24, Gram accuses himself of being among the "tepid ones" condemned in Revelations 3:16: "So because thou art lukewarm and neither hot nor cold, I will spew thee out of my mouth." Indeed, in his half-hearted wooing of Fanny Holmsen and Elise Berner and, we suspect, of a faceless Eline in the past, Gram has been lukewarm, and (with some self-insight) he realizes it; now, though, he applies the charge of lukewarmness to his growing but still tepid faith. Gram's twisted rendering of the Beatitudes reveals, in some of its passages, the fear of revolution which besets him, pseudo-aristocrat that he is: "Blessed are the oppressed, for when the revolution comes . . ." But the majority of his mock Beatitudes show the sourness of his own heart, his selfishness, his decadent nature: "Blessed, blessed are all who suffer and want, for they still possess the illusion of happiness," while "the rich, powerful, and healthy are no longer sheltered against the consuming sun called truth." The deterministic view of life Gram holds ("Life is arranged for us") is illustrated by the words of Jesus to Simon in John 21:18, of which he quotes only a portion: "Another shall gird thee and carry thee whither thou wouldest not." A reader of Gram's diary familiar with Scripture (as Gram's early readers no doubt were) would have remembered that Jesus also alludes here to the problems of the old: "But when thou shalt be old, thou shalt stretch forth thy hands, and another shall gird thee." As a child, these verses filled him with terror, Gram remembers; in his gnawing awareness of his age, his decrepitude, they must be more terrifying still, so terrifying that he cannot write them down in full.

The most important of Gram's biblical texts, though, appears, like Sven Brun's mélange from Genesis, at a religious ceremony, near the book's end. It is from Ecclesiastes, the Book of the Preacher, and Pastor Løchen uses it at Dr. Kvaale's funeral. "Vanity, vanity, all is vanity" — to which Løchen adds, "And the destruction of the soul." The text pushes Gram still further along the road to his (apparent) religious conversion. "It shows us the need for salvation in an inspiring way," Gram piously writes, "by presenting the world to us as it is seen from the standpoint of the godless. A world without hope, without any deeper explanation, nothing, nothing." The line from Ecclesiastes and its expansion ("I have seen all the works that are done under the sun, and, behold, all is vanity and a striving after wind") appeals mightily to the decadent mind; the comically decadent prince in Eça de Queirós's *City and the Mountains* reads Ecclesiastes as he rides through Paris in his wonderfully appointed carriage. Gram is reminded, and reminds his diary, constantly of the emptiness of his existence: "Oh, emptiness, emptiness. And this aching tiredness in my forehead." Even more shockingly, Gram sums up the sensation of emptiness at the end of the third chapter in Part 2, where — fearing the disease of the brain which began to affect an uncle of his at about the same age as his present one, and seeing himself, again, as "a reservoir of all possible inherited family sins and sicknesses" — he cries: "Oh God, the world is like a huge black hole."

Gram tries to alleviate his awareness of the abyss, at times, by romanticizing it, enjoying it: "Autumn is my time, especially when it is rainy and foggy," and he describes "a rainy-weather mood, mists hanging over ridges and hills, autumnally romantic." These autumn moods temporarily console him, yet they readily slide over into the arctic despair of winter. He tells Fanny Holmsen on one of their walks: "That is precisely what life is . . . an open, empty, frozen snow-chasm, twilight, and a gray snow sky," and, "Life lies before me like an icy wasteland, a black, frozen plateau with snow drifts and ice cliffs," and, "Existence is this black icy wilderness, where . . . there is weeping and gnashing of teeth." Gram is fully in the decadent tradition as he thinks in arctic images (from which, he sometimes reasons, marriage will save him): Huysmans's Des Esseintes had Poe's antarctic vision of loneliness, *The Narrative of Arthur Gordon Pym,* as one of his favorite books, and the adolescent Finland-Swedish poet Edith Södergran wrote, later on, a four-line poem in German called "Decadence": "I am in a great field of snow, / The moon trembles above me. / Everything is white / I am alone, freezing."

Oddly, in the midst of his besetting fear of nothingness, as if to escape from it, Gram takes comfort in fantasies of his own death: he advertises for a murderer skillful enough to do away with him (part of the book's clever opening); he calls up fantasies of several modes of executions, each followed by a description of the relief and comfort it will bring him. "This picture in my mind is of a very long and supple sword that sinks quite slowly into my heart," a sword that "cools and comforts," guided by a "large, white elegant hand"; "a kind of beheading machine" appears to him, "formed like a large bread knife . . . oh, delightful" (it is operated by an "older, pleasant, motherly woman"). "Then there are the fantasies of hanging . . . every moment, involuntarily, I stroke my throat where the rope would lie . . . I imagine that I am hanging, gasping, my tongue out of my mouth. This view pacifies and cools." (Later, he has a similar notion of his uncle hanging and twisting on the cord; he suspects that the uncle has committed suicide.)

Of course, for Gram, death is not the only way out, before he finds religion. The entire first book is the desultory account of his search for a salvation bestowed by woman—or, to put it directly, his pondering the question of whether he should propose to Fanny Holmsen. These arguments he has with himself are in part an expansion of the aesthete A's "ecstatic lecture" on marriage in the Diapsalmata of *Either-Or:* "If you marry, you will regret it; if you do not marry, you will also regret it"; much of Gram's discourse has a Kierkegaardian tone, just as Kierkegaard is a major contributor to Gram's style, the figure of the aesthete of *Either-Or,* selfish and hesitating, is clearly Gram's emotional forebear. The several marriages, mostly unhappy, that Gram examines in the diary—Kvaale's, the composer Brun's, Lunde's, and so forth—are examples chosen under the Kierkegaardian aegis. Gram intends them as a part of his campaign of persuading himself not to propose to Fanny; and, for this effort, he adduces other arguments. He is not, he insists, erotically drawn to her (he feels "this iciness when I am with her"), and he suspects variously and illogically that she "is not erotic" and that she has had an active erotic past. In actual fact Gram is strongly if perversely attracted by her—not least by the elements of physical illness betrayed in her appearance: she has "large, dark, slightly tubercular eyes" and "an almost sweet face with the almost too tumultuous curls and the almost too protruberant shining eyes— those large, sick, langorous eyes, swimming, absent eyes" without a goal; she has, as well, "snow-white, blue-veined temples." (We remember Ola Hansson's description of decadence itself as a woman lovely but ill, with blue veins visible in her temples; we remember, too, Elena Muti on her sickbed in the first seduction scene of *Il piacere.*) In order to ward off Fanny's curious allure,

Gram tells himself that she, as a schoolteacher, with somewhat shabby colleagues and friends, is "not sufficiently first-rate; inferior" — Gram is a snob like his father.

Nonetheless, once Fanny becomes inaccessible to him because of her marriage, he turns into a nympholept, like the subject of Browning's poem, imagining that he sees her everywhere, having hallucinations about her. And then, when he meets her after her return to Christiania, he suddenly is ready to admit to the existence of her sexuality — he perceives her as a bacchante, with men chained before her chariot (another betrayal of his fears of sexual inadequacy). At length, the woman of the vision can no longer be specifically identified as Fanny Holmsen; after a fantasy of a funeral, and of "a large black hole with earth on top," Gram suddenly sees a nymph, "white-skinned and leaping between fauns and satyrs . . . I can see her sweet, dangerous smile, painfully voluptuous," and he beholds himself as a "wet animal skin and a dead sheep" — that is, perhaps, as a dead satyr. The climax of the passage is made up of Gram's telltale thoughts of woman as "the infernal and the heavenly in one person, sinner and mother, Eva and Madonna." At this point, he notes, he must appeal to Dr. Kvaale for a "sufficient" dose of morphine. The vague attraction Elise Berner has for him comes from her equally vague fulfillment of the motherly role alone, in making no sexual demands upon him; refined, patrician, musical, she has a "remarkable intuition of how to treat a weary man," an allusion to the title of the book. The "marriage of reason" with her that Gram imagines for himself does not take place; she rediscovers an old flame and goes off to marry him. In this case there is no imaginary pursuit of a voluptuous Miss Berner by a tormented Gram.

As for the sometime alluring sick woman, bacchante, and nymph Fanny Holmsen, Gram encounters her again in actual fact. After the dinner at Pastor Løchen's, to whose pastoral care he has found his way, he attends Løchen's sermon and sees Fanny in the congregation, "pale, thin, with traces of much suffering and an ethereal glow in her dark eyes." Fanny — now Mrs. Ryen — has become a born-again Christian, we are told, under the influence of Løchen and the helpful second physician in the tale, Dr. Thisted, who employs faith as a useful medicine (he is a pragmatist, unlike the eventual suicide, Dr. Kvaale): Mrs. Ryen offers, Dr. Thisted says, " 'a strong proof of the effectiveness of the psychological method . . . In fact, she was rather exhausted [and] had already begun with morphine injections; on the whole the nervous system was in rotten shape. Now she is really quite well.' " We do not know, however, if Gram remains a member of Løchen's Lutheran flock; he says directly that he is happiest in the Roman Catholic Church with its special atmosphere and its Madonna. He is attracted, as well, to a new pastor figure, Pastor Holck, the black-clad man he has taken as Dr. Kvaale's revenant. "He is a very fine and intelligent man . . . He is going to attend a meeting with Mrs. Ryen and some other ladies in the Association for the Feeding of School-Children-Living-on-Communal Welfare; I immediately had myself enrolled in the association." Does Gram do this to be near Fanny? He has just written: "We shall meet, she and I, and in a better manner than we thought, once upon a time." Has he developed a sort of minimal social awareness, or human charity, at last? (He has just made a very un-Gramian notation in his diary: "To pat a dog, to get a child to smile from ear to ear, to make an old woman breathe more easily for a time by giving her a crown, and so forth" — but this is merely advice that Dr. Thisted seems to have given him: "Won't it weigh more heavily on Judgment Day than twenty volumes of disgust with life?") We do not know if Gram has indeed learned charity; not enough information is provided about Gram's future. We do know that he feels better; his visions have vanished, "as though the new physician had hypnotized them away." The decadent may have been cured, or he has found at least a refuge in church, and in small good works.

The epilogue of the novel has received much attention from critics and scholars; it contains Gram's last conversation with Georg Jonathan. Throughout the diary, in Gram's reports, Jonathan has been the main speaker against decadence, viewing it as one more symptom of the decline of bourgeois culture: " 'When ancient Rome began to rot, then, too, people ran around after hypnotists and magicians.' " When Gram expresses his interest in Huysmans, Bourget, and company, Jonathan condemns them " 'as tepidly sweet, weepy effeminates . . . [who] have given themselves a name worthy of them: "decadent," destruction, and the rotting process," and explains, " 'freely translated, decadence is putrefaction." Jonathan promises to do all he can to combat the phenomenon. (Probably Jonathan is the optimist with the world dream of ever-improving races, to whom the pessimist — Gram, the reader of Ecclesiastes — has retorted: " 'And then the sun will die.' ") In the last interview, Georg Jonathan, the inventive and practical optimist, offers his vision of the "evening party of the future." He intends to spread culture to the masses through a kind of television: " 'The screen picks up the instantaneous photographic images of the play in question.' " (Villiers de L'Isle Adam, in *L'Ève future,* and H. G. Wells made similar predictions of the technological future.) In Jonathan's opinion absolute happiness is neither attainable nor desirable for the human race: happiness is boredom; dissatisfaction carries men forward. To these remarks, and to Jonathan's ominous statement that, for those in despair, he has a program called "The Festival of Death," Gram gives the answer of someone who has put off the old man and put on the new: " 'All this masked despair is indifferent to me,' " and " 'For deeper, finer natures, these fantasies are just tiresome.' " An odd shifting of positions has taken place; the antidecadent Jonathan now plans to incorporate the decadent play-acting of despair into his program, " 'Hamlet's and Faust's despair,' " in order to keep mankind's dissatisfaction alive — so that mankind will not become too happy, and those who fall into absolute despair will simply have to die in "The Festival of Death." Gram, although he has been "saved," still retains the exclusiveness of the decadent — like Des Esseintes and Sperelli, he abhors mass culture to the end and rejects Jonathan's mass solution. He leaves Jonathan, saying, " 'I have bent because I did not wish to break. Go thou and do likewise.' " Behind him he hears Jonathan's mocking laughter: "It seemed to ring out of the depths of hell."

The ending of the novel confused many readers; they assumed that Garborg recommended Gram's individual religious (yet still decadently colored) salvation, and rejected Jonathan's all-too-rational plan to make "life human, worthy of humans" (with a dollop of the decadent method of assuming a role). Georg Brandes himself made this mistake. This was not the case. Jonathan had a record of admirable behavior in Garborg's earlier books; he had not suddenly become the Satan Gram perceived in him. The democratic Garborg apparently approved Jonathan's plans for the future and disapproved of the way out that Gram had found. The book's readers cannot be blamed for their misapprehension; decadence had appealed to Garborg — the passages about overrefined nerves, about the mystique of the old church, about thanatophilia, the love of death, seem to come from the authorial (and not just the diarist's) heart; they are the book's most memorable sections. The acute young Swedish critic Hjalmar Söderberg, in an essay in *Ord och bild* for 1893, said that Garborg's *Weary Men* might very well (à la *Werther*) cause an epidemic of mysticism in Norway, and continued: "Gram is the personality that an author escapes becoming in reality by letting him live on paper."

In one more respect, to be sure, Garborg is different from his Gram. Throughout the diary, Gram hints that he will turn his experience into a novel. He notes down the "characteristic replies" of Jonathan and Kvaale for the novel (or a drama, *Married Men*), he writes "studies and impressions" for his novel, and he says that "in my future novel [Jonathan] will appear as a typical representative of the cold, dull, matter-of-fact, prosaic period known as the present" (Des Esseintes would have called it le siècle, Sperelli would have talked of "today's gray democratic mud"). "Now it might be time to try the novel," Gram finally says — but he never does. Garborg does write the novel: he creates a classic of decadent literature, and one of the decadent canon's most difficult and complex texts.

8

Belgium

GEORGES RODENBACH

At Berlin's Café Bauer, on April 11, 1900, Rainer Maria Rilke wrote in his diary that he was reading Georges Rodenbach's *Le Mirage*, the Belgian's dramatization of his short and immensely popular novel *Bruges-la-Morte* (1892), "with deep emotion, in breathless hearkening." In September the same year, at the artists' colony of Worpswede, Rilke recorded how he and his friends had sat talking, "a rich community in conversation and silence," about Tolstoy, death, Georges Rodenbach, and Gerhart Hauptmann's play *Friedensfest* and "about life and the beauty of all experience, about being able to die and wanting to die, about eternity and why we feel related to eternity." The passage (which goes on) is a good example of fin de siècle sensibility and shows, as well, the stature that Rodenbach (1855–98) had in the literary world of the time. Two years later, *Bruges-la-Morte,* translated into German by Friedrich Oppeln-Bronikowski, a champion of Francophone Belgian letters (for example, of Charles de Coster and Maurice Maeterlinck), appeared in the popular Reclam series, and it has remained in print there ever since. *Le Mirage* was also translated as *Die stille Stadt* (1902) by the Viennese man of letters (and translator of Shaw), Siegfried Trebitsch, together with another short Rodenbach play, *Le Voile,* as *Der Schleier.* In 1920, the opera *Die tote Stadt* by the prodigy Erich Wolfgang Korngold (1897–1957) had its double premiere in Hamburg and Cologne, composed to a libretto by Erich's father, the Viennese music critic Julius Korngold.

The Korngold opera, premiered at the Metropolitan in 1921 with Maria Jeritza, may have made a broader American public aware of Rodenbach's novel, although the opera offers a bad distortion of the novel's text, including dream episodes and a happy ending. Marietta, Jeritza's role, has very little to do with the vulgar Jane Scott of the original. Interested Anglophones who did not know French had to have recourse to the stilted translation of 1903 by Thomas Duncan. The little book then waited until 1987 for a more congenial rendering by Philip Mosley, which appeared at a small press in Paisley, Scotland; a revised version of the Duncan text, by Terry Hale, came out in London in 1993. The English-language fate of *Bruges-la-Morte* has been as checkered as it has been fortunate in German.

In Paris, where Rodenbach had moved in 1888, out of discouragement at the narrow horizons of his "petite patrie," he became a friend of Stéphane Mallarmé, with whom he corresponded (Mallarmé gave *Bruges-la-Morte* great praise in a letter: "J'apprécie en ce livre le poème, infini par soi mais littérairement un de ceux en prose les plus fièrement prolongés"); he knew Alphonse Daudet, Edmond de Goncourt, Leconte de Lisle, and Villiers de L'Isle-Adam. In the introduction to Rodenbach's collected poems (1923), the Belgian poet Camille Mauclair recalled: "Son charme personnel était de ceux auxquels nul ne résiste," and he was "une des figures les plus sincèrement chéries par l'élite de son époque." After his death, he received the tribute of a portrait, with Bruges in the background, by Lucien Lévy-Dhurmer, and the essay "Le Pasteur des cygnes," in *Diptyque de Flandres* (1921), by Robert de Montesquiou-Fezensac (1855–1921), the wealthy dandy assumed to have been the model for Huysmans's Des Esseintes and Proust's Baron Charlus.

In Scandinavia, *Bruges-la-Morte* was lucky enough to receive a superior translation into Swedish by Agnes Palmgren (1874–1957), whose husband, Alexis Kraemer, a Romance scholar, was a member of Helsinki's internationally oriented Euterpe circle. For Palmgren—who later translated Rodenbach's *Le Carillonneur* (1905) and *La Vocation* (1916)—Rodenbach was "a pulse in the crisis of psychological and aesthetic decadence which characterizes the fin de siècle in Europe, a pulse which has throbbed with the tired but palpable strokes that come in the presence of death. In that autumn of thought and language which lends such a hectic splendor to the literature of decadence, Rodenbach stands as one . . . of the most subtly nuanced and evanescent phenomena." Shortly before his own premature death in 1906, the Swedish critic Oscar Levertin wrote a review of the Palmgren translation, intended to introduce it to readers (the translation had appeared at a small publishing house in Helsinki); Levertin began by observing that *Bruges-la-Morte* "has already won a circle of friends in every country, not large but devoted."

For a long time, authors and critics stood under the spell of *Bruges-la-Morte* and of the beautiful dead city Rodenbach seemed to have created; as late as 1929, Camille Mauclair in *Le Charme de Bruges* wrote about Rodenbach's "immobile city, half empty [*cité immobile, à demi vide*], beside a highway where no one passes," and remarked that "Venice has never known this sort of stupor, [this] opacity of spirit," and even Henry Miller, of all people, loved "the miracle and the mystery of Bruges" (1953). Recently, Francophone Belgian scholars, notably Paul Gorceix, have made subtle interpretations of what, for them, remains a chief ornament of the symbolist canon. These interpretations have been followed, in English, in Philip Mosley's symposium by various hands, *Georges Rodenbach: Critical Essays* (1996).

The great admiration accorded *Bruges-la-Morte* was a result not only of the hypnotic quality of what (as Mallarmé quickly noticed) was a long prose poem rather than the "novel" of the first edition's title page. The admiration also grew out of a long tradition of the city's literary fame. Throughout the nineteenth century and later it had been, like Venice, a goal for travelers: Wordsworth (1820: "Bruges I saw attend the golden light"), Longfellow (1843: "The Belfry of Bruges"), Baudelaire (1864: "Ville fantôme, ville momie, à peu près conservée"), Dante Gabriel Rossetti (1849: "Antwerp and Bruges" and "On Leaving Bruges"), Mallarmé (1893: "Le jamais banal Bruges multipliant l'aube au défunt canal"), Ernest Dowson (1894: "This autumnal old city . . . it is always autumn in Bruges"), Stefen Zweig (1901: "Hier sind die Häuser wie alte Paläste"), Rilke (1907: "Quai du Rosaire" and "Béguinage"), Émile Verhaeren (1907: "cette gloire en cendre et or: Bruges!"). Antonio Fogazarro's *Il santo* (1906) begins in Bruges, grand, mysterious, and dead, with its "silenzio di anticamera dell' Eternità." In his Bruges essay, Huysmans wrote, after rereading *Bruges-la-Morte,* that Bruges was "à la fois mystique et démoniaque, puerile et grave," and that "le satanisme fleurit à Bruges." (The real-life model of the satanist priest, Canon Docre, in Huysmans's *Là-bas* is supposed to have resided in Bruges.)

A main supporting factor in the popularity of *Bruges-la-Morte* is that the little novel provided a perfect example of a theme that fascinated the aesthetic, conservative, and thanatophiliac authors of decadence — the dead city, the city as museum piece, the city as it were under glass. In 1895, Levertin had published his own essay on Bruges: "When I dream of Bruges, I behold . . . a fairytale city, overgrown by withered moss, and with gables, circling walls, and battlements that disappear in a green mist." The Hispanist Hans Hinterhäuser in the essay "Tote Städte" (Dead Cities) lists four literary examples: Bruges; Venice (particularly as represented in the poetic essay "La Mort de Venise"), in Barrès's *Amori et dolori sacrum* (1902); Toledo, where Hinterhäuser's main specimen is Barrès's *Greco ou le secret de Tolède* (1912); and, somewhat surprisingly, "die Stadt Perle" in Alfred Kubin's fantastic novel *Die andere*

Seite (1909) — a town built by an American millionaire somewhere in the steppes of central Asia, out of buildings taken from Austrian towns of the Biedermeier. (It is then destroyed amid hideous atrocities.) The list of appearances of the dead city can be lengthened: Barrès's Aigues-Mortes in *Le Jardin de Bérénice* (1891), Toledo again in his story "Un Amateur des âmes" (in *Du Sang, de la Volupté, et de la Mort*, 1894), the town in ruins Linturno, in D'Annunzio's *Le vergini delle rocce* (1895), the anonymous Argive ruin of *La città mortà* (1896), and the Venice of *Il fuoco* (1900), the Toledo setting of the conclusion of Stanisław Przybyszewski's *Androgyne* (1906). For the Galician Valle-Inclán in *La lámpara maravillosa* (1916), Toledo is "an old hallucinatory city," "a sepulcher," while Santiago de Compostela "seems immobilized in a dream of granite, immovable and eternal." Ravenna received its tribute "Dans le Sépulcre de Ravenne" from Barrès (in the collection of 1894), and from Louis Couperus, "a small, dead, as it were useless town, which enchants the visitor as soon as he enter its churches and museums" (1911). At the end of his review of the Swedish-language translation of *Bruges-la-Morte,* Levertin inserts an imaginary excursion through the cities of Europe, "which only live as relics from past times . . . and on which death has long since set its solemn seal of decay." They have always attracted him "with their magic of greatness fallen asleep and a fairy tale ended, their shadow world [is] stronger than that of living beings." He names three examples, and in all he notes the element of darkness and decay: Ravenna, "the mightiest, with a historical mood of tragedy beyond compare," Ferrara and "its desolate monumentality," and Bruges, "its lyrical mood of melancholy self-destruction, which is its special quality and no doubt comes from the dampness and the mist in the city with all its deep, stagnant canals."

The quality of being a dead city also has something to do with size. The spreading metropolis, Verhaeren's "ville tentaculaire," is too big and too vital. More or less contemporary with the florescence of writing about dead cities, there are novels about the *destruction* of a metropolis, Richard Jefferies's *After London* (1885), H. G. Wells's *The War of the Worlds* (1898), and, much later, Gustav Meyrink's Amsterdam (why Amsterdam?) in *Das grüne Gesicht* (1916) and Karl Hans Strobl's Vienna in *Gespenster im Sumpf* (1920). Huysmans's *À rebours* ended with a curse called down on "the cities of the plain," i.e., Paris; in Bram Stoker's story "The Invisible Giant," Paris lies in the distance, "the doomed city, where so many would perish in the midst of their sin." Gentle as he is, Eça de Queirós' prince imagines the destruction of Paris, "where such cruel injustices exist" — the homeless sleeping under the bridges of the Seine. In Bely's *Petersburg* (1913), the suburban islands are burning, a leitmotif of the novel.

Rodenbach had and has his detractors. In 1904, the young Swedish poet of

"dead cities' splendor," Anders Österling, visited Bruges on a literary pilgrimage and purchased a guidebook which, of course, mentioned Rodenbach:
" 'Whoever wants to get to know and enjoy Bruges cannot read Rodenbach's
Bruges-la-Morte, the work by this . . . born Walloon, who never beheld Bruges
save through the sick state of his importunate temperament and his wistful
soul, lacking all definite and elevated idealism.' " Born in Tournai and educated in Ghent, Rodenbach had never actually lived in Bruges; following his
death, the citizens of Bruges refused to allow a monument to be erected in his
honor. It was put up in Ghent instead. The reasons for this hatred of Rodenbach in the city to whose fame he had contributed were two: in the language
struggle between French and Flemish, Rodenbach, like Maeterlinck and Émile
Verhaeren, had chosen French as his means of expression, although his cousin
Albrecht Rodenbach (1856–80) had taken the difficult road of writing in
Flemish, for a small public. In *Bruges-la-Morte,* no mention is made of the fact
that the city, Brugge, is fundamentally Flemish-speaking. And far more incriminating, Rodenbach had depicted the people of Bruges as a petty-minded
and venomously gossipy bourgeoisie; in *Le Carillonneur,* they are quite unaware of Bruges as a museum-city of great beauty. The people of Ghent, who
had been given an almost equally hard time in Rodenbach's first novel, *L'Art
en exil,* were more forgiving.

Rodenbach's reputation did not survive undamaged. The simple mechanics
of Rodenbach's novels and their repetitiveness of theme could not be overlooked: the "dead city," the still waters and the ubiquitous swans, the persecution of gifted men, the oppressive Roman Catholicism, incorporated in the
béguinages, aesthetically alluring but symbolic of stunted lives. The same iter-
ation can be found in his verse, from *La Jeunesse blanche* (1886), *Le Règne du
silence* (1891), and *Les Vies encloses* (1896) to *Le Miroir du ciel natal* (1898).
By 1909, the once admiring Rilke had become doubtful; in a letter to Georg
Brandes, strongly recommending Gide's *La Porte étroite,* Rilke added that one
need only imagine how one-sidedly Rodenbach would have described the
erotic conflict (the heroine fears that marriage to her beloved will sully their
love), "in order, entranced, to observe the greater artist."

By the middle of the twentieth century, open fun was poked at magical
Bruges and Rodenbach's book. Pamela Hansford Johnson saw Bruges as a
tourist magnet for its sex-shows (e.g., Leda and the swan) and its nimbus of
satanism, in her comic novel *The Unspeakable Skipton* (1959) — Skipton is a
professional out-of-pocket guide to the town's ludicrously obscene pleasures.
In 1966, the German man of letters Alfred Andersch admitted that Bruges had
a steady stream of visitors who wanted to see the art of Hans Memling, and
that, thanks to the magic of its name, it had not escaped the curse of mass

tourism, like "Venice and Nürnberg, Pisa, and Chartres." Whoever, Andersch wrote, wanted to find the dead Bruges of Rodenbach would be disappointed; then he gave the famous little book a coup de grâce: "It is an unintentionally comic hodgepodge of pastel colors and demonism." For Hinterhäuser, in the essay "Tote Städte," *Bruges-la-Morte* is "heavy with mood and old-fashioned as a pathetic daguerreotype from our grandfathers' or great-grandfathers' days."

Before turning, at last, to Rodenbach's text proper, it may be useful to examine some other prose narratives of his which can cast light on the little classic. Rodenbach began his work as a novelist with *La Vie morte*, serialized in a Belgian periodical in 1886; it was revised and issued in book form as *L'Art en exil* in 1889. As said, the location is Ghent, but the stage apparatus will be familiar to any reader of *Bruges-la-Morte:* the béguinages, the "melancholy of the dead waters," the "rain of iron" from the bells of the town. Jean Rembrandt — quite aware of the weight of his name — is a poet who writes in French on Flemish themes about "bells, faubourgs, quais, and dead waters," thus creating an "art in exile." It is the only work of Rodenbach which directly broaches the country's language problem; Rembrandt belongs to the Flemish nationalist movement, and one of the novel's high points is the tribute to Charles de Coster (1827–79), the Francophone author of a historical epic, *Le Légende de Thyl Ulenspiegel et de Lamme Goedzak* (1868), distinctly Flemish-patriotic and by inference anti–Roman Catholic in its depiction of the Spanish Inquisition in Flanders under Philip II — a work unjustly forgotten, in Rembrandt's judgment, but "where all the soul of Mother Flanders is un- veiled." Rembrandt and his friends take up a collection to erect a memorial stone for de Coster at his neglected grave; only twenty people attend the dedication ceremony. Living with his mother, Rembrandt is captivated by the voice "sharp and frail" like that of a child in a religious procession, emerging from the chapel of a béguinage; curious about the color of the béguine's hair beneath her coif, he pursues the voice's owner; he persuades her to leave the order and marry him. (The theme of a béguine's *chevelure* returns in *Le Voile* [1897]: the bachelor Jean, who has taken Sister Gudule into his home to nurse a dying aunt, is similarly fascinated by the mystery of the hair beneath the *cornette,* and falls in love with her when he sees her by accident with her hair exposed, only to lose interest directly: " 'It is no longer she.' " His family servant Barbe, who like her namesake in *Bruges-la-Morte* has a nose for occa- sions of sin, says of Sister Gudule that she " 'does not walk, she undulates.' ") Rembrandt's marriage is a failure, because Marie cannot appreciate his artistic aims, yet he is reduced to still greater isolation when she dies, destroyed by the thought of her sin in marrying him. Rembrandt detests the "malicious city" where he lives; in a scene foreshadowing a key episode in *Bruges-la-Morte,* Marie's spirit has been broken when Rembrandt dares take her to a performance of Meyerbeer's *Robert-le-diable* at the local theater. A riot breaks out: the crowd chants: "'The béguine has gone to see an opera of the devil,'" and Marie, watching the ballet of the lascivious (dead) nuns, believes that she too is damned. The couple runs away through the "black streets of Ghent, sad like a drowned landscape." After her death, Rembrandt immures himself in a chamber of his home, with copies of works by Rembrandt van Rijn, a Flemish Bible of the sixteenth century, and an organ, "in a mysticism of the heart, of the imagination, of art."

Bruges-la-Morte came next, and then a collection of short stories, *Musée de Béguines* (1894), specimens, with connecting texts, about the sisters—unencumbered by permanent vows and living half in the world—who so entranced Rodenbach. It was followed by the short novel, *La Vocation* (1895). As a child, Hans Cadzand—a name take from a Dutch bathing resort, just across the border from Bruges—is fascinated by the rites of the church, and insists that his golden hair be clipped so that he can serve at the altar; his mother collects the locks and preserves them in a pillow—one more example of Rodenbach's hair fetishism. However, Hans's enthusiasm for a religious calling wanes (as might be expected of a character named after a bathing resort, given to sensuality). He has been cold toward the other sex; the efforts of his mother to interest him in a friend's daughter, on a skating excursion to Damme, a picturesque little town near Bruges, fail. Lacking in foresight, the mother hires the luscious Ursula as a housemaid and, according to the narrator, the infernal world makes its assault, for she is "an envoy of Hell," sent on the "secret mission of the devil," and readily seduces Hans. Discovered, Ursula is sent away, leaving Hans unfit for the vocation he once desired. Approaching thirty, he lives on at his mother's old house on the Rue de l'Âne-Aveugle, the Blinde-Ezelstraat, near the favorite goal of tourists, the Quai du Rosaire, the Rozenhoudkaai. What Rodenbach's intention may have been with *La Vocation*—a further ironization of Bruges's religiosity, an attempt to make further profit from the Bruges atmosphere?—is difficult to say; with the hints of the infernal surrounding the buxom Ursula, the novel returns, in the narrator's noncommittal voice, to the satanic subtext of *Bruges-la-Morte.*

The last and longest of Rodenbach's narratives is *Le Carillonneur* (1897), another Bruges novel, whose protagonist, Joris Borluut, wins a contest of bell ringers and is installed as the official occupant of the town's great belfry; a lover of the past glories of Bruges and its monuments, now falling into decay, he also becomes the town architect. (In the reworking of *Bruges-la-Morte* for the stage, the above-mentioned *Le Mirage,* Joris Borluut is a friend of Hugues

Viane; the latter's mistress, Jane Scott, attempts to seduce him.) A passionate man, a close observer of the obscene — or at least Rubenesque — engravings of the Bell of Lasciviousness in the belfry, Borluut makes the mistake of marrying Barbe, the "red-mouthed" daughter of his mentor in Bruges antiquities, Van Hulle, although his spiritual love goes to her sister, the quiet Godelieve, "with eyes the color of the canals." A social climber, Barbe wants her husband to improve his status by supporting a movement to make Bruges modern and thriving, connected by a canal to the sea, "Bruges-Port-de-Mer," which Borluut opposes, in his wish to become "the embalmer of the town," a place "where death becomes a work of art." Sexually frigid despite her appearance, Barbe succumbs more and more to unreasoning fits of anger, and Borluut seeks refuge in his belfry, "above life." After Van Hulle dies and Godelieve moves into their home, Borluut perceives the difference between Barbe, violent and "Spanish" in the joy she takes in causing pain, and Godelieve, "a Flemish Eve with the golden hair of the Van Eycks and the Memlings." A physician diagnoses Barbe's illness as "anemia and neurosis, the decline of old blood, the ill of the century, which prevailed even in these far-away towns," and she goes off to visit cousins in Germany; Borluut and Godelieve at last confess their love to one another and celebrate a secret "wedding." Borluut has wish-dreams of Barbe's suicide — as a corpse covered with blood from a fall, or surrounded by "the aquatic plants of an Ophelia." The happiness of the couple is brief. Barbe returns and is filled with suspicion; Godelieve believes that she is pregnant, a fear allayed only when her menstrual period returns as she watches the Procession of the Sacred Blood — which has already been incorporated by Rodenbach at the climax of *Bruges-la-Morte,* and is used here with heavy-handed irony.

Barbe confronts the lovers, Godelieve becomes a béguine, and Borluut throws himself into a hopeless effort to save old Bruges, giving a poorly attended speech on "the glory of being a dead city," instead of a rejuvenated place meant to attract "merchants and Jews." Having been removed from his post as municipal architect, he looks for Godelieve in Furnes, where she has gone to participate in the annual Procession of the Penitents; bearing a heavy cross, she turns away from Borluut. He goes back to Barbe and Bruges, but she despises him, and his house is stoned by the supporters of a "modern Bruges." From the belfry, now his only refuge, he finds Bruges still "more dead" and "more beautiful" than before; climbing to the top one last time, an ascent which, as Paul Gorceix remarks, is also a descent into his own death, he hangs himself inside the great Bell of Lasciviousness. Of Rodenbach's protagonists, Borluut is the most complex; surrounded by impossibilities, he rises "above life" like Ibsen's Master Builder Solness, the victim of his love for a dead city and of love for the nunlike Godelieve. He may or may not be what H. Juin wrote summarily about Hugues Viane in *Bruges-la-Morte,* "a case of neurosis." Plenty of quite unimpeachable cases of neurosis can be found in the stories published after Rodenbach's death, *Le Rouet des brumes* (1901) — in the tale, for example, of a man enamored of mirrors and mirroring, "L'Ami des miroirs."

Hugues Viane is a widower of forty, prematurely aged (in the manuscript he is fifty); blissfully married for ten years, he lost his wife five years before the beginning of the novel, and on the eve of her thirtieth birthday. He has chosen Bruges as a residence (they had visited it in happier days) because he felt "the need for a dead city to correspond to his dead wife." In the introduction to this "study of passion" Rodenbach points out that Bruges is, as it were, "almost human," and directly involved in the plot. (Amidst a literature as city-fixated as that of decadence, certain works stand out as portrayals of the city as an integral character: Rome in D'Annunzio's *Il piacere, Bruges-la-Morte,* Venice in D'Annunzio's *Il fuoco,* Stockholm in Hjalmar Söderberg's *Doktor Glas,* the city in Bely's *Petersburg,* New York in Huneker's *Painted Veils.*) Seeking a "resemblance of his sorrows," Hugues wanders in November through the rain-drenched town where, as Rilke wrote in one of the Bruges poems of *Neue Gedichte,* "Die Gassen haben einen sachten Gang," the slow progression of Bruges's interwoven streets.

More striking, or alarming, than Hugues's peripatetic activity is the practice he follows in his residence on the Quai du Rosaire. After his wife's death, he cut off her tresses of amber yellow, or "ageless gold," which death left intact, and installed them in a domestic shrine, two rooms containing bibelots, furniture, curtains from the happy past, with the hair itself as the centerpiece, "under the transparent cover of a crystal case." (In *Il fuoco* [1895], the poet Stellio Effrena tells his mistress, the singer La Foscarina — i.e., Eleonora Duse — that he imagines "dead Summer" enclosed in a glass coffin beneath Venice's lagoon, her body swirled about by "the continuous undulation of her voluptuous hair, awaiting the hour of return.") Hugues does not expect the dead wife's resuscitation; but her hair is to be preserved, like Bruges, dead and under glass. Further, in the layout of this set of prose poems, the calendar of the church year is introduced; the narration begins on the eve of November 21, the Feast of the Presentation of the Blessed Virgin, as Hugues's pious servant, Barbe, takes the day off to visit her cousin, Sister Rosalie, at one of Bruges's béguinages. The second of the religious festivals is Easter, and the third the special Bruges holiday of the Procession of the Holy Blood in May. The book also, correspondingly, has a seasonal structure, from late autumn — Hugues remarks that he is in the autumn of his life—past the winter (which Hugues spends besotted with passion, in cozy circumstances), to early and full spring. Despite the relative lack of interest of decadence in nature, the seasonal structure is often employed, usually because of the easy way it provides of demonstrating a decline into age and death, in Valle-Inclán's four seasons of the *Sonatas,* in Johannes V. Jensen's *Kungens Fald,* and in the decline of summer and the coming of the first snow in Söderberg's *Doktor Glas.* In *Bruges-la-Morte* the progression is reversed for melodramatic and contrastive effect; the story begins in autumn's decline and ends amidst the green branches of May which adorn the houses of Bruges on the day of the great procession, as disappointed passion blooms into murder.

Like his literary comrades in neurosis, Hughes is haunted by thoughts of suicide: see Garborg's Gram, Tavaststjerna's Klercken, D'Annunzio's Giorgio Aurispa, Söderberg's Dr. Glas; Strindberg's Axel Borg in *I havsbandet does* kill himself grandiosely, more grandiosely than Aurispa when he slays his mistress and himself, a grotesque *Liebestod,* suggested to him by his Wagnerism. These suicidal thoughts are called up in Hughes by his vision, as he walks, of the dead wife's "Ophelia face, passing, and by hearing her voice in the frail and distant song of the bells," and again by "a whispering voice rising from the water—the water coming toward him as it came to meet Ophelia, the way the grave diggers tell it in Shakespeare." These two references inspired Gaston Bachelard to his famous phrase about *Bruges-la-Morte* as the "Opheliazation of an entire city." The Ophelia passages may have influenced the artist Fernand Knopff's frontispiece for the first book edition (it had been serialized in *Le Figaro* in February 1892), where the dead wife, with flowing hair, on her bier, is superimposed on a Bruges canal, the Quai du Rosaire in the background. Ophelia turns up elsewhere, almost automatically, eleven times in Rodenbach's verse and other prose: in *Le Règne du silence* and *Les Vies encloses* (the dead girl is regularly surrounded by her flowing hair or aquatic plants), and in Joris Borluut's wished-for, imaginary suicide of Barbe: "The hair spread over the gray water." Did Bachelard attach too much importance to the Ophelia of *Bruges-la-Morte?*

Mallarmé praised the fine artistry of Rodenbach, comparing it to the lace and goldsmith work of Flanders, and it is apparent in the splendid synaesthetic effects throughout the text—e.g., the "small, salty notes of the parish bells [falling on Hugues's head] as if flung from an aspergillum for some absolution," or in the cadence of the bells at the end: "weary, slow little old women, who had the air of listlessly shedding—on the city, on a tomb—the petals of flowers or iron." (Rodenbach's text provides instructions for the composer of a film soundtrack.) However, there is an almost robotic quality to Rodenbach's

obsessive calling-up of images (swans, bells, béguines, canals) which may reveal failing invention. The aspergillum of chapter 2 returns in chapter 7: "the
chandelier, about his head, in the closed silence of the chambers, emitted from
its aspergillum of shivering crystal the drizzle of a tiny lament." But it is
important to remember that Hugues himself, Rodenbach's creation, is possessed by the same repeated impressions.

In order to find consolation in art, Hugues makes the first of his excursions
to the treasures of Bruges, the tombs of Charles the Bold and his daughter,
Mary of Burgundy in Notre Dame (Onze Lieve Vrouwekerk). Hugues compares them to himself and his dead wife: "Thus was his dead [wife] resting
forever on his dark soul. And the time would also come when he would stretch
out in his turn like Duke Charles, and would rest near her." The manuscript
has, after "Duke Charles," the clarifying "at the side of his daughter"; but in
the printing Rodenbach suppressed the phrase — the omission suggesting that
the statues of their catafalques are after all of man and wife.

These thoughts of the "good refuge of death" beside the late wife do not last
long. On his way home, Hugues sees a young woman, and entranced by her
resemblance to the departed, pursues her from street to street as he takes in a
great deal: "This pastel complexion, the eyes with the large dark pupil in the
pearl," and "this hair . . . amber-colored and silky," the same gait. The widower (with remarkably keen eyesight, or a remarkable gift of self-persuasion)
loses her at one of Bruges's many crossroads, and bursts into tears. Rodenbach's work is full of nympholepts: Jean Rembrandt in *L'Art en exil,* the
"friend KK" in "Le Chasseur des villes," Ronsart in "Une Passante," and
Montaldo in "L'Idéal" in *Le Rouet des brumes.* Once more: Rodenbach was
not inventive. Hugues stays on the lookout for the "stranger" with her "slow,
rhythmic walk" over the next days, finds her, follows her through locations
carefully enumerated (she is real, after all), and sees her enter the municipal
theater, where she disappears again. He buys a ticket, and the presence of the
notoriously sorrowful widower in the audience causes malicious comment.
The opera is *Robert-le-diable,* as in the episode in *L'Art en exil,* "one of those
old-fashioned operas of which almost unfailingly the repertoire of the provincial theater is composed."

Music makes Hugues cry, the sound of the hurdy-gurdy or the organ at
Nôtre Dame or Saint Walburga; his eyes grow moist as the overture begins.
"Presently the violins were unfurling the first measures." Either Hugues is
distracted by his fear of making a spectacle of himself ("the bowing of the
violins played on his nerves"), or Rodenbach himself is careless. The overture
to Meyerbeer's opera, the enormous success of 1831 and decades to come,
begins with two long rolls on the tympani and a forte unison passage in the
trombones and ophicleide. Berlioz was so impressed by the brilliant instru-

mentation and the vocal parts of the opera that he wrote an essay on it; there, he expressed fears about its fate in provincial theaters: "Quel monstreux chaos qu'une exécution sembable!" The opera Hugues unintentionally hears is employed as part of Rodenbach's depiction of Bruges as a backwater — yet *Robert-le-diable* had not yet become as old-fashioned as Rodenbach made it out to be: its persistent fame is indicated by the Degas painting of 1872, depicting — from the viewpoint of the orchestra — its most sensational event, the ballet of act 3, scene 7, in which, at an abandoned cloister, the spirits of "lascivious nuns" are summoned from their tombs by Bertrand, the opera's devil-figure, determined to win his son, Robert, for Satan. (The bass role of Bertrand was the inspiration of Méphistophélès in Gounod's *Faust* [1859].) Bertrand promises Robert that if he breaks a cypress branch from the sepulcher of Saint Rosalia, it will make him invisible and give him access to the bedchamber of his beloved, the soprano Isabelle. The long "ballet" begins with the dance of the nuns as they emerge from their tombs after Bertrand's invocation, "Jadis filles du ciel, aujourd'hui de l'Enfer, / Écoutez mon ordre suprême," lines that must have sent a chill through Jean Rembrandt's sometimes béguine, Marie. A "bacchanale ardente" ensues, and after Robert's arrival the prioress of the accursed band, Héléna, seduces him into carrying out his father's direction. Her long solo dance — once performed by the great Taglioni — awakens Hugues from his stupor; the resemblance to his wife of Héléna, danced by the stranger he has followed, again moves him to tears — remarkably, one might add, in consideration of the role's lasciviousness. "Head on fire," Hugues runs from the theater; the narrator ominously observes, at the chapter's conclusion, that Hugues is like Faust, excited and rejuvenated by the magic mirror. (The manuscript says: "In the poem of Goethe": the reference is to the Witches' Kitchen scene of *Faust*, in which Mephistopheles shows Faust the image of Helen of Troy.) The elements of sexual rejuvenation, and satanic temptation, in the finale of chapter 3, have been neglected by commentators. *Robert-le-diable,* with its numerous and spooky infernal scenes, was employed by other authors for sinister effect: in Leopold von Sacher-Masoch's story "Die Toten sind unersättlich," the vampire couple of the title are spotted at a performance of *Robert-le-diable* in Lvov; in Gustav Meyrink's "Der Albino" the innocent Corvinus sings the "Signal for the Tournament" beneath the window of his beloved before setting out to meet his particularly horrible death at the Albino's hands — in sinister Prague. For early readers of *Bruges-la-Morte,* the interjection of the ballet scene must have had a similar uncanny import. How popular the opera still was can be told from the fact that Oskar II of Sweden sang an aria from *Robert* to an entranced Stockholm throng on the twenty-fifth jubilee of his reign (1898).

Now that Hugues knows the dancer's name, Jane Scott (is the first name intended to suggest the celebrated Parisian cabaret singer, Jane Avril?), he easily makes her acquaintance, and she receives him "as if expecting their encounter," just as Mme d'Ottange, in Tavaststjerna's novel, looks at Klercken "as if they had known each other for a long time." In both cases, there lies a hint of supernatural preparation. Jane Scott's eyes and hair, for Hugues, already resemble those of his dead wife; "by the demon of analogy" ("le démon de l'Analogie"), the voice, too, is the same. (In *Il piacere,* Sperelli hears the tone of Elena Muti in the voice of Maria Ferres, as he seduces her.) The action moves quickly; suddenly energetic, no longer sad, Hugues spends happy evenings with Jane in her hotel room and, persuading her to leave the musical stage, sets her up in a house in the suburbs.

Only momentarily dismayed by the discovery that Jane Scott dyes her hair, Hugues no longer hears the "sorrow" of Bruges's bells; he abandons himself to the resemblance between Jane and the dead woman and ceases cultivating the resemblance between himself, in his former sadness, and the dead city. In his sexual satisfaction he is not aware of any infidelity to the memory of his wife: "Jane had brought back to him his former love," and every morning—the evenings are spent with Jane—he visits "the stations along the way of love's cross" in the sanctuary of his dwelling on the Quai du Rosaire.

A crack appears in Hugues's fool's paradise when he insists that Jane model the dresses of his wife; she laughs—laughter is a persistent characteristic of the femme fatale: see Rider Haggard's *She*—as she dances in the out-of-date garments. In a town as given to gossip as this Bruges (along with the Ghent of *L'Art en exil* and the Bruges of *Le Carillonneur*), the comings and goings of the former solitary have not escaped attention; his sinful life has become notorious, reaching even the béguinage where Sister Rosalie, the cousin of the servant Barbe, lives. On Easter Sunday (chapters 7–8), Barbe's festive dinner with the béguines is spoiled by the cousin's remonstrance at Barbe's remaining in the service of her fallen master. Hoping that her savings will win her admission to the béguinage, Barbe does not wish to give up her post, and her father confessor at Notre Dame offers a casuistical way out: as long as Hugues does not bring the evil woman into his residence, Barbe may continue to work for him without damage to her soul.

Hugues's disillusionment grows. The eyes and voice remain the same, but Jane's conversation has turned vulgar, as has her walk; she spends more and more time away from their love nest, and the prose poem assumes the traits of a novelette of love betrayed. Suspicious, Hugues returns to the sadness of Bruges, a "matched sadness" to his own, amidst the downpours and the sound of bells.

Chapter 10 and 11 are not in the manuscript but were added in the printing.

Rodenbach takes advantage of Hugues's returned melancholy, and his jealous desperation, as he attempts to reestablish his connection with the town and his self of the past: giving the text more body, the author interjects a series of art-historical cadenzas as "the influence of the town on [Hugues] was beginning again"; he takes "lessons in silence from the canals and their stately swans," "lessons in resignation" from the silent quais, as Hugues receives "pious and austere advice" from the towers of Notre Dame and Saint Sauveur (Sint Salvator) near his dwelling. They chastise him, reminding this "defrocked Priest of Sorrow" of his sin, and of the interpretation that the citizens of Bruges have put on his behavior; his passion was a sorcery of the devil, "un maléfice du Diable." Stories of the Satanism said to be festering in Bruges return to his mind; he resolves "to throw off this evil yoke," as he again becomes like Bruges, embracing the sadness of this "great, mystical city," this *soror dolorosa*. Rodenbach makes his often quoted statement that "every city is a state of the soul," a spiritual state to which Hugues returns, trying to escape the tyranny of his sexual fixation, prompted by the incessant bells and by the sight of the women of Bruges, clothed in their cloaks which resemble bells, as it were desexing them. (In *Le Miroir du ciel natal,* Rodenbach devoted a series of seven poems to bells, one of them beginning "D'autres cloches sont les béguines.") He makes his way (Chapter 11) to Saint Sauveur and its paintings by "Pourbus, Van Orley, Erasmus Quellyn, Crayer, Seghers," in a Baedeker tour of the interior's "many ancient treasures of art." A religious nympholept, he follows the cloaked old women to the small Jerusalem Church or Church of the Holy Sepulcher; he makes a special pilgrimage to the Hospital of Saint John, a sometime infirmary to which he goes in hopes of curing himself, and, in its former chapel, to Memling's great reliquary of Saint Ursula, "painted music." The strangely gentle paintings of the martyrdom of the eleven thousand virgins of Cologne move Hugues to a renewal of his own hard-won calm and to the thought of release in death. Finally, Hugues attends a Sunday evening sermon at Saint Sauveur on the theme of mortal sin, and the terrors awaiting sinners after death. (In *La Vocation,* Rodenbach lingers over the effect an evening sermon has on the boys of Hans Cadzand's graduating class, on "sin, hell, death"; it will one day determine Cadzand's withdrawal from the world after his adventure with the pretty housemaid.) The thought of his sin besets Hugues ever more strongly, and is reinforced by the bells and by the reproachful city itself; the bells are like the rooks around towers, shoving him, piercing his head, to pull out his wretched love, to tear out his sin.

Chapters 12 and 13 turn from the city's consolatory and minatory shrines and sounds to the jealous sufferings of Hugues: "Il souffre" becomes the verbal leitmotif. The details are no longer grand in their melancholy but pettily domestic, rather as the way the grand Swiss landscapes of Klercken's sufferings in *I förbund med döden* switch to the Strindbergian skirmishes of marriage. Jane spends Hugues's money; extraordinary bills come from Bruges tradesmen; Hugues receives anonymous letters about Jane's other affairs; he spends much time spying on her as he stands before the rented house, like the lover weeping before a closed door in a *paraclausithyron*. Confronted by Hugues, who is still drawn to her in the "sad October" of his passion, she threatens to leave him, and fearful of new solitude, he begs her to stay. On his way home, after these sordid and quite unpoetic quarrels, he meets still another symbolic element of Bruges (after the bells, the towers, the béguinage, the canals, the rain) — the swans, held back for this climax, the stately, silent birds ubiquitous in the poetry, the music, the art of the fin de siècle. The swan, as in Sibelius's "Swan of Tuonela," becomes the bird of death, whose song presages its passing. Juxtaposed to this lyrical inset in chapter 12 is Jane's scheming in chapter 13: she thinks that Hugues, "ill as he was," does not have long to live, and so she attempts to persuade the wealthy *rentier* to name her as his heir. She limits her escapades, a reduction made all the easier because, as the manuscript says, "one of her lovers, the cavalry officer to whom she had become a little too publicly attached," is transferred. She conceives the idea of visiting Hugues's mansion, to make an estimate of what will someday fall into her hands. The famous Procession of the Holy Blood is about to take place — she demands to see it from the windows of his house. He consents, although (the satanic hint again) he fears that Barbe will regard her as "a devil's messenger," "une envoyée du diable." In the dramatization of *Bruges-la-Morte*, Hugues's concern with the supernatural is still more developed. To his friend Joris he divulges that, in his yearning for his late wife, he has indulged in "magic, spiritism," and Sister Rosalie makes no bones to Barbe about Jane Scott: "She is one of those women of hell." As for Joris, who has been tempted by Jane, offering herself to him as a nude model, she is more mundanely "a vicious woman," bearing the dental characteristic of the femme fatale — as in Strindberg's Maria in *I havsbandet:* she has "the teeth of a beast of prey in her face of dreams." Rodenbach no doubt thought that these additional details about the satanic world and Jane's animal nature would appeal to his theater audience.

On the great day, Barbe prepares Hugues's house for the passing of the procession, inspired to even greater piety by the tolling of the city's whole battery of bells. Told to prepare dinner for a visitor, she immediately guesses who is meant, refuses, and is dismissed by Hugues. As she goes, she feels a tinge of sympathy for her suffering master. The last chapter is a skillful piece of melodramatic writing and is fairly closely followed in the stage version. Jane arrives, shows herself at the window of the mansion she intends to inherit, is chided by Hugues, and lies sulking on a sofa as Hugues watches and listens to the parade—the synaesthesia here, as elsewhere in the prose poem, is carefully worked out; the "extended watered silk of the canticles," the innocent songs of the children, the bands strangely made up of curved winds, "serpents and ophicleides"—words out of a hat of instrumentation or shapes that recall the endless curving of the streets of Bruges through which Hugues has so often wandered? A historical pageant follows, the roles played by "the young men, the young girls of the noblest families of Flanders," figures calling up the age of the Crusades and Theodoric of Alsace, who brought the Precious Blood to Bruges; clergy of all ranks; and the portable shrine itself. In *Le Carillonneur,* Rodenbach repeated the effect in his lengthy and equally effective description of the Procession of the Penitents at Furnes.

Jane, who has not watched the sacred procession (a meaningful satanic detail?), sneers at Hugues's signs of piety as the shrine passes, puts on her hat, goes downstairs, and, out of curiosity, enters the rooms of the sanctuary, but feels both unwelcomed by and hostile toward the old furniture (this mutual repulsion is like Marie Holzer's reaction to the furniture in the Malcorns' apartment in Rilke's "Die Letzten"). Gazing at the pictures of the dead wife (" 'one of them looks just like me' ") and laughing, she pulls out the holiest object of all, the chevelure, putting it around her neck. Hugues throttles her. In effect, Jane has turned the hair into an adornment and weapon of the femme fatale, a boa, the hair as noose. But, after Jane's death, Hugues sees that the victim of the "profaned and vengeful hair" once again resembles his dead love: he cannot tell one from the other. In Hugues's choice of a murder instrument too, the sensual—or simply necrophiliac—aspect of Hugues's cult must be remembered, the sensuality of a woman's hair, of which Baudelaire was so aware; the last lines of Baudelaire's "La Chevelure" could be applied to Hugues's preservation of the relic: "N'es-tu pas l'oasis où je rêve, et la gourde/ Où je hume à longs traits le vin du souvenir?" In an age when shops for the sale of women's hair were common (see O. Henry's "The Gift of the Magi," Rodenbach's "L'Idéal"), the fascination with women's hair is everywhere: from the living and sexually consolatory hair of Maria Ferres in *Il piacere* to the long, long hair of Maeterlinck's Mélisande, to Mallarmé's "joyeuse et tutélaire torche," to the "waves of long brown hair" of the imaginary girl in the cupboard of Mann's "Der Kleiderschrank." The lunatic in Maupassant's "La Chevelure" (1884) has found a bunch of "luscious hair" in a chest of drawers, which looks like "un oiseau d'or"—words also used by Rodenbach to describe the "boa d'un oiseau d'or."

The sound of the bells of Bruges rushes in through the windows, and

Hugues — like Klercken with his obsessive refrain of "a sick soul in a sick body" — repeats "morte . . . morte . . . Bruges . . . la . . . Morte," attempting to match the cadence to that of the bells, those "weary, slow little old women." (The ending of *Le Mirage* is more crassly melodramatic. Barbe enters and discovers the corpse, as the sound of "serpents and ophicleides" is heard; Hugues, kneeling and sprinkling petals on Jane's body, cries: "It is not I — it is the chevelure.") *Bruges-la-Morte* is a cascade of resemblances or analogies: "Bruges was his wife, while she was Bruges," and before his affair with Jane, Hugues has rejoiced in the resemblance between himself and the melancholy city. Jane Scott, to Hugues, resembles the dead wife — the peg on which the whole and somewhat flimsy plot of the love affair and the murder is hung. The many and subtle interpretations of *Bruges-la-Morte* as a symbolist text should be taken into account, but fascination with that aspect of the little work has diverted attention from its quality of classic decadence: the dead city, the heavy hints of an infernal plot, and the portrayal of the decay of a fragile neurotic: Hugues has many brothers: Gabriel Gram, Couperus's Frank, Tavaststjerna's Klercken, Rilke's Harald Malcorn, Andrian's prince, Lucian in Machen's *Hill of Dreams,* Söderberg's Glas, and, on larger or better-known stages, Des Esseintes and Dorian ad finem.

9

Poland/Prussia

STANISŁAW PRZYBYSZEWSKI

In his autobiography, *Moi współcześni — Wśród obcych* (1926, My Contemporaries — Amid Strangers), translated into German in 1965 by Klaus Staemmler, Stanisław Przybyszewski (1868–1927) makes a sneering aside about Joseph Conrad: "With what greed is Joseph Korzeniowski-Conrad, who however cannot hold a candle to Nietzsche, demanded back for Poland." The remark comes in the course of Przybyszewski's argument that Nietzsche was of Polish origin, and in his style essentially Polish. Both Conrad and Przybyszewski had won their reputations writing in a foreign tongue, Conrad's in the English acquired in the British merchant marine, Przybyszewski's in the German learned at the gymnasium in Toruń (Thorn). The first part of Przybyszewski's literary career takes place in Berlin; he reverted to his native tongue after his return to Poland (1897), although he published several works in German later on. Histories of German literature during the fin de siècle occasionally mention Przybyszewski as a "typical representative of the decadence literature of the 1890s" (Klaus Günther Just, "Nihilismus als Stil," 1969); the conscientious Albert Soergel also detected that he was a forerunner of expressionism. His work fairly swiftly became old hat in Germany. In a poem, "Ghosts," from 1914, Ferdinand Hardekopf wrote: "We are left over from the time of Przybyszewski, / Ghosts who love Lautrec and despair," and, two years before, in 1912 the same Hardekopf reviewed a performance of Przybyszewski's play, *Das goldene Vließ* (1902, The Golden Fleece), which he praised

as "something for us unmodern beings, those facing backward, the neurasthenics and decadents."

Przybyszewski was from the region of Kuyavia (Kujawy) in northwestern
Poland, then under Prussian administration; he spent the first fifty years of his
life as a not altogether unwilling subject of the Kaisers. His father was a well-
to-do peasant and elementary school teacher, his mother, the father's second
wife, claimed to be descended from an old and impoverished noble family; in
Totenmesse (Mass for the Dead), he describes her as "the slender, fragile
woman . . . to whose features centuries of refinement and the most careful
choice of blood had given an ineradicable stamp." The decadent pattern of the
ancient family appears once more; the father is pushed into the background of
Totenmesse, except as a man in whom a sense of social justice and a stubborn
Protestantism persisted — in other words, the source of the author's own social
concerns, cultivated desultorily throughout his life.

After three years at Toruń (1881–84), Przybyszewski transferred to a small
gymnasium at Wagrowice (Wongrowitz), earning his *Abitur* there in 1889. He
seems to have been a mediocre student, worst in mathematics and "very good"
in Polish; he was interested in fashionable topics and figures outside the curriculum — naturalism and socialism, Dostoyevsky, Zola, and August Bebel. In
Wagrowice, too, he gained extra income (which he needed: his father showed
signs of mental illness) by giving piano lessons to a daughter of the wealthy
Jewish family Seligsohn, and to a daughter of a merchant named Foerder.
Her younger sister, Marta, would shortly become Przybyszewski's lover and
common-law wife.

Going to Berlin in 1889, with a stipend to study architecture (his time in
Toruń had aroused an interest in the Gothic), he shortly transferred to the
medical faculty but was eventually expelled because of his work for a Polish-
language socialist newspaper. (According to his autobiography, "the police
pursued me with great zeal.") A gynecologist, Max Asch — to whom he had
been recommended by the widow Seligsohn — became his Maecenas and introduced him to literary circles, in particular the so-called Friedrichshagen
group. Among them, the autobiography mentions the "Tyrtaeus of anarchism," the poet Karl Henckell; with Asch, he attended performances of
the plays of Gerhart Hauptmann, for which he had nothing but contempt. He
also met and, in retrospect, mocked John Henry Mackay, the affluent Scots-
German, the "salon anarchist," as Przybyszewski called him. Not without a
gift for self-advertisement, Przybyszewski impressed the critic Franz Servaes,
who found a publisher, Friedrich Fontane (the son of the subtle Prussian
novelist Theodor Fontane) for Przybyszewski's manuscript on Chopin and
Nietzsche, the first part of his *Zur Psychologie des Individuums* (1892). A

warm, lengthy, and anonymous review in the journal *Freie Bühne* caught the attention of the teenaged Hugo von Hofmannsthal ("Loris") in Vienna, who noticed a kinship between Przybyszewski's detection of Chopin's "art of the nerves" and Nietzsche's "keen eyesight of the degenerates," as well as with Hofmannthal's own sense of decadent hyper-refinement and hypersensibility.

Even more important for Przybyszewski was the Swedish (or more precisely Scanian) man of letters, Ola Hansson, who, together with his wife, the Baltic German Laura Marholm, lived just then in Friedrichshagen. The Pole was captivated by Hansson's "unbelievable intuition," his "astonishing empathy," and learned from him about Barbey d'Aurevilly and Huysmans. Hansson, this "interpreter and visionary" (an allusion to the title of an essay collection by Hansson from 1893, *Tolkare och siare,* or *Seher und Deuter* in the simulta-neous German translation), "showed the timid sheep — my thoughts — the way to their pasture." The second part of *Zur Psychologie des Individuums* (also 1892) was mostly devoted to Hansson's short erotic novellas, *Sensitiva amorosa* (1887, translated into German by Laura Marholm in 1892). A sign of Przybyszewski's literary education by Hansson, the title, *Zur Psychologie des Individuums,* echoed Paul Bouget's *Essais de psychologie contemporaine* (1883/1886), its essay on Baudelaire and the "Théorie de la décadence."

Another physician, the surgeon Carl Ludwig Schleich, to whom Przybys-zewski was presented by Dr. Asch, remembered the Pole in his memoirs as "the bloody physiologist" on account of his medical drawings, "a genius of as-tounding spiderlike imagination like Félicien Rops, Callot, or E. T. A. Hoff-mann." Through Schleich, evidently, Przybyszewski got to know the poet Richard Dehmel, who remained a lifelong friend; *Totenmesse* was dedicated to him as the author of *Die Verwandlungen der Venus* (The Transformations of Venus), the sexual-sensational portion of Dehmel's collection of 1893, *Aber die Liebe* (But Love). Both Schleich and Dehmel were bewitched by Przybys-zewski's playing of Chopin: in the autobiography, Przybyszewski — with un-usual modesty — admitted his technical shortcomings, but added that alcohol made "the Germans" more receptive to the spirit of the composer, a Chopin they had not known before, "the pain of a soul revealed with nakedness . . . a true suffering." The Chopin of Przybyszewski's pamphlet of 1892 is much more a decadent, a "creature of the most sensitive nerves," than the heroic figure presented in the memoirs written during the early years of the Polish Republic.

Przybyszewski's Chopin performances became star numbers in the gathering of the coterie which gave Przybyszewski, as biographical object, his greatest international reputation — at the restaurant "Zum schwarzen Ferkel" (At the Sign of the Black Pig), the new center of Berlin bohème, repeatedly described in

Swedish, German, and English literary histories and biographies because of the presence of Strindberg. (For more detail, see the chapter in Tavaststjerna's *I förbund med döden*.) The Norwegian Dagny Juel, who had gone to Berlin to study music and had fleetingly been the lover of Strindberg and Edvard Munch, was instantly drawn to the exotic Przybyszewski, and they were married on August 18, 1893. (At the Black Pig, Przybyszewski was at first almost embarrassingly devoted to Strindberg, but the relationship went sour in due course.) She was not aware that her husband maintained a Berlin household with Marta Foerder, by whom he already had two children; a third was born of the loose union in 1895.

From 1894 to 1897, Przybyszewski and Dagny lived in Berlin, and in Norway with her parents. For reasons of language and temperament, Przybyszewski did not feel at home among the Norwegians, but through the medium of German he grew fairly familiar with the work of some of his Norwegian contemporaries—Garborg, Hamsun, Obstfelder, and perhaps Hans Jæger of *Fra Kristiania bohêmen* (1885, From Christiania's Bohème); *Totentanz der Liebe: Vier Dramen* (1902, Love's Dance of Death: Four Dramas) and *Schnee* (1903, Snow) were influenced in their economy of characters and structure by Ibsen. Przybyszewski gave a keen analysis of two Ibsen plays: "The degenerated Danish-noble blood expresses itself in *Ghosts* and *Rosmersholm*. Yet, above all, there prevails in [Ibsen's] soul the cold calculation of the German Hanseatic."

The Przybyszewskis had two children, born in 1895 and 1897; when Przybyszewski returned to Kraków in September 1897, Dagny Juel-Przybyszewska followed him, but—as her husband had been in Norway—was isolated by language; Przybyszewski's constant affairs strained the marriage, and Dagny briefly abandoned him for the poetic Wincenty Brzozowski. In April 1901, at the invitation of a well-to-do admirer of Przybyszewski's work, Władysław Emeryk, Dagny and her elder son set out for the Caucasus, and on June 5, 1901, Emeryk shot Dagny and himself in a Tiflis hotel room. (The story of Dagny Juel has been carefully told in English by Mary Kay Norseng, 1991.) Przybyszewski does not mention her in the autobiography. The role she played in his German prose will be described later.

In the autobiography, Przybyszewski says that "in none of my five poems, if we want to call these exploding rhapsodies thus (*Totenmesse, Vigilien, Androgyne, De profundis, Am Meer*), does that which we ordinarily call woman appear; they are planets, torn from the glowing sun, from one's own soul in its most powerful arc: wild, sometimes terrible visions in parthenogenetic births, volcanic eruptions, where the soul tries to reveal from its own fiery lava that for which, perishing, it strives in desperate yearning: Androgyne!"—a typical specimen of Przybyszewski's dithyrambic prose. Przybyszewski's concept of the androgyne became his trademark in these works; simply, the female elements in the male seek the male elements in the female, thus creating the perfect union. Przybyszewski was not interested in arguing or searching for a genuine physiological androgyne, or in emphasizing the female elements in the male. Instead, his search for the perfect female mate consists largely of attributing boyish qualities to the woman: slenderness, slim hands, small breasts — see his description of Dagny in her various appearances in the dithyrambs, of the protagonist's sister Agaj in *De profundis,* or the child bride Bronka in *Schnee.* The elderly Przybyszewski admitted that the concept might well be unclear, "only sensed in anticipation, clumsily expressed, conceived in the birth pangs of the chaos which bears the stars — in this little monster of my thought, stretched to the uttermost boundaries accessible to me, the key lies hidden, not only to my poems but to my whole work." The statement was an ennobling apologia for his oeuvre, which makes constant use of his own sexual obsessions.

Przybyszewski's ambition, never realized, was to have his five prose poems published in a single volume, called *Pentateuch, oder fünf Bücher von erhabenen und niederen Sachen* (Pentateuch, or Five Books Concerning Matters Exalted and Base). The first, *Totenmesse* (1893), is a determined effort to join the growing body of European decadent literature. It opens with a definition of the decadent which fits neatly with Huysmans's Des Esseintes or Hofmannsthal's hemeralopic shadows. Taking (and singularizing) the title of Huysmans's art criticism *Certains* (1889), his central figure Certain is "one of those who fall broken by the wayside, like sick flowers, one of the aristocratic race of the new spirit, of those who perish from excessive refinement and the all-too-luxuriant growth of the brain." Yet the reader "should not be frightened by the neuroses that ultimately mark the road which the progressive development of the human spirit seems to follow." Calling on his medical training, Przybyszewski observes that physicians have long since ceased to regard neurasthenia as an illness. It appears rather to be "the latest and absolutely necessary phase of evolution, in which the brain becomes more capable of action and much more productive, thanks to its greater sensitivity." Moreover, "it is precisely in neuroses and psychoses that the germ cell of a new sensibility lies, not yet classified; studies in the emotional life of such apparently unimportant 'Certains' will provide the most illuminating revelations of the most intimate and hidden elements of the human soul"; they are "lightning bolts, which cast a bright even though elementary light into the great unknown, into the strange land of the subconscious." (Przybyszewski has been called a proto-Freudian.) It is neither surprising nor sad that "these 'Certains,' these intellectual migratory workers [!] of the spirit, with their homeland everywhere and nowhere, are destroyed." Przybyszewski's homely phrase "geistige Sachsengänger" ("intellectual travelers to Saxony") comes from the land of his youth; workers leave the Polish regions of Prussia to take part in the turnip harvests of neighboring Saxony.

An account of the existence of one of these "Certains" follows, in a first-person outpouring. It starts: "In the beginning was sex," the basic material of life, the innermost being of the individual. "Sex finally created the brain . . . That was the birth of the soul." Spurred on by sex, the male soul searches for the androgynic woman, a search made more difficult by childhood memories — in particular the mother's disgust at the sexual aspects of her marriage — which have given rise to the "sick swamp-flowers of [the narrator's] expression of life." Przybyszewski acts as his own psychoanalyst; he does not hesitate — or his "Certain" does not — to speak about his "phenomena of degeneration." Among these are the "hidden secret of a satanic black mass," a devotion to music as a "horrible, grim symphony of torments" and "an orgiastic cadenza of brutal deliria of suffering," and a necrophiliac dream of a dead woman, disgusting and fascinating: "hyena-lust reared up within me," "I tugged and pulled at the dead flesh," and "laughter, in which every muscle of my body cried out in wild erethisms, choked me," until the dead woman, "in fearful majesty," rises up in her coffin and strikes the "Certain" with terrible power. Later, after memories of the vain cries of the faithful in a village church and thoughts of suicide, the heavens open, and an "apocalyptic woman's body appears," Astarte, come to fetch her victim. The masturbatory quality of these many pages is made clearer still by the description of Astarte, "who caused Onan to discover new orgies of pleasure and lust." This night when nature has become "an apocalyptic apotheosis of the eternally erect phallus, which in boundlessly crude profligacy pours out streams of semen over the whole of the universe," closes at the inception of the rule of "my free asexual soul" and "its serenity of eternity without end"; a vision comes, or "the holy, conquered victrix," the true beloved in whose lap the "Certain" will press his forehead and kiss her "beautiful, long, fine hands," casting at her feet the heavy burden of his rule over the world and all its creatures.

Vigilien (Vigils), printed first in *Neue deutsche Rundschau* of 1894 and as a book in 1895, has a more distinct narrative line. (One can only wonder what Fontane *père* thought of the little books his son was publishing.) The narrator witnesses the adultery of his wife, who leaves him; he falls into memories of the village stork, the bird known for "marital" fidelity, which murders its rival and then, aided by other storks, kills its faithless mate. (Przybyszewski was influenced by Tolstoy's *Kreutzer Sonata* of 1889, to which he had also alluded in *Totenmesse*.) On All Souls' Day, the wronged husband, who has taken perverse pleasure in his wife's infidelity, feels grace descend upon him, and a new — not yet quite real — woman comes before him, "woman, you in me, I — you. You — I." It is the Androgyne, with her boy's breasts, "my timid presentiment, a holy paraclete of the love whose empire of a thousand years will come." In a startling and enigmatic epilogue, "the brother of my heart," Abel appears, "the strong, virginal element of affirmation in me," whom the speaker, now a Cain, has had to kill, but who comes to life again. The brothers will be reunited as a single, perfect male being. A second almost equally surprising apparition ends the poem: he remembers the little blond son he has fathered with the adulteress, "my tiny piece of immortality." "You, me, and a white, red-eyed rabbit." Woman, it appears, is no longer necessary after all. The baffled reader may want to look forward to the intimations of homosexuality in the novel *Satans Kinder*.

Vigilien seems to be an erotic novella about a betrayed man who comes out of the crisis strengthened. It is impossible to determine how much the book contains of jealousy toward Marta or Dagny, and of affection toward the first two children by Marta, born in 1892 and 1893. Dagny's first child came in the year of *Vigilien*'s publication as a book. (George Klim, the biographer (1992) of Przybyszewski's German years, sees in *Vigilien* Przybyszewski's bad conscience toward Marta, his jealousy of Edvard Munch, and his fear of Dagny's future unfaithfulness, as well as his confidence in his own "great, holy art.") *De profundis,* which first appeared as a private printing at the house of Hugo Storm in 1895 (had Fontane been made nervous by its incestuous theme?), is told in the third person, alone among the works of the *Pentateuch*. It is dedicated to "My friend, My sister, My wife, Dagny," and is preceded by a defense of his material, "Pro domo mea," likewise privately printed and issued separately, just before the book itself; Przybyszewski claims that he does not offer the tired eroticism of de Maupassant or the sweetish but disgusting "lingerie-writing" of the Danish author Peter Nansen (the friend and colleague of Herman Bang and the author, inter alia, of *Julies Dagbog* [1893, German translation, 1895]), but the "painful, tormented awareness of a nameless, terrible force." A husband has been away from home a week, for a visit of reconciliation to his mother, with whom — for reasons never spelled out — he has been at daggers drawn, one of Przybyszewski's many loose narrative ends. He will also see his sister Agaj, a "splendid girl," according to his wife's letter, "whom I [the wife] love almost as much as I do you." (Georg Klim proposes that Agaj's unusual name is an anagram of "Jaga." as in Polish and Russian *Baba Jaga*, witch. He might have bolstered his argument by adding that, in Slavic mythology, the figure has a strong sexual import. "La sorcière Baba Jaga," as Tchaikovsky called her in the title of an early piano piece, is known to the general musical public from "Baba Yaga's Hut" in Mussorgsky's *Pictures at an Exhibition*.) The letter hints that the wife suspects an abnormality in the relationship between brother and sister. "I have often reflected on her love for you. In fact, she does not love you like a sister at all. I have never seen anything similar between siblings." At his rooming house, the nameless protagonist, "He," is beset by visions of mass sexual pairings and especially by the "fevered fear of incestuous lust." (Przybyszewski praised the sexually intertwined sculptures of Gustav Vigeland in the pamphlet *Auf den Wegen der Seele* [1897, On the Ways of the Soul].) As a respite—dream or reality?—he encounters a young girl, a prostitute, who offers herself to him. The next day, meeting Agaj, he reveals the source of his past sexual passion for her: when she was twelve, she crept into bed with him during a storm and, as she slept, he saw her naked. Then, at a meeting a year ago, drinking heavily, she bit his lips. Agaj makes fun of him ("'Are you going to write a novel?'"), but adds that she does not fear incest, and, as he goes on with his confession ("'I love your cruel soul...I see your little breasts and feel them glowing their way into my body'"), she grasps his hand, and "they plunged senselessly into the cruel maelstrom of sexual ecstasy." (By this overheated phrase, Przybyszewski must have meant mutual fondling; after all, they are in a public place.) When he tells her, to "her sphinxlike face," that he intends to set out for home, she commands him to stay.

The next day, Agaj does not come to their rendezvous, and he is relieved that he is freed from "this vampire," but she suddenly appears, wearing red gloves. He tells her that she looks "very perverse...like a figure of Rops." At a café, her leg presses against his, and she does not object when he recalls another pubertal scene: she was twelve and they went swimming together in the nude. Nonetheless, she tells him to return to his wife. (In her teasing, Agaj resembles Edvarda, another boyish heroine, in Knut Hamsun's *Pan* [1894]; Przybyszewski praised Hamsun's *Mysterier* in an essay for *Die Zukunft* [1894].)

At his room again, "He" falls prey to the hallucination that a double pursues him; a telegram in his own handwriting, asking his wife to come to him, lies on his desk. He flees, and imagines that he meets Agaj, who tells him that she has waited for him the whole night through. Back at the fragile refuge of his room, he is joined in bed by a fantasy Agaj, who wraps him in her hair. At noon the next day, Agaj in fact appears, and after having accused him of being unfaithful to her with the little prostitute (about whom he has told her), she makes approaches to him and accuses him of coldness (or impotence): "'Your nerves are too weak for the erethism in which you constantly live.'" He thinks of murdering her, but she leaves, commanding him to come to her at ten o'clock. His double returns, terrifying him, and he falls into a faint, awakening when it is night. He rushes to Agaj and finds her in a gown of black silk, her red gloves on her naked arms. Like the mother in Rilke's "Die Letzten" she has adorned herself for a night of love, but she tells him that it will be "a festival of departure." She confesses her passion for him at length: " 'I have grown up on you — in the salty bather's heat of your body — you, you, my blood, you, my husband.' " Both surrender to a "visionary, somnambulistic ecstasy," yet Agaj fears, she says, the power of his will, "which swells so terribly." She proposes that they drown themselves in the nearby sea but quickly drops the thought, arguing that their death together, in an embrace, would offend his wife. She walks into the water alone; before going, she bites his neck, inflicting a deep wound. Back in his room for the last time, he once more beholds the vision of indiscriminate sexuality he had seen at the beginning of his adventure with Agaj. Hearing a mystical chorus that sings of sexual suffering, "de profundis," and seeing the orgy in its full "filth and disgustingness," presided over by a giant woman — Agaj? — in a scarlet cloak, he goes mad. At dawn, he reverts to childhood memories of Agaj, thinking she has hidden herself "behind the garden . . . in the sea . . . *is* the sea!" and throws himself out the window.

In the interplay between "He" and Agaj, *De profundis* has a dramatic tension lacking in the two preceding prose poems; *De profundis* is not unworthy of being placed beside Rilke's "Die Letzten," Élémir Bourges's *Le Crépuscule des dieux* (1884), and even Thomas Mann's *Wälsungenblut* as a document about a forbidden drive which fascinated the writers of the century's end, for whom the taboo had been broken by *Die Walküre*. As a matter of fact, in its account of erotic attraction, it stands on its own, without the heavy Ibsenian trappings of Rilke's tale or the Wagnerian allusions of Bourges and, however skillful, the young Thomas Mann. The critic Arthur Moeller-Bruck, devoting a whole essay to *De profundis,* wrote: "In this book, Przybyszewski has added an element of infinite enrichment to his art, this art of nuance, which preserves each movement of the soul as a mood of the soul, and refines it into the most unlikely and subtlest tones."

Epipsychidion was issued by Fontane in 1900; according to a note at the end, its final part, "Am Meer," was written at "Christiansfjord and Plaza dela Mera" (i.e., Playa de Mera) in 1898 and 1899. Przybyszewski and Dagny had visited Spain as the guests of the philosopher Wincenty Lutosławski in the late winter of the former year. The puzzling title of the German version, also used for the Polish periodical publication in *Życie* (Life), is from Shelley's long autobiographical poem (1821) in defense of free love. The Greek coinage means — after the model of *epithalamion,* a poem about or for a wedding — a poem about or for the soul. Przybyszewski got the word, and knew the poem, from a translation by Jan Kasprowicz in *Życie*. (By coincidence, D' Annunzio, who read it in the original, employed it in *Il trionfo della morte* to describe the erotic turmoil of Giorgio Aurispa: "Had he not too, like the poet of *Epipsychidion,* perhaps loved Antigone in a previous existence?") The opening consists of a conciliatory dedication to Dagny: "This book, written and experienced by us both," and a brief introduction, "Introibo," which makes several references (in the anaphoras with which the subsequent main text is filled) to an apparent parting: "Many moons have passed since I beheld you, but still my heart shines above the stars that you have sown in my life"; "Many moons have passed since you sang of my deepest sorrow and my greatest happiness"; "Many moons have passed since your final glance painfully burrowed into my blood, and I still see your moonlight-pale countenance." The first tale, "Sonnenopfer" (Sun Sacrifice), initially published in *Pan* in 1897, concerns "the Son of Light," a monarch who, like Ludwig II of Bavaria and Stefan George's Algabal, can create "paradisiacal wonder-gardens." "[T]hrice each day [he] sacrificed to the sun": his warriors are sent in search of new victims to the north, where the sun does not warm, "hanging like a giant topaz in the sky." (The language is studded with the jewels of which Huysmans was so fond in *À rebours:* "holy emeralds," chrysolites, agates, chalcedons, "treacherous onyx," and so forth.) Returning, the expedition brings him a beautiful slave girl, "pale as a moonless night." The monarch is bewitched by her: "You are like a beam which, after years of wandering, has made its way from a strange star to the earth"; "You came like dreams upon the heart exhausted with pleasure"; "You came like a sad fading-away"; "You came with the stillness of the night, when it pours out its melancholy over the earth." Sensing the slave girl's discontent in his realm, the Son of Light begins to hate the sun. All the gifts brought to her (some of them the jewels listed above) do not satisfy her; he decides to renounce his solar service, since "your love [is] white and pure and soft as the wings of an arctic seagull." The monarch himself grows pale, and pestilence, caused by the neglected and vengeful sun, besets his empire. His people, "howling like a thousand-headed hyena," attack his palace and demand the life of the slave. She is crucified (only by her arms, as in a Rops drawing) and dies; the ruler takes "a fearful revenge" on his subjects by means of mass crucifixions. Yearning for his lost beloved, he sets out for a new "homeland of moonlight." The verbal overloading gives "Sonnenopfer" considerable unintentional comedy.

The next section, "Helle Nächte" (Bright Nights), is a kind of sequel. The mood is again one of sadness and regret: "So sad I once beheld the black fields of All Souls' Day"; "So sad I beheld the sun descending on an autumn evening"; "So sad I once heard a song, shredded by the icy wind," at the grave of a child. The speaker has searched for the "white moonlight homeland" of the

beloved in vain. Once they were happy together, in sadness, their souls intertwined, dreaming — among other things — of "dead cities, which lie in shad-
owless silence from the reflection that invisible stars cast beyond the seas."
(Przybyszewski will take another look at the dead cities of decadence in *Androgyne.*) True decadent worshipers of the past, "we sat in contemplation,
estranged from life. . . . For there is no greater beauty than dead splendor,
wrapped in spiderwebs, than old, rust-eaten crowns and the pale glow emitted
by things that have died."

The lengthy epilogue to these recollections of the happy sadness the lovers
once experienced is an account of how the speaker, "the god," re-created the
lost beloved out of his dreams. However, the dreams vanished: "You: you were
extinguished like a willow-the-wisp, like mist in the first hour of spring." Yet
she persists in his visions, seascapes (as in Arnold Böcklin) are painted in
which she becomes a mermaidlike creature; her golden hair, repeatedly mentioned, indicates her (imaginary) presence. The visions are all in vain: "I have
sought you on all the seas; I have looked through all lands for you, and could
not find you." The conclusion of this grandiose lament is a calling up of the
couple's course through history: "I had cities leveled so that you could see my
ships, as they entered the harbor amidst fanfares"; together they beheld the
dying Nazarene; the sometime Son of Light carried her away from the Eternal
City as it was set ablaze by the "hordes of barbarians"; she rode beside him "as
he set out to consecrate the Holy Grave with his blood." Finally, the narrator
speaks of their comedown to simple happiness. "On the beach we knew our
greatest joy, like proud children of kings." If *Epipsychidion* is a plea to Dagny,
it may have been difficult for her to resist it; but by the time of publication of
the German text (1900), the split was at the door, and can be sensed *passim.* In
Przybyszewski, the personal element is never far away.

In the finale of *Epipsychidion,* "Am Meer" (By the Sea), the narrator,
during a presumptive Baltic crossing, is captivated by the sight of a "small,
moonlight-pale woman's face, with eyes . . . eyes." A nympholept — as so often
in Przybyszewski's *Pentateuch,* and as in Rodenbach — he attempts to find the
face again after landing, and does; he and she are mystically united in their
love for the sea. Then, once again, his happiness vanishes: "The joy had passed
away in foam, the pleasure had sunk away . . . Yet the sea remains and my love
remains, which from the depths of its misery tosses out flaming bonds of
dreams." By the time he wrote his autobiography, Przybyszewski regarded
only "Am Meer" — "Nad morzem" in Polish — as a part of the *Pentateuch,* and
listed its title instead of *Epipsychidion.*

Probably in order to make money, Przybyszewski used the same "Am Meer"
again as the first part of another collection of three prose poems, *In diesem*

Erdenthal der Thränen (1900, In This Vale of Tears), complemented there by two further outpourings of despair at separation. "In hac lacrimarum valle" (given the Latin title in the body of the text and printed with it in *Pan* in 1896) ends: "I no longer love you, but I love the memory of you." "Himmelfahrt" (Ascension), first printed in Otto Julius Bierbaum's *Moderner Musenalmanach auf das Jahr 1894,* was thus immediately preceded, in the chronology of Przybyszewski's production, by *Totenmesse,* with *its* sexual extravagances and Astarte. Following a particularly turgid recital of passion, jealousy, and parting, Przybyszewski adduces a vignette from his youth: A Whitsuntide service in a village church calls up the memory of the death of the speaker's pure mother during a terrible thunderstorm, interrupting the litany of "the holy virgin of Loreto" in praise of Mary — "tower of ivory," "ark of peace," "consolatrix of the dying." The search of the first part comes back, transformed, as lightning bolts shoot through the speaker's brain, into an obscene tableau: the devil sits on a crescent moon, playing the violin, and beside him is "the Woman of the Fall of Man," rubbing her naked body against the devil and laughing. She announces: " 'Here [am] I, the goddess of your Dionysian yearning, the tabernacle of your holy criminality!' " Like other representatives of decadence (e.g., Huymans, D'Annunzio, Wilde, Valle-Inclán), Przybyszewski made free with juxtapositions of the spiritual and the sexual and plainly had a weakness for scriptural or liturgical titles: *Pentateuch* itself, *Totenmesse,* "Himmelfahrt," *Vigilien, De profundis,* "Introibo" (in *Epipsychidion*), "in hac lacrimarum valle."

   In diesem Erdenthal der Thränen may be regarded as a patchwork sewn for money's sake, a pendant to the true *Pentateuch,* adorned with an epigraph from Maeterlinck's *Serres chaudes:* "Et la tristesse de tout cela, / o mon âme, et la tristesse de tout cela," the conclusion of Maeterlinck's especially dispirited poem "Âme." The dedication is to the pianist and composer, Conrad Ansorge (1862–1930), a sometime student of Liszt, about whom Przybyszewski had published admiring essays in *Die Kritik* and *Pan* for 1897; in Ansorge's performance of Chopin's B minor Sonata, Przybyszewski found a magnificent interweaving of "horrible visions of death and . . . sobbing laments."

   The last of the *Pentateuch*'s prose poems, *Androgyne,* came out in German in 1906 at the house of Fontane, but had had partial or full printings in Polish from 1899 on. An amusing detail about the Warsaw edition of 1902 was that the title was changed, under the prim censorship of Russian Poland, to *W godzinie cudu* (In the Hour of Wonder) from the *Androgyne* of the Austrian-Polish edition (Lvov, 1900). Likewise, the subtitle of the conclusion was not the suspect "Androgyne" but "Miasto śmierci" (The City of Death), after the anonymous Toledo setting. Knowingly or not, Przybyszewski had followed in the footsteps of Maurice Barrès in the Toledo story in *Du Sang, de la Volupté, et de la Mort* (1894).

After a performance, a pianist has received a bouquet with a card bearing "a mysterious woman's" name in "golden letters." (The reader never discovers her name or his.) Immediately, his imagination is touched off; convinced that the giver of the bouquet loves him, he has seemingly endless visions of flowers: giant fairy-tale roses, tuberoses, "primal trees of white and red," azaleas, "orchids on hotly opened lips, poisonous, pleasure-demanding lips," and "lilies with wide-opened maternal vaginas of chaste lusts," narcissi, peonies, begonias and camellias — "a whole deluge of intoxicating color-poison[s], enchanting, sucking perfumes streamed over his spirit." The next paragraph continues the botanical-sexual inventory surely inspired by the vicious flowers collected by Des Esseintes. A dream of his childhood village and its religious festivals, "the paradise of the home earth," comes over him (as often before), and is combined with the treacherous magic of the exotic flowers; a storm arises, the face of a girl appears, and he awakes from his dream. Remembering the concert, at which a girl in the front row (the reader now learns) had handed him the bouquet, he conflates her with the tuberose, "slender and pliant as the stem of the tuberose," and her eyes are "as pure as white Bethlehem stars." She is "half child, half woman, like unto a tuberose," which word appears eight times in the text. (Tuberoses had acquired a peculiarly erotic aura toward the end of the century, perhaps because of the Dane J. P. Jacobsen's "Arabesque for a Sketch by Michelangelo," about sexual desire, translated into German by Stefan George and Rilke, among others. In Jacobsen, a "glowing night" is made aromatic by laurels, myrtles, magnolias, "secretly whispering irises, geraniums," and "by the heavy-breathing perfume of tuberoses and jasmines.")

Descriptions of the pianist's nympholepsy alternate with fantasies in which there are, again, palpable echoes or even cribbings from *À rebours* ("from the syphilitic maw of incredible orchids, tongues stretch forth, monsters sprinkled with purplish red fever spots"), ancient forests ("carbonized fern trees, isaurian palmshrubs, coco-and-breadfruit trees, . . . a monstrous nest of vipers, creeping upwards from the primeval magma"), as in the jungle visions of Richard Beer-Hofmann's *Der Tod Georgs* (1900) and, later, Thomas Mann's *Der Tod in Venedig.* Wagnerian flower girls are lifted from *Parsifal* ("those whose arms hang down like withered lilies, or those, who in their seductive hands hold the lustful grape bunches of their body . . . or those who arise from the womb of a lotus"), and Przybyszewski's own production is also plundered: the tale of the mighty king and the slave girl (now amidst other slave girls) from *Epipsychidion* is served up again. The pianist's "night of unsatisfied lust" ends with the appearance of Astarte-Ashtoreth from *Totenmesse.* After another fit of walking the streets — the directionless wanderings function as perambulatory *textes de liaison* between the erotic visions — he gives a shortlist of the women he has possessed, all of them lithe, pantherlike, gazelle-like, and with the form of "a divine ephebe," comparable to a blade of Damascene steel. The visions take up Huysmans's material once more, now from *Là-bas:* Satan with a bifurcate phallus appears, a black mass is celebrated, and then, not to be avoided, Ashtoreth, as if Przybyszewski were attempting to outdo himself in these triple fortes of "whole tempests of mad erethism." (It was the age, after all, of Mahler.) At a temple of lust, a whole band of naked women, all with the same head, throw themselves upon him "in the crazily raging orgasm of a hellish passion let loose," a "mad sabbath of blood and sperm." The Rops-inspired nightmare of the beloved crucified returns, "tied to the cross, displaying the whole splendor of her nudity," in a gigantic palace court, somewhere in Sais or Ekbathana.

Leaving his bed, the pianist at last finds the giver of the bouquet and confesses his love to her, but when he tells her that he will have her fastened to the cross, she flees. After many nights and days, he gives a second concert, which she evidently attends; finally they fall into each other's arms, to experience "the hour of wonder," which provided the alternative title of the book. As he sleeps, exhausted, she slips away, leaving a note, in which she says that she returns to the (emotional) cross on which he has nailed her. He falls asleep again. "The hour of wonder has been fulfilled and will never return."

Nonetheless the search continues: the speaker, clad in armor, rides like a knight, then becomes a frenzied walker again. In his memoirs, Przybyszewski tells how he spent "five days and five nights" wandering through the intertwined arabesques of the streets of Toledo during his and Dagny's visit. In *Androgyne* the place lacks a name, and is simply "the city of death," the "catacomb-city," "this terrible catacomb-city," identifiable by the repeated mention of the Alcazar and the sound of the rushing river — the Tagus — in its gorge. Confronted by this midnight phantom-place, he yearns for his homeland, "the city in the deep valley [i.e., Kraków]" and the holy earth of his homeland. (He moved to Kraków a few months after his Spanish trip.) He becomes absorbed by sounds and colors, a "mad Te Deum of color orgasm," and by a dreadful cacophony of "melting bassoons, howling basses, shrieking violins . . . horns, which howled like apocalyptic beasts, clarinets whinnying like the stallions of hell." (The orchestral passage may well be a hapax legomenon for Przybyszewski, whose musical descriptions, like those of cities, consist rarely of details but rather of verbal explosions.) He beholds the beloved, walking like the white "shine of silver poplars in the magic of Good Friday" (*Karfreitagzauber*): is she Wagner's penitent Kundry and he Parsifal?

The voice of the beloved tells him that "his love is not of this world," a statement directly contradicted by the speaker's reply in their love duet, in which he lists one last time her physical charms: her eyes, her "precious mouth," her "beloved hair with the golden stream of its richness." His instructions are physical and unambiguous: "Hide yourself once more in my lap; pour over me the starry flood of your hair," the favorite love posture of Sperelli and Elena Muti — and for that matter, of D'Annunzio and Barbara Leoni. They will be united in the womb of eternity, as "He-She! Androgyne!"

The reading of *Pentateuch* is tiring, most of all in *Androgyne,* where Przybyszewski attempts to repeat the (relative) success of the earlier parts, and to outdo himself not only in his employment of his solipsism, but in his repeated interjection of the cumulative lurid details from literature (Huysmans), illustrative art (Rops, perhaps Böcklin), and music (Wagner) of the fin de siècle. But amidst what may be called standard decadent apparatus, or gimcrackery, Przybyszewski falls outside the realistic tradition of decadent literature — the sense, albeit concentrated on central figures alone, of character, the sense of larger place, the sense of intimate setting: Huysmans's Des Esseintes and his thébaïde at Fontenay-aux-Roses, D'Annunzio's Sperelli and his rooms beside Rome's Spanish Steps, Wilde's Dorian and his house on Grosvenor Square, Hugues's Bruges and his house on the Quai du Rosaire are still alive today, and even Tavaststjerna's Klercken, wracked by his obsessions, is distinctly aware of the topography of Lugano and its environs, and his hotel room, facing San Salvator.

Perhaps, to read the *Pentateuch* with any pleasure today, it would be necessary, relaxing, carried along by the flood of words, to regard its segments as garish and extremely self-revelatory fairy tales — something like the chaster fantastic legends written simultaneously by Louis Couperus, *Psyche* and *Fidessa.* To be sure, Couperus is esteemed not for them but for his intricate novels about society in The Hague. Przybyszewski also had ambitions as a realistic novelist and wrestled, even while completing the *Pentateuch,* with this commercially more viable form. Just's opinion, that Przybyszewski "renounced not only time as a constituent element of narration but place as well," is surely correct as far as the *Pentateuch* goes. It is slightly less accurate when applied to his novels.

Finland

KARL AUGUST TAVASTSTJERNA

The Finland-Swede Karl August Tavaststjerna's early promise was never quite fulfilled. He established himself as Finland's leading "realistic" novelist with *Barndomsvänner: Ett nutidsöde* (1886, Childhood Friends: A Present-Day Fate), the story of a singer's try at a continental career, and his return to a stationmaster's post somewhere in Finland's interior; with *Hårda tider* (1891, Hard Times), an account of the Finnish famine of 1867–68 and of the contrast between the Swedish-speaking aristocracy and Finnish-speaking refugees from the north of the country; and with some short stories, a form which forced him to control his weakness for digressions; yet he never won the German public he hoped for, despite the championship of the well-connected critic Ola Hansson and the German essayist and translator Ernst Brausewetter. Hansson, in *Das junge Skandinavien* (1891), hailed him as one of the great hopes of Nordic literature and, in *La Revue des Revues* (June 1, 1894), made a presentation of *I förbund med döden* (1893, In Alliance with Death), "La Maladie dans la littérature actuelle"; neither effort attracted German or French attention. A main cause of Tavaststjerna's failure—unlike Ibsen, Bjørnson, Lie, Alexander L. Kielland, admired by Thomas Mann, and Arne Garborg—to find publishers may have been the specific and not very picturesque local details of his works, which dealt much with the Swedish-speaking minority, its occupations, and its quirks. *En inföding* (1887, An Aborigine) takes up the clash between a dreamy and introverted Finlander from the countryside and an elegant, cosmopolitan official (significantly named Hård, "hard"); *Kvinnoregemente* (1894, Rule of Women) turns to the silly exaggerations of zealots for the Finnish-language cause; *En patriot utan fosterland* (1896, A Patriot without a Homeland) deals with a Finlander's loss of national identity in Russian service. Of Tavaststjerna's narratives, only two were eventually translated into German, *Finska Vikens hemlighet* (1895, The Secret of the Gulf of Finland), the notebook of a Russian naval officer trapped in the sunken monitor *Rusalka,* based on a historical event, and the author's memories of his childhood on a Finnish estate, *Lilla Karl* (1897, Little Karl).

In November 1892, Tavaststjerna and his bride, the Swedish actress Gabrielle Kindstrand, whom the blindly enamored Tavaststjerna called Nixe, had set out on a long European tour, in whose course he hoped to conquer German letters, and she the German stage. After stops in Berlin, Weimar, Geneva, Montreux, and an Alpine resort, Leysin, described fancifully in an epistolary novel, *Korta brev från en lång bröllopsresa* (1893, Short Letters from a Long Wedding Trip), the couple parted company, Gabrielle for Berlin, in pursuit of her fata morgana, Tavaststjerna for Lugano, where two-thirds of *I förbund med döden* takes place. The summer of 1893 was spent on the island of Rügen; before Nixe — who had been improving her German in Bavaria — joined him in August, he had the occasional company of Strindberg and Strindberg's Boswell, Adolf Paul, "the friend of great men" (Sibelius principal among them). The Tavaststjernas' first meeting with Strindberg in Weimar caused Strindberg to tell Paul that "Tavaststjerna's wife is dangerous for my peace of mind." On Rügen, Tavaststjerna composed *I förbund med döden,* which came out at Bonnier's in Stockholm in 1893; about the Rügen stay, Tavaststjerna wrote: "This summer misery is the worst and deepest I have ever known in my life."

For Tavaststjerna the autumn and winter of 1893–94 in Berlin were at least equally miserable: he was tormented by his increasing deafness and by Strindberg's attentions to his wife. The Swede was the center of the company foregathered at Türck's tavern on Unter den Linden, dubbed Zum schwarzen Ferkel by Strindberg. Among the main participants were the Norwegian painters Edvard Munch, Christian Krohg (also the author of *Albertine* [1886], about the making of a prostitute), and Fritz Thaulow, the Norwegian dramatist Gunnar Heiberg (in love with Krohg's wife), occasionally Knut Hamsun, the Dane Holger Drachmann, and the Germans Richard Dehmel and Otto Erich Hartleben. The most colorful members, next to Strindberg, were Stanisław Przybyszewski and his wife-to-be, the Norwegian Dagny Juel, who achieved a reputation as the "Aspasia" of the group — Gabrielle paled beside her. In his memoirs, Przybyszewski mentioned "a Finnish author, elegant but only moderately gifted," together with his wife, who "stormed the German stage in vain."

By the spring of 1894, Tavaststjerna went to Sweden, to live for a while on an estate in Närke, making a translation of Gerhart Hauptmann's *Hanneles Himmelfahrt,* in which, thanks to her childlike appearance, Nixe toured successfully in Sweden and Finland. For economic reasons, Tavaststjerna — semi-abandoned by Nixe — returned to Finland in September 1895, to become the editor of "Finland's smallest newspaper" at the new ice-free port of Hangö (Hanko). The post turned out to be a bitter disappointment; in Hangö, he wrote one of his darkest lyrics, "Homeward in autumn rain, homeward at nighttime." By New Year's Day, 1896, he was the editor of the Swedish-language paper in the overwhelmingly Finnish-speaking town of Björneborg (Pori). His unabating depression informs the poem, "Burial bells ring on New Year's Days."

What he regarded as the major literary product of these last years was the epic-and-lyric cycle *Laureatus* (1897), which ends with Laureatus's vision of himself as the suffering Christ. The book was inspired by the poet's love for Aline Borgström, the wife of his Maecenas, a shipping magnate and industrialist; as "Diane," she was the object of a sonnet cycle, the most convincing (and most often quoted) content of the mixed bag. In the winter of 1898, exposed in a snowbank after a drunken evening, Tavaststjerna contracted pneumonia and was admitted to the town hospital, where he died on March 20, 1898; in 1960, it was revealed that he had died not of his infection but of a dose of Lysol, administered instead of his medicine by a careless nurse.

During the last summer of his life, on the island of Visby, Tavaststjerna met the Swedish novelist Selma Lagerlöf and her companion Sophie Elkan. Speaking at the Swedish Literary Society in Finland on February 5, 1912, the birthday of the national poet, Johan Ludvig Runeberg, the celebrity Lagerlöf — she had won the Nobel Prize for Literature in 1909 — confessed that she had never read a line by Tavaststjerna before the chance meeting; she had caught up on his life and works by looking into Ernst Brausewetter's *Nordische Meister-novellen,* which she had in her luggage. She was at first disappointed by his appearance; the *Meisternovellen* had contained a youthful portrait of the aristocrat, but what she saw was a face with "features grown heavy and coarse — the fine, chiseled quality was gone. His whole face was gray, not pale or colorless but truly gray." Conversation would have been impossible, because of his deafness, had it not been for Sophie Elkan's patience. Lagerlöf liked Tavaststjerna's gentlemanly manners, but was startled at his megalomania. He was finishing, he said, a poem (i.e., *Laureatus*), which would be "like *Faust* or *King Fjalar* [Runeberg's masterpiece of verse technique] and which, with a single stroke, would raise [Tavaststjerna] up among the greats of world litera-ture." A somewhat condescending wish was injected into Lagerlöf's perora-tion: "If we had only had sense and courage enough to force him to work more carefully and slowly." Yet such a calm mode of work was impossible for him, he lived in constant emotional crisis. His longtime friend, the psychiatrist Jarl Hagelstam — who, a month before Tavaststjerna's death, had advised him to take a cure at Hagelstam's sanatorium — characterized him as "[a] creature of moods and [a] psychopath."

I förbund med döden has baffled its rather few commentators from the start. The Swedish critic and poet Oscar Levertin, writing a review of Werner Söderhjelm's memorial biography (1900), said that the "novella," the generic term on the title page, was a "gloomy and mysterious confession"; the author was "still young in years but already aged in spirit and experience, absorbed by the thought of death." Söderhjelm himself had noted, without specifics, the autobiographical nature of *I förbund med döden,* "not so much a narrative as a psychopathological study of character or a personal confession and personal analysis." Erik Kihlman, in a life-and-works volume (1926), and E. N. Ti-gerstedt, in an exploratory study of "Tavaststjerna's Christ neurosis" (1938), were disturbed by the swerve away from the concept of the protagonist's "union with death" to a bitter story about marriage in the style of Strindberg's *Giftas* (1894–96, *Married*). Erik Ekelund, a later biographer (1958), found the novel's conclusion to be a "jangled chord" and "grotesque." The mag-isterial Gunnar Castrén, in a general history of Swedish-language literature (1957, revised 1967), decided that the novel was not a "finished literary work," but the story of a neurotic which turns into the tragedy of marriage. In an informative monograph on decadent traits in Swedish literature of the fin de siècle, Claes Ahlund (1994) again concluded that the novel was confusing in its intentions. Tavaststjerna himself admitted that the book did not hang together; he implored Nixe to hypnotize him so that he could write as "fine an ending" to the story as its beginning. "So far I can't compose the conclusion; my brain says stop to the effort."

Lecturing on Tavaststjerna in Helsingfors (Helsinki) in 1897, the Swedish novelist Gustaf af Geijerstam stated that the very air of the 1890s was in the book, "a mood of tired overstimulated senses, religious mysticism, and talk about sympathy between souls." Sixty years later, Ekelund made much the same point, more specifically, about Tavaststjerna's Gustaf von Klercken: he belongs to "the same decadent race" as Huysmans's Des Esseintes, with the same nervous illness, never quite defined. Both are in their thirties (Klercken is thirty-six), fragile representatives of a dying century (Klercken reflects that "the century is nearing its end"); both are tired and nervous (Klercken is "an oversensitive compass needle"); both belong to the nobility which, they lament, is dying; both despise the masses, as they despise vulgar materialism. Klercken's surname provides an interesting ambiguity. It can mean a member of the medieval clergy or, in a modern sense, simply a clerk; as "Klercker," it is also the name of a historical Finland-Swedish noble family. In a review, Arvid Järnefelt, a subscriber to Tolstoy's doctrine of the humble life, thought Klercken was possessed by a boundles egoism, surely a characteristic of Des Esseintes, Sperelli, Dorian Gray, and D'Annunzio's Giorgio Aurispa in *Il trionfo della morte*. Determined to kill himself, Aurispa, jealous of his mistress Ippolyta's possible future lovers, wants her to die with him and employs an aesthetic strategy to persuade her, playing the *Liebestod* from *Tristan und Isolde* on a piano hauled up to their "hermitage" overlooking the Adriatic. Unwilling, Ippolyta wrestles with Aurispa, crying, "Assassino!" as the two of them fall to their deaths. But Klercken does not include his wife in his thoughts of death and, an impoverished bank clerk, is concerned for her and her two children. A sense of duty takes him back to the small gray house in Helsingfors and the monotony of his job.

If Klercken's place among the *decadenti superiori* is only conditional, the novel's title is secure enough in the titrology of the period. Tavaststjerna himself — perhaps in an indication of his own confusion about the meaning of his book — offered several proposals to his friend Söderhjelm and to his publisher Bonnier. "A sick soul in a sick body" is the refrain which has taken residence in Klercken's mind and ears even before he sets out on his trip south, heard in the passage of train wheels over ties and fishplates, and in the slap of a steamer's paddles. (It appears to be an auditory hallucination, like the high E which tormented Bedřich Smetana.) "Asra," another rejected title, was a reference to the desert tribe in Heine's poem, "who die when they love" — if the disheartening phrase was clumsy, the Heine allusion was relatively obscure and might have overemphasized the novel's erotic component. "På hetsjakt undan dödan" (On a Chase away from Death) and "Timglaset vändes" (The Hourglass Is Turned) may have seemd too sensational and, in the former case, again misleading: Klercken does not flee death. Tavaststjerna's final title, calling attention to the imaginary meeting with death in the first chapter, found favor with Bonnier, who was quite aware how modish it was.

It was preceded by Edmond Rod's *La course à la mort* (1880), Tolstoy's *Death of Ivan Ilyitch* (1886), the Dutch author Marcellus Emant's *Dood* (1892), Rodenbach's *Bruges-la-Morte* (1892), Hofmannsthal's *Der Tod des Tizian* (1892), and it was contemporaneous with Schnitzler's *Sterben* (1893) and Hofmannsthal's *Der Tor und der Tod* (1893). Death titles came thick and fast in those days: D'Annunzio's *Il trionfo della morte* (1894), Maurice Barrès's essay "La Mort de Venise" in *Du sang, de la volupté, et de la mort* (1894), Thomas Mann's story about another death-possessed middle-aged man, "Der Tod," was from 1897, D'Annunzio's play, *La città morta* and Ibsen's *Når vi døde vågner* (When We Dead Awaken) from 1898, Stefan George's *Der Teppich des Lebens und die Lieder von Traum und Tod* from 1899, Maeterlinck's puppet play *La mort de Tintagiles* from 1899, Richard Beer-Hofmann's short novel *Der Tod Georgs*, the Dutch psychiatrist Fredrik van Eeden's fictionalized case history of a suicidal woman *Van de koele meren des doods* (Concerning the Cool Meres of Death), and Rilke's "Ein Märchen vom Tod" in *Vom lieben Gott und Anderes* were all from 1900, Strindberg's *Dödsdansen* from 1901, Richard Schaukal's *Von Tod zu Tod* from 1902 and his *Eros Thanatos* from 1906, Jiři Karásek ze Lvovic's *Hovory se smrtí* (Conversations with Death) from 1904, Arvid Järnefelt's play, *Kuolema* (1902, Death), about a woman obsessed by the thought of death, is familiar to every concertgoer, because of Sibelius's incidental music, in particular the "Valse triste." The fad played out, it can be argued, with Thomas Mann's *Der Tod in Venedig* (1912); alongside the mass slaughter of the First World War, thanatophilia — the romantically absorbed contemplation of death, whose nineteenth-century history goes back to Novalis's *Hymnen an die Nacht* and which was enormously encouraged by Wagner's *Tristan und Isolde* — was no longer as attractive or literarily effective as it had been, particularly during the last years of the dying century.

For all the interpretive problems that emerge from *I förbund med döden*, its composition is lucid enough: chapter 1 tells about Klercken's journey to Lugano, 2 through 7 about his stay at the Pension Bellevue, 8 about his return to Helsingfors, 9 about his life at home, 10 about his ultimate collapse. The opening is a wonderful if sometimes turgid presentation of Klercken's mental and emotional torments, his immediate past, and the vision which gives the novella its name. Directly, Klercken hears the familiar refrain, "a sick soul in a sick body," from the paddle wheels of the steamer bringing him to the resort town in Ticino. The slogan has made him a "helpless slave of the teachings of medicine"; it has sent him into the hospital (where it momentarily abates), only to return when lack of money forces him back to his desk at the bank. The previous autumn, he left home and income (thanks to his wife's sacrifices) to seek relief in "the sanatoria of the Alps." Klercken can scarcely be given any effective medical treatment, for — the information comes up later in the chapter — he reveals the nature of his torment neither to wife, friends, nor physicians. Abruptly, he sets out on a two-month journey through the "grave monuments of dead cultures in Italy," and his itinerary resembles that of an ordinary tourist — Vesuvius, the Blue Grotto on Capri, the canals of Venice. (In chapter 2, Klercken recalls his "feverish weeks" in Venice, and his efforts to put his hodoeporic impressions in some order: "It was no pleasure trip but rather a journey through the dark pages of history, which, of course, were opened before him.") He resolves to commit suicide, "to experience death without fear or hatred"; the thought of death becomes his fast companion and the "previously cruel voice" (the auditory hallucination) becomes "a gentle, melancholy woman's voice." On the steamer to Lugano, the voice speaks "with undiminished force" but has grown "friendly and kind, as if it too desired rest."

At this juncture, Klercken is snapped back into an examination of his surroundings, viewed with "a painter's and an observer's sharp eye," as he catches sight of the white stone marking the boundary between Italy and Switzerland. Quite scientifically, Klercken notes the currents and colors of the water, the effect of the northeast breeze, and he is even able to estimate the height of the mountains he sees as he sails toward Lugano: Monte Bre on his left, Monte Generoso some distance to the south on his right, the Veltline Alps still farther away. But the amateur topographer falls back into a quasi-mystical mood at the sight of a villa and a tower on the slopes of Monte Bre, for he feels he has beheld them before, in some "preexistence." In his persistent vacillation between dream and reality, he realizes that he had seen the same landscape, the same peaks in the background and the same villa, on a painted tea set in his parents' home when he was a boy. Life, then, has no mystical experiences to offer him (he is forever on the lookout for them), but only "disillusioning reality." The steamer ties up briefly at Gandria at the foot of Monte Bre, and again the observer notes the effect of the northeast wind, the *bise,* coming down the Cassarate gorge, as the steamer slowly churns on toward its destination, Lugano. All details are carefully registered.

Klercken falls out of reality once more as San Salvatore, just south of Lugano, comes into view, "resembling a gigantic cat of the primeval world, arching its back, with the old white pilgrimage church on top, like a toy house." His great vision begins: Death, with his hourglass, comes to meet him, leads him upward through the chestnut groves on San Salvatore's slope, and takes him, "without difficulty," to the "pinnacle of the temple," from which Klercken — the topographer again — can see the plain of Lombardy and the Apennines in the far distance. Death's words seem familiar enough: " 'Cast yourself down from here, and all this shall belong to you!' " What Death says is a mélange of Satan's words to Christ on the pinnacle of the temple in Matthew 4:6, " 'If thou be the Son of God, cast thyself down,' " and Matthew 4:8, where the persistent devil takes "Jesus up into an exceeding high mountain, and sheweth him all the kingdoms of the world, and the glory of them," and (4:9), "saith unto him, 'All these things will I give thee, if thou wilt fall down and worship me.'" Tavaststjerna's Death also seems to remember the alternate version of the story in Luke 4:5-9.

Klercken, baffled by Death's scrambling of Scripture, asks: "'Why do you tempt me with life, Death?'" Actually, as Ekelund noticed, what Death offers Klercken is suicide and, in his physical destruction, a return to nature; but Klercken's question shows that he has ignored the lethal first part of Death's command, grasping only the second, as Death shows him the beauties of the world. Death clarifies his offer, saying that he is not tempting Klercken, but giving him a "free choice between me and life." Since Klercken has had the courage to look, as Death says, straight into his face, and since Klercken evidently loves life after all, Death, compromising, will allow him a return to life. Klercken makes a "concessive and thoughtful speech," life tempts him no longer, for Death has shown him "another and fairer world," to which Death retorts, reasonably, "'And then you will be mine,'" and Klercken replies: "'Rather belong to you than to pettiness." Pettiness, in Klercken's rambling psychomachia, is a word for the present world, Des Esseintes's "le siècle," whereas a noble spirit welcomes the end; Klercken accuses himself of pettiness for having hesitated to accept Death's offer, "my only, sure, and dependable friend." (Death says "pettiness" has also transformed him — Death — into a "demonized bogeyman, a skeleton," made ridiculous by mankind out of fear.) Ending the conversation, Death informs Klercken that, because he has humbled himself before him, he — Death — has turned the hourglass over, giving Klercken an extension of life. Yet he must never forget their meeting — he must never flee, a coward, when Death offers him "his great peace." "'Only by your having become my friend can life have value for you. Behold my hand! Take it as a seal upon our union.'" Although San Salvatore resembles a "giant cat of the primeval world," and although Klercken is aware that Death's words "have been uttered by the Tempter to the Divine One Himself," he represses these hints that his Death is a satanic figure. What Tavaststjerna has offered is a clumsy and self-contradictory *monologue intérieur,* five years after Dujardin's *Les Lauriers sont coupés* (1888). Small wonder that reviewers and commentators were puzzled.

Klercken comes to himself on the steamer's deck, and the words of Death fit themselves to the rhythm of the paddle wheels, replacing the old and tormenting refrain — which, however, directly returns: "A sick soul in a sick body." As the steamer glides into Lugano, Klercken's imagination shifts to a consolatory fantasy — of a deathbed amidst the white houses and green trees of the town, amidst "benevolent, sympathetic strangers, who will not be much concerned about his death." The deathbed fantasy is given a specific detail: Klercken's bed must be placed so he can climb, in his imagination, up San Salvatore, to the pinnacle of the temple, and "there he [will] make the final, decisive leap into space." Once more, reality seizes control of him, and the northeast breeze almost catches his hat. He feels a little foolish and takes a coach to his pension, sitting "with a vigorous posture, as though he did not look only for a clean, soft deathbed." Mockingly, the wind blows his collar up over "his poor, pondering head." The vision ends with its creator, Tavaststjerna, making not unsympathetic fun of his alter ego, as Huysmans made fun of Des Esseintes at the dentist's office and in the Miss Urania episodes of *À rebours*.

At the pleasant Pension Bellevue (chapter 2), Klercken gets a room, "bright, large, and cheerful," with a view of San Salvatore from one of its windows, Lake Lugano and the Veltline Alps from the other; aided by the chambermaid, Klercken moves his oaken bed so that, lying on it, he can contemplate the magic mountain. (Pension Bellevue is listed in the Swiss Baedeker for 1885, located in the suburb, Paradiso, southwest of Lugano's center, with a view of San Salvatore.) In the dining room, his attention is drawn to "a silent lady" for whom he immediately feels a lively "sympathy," i.e., affinity. She is dark — Russian, Italian, or from the south of France — and clad in a Russian shirt which "allows her generous bosom to swell freely." Her eyes and her mouth fascinate him — Klercken experiences the start of an erotic renaissance. (The reader of *Der Zauberberg* will not be able to repress memories of Clawdia Chauchat.) When he meets her glance for the first time, it is friendly, smiling, direct, as if she wished to say: " 'It is good to see you. I have long waited for you,' " the first of the quasi-supernatural qualities the suggestible Klercken will discern in her. A new light seems to have been lit in his soul, a perception modified, however, by his overriding concern with death: "He had found his last, idyllic sanctuary among the sheltering Alps, and he would never leave this sanctuary alive." Yet he also feels a desire never known before, to "initiate someone into his gloomy secret, and to make his final great confession before leaving everything behind." The inconsequence of Klercken's thoughts may have its cause in his drinking wine in great gulps, another real detail; analyzing his thoughts according to "hypochondriacs' custom," he convinces himself that his intoxication has nothing to do with alcoholic intake.

In the pension's garden, Klercken, customarily shy and withdrawn, makes himself the center of a group of guests: they play a game of guessing nationalities, at which he does well, and the others marvel at his perceptivity. But he fails in the attractive woman's case: she is not Russian, she says, but has associated much with Russians. One of his several guesses gives her a start. She perhaps has gypsy blood — onto which he tacks a long story, true or not, about the "gypsy features" of members of his family and about his childhood nurse, "a tamed gypsy": thus Klercken and the woman may share a connection with a particularly mysterious race. When they part for the evening after she has lavishly flattered him for his sensitive artist's soul, she reveals that she is from Provence, giving him her "plump white hand," letting it lie in his. Klercken sleeps soundly and long.

The next morning (chapter 3), Klercken takes a walk along the shore road leading toward San Salvatore, and notices that, even though a "candidate for death," he has regained his health. He also notices that the strange woman stands above him, gazing out over the lake's waters, as though in a trance; to his consternation, he realizes that he has been looking for the place where he met Death and has found her instead, perhaps "a mystical instrument in the hands of a higher power," put in his way for his salvation, so that Death will not have turned his hourglass over in vain. He catches up with her on the highway, and they resume their flirtatious conversation of the evening before, but he thoughtlessly smiles at her remarks about her own sensibility to shifts in the wind and the "beginning mystification" in her words; annoyed, she breaks off the conversation, leaving Klercken repentant. She will have nothing more to do with him that day, the second of his stay and of their acquaintance.

At the start of chapter 4, he lies on his bed at the pension, estimating the height of San Salvatore. Enjoying the sense of peace which, he thinks, his meeting with Death has given him, enjoying his superiority to those "thralls of materialism" (and of the crass materialism of "le siècle" that Des Esseintes despises) who nonetheless will take over the world in a great "internationale," he decides — now that he has been cured by Death from his fear of death — that he will return to the small joys of home and hearth and, impatient as he is, writes to his wife, telling her that he will hasten back to her, as a new man. Resting in the garden's bamboo glade, he feels "a hand pass over his soul's eyes"; the strange woman appears, extends her "plump white hand," and asserts that with her glance she has forced him to turn toward her. (The day before, she claimed she sensed his presence in his hiding place on the shore road.) At last, she tells more about herself: she is a translator, who regards it as her task to incorporate the new "spiritism and the supernatural" into French literature. Challenging Klercken, she says that he no doubt is a "well-placed, established, and salaried thrall of the age" who has accepted materialism, to which Klercken replies with his own challenge: that she try to convert him. Their budding friendship almost winds up on the rocks again when she accuses him of bullying and unimaginative heartlessness. This second spat of the incipient lovers is ended by her presentation of her visiting card with its crown, indicating her nobility, and her name: vicomtesse d'Ottange. Not to be outdone, Klercken later sends her *his* card with name and crown. It is not until chapter 8, in the vicomtesse's farewell note to Klercken, that her first name is revealed, Gabrielle, the same as that of Tavaststjerna's much adored and usually absent wife who had, we know, the ability to hypnotize her husband.

After lunch (chapter 5), the two aristocrats (bank clerk and translator) resume their talks; ever more charmed, Klercken feels pangs of conscience toward his wife in Finland, but manages to submerge them in his new sense of "bright life and health," and in the Sphinx smile of Mme d'Ottange and the persuasive rhetoric of her words about "our nervous age." He begins to speak about "the strange experiences within himself," which, she assures him, are shared by hundreds of other modern human beings, a number considerably expanded over what Hofmannsthal wrote almost simultaneously about the sensitive decadents: "we few." At this, he feels an inner happiness. But he cannot forget his fascination with death; indeed, he confesses that it has been his daily companion. Forever labile, he weeps like a child, drawing her hand, wet with his tears, over his lips, his hot eyes, and his throbbing forehead.

Back in his room, he continues to weep, and hears the familiar, tormenting refrain, as his gaze slides up the slopes of San Salvatore. Mme d'Ottange's influence on him reminds him of the story of Samson and Delilah, the tale of unmanning suggested to Strindberg's Axel Borg in *I havsbandet* by the oleograph in a fisherman's cottage: decadent protagonists are usually afraid of women when they take command, as Mme d'Ottange has just — almost — done. The only safe woman is the mother, who appears to Klercken now in the form of his wife, patiently waiting in Finland, and, in an effort to put Mme d'Ottange's consolatory remark (that he shares the malady of the fin de siècle with many others) out of his mind, he begins — like Holmes, leaping into action from his inertia — an ascent of San Salvatore, passing Mme d'Ottange on his way through the garden. Now he feels like a "conqueror, bound to vanquish the giants of the mountain." A native of the North, Klercken falls into a vague Nordic mythology: he means to bring the "goddess of health, a voluptuous blond Germania with flowing locks and a calm gaze, home to Finland" — or she may be his waiting wife. But, all of a sudden, she assumes the dark features of Provence, with laughing eyes and smiling mouth; this transformation is rejected in an "access of pride and strong will." Arrived at the top of San Salvatore, Klercken sees the whole topography of mountains and lakes spread out before him and he is tempted to follow Death's instruction, to cast himself down into the sea of air. Once more, he hears the words: " 'Cast yourself from hence, and all this shall belong to you.' " The thought gives him such pleasure that "the leap hardly should be called a suicide (*självmord*) but rather a murder with sexual pleasure (*lustmord*)." Still, switching as usual, he decides to reconcile himself to the thought of becoming Death's friend, accepting the gift of the reversed hourglass of life. Growing calm, Klercken resolves (again) to go home to Finland; he enjoys the mountain view like an ordinary tourist, eats dinner at the restaurant on the peak, and, having missed the last funicular, makes his way on foot down to his pension. He will leave for Finland early the next day.

He oversleeps and misses the train north. Meeting Mme d'Ottange in the breakfast room, he is reprimanded by her for breaking off their friendship so abruptly, "as her full breast touches his arm." He falls back into her power, as she shows "a manly boldness" in the demonstration of her strength. Now he is "the being carried off" (*den bergtagne*), repeating the masculine form of the word (*den bergtagna*) he applied the day before in his imaginary capture of the Germanic goddess of health during his ascent of the mountain. Flattering him again, Mme d'Ottange compares him to Christ: Klercken's bushy eyebrows resemble a crown of thorns. Further, she makes one of her several excursions into contemporary culture; she observes that Christ has become a popular figure in "art and literature," comparing herself, in her translator's efforts at spreading the message of a new mysticism, to Mary Magdalene "in need of an all-comprehending, all-forgiving master." The remark is likewise flattering to Klercken, and perhaps to Tavaststjerna himself, in his own toying with Christological motifs, and may, as well, be a reference to a painting from 1890, *Christ and Magdalena,* by Tavaststjerna's friend Albert Edelfelt. The conversation closes with Mme d'Ottange's injunction — almost a direct quotation from Death in Klercken's vision — " 'never to fear death. Live with death present before your eyes, and break the sting of its [*sic*] terror through your good and solid awareness that you have made him [*sic*] your friend.' " The epilogue is her expression of contempt for those who fear death. She respects the suicide Socrates and loves the martyred Christ. " 'Humanity's nobility will be dead and life will become a wretched parody when their last successors breathe their last breath. Pettiness will triumph, and the mob will rejoice, and after them the deluge will come.' "

As often in his meetings with Mme d'Ottange, Klercken is left in an "unbearable" state of confusion, exhaustion, and longing for this consolatrix or temptress who, during the afternoon, vanishes; trying to understand her control over him, he drinks heavily again, a half bottle of "Vesuvius wine" and thinks that, if she has given him back his life, she can take it away again — he does not say how. He decides, another of his *stante pede* decisions, instead of succumbing to a slavish dependency on a woman's will, to do what he knows is right, his duty, to choose not glorious suicide from the peak of San Salvatore, nor continued flirtation with Mme d'Ottange, but the living death waiting for him in Finland, his fate when he returns to wife, family, and bank. Once more, he plans for the morning train, and, inspired by wine, imagines he will receive Mme d'Ottange's thanks for the boldness of his decision. Going to his room to pack after his last supper, he is fetched by Mme d'Ottange to a farewell party, at which he lets slip that he has a wife and children to whom he returns. (He has been mum about them before.) Yet she does not give up: as he holds "her plump hand," she tells him: " 'There are natures involuntarily and fatefully drawn to one another.' " A warning is added: the wonderful power she has had over him (which he has confessed to her) will last only as long as their "sympathy," their spiritual affinity, endures.

After a sleepless night, despite the chloral he has taken, Klercken leaves at last; at the breakfast table, he finds a welcoming letter from his wife. Mme d'Ottange's "plump, beautiful hand" takes the letter from him, writes a message on the back inviting him to future correspondence, and repeats her words of yesterday, about " 'life-giving affinity.' "

The account of Klercken's homeward journey is compressed but effective: he thinks that he is "past, past, past, as the whole of life has become for him." (Is this an echo of the ending of Hans Christian Andersen's "Fir Tree"? "Now [its happiest evening] was past, and the tree was past and the story too: past, past.") Changing trains in Basel, he is astonished that other passengers do not notice him; the police ignore him, and he despises them for their inability to see that he is far more dangerous than all the pickpockets whose pictures hang on the station walls. From Frankfurt to Hamburg, Klercken pretends to the fat traveler sharing his compartment to be a businessman; on the way to Copenhagen he notices nothing because of the chloral he takes. He comes to his senses — first in deepest despair and then relief — as the ship passes through the Åland Islands, and he breathes the "peculiar, enticing aroma" of the homeland; he thinks of himself as a Dante who has been through the torments of hell and the pleasures of paradise during a long dream, lasting more than half a year.

The Strindbergian marriage drama, so long prepared, begins; his home, on a gray street, has been plundered to pay for his journey, his wife's rings have been pawned, in the dining-room closet the silver service is missing, as if "the cupboard had lost most of its front teeth." He returns to work, keeping his spirits up only by thoughts of the promised exchange of letters with Gabrielle d'Ottange, on which he works at night, pretending it is the bank's French correspondence. The smell of perfume from the letters of Mme d'Ottange arouses his wife's suspicions. He confesses to this innocent contact from abroad but, when his wife demands that the correspondence end, he refuses, since it is a "question of life" for him; lacking it, he would be "brought to an asylum." His wife leaves home, taking the children with her. He feels Christ's crown of thorns around his head, writes a farewell letter to Mme d'Ottange, and directly comes down with fever and chills: the *correspondante* has removed her power from him; "life's will has been extinguished." Klercken believes he is dying; he waits for Death, his friend, to take him away, but now fears that he has gone back on his pact with Death by fleetingly accepting the Frenchwoman's love. The doorbell rings, and Klercken, half clinging to reality, decides that Death would scarcely announce himself in such a mundane way. It is his brother-in-law, who believes that Klercken has poisoned himself, a belief in which Klercken readily concurs, imagining that, as the maid gave him a cup of warm milk, he, another Socrates, has been sent a cup of hemlock by Mme d'Ottange. Questioned by the family physician about the poison he has taken, he calls it "Socrates' bane!" Given morphine by the doctor, Klercken again believes that he is dying, and he sends a plea for forgiveness to his wife. When she returns, he is filled with shame at the suicide game he has played.

Klercken goes back to the bank, "filling column after column with numbers, never saying a word too much." On the wall of his study at home, he hangs a watercolor of San Salvatore; above it, on a shelf, he places an hourglass, in which "the sand can run down only on one side — a little flap prevents it from running down on the other." Two years pass; to an inquisitive colleague he explains the picture in his little sanctuary by telling him how Death once saved him for life. " 'Death is a better comrade than you may think.' " Concluding that Klercken has gone mad, the friend leaves, not wanting to be present when Klercken's wife finally apprehends her poor husband's condition.

A direct way to look at the story of Klercken is to regard it (as Klercken himself does on occasion) as a momentary healing of his schizophrenia through a flirtation with a sexually and intellectually attractive woman. Readers of Tavaststjerna's day may have made an association with chapter 12 of Jens Peter Jacobsen's *Niels Lyhne* (1880), then at the height of its popularity. At a resort in Riva, beside Lake Garda, shattered after an affair with his best friend's wife and the friend's sudden, drunken death, Niels is briefly restored to an interest in life by contact with a mysterious opera singer, Mme Otero — who then abruptly leaves him.

The imaginary pact with Death, the memory of which never leaves Klercken, is connected — on occasion — in Klercken's mind with Mme d'Ottange; she may have been, he thinks, "the instrument of a higher power," who looked as if she had been waiting for him when they first met, and who spoke Death's phrase to him. Mme d'Ottange is generous Death's instrument. Finally, in his debilitation, Klercken eliminates from his thoughts the life-giving, seductive woman, thinking only of friendly Death. (To be sure, Tavaststjerna's growing ambivalence toward "Nixe" may have played into those instances in the novel in which Mme d'Ottange, with her inscrutable smile, her omniscience and omnipresence, and her sometimes resented control over Klercken, is given a possibly sinister air. *La décadence* liked to imply — on the model of Wagner's Frau Venus — an infernal connection for its women who sexually rejuvenate men: see Jane Scott in *Bruges-la-Morte,* Mme Chantelouve in *Là-bas.* Klercken's stream of reflections, impressions, and fantasies is a muddled but nonetheless convincing picture of decay. *I förbund med döden* is one of those essentially confessional novels — like *Dorian Gray,* like *Noodlot,* like the Czech Julius Zeyer's *Jan Maria Plojhar,* like Andrian's *Der Garten der Erkenntnis* — in which the author grapples with his personal demons. Geijerstam, in his Tavaststjerna lecture, said that *I förbund med döden* was a "strange mixture of sharp, clear analysis and deep feeling. [Tavaststjerna's] observation of the shifts in the state of the spirit is so sure-handed [*sic*] that at times it almost has a chilling effect." His own novel about crippling psychosis and ultimate suicide, *Medusas hufvud* (1895, The Head of Medusa), was, it can be argued, a spin-off of Tavaststjerna's book.

In 1943, the aesthetician Hans Ruin published a long essay which borrowed Tavaststjerna's title as its own; Ruin wrote about the actual suicides of men of letters of his own generation in Finland: Erik Grotenfelt in 1919, the great novella writer Runar Schildt in 1925, and Ruin's friend the poet and novelist Jarl Hemmer in 1944. (Suicide has a particularly large role in Schildt's small body of work; but in his early "Mot skymningen" Birger Weydal, a member of Finland's decimated "Swedish" nobility, decides for familial duty on the day of his majority, and "with energetic steps and head held high entered into his fathers' house," doomed to financial ruin and "brilliant poverty.") Suicide is a rare occurrence in Tavaststjerna's oeuvre; an end in entrapment — the disappointed singer in *Barndomsvänner,* the ex-officer in *En patriot utan fosterland,* the naval officer beneath the waves in *Finska Vikens hemlighet* — is not unusual.

Ireland

EDITH OENONE SOMERVILLE AND
VIOLET MARTIN ROSS

Eight years after *A Drama in Muslin,* another novel dealt in a subtler way with the imminent decline of the Ascendancy, *The Real Charlotte* (1894) by the cousins Edith Oenone Somerville (1858–1949), from Drishane House at Castle Townshend in West Cork, and Violet Martin Ross (1862–1915), from Ross House in Galway. It was criticized at first because of its "sordidness"; when he got around to reading it, W. B. Yeats described it, somewhat bizarrely, as picturing "with unexampled grimness our middle-class life," although he recognized it as a near-masterpiece. In his *Irish Literature and Drama in the English Language* (1920), Stephen Gwynn called it "one of the most powerful novels of Irish life ever written." Its reputation has been maintained: John Cronin (1972) said it was "unquestionably the finest Irish novel of the nineteenth century, and there are not that many in the twentieth to challenge its primacy," and in *Anglo-Irish* (1995), Julian Moynahan argued that it was "a serious contender for [the] title of the best Irish novel before Joyce."

Like the less praised *Muslin,* it is planted in Galway geography; the country town of the action, Lismoyle, is Oughterard (known to readers of Joyce as the churchyard remembered at the end of "The Dead"), and the lake, Lough

Moyle, is Lough Corrib. Ross House lay on the way from Galway City to the little town. The time of *Charlotte* is slightly later than that of Moore's novel; it begins in Dublin, with a prologue from a summer in the 1880s, when the heroine, Francie Fitzpatrick, is fourteen; a second prologue takes place early in the next decade, as old Mrs. Mullen, the owner of Tally Ho Lodge, impatiently attended by her niece, Charlotte Mullen, passes away. The remainder of the book stretches from a garden party (chapter 3) at Bruff, the grandest house in the neighborhood, on June 15, 189- (one may guess 1891 or 1892, the year of the completion of the manuscript) to June 1 of the next year, when poor Francie is killed in a riding accident (chapter 50). The new decade is far calmer than that of the immediate past, the time of the agrarian murders and Dublin unrest mentioned by Moore. We hear little of the difficulties between Roderick Lambert, the agent of the Dysarts and the tenants of Bruff; the noble family itself enjoys tranquillity. The Land League appears only for comic effect. At the garden party, Charlotte, a fine storyteller, making use of Irish brogue with an actress's skill, amuses the English-born Lady Dysart of Bruff and her guests, telling how she "served Tom Casey, the land leaguing plumber": as he was mending a tank at the lodge, she removed his ladder, keeping him "up to his middle" in the cold water until he sang "God Save the Queen." At the same party, Charlotte reminds Christopher Dysart, the family's scion, shy, short-sighted, and stammering, of the days when her "poor father" was the agent of Christopher's father, the now daft Sir Benjamin. He retorts that he wishes Charlotte, who helped Mullen out in the estate office, were there still: " 'If anyone understands the Land Act, I believe it would be you.' " Lambert himself finds a Land League meeting of Sir Benjamin's tenants — at which, egged on by the local priest, they pledge themselves to the Plan of Campaign — annoying and no more: "He had no objection to their amusing themselves as they pleased during the summer," in fact, "a certain amount of nominal disturbance might not come amiss."

For some time Lambert, enjoying "the brevet rank as a country gentleman" that the Dysart agency confers upon its holder, and with high tastes, has been embezzling part of the payments made to him, detected neither by the incompetent Sir Benjamin nor by his dilettantish and distracted son. On the occasion of Christopher's twenty-first birthday, six years ago, Sir Benjamin suffered a stroke, and he is now confined to a bath chair, tended by his lunatic body servant, the ex-school teacher James Canavan. A matter hinted at, but never fully stated, is the possibility that Sir Benjamin's bullying, during Christopher's boyhood, has rendered him timorous and indecisive: Lambert treats him with a contempt barely concealed. Christopher's sister Pamela, well-meaning and tentative, is also incapable of action, not even a response to the — admittedly unspoken — wooing of Captain Cursiter from the regiment stationed nearby.

The tenants of Bruff are mostly invisible. Roman Catholics are present in the book as Charlotte Mullen's kitchen help — i.e., Norry the Boat, so named because her father was a ferryman, and Bid Sal, Nance the Fool, the female beggar of Lismoyle, and the half-witted messenger Billy Grainy. A "Protestant orphan girl," Louisa, is also on the Mullen staff; Charlotte — who sings noisily in the Church of Ireland choir and can even fill in at the organ when Mrs. Gascogne, the archdeacon's wife, is absent — has presumably taken Louisa into her employ to strengthen her position among Lismoyle's Protestants. In contrast to the Protestants, as far as we know middle-class and cleanly, the Roman Catholics (and even Charlotte's staff) are dirty. Dirtiness is also a quality of the tenants of Charlotte (who has her own private enterprise), washerwomen and a tailor of Jewish appearance, Dinny Lydon; the author-cousins take some snobbish and sectarian pleasure in describing Roman Catholic dirt (as did Moore). But dirtiness is not exclusively a Roman Catholic condition; it also pertains in shocking measure to Julia Duff, the aging proprietress of Gurthnamuckla. The daughter of a drunken Protestant farmer and his servant-girl wife, and the granddaughter of a local squire, "all but a gentleman," Julia, like her property, has come down in the world and is too poor and proud to attend a proper Church of Ireland service.

Gurthnamuckla has caught the eye of Charlotte and, before the end of the novel, will replace Tally Ho Lodge as her seat of operations. Julia Duffy in her youth has been a "good friend," as James Canavan lets slip, to a much younger Sir Benjamin and has been promised the title to Gurthnamuckla in perpetuity; at Charlotte's instigation, she is dispossessed by Lambert for failure to pay rent. She makes a terrible pilgrimage in summer heat to Sir Benjamin but is driven away by the old man and ignored by Christopher, to whom she appeals; she suffers a stroke by the roadside and is committed to the asylum at Moore's Ballinasloe. The parallel with the fate of Sir Benjamin is striking enough; Sir Benjamin will die in the early spring of the next year, Julia Duffy at the end of May. Julia Duffy is the saddest case of decline in *Charlotte;* Gurthnamuckla shows traces of past glory even now ("the lawn-like field was yellow in spring with the daffodils of a former civilisation"), and Julia Duffy can still speak in a cultured voice when she wishes. She has earned a reputation among country folk by her talent for "doctoring," and is praised by her cousin, Norry the Boat, related to her through her dairymaid mother, "as wise a woman and as good as scholar as what's in the country.'" In this quasi-medical talent, as in her ability to change voices and her desire to hold on to property, she bears a resemblance to Charlotte, save that Charlotte's medical arts are used on people of the class into which she has ascended. At the garden party of chapter 3, teased by handsome Lambert, for whom, ugly as she is, she has a weakness, she retorts that she has restored hair to his head, and she acts as a lethal nurse to Lucy, the "peenie-weenie" wife of Lambert, Lucy's second husband. In both cases, Lucy, "the turkey hen," as Charlotte calls her behind her back, has been wedded for her money, and Lambert enjoys some sympathy from the Lismoyle townspeople for the sacrifice he has made. The Lamberts live at Rosemount Lodge, where Lambert comports himself as the country gentleman he wants to be, going through his wife's money in an "absurdly short time." All oblivious, Lucy leaves the finances to him as she putters in her garden, pampers her pug dog, and grows ever more sedentary. She suffers from a heart condition.

Lismoyle town society, of which the Lamberts are prominent members, is wholly Protestant; this one-sidedness scarcely corresponds to the confessional distribution in the Oughterard of the time. It revolves around the religious establishment: the archdeacon Gascogne and his wife; Mrs. Corkran, the widow of the late rector; and her foolish son, the Reverend Joseph Corkran. All have more or less constant contact with the Dysarts, through choir practice, and, like Charlotte and Lambert, are welcome at Bruff. On the acceptable commercial side, there are Mr. Baker, the banker, his wife and daughter, the grocer Mr. Beattie, his wife and six daughters, the lawyer, Mr. Lynch, his spinster sister and his clerk, Mr. Redmond, "who came in thick boots and a suit of dress clothes so much too big for him as to make his trousers look like twin concertinas." These second-line notables of Lismoyle are put on display at the raspberry party held by Mrs. Beattie. The narrative takes great care to make fun of the party, which ends in noisy dancing, described by Charlotte as "great high jinks": windows and teacups rattle. The Dysarts — who come from the same social class as the narrators — do not attend.

As usual in Lismoyle, much gossip is bandied back and forth at the Beatties' party, much of it fastened on Francie Fitzpatrick, "the first cousin once removed" of Charlotte Mullen. Pretty Francie, now nineteen, has been invited by her "Welsh aunt" (the working title of the novel, meaning "a first cousin of father or mother"), to spend the summer at Tally Ho, but not out of the kindness of Charlotte's heart; she has made her own interpretation of the late Mrs. Mullen's deathbed instructions "to take care of" Francie, who has grown up in Dublin with her aunt and uncle, Robert and Letitia Fitzpatrick, in poor and crowded circumstances. Francie was first seen (chapter 1) when she was fourteen; even then she had golden hair, a fine figure, and a pert Dublin accent that attracted men, but she seems "vulgar" (a key word in the novel) to both Lady Dysart and Miss Hope-Drummond, when they meet her. Miss Hope-Drummond has been imported from England as a possible bride for Christopher; but Charlotte means for Christopher to become enamored instead of the

Dublin girl, despite the glaring social difference. A marriage between them will give Charlotte a direct and permanent link to the big house at Bruff. To this end, she arranges for Francie to stay at Bruff while the "Welsh aunt" is in Dublin at the dentist's.

The plan backfires. Much drawn to the subaltern Hawkins in his red tunic, Francie creates a sensation by allowing herself to be closeted with him in an ancient brougham which serves as a theater box at the performance of a version of Scott's *Waverly* (starring young Garry Dysart, the Dysarts' last child, Kitty Gascogne from the clerical family, and crazy Canavan as Queen Elizabeth), held in the coach house at Bruff as entertainment for Lady Dysart's guests. The motto in Sperelli's carriage, it will be remembered, runs "Pro amore curriculum, pro amore cubiculum"; the petting becomes fairly advanced before the pair is discovered. The next day, to make matters worse, in another of those entertainments of which summer life at Bruff consists, Hawkins absconds with Francie in the steam launch of Captain Cursiter; the launch runs aground, and while they are marooned, their affair goes further still. (Somerville and Ross are circumspect about the details.) Having rendered herself impossible at Bruff, Francie returns in disgrace to Tally Ho; at the raspberry party, she gives Hawkins the cold shoulder, upon learning from Lambert (who has the information from Hawkins's batman) that the subaltern is engaged to a wealthy young woman in Yorkshire.

The erotic complications around Francie increase. She has known Lambert since her girlhood; in the opening Dublin chapter, he saved her during an escapade in which, running away from an importunate juvenile boyfriend, she commandeered a milk wagon, whose horse, in turn, ran away with her, a perhaps all too obvious foreshadowing of *The Real Charlotte's* end. Sixteen years her senior, Lambert impressed her then as "a country gentleman, a Justice of the Peace, and a man of standing"; subsequently, Lambert has carried on a correspondence with her. When Francie appears at Lismoyle, Lambert immediately pays court to her; she feels she does not like him as much as in her adolescence. Lambert's infatuation nearly comes to an early and sad end: during a picnic at Bruff, Lambert takes her on a cruise in his yacht, the *Daphne,* which, fortunately, has Christopher, an experienced sailor, for a crewman. Social backgrounds play a role; just as Francie, the Dublin girl, is a poor horsewoman, so Lambert is inept on the water. His purchase of the yacht has been one of the means by which he inserts himself into the world of the gentry. Refusing to listen to the despised Christopher's advice, he makes the *Daphne* capsize. Francis is almost drowned, not least through the efforts of Lambert (a poor swimmer) to save her. Both are rescued by Christopher, and by the arrival in the nick of time of Captain Cursiter in his steam launch — a moment of rare resoluteness for Christopher, who is about to fall in love with Francie.

This realization comes clearly to Christopher after the boating accident, and it is encouraged by the literary associations which he, an amateur poet, makes between Francie and water. Initially he ignored Francie in her vulgarity but reasoned that she must be "a nice girl somehow not to have been more vulgar than she was, and she really must have a soul to be saved." After the accident, Christopher thinks of her in watery terms: "There was something about her — some limpid quality — that kept her transparent and fresh like a running stream"; and when Francie is on Lough Moyle (again) in the runaway steam launch with Hawkins, he remembers the accident "with a shudder that he had not felt at the time, the white face rising and dipping in the trough of the grey lake waves"; she becomes a kind of Ophelia (although the name does not appear in his thoughts), like the Ophelias of Rodenbach and like the nameless drowned beloved of Dr. Glas's youth. He makes a specific literary association for Francie in the choice of the poem he reads to her outside Tally Ho Lodge on the afternoon of Julia Duffy's vain appeal to him, Dante Gabriel Rossetti's "The Staff and the Script." The lines describe the queen: "Her eyes were like the wave within,/Like water reeds the poise/Of her soft body, dainty thin:/ And like the water's noise/Her plaintive voice." (To which Francie, dreaming of Hawkins, says: " 'That's awfully pretty. It's a sort of religious thing, isn't it?' ")

Earlier, the narrators have indicated the difference between the inept spirituality of Christopher's affection and the possessive physicality of Lambert's by remarking on what Lambert does *not* think of as he looks at Francie. At another Bruff picnic (chapter 12), Francie vigorously fights flies, and "the colour [of] her face lent a lively depth to eyes that had the gaiety and the soullessness of a child." But her "Dryad-like fitness to her surroundings did not strike [Lambert], as it struck another more dispassionate onlooker," Christopher the aesthete. Lambert pays a call on Francie, seated under a lime tree at Tally Ho, and "the golden green light that filtered through the leaves of the lime moved like water over her white dress." He is annoyed with Francie because she cannot be "a little more grown-up and serious" and pay attention to his wooing, instead of inquiring about the health of "poor Mrs. Lambert." Lambert fails again, where Christopher would have made the mythological association: "If he [Lambert] had ever heard the story of 'Undine,' it might well have afforded him the comforting hypothesis that this delicate, cool, youthful creature . . . could not possibly be weighted with the responsibility of a soul." The several linkings of Francie with water, the mentions of her soul or soullessness, and her near drowning, suggest that Francie, too, may marry a mortal and get a soul, before returning to the water; but this pattern is never wholly worked out. She does marry a mortal, Lambert, but she dies, as we know, while riding; we do not know if she gets a soul or not.

After the pilgrimage of Julia Duffy that interrupts Christopher's reading of Rossetti to the perhaps soulless Francie (chapter 31), the novel's action moves more rapidly. Already suspicious of her husband's affection for Francie (they often go riding together, a skill of which the horse trader Lambert is a master), Mrs. Lambert is visited by Charlotte, who continues her tormenting of the turkey hen, compelling her to look through Lambert's letters from young Francie in Dublin. The effort of lifting the heavy dispatch box down from its shelf brings on the heart attack that has long threatened the feeble woman, and she dies, "asking for her drops," as Charlotte coolly rummages through the letters (chapter 32). Christopher is unhappy at his failure to listen to Julia Duffy, "the afternoon of four days ago" — Julia Duffy's parting shot was a revelation of Charlotte's plan to win Christopher (and Bruff) through the bait of Francie; but he absolves Francie of any part in the scheme, and he proposes to her, clumsily and diffidently as ever, forgetful of what he has perceived as her vulgarity. Filled, as usual, with thoughts of Hawkins, who has made matters up with her, Francie refuses him. Francie's passion for Hawkins will remind some readers of Marianne Dashwood's blind love for the worthless Willoughby in *Sense and Sensibility,* or Elizabeth Bennet's momentary rejection of Darcy for the unprincipled Wickham in *Pride and Prejudice.* Yet the world of Somerville and Ross is far crueler, and funnier, than Austen's, sometimes mentioned as one of their models.

Charlotte learns what Francie has done. An exchange of recrimination follows, Charlotte telling Francie that Hawkins will never marry her and that she will go " 'whimpering to Roddy Lambert . . . asking him to make ye Number Two.' " (Charlotte falls into her brogue.) With a sharp eye for Charlotte's weakness, Francie responds: " 'You may keep him all to yourself,' " and goes back to Dublin, or rather to the seaside town of Bray, down the coast, where the Fitzpatricks now live. Autumn comes, and the widower Lambert returns to Rosemount, having "honeymooned with his grief in appropriate fashion," while settling affairs with his late wife's relatives in Limerick, his own hometown: he speaks, we are told, with a vulgar Limerick brogue. Charlotte gladly helps him dispose of his wife's effects; they continue to plan the takeover of Gurthnamuckla by Charlotte, Lambert will let her "down easy with the fine" (rent), and will keep his young horses there. In the film version of the novel, Charlotte makes a gesture at seducing Lambert over sherry; the text somewhat supports this augmentation: "She was feeling happier than she had been since the time when Lambert was a lively young clerk in her father's office." Not responding, Lambert instead brings up Francie, and Charlotte's "hot face looked its ugliest as some of the hidden ego showed itself." The real Charlotte emerges.

At Bray's shabby Albatross Villa, crowded with her teasing cousins, Francie's misery is increased by an unfeeling note from Hawkins in England; her life passes in a "squalid monotony of hopelessness." Lambert's letters cheer her up only in some measure, as she dimly and illogically compares him and Hawkins to Christopher: "Some errant streak of finer sense made her feel [Christopher's] difference from the men she knew." Francie has had a good Church of Ireland upbringing, and her knowledge of Scripture has astonished Christopher; leaving church on "a rainy Christmas Day evening," she finds Lambert waiting for her. The last day of the year, they make an excursion to Kingstown (now Dun Laoghaire) and, by accident, meet the mail boat bringing Lady Dysart and Pamela back to Ireland; Hawkins disembarks too, and his greetings again are cold. Ever kindly, Pamela notices Francie's hurt, "something in [Francie's] voice made even the Dublin brogue pathetic." Quite as obliquely as Christopher wooing her on other occasions, Pamela tries to console her.

By March, Miss Mullen has taken charge of Gurthnamuckla, with the intent of sprucing it up and making it pay. "[H]er wakeful nights were spent in schemings in which the romantic" — she still believes she will catch Lambert — "and the practical were logically blended." Billy Grainy brings the post and a letter from Lambert in which he tells his "oldest and best friend" that he intends to marry Francie and set her up in Rosemount. She tears the letter to pieces with her teeth (the cousins like to emphasize her "dreaded temper" — she was "for the time, a wild beast"), smashes a cabinet photograph of Lambert recently sent from Dublin on "one of his plausibly explained visits there," and throws the picture into the fire. The Lamberts take a honeymoon trip to Paris; Lambert's heavy and unwelcome affection is interrupted by the news of Sir Benjamin's death: Christopher has inherited property and title. Charlotte plots an exquisite revenge; pretending to ready Rosemount Lodge for the arrival of the newlyweds, she compares Lambert's private bankbook and the bankbook of the Dysart estate. Armed with the primary evidence of his embezzlements, supported by further incriminating facts acquired from the tailor Dinny Lydon, she bides her time. Lambert and his bride return, to the perfect order Charlotte has created at Rosemount, and, almost simultaneously, Hawkins comes back, to close off his affairs before his regiment leaves for India, thereby providing Charlotte with one more instrument of torment. Initially speaking with "a newly acquired English accent," Francie is cool, but she soon weakens; Lambert, immediately suspicious, asks Charlotte to stay at

Rosemount as a duenna while he, the agent, is away on a collecting trip. She does, offering Francie and Hawkins every opportunity to be alone together. Charlotte has been particularly foresighted: when Francie and Lambert visited Gurthnamuckla, Francie was almost trampled to death in a lane by Lambert's young horses; Charlotte thought of stumbling as she ran to close the gate to their pasture, but decided against it. "It was fascinatingly simple, but it was all too simple, and it was by no means certain"; Francie is to be saved for a crueler revenge by means of Hawkins. Charlotte meets Lambert with "the smile of the benefactor broad upon her face."

Charlotte reveals Lambert's manifold thefts to Christopher, who does not want to listen but is at last convinced. Simultaneously, he—who so readily falls into self-abhorrence—"had time to despise himself for not being able to conceal his feelings from a woman so abhorrent and so contemptible." (Christopher's crippling self-contempt is revealed in a different way during an interview with his mother; defending Francie against his mother's charge that Lambert's bride is "an adventuress," he admits that he himself, a year before, proposed to her and was refused.) Lurking about Rosemount, Hawkins proposes that he and Francie run away together. The next day, Christopher comes to Rosemount to inform Lambert that he has been found out; once the owner of Bruff leaves, Lambert breaks down weeping, wanting Francie to console him, before he rides off to Gurthnamuckla, thinking to obtain aid from Charlotte. In the afternoon, Christopher reappears, to tell Francie, for whom he feels desperately sorry (the film gives an unnecessary sexual tinge to his emotions), that he will allow Lambert to keep the agency, and is again filled with self-recrimination for the pain he has caused by offering up Lambert as "an oblation to his half-hearted sense of duty." Even in his confession to Francie, the blubbering Lambert has made no bones about *his* contempt for Christopher, " 'a rotten, cold-hearted devil, you can't tell what he's at.' " Believing she is now freed of any obligation of sympathy toward Lambert, she rides off on her black mare toward Gurthnamuckla to bring her husband the good news; what she will do after that, she does not know, and her confusion is increased when Hawkins gallops up beside her, repeating his pleas: "She was giddy with struggle, right and wrong had lost their meaning and changed places elusively." They meet the funeral procession of Julia Duffy; the old woman's Roman Catholic relative, Norry the Boat, wants to "bury her like a Christian." Hawkins's pleas distract Francie; she is tugged at by the drunken Billie Grainy, and, still the child of Dublin, she is "heedless of the etiquette that required that she and Hawkins should stop their horses till the funeral had passed." As she comes beside the coffin, the keening of the "Irish Cry" is raised, and Norry the Boat, riding on the first cart, "flung out her arms inside her cloak, with a

gesture that made her look like a great vulture opening its wings for flight."
The cloak flaps across the black mare's face, it bucks three times, and Francie is
thrown to the ground and killed. In the epilogue (chapter 51) at Gurthnamuckla, Lambert finds Charlotte, ever industrious, cleaning the potato loft
and asks for help, but is mocked. Losing his temper, Lambert calls her refusal
her " 'dirty devilish spite, because you were cut out by someone else.' " In
complete control of her weapons, Charlotte asks him about Hawkins, " 'who
[has] made ye the laughing stock of the country.' " Norry the Boat appears,
screaming the news of Francie's death: " 'Her neck's broke below on the
road.' " *The Real Charlotte* is from the age of Verga's and Mascagni's *Cavalleria rusticana* (1880/1884/1891), and its horrifying scream at the end:
" 'They have killed Master Turiddu.' "

Setting out on their writing career, Somerville and Ross referred to their first
novel, *An Irish Cousin* (1889), as "The Shocker"; it contains, among other
things, extreme drunkenness, a woman made mute by shock, and hints of
incest. Their second, *Naboth's Vineyard* (1891), has a boycott, the burning of
the boycotted widow's house, and the unintentional murder of a gombeen
man, or usurer. *The Real Charlotte* likewise administers a series of shocks.
Charlotte does not listen to the final wishes of Mrs. Mullen, and, in effect, robs
Francie of her share in the inheritance; she brings about the stroke of Julia
Duffy by taking over Gurthnamuckla; she delays giving Mrs. Lambert her
drops; she sees to it that Hawkins has easy access to Rosemount Lodge during
Lambert's absence and thus contributes to Francie's confusion and death.
Charlotte is a multiple semimurderess, albeit no court of law could charge, let
alone convict her. The attitude of her creators toward her is mixed. They
realize very well that Charlotte's ugliness and dumpiness have been her curse;
had she been able to win Lambert long ago, she might have never followed her
course. Near the conclusion (chapter 46), the authors—having already entered so many terrible actions into Charlotte's account—make a single conciliatory statement. Charlotte knows how to be generous in small instances.
Eliza Hackett, the new cook at Rosemount Lodge, otherwise despised by
Charlotte as a convert to Roman Catholicism, wins Charlotte's approval for
her kitchen skills: "Charlotte, upon whose birth so many bad fairies had shed
their malign influence, had . . . the gift of appreciation, and of being able to
express her appreciation—a faculty that has been denied to many and good
Christian people." But the bad fairies have the upper hand. In the great altercation between Charlotte and Francie, the latter, who once thought Charlotte
"was queer, but very kind and jolly," realizes that she fears her: "She had
learned, like her great aunt [old Mrs. Mullen] before her, the weight of the real
Charlotte's will, and the terror of her personality."

Charlotte's father, the Dysarts' previous agent, had two brothers, a doctor and an attorney; these brothers had married two Miss Butlers. (Charlotte's paternal grandfather was also an attorney; as she and Lambert plot the expulsion of Julia Duffy from Gurthnamuckla, "the spirit of her attorney grandfather [gleams] in her eye.") She is extremely proud of the Butler connection; she tells the bemused Christopher—who observes, very rightly, " 'It's all very intricate' "—that "my father's brother [*sic*] married a Butler, and Francie's grandmother was a Butler too.' " And: " 'Your poor father would tell you, if he was able, that the Butlers of Tally Ho were as well known in their time as the Dysarts of Bruff.' " We are also told that Mrs. Mullen's foxhunting husband—a Butler—gave Tally Ho Lodge its name. Charlotte's boasting about her Butler relatives is an effort to connect herself, by roundabout implication, with one of the grandest and most ancient of Anglo-Irish noble families, the Butlers, earls of Ormond. To Christopher, Charlotte admits that she is "mad about family and pedigree," but Christopher thinks to himself that his conversations with his father were "of more stirring and personal topics [i.e., beatings] than the bygone glories of the Butlers." She concedes that Francie half belongs to a lesser breed, through the mismatch of "my poor cousin Isabella Mullen" with a Fitzpatrick, "no better than the dirt under [the] feet" of Isabella, who after all had Butler blood, and she continues to Christopher in doubtful French, " 'bong song ne poo mongtir' " (good blood cannot lie). The Butlers come up again when it is recalled, in the description of what Charlotte has brought to Gurthnamuckla from Tally Ho Lodge, that "the foxhunting prints dating from Mr. Butler's reign at Tally Ho hang above the chimney-piece."

Hints are sprinkled throughout that Somerville and Ross, mindful or not of Gobineau's theories about the curse of mixed blood, also have an eye on Charlotte's heritage. Just what this heritage was cannot be easily made out, although Lambert remarks that Charlotte is "a nailer at pedigrees." The Mullens, educated as they were, seem nonetheless to have had ties to the peasantry, but Charlotte never admits as much. At the Dysart parties, Charlotte is given to "a ponderous persiflage . . . the aristocratic foster-sister of her broader peasant feelings." Coming on Lambert in the gardens of Rosemount Lodge, on a warm summer day, he asks her why she wears a heavy coat; the narrators comment that "she had the Irish peasant-woman's love of heavy clothing and dislike of abating any of it in summer." She is glad to have moved into Gurthnamuckla, away from the empty room at Tally Ho Lodge in which "Mrs. Mullen's feeble voice had laid upon her the charge she had not kept." A "strain of superstition [was] in her, that, like her love of land, showed how strongly the blood of the Irish peasant ran in her veins." She startles the tailor Dinny Lydon by speaking fluent Irish.

Charlotte's streak of superstition has a contrastive source as well; she is up-to-date on "table-turning and spirit-rapping," which have "expanded for her the boundaries of the possible." Sophisticates in the great world shared these occult interests; see, among the literary evidence, Bang's *Sælsomme Fortællinger* (Strange Stories) and the remarkable chapter "Fragwürdigstes" (Highly Questionable) in *Der Zauberberg,* Mann's backward look at the time before the war. Of all the people in the novel, Charlotte is far and away the best informed and brightest; at the Beatties' raspberry party, "her big, pale face had an intellectuality and power about it that would have made her conspicuous in a gathering more distinguished than the present"; she is an insatiable reader, thoroughly acquainted with the classics of literature, and improvident — this woman so careful with money — in the purchase of books. Caught by Christopher browbeating a fishwife in fishwife's language in the Lismoyle marketplace, she revives, she believes, her status by using a Latin tag in a voice that "contrasted almost ludicrously with her last utterances." Her neighbors, much impressed by her subscription to contemporary periodicals, also hint that the bookshelves she has put up herself at Tally Ho Lodge contain "a large proportion of fiction of a startlingly advanced kind," and "many [of the books] are French."

Has Charlotte read any of the literature of decadence? We do not know, nor do we know how far the cousins' acquaintance with that contemporary literature went. Yet, willy-nilly — literally a femme fatale in her murderous way — she has one striking attribute of the literary fatal woman: she possesses an animal familiar, the tomcat, "Susan my bully boy," his gender mistaken by innocent little Francie on one of her childhood visits to Lismoyle. (The animal familiar goes from the sinister black cat, with red trousers, of the much read protodecadent *Sidonia von Bork, die Klosterhexe* [1847] of Wilhelm Meinhold, translated into English by "Speranza," Jane Francesca Elgee, Lady Wilde to-be, a translation which inspired a watercolor by Burne-Jones, to Salammbô's serpent and the wolfhound of Elena Muti in D'Annunzio's *Il piacere.*) The writing cousins do not attach any clear supernatural quality to Charlotte, but as she excites the suspicions of Lucy Lambert, she speaks with "Mephistophelean gaiety"; in their next novel, *The Silver Fox* (1895), the supernatural plays a more overt role. Similarly, Francie — by chance? — has an attribute of heroines in decadent novels: she has golden hair, caught in the branches on her arrival at Tally Ho Lodge, admired by Christopher, recognized by Tommy Whitty on the pier at Kingston. But she does not use it to kill men, like *La Belle Dame sans Merci* in Burne-Jone's painting. Instead, as the narrators carefully point out, Francie is a silly girl, constantly flirtatious, but with a "sincere and innocent heart."

Beyond doubt, Francie is prone to accident. The milk horse in Dublin runs away with her, her hat is swept off her golden hair by a bough of (golden) laburnum, and she foolishly snatches at the reins of Lambert's trap. Lambert says that she is " 'no great shakes as a horsewoman' "; Lucy Lambert fears that she will be injured if put up on the pony Paddy; Lambert entrusts her to the black mare instead, "a lady of character, well-mannered but firm"; getting ready to ride on her own, she tries to climb onto the black mare's back with the aid of a wheelbarrow. Fascinated by riding, she brings a new and expensive olive green riding habit with her to Galway; she also wears a skirt with pink horses on it, which she decides is "horrid" as soon as she sees Pamela's tasteful riding clothes; after her near drowning, Lambert gives her a "horse-shoe ornament with pearls on it," bought with money borrowed from Charlotte. Francie becomes a better rider during her summer in the country, but, when the Reverend Corkran tries to teach her to ride a "tricycle," it runs away with her. To Lambert she says: " 'I declare I thought I was killed.' " For the cousins, poor horsemanship was a sign of not belonging to their class; in Somerville's *The Big House at Inver,* Peggy Weldon, the daughter and granddaughter of agents, is " 'never any good to ride anyhow,' " although her father has given her " 'the best of ejication'!" Somerville and Ross were snobs, and Ross died a premature death in result of a severe riding accident.

One of the curiosities of *The Real Charlotte* is that the Dysarts do not engage in the gentry's foxhunting. Somerville was an enthusiastic hunter until late in life, and the hunt is a major element in *The Silver Fox,* as it is in their comic parade piece, *Some Experiences of an Irish R. M.* (1899) and its sequels of 1908 and 1915, as well as in *Dan Russell the Fox* of 1911. What would have seemed to be a ready-made opportunity to further demonstrate Francie's out-of-place-ness, and her vulgarity, is not taken, perhaps because it was not necessary for the novel's development; perhaps Somerville and Ross, attentive to Ascendancy detail, knew that the foxhunting season takes place in autumn and early winter, the season after Francie's expulsion from Tally Ho Lodge to the penuriousness of Bray.

Among the elements of the literature of decadence, the protagonists' concempt for the vulgar masses appears everywhere: Des Esseintes's disgust at the struggle of the children over the sandwich, Sperelli's contempt for the soldiers killed at Dogali, Aurispa's for the pilgrimage of the hopeful cripples, Dorian's and Bradomin's and Dr. Glas's easily irritated aesthetic sense. The Irish narrators make this contempt a class-conditioned social one and surely do not aim it at Francie alone; Lambert is another main target — Lambert's chewing a toothpick in a confrontation with Christopher, Lambert's falling into "the raw Limerick brogue, losing his air of gentlemanlike self importance," Lambert's "indifference to fresh air, common to his class." As the narrators point out,

Lambert has "raised himself just high enough from the sloughs of Irish middle class society to see its vulgarity," a perception which aids him in his dealings with the family at Bruff, but he does " 'not stand sufficiently apart from it to be able to see its humorous side.' " As for the Protestant merchant class of Lismoyle, their vulgarity has been put on display early; the Roman Catholics in their picturesque dirt and poverty are altogether beyond the pale. In his essay on Somerville and Ross in *Writers and Politics* (1965), Conor Cruise O'Brien remarks that the people on whom the terrible Charlotte wreaks destruction, Francie and Lambert, are "not well bred and therefore not quite human"; he does not adduce Julia Duffy, for whom the reader feels pity — yet one is never allowed to forget her filth, her dreadful air of having come down in the world — or the pitiful and comical Lucy Lambert, the turkey hen. The Ascendency condescension and contempt for most of the characters in the book "harm an otherwise splendid achievement."

Nevertheless, Cruise O'Brien detects an exception made for Charlotte herself, "who has attained a certain aristocracy of evil like Satan in Pandemonium." In reality, Charlotte's model belonged to the gentry. She was a cousin of Edith Somerville, one Emily Herbert, who cheated Edith out of an inheritance. In an early letter to Edith of May 19, 1886, Violet Martin Ross mentions the sale of Herbert's house at Castle Townshend after her death: "No one dared to enter Miss Herbert's room as there were 16 cats confined there." In St. Andrews after the publication of *The Real Charlotte,* Martin Ross admitted to a Mrs. Butcher — the wife of S. H. Butcher, the Irish-born professor of Greek at Edinburgh and Andrew Lang's collaborator in translating the *Odyssey* — that Charlotte was "drawn from life and [Martin Ross] told about an interview with her before she died," only to learn to her consternation that Emily Herbert was S. H. Butcher's cousin. A small Irish Protestant world indeed! In subsequent letters, Edith told of her surprise at learning that Emily Herbert had been desperately in love with a married lawyer, a case of authorial intuition, because the cousins had known nothing about it when they wrote their book. In a letter to Martin Ross of 1908, Edith gave the full story of the stolen inheritance. Emily was also "an awful drunkard and when she finally drank and cat-poisoned herself to death," her body was found with fourteen cats around it.

Somerville reported in *Irish Memories* (1917) that her mother had written to a sister that " 'Francie deserved to break her neck for her vulgarity.' " Still, the authors themselves seem to have fallen in love with their creation, vulgar Francie herself. Tempted by Hawkins, Francie had, after all, a "light, wholesome nature," and "her emotional Irish nature, with all its frivolity and recklessness, had also, far down in it an Irish girl's moral principle and purity."

About to kill Francie, the narrators seemingly forget — and want their audience to forget — Francie's adventures with the wretched Hawkins in the brougham and the steam launch. In her diary for June 8, 1892, Somerville noted: "Finished Francie . . . We felt her death very much . . . It felt like killing a wild bird that had trusted itself to you." Otherwise, the statement does not accord Francie any humanity.

T. P. O'Connor wrote a review of the novel called "The Shoneens," by which he meant lower-class Irish who try to raise themselves by hanging on to "the English-dominated class." (Joyce would use the word in "Ivy Day in the Committee Room" in *Dubliners*.) Writing to Somerville from Scotland, Ross praised the review: "One of the best, and best-written notices we have ever had." Unhappily, O'Connor supposed that the authors themselves were shoneens, and Ross's host at St. Andrews, Andrew Lang, remarked, according to Ross, "If there was one thing more obvious than another in the book it was that we were the reverse." Cruise O'Brien claimed that the Dysarts of Bruff are "a highly idealized Ascendancy family," as T. P. O'Connor had, decades before. Violet Powell took exception to this statement, in mentioning the "sinister goings-on" of Sir Benjamin, the "exquisite boringness" of Miss Hope-Drummond, and the "selfish villainies" of Hawkins. But Sir Benjamin is mad, and Miss Hope-Drummond and Hawkins are outsiders from England, the caddishness of the last-named offset by the gentlemanliness of the shy Captain Cursiter. In fact, Lady Dysart (from England but long resident in Ireland) and Pamela are kindly, and Christopher, the most wholly positive figure in the book, is unfailingly courteous, a forerunner of the narrator Major Sinclair Yeates of the *R. M.* stories, another English person (but with Irish blood) who learns — like Lady Dysart in her way — to accept Irish peculiarities. (Praising Christopher to Francie. Charlotte says that he is "a real gentleman" and, inaccurately, without "a drop of dirty Saxon blood in him.") Baffled, Miss Hope-Drummond thinks that "Irish society [is] intolerably mixed"; in the view of the authors, however, it is not so mixed after all: a tiny group not guilty of vulgarity, and a huge group which, in a variety of fashions, displays it constantly.

The Dysarts of Bruff are ultimately at the mercy of the main shoneens, Charlotte and Lambert. Christopher has reinstated Lambert almost immediately after putting him on notice, and — looking into the future of the characters — there is no reason to think that Charlotte, intelligent and unscrupulous, will not achieve more power in the county and over the manor house than ever before. Christopher does not want to hear the vulgar details of the embezzlement, and he is constantly weakened by his propriety and his endemic self-loathing. Lambert, who has no pride, will very likely appeal to the residual

affection in Charlotte, and to her realization that in him she possesses a splendid tool for involving herself in Bruff's finances. He may marry her.

What will become of Christopher—now Sir Christopher—some twenty-
five years later on, if he stays on the estate? What will become of Pamela, for
that matter, ever good-hearted and ever unmarried? Christopher's hobby has
been photography, which keeps him—behind his clumsy camera, in the red
light of his darkroom—at a distance from life; he is shortsighted, like Major
Yeates (who has the good fortune to live in an imaginary benign Ireland, full of
the dishonest but not malicious Irish servants, peasants, hangers-on placed in
his official care). What would have happened to a real Christopher, a real
Major Yeates, had they lived on into the time of the Anglo-Irish War? According to R. B. McDowell in *Crisis and Decline,* three resident magistrates were
among the "at least 130 civilians . . . shot by the republicans between 1919 and
the Truce." Nothing at all is said in *Charlotte* about the coming destruction of
the big house; will Christopher's kindness and sense of fair play protect it for a
time? Or, in his weakness, will he fall prey to Charlotte and her creature,
Lambert? Such conjectures and more are caused by "the novel in which Somerville and Ross realized with an unforgettable totality the dying world of the
Anglo-Irish Ascendancy" (John Cronin).

Martin Ross had experienced a semidestruction of the big house long ago.
As a young girl, she saw Ross House abandoned during the agrarian troubles;
the tenants of her father, James Martin, turned against him in the election of
1872, and he died two months afterward. His son went to London as a journalist, and Mrs. Martin moved the remaining members of the family to Dublin, an experience that was the source of Martin Ross's knowledge of the
milieu in which Francie was brought up. In 1888, the mother attempted, by re-
opening the house, to reestablish its past glory, an effort in which her daughter,
now an active writer, was much engaged; but after the death of her brother,
Robert, and her mother, Martin Ross moved to Drishane House in Castle
Townshend, to be near Somerville. Following Ross's illness and death in 1915,
Somerville continued their joint authorship through consultation with me-
diums (remember Charlotte's interest in spiritualism), and Ross's name appeared on the title pages of subsequent books, as late as *The Big House at
Inver* of 1925.

Of these, three in particular touch on the Ascendancy. In *Mount Music*
(1919), a feckless Anglo-Irish family falls under the control of a Catholic
physician, Dr. Mangan; having lost their house to him, the Talbot-Lowrys slip
away to England, but their daughter, Christian, marries a Catholic foxhunting
companion. A spirit of some tolerance turns up, to be detected occasionally in
the earlier production (for example, in the willingness of the selfish Lady Susan

to accept the criticisms and the help of the countrywoman Maria in *The Silver Fox*), and here in the love and marriage between confessions, and in the devotion of the crooked Dr. Mangan to his patients: he dies in a flood, riding to help one of them. In *An Enthusiast* (1921), the Troubles are in full swing. Dan Palliser, the innocent enthusiast of the title, a veteran of the World War, has had to turn over his big house to a wealthy Englishman but attempts to bring agricultural reform and political peace to his country, thereby becoming suspect to both sides. He is accidentally killed by one of the Englishman's guests while trying to save the big house (and his beloved, the trophy wife of the magnate) from an attack by the IRA. *The Big House at Inver* takes the house through generations of improvident landlords, until it is almost saved by Shibby Pindy, the Catholic and illegitimate child of one of them, in her great age. The family's faithful protector, she is a descendant, in literature, of Thady, the faithful servant of Maria Edgeworth's *Castle Rackrent*. The gentry is clearly degenerate and has fallen into Catholic commercial hands; Shibby Pindy has a strange nobility — and would have been thought vulgar by the Dysarts of Bruff. Somerville cannot resist the temptation to criticize Shibby Pindy's bad taste in furniture as she tries to save Inver from ruin, to no avail.

During the Anglo-Irish War and the Civil War, Somerville remained more or less safe in the Protestant enclave of Castle Townshend. She and a brother, Cameron, appealed to Michael Collins, the commanding general of the new Free State army, for protection during Collins's inspection tour of West Cork, in August 12, 1923; on the evening of the same day, Collins was killed by dissident forces, in an ambush on his way back to Cobh. Details of the meeting between Somerville (herself or her brother) and the peasant's son are unknown. Regrettably, Somerville, with her flair for the melodramatic and the tragic, never turned it into literature. Then, on March 24, 1936, another and favorite brother of Edith Somerville, Boyle, a retired vice admiral in the Royal Navy, was assassinated at the door of his house, The Point — once upon a time the property of "Charlotte," Emily Herbert, in Castle Townshend — presumably by members of the IRA. Like Christopher, Boyle Somerville was shortsighted and an enthusiastic photographer. Edith claimed to have made contact with him through her medium.

Austria

LEOPOLD VON ANDRIAN

RAINER MARIA RILKE

Leopold Baron (Reichsfreiherr, or "baron of the Empire") von Andrian-Werburg experienced a terrible misfortune at the very start of his life. The misfortune was the place of his birth: he was born in Berlin on May 5, 1875, the grandson of the German-Jewish composer of grand opera, Giacomo Meyerbeer; his father, Ferdinand von Andrian-Werburg, was from a distinguished Viennese family that had received the patent of nobility from Leopold I. As an adult, Leopold Andrian went to remarkable lengths to conceal the fact that he had first seen the light of day in the capital of the detested Prussia. (It has been proposed, as well, that Andrian's hatred of the mighty land to the north came not only from the defeat the Prussians had administered to the Austrians in the "summer war" of 1866, but from a disguised anti-Semitism; his father's family was devoutly Catholic, as was Leopold himself, while the Jewish component was, after all, at home in Prussian Germany.) The marriage of Andrian's parents was not a happy one; his mother, Caecilie, who had received a huge inheritance from her financially acute father, the composer, devoted herself to annual sojourns in Nice, Ouchy, Paris, Montreux, and Venice — that she is the mother in *Der Garten der Erkenntnis* (1895, The Garden of Knowledge) goes almost without saying; his father, an anthropologist, devoted himself to scientific studies and to his friendship with Crown Prince Rudolf, until Rudolf's death in 1889. (Everyone remembers the gruesomely romantic story—how the prince killed first his young mistress and then himself in a suicide pact at the hunting lodge of Mayerling in the Vienna woods.) Andrian senior died in 1914.

When Leopold was ten years old, he was sent to the Jesuit school at Kalksburg outside Vienna, an institution catering to leading families of the Austrian nobility; the reader of "The Garden of Knowledge" will see how much autobiography is in the book. Because of illness (was it really caused by his fellow pupils stuffing snow in his mouth during a tobogganing excursion?), he was eventually removed from school and was given as a private tutor Oskar Walzel, later to be one of the greatest stars of German literary studies. In his memoirs, Walzel remembered Leopold as "uncommonly mature" for his years—very few people "were on his level of intelligence," although his large store of information was somewhat helter-skelter. Also, wrote Walzel, "I was alarmed by the elegant smoothness of a thirteen-year-old who concealed gentle reproach beneath a heartiness that seemed quite credible . . . He knew that he was regarded as an extraordinary being, and let others know it." Walzel is disguised as the priest who accompanies Erwin to Bozen, the town near Meran in the South Tyrol, the latter the place where Leopold in actual fact was a kind of external pupil at the local lyceum. Later, pupil and tutor resumed residence in Vienna; there, in 1894, Leopold took the final examinations allowing him to enter the university.

A few months earlier, at the home of Walzel's parents, Leopold—or Poldi, as his few intimates called him—came across a comrade worthy of him, Hugo von Hofmannsthal, born in 1874; under the pseudonym of Loris, Hofmannsthal had already become the teen-aged literary sensation in Vienna, with his short verse dramas and his lyrics. Poldi and Hugo became fast friends, enjoying the intellectual gifts they held in common and their exquisite awareness of belonging to a culture that had entered a beautiful twilight; in his diary for April 23, 1894, Hofmannsthal tells how Poldi and he went for a twilight stroll in the gardens of the imperial palace at Schönbrunn. "We think that we sense the soul of this Vienna which perhaps, in us, vitally trembles [*aufbebt*] for the last time—we were triumphantly sad." Four years later, in a sonnet 'To the Brothers,' i.e., Poldi and Hugo, the German poet Stefan George (who had brought out a good many poems by Hugo von Hofmannsthal and a handful by Poldi Andrian in his exclusive publication, *Blätter für die Kunst* [*Leaves for Art*]) saluted the pair, telling them how "our love"—by the possessive pronoun George meant himself and his disciples—was given "to our, to your ailing Austria," and how "We—like you—showed simpler, happier barbarians/That a fair death was the highest pride." George went on to salute the "rich plentitude" of the brothers' work:

Denn dazu lieben wir zu sehr euch brüder
Um zu geniessen nur als spiel und klang
An euch die schwanke schönheit grabes-müder
An euch den farbenvollen untergang.

(For brothers, far too fervent faith we gave
To you, to savour as a sound, a sight
Your grace, enhanced by yearning toward the grave,
Your downfall, sheathed in iridescent light.

Trans. Ernst Morwitz)

In the winter of 1894–95, urged on by Hofmannsthal, Andrian wrote the book he first called *Das Fest der Jugend* (The Festival of Youth); the novelist and critic Hermann Bahr — another and older member of the Viennese circle to which Andrian, Hofmannsthal, Arthur Schnitzler, and Felix Salten, the author-to-be of *Bambi,* belonged — calling the attention of the Berlin publisher Samuel Fischer (the publisher of Arne Garborg's *Weary Men*) to the manuscript, suggested that it could be printed in Fischer's magazine, *Freie Bühne.* Misspelling Andrian's name as Andrean (but what else could be expected of a mere Berliner?), Fischer wrote back to Bahr, saying that his magazine presently was taking only longer works and, then, some "short, amusing tales"; however, he would be willing to publish the manuscript as a book, provided that the author would cover the costs of publication, "since I doubt that any larger group of purchasers will turn up for this work." Money was surely no object for Andrian; the book came out, sixty-two pages long (in large type) in 1895 — but with a new title, *Der Garten der Erkenntnis.* Twenty-six years later, in the introduction to a new edition, Andrian — employing the obscure style characteristic of him — explained what had happened; he had just passed through "the indescribable transition between two stages of life," the receptive, obedient being had become a striver, a thinker, a being who set up goals, and the new title came from "the light that seemed to darken all the others in the first days of [the author's] new phase of life."

Fischer was right, in a way; the *libellum* did not turn into a best-seller, but instead became a cult book for refined souls; as Hofmannsthal noted in his diary, "there are wonderful moments where a whole generation in various lands discovers one another in the same symbol." The "tractate" (as one reviewer called it) received mostly praise in the Austrian press. (Hofmannsthal's review was rejected by a German editor, however, who said that the book was not worth the extravagant praise Hofmannsthal had lavished on it.) Stefan George became deeply devoted to it, and wrote another little poem of four lines, "Bozen: Erwin's shadow". (Erwin is the name of the protagonist of Andrian's book.)

Stimmen hin durch die duftige nacht verschwommen
Der mauern zitterglanz wie der natur
Entzücktes beben: sind sie nur entnommen
Mein Erwin deiner zarten spur?

(Voices blurred in the fragrant night, the sheen
Which quivers on the walls, the tremulous
Pulse of the earth — was this accorded us
Because we go where, Erwin, you have gone?)

Erwin's book gave a similar thrill to others: ten years after the initial publication, André Gide read the book with evident enthusiasm — amusingly enough, at the same time as he was going through Robert Louis Stevenson's *Kidnapped* and the proofs of his own portrait of Oscar Wilde; and the Dutch poet, Albert Verwey, urged on by George, translated it into Dutch as *De Tuin van de Openbaring*. In an essay, Verwey classed "The Garden of Knowledge" as a text inaccessible to literary analysts: "It is but a little booklet, in prose, but it has the importance of a great poem . . . Its characteristic feature is that everyone who reads it with the wish to understand it will have taken his pains in vain . . . Behold, here is a symbolism for which interpretation would profit nothing." Richard Schaukal, who would later write his own little books about his childhood and youth at Brünn (Brno) in Moravia, confessed (1901) that he loved "this imperfect, dreamlike chapter from the sphere of the reactionaries — slender in form and gesture, refined and elegant — against the trivialization of our time, with its urge to uniformity."

Some others were less kind. Amidst friendly words, Felix Salten said that it "had not become a work of art, it consisted of parts which, to be sure, could turn into one." The viciously witty Karl Kraus (a Viennese but *not* a member of Andrian's circle) called it *The Kindergarden of Ignorance*. (For this remark, Hofmannsthal, usually reserved and diplomatic, said that Kraus should be struck dead.) Kraus went on: it was "a product of that intellectual limitation which, stuffed with all the notions connected with the word 'Viennese,' is familiar under the name of 'pure artistry.' " Schnitzler, who often told his diary things he would never tell his friends to their faces, observed that there were in it "traces of an artist, handsome comparisons. No ability to create forms; affectations, obscurities. Immature Loris [i.e., Hofmannsthal], not mature Goethe, as Bahr claims." (In his review, Bahr had found a Goethean wisdom in Erwin's search for "knowledge" about life's secret.) Even Loris himself, Hofmannsthal, confided to *his* diary that "Poldi entirely overlooked what was real . . . he tried to find the essence of things — he paid no heed to their other aspect; he intentionally refused to pay it heed." Nonetheless, Hofmannsthal continued to call attention to his friend's book; in 1900, when he went to Paris for the first time, he took along a copy to present to Maurice Maeterlinck, and in 1918, writing an essay about the future of Vienna's Burgtheater, he brought up the book again.

The remainder of Andrian's life is swiftly told, and anticlimactic. He wrote no more creative literature, save for a handful of poems; in 1896 and 1897, he went through a series of what simpler times called nervous breakdowns, apparently because of his feelings of guilt at his overriding homosexuality, and consulted Schnitzler, who still continued in psychiatric practice. (Herbert Steiner, later, trying to decipher the copious diaries Andrian kept at this time, called his handwriting that "of a young man on the verge of madness.") By 1900, though, Andrian had pulled himself together sufficiently to enter the imperial diplomatic service, and he served with distinction until 1918, when, very briefly, before the empire's collapse, he became the director of the Burgtheater; previously, as a specialist in Polish affairs, he had been an important member of the Austrian delegation at the signing of the Peace of Brest Litovsk, between Germany and Austro-Hungary on the one hand and Soviet Russia on the other. When the Republic of Austria was proclaimed in November 1918, Andrian fled to Switzerland, fearing that the Austrian noblility would be treated as the French nobility had been in the Revolution of a century and a quarter before; subsequently, he returned to his homeland from time to time, once his anxiety had been allayed. He moved about Europe continually, to Nice, to Fribourg in Switzerland, to Alt-Aussee in Austria, where the Andrians had had their summer place for generations. He wrote an unreadable theological tract, *Die Ständeordnung des Alls: Weltbild eines katholischen Dichters* (The Order of the Estates of the Cosmos: World Picture of a Catholic Poet, 1930), for which Hofmannsthal, just before his untimely death in 1929, aided him in finding a publisher; in France, he came to the attention of the Renouveau Catholique, whose conservative Catholicism was also congenial to him — he met Jacques Maritain and Marcel Brion, and Charles du Bos devoted a long essay, one of his *Approximations,* to "The Garden of Knowledge." When the Nazis annexed Austria in March 1938, Andrian's name was on their blacklist, and all the obtainable copies of his latest publication, *Österreich im Prisma der Idee* (Austria in the Prism of the Idea, 1937), were confiscated and destroyed; this was a Platonic dialogue, a "Catechism of the Leading Spirits," between Erwin, a poet, Heinrich Philipp, a statesman, and the Jesuit father Gabriel, about the Catholic and conservative essence of Austria. (Adrian also tried his hand at a novel continuing "The Garden of Knowledge," "Gabriels Lauf zum Ideal" [Gabriel's Course to the Ideal], but quickly abandoned the project.)

Luckily, Andrian was abroad at the time of the Anschluß; he went to Brazil, where he had been stationed as a young diplomatic officer, and after spending the war years there, returned to Nice in 1945. In 1948, a new edition of "The Garden of Knowledge," this time with its original title (together with some of his youthful poetry), appeared in Graz; it also contained the sonnet he had written to the late Hofmannsthal on the latter's fiftieth birthday: "We once were rich and now are poor, for our homeland disappeared." Andrian had married in 1923, the widow of a baron, as a cover for his erotic desires; after her death, he wed again, in 1949, this time the sister-in-law of the prime minister of Rhodesia, Sir Geoffrey Higgins, and on this account made a prolonged trip to South Africa. He died on November 19, 1951, in Fribourg, the site of the most Catholic of all Switzerland's universities.

There is a linguistic peculiarity in "The Garden of Knowledge" that refuses to be translated into English. Once Andrian has established the extremely blue-blooded background of the protagonist — the Andrian parents are transformed (and elevated) into a princess and a prince, "whose properties bordered on Germany" — their son, Erwin, is almost always referred to in the original as "der Erwin," literally, "the Erwin." In his review, Felix Salten noted this peculiarity, and explained it thus: the usage is the way "one speaks to acquaintances about acquaintances": Salten argues that it creates the atmosphere of a story — almost a fairy tale — told intimately. Even before mentioning this philological-social detail, Salten observed that Andrian does not bother to describe his prince (by whom he means Erwin), since all of the narrator's listeners know him — although there are descriptions galore, to be sure, of the persons who touch upon Erwin's life: his father as he lies dying, "his bracelets . . . too large for his wrists, and his rings too large for his fingers"; Lato at the boarding school, who has "quite light blond hair and quite light eyes"; the tubercular lieutenant from the Emperor's Light Infantry whom Erwin and his tutor meet on the train: "Very young and not very elegant, and of a shy and touching politeness, his manner of speaking was somewhat circumstantial and he stressed the unstressed vowels a little," a description perhaps implying that the officer was not a native speaker of German — a by no means uncommon phenomenon in the armies of the multilingual empire; the singer at the Bozen theater, whose mixture of magnificence and vulgarity frightens and fascinates Erwin; the ever polite Heinrich Philipp, who tells Erwin about Vienna but who, as it were, "speaks across Erwin, back to himself"; the "ugly boy with large eyes, who had difficulty in learning" whom Erwin notices among the other former comrades from his school; the coachmen with "their strong resemblance to young gentlemen" which, nonetheless, was "not a true resemblance." Of course, there is Clemens, the depraved and alluring poor boy: "Everything about his face was bright, save for the black rings around his eyes. In his fair hair, which had a dull appearance, as though it were powdered, in the soft riches of his face, and, in particular, beneath his eyes there lay the touching beauty of late ages. He had the voice of that officer with whom Erwin had traveled to Bozen"; Erwin sprinkles Clemens with perfume and showers him with expensive gifts and, at last, bids him farewell in a shabby hotel room at Bruck (an experience Andrian also described in an early, unpublished poem). As Clemens's female counterpart, there is the woman with whom (quite unbelievably) Erwin lives for a year, "beautiful, with the beauty of those late busts at whose sight we hesitate for a moment, not knowing whether they show us a young Asian king or an aging Roman empress." Later on, there are the entertainers in the suburban tavern where Erwin goes by chance, particularly the "young man, thin and rouged, with tired eyes, dressed in a tailcoat, his hair carefully waved," and, in the same scene, the equally odd young man at Erwin's table, "whose body seemed to grow smaller in wheedling, humble gratitude, while his eyes looked across to Erwin, imploring but calm" — he reminds Erwin of his dead mistress. Erwin will meet him twice more, once in the late summer, after his upsetting experience at a herders' hut in the mountains ("his face and his movements were as different from one another and as secret as on the first encounter"), and then in November a year after, directly before Erwin's illness and death ("his face was changed . . . [it] had become thin and inexorable and distorted"). To these figures that belong, many of them, to a kind of demimonde, Erwin's mother must be added, with whom he makes a trip to Italy, and whom he remembers as she appeared to him when he was ill as a child: she was "adorned with silk and flowers and jewelry."

Yet what Erwin himself looks like we never get to know; he is the Narcissus of the first of the book's epigraphs, "Ego Narcissus" — the others are important only as they pass before his eyes. Many of the objects of Erwin's attention are described in a way to leave no doubt about Erwin's sexual orientation; in this respect, the book (as has been argued by the German writer on literary decadence, Jens Malte Fischer) is related to Wilde's *Picture of Dorian Gray* — it is about erotic confusion and the winning-out of the male-to-male urge. (In his diary for January 1894, Andrian set down what he had told Hofmannsthal in conversation: "Perversion is charming, as long as it is a game — horrible, with foaming lips, imperious, [when it is] a disease.")

The affection of Erwin for persons below him on the social ladder may also be noted as a component of his homosexuality: the unsure young officer, the coachmen, Clemens, the herdsmen in the Alps, the stranger in the tavern and on the streets of Vienna. The three women in Erwin's life, too, can be fitted into the homosexual pattern; they are all old enough to be Erwin's mother —

the aging actress, the aging mistress (evidently an actress too), his mother de facto. With the last he shares notable features: "Erwin had her hands and her voice," we are told twice, early and late in the tale; this resemblance makes his mother uncomfortable. Furthermore, in the catalogue where sexual aberration and decadence are blended, it is twice noted that the objects of Erwin's love belong to "late times," Clemens with "the touching beauty of late times," and his mistress—who has an hermaphroditic quality (like "a young Asiatic king"—Heliogabalus?—or "an aging Roman empress"). As Erwin looks at the stranger in the café, the memory of her comes back to him, seen the way she looked in death, with what may be a masculine attribute: "with her closed eyes like a mask beneath the helmet of her hair." The hermaphroditic role Erwin plays in his mother's company (and which makes her uncomfortable) may also be emphasized by his noticing, once he has left her, the youth and the girl on the square in Venice who look alike; he "remembered them and knew that they were meaningful for him, and he would almost have turned around, but he did not know their name."

The novel—and reviewers called it just that, in remarking upon its resemblance to the traditional German *Entwicklungsroman,* a novel of development like *Wilhelm Meister,* detailing the course of a young man's emotional and intellectual formation—has, in addition to its patently erotic layer, another which is typical of decadence; like D'Annunzio's *Il piacere* and *Il fuoco (The Flame),* like Rodenbach's *Bruges-la-Morte,* it takes place mostly in a city which is a wonderful museum, a museum which, however—unlike Rodenbach's Bruges or Thomas Mann's Venice—seems at first to be very much alive. The tributes to Vienna, the depictions of it, are many: its spectacles (including the Spanish Riding School), its festivals (with their religious processions: "especially Corpus Christi Day, on which the Blessed Body of Our Lord and Savior Jesus Christ came to it with no less splendor and with no less jubilation than on those glorious other days of Charles VI, when, returning from his Spanish lands, he made his way into Vienna, his most humbly devoted imperial city, his capital and his residence"), and its places of amusement, "the Sophiensäle and the Ronacher and the Orpheum and the circus." The eye of the peripatetic Erwin sees the "meaningful beauty" of its "cathedrals of the middle ages" and its "baroque churches" and the "the little medieval churches" tucked away in the side streets, and the "poor churches of the 1820s," its palaces and gardens and its statuary, "the golden carved statues whose pedestals are never empty" (i.e., they are covered with flowers and wreaths), and the "saints on the noisy bridges" (a reference in particular to St. John Nepomuk, the patron saint of Bohemia who was cast from a bridge into the Moldau). At Schönbrunn, on a January evening, Erwin feels "the unutterable charm of a group of statuary in which two women embraced one another" — does he see in this a confirmation and expression of his homosexuality? (The unity of the stone women may be contrasted with the strain, mentioned in his next paragraph, which has entered into his own relationship to the beloved Clemens.) Another great Vienna passage treats the Erwin's excursion to the suburbs (which concept means a lower-class side of Vienna, as in Schnitzler's plays); we may be gently reminded of Dorian's excursions to the London docks, a locale which, nonetheless, is infinitely less appealing and more horrifying. There, Erwin comes into direct contact with a world that attracts and frightens him; he has already gone in summer to the wine restaurants with Clemens, where both of them were grasped "by the music of the waltzes with their eternal monotony, made up of sweetness and vulgarity." Now, he hears the waltzes again just before he notices the stranger with his "base countenance."

The celebration of Vienna, too, shades over into a celebration of Austria proper; the several geographical references in the text are — quite apart from possible erotic overtones, as the destination or home of a person that has attracted Erwin — a delineation of the very expanse of the empire and its many nations: the lieutenant is on his way to Riva, in the empire's southernmost part, and the Bukovina, which Erwin suddenly and madly desires to visit, because of a comrade who has come from there, lies far to the east. (In his childhood, Erwin's mother has read to him about the "betrayal" of Austria in 1859, the failure of the German Confederation to come to the aid of the empire in the war against France and Sardinia.) In addition, Erwin is keenly aware of the great regiments of the Austrian army, the Kaiserjäger and the Imperial Guards and the Hoch-und-Deutschmeister Number 4, the house regiment of Vienna. Erwin catalogues the various nationalities of the troops he sees in Vienna: "and all the soldiers and especially the tall, somber, tragic Bosnians, and the faces of all the peoples of the empire, the loyal Bohemians, sometimes with a tinge of gentle suffering in their faces, and the Slovakians with their fixed, deep, yearning eyes." The Bosnians return in the café scene; they are the only members of the audience who remain earnest — that is, save for the stranger at Erwin's table. The military passages may remind us of how young Andrian was as he wrote (they give "The Garden" the passing air of a boy's book), and they may remind us, again, of Andrian's erotic interest in men and boys of a lower social status; certainly, the sight of soldiers seems to console and strengthen him. His unhappiness after the experience in the Alpine barn and the sensation of fear that assails him in the hot streets of Vienna is dispelled or alleviated only once, before he leaves for his meeting with his mother in Italy. "He was deeply moved only once before his departure. It happened at a little station near Vienna: a train passed through the station, from whose windows young men looked out; they were on their way to military service. Their pale faces shone and they sang, and they had bright sprigs attached to the blue caps of the Deutschmeister regiment." They have achieved a sense of community denied to Erwin, but for which he still hopes.

All these impressions, and more, comprise the world that bears in upon Erwin during his brief existence, the particles of life that give him, mostly, a sensual pleasure in their perception and are a part of that "Festival of Life" which was the book's initial title — Hermann Bahr, in his first essay on decadence, had said that for the decadent, life is made up of impressions, not emotions. Erwin's trouble is that in his search for a meaning to life, he cannot form a deeper emotional attachment to any of it; when his admired Lato dies, he goes out to the funeral, "surprised that he remained quite cold, even at the sight of the corpse." The festival of life itself calls up another death-imbued image, or at least one of a profound human estrangement: "It resembled those festivals which were so grand and solemn that, in the experience, joy was forgotten; those festivals of the seventeenth century on dark winter nights, between mirrors and lights, those festivals at which the participants met but once and, with fingertips affectedly entwined, slowly circled about one another and smilingly looked into another's eyes and then glided away with a deep and admiring bow." (The passage calls up memories of a similar one in *Il piacere,* the image elicited by Maria's playing of the Rameau gavotte: the lovers dance in a deserted park, on the point of ceasing to love one another.) Earlier, Erwin has told the tale — with a Huysmanian display of jewel names — of the youth in the cavern, who waits in vain for the "pious ancient" to tell him the magic word necessary to give some sense to all the impressions of life. Now, realizing that he does not possess that word, Erwin undertakes the journey with his mother on the same quest, a quest that again does not succeed: "But the two of them did not find the secret of life." (The reviewers referred frequently to this element of the fairy-tale quest in the story; we may think of Hans Christian Andersen's *The Bell,* in which two friends follow the sound of a distant bell, hoping forever to learn its meaning.) The blood relationship of mother and son should perhaps give them mutual aid on the quest; but it is all in vain. They are indeed joined together like the frog embryos in the old priest's experiment in Bozen, but "painfully and dully and senselessly." Between Erwin and his mother, as between Erwin and his lovers, there is a bond of some sort of human relationship, but no way of overcoming life's essential loneliness: "I believe that the key to the secret lies here: we are alone, we and our life, and our soul creates our life, but our soul is not in us alone." We may sense a spiritual kinship with other humans — "the soul is not in us alone" — but that sense of kinship is not sufficient to dispel the individual's isolation—an isolation that has been still more radically developed in Erwin ever since, as a boy, he knew fear, at the boarding school, of the hostile others who encroached upon his life, even as he tried to ward them off. In his review, Hermann Bahr compared the boy Erwin to the protagonist of Maurice Barrès's trilogy *Le Culte du moi* and applied the title of its first part, *Sous l'oeil des barbares,* to Erwin: he has "a sense of rage and bitterness toward everything that is different from him, that is not he, that is different from himself and thus dangerous or at least harmful to him—Barrès called [this force] 'the barbarians.'" As Bahr points out, a flattering sense of his own "otherness" begins to exert its charm upon Erwin, and he succumbs to it now and again—but simultaneously, he never loses a painful awareness of his isolation, arising from his boyhood, not even on that trip to Italy which, in its way, is an effort (as the childhood memories of his mother, consoling him, show) to recapture a feeling of trust. After the failed trip is over, he sees the youth and the girl in Venice who resemble each other, in a kind of familial community; he sees the statue of Mithra-Helios, with the "people," the worshipers of the light-bringing deity, sculpted at its base, another community or congregation. Yet Erwin remains alone. About to set out for Vienna, he drinks "tea and cognac," and remembers Clemens and the parting in Bruck and the "measureless charm of his friend, who [was] lost for him." Once again, "the early morning lay over the houses, and they were painful and eternal, like things from which one takes farewell."

Erwin is possessed by a narcissism which receives its most telling expression in the passage about the excursion to the mountains, following upon the ambiguous praise of "The Festival of Life." Erwin nods off in the loft of the barn but soon awakens and is overcome by "that madness of experience that the hot nights bring"; he looks at the slumbering cowherds and mountain guides, then returns to his loft, after having observed the cold serenity of the nocturnal landscape, and starts to fall asleep again. Yet, as he does, he is assaulted a second time by images that become "more and more physical and sensual." The waltzes that he heard with Clemens at the wine restaurant, the ceremonial dances of the baroque that had been a part of the "festival of life," return to his mind: the images "moved their limbs and made enticing gestures and smiled and began to dance, and the change in the configuration of their dance was mingled with the change of the houses and the rooms in which they had given themselves to him." Then he thinks that there is a window in the loft, and a "human figure [standing] by the window, and this form had come on his account and it waited for him." But the window and the figure do not exist; a reflection in a cheap mirror from Goisern has tricked him—the mirror is the surface in which Narcissus sees himself, the mirror "across whose gilded frame the moonlight had passed, as the gentle wind which had arisen cast the frame against the wall." "No, he did not want to lie down again . . . Trembling with desire, he leaned against the wall, and his soul enjoyed the memory of the pleasure of his body and confessed that it was the truest urge of human being to press its body against another, since this mysterious destruction of existence gives us knowledge." In the sexual experience, Erwin has been freed, or so he believes, momentarily from his Nietzschean "principle of the individual," from his narcissistic captivity. "Then he climbed down and awakened the guides; in the night their faces [had been] mighty and full of secrets," but, by daylight, they "became ugly and repugnant." "The memory of the night was unpleasant for Erwin . . . ; it was as if his soul had fallen, and yet, for someone who measured life by the measure of life, there could be no fall."

Music, the art and the sound with which Vienna is filled, the accompaniment of the dances, becomes hateful to him, as does the city itself. "The city was transformed for Erwin; . . . its diversity, which formerly had moved him, now confused and threatened him. On a very hot day he was afraid of the music which was in the streets; it seemed to him as though it impregnated the city with a treacherous poison, meant to make the listener feel sleepy [as in the Alpine loft] and defenseless." Erwin is afraid, but he seems reassured as he beholds the train with the young recruits, and he conceives the idea of the reunion with his mother. After his next return to Vienna, a year passes: "He was always alone." Then, in the November rain, he meets the stranger again, and in the stranger "there was nothing save a single and terrible threat." Suddenly, Erwin thinks he knows who the stranger is: "his enemy, who had sought him from his very birth and had found him in the intoxication of springtime and who since then had pursued him and followed him, and who came ever nearer to him, and who would finally catch up with him and place his hand upon him." For Erwin, the stranger signifies death; it is not out of the way to see, in this progression of the stranger's meaning, Andrian's and Erwin's sense of guilt at homosexuality — "for the wages of sin is death." "On the third day" (instead of rising from the dead, like Jesus) "Erwin fell ill; when he had gone to bed, the stranger appeared to him no longer; the fear of death had also vanished from his soul"; Erwin has resigned himself to his end, and all that remains is "the old yearning for knowledge, but dry and tormenting." Friends visit him, including Clemens, "who had become a lieutenant" (we remember the voice-association between the lieutenant in the train and this most important of Erwin's lovers). "But his visits in particular were painful, for Erwin felt all the colors of his charm, but not with the value of before, but in a strangely indifferent way, as if Clemens did not concern him." The last vestiges of his love for Clemens are impressionistic; whatever there was of deeper affection has passed away. Burning with fever, Erwin experiences a "drought of his soul"; this dryness should be contrasted with the rain that fell the first and third times he saw the stranger; the rain that had fallen in the springtime was fructifying, the chance at the start of a new life for Erwin (had he been able to surrender himself); and even in the autumn rain, he felt "a yearning for the experiences that lay within him." (A perceptive commentator, Jens Rieckmann, has argued that the stranger is a kind of rejected Dionysus; Erwin cannot abandon himself to him, and so comes to fear him as death itself.)

The rain, on this third occasion, actually turns lethal; Erwin (prone to colds, as we know from his experience on the toboggan slide, long ago) is soaked through, and the rain, rejected, leads to his parching fever. On his deathbed, Erwin is tormented by dreams, of a being who may be Clemens or the lieutenant (it refuses to give its name) and then of a railroad station; the basis in reality is the sighting of the train with the recruits. "Many people were gazing from [the train's] windows, they had the faces of those who travel, their color was white and their eyes were shining, but beneath their eyes coal dust lay. [We may recall the blackness—of cosmetics or depravity—beneath Clemens's eyes.] There were many of them, very many, and everyone he had known was among them, but not the women." Of a sudden they call him by name, summoning him, "and he became very happy": he has been called (in the dream) into a community where, significantly, "there were no women." But his dreamed-of joy is interrupted; someone lights the stove in his room, increasing, we should guess, its dryness; "since he had a high fever, he did not know whether he was waiting for the rain, for which he yearned, or for sleep, in order to find knowledge in the dream. But it did not rain, nor did he fall asleep. Thus the prince died, without having known." (Erwin is called "the prince" here—the title he inherited from his long-dead father—for the first and last time in the tale.) In this painfully autobiographical work, no solution exists for the prince's conflicts, or for his creator's, no way out of or into his homosexual urges (wholly giving way to them might, it is implied, have saved him), no way out of his narcissism, no answer to his search for the answer to the mystery of life. No path exists, for Andrian or Erwin, to the "measureless joy of the truly great festivals," the joy "as holy as pain, of the festivals of Alexander the Great at Persepolis and at Babylon." These were, to be sure, festivals to celebrate Alexander's conquest of these cities and their destruction.

Rilke's story "Die Letzten" ("The Last Ones") will not require a retelling of the author's life. It is a fairly early work, written when Rilke was twenty-four, before he had begun to achieve his great fame as a lyric poet with *Das Buch der*

Bilder (*The Book of Pictures*), *Das Stunden-Buch* (*The Book of Hours*), the *Neue Gedichte* (*New Poems*), and later works. At first, Rilke was very fond of "The Last Ones"; it appeared in November 1901, in a volume of the same name which also contained two other, slighter tales. He told his then publisher, the Danish-German Axel Juncker, that it was, for him, among the dearest things he had written; but he soon turned sharply against it, perhaps embarrassed by its sensational close, and, by 1912, offered the opinion to his new and permanent publisher, Anton Kippenberg, that "the little book is quite unimportant." Early reviewers praised it, one of them stating that it was a book of novellas by a decadent lyricist, in whom the decadence was not a borrowed and modish trait, but an authentic part of his artistic being; others thought that it seemed very Scandinavian: "If Rilke had not attached his own name to the work, one could believe that it was a piece of tender, nervous, Danish art, perhaps by an over-refined Copenhagener." (The reviewer may well have been thinking of Herman Bang.) Rilke's mentor and friend Professor August Sauer of the German university in Prague simply assumed that the Malcorn family was "a Nordic clan that had come down in life." Since Rilke was a member of Prague's German-speaking minority, the book, it would seem, could scarcely have contained any autobiographical elements; but we know that in his novel *Die Aufzeichnungen des Malte Laurids Brigge* (1910, *The Notebooks of Malte Laurids Brigge*), Rilke took an imaginary young Danish nobleman to be his mouthpiece or diarist. In "The Last Ones," he had in fact conjured up a suggestion of Nordicness by means of Harald Malcorn's first name, and a plot that, subliminally or not, must have reminded readers of Ibsen's *Ghosts*. Oswald Alving returns to the family estate and to his mother from Paris a sick man, and he loses his mind at the end of the play; Harald, already tubercular and likewise returned to his mother's care, falls into a fit of paralysis at the story's end. The healthy girl who might have been Harald's savior, Marie Holzer, has an equivalent of sorts in Ibsen's Regine Engstrand; in Ibsen, Regine is ousted not by Oswald himself but by Mrs. Alving, whereas at the close of "The Last Ones" Harald turns erotically to Frau Malcorn.

Beneath these Nordic suggestions, there lie elements of the personal mythology that Rilke was busily constructing about himself. He liked to think and to announce that his family had come from the ancient nobility (*Uradel*) of the Austrian province of Carinthia and, more recently, had owned castles in Bohemia; his own father was a former warrant officer in the Austrian army and a railroad inspector, but his father's brother, the prosperous Uncle Jaroslav, had spent time and money on perhaps spurious genealogies in which his nephew delighted. In the story itself, Harald repeats names (Tschakathurn, Hallpach, Indichar) somehow connected with the Rilke family history; Castle Skal

(Czech "skála," rock) has a name that is appropriate enough, and a noble family, the Freiherren von Skal, had large Bohemian properties in the nineteenth century. That the ancient Malcorn family has once been mighty, emerging from the very mists of history, and has fallen on hard times is made abundantly clear; moving down socially, they have, as the realistic intruder, Marie Holzer, observes, literally moved upward, into an apartment, crowded with family heirlooms, over the heads — according to Marie — of "sensible, unimportant people," in the same building. The theme of the people "down there," to whom Harald has given so much of his energy, and whom he comes to despise, returns again and again in the tale.

The Malcorns have lost their money, and Harald has become involved in a kind of social ministry (of three years' duration, like the ministry of Christ), trying — the program seems very vague — to bring a sense of beauty to the masses. (Rilke may have thought of his callow efforts to bestow his pamphlets of verse on the common people, with *Wegwarten: Lieder dem Volke geschenkt* [1896, Wild Chickory: Songs Given to the People] — people who in Prague spoke Czech; the city's German-speaking minority was largely made up of officials and members of the professions.) The hearty and talkative Marie Holzer (using the big words for which Harald criticizes her) has met Harald in the course of his public activity and has been captivated by his hypnotic style: he lifts his hands, she reports to Mrs. Malcorn, to the audience and cries: " 'Oh ye of little faith!' " — messianic behavior indeed. She wants him to continue in this calling, as she repeatedly says. (There is a good deal of insensitivity in Marie, the "young," the "new" person; the daughter of a peasant, she may well be the sister of Hermann Holzer of the story "Der Liebende" [The Lover] in the same volume; the male Holzer, boisterous and apparently good-hearted, has taken the fragile Helene away from his friend Ernst Bang, another sensitive soul, whose last name means "afraid" or "anxious" in German, a name that may allude, as well, to Herman Bang.) Harald returns in the middle of a conversation between Marie and Mrs. Malcorn during which, despite the mutual affection and respect on its surface, a rivalry has emerged between the two women for Harald, over the love he appears to have withdrawn from his delicate mother and bestowed on his robust friend and on his task. But he has grown weary; he believes that he has given away too much of himself, offering "unripe fruits" to an audience that cannot appreciate his message of a "festival of beauty." (Beneath his attitude of caring for his flock, Harald is a snob; see his remark about trousers that are too short and shawls that smell of camphor.) At the end of the story's first half, Marie has lost the contest for Harald, who falls back into his mother's hands; he has long resisted Mrs. Malcorn's efforts to make him " 'sit by the fire, sit by the fire, snuggle up to it if that were possible,'" but now, exhausted, ill, and gnawed by the thought that he might have an artist's calling (he would like to give himself over to Mrs. Malcorn's task of embroidery, carrying it on into infinity), he says "I am tired." Meanwhile, Marie Holzer, who has admired the fine old things in the Malcorn's apartment without understanding their essence, the memories stored within them, "watches as he falls into the easy chair; she sees the fragile woman bend down over him and cover him, wholly. And she says no more; nor would her words have been heard, for Harald's cough is very loud."

Rilke had written several plays and was a badly disappointed dramatist; when his last play was laughed off a Berlin stage (the audience did not appreciate his manifold, Maeterlinckian silences), he resolved to compose no more for the theater. In "The Last Ones" (which in its first, magazine publication had the subtitle "Ein Schlußakt," "A Final Act"), he created a substitute for the stage drama, a narrative drama in which he, as the narrator, had complete control over his imaginary theater — he had railed in an essay against the interference of directors. All the elements of a drama are present: the long stage direction at the opening; the long conversational tussle between the two women as they wait for the appearance of the men they both love (as in Ibsen's *John Gabriel Borkman,* in whose first act two sisters battle, subtly, over the married woman's son, and more importantly, over the husband of the one and the former beloved of the other); the repeated use of the word *pause;* the melodramatic appearance of Harald; the equally melodramatic ending of the first part, with Mrs. Malcorn's symbolic covering of Harald. Then there comes the entr'acte, during which Harald's illness flares up and his apparent convalescence begins; when the curtain rises again, Harald and his mother are alone in the apartment, and Harald speaks of Marie as an intruder to whom he has given walking papers. The dialogue leads into Harald's inchoate thoughts of clouds and of his own childhood, when he and his mother shared melancholy artistic experiences; these thoughts pass gradually over into the fragmentary narrative of Mrs. Malcorn's adultery of the past. As a child, Harald was given the pet name Jerôme by his mother, evidently her young lover's name as well, and Harald himself uses a language about his father which reproduces Mrs. Malcorn's reasons for her unfaithfulness: "'He had a long white beard. He was old. He had strangely wild hands.'"

The plan to go out to an uncle's castle, Skal, is abandoned because of Mrs. Malcorn's superstitious fear of the "white lady," the original adulteress in the family's history, who always appears before a Malcorn dies. (Is she afraid that Harald will die at Skal, or is she afraid of memories of her own past unfaithfulness?) At any event, the introduction of "la dame blanche" — reminiscent of the family curse Max Beerbohm used to such wonderfully comical effect in

Zuleika Dobson — is risible, although Rilke did not intend it to be so. After the legend of Lady Walpurga is threshed out between mother and son, Harald returns to his diffuse artistic plans: he will paint clouds, he will write a book called *Kunst und Kindheit* (Art and Childhood) — Rilke believed that all art is born of childhood experience — and so Harald is led back to childhood evenings with his mother, when he was "Jerôme." A web of eroticism is woven more and more closely around the pair in the apartment: she approaches his chair and is fondled by him, she retreats, clinging to the black family clock (as a symbol of her own age?) for protection; Harald tells her that he wants to paint her in a gown of clouds, but with hot red flowers, a red like that he found so abhorrent in the runner on which she worked in the first act. He is terribly forgetful, claiming that he cannot remember her name; it does come to him, at last, Edith, but then he wants to know her *nom d'amour,* by which her lovers called her, and learns that it was Edel, "Noble." (Rilke may have taken the name from the Danish heroine of a narrative poem by Paul Bourget, where a decadent, the last of his line, loves a fragile girl, or from Edele Lyhne, the erotically attractive aunt of the adolescent Niels Lyhne in the novel by Jens Peter Jacobsen, whom Rilke so much admired.) Harald has already told his mother how beautiful she is, and how youthful her walk; he finally urges her to put on her white gown, to reappear as "white Edel" (her virginity restored) for the festival of beauty. " 'Why should we wait? Beauty will come upon us.' " He stands up for a last time, stretching out his arms in his hypnotic gesture: "Strong and mighty, his arms [are] like wings, and he laughs to her." She obeys and goes off stage. He is in ecstasy.

But once she is gone, he realizes what he has done and, exhausted by his efforts at persuasion (or seduction), falls asleep in his chair. "When he awakens, it is night," and he beholds a woman, clad in white, in the moonlight. This time Harald thrusts out "his thin arms" as if to ward off "the white lady," and cries, " 'Not yet, Walpurga!' " Does he believe that the family curse has gone into effect again? Someone turns on the electric light: who we do not know — Mrs. Malcorn herself, in an effort to calm her son, or Marie, returning for a final try at reconciliation? (The text makes it clear that Marie is a creature of light; Harald complains that she has "too much light" — or reason and practicality — about her.) While Mrs. Malcorn stands before him, withered, Harald's once effective hands, his instruments of public oratory and private seduction, fall to his sides, paralyzed; her hands are in gloves, as though readied for a ball. "And, with awful strangeness, they looked into one another's dead eyes."

The incestuous near-union between the surviving members of the old house has resulted in death, real or spiritual, for them both. (Has Harald had a stroke? A vein in his neck throbbed ominously as he cajoled his mother.) The story would imply that, however one may long to be young, whether in the social action Marie praises, in the youthfulness of a new art, or in the youth that Mrs. Malcorn so briefly recaptures, decadence, the world of the old, the burden of the past, cannot be overcome. (In Rilke's contemporary and subsequent literary production, he repeatedly returns to the importance of youth, of creating something new for the new century superseding the overwhelming burden of the old, the spirit of the fin de siècle, the fin du globe.) What the story may tell about Rilke's relation to his own mother, it is impossible to say; he disliked her intensely, because of her affected and stagy Catholicism (he left the Catholic faith of his youth, and never returned), and wrote a hateful poem to her, fifteen years later, when she announced that she would visit him in Munich: "Oh woe, my mother is destroying me." He was forty at the time. Yet he was a dutiful son (most of the correspondence with Phia Rilke has yet to be published), and his early poetry and *Malte* are filled with appearances of a lovely, young mother figure. This much is sure: in good part, the story is an account of a failed effort to conquer decadence, and a *conte cruel* or a *conte morose* as shocking as anything by Villiers de L'Isle Adam or Jean Lorrain.

13

Poland/Prussia

STANISŁAW PRZYBYSZEWSKI

Przybyszewski wrote seven novels in German. The first three compose a trilogy under the collective title *Homo sapiens* — *Über Bord* (1896, Overboard), *Unterwegs* (1895, Under Way), and *Im Malstrom* (1895, In the Maelstrom); the second part, published first, was issued by Fontane, who probably believed that its simplicity and somewhat unusual setting would appeal to the reading public. The other two were published by the smaller house of Hugo Storm. *Über Bord* has as its background the Berlin *Bohème* of the early 1890s and the restaurant Zum schwarzen Ferkel; Strindberg figures as the detested "Iltis," "Skunk," and the restaurant is renamed Zum grünen Nachtigall (At the Sign of the Green Nightingale). The protagonist is the enormously self-confident Erik Falk, an author whose name Przybyszewski may have taken from the bumptious hero of Ibsen's *Kjærlighedens Komedie* (1862, Love's Comedy) or from the skeptic Arvid Falk of Strindberg's novel, *Röda rummet* (1879, The Red Room). Falk is not a Scandinavian (although he has Scandinavian contacts, and an acquaintance with the work of Arne Garborg), but from "Congress-Poland," the part of the country controlled by Russia. The novel is a roman à clef; Falk steals the fiancée, Isa, of his friend, Mikita, a promising painter, who kills himself. Mikita is a much disguised version of Edvard Munch, of whom Przybyszewski was jealous, and Isa, albeit from Paris, is Dagny Juel. Falk has long had a partner when he marries Isa — Janina, Marta

Foerder in real life. The title refers to Mikita, the rival gone overboard.

The second part, *Unterwegs,* takes place a few years later, and was presumably inspired by the efforts of Przybyszewski's mother to interest him in a local governess, Bogumiła Łukomska, to whom he dedicated a lyric diary. Now twenty-four, on a visit to home ground, Falk falls in love with and seduces a pious sixteen-year-old, Marit Kauer. She drowns herself on hearing his confession that he has a wife (Isa) in Berlin; earlier, he has told her that he has had a child with an artist's model (Janina/Marta). Among the novel's memorable features are the incisive political discussions carried on by Falk with Marit's father and other prominent people of the provincial backwater; he does not conceal his contempt for the Bismarckian policies followed in the province of Posen, a topic to which Przybyszewski returned decades later, after Poland's independence, in the second, incomplete part of his memoirs: the Prussians are a "bastard" race, fearful — unlike the true Germans of the west — of the pure-blooded Poles. Another notable inset is the story Falk tells the impressionable Marit of a "truly great man" he has met in Norway — the poet Sigbjørn Obstfelder (1866–1900), later to be identified by Rilke's French translator, Maurice Betz, as a model for Malte Laurids Brigge. (Dagny translated Obstfelder's story, "Liv," into German for the periodical *Pan* and, further, turned *Unterwegs* into Norwegian for simultaneous publication with the German edition.) The brief portrait of Isa/Dagny in *Unterwegs* is flattering; hearing that Falk has fallen ill (after the seduction of Marit, of which Isa is unaware), she travels to Kuyania to nurse him back to health.

Im Malstrom takes place in Berlin, three years after Marit's death. Falk has become involved with radical socialist or anarchist circles; in *Unterwegs,* he had already interpreted the anarchist Émile Henry — who reached the climax of his career by throwing a bomb into the Café Terminus at the Gare Saint Lazare — as "a criminal from a sense of revulsion, a criminal of indignation," making his gesture against a hypocritical bourgeois society. Falk has fathered a second child with Janina and is gripped by the fear that his second family will be revealed to Isa by his fellow "Social Democrat" Czerski, for whom Falk, formerly admired, has become a "small man." Once upon a time Janina's suitor, Czerski now demands that Falk divorce Isa to marry her. In the maelstrom of erotic ties and conspiratorial pullings and tuggings, Falk — the quondam superman — becomes more and more anxious, fancying that Marit's father pursues him and that the police are after him for his political activities. (His fellow socialist Grodski has committed suicide, a death which a mysterious stranger, an agent provocateur, tells Falk was caused by Grodski's disgust at Falk's "experiments in decadence and degeneration" with the lives of others.) Temporarily filled with self-loathing, Falk challenges the anarchist

Kunicki—much feared because he has killed a fellow conspirator in a duel at Zurich—to a duel; assuming he will likewise be killed, Falk asks a friend, Olga, to look after Janina. Kunicki misses him and is shot in the kneecap by Falk: "The *citoyen cosmopolitique* with the limping principles must now limp himself"—Falk has been envious of Kunicki as a "citizen of the world." Kruk, Janina's brother and an accomplice of Czerski (now a proponent of nonviolence, so that he himself cannot punish Falk), reveals to Isa the secret of Falk's other life. On the eve of the duel, a terrible scene between Falk and Isa takes place, in the course of which Isa also accuses him, "you proud monogamous man," of having caused Marit's death; when Falk returns from the duel, unharmed, Isa has left for Paris with their child. As usual in moments of crisis, Falk falls ill, and the devoted Olga cares for him; he proposes that she follow him in *his* new life program of nonviolence, lifted from Czerski. The cluttered novel's last line is Falk's "Vive l'humanité," intended, Przybyszewski argued in his memoirs, as a sign of Falk's "complete bankruptcy of heart and mind." In a dissertation of 1938, Maxime Herman called Falk a decadent, a correct classification on the evidence of his egomania, and his abuse of others (like Sperelli, like Dorian, like the marquis de Bradomín). Yet in Falk, the decadent trappings of aesthetic inventiveness or of constant literary and artistic allusion are altogether missing. Falk has no refined ambiance, or, for that matter, genuine perversity; Przybyszewski had used up that ammunition in the *Pentateuch*.

A Polish version of *Homo Sapiens* appeared at Lvov in 1901, during Przybyszewski's residence there. This was translated into English by Thomas Seltzer in 1915 and published by Knopf. A translator's note runs: "It is universally conceded that Stanisław Przybyszewski is Poland's greatest living writer; *Homo Sapiens* is his most famous book." In an effort to present Przybyszewski to an American public, Knopf also brought out a pamphlet about the *Pentateuch* and its "poetic charm." No further attempts were made to bring Przybyszewski to the English-speaking world; perhaps the devotion of Przybyszewski to Germany during the First World War put a damper on other translation projects. Moreover, Przybyszewski was in the shadow of Henryk Sienkiewicz, the Nobel Prize winner (1905) who died a year after the publication of the English *Homo Sapiens*: Sienkiewicz, the author of *Quo Vadis,* had attracted an audience altogether different from Przybyszewski's putative readership. In his encomiastic survey of Poland's literature from 1917, Przybyszewski gives Sienkiewicz grudging praise as "not one of the greatest, nor a prophet and interpreter, nor an outstanding artist, but one whom a friendly fate has chosen as the executor of [Poland's] mighty heritage."

Przybyszewski's other novel from the fin de siècle, *Satans Kinder* (1897, Satan's Children), will be discussed presently. (It appeared in Polish at Lvov in

1899, as *Dzieci szatana*.) In September 1898, Przybyszewski moved to Kraków, his base until 1900, when he went on to Lvov and then to Warsaw and Torún, returning to Germay in February 1906, where he would remain until the establishment of the Polish republic. His later German-language novels are *Erdensöhne* (1905, Sons of the Soil), *Das Gericht* (1913, The Judgment), and *Der Schrei* (1918, The Cry). The first two were parts of a planned trilogy (Fontane's title page for *Erdensöhne* calls it a "novel in three parts"), which, under the general title *Synowie ziemi* (Sons of the Soil), was completed with *Zmierzch* (1911, Twilight), never translated into German. The Polish originals of Parts 1 and 2 had come out in 1904 and 1909.

The central figure of *Erdensöhne* is another Przybyszewski alter ego, the successful dramatist Czerkaski, surrounded by adoring friends at a Kraków restaurant, At the Sign of the White Peacock; he dazzles them with his accounts of reading in Petrus Borel, the self-styled lycanthrope, and the marquis de Sade's *Justine*. The city itself — as customarily in Przybyszewski — is only vaguely described; it is in the grips of an epidemic of malaria from the bogs along the Vistula. Czerkaski is deeply in love with Hanka, the wife of his friend Glinski; in the novel's finale, he seduces her and the two plan to flee together to "the land of a thousand lakes" — Finland, perhaps, with which Przybyszewski had no connection whatsoever, thus a dream land — or into a love death. Having used the story of his own affair with and eventual marriage to Jadwiga Kasprowicza, the wife of Przybyszewski's friend and mentor, Jan Kasprowicz, for the main material of the novel, the obsessive confessor Przybyszewski also tells another tale about himself through the composer Szarki: he has been imprisoned on suspicion of having poisoned a woman. On June 9, 1896, Marta Foerder, who by now had borne three children to Przybyszewski and was perhaps pregnant with a fourth, took poison; accused of implication in her death, Przybyszewski was detained by the Berlin police for two weeks. In one of the novel's most impressive passages Szarki imagines his own execution; his cell-mate, sentenced to twenty years for burglary, does kill himself, even as Szarki does after his release. Like Oscar Wilde and Herman Bang, Przybyszewski lived in fear of the law.

Das Gericht, a sequel to *Erdensöhne,* reports on the subsequent marital troubles of Czerkaski — his wife Hanka leaves him, in an effort to find her child by her former husband, Glinski; her addiction to opium, fed by the sinister Korfini (an admirer of Czerkaski, who wants to keep the dramatist for himself), almost destroys her, but she is saved temporarily by (and perhaps has a night of love with) the noble-hearted composer Milosz Zaremba. Her search for her daughter leads to the High Tatra, where, gone astray in a storm, she may — or may not — kill herself. The meaning of the title is that a judgment is passed on both Czerkaski and Hanka; *Das Gericht* is dedicated, with some irony, to "My wife Hedwig [Jadwiga], in deep love." In fact, the relationship between Przybyszewski and this second wife — to whom he stayed married — was complicated from the start by the jealousy Jadwiga bore toward Stanisława, Przybyszewski's illegimate child by still another of his lovers, Aniela (Nelly) Pająkówna, to whom Przybyszewski wrote: "I have never borne so pure an image of a woman in my soul . . . I did not know that a woman could be like you." Przybyszewski did not make fiction out of this subsidiary adventure, a surprising omission, although, tormented by guilt as usual, he remained devoted to his daughter by Nelly, his "dearest, sweetest Stachulina," to whom he dared to write only when "the woman who calls herself my wife" was away from home. The sentence is from a letter of May 1927, a few months before his death.

In his correspondence Przybyszewski had long complained that he was old and tired; his last novel, *Krzyk* (1917) or *Der Schrei* (1918), was written in Munich, at a time when he gave vent to his strongly pro-German views on the First World War in *Polen und der heilige Krieg* (1915, Poland and the Holy War) and *Von Polens Seele* (1917, On Poland's Soul). In the first of these polemics he expresses the hope that a nation with such a strong sense of justice as Germany would recognize the "terrible sacrifices" the Poles had made as a vanguard of the Central Powers; the second is an effort to describe the Polish cultural world to the Germans. *Der Schrei,* whose original may have been in German (nearing completion in 1914–15), was an effort to reawaken an awareness of his presence in the German cultural world; it clearly belongs to German expressionism, as the title and the contents indicate. The artist Gasztowt wants to paint the cry of a woman whom he first saves from drowning and then, to recapture her cry, again throws into the waters of an unnamed river. (Gasztowt is also obsessed by the project of painting the horrors of "The Street.") *Der Schrei* has elements, too, of the literature of an earlier age — recollections of Knut Hamsun's *Sult* (Gasztowt is starving) and of the remarkable violin performance of Nagel in Hamsun's *Mysterier:* gorging himself on a restaurant meal for which he cannot pay, Gasztowt amazes the other guests by his virtuosity on the borrowed instrument of a café musician. Further, in Werylho, the somehow supernatural controller of Gasztowt's life, one may sense a satanic figure possessing supernatural powers (like Dracula, he changes at need into a coachman), and of strong aesthetic tastes (the owner of a marvelous apartment, filled with precious jewels and rare weapons). A tempter, Werylho wants, he says, to make Gasztowt, through the latter's art, into God. Dream or reality, Gasztowt shoots him with an ordinary sort of pistol, perhaps a statement of Przybyszewski's renunciation, finally, of his overreaching and altogether undisciplined artist ambitions.

During the second half of the nineteenth century, in Germany and elsewhere, what passed for calm was disturbed by an epidemic of political assassinations and terrorist bombings: the attempt of Felice Orsini to assassinate Napoleon III and Eugénie in Paris on January 14, 1858 (the bombs thrown at their carriage killed 10 spectators and injured 150); the two attempts on the life of the Emperor Wilhelm I in May and June 1878, which caused Bismarck to put through the so-called Sozialistengesetz (albeit neither would-be perpetrator was a Socialist); the assassination of Czar Alexander II in 1881; the Phoenix Park murders in Dublin in 1882; the planned killing of the assembled German princes, including Wilhelm I and Crown Prince Friedrich, at the unveiling of the Niederwalddenkmal (the Germania Monument) in 1883; the casting of bombs into residences of judges who had officiated at anarchist trials in Paris, by François-Claudius Koenigstein, alias "Ravachol," in 1893 (a deed sending "pious citizens into Abraham's bosom," according to Falk in *Im Malstrom*); Edmond Vaillant's bomb thrown in the Chamber of Deputies in 1893 (his execution was transformed in Zola's *Paris* into the guillotining of Salvat); Émile Henry's ghastly deed against "peaceful and anonymous persons" in 1894, generously interpreted by Falk in *Unterwegs;* the stabbing of President Sidi Carnot of France by the Italian anarchist Caserio at Lyon in 1894; the murder of the Spanish minister of state Canevas del Castillo in 1897, again by an Italian anarchist; the stabbing of Empress Elizabeth of Austria by the anarchist Luccheni on the Geneva pier in 1898, a violent death of this "Goddess of the Dream" memorialized by D'Annunzio in a splendid oration, then translated by Loris (Hofsmannsthal); the shooting of Umberto I of Italy by the anarchist Cresci in 1900; the slaughter, by army officers, of Alexander I of Serbia and Queen Draga at Belgrade's royal palace in 1903; the assassination (with dumdum bullets) of the Russian governor general Bobrikoff on the staircase of Finland's senate on June 17, 1904; the killing of V. K. Plehve, Russia's minister of the interior, on July 28, 1904; the killing of Grand Duke Sergei, the czar's great uncle, by a bomb thrown in the Kremlin on February 17, 1905; the killing of Carlo I of Portugal and the heir apparent in Lisbon in 1908; the shooting by the socialist Hjalmar Wång of the Swedish major general Otto Beckman in Kungsträdgården as he accompanied Nicholas II of Russia and Maria Alexandrovna on a tour of Stockholm in June 1909; the fatal shooting of Peter Stolypin, the president and minister of the interior, in the czar's presence at the Kiev City Theater in September 1911 (after a bomb attack on his country home in 1906, in which twenty-seven people were killed); the assassination of Archduke Franz Ferdinand and his wife at Sarajevo by Gavrilo Prinčip on June 28, 1914 — and the list could be amplified. Some of the deeds were the work of patriots, Orsini in Paris, the "Invincibles" in Phoenix Park, the Finlander Eugen Schauman, the Serb Prinčip; the majority were attributed to socialists or anarchists, words often and loosely interchanged, and seemed to be part of a vast European conspiracy.

Such public murder was fascinating, as might be expected, to literary men: its hallmarks, apart from sudden and violent death itself, were the mentality of the killer(s), slaying as it were impersonally, and the suspense, the waiting for the shots to be fired, the bombs go to off. The reader, further, knows something that the intended victim does not know, yet cannot be sure that the deed will take place. In *The Devils* (1871), Dostoyevsky, creating the fountainhead of the subgenre, is principally interested in the nature of the conspirators; he was able to make numerous and quite distinct portraits, not only of the enigmatic Stavrogin and the vain Verkhovensky, but of the other members of Verkhovensky's inner circle, Liputin, Virginsky, Lyamshin, Shigalov, Erkel, and the main disciples of Stavrogin, the engineer Kirillov and the principled Shatov, eventually murdered by the conspirators at Verkovensky's orders. In Alphonse Daudet's *Tartarin sur les Alpes* (1885), the bumbling hero becomes involved with Russian "nihilists" plotting the murder of Czar Alexander III. Henry James's *Princess Casamassima* (1886) moves slowly through anarchist circles, and ends with the suicide of the sensitive designated assassin, Hyacinth Robinson. In Germany the salon radical Mackay employed *Die Anarchisten: Ein Kulturgemälde aus dem Ende des 19. Jahrhunderts* (1891, The Anarchists: A Cultural Portrait from the End of the Nineteenth Century) to allow his main characters to debate at great length — the thoughtful Carran Auban, converted to peaceful resistance while in prison (like Przybyszewski's Czerski later on), and his friend and opponent Otto Trupp, the unrelenting advocate of violence. (Mackay's anarchists closely follow the trials and executions coming out of the Chicago Haymarket bombings of 1886; a chief event in the novel is "Bloody Sunday," November 13, 1887, when police and troops attacked peaceful demonstrators at Trafalgar Square — an event which, in its fictional turn, brought about the great change in England described by William Morris in his utopian romance *News from Nowhere* [1890].) Another German work, *Roman aus der Décadence* (1901, Novel from the Decadence) of Kurt Martens, has as a secondary theme to the would-be decadents alluded to by the title's key word, the Russian anarchist Dimitri Teniawsky, who cannot bring himself to hurl a bomb into the audience at Leipzig's Gewandhaus. Martens is very skillful at recreating Teniawsky's torments; the Russian decides to work for a bloodless and peaceful revolution. In his two novels about the decline of royalty, *Majesteit* (1893) and *Wereldvrede* (1894), Louis Couperus inserted a subplot about the activities of an anarchist, including the assassination of a monarch during a performance of *Aïda;* like Mackay and Martens, Couperus treats the serious aims of the anarchists respectfully, and their revolution almost succeeds. Andrei Bely's *Petersburg* (1913/1916/1922) hinges on the death of Plehve, and the half-hearted efforts of the son of a highly placed official to fulfill his promise to plant a bomb in his father's room — a summary that hardly does justice to what Nabokov numbered among the "greatest masterpieces of twentieth-century prose."

In English literature, where the suspense-and-detection potential of the theme was cultivated by major talents, but without the sympathy (Morris's *News from Nowhere* is an exception proving the rule) to be found in the continental works adduced, the examples are numerous. *The Dynamiters* (1895), partly by Robert Louis Stevenson, mostly by his American wife, Fanny de Grift, laughs nervously at the bumbling Fenians. For whatever reason, Sherlock Holmes confronts neither anarchists nor Fenians, although, in a single instance, "The Golden Pince-Nez," in *The Return of Sherlock Holmes* (1905), he becomes involved with Russian "reformers — revolutionists — Nihilists," the passionate and unwittingly murderous Anna and her treacherous husband, Professor Coram. In *Raffles: The Further Adventures of the Amateur Cracksman* (1901), by E. W. Hornung (Conan Doyle's brother-in-law), the evil foe of Raffles, Carollo — another Professor Moriarty — turns out to possess "the infernal apparatus revealing the fiendish acts of the anarchists." G. K. Chesterton created anti-anarchist comedy of a very high order in *The Man Who Was Thursday: A Nightmare* (1908), a fantastic spoof on the side of loving-kindness and order.

But not everything was entertainment, complacent or not, in the anarchist-inspired literature written in the British Isles. The attempt of a clerk, Martial Bourdin, to blow up the Greenwich Observatory, and Bourdin's mortal wounding, were turned, in Joseph Conrad's *Secret Agent* (1907), into the death of the simple-minded Stevie, persuaded by his foster uncle, the agent provocateur Verloc, to attempt to deliver the bomb. Verloc is murdered by Stevie's sister and Verloc's wife, who then commits suicide — carnage in the best tradition of *The Devils* and Przybyszewski's *Satan's Kinder.* Conrad's *Under Western Eyes* (1911) begins with the assassination of a Plehve figure and ends with the cruelly inventive revenge the conspirators take (in Geneva) on an informant. Martin Ross's Fenian story, "Two Sunday Afternoons," published posthumously in 1920 but written at least two decades earlier, concentrates on the terrorist act and its innocent victims; H. H. Munro's ("Saki's") bomb story "The Easter Egg" (1911) does the same.

During the First World War the anarchist terrorist is transformed, in entertainment literature, into the German spy, in John Buchan's *Thirty-Nine Steps* (1915) and in Christopher Morley's *Haunted Bookshop* (1919): President Wilson, sailing to the Paris peace conference, is to be given a copy of Carlyle's *Cromwell,* hollowed out, containing a bomb. Horne Fisher, G. K. Chesterton's *Man Who Knew Too Much* (1922), dies crying, "God Save England," as the island nation is first made rotten and then invaded by "dirty foreigners," Jews and Germans. However, we are asked to believe that England will be rescued by Irish regiments, who march into battle with the English, singing Fenian songs. Earlier in the same book, Chesterton — who became a Roman Catholic in the year of its publication — inserts a tribute to the "vanishing prince," Michael O'Neill, that is, Michael Collins. The villain of the piece is a Cockney police officer; *The Man Who Knew Too Much* is filled with intimations of British decay, high and low. In the more firmly patriotic Buchan's *Three Hostages* (1924), the intrepid Richard Hannay (from *The Thirty-Nine Steps* and *Greenmantle*) rescues the hostages kidnapped by "the handsomest being alive," Dominick Medina, "déraciné Irish," no "common anarchist" but a mastermind intending to achieve world control or world destruction, "whose hatred of Britain was only part of his hatred of all that most men hold in love and repute." The anarchist terrorist of long ago has lost his roots altogether, eventually to be replaced by Ian Fleming's Dr. No and Goldfinger (Sax Rohmer's Dr. Fu Manchu is a way station on the path to them), while Hannay (and Chesterton's chaste-mannered Gabriel Syme and Rohmer's Shan Greville) have been replaced by the supervirile James Bond.

Before writing *Satans Kinder,* Przybyszewski had studied *The Devils,* as Maxime Herman proved (1939), and was no doubt aware of Mackay's *Die Anarchisten.* In the anarchist-terrorist novel's heyday, common features were the persuasive will of a leader and the hesitation, fear, and incompetence of his followers. The organizer Gordon's forces consist first of all of the siblings Stefan Wronski and Pola Wronska; both are slavishly devoted to the imposing Gordon — Pola has become his lover, and murmurs, " 'You, you, my god,' " as he distractedly embraces her. A sometime student of municipal archaeology, Wronski shows a similar adoration: " 'For me you are the greatest being — you are a god,' " and, " 'My lord, my master.' " His abject devotion — his language resembles that of Renfield to Dracula — comes in part from Gordon's encouraging him to carry out his old plan of revenge against a society that has abandoned him: he is in the last stages of tuberculosis. The plutocrat Cortum has refused him the money to have his illness treated and to carry on with his studies. But he is still more in awe of Gordon because of his notion (" 'You, you are the great prince of darkness' ") that Gordon is Satan himself. Hesitatingly, he questions Gordon about satanic rites, but Gordon's answers are evasive: " 'I speak only aesthetically.' " In his curiosity, Wronski asks Gordon if the "Palladists" practice " 'unnatural sexual intercourse as a kind of sacrament.' " (Wronski alludes to the polemics, carried on in numerous widely read publications, by "Léo Taxil" [Gabriel Jogand-Pagès], against the Freemasons, charging that a secret Masonic body, "the Order of the Palladium," worshipped Satan and conducted human sacrifice and sexual orgies as a part of its ritual. At the ball in Bely's *Petersburg,* an anti-Semitic editor holds forth on his notion that "Jewish Freemasonry" belongs to the Palladists and is planning to sacrifice Russia to Satan.) Deflecting Wronski's specific query, Gordon — citing the title of the novel — admits to a central, nominal satanic element in his beliefs: " 'We are all Satan's children . . . Life itself is Satan's empire,' " and " 'those who are afraid, in despair' " will be his followers. Although Wronski, growing briefly restless, charges Gordon with aestheticism in his satanism (to which Gordon admits) and a vague mysticism, he says that he will remain loyal to his master all the same, who has made him a " 'priest of atheism.' " His one plea to Gordon is that the master will allow him to participate in the "great destruction" of the city where they live, and to be annihilated with it.

The same year as *Satans Kinder* appeared, Przybyszewski published a historical account of satanism, *Synagoge des Satan: Ihre Entstehung, Einrichtung und jetzige Bedeutung* (The Synagogue of Satan: Its Origin, Arrangement, and Present Meaning), a brief and dryly informative account of the result of Przybyszewski's studies of the complex phenomenon. His respectable publisher, Fontane, must have thought of the pamphlet as a profitable ancillary text. Like Gordon, Przybyszewski — the great poseur — put on quasi-diabolical attitudes and gladly displayed his knowledge of the field; but in *Satans Kinder* there are no detailed references to the cult, except in Wronski's leading question about the homosexual practices of the "Palladists"; there are no black masses, none of the revelations which made Huysmans's *Là-bas,* well known to Przybyszewski, such sensational reading. Gordon's Satan's Children are simply the disadvantaged or abused masses whom he plans to employ in his program of destruction of the city. Gordon's satanism is play-acting before his handful of adherents — as is his reductionist Superman pose: " 'I am I.' "

Gordon's other locally recruited aide is Ostap, whose father is a bookkeeper at the city hall; from him, Gordon wants models of the keys to the municipal safe. Terrified of arrest, Ostap is as much a fragile reed as Wronski;

like Wronski, he admires Gordon, but at the same time detests him. An erotic motive, never far to seek in Przybyszewski, lies at the root of his hatred: Ostap is in love with Hela Mierzeska, a physician's daughter, but knows that during a stay at anarchist headquarters in London, she has been Gordon's mistress. However, Gordon has cast Hela aside, for reasons he quite willingly reveals to Ostap and to Hela herself: she has belonged to someone else before becoming Gordon's lover, and so, in Gordon's mind, is polluted. Ostap attributes Gordon's sudden revulsion to his " 'yearning for beauty.' " Gordon agrees: " 'The woman always belongs, unconsciously or consciously, to her first [lover] . . . and to take a woman in whose soul the first lover remains, is ugly.' " Meeting Hela in her apartment, Gordon repeats his argument, more brutally still: " 'What you gave me was really no gift . . . It cost you nothing — you soul is evil.' " He suffers under the rupture, but " 'only aesthetically' " — from a sense of aesthetic loss: turning a girl into a woman in her initial act of love, is " 'for me the highest beauty,' " but, he tells her, " 'You do not know what beauty is.' " At the end of this third conversation, after those with Wronski and Ostap, Gordon — "indifferently," a word repeatedly used to describe his behavior — says he will marry Pola. Hela slaps his face, a blow that will have consequences; Hela tells Pola what she has done to the latter's god, and Gordon directly loses his aura of greatness in Pola's eyes.

Gordon's plot, slovenly hatched, succeeds, and the provincial city where the events take place is, if not destroyed, very badly damaged. The city itself seems to be Gnesen (Gniezno) or Posen (Poznań), so identified through the references to the cult of St. Adalbert (Wojciech), whose putative remains are an ornament of the cathedral in Posen. A special appeal is made to the saint by a zealous young priest as the catastrophes in the unnamed city mount up. Topographical details are few and far between; the social structure of the town is hastily sketched. The holders of power are the ineffectual mayor (the uncle of the principal plotter, Gordon), the factory owner Schnittler, who routinely seduces the young girls he employs (quite like the factory owner in Bang's *De uden Fædreland*), and Cortum, whose mansion, like the Schnittler factory and the city hall, will fall victim to the revolutionaries. Gordon himself, wealthy in his own right, maintains an apartment in town and an estate nearby. He has no first name, but his patronymic alludes to George Gordon, Lord Byron, to whom his accomplice Ostap compares him; he has been an amateur poet and likes to give himself a dramatic and romantic air. By torching the city, Gordon intends not to effect the end of an old and rotten social order, but to bring about destruction for its own sake. " 'I mean to destroy not in order to build up again, but only in order to destroy . . . Destruction is my dogma, my belief, the objection of my veneration.' " Later, as the city burns, he hopes for: "Still more! Still more! To destroy whole cities, whole provinces, a whole country, the world. That would be great joy."

His intentions collide with those of Hartmann, an engineer and terrorist who, come from abroad (Gordon has met him through anarchist circles in London), has obtained employment in Schnittler's factory; Hartmann claims that he is not in fact an anarchist (they are "people of emotion"), but a reformer, a man of sheer reason who loves "all human beings": "'I believe in the power of the brain, and the power of the conscious will, which can introduce new economic systems.'" Gordon retorts: "'You want to destroy what exists because you have a new system.'" Once the existent social world has been done away with, Gordon will gladly leave it up to Hartmann to shape the future according to his principles. But the process of destruction will continue forever. Gordon destroys because he hates: "'And my hatred is holier than your love, for you have love in your brain. My hatred is older and deeper, because it existed before all love. Lucifer existed before the world, which has arisen from love.'"

The terrorists from the outside, the rational Hartmann and the professionally cool Botko, are not affected by Gordon's satanic posing, in contrast to the credulous members of Gordon's local circle. Ostap's emotional lability — he repeatedly falls into fainting fits, like Falk, after moments of excitement — may have its source in a terrible event hinted at by Gordon in their initial interview as a cause of Ostap's paralyzing fear of punishment. No more is told until well along (Book 2, chap. 7), when the drunken Ostap, at a rendezvous with Gordon in a brothel, confesses: "'Gordon, I have killed a child . . . my own child.'" Still later (Book 3, chap. 5), Ostap recalls that the cry of "a child" cut into his ears, and so he decided to kill it, pouring a pitcher of ice-cold water over it: "The child stopped screaming." The passage bears a startling resemblance to the deed of Tullio Hermil in D'Annunzio's *L'Innocente* (1892), who kills his child, on Christmas Eve, by exposing the boy on a windowsill to the night air. (*L'Innocente*, translated into French by Georges Hérelle, was published as *L'Intrus* in 1893.) Whether or not Przybyszewski took the episode from D'Annunzio cannot be determined. After recalling the murder, Ostap falls into the longest of his several syncopes. Awakened by Hartmann, come to congratulate him on the success of their joint venture in stealing the funds at city hall, he listens to Hartmann's story of a friend in London who experienced a similar fit of what Hartmann calls lethargy; two days later, the friend kills himself. Does Hartmann intend, by suggestion, to get this half-demented and drunken accomplice out of the way? The same evening, amidst the fires and outbursts of violence that have swept over the city, Ostap hangs himself at Gordon's estate.

The nature of Ostap's love-hate relationship with Gordon (why has he gone to Gordon's estate to end his life?) requires some further elucidation. In the continuation of the brothel scene (Book 2, chaps. 7–8), Ostap remembers a "beautiful" poem written by Gordon during their schooldays together, in which the youthful poet asked God for a " 'suffering greater and holier than that of His great son' . . . 'You love beauty, You yourself are beautiful in your dreams,' " and " 'In you there is something of Alexander the Great, of Byron, of Charles XII.' " The last name in the quasi encomium particularly fascinates Ostap: he calls Gordon " 'a degenerate criminal genius . . . a Charles XII.' " He has long thought, he adds, about "the riddle called Gordon" before solving it, uttering a historical cadenza about the Swedish warrior-king (1682–1718): he was the " 'poor aesthetician' " who ruined his country and others with his love of destruction, who was an incendiary, writing to his sister that he had " 'just roasted a couple of thousand people in Stralsund.' " Ostap's thoughts swerve off into the question of the king's sexuality, bringing up his " 'little, painted girl's face, precisely like yours' " (Gordon's) and Charles's famous virginity. (Ostap's cataloguing of the peculiarities of Charles is directly contemporary to Verner von Heidenstam's ambiguous novella cycle, *Karolinerna* [1897–98, *The Charles Men,* 1920], and precedes Strindberg's play about the cruel and demented Charles [1901] and Rilke's "Charles XII of Sweden Rides in the Ukraine" [1902] about Charles's aesthetic love of war and killing. The theme lay in the air.) Babbling, Ostap comes close suggesting that Gordon is homosexual: " 'And do you know he never had a woman, I mean physically. Do you know that? I'm not sure whether you . . . Hela, ha, ha, Hela! That was a sort of mystical marriage.' " These aspersions may arise from Ostap's jealousy, or from the same suspicions which may be read into Wronski's questioning about the practices of the Palladists.

Przybyszewski has made a case for Gordon as an almost classic decadent with traits of Des Esseintes's, Sperelli's, and Dorian's cruel manipulations, with the sudden fits of inertia like those characteristic of Dracula and Sherlock Holmes, with his often stated and observed "aestheticism," with the whiffs of homosexuality (looking at Hartmann's hands, Gordon notices how "slender and beautiful" they are). Gordon also has a (barely indicated) decadent life style, in the manner of Des Esseintes at Fontenay-aux-Roses: well-heeled, Gordon maintains his principal residence at the estate outside the city, taken care of by two elderly servants. Yet, perhaps because of Przybyszewski's aversion to detail, other facets of the decadent protagonist are lacking: there is no demonstrated interest in the artifacts of decadence (furnishings, paintings, literary or ecclesiastical works), not even in Przybyszewski's favorite illustrator, Rops. The possible borrowing of lethal behavior from *L'Innocente* falls to Ostap, not Gordon. Quite as in the case of his predecessor Falk in *Homo*

Sapiens, there are no indications of how Gordon dresses, what his rooms look like, what his reading has been. Gordon is consumed by his desire for destruction, an aesthete of anarchism, an "evil philosopher," in the words of Gabriel Syme, the nemesis of the anarchist band in *The Man Who Was Thursday,* conspirators "not trying to alter things but to annihilate them."

"Die Tat" (The Deed), the novel's third megachapter, is a topsy-turvy chronicle of the conflagrations, explosions, and ensuing popular uprising planned by Gordon; but now Gordon is only a spectator, enjoying what he sees. The city hall burns and Wronski with it, the Cortum villa is ignited by Wronski's cousin Franz, a cheerful extra of whom nothing else is learned, the factory of Schnittler is likewise burned by Franz or Hartmann, the workers take over the center of the city, a shopkeeper is lynched, the red flag is raised, and fire departments and troops from the outside are summoned too late — echoes of the fire which consumes a whole suburb near the end of *The Devils* can be heard here. As for Gordon, doing nothing, "an animal joy filled him," he had "the feeling of destruction." But a second, smaller fire will be set by Gordon himself at the barn on his estate; he and the external agent Botko carry the suicide Ostap's body into the barn to incinerate it. Botko is dispatched to London with a message: " 'Tell the idiots . . . that my only dogma is destruction.' " The stage is strewn with corpses: Pola, who has fallen ill, is brought to the estate and dies from the shock of seeing Ostap's dangling body; another tool of Gordon, Okonen, who has delivered a revolutionary speech to the mob (written by an unknown hand, perhaps Gordon's) comes under suspicion from Botko, who assumes that he will reveal all if arrested and interrogated. Okonen is told by a stranger (Botko) that Gordon will meet him in the woods with a passport and money. Instead — no longer the supreme manager of events but afraid for his own hide — Gordon beats Okonen and drowns him in a swamp. Gordon is not "the last aristocrat" the cool-minded Hartmann once thought him to be. After learning from Hela that Pola is dead, Gordon, relieved, looks at the barn which will be Ostap's crematorium, and his spirits perk up: " 'Then I shall be free for a new deed.' " With Botko, Gordon has discussed a new effort at destruction " 'next year,' " this time probably without the aid of the oppressed masses. Gordon will call on the "children of Satan" only as he needs them.

Richard Schaukal wrote that Gordon "rules and conquers like a demon, piling up atrocities which do not move the reader. Here, an author, out of control, has come a cropper." (However, *Satans Kinder* got a strange sort of compliment from the proto-expressionist poet Ferdinand Hardekopf, who took "Stefan Wronski" as his nom de plume.) Much in *Satans Kinder* is frustrating: the loose ends (e.g., a Father Sciegenny, to be enlisted for next year's effort, is mentioned in passing), the insubstantiality of the city, the incomplete portraits (Hela, Pola, Ostap, Botko, Hartmann, Franz, and Okonen), the repeated outbursts of extreme emotion — the fits of fainting or narcolepsy of Gordon and Ostap, Ostap's biting the throat of Hela and Wronski's fear that Ostap will bite *him* as well, the ubiquitous foaming at the mouth. The root of the egomaniac Gordon's overwhelming urge "to destroy" is left, perhaps intentionally, in the dark. If he is a Satan, then he becomes a notably timorous one. All the same, in his plans for the future, there lies something of the prayer at the close of the Tridentine mass: that Saint Michael the Archangel will thrust into hell "Satanam aliosque spiritus malignos qui ad perditionem animarum pervagantur in mundo" ("Satan and the other evil spirits who wander about in the world, seeking the ruin of souls"), a text Przybyszewski had repeatedly heard in his Roman Catholic boyhood. Also, less infernally as far as Gordon is concerned, Przybyszewski had read Émile Henry's widely disseminated speech in the dock before his execution, paraphrased in *Unterwegs;* Henry told how, having failed to prevent the guillotining of Ravachol, he went to London and Brussels before the bombing at the Gare Saint Lazare.

Like so many other authors of the decadence, Przybyszewski was a master of self-dramatization, quite in the fashion of D'Annunzio, Wilde, Bang, Valle-Inclán, and even Couperus; like Wilde, like Bang, he became a figure of fun, much caricatured by his contemporaries: for the poet Detlev von Liliencron, he was the "Chopin pianist," "Mr. Prrttttczrczczrczrczrczrrrzzewski" — his unpronounceable name was a source of primitive merriment to Germans. For Strindberg, he was the ubiquitous Popoffsky in the writings of the so-called *Inferno* crisis, entertaining designs on Strindberg's life, even turning up as late as *Svarta fanor* (1907), where he was reduced to an accessory bogy, overshadowed by new objects of Strindberg's obsessive hatred, Gustaf af Geijerstam and Ellen Key. For Otto Julius Bierbaum in the Berlin-Bohème section of *Stilpe: Ein Roman aus der Froschperspektive* (1897, Stilpe: A Novel from a Frog's Perspective), he was "Kasimir, the fugue organist," an "altogether wild Pole, full of demonism as well as the arts of hot air." For Arno Holz in the comedy *Sozialdemokraten* (1896, Social Democrats), he was the cigarette-cadging journalist Styczinski; for Wilhelm von Polenz, in the anti-decadent *Wurzellocker* (1902, Rootloose), he was Michael Chubsky, an author in French, German, and Polish, a friend of Oscar Wilde and Félicien Rops, an "intellectual companion" to Strindberg, Ola Hansson, and Hermann Bahr, an imitator of Verlaine, Poe, and Huysmans, and an essayist on sexuality (investigating "the perverse in all directions, especially where it bordered on the religious") as well as on sadism, Satanism, and the occult. An absinthe addict, epicure, and deadbeat, Chubsky visits the protagonist of *Wurzellocker* — who has just made his own debut with a novel called *Das Geschlecht* (Sex) — while on his way to Kraków, and orders a huge gourmet dinner, for which his host has to pay. For Max Dauthendey in *Maja: Skandinavische Boheme-Komödie* (1911, Maja: Scandinavian Bohème-Comedy), he was Loge (after the tricky Wagnerian god of fire), "a Bohemian writer," and a compulsive womanizer; for Bruno Wille, in his reminiscence of early Berlin days, *Das Gefängnis zum preußischen Adler* (1914, The Prison at the Sign of the Prussian Eagle), he was "the noble Pole from Polackia," drunken but ever gallant (in contrast to Strindberg). For Thomas Mann in the penultimate chapter of *Der Zauberberg* (1924), "Die große Gereizheit" ("The Great Irritation"), he was the hypersensitive Stanisław Zutawski, enraged at the insulting remarks made by another Pole about the morals of his wife Jadwiga. Considering Przybyszewski's own extensive use of himself, his wives, and his acquaintances in his creative work, it seems only fair that he should have had to endure this second, parodied life in Swedish and German letters.

14

Wales

ARTHUR MACHEN

Arthur Machen (1863–1947) was the son of John Edward Jones, an Anglican clergyman; his mother's maiden name was Machen, and by the terms of an inheritance, Reverend Jones added her name to his, thus Jones-Machen. The author dropped the nondescript first element. Machen's birthplace was Caerleon-on-Usk in Monmouthshire, from 1974 officially called by its Welsh name, Gwent, after the post-Roman kingdom between the Usk and the Wye, the border with England; his father was rector of the little church at Llanddewi Fach, within easy walking distance of Caerleon. In *Far Off Things* (1922), Machen wrote: "I shall always esteem it as the greatest piece of fortune that has fallen to me, that I was born in that noble, fallen Caerleon-on-Usk, in the heart of Gwent . . . When my eyes were first opened in earliest childhood they had before them the vision of an enchanted land." Returning from London in 1884 to spend the summer in Gwent, he visited Caerleon, "drank old ale at the Hanley Arms . . . a medieval hostelry, close to the Roman tower by the river," and walked to the hamlet of Usk, "over the river; on the right are King Arthur's Round Table and the relics of the Roman wall of Isca Silurum, as the Second Augustan Legion, garrisoned at Caerleon, called the place." In the autobiography's continuation, *Things Near and Far* (1923), Machen again remembered Caerleon, "shining, beautiful, a little white city in a dream"; in *Dog and Duck* (1924) Machen boasted that "the Second Augustan Legion . . . made a tiny

Rome of the place, with amphitheatre, baths, temples, and everything necessary for the comfort of a Roman-Briton . . . I suppose the Second Augustan
was recalled somewhere about A.D. 400." In *Notes and Queries* (1926) he
announced — if his readership did not know it already — that he was "a citizen
of what was once no mean city . . . Caerleon on Usk, once the splendid Isca
Silurum, once the headquarters of the Second Augustan Legion. And, then,
again a golden mist of legend grew about it, it became the capital of King
Arthur's court of faerie and enchantment." The same year, Machen confided
to his fellow transplanted Welshman, Ernest Rhys, that his native town had
become "an agonising spectacle . . . It has a training college, three stink factories, and a madhouse . . . It is, in fact, as a man told me, 'a progressive little
place.' It is, indeed, it progresses swiftly to *uffern du* [black inferno]." Machen
liked to show off his fragments of Welsh.

Geoffrey of Monmouth, in the twelfth century, celebrated Caerleon as the
place chosen by Arthur for placing the crown of Britain on his head: "By the
gold painted gables of its roofs it was a match for Rome"; Giraldus Cambren-
sis, passing through the "City of the Legions," recorded that many vestiges of
its sometime splendor could still be seen; it is mentioned time and again in the
Mabinogion as Arthur's chief court. Tennyson stayed at the Hanley Arms,
seeking local color for *Idylls of the King,* but "old Caerleon" was shouldered
out by imaginary Camelot. A couple of years before Tennyson's unproductive
visit, George Borrow, working on *Wild Wales,* left Caerleon out of his itinerary, and stayed instead at Newport, which "stands some miles below Caerleon, and was probably built when that place, at one time one of the most
considerable towns in Britain, began to fall into decay." Machen revived the
reputation of Caerleon with *The Hill of Dreams,* but the little town hardly
achieved the stature of Venice or Bruges; it was out of the way and had too
little to offer. Its rank among the magic sites of decadence is like that of Aigues-
Mortes, which got its small nimbus through Maurice Barrès's *Le Jardin de
Bérénice.*

Reflections of Machen's Caerleon youth are readily spotted in the first chapter of *The Hill of Dreams.* Lucian Taylor, twelve years old and the son of an
impecunious clergyman in the Welsh countryside near Caermaen (Caerleon),
is on Christmas holiday. His school experiences have not been unhappy, except for teasing by his classmates because of his Latinate name, hypocorized
into "Lucy"; his out-of-the-way literary interests, in medieval Latin and Vil-
lon, are criticized by his teachers: "Healthy English boys should have nothing
to do with decadent periods." (Machen attended the Hereford Cathedral
School from eleven to seventeen and thrived; however, in *The Secret Glory*
[1922] Ambrose Meyrick, a later Lucian, is badly treated by his headmaster

for his aberrant tastes in letters and his passion for the relics of the long vanished Celtic church.) On a stormy January afternoon, Lucian discovers a "narrow lane" that leads to an old Roman fort, but he does not take it. At fifteen (there is no chapter break), Lucian goes home in August at "a time of great heat." The white Welsh farmhouses "blaze . . . as if they stood in Arles or Avignon or famed Tarascon by Rhone," the town of Alphonse Daudet's *Tartarin de Tarascon*. Lucian has just purchased De Quincey's *Confessions of an English Opium Eater* at the railway station in Caermaen; fetching him, Reverend Taylor says he knows the book well — he read it many years before. "Indeed, he was almost as difficult to surprise as that character in Daudet, who had one formula for all the chances of life: 'J'ai vu tout ça,' " in other words old Jean Réhu in Daudet's *L'Immortel,* who has just seen his grandson-in-law, a member of the Academy, dragged out of the Seine, a suicide. The pair of allusions (to De Quincey and Daudet) has some significance; Mr. Taylor receives the news of his son's reading matter, which will turn out to be lethal, with the phlegm that characterizes his reception of Lucian's other, later revelations.

Lucian's "one adventure of the holidays" is a visit to the Roman fort; after the steep ascent in the heat of the day, Lucian strips off his clothes and lies down: "Suddenly, it seemed, he lay in the sunlight, beautiful with his olive skin, dark haired, dark eyed, the gleaming bodily vision of a strayed faun"; he feels both ecstatic and frightened. (*Ecstasy* would become a key word in Machen's literary criticism: see *Hieroglyphics* [1902].) He falls asleep and, on waking up, has a dim memory of a "visitant" with "dark eyes" and "scarlet lips that kissed him." Running home, he shows his father a nettle that stung him on the way up to the fort; Mr. Taylor identifies it as a Roman nettle, *urtica pilulifera*. Lucian does not dare to approach the fort again, but in his wanderings turns in at Mr. Morgan's White House Cottage and is hospitably received by Annie Morgan, the daughter of the house; on the January afternoon of the book's beginning, he thought he saw her in the woods. She is now eighteen, a "grown woman," and he wonders if he would have the courage to kiss her. At seventeen, like Machen, he is removed from school by his father, who is unable to afford the fees. He spends his time at home, musing and reading, but still avoids the fort; the "vision of such ecstasies frightened him." He begins to write, but it seems impossible for him "to win the great secret of language": the struggle will torment him for the remainder of the narrative.

By the second chapter, Lucian is twenty-three, still at home; his manuscript, submitted to a publisher, has been issued as *The Green Chorus,* under the name of a well-known author: of the two hundred pages in the "pretty little volume, about ninety were Lucian's". (At this point, Machen leaves autobiography behind for a time; he moved to London at nineteen, to try his hand as a literary free-lance, going to Caerleon only on short visits. His father declared bankruptcy the next year, and Machen lived in London from hand to mouth.) On his way back from the Caermaen postoffice, Lucian is shown a shortcut across the fields by a friendly doctor on his rounds; at a distance, he sees the amphitheater and the wall of the cantonment and, hearing a bugle somewhere, has a vision of Roman legionaries on the march; "As the trumpet sounded, the hill fort above the town gave up its dead" (an effect to be used by Vaughan William in the *London* Symphony [1911–18] and by Respighi in *The Pines of Rome* [1923–24]). The Roman trumpet is described as " 'tuba mirum spargens sonum,' " a line from the thirteenth-century *Dies irae* that is chronologically jarring but effective. Once again, Lucian is seized by panic and the memory of "the hour in the matted thicket" of eight years before; he feels the sting of the Roman nettle. He encounters Annie Morgan, who embraces him, saving him from his sense of having "sinned against the earth." A strong hint of guilt about a boyhood masturbatory experience lies in his memory of himself in the fort: "A faun with tingling and pricking flesh [who] lay expectant in the sunlight, and . . . also the likeness of a miserable shamed boy, standing with trembling body and shaking, unsteady hands." Now, his black hair is already graying, although his skin is still olive, like Annie's. When he comes home, his father is mildly concerned about his son's purloined manuscript and, as mildly, admires his good looks — he was "very handsome; he had such kind, gentle eyes and a kind mouth, and his pale cheeks were flushed like a girl's." Mr. Taylor does not know that Lucian's excitement derives from his intimacy with Annie.

The third chapter consists of the aftermath of that very brief affair; Annie leaves to visit a married sister, and Lucian will never see her again. He constructs a cult, of abject adoration and self-flagellation, sleeping on "a bed of thorns and spines." "The pale skin was red with the angry marks of blood, and the graceful form of the young man appeared like the body of a tortured martyr." In chapter 5 he will learn that Annie has wed a farmer to whom she has long been engaged; he takes the news at first with "amusement, mingled with gratitude," and, in his clumsy bookishness, makes "an analogy between [Milton's *Lycidas*] and Annie, loving poem and woman alike, despite their faults." At Caermaen, he is seized by a hatred of humanity, with which he has "almost lost his sense of kinship," a hatred increased by the hanging of a puppy, for amusement, by a group of town boys. He takes up the monastic "limner's art," re-creating medieval manuscripts, and longs for some "hermitage in the mountains, far above the stench and the sound of humanity." In his exalted repugnance, he makes repeated visits to Caermaen's Roman remains, the amphitheater and the museum, although not to the dangerous fort, and attempts to rebuild, in his mind, the "splendid and golden city of Siluria," even drawing a map of the town, "which he proposed to inhabit, in which every villa was set down and named." Chapter 4 provides a detailed view of his late-Roman paradise, laid out for "the delight of his sweetheart and himself." In London (chapters 5–7), Lucian, whose "sense of external things" has grown "dim and indistinct," faces up to the reality of a bed-sitting-room in a western suburb, "neither town nor country." His move to the metropolis has been made possible by an inheritance of two thousand pounds from an unknown cousin on the Isle of Wight. Repressing the experience of the fort, he shelters himself in the modern suburb against the siren voices of the "old wood whisper . . . or the singing of the faun"; grandiloquently, he sets out on the Great Adventure of Letters. Some time has passed since his imaginary summertime escapes to Siluria; he received the inheritance the next March and went to London in May, but by December he has accomplished nothing. He abandons verse (on the model of Coleridge's "Kubla Khan" and Poe's "Fairy-Land") for a "prose in which the music should be less explicit, of neumes rather than notes" (the alliterative reference is to notations in Gregorian chant), "a prose which should sound faintly, not so much with an audible music, but with the memory and echo of it."

In his autobiographies, Machen described his "cell," to which he withdrew after his "senseless wanderings" through London, still looking for the spark of his Great Romance. His *Anatomy of Tobacco* (1884) had been written in a "ten by six cell on Clarendon Road, Notting Hill Gate," the "well-remembered cell on Clarendon Road." Painstakingly, Machen totted up his moves from address to address (Wandsworth, Turnham Green, Bayswater); London had begun to "assume for [him] its terrible aspect. It was rather a goblin's castle than a city of delight; if it indeed had not become a place of punishment wherein I was condemned to hard labor through many dreary and hopeless years." All this is condensed in the later chapters of *The Hill of Dreams*. Neither the suburban streets nor his "hermitage" is a refuge; Lucian's "ruin and his grief were within," his inability to write, and in desperation he ventures out into the country, making for "remote and desolate places." He realizes that he has "lost the art of humanity forever"—he is "foreign and a stranger in the world," like Moses in Egypt, "a stranger in a strange land.'"

A severe winter descends on London; in this frozen world, Lucian "felt the approaches of madness," "convinced of his utter remoteness from all humanity." His gesticulations in the icy fog frighten a woman, who runs for dear life, children shout after him as he staggers like a drunken man, and back in his room he has to force himself to look into the mirror. No possibility of a textual connection exists, but Lucian's symptoms are like Borg's in the last chapter of *I havsbandet.* Also as in Borg's case, the sexual element in Lucian's dissolution becomes plain as he hangs about the road where he terrified the woman: "Her scream was a thing from the nocturnal Sabbath," and "he had perhaps repulsed a sister who would have welcomed him to the Sabbath," "the marriage of the Sabbath," the Witches' Sabbath. A Christmas letter from his father momentarily saves him from "such an obscene illusion, that he had gloated over the recollection of that stark mouth, filled him with disgust"; in the country, he is about to ask a farmer "driving his cattle home from the hill" to take him as a lodger, but, when he stretches out his hand to a little girl, she too runs away screaming. He returns to a London still in the grip of the great frost, as if "he strayed into a city that had suffered some unconscionable doom."

Despite his misery, Lucian keeps track of the calendar; February comes, the great frost lets up, and deciding that he is "wretched because he was an alien and a stranger amongst citizens," he goes out into the streets on a Saturday night. Shocked, he wonders if "De Quincey had also seen the same spectacle and concealed his impression out of reverence for the average reader." (Mark Valentine, in his biography of Machen, suggests that Machen may have drawn on James Thomson's *City of Dreadful Night* [1874]; the imagery also resembles that in a text published some twelve years after the composition of *The Hill of Dreams,* the Mardi Gras episode in Rilke's *Die Aufzeichnungen des Malte Laurids Brigge:* the Parisian crowds seem to copulate standing.) Instead of the English working class on its way to shop, Lucian finds "wonderful orgies, that drew out his heart to horrible music," "the Bacchic fury unveiled and unashamed," and he imagines that the revelers recognize him "as a fellow . . . in on the secret." Approached by a tall woman "with bronze hair," whose cheeks are "illuminate as she views the orgy," "with dark brown eyes . . . brightened with an argent gleam," he flees: "There was death in the woman's face, and she had indeed summoned him to the Sabbath." Abruptly, the narrative again praises Lucian's good looks, emaciated but with the "suggestion of a curious classic grace, and the look as of a faun." He spends a restless night, dreaming of what he has refused.

Sunday morning, the "horrid trams filled with impossible people" sober him. He returns to his desk. The jumble of Lucian's emotions — the awful Saturday night is turned into an antique drama in which "that woman was the consummation and catastrophe of it all" — is brought to earth as Lucian practices some private literary criticism. He could write another *Romola* but shuns "the shabby trick of imitating literature." Machen disliked George Eliot; *Romola* had made "the great host of the serious, the portentous, shout for joy"; the real historical novel, *The Cloister and the Hearth,* had been a comparative failure. Sometimes, particularly with the literary-critical digressions

(see *Lycidas* and Annie), the third-person account of Lucian's decay veers off
into De Quincey–like meandering.

The last chapter (7) opens as Lucian wakes from a "long and heavy torpor,"
the source of which has been half revealed at the end of chapter 6: a bottle of
dark blue glass stands on his mantle, before which Lucian "trembled and
shuddered as it were a fetish." Lying in bed, he reviews, piecemeal, the settings
of his pre-London life, the "dearly loved" and "beloved land" of Gwent, the
graves where the legionnaires wait for the trumpet, the "strange deserted city
mouldering into a petty village"; the experience on the hot day atop the "vast
hill" comes back as "the horrible Sabbath." He gets up and labors in despair at
his writing, "every line . . . doomed as soon as it was made"; he returns to the
resurrected legions — the trumpet blows: "The array was set for the last great
battle, behind the leaguer [i.e., camp] of the mist," a reminiscence of one of the
best-known lines in *Idylls of the King,* about the death of Arthur in "the last,
weird battle in the west." (Otherwise, Machen pays little attention to the
Arthurian legends attached to Caerleon, fixed as he is on the Roman-Celtic
past.) He goes on his final walks past "the last sentinel wavering lamp . . . the
edge and brim of London" and chances on "a poor and desolate house,"
surviving amidst the "vulgarity . . . greasiness . . . squalor" of the new London.
It appeals to him by its "sense of doom and horror." (Machen had a weakness
for the word "doom" as he did for houses that "bore outward signs of evil,"
the evil house in "Strange Occurrence in Clerkenwell" and the house where
"The Young Man with Spectacles" is tortured to death in *The Three Impostors.*) In his room he "images" the "old mouldering house in the field," remembering its "odor of decay, of the rank soil steaming, of rotting wood," and
almost "imagines" that the "air in his room was heavy and noisome, . . . with
some taint of the crypt." He finds another old house near his quarters: it has a
garden similarly decayed: "the laurels had grown into black skeletons, . . . the
ilex gloomed over the porch," and so forth. For Mark Valentine it is an ana-
logue, corrupted and dying, to the Garden of Avallaunius of chapter 4, and he
could have supported his argument by attention to the trees (laurels, ilex)
common to both places.

Lucian tries to put aside "the rich efflorescence of horrible decay" by means
of a fragment of the story of the Amber Venus, described with all the preciosity
of Huysmans in *À rebours:* one of her worshipers, "who has a fire of bronze
hair" like the street woman of February, empties her silver box containing
"chrysoberyl and sardonyx, opal and diamond, topaz and pearl" at the feet of
the goddess, before she disrobes. (It appears that Lucian has found a public,
however unfriendly. The "little tale of *The Amber Statuette,*" "by an author
utterly unknown," has been issued "in the springtime after his father's death

by a wholesale stationer and printer." The reviewers were "sadly irritated." Lucian's father died a year and a half after his son came to London, a blow that prostrated him. Machen's juvenile poem, *Eleusinia,* had been privately printed at Hereford in 1880, in one hundred copies; but Reverend Jones-Machen did not die until 1887. The whole passage is a semiautobiographical interjection.)

The offering to Venus brings back the orgy witnessed in February, and (Lucian's associations move fast) "the sad and sinister house" in the fields, followed by the Roman fort, which "surged up" with "hideous shapes" in the surrounding oaks. The memory of Annie, hitherto worshiped, begins to turn evil; he let her "drink his soul beneath the hill." The preposition "beneath" is accurate enough, meaning "at the foot of," "below," but it may also be a Venusberg echo from Beardsley, whose superdecadent tale of Venus and Tann-häuser, "Under the Hill," appeared in *The Savoy* in 1896. Lucian's visions and his physical state grow worse; he cannot move, "a heavy weight was on his head," and in his mind he wanders through the avenues of a city (his ideal Siluria) "ruined from ages," lying "desolate forever in the accursed plain" (a city of the plain, as in the Old Testament and Huysmans). Trying to get up from his chair, he beholds the Roman fort, with "the writhing boughs in a ring, and behind them a glow of heat and fire," the moment of Annie's transmogrifi-cation — "jets of fire issued from her breasts" — into the Queen of the Sabbath. Jovial Dr. Burrows in Caermaen — who in chapter 2 sent Lucian off on the shortcut through the fields to encounter Annie — returns to Lucian's imagina-tion in his last hours, whispering about the witch and mistress of witches, old Mrs. Gibbons, who, naked, accompanies the flame-shooting Annie as they urge Lucian "to mount the hill." (Before Annie met and "saved" him in the second chapter, "two unknown figures stood together in the darkness and tried the balance of his life and spoke his doom." Were they Annie and Mrs. Gibbons?) Lucian enters "the sanctuary of the infernal rite . . . to celebrate the wedding of the Sabbath." Annie becomes the woman with bronze hair and "argent flame in her eyes" and a "smile that froze his heart," whom he pursues into the "matted thicket" of the fort: "they writhed in the flames, insatiable, forever," and "in the sight of thousands." Lucian is overwhelmed by a great silence: he dies from an overdose of opium. In chapter 6, Lucian has "yielded to a temptation without having knowing that he had been tempted and in the manner of De Quincey had chosen the subtle in exchange for the more tangi-ble pain," that is, "he had yielded to the poisonous anodyne which was always at his hand," and he may have taken opium to encourage inspiration. Ma-chen's bête noire, the Puritan Dr. Stiggins in the polemic of that name (1906), despises "the distorted and unhealthy landscapes that presented themselves to the opium-drugged minds" of Poe and Coleridge.

In a coda, Lucian's landlady appears, her "splendid bronze hair" let down, her cheeks flushed, an "argent gleam" in her eyes. A leading motto of Machen's work is "Omnia exeunt in mysterium" (at his wish it was put on his tombstone), and the reader is left to guess that lonely Lucian has lusted after her and given her some physical features of the woman in the street. The landlady tells her companion or husband, Joe, that she has heard Dr. Manning — like herself mentioned only here — say that "he'd kill himself one of these days." The final sentence suggests another mystery: Lucian may still be only moribund: the light of the lamp "shone through the dead eyes into the dying brain, and there was a glow within, as if great furnace doors were opened."

The furnace doors are a reprise of the "great furnace doors" of the winter sun seen by twelve-year-old Lucian when he approached the fort for the first time: "Here and there it looked as if awful furnace doors were being opened"; before meeting Annie Morgan when he is fifteen, "a furnace fire shot up on the mountain"; after the physical contact with Annie, he wrote that "[he] burnt and glowed 'like coals of fire which hath a most vehement flame.'" (Lucian takes recourse to the Song of Solomon, 8:6, about love and jealousy.) Envisioning the Roman fort, it seems to Lucian "as if great furnace doors were opened"; when twilight changed the "huddled squalid village [Caerleon] into an unearthly city," the last "red light . . . blazed up from the furnace on the mountains." The prefinale, presumably born of Lucian's sexual deprivation and his opium addiction, pulls out all the stops; the Witches' Sabbath is even filled out with a repetition of the story of the Amber Venus: the woman with the bronze hair "drew out her hair pins of curious gold, and glowing brooches in enamel and poured out jewels before him from a silver box . . . Then she stripped from her body her precious robes, and stood in the glowing mist of her hair and held out her arms to him." According to Malcom Cowley, Harvard undergraduates thrilled to *Marius the Epicurean* and *The Hill of Dreams* in tandem; following on Pater's cool prose, the latter must have seemed an erethic extravaganza. Machen claimed to have read *Marius* only late in life and to have been disappointed.

The original title of *The Hill of Dreams* was *The Garden of Avallaunius*, the Latinate-Celtic name Machen gives his alter ego of chapter 4, derived from Avalon, the realm of the blest. The book was written in 1896–97, in London, during Machen's marriage to the amateur actress Amelia Huddleston; she died of cancer in 1899 and was apostrophized by Machen in the third volume of his autobiography, *The London Adventure, or The Art of Wandering* (1926), as "dear Cinara," from Horace's "Non sum qualis eram sub bonae regno Cinarae," lately popularized by Ernest Dowson's "Non Sum Qualis Eram." The years of the marriage had been productive; *The Great God Pan,* Machen's first popular success, was published in 1894, to which the similarly horrifying but shorter story "The Inmost Light" was added at the request of Machen's publisher, John Lane, who then brought out *The Three Impostors,* an amateur-detective novel, or set of novellas, the next year in his Keynote Series. However, Machen had difficulty in placing *The Garden of Avallaunius* (or *Phantasmagoria,* the working title). Finally, it came out in serial form from July to December 1904, in *Horlick's Magazine,* the house organ of the malted milk company — of all places: in 1935, the French comparatist Madeleine L. Cazamian called it "sans doute le livre le plus décadent de toute la littérature anglaise." The title was changed for book publication, in 1907, to *The Hill of Dreams* because, Machen claimed, he feared the public would mispronounce *Avallaunius.* Had Machen, and his new publisher, Grant Richards, stuck with the garden title, they would have partaken of a mode in titrology — Maurice Barrès's *Le Jardin de Bérénice* (1891), Andrian's *Der Garten der Erkenntnis* (1895), Stefan George's *Die Bücher der Hirten und Preisgedichte der Sagen und Sänge und der Hängenden Gärten,* Octave Mirbeau's horrific *Jardin des supplices* (1898), and Valle-Inclán's *Jardín umbrío* (1903). Elizabeth von Arnim's *Elizabeth and Her German Garden* (1898) was an innocent member of the company. The title word entered children's literature in Stevenson's *A Child's Garden of Verses* (1885) and reappeared in Frances Hodgson Burnett's *Secret Garden* (1911) and even, less innocently, reached distant Finland in Aino Kallas's verses *Suljettu puutarha* (1915, The Closed Garden).

Machen regarded the youth Avallaunius' description of "the splendid and golden city of Siluria" in chapter 4 as the heart of his novel; Lucian can now walk the streets of Caermaen, "confident and secure, without any dread of interruption, for at a moment's notice the transformation could be effected." The reconstruction of the late Roman-colonial world suggests popular paintings of the time, for example by Sir Lawrence Alma-Tadema, e.g., *Strigils and Sponges, In the Tepidarium, The Rose Garden, An Oleander,* and *The Shrine of Venus,* with their exactness of detail and their (sometimes) veiled eroticism. Machen's Siluria is warm, almost Mediterranean. Avallaunius takes refuge from the sunlight beneath the ilex trees in his garden outside the city walls, "filled with strange and brilliant flowers . . . filling the hot air with their odor." (Machen's repeated mention of the ilex, the holm oak, is probably a holdover from his schoolboy training, it appears in Horace's Odes, III:13, on the Fountain of Bandusia, in the setting of Vergil's Seventh Eclogue, and in Ovid's Golden Age.) Sitting in his garden, beneath the ilex's purple shadows, he listens to the sound of a double flute, played by a girl, while a nude boy ("the perfect white body") sings one of Sappho's love songs, in a voice as "full and pure as a woman's." (Intimations of bisexuality will return in a later section.)

The boy is "unconscious of the songs' meaning," but the girl smiles. Surrounded by odors of even greater delicacy, which modern man cannot perceive, Avallaunius watches "the girl's desire and the unripe innocence of the boy ... as distinct as benzoin and myrrh," as he leans against cushions covered with "glistening yellow silk," brought up the Usk to Siluria from the exotic lands of the east. Like Des Esseintes and Dorian, he seeks for "new and exquisite experiences."

Four more set pieces follow. The first consists of "strange entertainments," nocturnal performances of tales such as *Daphnis and Chloe* and *The Golden Ass*. Machen chooses an episode from Book 2 of Apuleius' novel about the misfortunes of Lucius, naming Byrrhaena, the lustful wife of Lucius' host at Hypeta, and the servant girl, Fotis, with whom Lucius (not yet turned into an ass by Byrrhaena's misfiring magic) has a series of stands, in accounts including copulative postures: one assumes that Apuleius was not read at the Hereford Cathedral School. Machen quotes the line (in "singing Latin") in which Lucius encourages Fotis in her preparations for Byrrhaena's banquet and their own first night together: "Veneris hortator et armiger Liber advenit ultro" (The encourager and squire of Venus, Liber [Bacchus], has also come). The second scene takes place in a vineyard, where Avallaunius spends the whole day, "looking out over the town," "a charming piece of mosaic," "a curious work in jewelry"; its "preciousness" reminds him of "a beautiful bowl in his villa," the city as work of art, a decadent ideal. Odors were a main constituent in the boy-girl overture; colors and plants — "scarlet flesh of poppies," purple grapes running through the green, quiet red brickwork, "dark groves of ilex," "cypress, and laurel, glowing rose-gardens" — are the essence of this vision. The third scene is set in a crowded tavern — priests of Mithra and Isis, actors from the theater, officers of the local legion, dancing girls, serving boys, bearing a variety of cups. Color and odor are mixed, some glasses are of "rich gamboges yellow," women are scented "with unctuous and overpowering perfumes," and the company "drank its wine and caressed all day in the tavern" (something like Thomas Couture's "Romains de la Décadence"). Listening to the medley of voices, Machen-Lucian-Avallaunius decides that "[language] was chiefly important for the beauty of its sounds . . . and *Lycidas* [again] was probably the most perfect piece of pure literature in existence." Arthur Symons, in *The Symbolist Movement in Literature* (1899), said: "[Verlaine] paints with sound, and his line and atmosphere become music."

This flight into Verlainesque poetics is interrupted by Avallaunius' search for "more exquisite things of which he might be a spectator"; he becomes avowedly the amoral seeker after sensation, "not concerned to know whether actions were good or evil but content if they were curious." The finale is a "singular story of corruption," introduced by a sketch of contacts between women and fauns, a notion to which Machen gave a quasi-Celtic form in "The Ceremony" of 1897 and *The White People* of 1899. Avallaunius hears the story, "from [a] woman's full red lips" as he watches her face, "full of the ineffable sadness of lust," of how she fell in love with a boy, "bought in the market of an Asian city," and tempted him for a full three years in vain. The pattern of temptress and boy returns—Annie and Lucian, flute player and innocent singer; in chapter 5, Lucian decides that Annie "has simply willed to satisfy her own passion." The sad woman's strategies are listed: at her command, her slave girls undress the boy and bathe him, then they undress and fondle one another, she herself undresses and has her girls caress her, and she experiments with "curious odours, soft dresses, delicious banquets." Finally, she succeeds but wins only a "green crown," "fighting in agony against his green and crude immaturity." She sends him to the theater, to "amuse the people by the splendor of his death"—that is, he is publicly tortured to death. The woman's story must have confirmed Cazamian in her judgment about the excessive decadence of *The Hill of Dreams;* she no doubt remembered the aesthetic sadism of the slave girl's crucifixion in Pierre Louÿs's *Aphrodite,* Félicien Rops's numerous crucified beauties, and the quasi-botanical executions of Mirbeau. In other works, Machen is more specific about methods of death: there are the instruments of torture in "Novel of the Iron Maid," in *The Three Impostors,* a wholesale lynching in "Novel of the Dark Valley," the deliquescence of "The Recluse of Bayswater," and the horrible discovery at the end of the "Adventure of the Deserted Residence." In *Things Near and Far,* Machen lingered over saints' martyrdoms; in the epilogue to *The Secret Glory* the Grail-seeker Ambrose Meyrick is crucified by "the Turks or the Kurds—it does not matter which." T. E. Lawrence, in his introduction of 1927 to Richard Garnett's minor antiquarian classic, *The Twilight of the Gods* (1888), recommends its "delightful callous cruelty, of the playful sort which thrills bookish men."

The question of Machen's knowledge of contemporary French decadent literature remains tantalizing. For bread and butter he translated three large works from earlier periods, Marguerite de Navarre's *Heptaméron* ([1558] 1884), Béroalde de Verville's *Le Moyen de parvenir* ([1610] 1890), and Casanova's *Mémoires* ([1786] 1894); from the nineteenth century, there is only the double reference, in *The Hill of Dreams,* to Daudet, which may well be a diversionary tactic. As Mark Valentine says, it is impossible that he had not read Huysmans's *À rebours.* A proof in point (among many) is Huysmans's repeated use of the catalogue, as in chapter 10 of *À rebours,* on perfumes, and Machen's listing of odors, plants, goblets, and so forth. Also, the probability of Machen's having known Maurice Barrès's tripartite *Le Culte du moi — Sous l'oeil des barbares* (1888), *Un Homme libre* (1889), and *Le Jardin de Bérénice* — cannot be ignored.

The overriding theme of the Barrès trilogy is the sensitive protagonist's perception that he lives his life "beneath the eye of the barbarians," in school, in a Paris lying on the immense plain where the barbarians are encamped, in the city itself amidst "sensual and vulgar barbarians." He declares, "I must free myself from the allures which the filthy river of the barbarians throws off wholesale" (Part 1). In Part 2, amidst numerous appearances of the key word, the protagonist means to employ "the same energy, the same perseverance, to protect [himself] against the strangers, against the barbarians, then [he] will be a Free Man." In *Le Jardin de Bérénice,* which gave modest literary fame to Aigues-Mortes as a "Venice more advanced in its development, [on] a dead lagoon," the protagonist (who at last has taken a name, Philippe) defines the core of his life: "As far as I am concerned, from my first reflections of childhood, I have feared the barbarians who reproached me for being different, I had the cult of being different within me." Philippe has come to Aigues-Mortes to be a companion to his sometime mistress, Bérénice, in her closed garden; on his mistaken advice, she marries the "Adversary," Charles Martin, an engineer who, according to Bérénice, " 'would substitute for our swamps filled with beautiful fevers some carp pool or other.' " Shortly, she dies, just as Aigues-Mortes will perish under Martin's plans — the ruin by means of renewal of an old and lovely town is also central to the intrigue of Rodenbach's *Le Carillonneur.* The fate of Bérénice and her crusader port has already been prefigured in *Sous l'oeil des barbares.* The protagonist imagines he is transformed into the Roman Lucius, who with his mistress Amaryllis witnesses the storming and destruction of the library of Alexandria, and the murder of Athéné, the priestess of Minerva. "Thus perished, for her illusions, under the eye of the Barbarians, . . . the last of the Hellenes." The Barbarians are legionaries of the empire, "helmeted in bronze," assigned to protect the old city; for its sake "they sacrifice the Serapion to the fanatics who assemble, ferocious, in the skins of animals, with their spears," in other words, the destruction, by the Patriarch Theophilus and his monks, of the Serapion at Canopis in 389 and of the great temple in Alexandria proper in 391, together with its library. (The last stage in the annihilation of pagan Alexandria occurred in 415, with the tearing apart of the learned woman Hypatia by the monks; Charles Kingsley turned the murder into an act of male sexual repression in his *Hypatia* [1854] for a shocked Victorian audience.)

An obsessive element in Lucian's vocabulary is *barbarian, barbarous.* Its employment begins harmlessly enough. His classmates were "very kind to him in their barbarous manner"; when he leaves school to live at home, he is more isolated still, "lacking even the company of the worthy barbarians who had befriended him" at school; going into Caermaen, he passes along backstreets, "to avoid the barbarians (as he very rudely called the respectable inhabitants of the town)." (It is not likely that Machen is thinking of Matthew Arnold's division of English society into "an aristocratic class, . . . the Barbarians, the middle-class Philistines, and the Populace": the people of Caermaen are pretty plainly Philistines through and through.) In London, receiving a letter from his cousin Miss Deacon—who disapproves his decision to live by his pen—he pigeonholes it "solemnly in the receptacle lettered 'barbarians.'" And in London his sufferings on his long walks—when he sees "a barbaric water tower"—and in his "hermitage" during the great frost "were so piteous that the barbarians themselves would have been sorry for him." He almost concludes that the "barbarians were in the right" when he cannot produce his work of great literature. Then the word *barbarian* is expanded to include not just school companions and the people of Caermaen but the whole of nonartistic humanity. The "enthusiasm of literature . . . dissevered the enthusiast from his fellow-creatures"; "the barbarian suspected as much, [so] that by some slow process of rumination he had arrived at his fixed and inveterate hatred of all artists." "Lucian was not especially interested in this hatred of the barbarian for the maker," except that it "confirmed him in his belief that the love of art dissociated the man from his race." However, a difference exists between Lucian and Barrès's protagonist. Less strong than Anonymous-Lucius-Philippe, Lucian longs for contact with despised humanity—his landlady recalls how, before his death, "he stood before the gate of a house, calling out that it was his home." The aim of Barrès's Anonymous is his cultivation of himself or his variety of selves; he rejoices in his quality of being "Alienus: foreign to the exterior world, foreign even to my past, foreign to my instincts, knowing only the rapid emotions which I shall choose: truly [a] Free Man." (Another possible offspring of Barrès's *Le Culte du moi* is *Hans Alienus* [1892] by the Swede Verner von Heidenstam, who would receive the Nobel Prize in 1916; Alienus, an egomaniacal traveler, follows his love of beauty through Renaissance and classical worlds, and falls dead on the shattered image of Jupiter.)

With some slyness or diffidence, Machen puts the possibility of Lucian's (or his own) knowledge of contemporary French literature at a generational remove. Noticing his son's strange behavior, Mr. Taylor fears that the young man has "become like some of those mad Frenchmen of whom he [the elder Taylor] had read, young fellows who had a sort of fury of literature, and gave their whole life to it, spending days over a page and years over a book, pursuing art as an Englishman pursues money" — precisely what Lucian will do, without success and with a deadly outcome. Lucian's teachers have long since put their finger on the boy's "decadent" literary tastes; Lucian characterizes himself as "degenerate, decadent," when he is struck by fear, hearing the voices in the darkness (just before Annie Morgan emerges, and their encounter takes place); but here the word seems to be used as the equivalent of *weak:* his exhaustion and his terror at the voices would have been laughed off by "a stronger man." (Machen also uses the word in a sense of cultural comedown in "The Decorative Imagination," the preamble to the "Novel of the Iron Maid." Dyson says: " 'Certainly, I agree with you that the times are decadent in many ways . . . Australian wines of fine Burgundy character, the novels alike of the old women and the new women, popular journalism — these things, indeed, make for depression.' ") Machen hints at his membership in the literature of the decadence, and the text itself contains manifold evidence of that membership; but he is leary of admitting such a membership *expressis verbis*.

Writing in *Things Near and Far* about the genesis of *The Hill of Dreams,* Machen claimed that at first he had no idea whatsover of what "the Great Romance" was to be about, but then he received a spark from the introduction to a new edition of Laurence Sterne's *Tristram Shandy* by one Charles Whibley. (In London, Lucian tries out some possible remedies for his writer's block, "The English *Don Quixote*" and Smollett's *Roderick Random;* subsequently he enjoys the "burlesque and gross adventures" of *Don Quixote* once more, the "Tourainian sun" of Rabelais, and, surprisingly, "the magic by which Hawthorne had lit his infernal Sabbath fires" in *The Scarlet Letter.* With "Sabbath fires," Lucian evidently means sexual sin.) For Whibley, "*Gil Blas* represented the picaresque of the body, *Don Quixote* the picaresque of both mind and body," and *Shandy* was "picaresque of the mind alone." Machen decided to write a "Robinson Crusoe of the mind," to represent "loneliness of soul and mind and spirit in the midst of myriads and myriads of men," in other words the material of chapters 5 to 7; he had had plenty of experience, as a "mere lad," more than a decade before, of "the *inextricabilis error* of the London streets," of isolation in "the tremendous and terrible London." In the 1920s Machen recalled that, in the 1890s, he had taken up his walks again as he worked on *The Hill of Dreams,* carrying with him "the problem of this great book . . . that was to be the better part of me." He fought a three-week battle with the second chapter (in which Lucian's manuscript is expropriated and he has his encounter with Annie Morgan); the fifth chapter — the arrival in London — made him lose his way and write "many thousands of words that had to be rejected." After a summary sentence about his "doubts and trials and questionings," Machen gives an extended account of a trip to Provence and

Languedoc in the summer of 1896, which is reflected in the Siluria of chapter 4—the "southern sun shining on white rocks, on the dark cypresses," the "scented rosemary," the monuments from Roman antiquity—he felt he had made "a journey rather in time than space." Back from Mediterranean France, he discovered that "the labour of months had been wasted, and set to work to break and remake." The book was finished in March of 1897 and was quickly rejected by John Lane and Grant Richards, who judged that "it would do him no credit." Richards wanted something like *The Three Impostors* and its factual prose; that book's horrors were permissible, whereas the extreme eroticism of the "Phantasmagoria" was not. It was published by Richards ten years after its completion.

In his third autobiographical volume, *The London Adventure, or The Art of Wandering* (1924), looking at an old notebook—and, always the cunctator, delaying "the Great Work on London"—Machen found "a great bulk of notes and suggestions" for *The Hill of Dreams,* which make "altogether the impression of a man who didn't know where he was going, losing his way in his endeavour to get there." As a postscript, he admits that he would like to revive another old recipe, the book on which he had set his heart in the 1890s, "the symbolizing of a story of the soul by the picture of exterior things," apparently a transposition of *The Hill of Dreams* into a major key, in which "a man on summer holidays," in Caerleon and the reaches of Gwent has his soul "renewed within him." The book was never written: "Dear Cinara's reign is ended." But still, thinking of the effort to write *The Hill of Dreams,* Machen tells how he plunged into the difficulties of "The Roman Chapter," where "the hero—or *idiot* [italics added]—of the story is rapt into the Roman world of Caerleon and listens to the music of those corrupted flutes," an interesting disparagement of Lucian. Linda Dowling has argued that Lucian is a Dorian Gray of the imagination; yet he is also a deluded and belated adolescent, and an exceptional decadent who never manipulates others, doing harm only to himself.

During the brief outburst of would-be decadent literature in the United States after the First World War, Machen acquired a substantial following. James Branch Cabell included a tribute in *Beyond Life* (1919); reviewing *Far Off Things* in 1922 ("Arthur Machen, Dreamer and Mystic"), Carl Van Vechten mentioned "this solitude which gave the boy his opportunity to dream his dreams," and a year later, about *Things Near and Far,* Van Vechten again brought up the "loneliness and solitude of the formative years, a loneliness that early found expression in his masterpiece, *The Hill of Dreams.* Did ever, one wonders, another literary artist have so few contacts with his fellow men?" Also, in Van Vechten's novel, *Peter Whiffle* (1922), Peter, a frequent visitor to Paris and a reader of Huysmans, exclaims to the narrator that Arthur Machen is "the most wonderful man writing English today and nobody know him." It was not true; in 1918 the Chicago journalist Vincent Starrett had published the perfervid *Arthur Machen: A Novelist of Ecstacy and Sin;* Starrett continued to praise Machen in *Buried Caesars* (1923) and put together a collection of Machen's short pieces in *The Glorious Mystery* (1924), which emphasized Machen's studies of the San Graal, a fancied possession of the "Celtic church." David Punter in *The Literature of Terror* (1980) called *The Hill of Dreams* overlush, and remarked, "The baroque quality of Machen's prose sometimes becomes absurd . . . Yet its continuing power derives from Machen's never separating Lucian wholly from reality," and his views of London are "comparable to Baudelaire's urban nightmares in intensity, if not in execution." The narrator of Iaian Sinclair's *Landor's Tower* (2001), a Welshman resident in London, apostrophizes Gwent and Machen: "These Welsh borderlands, as Arthur Machen knew, are passages where sights and sounds break through the mantle of unconvinced reality with grail hints, chthonic murmurings, earth spirits and strange atavistic impulses. I feared, shading my eyes against the autumnal clarity of the light, the savagery that counterbalanced Machen's sense of the blessedness of the countryside around Caerleon."

15

England

BRAM STOKER

It may not be coincidence that the three 'English' authors mostly closely associated with the phenomenon of literary decadence — George Moore, Oscar Wilde, and Bram Stoker — were all Anglo-Irishmen of a sort: Wilde and Stoker were born into the Church of Ireland, while Moore, from a wealthy Roman Catholic family, was converted to Protestantism amidst much publicity. Whether this common background gave them a sense of decay (stemming from their own local culture) or whether their "outsider" status in England, where all three spent their literary careers, made them aware of the possibility that the British Empire did not have the permanence the late nineteenth century was inclined to attribute to it — these questions cannot be answered here. Abraham (Bram) Stoker was the eldest of the trio of authors in question, born at Dublin in 1847: he studied at Trinity College, Dublin, like Wilde, whom he put up for a literary club, and entered the Irish civil service, following in his father's footsteps; at the same time, he became a drama critic for the *Dublin Mail*. A major experience of his college years had been seeing the great British actor Henry Irving on the stage of the Theatre Royal in Dublin in 1866; in 1876 he met Irving, in 1877 he published the dry-as-dust manual *The Duties of Clerks of Petty Sessions in Ireland,* and in 1878 he married Florence Balcombe, whereupon he moved to London as manager of Irving's Lyceum Theatre. (Oscar Wilde also appears to have been in love, or so he thought, with the beautiful Florence, and was disappointed to learn of her choice.) The London appointment meant that Stoker became the manager of Irving's career—a post he held until 1905, when Irving died at Bradford, Yorkshire, still on tour. Stoker told the story of his self-effacing life with the actor in *Personal Reminiscences of Henry Irving;* it has been conjectured that Irving—melodramatic, forever clad in black, shifting between demoniacal energy and exhaustion, sucking the strength from all around him—was to some extent a model for Stoker's count: Stoker did devote overwhelmingly much of his time and strength to the actor's career, and he arranged the several American tours on which he accompanied the star. Stoker liked America and was in particular an admirer of Walt Whitman, with whom he had begun to correspond, "uninhibitedly," as Whitman said, when he was still an undergraduate. (Again like Wilde, Stoker visited Whitman in Camden, New Jersey.)

Ever since the 1870s, Stoker, in odd moments, had tried his hand at horror tales; Charles Maturin of *Melmoth the Wanderer* and Sheridan LeFanu of *Green Tea* had been his Anglo-Irish predecessors in uncanny narratives. (LeFanu's story about female vampires, *Carmilla,* had come out in 1870; it will be recalled that Wilde's *Dorian Gray* is also a story of the supernatural. In his essay "Protestant Magic" [1989], the cultural historian Roy Foster argues that the bent for the supernatural of Maturin, LeFanu, and Stoker, culminating in W. B. Yeats's almost ridiculous concern with necromancy, may have grown from the disorientation and sense of dispossession experienced subliminally by late-come members of the once all-powerful Ascendancy.) In 1890 Stoker published the first of his full-length novels, *The Snake's Pass;* this was followed by *Dracula* in 1897, *Miss Betty* in 1898, *The Mystery of the Sea* in 1902, *The Jewel of Seven Stars* in 1903, *The Man* in 1905, *Lady Athlyne* in 1908, *The Lady of the Shroud* in 1909, and *The Lair of the White Worm* in 1911. Of these, *Dracula* has maintained itself over the decades and has given rise to numerous plays, movies, comic strips, and Halloween masks; *The Jewel of the Seven Stars,* about an English girl who somehow shares her body with the soul of the ancient Queen Tera of Egypt (shades of Théophile Gautier's *Roman de la momie!*), has been made into a film with Charlton Heston as the heroine's archaeologist father. Stoker's crazy last novel, *The Lair of the White Worm,* has also reached the screen; in it, Lady Arabella March, resident at an ancient farm called Diana's Grove, keeps an enormous white serpent in a cistern in the basement and enjoys a symbiotic relationship with the beast. The film was directed by Ken Russell, whose previous "decadent" film was based on Wilde's *Salome.*

After the death of Irving, Stoker entered a period of intense literary activity; to the three last novels may be added his memories of Irving and a series of studies of *Famous Imposters*. Then Stoker's health rapidly declined, and he died on April 20, 1912; the sinking of the *Titanic* pushed the report of his death to the back pages. The story of Stoker's physical well- or ill-being is an interesting one; he had been an invalid the first eight years of his life and was not expected to survive: in prepuberty he suddenly recovered, growing into a stalwart figure, so that he was chosen university athlete at Trinity. Stamina was essential during the hard years of touring with Irving; the illness which is supposed at last to have laid him low was Bright's Disease, coupled with "exhaustion." However, his descendant Daniel Farson, who published a Stoker biography in 1976, discovered a death certificate which contained the phrase *locomotor ataxy*. Farson concluded that the term was a synonym for *tabes dorsalis* and *general paresis*, and that Stoker had contracted syphilis sometime around the turn of the century, having been driven to unfaithfulness by the frigidity of his wife, who had refused to have relations with him after the birth of their only son, Noel, in 1879. The theory adduced by Farson is of some importance, since Stoker's enforced celibacy, and his sense of guilt, would help to account for the strongly sexual nature of many episodes in *Dracula*; the possibility of growing mental degeneration on Stoker's part could be the cause of the disorder of *The Lair of the White Worm*, whose construction is as loose as that of *Dracula* is tight.

It is not known precisely what attracted Stoker to Dracula; having already established himself as a writer of spooky fiction, he was no doubt always on the lookout for new topics. His first notes for the novel are from March 8, 1890, and on April 30 of that year he met Hermann Vambery, of the University of Budapest, through Irving. From the Hungarian he may have received some of the ethnographic and folkloristic material he needed — Vambery is the Arminius of Buda-Pesth twice mentioned by Abraham Van Helsing as an excellent informant about Dracula. As Van Helsing says in his comically fractured English: " 'From all the means that are, [Vambery] tell me of what [Dracula] has been.' " A visit to Whitby on the Yorkshire coast in August 1890, seems to have been of particular importance: there Stoker interviewed a coastguard about a Russian schooner that had come into the harbor, "all sails flying" while its crew huddled below; and in the records of the coastguard station he found a notice about another Russian ship that had been driven into the Whitby harbor "by pure chance," laden with silver sand from the mouth of the Danube. More important, on one of his Whitby vacations Stoker read and took notes on a book by William Wilkinson, "late consul of Bucharest," called *Account of the Principalities of Wallachia and Moldavia* (London, 1820), from which he made jottings about the name Dracula ("In Wallachian language it means devil. Wallachians were accustomed to give it to any person who rendered himself conspicuous through courage, cruel action, or cunning"); he also found information in Wilkinson about the "Voivode Dracula," who "has crossed the Danube and attacked the Turkish troops," but "with only momentary success." Later, he used an article by Emilie Gerard, "Transylvanian Superstitions" (1885) and her book *The Land Beyond the Forest* (1888) for further information. Stoker was never in Transylvania, the place he conjured up with such skill, but an American connection with the genesis of *Dracula* possibly exists; among Stoker's papers there is a clipping from the *New York World* of February 2, 1896 (he was there at the time on tour), called "Vampires in New England," dealing with several cases of vampirism in Rhode Island: " 'It appears that the ancient vampire superstition still survives in that state, and within the last few years many people have been digging up the dead bodies of relatives for the purpose of burning their hearts.' " (Later, Stoker told a seventeen-year-old Harvard undergraduate, Roger Sherman Hoar, that he planned to revivify Dracula and bring him to America. Hoar grew up to be a writer of horror stories himself, working for the pulp magazine *Argosy*.)

The historical figure with whom Abraham Van Helsing (and Vambery) associated the nineteenth-century Dracula was once called, in a *New York Times* travel article, "The George Washington of Romania"; certainly, Dracula has done as much for the reputation of Romania (although he is often called the Hungarian count) as Ibsen for Norway or Sibelius for Finland. " 'He must have been,' " Van Helsing says, as quoted by Mina Harker in her journal for September 30, " 'that Voivode Dracula who won his name against the Turk, over the great river on the very frontier of Turkey-land. If it be so, then was he no common man; for in that time and for centuries after, he was spoken of as the cleverest and the most cunning, as well as the bravest of the sons of 'the land beyond the forest.' That mighty brain and that iron resolution went with him to his grave, and are even now arrayed against us. The Draculas were, says Arminius, a great and noble race, though now and again were scions who were held by their coevals to have had dealings with the Evil One . . . In the records are such words as 'stregoica' — 'witch,' 'ordog' and 'pokol' — 'Satan and hell'; and in one manuscript this very Dracula is spoken of as 'vampyr,' which we all understand too well.' " Abraham repeats, in reduction, what Dracula has said about his forefathers and himself as recorded in Jonathan Harker's journal of the previous May: " 'Who was it but one of my race who as Voivode crossed the Danube and beat the Turk on his own ground. This was a Dracula indeed. Who was it that his own unworthy brother, when he had fallen, sold his people to the Turk and brought the shame of slavery on them! Was it not this Dracula indeed who inspired that other of his race who in a later age again and again brought his forces over the great river into Turkey-land; who, when he was beaten back, came again and again and again . . . since he knew that he alone could ultimately triumph?' " The passage is again alluded to by Van Helsing on October 3, and quoted by him (in Seward's journal) at Varna on October 28, as he lists for his companions the strengths and weaknesses of the count.

The original of our Dracula was born in 1430 or 1431 at Sighişoara (German Schässburg) in the region called Siebenbürgen in German and Transylvania in English and Romanian; however, he was not one of the "Transylvanian Saxons" who had come to "the land beyond the forest" in the twelfth and thirteenth centuries from northwestern Germany, at the invitation of King Geza of Hungary. (The story of the Pied Piper of Hamlin refers to the recruiting of these German pioneers for the underpopulated mountainous lands, five hundred miles away.) Dracula was a Romanian-speaker and a member of the Romanian (or Wallachian) royal house; he was not, in contradiction to what Stoker's Dracula says, a member of the Székely, a tribe related to the Magyars. Dracula's real name was Vlad, like that of his father, who was the voivode of Wallachia from 1431 to 1447. The same year as this elder Vlad ascended the throne and became little Vlad's father, he was named a knight in the Order of the Dragon, a Hungarian society founded by the Emperor Sigismund with the aim of fighting the Turks. Thus, Vlad senior received the sobriquet Dracul, "dragon," which, by happy coincidence, as we know, also means "devil" in Romanian; his son was called Dracula, "the son of the dragon." According to the late nineteenth-century Romanian historian Nicolas Jorga, the son — the object of our investigation — was only "a weak dilettante when it came to impaling foes, subjects, and animals"; in this case, the deeds of the father must have beggared description. The younger Vlad and his brother, Radu the Handsome, were eventually given as hostages to the Turkish sultan, Murad II; at his court, Vlad picked up his own taste for impaling and Radu learned other bad habits. In 1447, Vlad the elder was murdered by the Hungarians; Vlad-Dracula escaped from his golden captivity and returned to his homeland. After having gotten rid of a rival for the post of the voivode, Laszlo the Unfortunate, Vlad took his father's place, ruling from 1456 to 1462. During this time, Vlad Dracula — now also called Vlad Ţepeş, the Impaler — committed the majority of the atrocities for which he became so notorious in his day; meanwhile, he carried on his valiant campaigns against the Turks. Finally, his back to the wall, he sought refuge with Matthew Corvinus, the king of Hungary, who imprisoned him, but time did not hang heavy on his hands — he converted to Roman Catholicism from the Orthodox faith, married a sister of the king, and sired with her, while in durance vile, three sons, Vlad Ţepuluş ('the little impaler'), Mihnea the Rotten, and the colorless Mircea. He also amused himself by impaling mice, birds, and other small animals. After twelve years, he was freed and returned to Wallachia, where he was killed in battle in 1476, either by his own boyars or by the Turkish foe.

Vlad Țepeș, or Vlad Dracula, got his original international reputation not for his military exploits (for example, he almost captured Sultan Mohammed II in bed), but for his love of mass impalements. The Turks, themselves no pikers at impaling, called him *Kasikli-voda,* stake prince, and he had slain so many Turkish prisoners in this fashion that even Sultan Mohammed grew ill when he came across a valley filled with a forest of pales topped by his Turkish compatriots and his Bulgarian allies. However, the majority of Vlad's atrocities were committed against the neighbors of his childhood, the Transylvanian Germans, from Kronstadt and Hermannstadt and Klausenburg (which last-named town Harker visits). For example, on Saint Bartholomew's Day in 1460, he is said to have had the inhabitants of Kronstadt impaled and left to die in agony. The reasons for his hatred of the Germans seem to be plain: they had money, they maintained close contact with the West (and Vlad suspected that recent arrivals were spies), and, economically adroit, they enjoyed more favor with the Hungarians than the simple Wallachians did. However, in the Germans, Vlad had chosen the wrong victims; the printing press had been invented, and by 1476, the year of Vlad's death, some eleven chapbooks had appeared (with woodcuts), detailing the Romanian's cruelty, and, at the same time, calling attention to his good looks: a papal envoy, who had seen him in his Hungarian captivity, said he was a man of particularly fine appearance. Until the seventeenth century, at least, Vlad's name, or Dracula's, stood in Germany, High and Low, for a bloodthirsty tyrant, another Nero or Diocletian. In a poem from 1576 which with heavy wit described the warfare between fleas and their natural enemies, women, *Flöh Hatz, Weiber Tratz (Fleas' Hew and Cry/Women's Bold Defy),* Johann Fischart tells of a market vendor who eats her picnic lunch while she murders the fleas that annoy her: "Da dacht ich an den Traculam/der sein Mal unter Toten nahm" ("To Dracula my thoughts were led/who ate his meal among the dead"). The reference is to Dracula's habit of banqueting among the impaled bodies of his victims. In time, to this monster, stories of a league with Satan and of vampirism accrued: his conversion to Roman Catholicism had not sat well in Romania, and he did, after all, bear the sobriquet the Devil. Stoker never mentions the atrocities for which Dracula was known in his own day. The author's artistic instinct was correct: the inhuman practice was grotesque and would have taken away from the seductive smoothness of Dracula — who, in addition, a typical decadent, operates alone, as Van Helsing emphasizes, whereas an impaler needs many helpers. Impalement, too, has a crude implication of sexual spectacle about it; the sexual implications of vampirism are subtler, more private.

Some of the causes for the instant and lasting popularity of *Dracula* (it has never gone out of print in more than a century of existence) lie very close to hand. For one thing, it is a supremely good horror story, as Charlotte Stoker, Bram's energetic and liberal-minded mother, realized: "It is splendid, a thousand times beyond anything you have written before, and I feel certain it will place you very high in the writers of the day — the setting and the style being deeply sensational, exciting, and interesting . . . No book since Mrs. Shelley's *Frankenstein* or indeed any other at all has come near yours in originality and terror — Poe is nowhere!" Professional reviewers were similarly enthusiastic: the *London Daily Mail* compared it to "classics of horror fiction," such as Ann Radcliffe's *Mysteries of Udolpho* and *Frankenstein,* and the *Pall Mall Gazette* said it was "horrid and creepy to the last degree." The horror of it all was enhanced by the fact that the count (unless one looked closely) was not a physical monster, but a "handsome old man" of supreme athleticism, strength, and intelligence — in his elegant get-up, never changed when he as human form, he is a dandy. (Albeit he is a dandy to whom a certain necessary rough-and readiness of toilet attaches; remember the description, after the searchers have run him to ground in Piccadilly, of his dressing room: "There was also a clothes brush and a comb, and a jug and a basin — the latter containing dirty water which was reddened as if with blood." The dandy Sherlock Holmes in *The Hound of the Baskervilles* has similar basic instruments for keeping neat and clean in his hideaway on the moor, as he tries to find out the murderer of Sir Charles and the nature, real or supernatural, of the hound.) There is also the strange straw hat which the count, who has lost his top hat, wears when he negotiates for the loading of his boxes of earth at the London docks: a gentlemen does not venture forth without a head covering. Before that, the count is seen as a lustful boulevardier, beheld in a broad daylight by Harker and Mina, ogling a "very beautiful girl in a big cartwheel hat, sitting in a victoria outside Giuliano's." To Mina, the count is "a tall thin man, with a beaky nose and a black mustache and pointed beard . . . His face is not a good face . . . and his big white teeth looked all the whiter because his lips were so red [and] parted like an animal's." The would-be seducer has grown younger, as Jonathan, who knew him all too well before, remarks. And just as the count fits easily and discreetly into the London street scene, so his appearances in the novel are discreetly limited, although his presence is ever felt — the novel is kept from being overladen with horror; the horror is held under control. The details and datings of the various entries and the newspaper accounts (and, less successfully, the humorous scenes with representatives of the "lower classes") also contribute to this moderation in the book; all is not uncanny, by any means.

Another attraction of *Dracula* was its quality of being at once a travel book and an adventure tale, and a detective novel. The first of the episodes leads us, very skillfully, into the polylingual and polyethnic world of southeastern Europe's reaches, as Jonathan makes his way, in the service of his chief, Hawkins, from Munich to Vienna and Budapest ("the impression I had is that we were leaving the west and entering the east"), and down to Klausenburg (Cluj) in Romania, then up to Bistritz and on to the Borgo Pass where he has the rendezvous with the count's coachman — that is, the count himself. (A whole opening chapter was omitted from the manuscript, about a preparatory vampire encounter in the Bavarian countryside, during which a communication from the count saves Harker: he is to be spared for worse things.) Harker (and Stoker) give a careful account of dress and accommodations and, particularly, food and drink (as the overture to a novel which is about the nourishment of vampires); the menus of the meals Jonathan has at Klausenburg and Bistritz and even at the castle itself are presented, and they sound very tasty. The effect is that of a culinary Baedeker. Likewise, the novel's final episode, the chase of Dracula to his lair, has the qualities of high adventure; again, the multitude of nationalities is mentioned and, above all, the sweeping panoramas of the mountains as the autumn cold tightens around pursued and pursuers. The account of the transport and the arms of the crusaders, the layout of the ambush of Dracula at the end, with the disposition of the various forces, call to mind the Himalayan scenes of Kipling, for example, in *The Man Who Would Be King.* (Major E. C. Johnson, whose book *On the Track of the Crescent* Stoker used in his preparations, remarks on the resemblance between Carpathian and Himalayan scenery.) In between these episodes, of course lies the bulk of the novel, the British sections: the spooky and yet splendid setting of Whitby with the dissolving churchyard and the ruin of the abbey (to which Mina, the sometime schoolteacher, immediately attaches memories of Scott's *Marmion,* and of Constance, the nun seduced by Marmion, who was walled up there), and the promenade concerts and the stormy harbor (and the almost unintelligible dialect of ancient Swales, telling the story of Geordie, the hunchback who committed suicide in revenge for his mother's hatred of him). The middle portions, at the lunatic asylum and Carfax estate next door, at the Westenra residence in Hillingham, and in London proper, have the air of Sherlock Holmes stories. As in the Holmes corpus, much attention is given to the gloom of the places (the grounds of the asylum, the churchyard where Lucy is laid to rest, only to rise again, placed against the background of the glow of London, "the wonderful smoky beauty of the sunset over London, with its lurid lights and inky shadows"). These locales are interlocked through constant communication by means of telegrams, and by public transportation, as in Holmes and in E. W. Hornung's *Raffles* novels—the use of cabs and trains to get around the London sprawl. Furthermore, preparatory to the Piccadilly episode, we come across a careful, Holmesian gathering of evidence; subsequently, like Holmes, the searchers confront the problems of dealing with the police. Another Holmesian device is that of introducing cabbies and draymen and zookeepers, speaking substandard English, and possessed by a powerful thirst and an equally powerful desire for a tip. As in Conan Doyle, these details are meant to bring a superior smile to readers' lips.

Victorian audiences, too, must have liked the moralizing of the tale: the fact that the count and his voluptuous ladies are patently evil; that the members of the pursuing band are good (they kneel down four times in the text to sanctify their allegiance to their purpose); that Mina — who has suffered the most from the count—is willing to forgive him. Seward records the words she speaks on October 3: " 'I know that you must fight—that you must destroy even as you destroyed the false Lucy so that the true Lucy might find life hereafter; but it is not a work of hate. That poor soul who has wrought all this misery is the saddest case of all. Just think what will be his joy when he too is destroyed in his worser [!] part that his better part may have spiritual immortality. You must be pitiful to him, too, though it may not hold your hands from his destruction.' " Her husband, Jonathan, is not moved by her argument, but, at the novel's conclusion, Mina's Christian charity in fact prevails: "I shall be glad as long as I live that even in that moment of final dissolution there was in the face a look of peace, such as I never could have imagined might have rested there." Similarly, as Van Helsing does away with the three women at the castle, he thinks: "The poor souls, I can pity them now and weep, as I think of them placid each in her full sleep of death, for a short moment ere fading." Readers could be proud of a Christian culture that had produced such forebearing folk as Mina and Van Helsing — both of whom might also have said, "There but for the grace of God go I." Good has triumphed, and good is never vindictive; good is forgiving, and good also knows its own fragility.

The Victorian audience could also feel flattered on another score: the courageous white people conquer the minions of darkness. Dracula is seen by Mina as "the dark man," and earlier Lucy makes a strangely racist remark, before Dracula has sailed into Whitby's harbor. She recognizes, it would seem, the seductiveness of the "black man"; in the midst of her account of the three suitors, she says — the reference seems strangely incongruous — "I sympathize with poor Desdemona when she had such a dangerous stream poured into her ears, even by a black man." (Like other authors of his time, Stoker associated "the black man" with lust unbridled.) Stoker makes it quite plain that Dracula is a product of a nonwestern world, an alien world. This may be a reason for Stoker's changing Dracula from a Wallachian, the speaker of a Romance tongue and a descendant of the inhabitants of Roman Dacia, to a Székely, a kinsman of Attila the Hun, come raging from the East to destroy Western civilization — which is, we remember, Dracula's own plan, when he can get at "the teeming millions of London." The main henchmen of Dracula are again from the East, the Gypsies: "there were thousands of them in Hungary and Transylvania, who are almost outside all law . . . They are fearless and without religion, save superstition." Dracula's other helpers are the servile Slovaks, "more barbarian" than the other inhabitants of Transylvania: "On the stage they would be set down at once as an old Oriental band of brigands," in their "great baggy dirty-white trousers," or their "dirty sheepskin" — appropriately enough, since their job is to move boxes for the transport of dirt.

Opposed to these creatures of the East are the crusaders whom the awful fate of Lucy Westenra has brought together. They are a white company, all from the Anglo-Saxon-Germanic cultural world, and men who, in some instances, have dealt with lesser breeds without the law before. Arthur Holmwood, later Lord Godalming, Dr. John Seward, Quincey Morris, have hunted together in the wilds of South America; although we know nothing of the background of Jonathan Harker (who possesses the same physical vigor as the others and, through his inheritance, lands financially in the class of Holmwood and Morris as well), a detail of his weaponry may make us think that he, like John Watson, M.D., has served with the British Army in India: his Gurkha knife, his *kukri,* with which he attempts to slay Dracula in Piccadilly, and which he uses to decapitate the villain at the castle's approaches. The composition of the group would have pleased Cecil Rhodes; three are Englishmen tried and true, the mysterious and learned Van Helsing is a Dutchman, and Morris, with his funny lingo and his great bowie knife, is the Texan, who pries open one side of the coffin as Harker used his kukri to open the other. After plunging the knife into Dracula's heart, Morris is allowed his series of curtain speeches, worthy of the representative of the great nation in the West: " 'I am only too happy to have been of service,' " and " 'Oh God,' " he cried, gazing at Mina, who no longer bore the mark of her pollution on her forehead, " 'It was worth this to die . . . Now God be thanked that all has not been in vain! See! The snow is not more stainless than her forehead! The curse has passed away!' And, to our bitter grief, with a smile and silence, he died, a gallant gentleman." (Morris shares a death date, by the way, with Gustaf

Adolph, the Christian Lion of the North in the Thirty Years' War, who fell at Lützen on November 6, 1632.) The crusaders have the same sense of duty as soldiers in Kipling (Van Helsing exhorts them to "do their duty"); the Whitby newspaper reporter also puts down the last words of the devout Russian captain of the *Demeter*—evidently more pious and conscientious than his Romanian seamen, who are hysterical with fear: "The saints help a poor, ignorant soul trying to do his duty." The captain, incidentally, wants "to die like a man," the wish expressed by Harker at the castle; all the crusaders are gentlemen, gentlemen brave in their manliness. It was the age in which "Onward, Christian Soldiers" of Sabine Baring-Gould and Sir Arthur Sullivan had its greatest popularity.

Two further details may be added to the pattern of subtextual suggestion in this novel of the virtuous West battling against the vicious East. The one is the request Mina makes of Jonathan to kill her before she becomes wholly the victim of Dracula: the request is uttered in Galatz, before the expedition starts up river: " 'Think, dear, that there have been times when brave men have killed their wives and their womankind, to keep them from falling into the hands of the enemy.' " The allusion would have quite clear to the Victorian readership; in the Sepoy Rebellion forty years back, incidents occurred of Englishmen killing first their wives and then themselves, lest they should fall into the hands of the priapic foe. Christina Rossetti wrote a well-known poem on just such a scene, "The Death of Capitan Skene and His Wife":

> A hundred, a thousand to one, even so,
> Not a hope in the world remained;
> The swarming, howling wretches below
> Gained and gained and gained.

And newspaper readers, even as *Dracula* came out, could come across events in every British paper that paralleled those in the novel. Young Winston Churchill wrote about them in *The River War*. Two British forces were invading the Sudan, one on the Nile, one over land (just as in the last episode of *Dracula*), to avenge the death of the Christian gentleman Charles "Chinese" Gordon and to defeat the dervishes. They would succeed, in 1898, at the Battle of Omdurman; the "ghoulish practices" of the dervishes were ended, and the city that had been "a monstrosity of African lust" was taken. Young Churchill, however, in his book criticized Kitchener's order that the tomb of the Mahdi be opened, systematically defiled, and the head cut off. Obviously, Stoker could not know of these stirring deeds, which lay in the immediate future. But his readers were ready for his implications of the imperial mission, R. N. Bennett, of *The*

Westminster Magazine, wrote: "The cause of western civilization was advanced by British arms. Mahdism has proved the most shameful and terrible instrument of bloodshed and oppression the modern world has witnessed."

To readers who had been following the currents of contemporary, decadent literature, the novel *Dracula* contained much that was familiar: it was in fact a vulgarized and popularized example of decadence. Dracula himself is the last of a long, long line; as he tells Harker, he lives in an old house (" 'I myself am of an old family, and to live in a new house would kill me' "). He "loves the shade and the shadows," he is alone, he has untold wealth at his disposal (except on that occasion in Piccadilly, when he seems to have run out of funds and scoops up banknotes from the floor), and his vampirish tempo of life compels him to alternate between decadent languor and excessive activity (once, when he is awake, Harker finds him lying on a couch, reading *Bradshaw's Railway Guide*). He despises the masses (he repeatedly tells Harker about his contempt for the peasants: " 'Your peasant is at heart a coward and a fool," and " 'Bah, what good are peasants without a leader?' "). He despises, equally, the upstart royal houses of Europe: " 'Ah, young sir, the Szekelys—and the Dracula as their heart's blood, their brains and their swords—can boast a record that mushroom growths like the Hapsburgs and Romanoffs can never reach.' " Dracula is aware, like other decadents, that the world has declined, has become humdrum: " 'The warlike days are over. Blood is too precious a thing in these days of dishonorable peace; and the glories of the great races are as a tale that is told.' " (Rudyard Kipling's great and ominous "Recessional" [1897]— "The captains and the kings depart" and young Rilke's "Die Könige der Welt sind alt" [1901] in *Das Stunden-Buch* are other statements of similar themes.) In short, Dracula is a typical decadent *laudator temporis acti.* The men of the past were stronger than the men of the present, and Dracula, decidedly, is a man of the past. He is coupled, too, with another character type of decadent literature: the *femme fragile,* Lucy Westenra, the blood slowly sucked out of her at Whitby and Hillingham, becomes, in her undead condition, the most aggressive of femmes fatales.

Dracula has a prime characteristic of decadence in his desire and ability to use others, horribly; Mina notices this. She has read, she says, her contemporary critics of decadence, Max Nordau of *Entartung* (*Degeneration*) and Cesare Lombroso, and has decided they would classify Dracula as a degenerate criminal ("and, *qua* criminal, he has an imperfectly formed mind"). Or, as Abraham Van Helsing says: " 'He be of child-brain in much' "—like other decadents, Dracula works empirically, by his experiences, not on principle, principle which, as the narrator of *Il piacere* says, is also sadly lacking in

Andrea Sperelli. However, there is one principle by which he does operate, not so far away from Sperelli's *habere, non haberi* and identical with Dorian Gray's selfishness; bright little Mina describes it very clearly: " 'Then, as he is criminal he is selfish, and as his intellect is small and his action is based on selfishness, he confines himself to one purpose . . . His own selfishness frees my soul somewhat of the terrible power he acquired over me on that dreadful night'." Van Helsing listens, approves, and takes up the theme of Dracula's selfishness that will bring him to a fall. Then he says, "We [the crusaders, about to land at Varna, where, in 1444, the last historical 'Crusade' ended] are not all selfish, and we believe that God is with us through all this blackness." The theme of selfishness has come up earlier; Dr. Seward, back in April, observed that the madman Renfield is "probably dangerous if unselfish." The latter quality is Renfield's source of final grace — he tries to sacrifice himself to save Mina. In between, though, Seward thinks for a while that Renfield has "certain qualities very largely developed: selfishness, secrecy, and purpose"; he has come under the influence of Dracula and has started to resemble him. The count, like Dorian Gray, seems to have made a pact with the devil in return for a prenaturally long life (in which he can become younger from time to time, and in which he never loses his good looks); he — like Henry Wotton — is associated with the devil in his appearance, and he speaks to Renfield in a parody of the words Satan used to Christ in the wilderness: " 'All these lives will I give you . . . , and many more, and greater, through countless ages, if you will fall down and worship me' " — at least, this is what Renfield remembers. But, as usual in decadence, the direct connection with the infernal is left intentionally vague. Looking Dracula over, we could say that the only salient features of the decadent he lacks are indolence, neuresthenia, and a taste for the aesthetic; his large library is of a practical nature, and he is not a collector of fine objects or handsome books — only a collector of victims whom he can turn into his puppets or his slaves, or simply slay.

Yet Stoker's Dracula is a decadent with a difference; he is at once the decadent and the barbarian who has entered the Western atrium, who wishes to destroy the New Rome of Britain. He has the animal facial (and dental) features of his vampire kind, he has hairy palms, he has laid out a plan to place London and the world under his control, and Western Europe must fight back. (John Buchan, who in his adventure books wrote about a similar constellation, applied it to Bolshevism: "The European tradition has been confronted by an Asiatic revolt . . . an ugly pathological savour as if a mature society were being assaulted by diseased and vicious children." In Buchan's *Greenmantle* [1916], a major novel about the struggle between West and East, his "missionaries," going out to Turkey in the First World War, have a composition much like Stoker's: the Scots South African Richard Hannay, the Boer Peter Pienaar, the Anglo-Scot Sandy Arbuthnot, and the American John S. Blenkiron of Indiana.) This barbarian primitivism of the count, his elementary and single purpose of creating "a new order of human beings, whose road led through Death, not Life" (an echo, perhaps, of the plan of Rider Haggard's semi-immortal *She*, of 1884, to take over the British Empire), is opposed not only by the will of the crusaders but by their marvelous and modern technology. Jonathan Harker has the shorthand which he has learned from Mina, the product of some very up-to-date business school; Mina has her portable type-writer; the coastguard at Whitby has its new searchlight that illuminates the harbor (as the giant dog escapes from the *Demeter,* a hound in which the SPCA then take a touching interest); Seward has his wax phonographic cylinders to which he dictates; the telegraph keeps Godalming informed of the whereabouts of the schooner *Catherine:* the friends go east with the Orient Express, while Dracula takes sailing ships; in Romania, Godalming and Seward travel by steam launch, while Dracula must bounce along on the Gypsies' *Leiterwagen;* the friends, on the counsel of Quincey Morris, have the best in modern weaponry, Winchester repeating rifles. These technical advances sometimes foil the count, even though he has supernatural aids at his disposal (appearing as a dog, a wolf, a bat, and, Zeuslike, as a cloud); when he destroys the records of the group at the asylum, he does not know that they have copies in the safe. The friends use the tools of "this enlightened age" (as Van Helsing says), although the rational thinking of enlightened men, who cannot believe a Dracula exists, is the strongest weapon on the creature's side. Dracula mocks his pursuers (" 'You think to baffle me, you — with your pale faces all in a row like sheep in a butcher's' "), but he succumbs in the end. To be sure, as Stoker has his several good characters make abundantly clear, God — not just technology and valor — is on their side. Van Helsing closes one of his many exhortations to his companions thus: " 'We are willing to peril even our own souls for the safety of one we love — for the good of mankind, and for the honor and glory of God' " — in which the Catholic Van Helsing uses the formula of the minor elevation in the Latin mass, "Omnis honor et gloria."

No reader of *Dracula* has escaped noting how much of the Bible and of Christianity is in the book, both on the side of evil and of good; to make a long story short, Dracula's drinking of the blood of his victims is a blasphemous parody of the central symbolic act of the Christian ritual: the drinking of the blood of Jesus at holy communion, blood that strengthens and purifies, Stoker must have known William Cowper's wonderful hymn:

There is a fountain filled with blood
Drawn from Emmanuel's veins,
And sinners plunged beneath that flood
Lose all their guilty stains.

The blood is the substance that, taken selfishly, keeps Dracula alive, and blood is the substance with which he pollutes others. For himself and his creatures, Dracula offers a version of the words of Jesus in John 6:54: "He that eateth my flesh and drinketh my blood hath eternal life, and I will raise him up at the last day." What the Church Father Tertullian (beloved reading of Jean Floressas Des Esseintes) says about the supply of New Christians could also apply to Dracula's putative army of the Undead (he does not intend to remain as supremely alone as he has been): "We are made the more as often as we are hewed down by you; the seed is the blood of Christ." Renfield, Dracula's vocal congregation of one, tells us about another biblical verse that Dracula has appropriated, Deuteronomy 12:23: "The blood is the life." But Dracula is up against Christian gentlemen who likewise have Holy Scripture at their sincere beck and call: Quincey Morris, in his homespun way, refers to "the seven young women with the lamp" (Matthew 25:1–10, the wise virgins of whom there were actually only five), the reverent Van Helsing quotes from Luke 8:58: the Parable of the Sower, to make a point to his friend and former student John Seward. At the end of the novel the Christian home of Jonathan, Mina, and little Quincey has been established: the promise of the novel's opening has been fulfilled. Jonathan began his Draculan experience, we are told, on the Eve of Saint George's Day, May 4, in the Old Style calendar used in Romania at the time (in the Anglican Church, Saint George's Day falls on April 24). (For his omitted chapter, "Walpurgis Night," the vampire episode near Munich, Stoker uses the Western calendar, the night from April 30 to May 1.) The several Saints George of the band have slain the dragon, Dracula, in his lair, and saved the "maiden," Mina, revirginized or at least purified by Dracula's death.

The religiosity and the implied Western patriotism of *Dracula* may have blinded contemporary reviewers to its obvious and shocking sexuality, which has recently been the object of much comment: C. F. Bentley's "The Monster in the Bedroom: Sexual Symbols in Dracula" (1972), Phyllis Roth's "Suddenly Sexual Women in Bram Stoker's Dracula" (1977), John Allen Stevenson's "A Vampire in the Mirror: The Sexuality of Dracula" (1988); these are some specimens, but many more could be adduced, among them Christopher Craft's "Kiss Me With Those Red Lips: Gender and Inversion in Bram Stoker's *Dracula*." The themes of these papers have to do, among other things, with the circumstance that, for Stoker's Victorian mind, pious but prurient, women with clearly pronounced sexual urges are instruments of the devil or of Dracula; that Dracula attempts to form one big incestuous family, in which he is both the father and chief lover; that Stoker excites the male Victorian libido with images of the rape of purity (see Gail Grafton's " 'Your Girls That You Love Are All Mine': Dracula and the Victorian Male Sexual Impulse" of 1980); and so forth. It cannot be denied: the book *is* full of scenes that indicate, through and in their horror, a sense of "perverse" sexuality. At the castle, Harker is almost seduced by the three vampire girls who cluster around the couch where he lies, and he likes the prospect; as he confesses to Mina: "I felt in my heart a wicked, burning desire that they would kiss me with those red lips," and he hears them say: " 'He is young and strong, there will be kisses for us all' . . . I lay looking out under my eyelids in an agony of delightful anticipation . . . I closed my eyes in a languorous ecstasy and watched — watched with beating heart." In this instance, Harker is saved by the count himself; Harker redeems himself by his daredevil and desperate escape from the castle, down the wall: he recovers the manhood he almost lost in his passivity toward the girls: "At its foot man may sleep — as a man. Goodbye all! Mina!" The experience is so trying for Harker that, at Budapest in August, as he convalesces, he is a "wreck of himself . . . All the resolution has gone out of his clear eyes, and that quiet dignity which I told you was in his face was vanished," Mina writes to Lucy. At the wedding ceremony, he has "poor weak hands." "He has begun to doubt himself." This last report is from September 18, but by September 26, he has recovered; he had felt "impotent" because he "doubted the reality of the whole thing," but "now that I know, I am not afraid, even of the count." He maintains his courage from then on in the novel, though his hair turns white during the hour when Dracula invades the Harkers' bedroom; Harker gains in strength, and he is in the forefront at the kill. He has feared, it seemed, not for his sexuality but for his sanity, but his language was surely sexual.

Lucy likewise had a triple erotic experience when she wished that she could be married to three men at once, a thought she confided to Mina; in a way, she is punished for this departure from the straight and narrow (in her imagination) when she becomes the victim of the flying count, and, then, in the subsequent transfusions (without thought for blood types) gets her wish of triple husbands and more: there are four transfusions, one of them from the fatherly Van Helsing, the others from the suitors. She becomes symbolically married to four men, as Van Helsing clumsily points out. That Lucy was attracted to the count, even as she was seduced by him, is made plain in the record of the erotic dream she gives to Mina: " 'Something very sweet and bitter [was] around me all at once." After her death, she turns into the voluptuous temptress who makes a clearly sexual advance to Arthur (and, startled, he is about to succumb); her virginity is restored (another instance of that process) when the devampirizing ceremony is carried out on her body by Van Helsing and Seward. (In the meantime, she has been molesting children.) A telltale sexual detail, or a slip of the pen by Stoker, occurs when the "sperm" of the candle falls on her coffin in the mausoleum; she has been defiled by Dracula. Brave little Mina—who has been excluded, despite her knowledge and fine brain, from the deliberations of the men—is left alone by that thoughtless band and herself falls prey to Dracula; her dream, when Dracula visits her for the first time, also has sexual components: "I lay still and endured," like the apocryphal Victorian wife, unlike her fiancé Jonathan at the castle, whose passivity was marred by sexual anticipation, or her friend Lucy. She succumbs because she cannot do otherwise: "The last conscious effort which imagination made to me was to show me a lurid white face bending over me out of the mist." She is stronger, and less pleasure-prone, than Lucy, with the latter's fantasy of three husbands: she is faithful to her one, to the extent she can be. She becomes Dracula's partial slave during that awful night when, having been vampirized by the count, she is forced in turn to drink his blood—after he has threatened to kill Jonathan. (That she is turned into a kind of Fifth Column in the crusaders' midst, while still serving as their brain, not outdone even by Van Helsing, adds an exceptional tension to the pursuit; it may, as well, point to Stoker's own ambivalent attitude toward woman: on the one hand frail and undependable, and on the other brighter and even more loyal than man.) She is terribly conscious too, of the nature of the rape, and cries repeatedly "unclean, unclean"; but she is made of such resilient stuff that she pulls herself together immediately and plunges into the expedition's effort with renewed vigor. Likewise, despite what has happened, Harker also recovers quickly: the experience of the castle has steeled him; he emerges from his stupor, and "all the man in him awoke at the need for instant exertion."

These several scenes, with their implications of group sex, of polyandry, of rape and oral sex, and their concomitant implications of the constant frailty of the human flesh (only Seward, Quincey Morris, and Van Helsing are not exposed to temptation), are all the more surprising because of Stoker's own attitude about "indecency" in literature. In an essay "The Censorship of Fiction," from 1903, he fulminated against "catering for . . . base appetites" and "the exposition of lewd suggestion" and called such writing "a startling fact of decadence." He demanded a strict censorship, "constant and rigid," because the seed of evil, the sexual urge, lies in everyone. "The force of evil, anti-ethical evil, is the more dangerous as it is a natural force." (Remember Dr. Kvaale's

Horatian quotation in *Weary Men* about trying to drive nature out with a pitchfork!) By his lights, Stoker was a painfully moral writer who, in *Dracula*, recognized sex as a pernicious force which, uncontrolled, ruins all those who enter into its power; his Dracula — like the devil in the mass — is the spirit that roams throughout the world, seeking the ruin of souls, and sometimes almost succeeding. In this essentially antisexual attitude, Stoker also shows himself to be closely related to the other decadents of the canon, who, again and again, in the midst of their orgies and perversions, are actually bent on asceticism. Stoker is too much the profeminist to see woman, though, as the sole root of all evil; the count is the main tempter, the novel's *homme fatal*. For either gender, sex is alluring but brings misery and death, save when it is safely anchored within a marriage, and not practiced in the evil and illicit relationships the count fosters, and which Lucy innocently imagines for herself. Harker enters upon his husband's and father's role fully at the novel's end; Morris is a martyr, stabbed in the side like Jesus; Seward and Godalming, worshiping Lucy's memory, may very well remain celibate for the rest of their lives; Van Helsing — the widower and the good parent, who shares Stoker's first name, and who speaks of "my children" and "my boys" — will return to his research and his church, in which he has been so secure; entering Carfax on the night of September 30, for the great fight with the rats, he says, in Latin, " 'In manus tuas, Domine' — 'oh Lord, into thy hands I commend my spirit.' " The church which decadents so often saw as their final refuge has triumphed here, aided by northwest European and American good intentions and goodwill and pluck and a sense of duty. Mina is saved, as is the world.

Despite all the careful detail work, much about *Dracula* remains fuzzy, probably because Stoker could not directly confront all the problems of the human condition he dredged up. Can the Good Man (Harker) resist sexual temptation? The answer seems to be no, and Harker suffers for it. (He would have succumbed when "the fair girl" bent over him, had not evil's own messenger, Dracula, appeared.) Is the Good Woman (Mina) to be trusted or not? Can the Good Woman be safe from her sexual impulses? Mina records on August 8 that she and Lucy, returning from their country walk, are afraid of the "wild bulls." And Mina herself prefigures her own defilement when she dabs her feet with mud after she has come to save the somnambulistic Lucy from the shadow bending over her; Lucy's feet have also grown dirty from her nighttime promenade. Still, the drift of Stoker's book remains clear: that goodness and purity of heart must finally win out, unless the count comes back.

16

Portugal

JOSÉ MARIA EÇA DE QUEIRÓS

A cidade e as serras (*The City and The Mountains*) is the last book of the great Portuguese novelist José Maria Eça de Queirós, who died on August 16, 1900, while reading the proofs; at the time, Eça was Portuguese consul in Paris. He had been born in 1845, the illegitimate son of a young official and an officer's daughter. The parents were married four years after his birth, but the boy was brought up separately from his three legitimate younger brothers, at boarding schools, from which he went on, at sixteen, to the University of Coimbra. After a failure as a practicing attorney, he entered the diplomatic service; he had also undertaken the start of a literary career, as a member of a coterie of young writers who styled themselves *Os vencidos da vida* (Those Conquered by Life) and who combined predecadent, Baudelairian attitudes with a strong devotion to liberal ideals in politics. (A spot of color was added to Eça's life by a trip to the Near East, which he described in articles for a Lisbon newspaper; he was present at the opening of the Suez Canal.) He made his start as a novelist with a tale of irresistible passion, *O crime do Padre Amaro* (1875, *The Crime of Father Amaro*), the crime being the overwhelming lust of a young priest for a girl, a book reflecting Eça's views on what he considered to be unnatural celibacy, his dismay at clerical corruption, and his larger fascination with erotic themes; that he twice revised the book, after its initial publication, shows how close a student he was of Flaubert's careful stylistic art—he regarded Flaubert's *Madame Bovary* as the book of books. His diplomatic career led him to Havana (which he disliked, but where he interested himself in the plight of the Chinese laborers imported to work on Cuba's large estates), and on a trip through the United States, of which he scarcely conceived a better opinion; then he was posted to Newcastle-upon-Tyne, where again he was unhappy, because of both the coal capital's ugliness and the contrast between the city's "five hundred employers" and the "150,000 wretched laborers" whom they exploited. Thereafter he was sent to Bristol, in 1878, which he found but a little more attractive, although his affection for English letters was founded there, rivaling for a while his cultural devotion to France. His *Cartas de Inglaterra* (*Letters from England*), published in Rio de Janeiro's *Gazeta de Noticias* from 1879 on, made comment after comment on the oddities and the institutionalized injustices of British life: he wrote that engravings or lithographs of the English Christmas invariably depicted a snow scene, in which the solid walls of a castle, "its windows agleam with the brightness from within and the gaiety of those who live there," form the background to a group at the park railings in the foreground, "a woman and two children in their rags, huddled, holding lanterns in their hands and singing carols." On the subject of riding to hounds, Eça waxed particularly ironic, noting that the men almost always fall asleep after the day in the open; they collapse, "lulled . . . by one of Chopin's nocturnes, which a golden-haired angel is playing at the end of the drawing room; for all the use they are at a flirtation, an amorous intrigue, or a cultured conversation, they might as well be stuffed with straw."

Eça began to plan a series of twelve short novels, meant to depict the development of Portuguese society since the 1830s, something in the manner of Zola's Rougon-Macquart series. *O primo Basilio* (1878, *Cousin Basilio*) was a step in this direction, an upsetting but amusing picture of an affair between the not altogether bright wife of a good-natured and good-looking agricultural official and her vain and superficial cousin—eventually, she becomes the veritable slave of a scheming servant woman who has discovered her poorly guarded secret. Eça's grand plan foundered on the fact, he subsequently argued, that his diplomatic calling kept him far away from the scenes he meant to depict; his masterpiece, *Os Maias* (1881, *The Maias*) puts into a single large book his observations on the tired, effete, but almost always charming world of the Lisbon nobility and its retainers. Other works, however, veered away from the major intention: *O mandarino* (1880, *The Mandarin*), about a Portuguese who, in China, comes quite accidentally into a fortune and lives to pray that he might be freed from the burden of riches, and *A reliquia* (1887, *The Relic*), in which the opportunist and gifted liar Teodorico Raposo, sent by his pious aunt to the Holy Land to obtain a relic, comes back with what he announces to be the original crown of thorns, but mixing up his crates, he gives the old lady the lacy nightgown of the English semiprostitute with whom he has spent many happy nights in Alexandria.

In 1888, finally, Eça was granted the Portuguese consulship at Paris, a post he long had coveted and in which he remained until his death; during these later years, he worked at *A correspondencia de Fradique Mendes* (The Correspondence of Fradique Mendes), a novel in whose first part a portrait of the elegant aristocrat Mendes is given, a dandyistic ironist who has a good many points of resemblance with his creator; the second part consists of sixteen letters from Mendes to real or fictive members of society, to friends, to a sometime mistress. The book came out in 1900, the same year as *A ilustre casa de Ramires* (*The Illustrious House of Ramires*), about the soft and pleasant Gonçalo Mendes Ramires, apparently the last of an extremely long line of noblemen, who is incapable even of the courage to deal honestly with the farmers on his tumbledown estate or to stand up to local bullies (it would have been an ideal movie role for Marcello Mastroianni); the novel was followed by *The City and the Mountains,* published posthumously in 1901. The short *Alves & C.a* (*The Yellow Sofa*), about the brief cuckolding of a complacent businessman by his partner, and his eventual reconciliation with his not too nimble-witted wife, was put together by Eça's son and published in 1925.

While Eça deals with members of a decaying nobility and a middle class ready for every compromise, most of his novels, characterized by his irony, his sly humor, and his genuine and constant love of what he viewed as the essential gentleness of Portuguese life, do not specifically confront the problems of decadent characters but present more common human frailties: abandonment to heterosexual passion, greed, hypocrisy, venial weaknesses of all sorts. Only in his last books did he choose directly to employ features of the phenomenon of decadence which he had been able to observe for more than a dozen years at the Parisian fountainhead, a Paris with which he had become steadily more disenchanted. The extravagance and sometimes almost burlesque humor with which he assails decadence in the first part of *The City and the Mountains* leaves no doubt, apparently, about his attitude toward it; he finds it immeasurably funny, and immeasurably harmful, and his decadent is, it seems, so inherently sound that a cure is quickly achieved.

Jacinto, "my prince" to the devoted (but not blindly devoted) and commonsensical narrator and friend, Zé Fernandes, is given, to be sure, decadent attributes in large—but not complete—measure. Like Gonçalo Ramires before him, he comes, as the opening pages make clear, from an old and once vigorous line: "The ancient family . . . was already producing grain and planting vines in the time of King Dom Dinis" (that is, in the thirteenth century). For Jacinto's grandfather, though, the vigor has been concentrated in an enormous stomach, an enormous purse, and a weakness for lost causes: he follows his admired leader (who in fact went to Brazil and became emperor there) into a very comfortable Parisian exile, refusing to live in the "perverse country" from which "the Good King of Portugal," the absolutist Dom Miguel, had been forced to depart. (The little episode in which the courteous monarch picks up the overweight forebear after he has slipped on an orange peel is typical of Eça, in whose work small events often have large consequences.) The grandfather, having bought the palace at 202 Avenue des Champs-Elysées from a Polish prince, dies, like Henry I of England, of indigestion from a pickled lamprey; his son Cintinho, who displays the physical degeneration often characteristic of the decadent, does not survive long enough, shadowy and tubercular, to see the birth of his only child, our Jacinto. The offspring seems to have regained the family's old strength, shown in his excellent mind and corporeal well-being; he is a veritable "Prince of Good Fortune" ("Príncipe de Grã-Ventura").

Nevertheless, he has a streak of egoism which Zé Fernandes notes, as it were, in passing: "Without enough heart to fall strongly in love, and quite content with this incapacity which freed him from responsibilities," he experiences only "the sweetness of love without its bitterness." He has but one goal in life, we are told, to be "strong, rich, indifferent to the laws of men," which does not mean, though, that the good-mannered millionaire can become as hateful as Des Esseintes or as cruelly egocentric as Sperelli; "we never saw him with any other ambition than thoroughly to understand general ideas." It is his drive for an access to all knowledge, in fact, that leads him to his peculiar decadence: he is the most abstractly intellectual (if not the most aesthetic) of all the members of the decadent clan we have met; in the most civilized place in the world, Paris, with all the advantages of modern technology at his well-heeled disposal, he believes he will somehow be able to collect and consolidate all the information he wants to have — the specific urge for a final frisson on the part of the jaded Des Esseintes, and the hunt for constant pleasure of the cynical Sperelli, have been turned into a diffuse search for total cognition. Yet he immediately reveals traits that put him more directly into the decadent tradition: primary among them is his fear of nature, which he cannot control — the grass, in its changing, reminds him of human mortality, the stile in a fence makes him engage in what he considers to be unbecoming behavior, sending him back "to the original apes." (Like all Eça's protagonists, he is sedentary.) The not always perceptive Zé Fernandes, while recording this and other symptoms, decadent to our trained eyes, cannot interpret them as such;

before the sturdy countryman leaves for his seven years in the homeland, he sees Jacinto as "a superbly built young man in whom appeared the strength of generations of ancient, rural Jacintos." Indeed, Zé Fernandes says that he finds only one characteristic of the "nineteenth century," for which read decadence: "Only by his sharp nose with its delicate, pale nostrils restlessly mobile as if savoring perfumes did he appear to belong to the nineteenth century at all." Still, Zé Fernandes goes on to list other features that predict the young man's decadent fate: his dandyism (the "cravats of dark satin and his gloves of white doeskin . . . all ordered from London in boxes of cedar"), and the floral detail that could make us think Jacinto had been reading *À rebours* if the year (in Eça's book) were not 1880 but 1884, the date of the decadent breviary's publication: "He always wore in his buttonhole a flower which was of no natural growth but had been synthetically composed by his florist of petals of different flowers." Naturally or unnaturally, the fictional Des Esseintes will go the fictional Jacinto one better, trying to find those flowers which are actual growths, but look artificial in their horrible conformations. (Jacinto never acquires Des Esseintes's — and how many other decadents' — genius for the genuinely perverse.)

Coming back to Paris, Zé Fernandes finds Jacinto much changed. Now thirty, he is stooped, and his face has developed two wrinkles, "like those on the face of a tired comedian." His fascination with technology (related to that of Des Esseintes and Bavaria's mad king Ludwig) has turned his palace into a treasure house of exotic comfort: the unnecessary elevator is the most mundane of the improvements. "Perfuming pans . . . steamed a vapor which aromatized and maintained that delicate and superfine atmosphere." In Jacinto's artificial paradise, his books have increased, in the outer rooms, to thirty thousand in number, handsomely bound; his study is done in shades of green, the familiar green of decadence; his desk is covered with gadgets (one of which pricks the inexperienced Zé Fernandes's finger); acoustic tubes carry his messages throughout his household; he has an electric fountain pen; the library contains another thirty thousand volumes; Zé Fernandes is startled by a "man speaking from inside a box," the lecture-phone ("o conferençofone"), which has an equivalent, of course, in the theater-phone, put on particular display at the banquet for the grand duke. We have come upon an equivalent in its communicational aspects of the world of machines predicted by Georg Jonathan in *Weary Men,* but here devoted not to the service of humanity but to the whims of a single man, the enormously wealthy "Prince of Good Fortune." Yet Jacinto — on his way to his warm shower, at seventeen degrees Centigrade, and his "massage of geranium juice" — utters a lament to be heard again and again from his lips: " 'It's a bore' " ("é uma seca"), his verbal signature. After a glance into the dining room with its sets of water and its more-than-extensive place settings, Zé Fernandes learns that Jacinto suffers from thirst (he cannot find any water that suits or satisfies him) and he has "lost his appetite," lost it long ago. The life of Jacinto has become a routine of being dressed, of accomplishing his toilette (his brushes are legion and he has a special need of daily pedicures), of holding membership in boards of directors and esoteric clubs, of pointless visits, regulated by an "agenda book . . . bound in leather of a tender, faded rose color." In the midst of all this, the prince lies on his divan, "his eyes miserably half-closed," hugely yawning. The admirer of the city, too, when he goes out, is "afflicted by the brutality of [the] haste, egotism, and noise" of the scores of people in the streets. He seeks to excuse the "furrows, wakes, or tracks which people leave behind" as " 'only the petty miseries of an otherwise delightful civilization.' " " 'It *is* ugly, very ugly,' " he says, but he refuses to condemn it, as Des Esseintes did; it is an unavoidable part of the civilization he has accepted as his particular nest. (He has managed to incorporate nature, of a kind, into his acceptance of Parisian life: he has developed a love for the Bois de Boulogne — as a social meeting place of the cream of society, which he views from the window of his carriage — on outings that he regards as acts of "conscience and duty,' but which, nonetheless, quickly put him into another fit of boredom.)

The technical world turns against him: the electric pens leak, the bathroom plumbing explodes, the lights in the palace go out, and, a little later on, bearing the grand duke's fish, the dumbwaiter gets stuck. Jacinto's erotic life has become arid in a strange way; he owns a share of the great cocotte Diane de Lorge (sharing her with seven members of his club), but "lower than her shoulders [he does] not know the color of her skin." He does carry on — a Parisian custom — an adulterous affair with Mme Oriol, a flower of society that, it seems to Zé Fernandes, has "something in her petals that seemed about to fade and wither"; in her stagy piety, during Lent, she puts onto her velvet hat "a perfect little crown of thorns," made of the finest jet. (The telling detail, from chapter 3, comes back in chapter 7, where this time the ornament is worn specifically during Holy Week.) Mme Oriol is a member of Jacinto's set, portrayed during the banquet for the grand duke centered around the "very delicious and rare fish . . . caught in Dalmatia," which the guests try to catch with bent pins and never get to eat. Eça takes the occasion of the banquet to parody what D'Annunzio portrayed with all seriousness in *Il piacere*, the high society in which the princely aesthete lives. The lights fail, again, before the banquet begins and are repaired in the nick of time (Zé Fernandes, forever leary of civilization, stuffs "two stout stumps of tallow" into his pocket); then the guests arrive. Among these the most notable are the comtesse de Trèves, whom her husband shares with the "terrible banker Ephraim" (she compliments Jacinto on his electric stamp-licker vacuously, as a part of her Art of Charm — to Zé Fernandes, she seems a "falsehood of towering sublimity"); the Psychologist, a somewhat inaccurate portrait of the novelist and essayist (on decadence) Paul Bourget, who is exposed as a bumbler by the dandy Marizac (a name that suggests the dandy Robert de Montesquiou-Fezensac, the model for Des Esseintes in his pre-thébaïde existence) — in his novel *The Cuirass*, the Psychologist had blundered, writing that its heroine, a duchess with notably good taste, nonetheless wore a "corset of black satin"; the fat Dornan, the "mystical poet"; the undulating Mme Verghane, with the "fecund rotundity of her hips" and a waist so tiny that Zé Fernandes fears she "will break in two." The grand duke himself, evidently well read in the literature of decadence, picks an orchid — the "wicked flower" of *Il piacere* — that resembles a "greenish scorpion," so that Mme Oriol can fasten it onto her "lustrous breast, whose beauty the venomous deformity of the flower seemed perversely to spice and flavor." Perhaps the most thoroughly decadent member of the whole company is the youth with the "pale maize-colored beard as flimsy as thistle down," who imagines that a dynamite bomb "could be thrown from the door": " 'What a fine ending for a dinner, for the end of the city.' " Not having read *À rebours* (where the vengeful God of the Old Testament is enjoined to destroy the Cities of the Plain) or *Dorian Gray* (with its conversation about "fin de siècle, fin du globe."), Zé Fernandes is shocked, but the youth continues, declaring that "nowadays the only sensation left which [is] really a fine on, would be to annihilate Civilization . . . All the pleasure to be got out of creating [is] already outworn. The only pleasure left [is] the divine pleasure of destruction." As the dinner goes on (Zé Fernandes, the natural man, always has a superb appetite) and the "frosted ortolans" are served, the "downy cheeked youth" continues "lyrically crooning about the destruction of the world," and Zé Fernandes agrees with him: decadent and natural man are in harmony on this point, more or less, but the former is so surfeited with thrills that there remains for him only the greatest and last thrill of all, the absolute end, while the latter would like to see only a destruction of the city itself, as the breeder of rottenness.

For Jacinto, "it is all a bore." He has not even been struck by the "heavings of the vast bosom of Madame Verghane," for which Zé Fernandes (ever the natural man) has had an eye even in his postprandial exhaustion: " 'A superb woman — that Verghane.' " Nonetheless, however bored he has been, Jacinto does not abandon his banquets; during the next winter season, the last he will spend in Paris, he tries still harder to lead the decadent life: "He imitated the Feasts of Color, following the example of Heliogabalus as recorded in the

Historia Augusta, and offered his female friends that sublime rose-colored dinner at which everything was colored rose . . . while from the roof, covered with rosy veils, fell showers of fresh rose petals." This performance bores him too. Nevertheless, lacking the superb cruelty of the true decadent, Jacinto does not finish the banquet quite as Heliogabalus did. The emperor saw to it that his guests were smothered to death in the rose petals, the scene painted by Lawrence Alma-Tadema and given poetic form by Stefan George in his verse cycle from 1892 about Heliogabalus, *Algabal.*

The structure of *The City and the Mountains* is symmetrical and crystal-clear: chapters 1 through 3 lead up to the banquet for the grand duke, presented in chapter 4; chapters 5 to 7 depict the spiritual unraveling of the prince, chapter 8 describes the farewell to Paris and the journey to Portugal, and the remainder, chapters 9 to 16, deals with the prince's healing and his projects conceived in his newfound strength. The mechanical jokes abate (among the last of them are the salad mixer "that spattered vinegar into the eyes of my Prince, who fled yelling" and the planned machine for buttoning drawers); the piles of books increase — so radically that Zé Fernandes has a dream of an avalanche of books covering the streets of Paris, and an ascent into Heaven, where he finds the All-Highest, smiling, reading a cheap new edition of the atheist Voltaire; the dream ends as Jacinto, bearing "three spicy novels" under his arm, appears. The blunt and faithful servant Cricket ("o Grilo") decides that Jacinto (like Thomas Mann's Siegmund Aarenhold) suffers from surfeit, pure and simple; the "warlock or wizard" Maurice de Mayolle, encountered on Montmartre, recites the catalogue of the intellectual fads he (and so Jacinto) have encountered in Paris: Wagnerism and Wagnerian mythology, Pre-Raphaelitism, Renan, the Cult of the Ego (a reference to Maurice Barrès's *Culte du moi:* Jacinto admits that he himself has followed it for a time), Eduard von Hartmann and the Unconscious, Nietzschianism, Tolstoyism, Emersonianism, "and the worst plague of all . . . Ibsenism," diabolism, phallism, Ruskinism, the last a concept that not even Jacinto understands until it is explained to him as "the Cult of Beauty"; the list ends with de Mayolle's baffling description of his own Indian cult, which has "verified the waves and vibrations of the Will . . . We work. We are seekers.'" Once the catalogue is over and de Mayolle has departed, Jacinto adds an epilogue of his own, trying to explain what that " 'strange fellow, very rich and descended from the Duke of Septimania' " is up to at present: " 'Theosophy. Esoteric Buddhism. Aspiration. Disillusionment. I've tried it . . . and it's a horrible bore.' " But he is not yet cured. He decides to build a house, with a tower made of glass and iron, on the heights of Montmartre, "where I can rest and dominate the city." He does not carry out the plan; instead, he becomes a Prince of

Melancholy, and, surrounded by his multiplying books, he concentrates on two of them — as he fingers his face, "as if to encourage and coax the skull from beneath its covering." The one is Ecclesiastes, Gram's favorite biblical text (Jacinto is driven around Paris, holding Solomon's lament in his hand, crying " 'Vanity of Vanities, all is Vanity' "), the other is Gram's Schopenhauer, read as the prince has his toenails done by his pedicurist and sips the mocha sent to him "by the Emirs of the desert, but which he never finds satisfactory."

Zé Fernandes goes on a European tour after two experiences that contribute in some measure to Jacinto's conversion. The first is the Natural Man's sexual encounter with a very vulgar handmaiden of the decadent life, Mme Colombe, which serves to inoculate him (if he needs inoculation) against a possible decadent infection. Scarcely virginal, at the opera with the prince, he does not enjoy *Lohengrin*, "his white soul, his white swan, and his white arms, or his white armor." After "his incessant and perceptible despoilment" by Mme Colombe he learns from the concierge at 16 Rue Helder that she " 'has run away with some other pig.' " Hungry as ever (nothing can spoil his appetite), he eats his feast of lobster and duck with pimientos, drinks his Burgundy, and then throws it all up. He throws up the vampiristic Mme Colombe as well: appearing out of the flame of a candle during his nightmare of indigestion, she "sunk herself into my breast, put her mouth to my heart, and began to suck my blood from it in long, slow gulps" — naturally enough, Zé Fernandes cries out for his Aunt Vicencia in distant Portugal. He concludes that he must have got a fever, "a fever of the imagination, caught in a dirty puddle of Paris — one of those puddles . . . formed around Paris by the stagnant waters, slime, dirt, fungi, and worms of a civilization that is rotting away."

The second experience is shared between Zé Fernandes and his prince, the Prince of Surfeit. The friend persuades the prince to go up to the Basilica of Sacré Coeur on the heights of Montmartre, and here — playing, in radical transformation, the role of Satan tempting Christ, on "the exceeding high mountain" — he tempts Jacinto to abandon "the city of the ash-gray plain": readers of the time may have caught the echoes of the anathema Des Esseintes hurls at Paris at the end of *À rebours*. Suddenly become a very persuasive preacher, Zé Fernandes tells Jacinto at length about the dehumanizing effect of the City. Part of what he says belongs to those many complaints about the metropolis that turn up in literature around the turn of the century, from Arthur Conan Doyle's drab and awful London in *A Study in Scarlet* to Émile Verhaeren's "ville tentaculaire" and Rilke's outcry in The Book of Hours: "Denn, Herr, die großen Städte sind/Verlorene und Aufgelöste" ("For Lord, the mighty cities are/Lost beings, beings in decay"). Part of what Zé Fernandes says, too, is a reflection of a topos from classical antiquity, which the German scholar Friedrich Sengle defined as "Wunschbild Land und Schreckbild Stadt" ("ideal image of the country, horrible image of the city") — the praise of country life, as opposed to city cares, which we find in Horace's "Beatus ille, qui procul negotiis." (With his classical upbringing, Zé Fernandes is perfectly aware of this element in his argument: "Before these hoary and antiquated invectives let fly by every bucolic moralist for centuries, since the time of Hesiod — my Prince meekly bowed his head.") Sandwiched between these more general warnings lie specific references to the City as the breeding ground of decadence: in it, "man is imprisoned either within the pale of banality" or else "in the wastes of eccentricity and extravagance." (The particularly antidecadent section of Zé Fernandes's sermon follows directly on his condemnation of homosexuality, "the dismal recesses or Sodom and Lesbos.") For the captive of the city, every experience must be at second hand: he "can only express what already has been expressed": he must live by analogy, he is barren. (Precisely: Jacinto has gotten his idea for his rose banquet by reading the *Historia Augusta,* or maybe Jean Lombard's shocker on Heliogabalus, *L'Agonie* of 1888, or, possibly, too, the account of the black banquet in the first chapter of *À rebours.*) Thus the captive of the city must invent, as a decadent, "some novel deformity, at the cost of much groaning effort, which will shock and arrest the crowd like some freakish monster at a fair."

In the coda of his sermon, Zé Fernandes turns to a topic which has variously troubled the horizons of a Sperelli, of Mann's Aarenhold twins, of Harald Malcorn in Rilke's "Die Letzten," in these instances, however, eventually to be put aside with contempt — the presence of the poor, the disadvantaged. It is probably indicative of Zé Fernandes's essentially feudal turn of mind that he ignores the bourgeoisie whom Des Esseintes wished to shock; Zé Fernandes divides the population of the city, instead, into but two groups: "Only a very small and brilliant caste enjoys in the City any of the pleasures which derive from city life. The rest, the obscure, immense plebs, can only suffer and they can only suffer the special sufferings that are derived from city life . . . There they lie scattered about the City like vile manure which fertilizes the City." It is not the only time that Zé Fernandes entertains thoughts about "the tatters [which] the ragpickers" wear so that "Madame Oriol can undulate sweetly up the stairs of the Opera in silks and laces," thoughts about the "whole people and its little ones weep[ing] with hunger" — so that the Jacintos, in January, "might toy yawningly, on plates of Dresden china, with strawberries frozen in champagne." Zé Fernandes conjures up Mme Oriol preparing her skating costume while, "under the arches of the bridges shelterless children begin to die of the cold"; he thinks, on the rainy winter night of Jacinto's birthday as the two drink to the *manes* of their dead, about the "ten thousand poor who nightly roam through Paris, without food or shelter," and then adds, again, his feudal thought — that, in the Portuguese countryside, under a patriarchal system, the poor are much better off, "sheltered by their own roof, sure of their pot of rice and cabbage . . . Oh, little Portugal, still so good to the little ones, the humble, and the poor." (We shall presently see how accurate this view of Portuguese poverty is.) Zé Fernandes finishes his sermon with the charge that Jesus was ineffectual in his mission on earth, "the adorable Son of God was in too much of a hurry to return to the House of His Father," and his clergy has become venal — a line of argument not so far removed from that of Des Esseintes in the last chapter of *À rebours,* although Des Esseintes, with his grand contempt for humanity, is more concerned about the clergy's adulteration of the articles of the church than about its failures in social care.

These experiences and others bring Jacinto to his decision to go to the land of his fathers; the direct cause is the news of the imminent removal of the bones of his noble ancestors from the Church of San José to the newly rebuilt chapel of Tormes. (The property, Tormes, lies near the hill town of "Guiàes"; one wonders if this is Guimaràes, north of Oporto, where Portugal was born.) Certainly, Jacinto's sense of family history (aroused on the night of the melancholy birthday party, when "sweet rice, Portuguese rice" turned out to be an overflavored and overadorned horror) had a part in spurring the decision: standing in the midst of his thousands upon thousands of volumes, his attention is briefly caught by "the splendor of the Byzantine Empire," and, tentatively announcing his intention to Zé Fernandes, he recalls that " 'one of [my] properties dates from 1410 . . . when the Byzantine Empire was still in existence.' " The decision is taken in the very nick of time: "Thus it seemed was going to end the mighty, mountaineering race of the Jacintos — in this super-refined, over-domesticated spindle-shanks." The forebears had been mighty, but "now this last of the Jacintos, this Jacintulus, with his smooth skin soaked in perfumes, his narrow soul choked with philosophies, stood fettered in trivial indecision before the mere prospect of going on living." (The diminutive "Jacintulus" recalls the name of the last emperor of the West, Romulus Augustulus.)

The story of the vastly complicated preparations for the journey and the story of the last season in Paris make easy and amusing reading. Having uttered his announcement in a "deep, urgent voice," Jacinto begins to backslide, loving the city one moment and thinking the next of a "rapid painless death by prussic acid," as he lies on his divan with crossed arms, "like a statue on a tomb"; he takes his last ride through the Bois ("Not a single untidy branch or shoot disgraced the smooth undulations of greenery"), and meets — not unwillingly — several of the effete snobs who participated in the dinner for the grand duke. The slow farewell is followed by the trip in the special railroad coach (and then shabbier public coaches) through France to Spain and Portugal, the first sight of the estate, the revivification of Jacinto and the taking of his next decision: " 'I even prefer to sleep at Tormes, in my own house in the mountains,' " his slow absorption into the tempo of country life, his acceptance by his manager, his farmers, and his neighbors. The episode of Jacinto's reading, when he has come home, summarizes what has happened. Like Siegmund Aarenhold, Jacinto has never been able to give himself wholly to a book (save for the two classics of pessimism noted above); otherwise, he has been surrounded by books, "without ever having tried the matter of a single one of them." Now, "since his resurrection," he plunges heart and soul into *Don Quixote* (Zé Fernandes has remarked that he plays the role of Sancho Panza to Jacinto), and then the *Odyssey,* with its "wideswept, health-giving saline fragrance." Meanwhile, the prince dismisses Schopenhauer (who abandoned pessimism when he became a celebrated author) and Solomon (who grew pessimistic when his power was slipping from him, and "his seraglio of 300 concubines had become ridiculously superfluous"). Now, too, Jacinto has a "strong tread" as he enters the province of Nature, and forges his impractical and practical plans for improving his farm. (One scheme is so complex that Zé Fernandes fears Jacinto is sliding into his old decadent ways again, "a prey to his old passion for accumulating sensations.") His discovery of Portuguese rural poverty (which gives the lie to Zé Fernandes's own dream of an idyllic Portugal where no one starves) and his bravery in entering the house that contains smallpox are signs of the new, socially concerned Jacinto. Having repeatedly called himself the last of his line, he marries the plump Joaninha and fathers the children who, later on, come to the station to greet Zé Fernandes as he returns from an excursion to Paris, throwing aside — at Jacinto's command — the refuse of a "putrid Civilization" he has picked up under way: newspapers "full of ladies in different stages of undress, dirty stories, Parisian jokes and eroticism." Jacinto has been saved, we have known it for a very long time, and we are not surprised when the little band, young Jacinto's flag flying, makes its way, "serenely and securely toward the Castle of Great Happiness ("o Castelo da Grã-Ventura")."

The completeness of Jacinto's transformation (which resembles the sudden transformation of Gonçalo Ramires into a man of action, somewhere in the African colonies, near the end of *The Illustrious House of Ramires*), and the happy ending of the book have caused commentators a great deal of pondering: some have taken the change at face value, others have not — it has been proposed by Maria Lúcia Lepecki (1974) that Jacinto is still another of the "deluded men" of Eça's earlier novels: what he does at Tormes is a "desperate attempt to survive in a time and in a place that are no longer his, and in a reality that has never been his" (quoted by Alexander Coleman in *Eça de Queirós and the European Realism* [1980]). His turning into a benevolent country squire, of the feudal cut of his ancestors, is an example of fantasy become real. V. S. Pritchett wrote that the book's last chapters "have the absurd beauty of Oblomov's dream" of pastoral happiness. Jacinto can realize his dream because of his untold wealth — with his model dairy farm, his Tolstoyan school, his concern for public health, and so forth, he has given his tenants a new life; they admire him as a savior, as a reincarnation of the Portuguese national hero, Dom Sebastião. (The comparison is surely undercutting; Dom Sebastian, perhaps insane and surely deluded, invaded Morocco [1578] and was lost, together with his army of twelve thousand men, a catastrophe leading the kingless country to sixty years of Spanish domination.) The argument of Pritchett and others could be refined a little by putting the book into the tradition of literary decadence on which, in its first part, it so obviously draws; Eça has taken pains — all too many, it might seem — to list, underline, and emphasize the decadent traits of Jacinto; however, as has been proposed above, he lacks some essential features — he is only superficially aesthetic, he is never cruel, and he is never perverse, albeit surrounded by perversities. But he has been, and remains, a decadent in a certain hidden yet obvious way: he has played, to the point of self-destructive boredom, the decadent role in Paris, with the "face of a tired comedian." In Portugal, he plays, very brilliantly, another role, that of the good master, surrounded by his admiring vassals. The tired comedian, having become filled with energy, still uses, reasonably now, the technology of which he was so insanely enamoured in Paris; his world, as said, is a small one, a medieval fiefdom, as in a comic operetta, in which he acts out his notion of what his ancestors were — who went in their armor to the fields of their estate: his armor is his money and his (still sometimes very far-fetched) inventiveness. And Zé Fernandes is as much a feudalist as the prince: both have refused to join the twentieth century and have gotten away with it. How long the vassals, educated and enlightened, will be happy to tug their forelocks is another story, not told here. Probably the friends' Portuguese country world (which they also see as resembling the estates of ancient Rome, as they vie with one another in quotations from Vergil's *Eclogues* and *Georgics*) will end too, but in all likelihood they will not witness the ending. That lot may fall to little Jacintinho, the boy carrying the white flag, when he grows up. What would the royalist Prince of Good Fortune have thought of the assassination of King Carlos I and the crown prince in 1908, and the abdication of the surviving son, Manuel II, two years later?

Just the same, if we wish, we can take Jacinto's cure as a real one; the cure *has* taken place, and even religion (that aid for which decadents have so often longed) has something to do with it — not that Christianity overtly plays much of a role in the novel. Zé Fernandes's Sermon on the Mount has shaken Jacinto (or tempted him, if we wish to see here a benevolent parody on the stories of Satan's efforts to tempt Christ on the pinnacle of the temple and on "an exceeding high mountain"). Like Philip in Acts 8:26–41, Jacinto has arisen and gone to the south at the injunction of the angel; he has lifted up his eyes, in accordance with the Psalmist's words, until the hills, whence cometh his strength. Zé Fernandes, the seemingly hard-headed man, has aided and abetted him, we might guess, in another way too — Zé Fernandes, who in his accord with Nature (an intimacy into which he also leads Jacinto), has spoken in the tones of Saint Francis of Assisi as they ride along to Tormes for the first time: " 'Thank you brother blackbird! Thank you, brother vines! Here we come.' " (Earlier, in his account of Jacinto's fear of nature, the narrator-friend has already alluded to Saint Francis: unlike the saint, the timid and selfish Jacinto would not stretch out his arms to the Wolf of Agobbio). The affection for Saint Francis, the lover of Nature, was by no means unusual among others who had gone through the decadent illness: Johannes V. Jensen, after his early decadent novels, became the saint's indefatigable biographer and eulogizer, Rilke apostrophized the saint in the conclusion of *The Book of Hours*. Zé Fernandes — at once natural man, Sancho Panza, and a kind of saintly Christian persuader — has saved his friend.

17

Spain

RAMÓN MARÍA DEL VALLE-INCLÁN

The *Sonatas* of Ramón María del Valle-Inclán (1866–1936) fell outside the loop of international decadence when they appeared. The tetralogy of short novels was begun in 1902 with *Sonata de otoño* (Sonnet of Autumn), *Sonata de estío* (Sonnet of Summer) followed in 1903, *Sonata de primavera* (Sonnet of Spring) in 1904, and *Sonata de invierno* (Sonnet of Winter) in 1905. Attention had been called to contemporary Spanish literature by the ill-founded award of the Nobel Price for Literature in 1903 to the fecund dramatist José Echegaray (1832–1916), and by the representation in German — that major translation language — of the great novelist, Benito Pérez-Galdós (1843–1920) with *Doña Perfecta* (1876, German translation 1886) and *Gloria* (1877, German translation 1880); such younger writers as Valle-Inclán passed largely unnoticed outside the Spanish-language realm, perhaps because of the cultural isolation of Spain of which Valle-Inclán would later complain, calling his country a "deformation of European civilization." Neither the stylistic brilliance of the tetralogy nor the occasional perversity of its themes attracted attention. In transmission Eça de Queirós was more fortunate: his novel about adultery *O primo Basilio* (1877) appeared in German in 1880 and *A cidade e as serras* (1900) as *Stadt und Gebirg* in 1903, and Eça also attained early translation into French. Valle-Inclán was a translator of Eça into Spanish; *La reliquia* (1902) and *El crimen de Padre Amaro* (1904) were done for money — Valle-Inclán was always hard up — but their send-up of Catholic cults and criticism of a lustful and hypocritical priesthood must also have appealed to him. Valle-Inclán himself languished without notable translation for years; the *Mémoires aimables du marquis de Bradomín* appeared in a private printing in 1910, the *Sonates de printemps et été* in 1928, but a partial *Sommersonate* in German had to wait until 1958. The silence around Valle-Inclán should be compared to the ease with which Bang, Couperus, Garborg, and Jacobsen moved into German. The *Sonatas* entered English in 1924 as *The Pleasant Memoirs of the Marquis de Bradomín,* by May Heyward Broun and Thomas Walsh, perhaps riding on the coattails of belated decadent writing in the United States; it was accompanied, the same year, by a translation of a novel in some respects a spin-off of the *Sonatas,* the Argentinian Larreta's *La gloria de Don Ramires: Una vida en tiempo de Felipe II* (1908). The Broun-Walsh translation omitted some passages and contained a good many errors. A full version of the *Sonatas,* by Margaret Jull Costa, was published in 1997–98.

Overlooked in the few general studies of European decadent literature, the *Sonatas* are mentioned only in passing in the addenda (1951) to Mario Praz's classic *La carne, la morte, e il diavolo nella letteratura romantica* (1931). Hans Hinterhäuser rescued them in an essay of 1972, placing them in the vicinity of *Il piacere* and *The Picture of Dorian Gray.* Specialists in Spanish letters had produced a huge secondary literature on Valle-Inclán's whole output, which, however, largely failed to put it in the European context. Recently, in Hinterhäuser's wake, German scholars and translators have compensated for the neglect of a century ago by a burgeoning industry of texts by and on Valle-Inclán.

Had the *Sonatas* been known to European criticism in the heyday of decadence, it would have been easy enough to spot resemblances between the marquis and Andrea Sperelli, and, somewhat more distantly, Des Esseintes and Dorian. The marquis is a prideful and destructive seducer, and, not unimportantly, shares a sense of self-irony with Des Esseintes. He comes from the well-known long ancestral line; his "uncle" Don Juan Manuel de Montenegro in *Sonata de otoño* claims that, like the Montenegros, the Bradomíns are sufficiently ancient to have descended from Roland, who did not die at Roncesvalles. Like Des Esseintes and Sperelli, though to be sure on a much smaller scale, Bradomín knows art, as demonstrated in the several painterly allusions of *Sonata de primavera;* his main musical statement, however, is directed against Wagner, whose compositions he can appreciate as little, he says, as homosexual love.

Like Des Esseintes, and Sperelli and other protagonists of D'Annunzio, he is extremely well read. He gets his information on homosexuality, he claims, from reading "that amiable Petronius" at the Seminary of Nobles. He bears his learning more lightly, as a man of action, than does Des Esseintes, and — a rival to Sperelli and his Latin and Italian verses — he is creative, as the author in old age and "in exile" of his memoirs. Valle-Inclán himself criticized the *Sonatas* as "literature made of literature," a statement often quoted, and Bradomín freely throws about the great names of his predecessors in memoiristic literature, St. Augustine, Saint-Simon, and Chateaubriand, although the last reference is to *Atala,* and not to the *Mémoires d'outre-tombe.* He is especially indebted to Casanova's *Mémoires,* like Bradomín's written in old age during the great lover's "exile" as librarian at the Bohemian castle of Dux.

At the outset of *Sonata de primavera,* Bradomín implies that his noble lineage is a justification for his having been chosen, a young captain in the papal guard at Rome, to bring the announcement of a cardinalship to Monsignor Estefano Gaetani in Liguria. Bradomín's paternal grandmother was a "Bibiena di Rienzo," the daughter of the Prince Máximo de Bibiena poisoned in 1770 by the famous actress Simonetta la Corticelli, an event "which gets a long chapter in the Memoirs of the Chevalier de Seingalt" or Casanova. This is a fiction on Bradomín's part; while the actress Maríana Corticelli was among Casanova's loves (see Book 2 of the *Mémoires*), Simonetta and the poisoning story do not appear. In a key passage of *Sonata de invierno,* after Bradomín has lied to the priests of the church at Estella about his stay in a monastery as penance for his many sins, he utters an apostrophe to the " 'winged and laughing lie. When will men be persuaded of the necessity of your triumph?" and to the "smiling lie, you bird of light that sings like hope itself.' " The apostrophe comes later than Wilde's "Decay of Lying" — no evidence exists that Valle-Inclán knew that essay — and a few years before Rilke's portrait of the great liar Saint Germain, in *Die Aufzeichnungen des Malte Laurids Brigge.* Casanova, an admiring acquaintance of Saint Germain, has also been accused of lying, for example, about his trip to Constantinople and, of course, about his startling sexual feats.

Having set the tone for a specious veracity with the flourish of his first entry, Bradomín continues to employ Casanova in his advances to María del Rosario — the eldest of the daughters of his hostess, the Princess Gaetani, she is about to enter the convent. The widowed princess lives at the fictional town of Liguria near the Tyrrhenian Sea. Her brother-in-law, Monsignor Gaetani, "the bishop of Betulia," has an ecclesiastical title that may be an author's joke: Betulia in the Vulgate is the home of the beautiful widow Judith who seduces Holofernes, makes him drunk, and decapitates him. (Just so, another churchman in the tetralogy is "the bishop of Corinth," notorious in antiquity, and to St. Paul, as egregiously licentious.) The marquis finds María del Rosario reading a devotional book, the *Mystica ciudad de Dios,* whose content is revealed in its subtitle, *Historia divin, y vida de la Virgen Madre de Dios,* by Sister Coronel de Jesus de Agreda (1607); Bradomín says that he knows it too, because his "spiritual father" read it when a prisoner in the Leads at Venice. Surprisingly, this claim is true; Casanova was given the *Mystica ciudad* as reading matter during his solitary confinement there. Asked by María del Rosario who the spiritual father was, Bradomín identifies him, truthfully again, as Casanova, of whom the pious girl has never heard. Bradomín informs her that he was a Venetian adventurer who repented at the end of his life, writing his confessions, to which María del Rosario asks " 'Like St. Augustine?' " " 'The same, but humble and Christian, he did not wish to compare himself to the father of the church and called them memoirs.' " Asked if he has read them, Bradomín lures the girl on by adding, correctly, that they are his favorite reading matter, and that she could " 'learn much in them.' " Bradomín continues his efforts at oblique literary seduction: "Jacopo de Casanova" was " 'a great friend of a nun of Venice,' " i.e., the beautiful "M. M." of the *Mémoires'* first book, with whom Casanova carried on a long affair, not described by Bradomín. But he adds one more religious detail: she was a Carmelite, to which María del Rosario, rising to the bait, replies that she too will become a member of that order. She is led, in sly and easy steps, toward the passion for Bradomín which will end with the accidental death of her youngest sister, María de las Nieves, as María del Rosario is distracted by Bradomín's advances.

Still other episodes or details from the *Mémoires* or about their author have been put to work by Valle-Inclán. The brief introductory note to the *Sonatas* states that the marquis was "ugly, Catholic, and sentimental"; the ancient Marquesa de Tor repeats the phrase to him at the tetralogy's end. The memoirist Charles de Ligne, the uncle of Casanova's long-suffering employer at Dux, reports that Casanova would be "a good-looking man if he were not ugly." Casanova himself emphasizes in his introduction that he is a Christian; Bradomín remarks that he possesses "the soul of an adventurer, a nobleman, a Christian." Occasionally pious and a self-styled nobleman, Casanova gives plenty of evidence of his sentimentality: he weeps upon leaving Venice after his escape from the Leads (Book 1, chap. 53: "La matinée était superbe, l'air pure, les premiers rayons du soleil magnifiques . . . tout cela m'émut si violemment que, plein de reconnaissance envers Dieu, je me sentais suffoqué par le sentiment et je fondis en larmes"). He weeps again upon learning that one of his most enduring loves, Manon Balletti, has rejected him (Book 2, chap. 36). Bradomín often weeps, sometimes for effect, sometimes not. Remembering María del Rosario, his "dry, almost blind eyes fill with tears." Like Casanova, Bradomín is painfully aware of having grown old.

The episode in *Sonata de primavera* in which a mysterious Capuchin monk tells Bradomín that he is in danger and must get back from a witch his ring, stolen for magical purposes, is taken directly from an adventure of Casanova at Milan (Book 2, chap. 42); there, more explicitly than in the *Sonata,* the witch has made a waxen image of Bradomín by which she means to rob him of his manhood ("Les parties de la génération étaient monstrueuses de disproportion"). Bradomín's ambiguous attitude toward homosexuality is likewise twice borrowed from Casanova: in the *Sonata de primavera* he regrets his constitutional inability to experience "that beautiful sin, gift of the gods and temptation of the poets," a phrase repeated expressis verbis in *Sonata de invierno.* In the second instance, the thought is directed at a handsome Russian youth who appears in the company of another, older Russian, a giant, whom Bradomín has already met and disliked for the latter's attentions to La Niña Chole on the way to Veracruz in *Sonata de estío.* (La Niña Chole calmed Bradomín by calling attention to this Russian's homosexuality.) The episodes are based, in a roundabout way, on the *Mémoires,* (Book 3, chap. 19): in Petersburg, Casanova becomes enamored of the Russian officer Peter Michaelovitch Lunin, but physical contact between them is prevented by the jealousy of Casanova's female lover of the moment, La Rivière. Lying in a military hospital in his old age, seeing the "son" of the man who he thought was his rival for La Niña Chole, Bradomín, addressed by the younger Russian in Latin, thinks of the happy time when "other ephebes, his brothers, were anointed and crowned with roses for the emperors." "Were he so inclined, he could take the youth as booty of war."

Another taboo is also brought up in the *Sonata de invierno,* Bradomín is informed by a former lover, the duchess de Uclés, that they have a daughter, Maximina, who has become a novice. He meets the "very homely" girl and tries out his dilapidated arts of seduction on her with some success. Casanova, growing older, falls in love with and almost marries "Leonilda," then learns that she is his daughter by a sometime mistress, Lucrezia Castelli, and eventually fathers, in place of the impotent husband, Leonilda's child (Book 2, chap. 32, and Book 3, chap. 35). When the obstinately heterosexual Bradomín arrives at a Mexican convent with the readily seduced Chole in *Sonata de estío,* the couple, a bogus man and wife, celebrates fake nuptials "with seven rich sacrifices which we offered to the gods as the triumph of life." The passage is either an intertextual challenge to Eduardo Tiretta, the "comte six fois," so enviously described by Casanova in the *Mémoires* (Book 2, chap. 3), or a replication of Casanova's seven hours of marathon lovemaking with Mimi van Groote, the wife of the lord mayor of Cologne (Book 2, chap. 13). At the convent, in Casanova's typical fashion, Bradomín has established his legitimacy by a virtuoso display of possible truth and certain fiction. He informs the prioress, a noble Spanish lady, that the marquis de Bradomín she once knew was his grandfather, and that he himself is a knight of the Order of Saint James, which founded the convent. To the unverifiable facts he adds a "chivalrous and whole legend of romantic love" about himself and Chole.

The phrase, "el trionfo de la vida," may be an allusion to the title of D'Annunzio's *Il trionfo della morte,* which ends with the grotesque love-death of Giorgio Aurispa and his mistress Ippolita. Scholarship has long recognized Valle-Inclán's debt to D'Annunzio; he may have fashioned María del Rosario, about to take the veil, after Massimilla, the third sister in *Le vergini delle rocce* (1891). Andreas Sperelli in *Il piacere,* haughty and gifted, employs literature, as Bradomín does, for his slow seduction efforts, by giving a book of Shelley's poems to Maria Ferres at Schifanoja, and, when he is getting closer to his goal, reading lines of Shelley, "killing the senses with passion," to her at the Villa Medici in Rome. For the second night of love with La Niña Chole on their way through Mexico, Bradomín recites, "like prayers," seven Italian sonnets by Pietro Aretino, "a different one for each sacrifice," a part of Aretino's erotic-pornographic cycle *I modi,* often referred to by Casanova. Bradomín cannot make love without literature; "I repeated the last one twice." In the *Sonata de otoño,* recalling his erotic education of Concha, still virginal despite her marriage to an older man and the birth of two daughters, Bradomín has to teach her, "line by line," the whole of Aretino's thirty-two sonnets.

Bradomín feeds on literature; he also feeds on historical analogy. Perceptively, Concha says, when he returns to her after a two years' absence in *Sonata de otoño,* " 'I won't permit you to pose as an Aretino or as a Cesare Borgia.' " About to invade the bedroom of María del Rosario, he feels an "ardent impulse" and then "the boldness one admires in the lips and in the eyes of that divine portrait of Cesare Borgia painted by the divine Rafael di Sanzio." Bradomín wants to look like the treacherous and murderous son of Pope Alexander VI. The "aesthetic admiration" he felt "in his youth" for Cesare Borgia frightens Concha, the pale princess of the Palacio Brandeso, "as if it were the cult of the devil." Writing in *Dorian Gray* about "that wonderful book which so much influenced Dorian's life," Wilde plundered John Addington Symonds's *Renaissance in Italy* for, among other Renaissance killers and debauchees, "the Borgia on his white horse, with fratricide riding beside him." Even more often than with Borgia, Bradomín makes an identification with the conquistador Hernán Cortés, who — unnamed — comes to his mind as his ship anchors off Veracruz in *Sonata de estío:* "The adventurer from Estramadura setting fire to his ships"; the bandit Juan de Guzmán, whose life Bradomín saves on impulse at the convent, is "as handsome as a bastard son of Cesare Borgia," and, in the sixteenth century would have fought "under the banner of Hernán Cortés." In the *Sonata de invierno,* before attempting to reconquer his old flame, the dancer Carmen, now the widowed duchess of Uclés, he sees paintings on the walls of her house that depict the love affair between the Cortés and Doña María, the Aztec princess. Defending the brutality Carlist soldiers display even in a loyal Carlist town, he apostrophizes "the proud duke of Alba" (and his bloody rule in the Netherlands); the "glorious Duque de Sesa" — i.e., "el gran capitán" Gonzalo Fernandez de Córdoba, who took Granada from the Moors and gave Naples to Ferdinand of Aragon — and, as a climax, the "magnificent Hernán Cortés," under whose banner Bradomín would glady have marched as an ensign. "I too feel that horror is beautiful, and I love the glorious purple of blood, and the sacking of cities and cruel old soldiers and those who rape maidens and set crops ablaze and those many who commit outrages in the name of military ardor." He subscribes fully and approvingly to the Black Legend of Spanish cruelty. Landing at Veracruz, Bradomín thinks of the Spanish caballeros who first came there, sons of Alaric the Barbarian (Alaric the Goth), and Tarik the Moor, the leader of the Muslim invaders of the Iberian peninsula. On his first sight of the New World, he remembers the adventurous tradition of his own forebears, "like a Homeric song," the fictitious Gonzalo de Sandoval, the founder of the "Kingdom of New Galicia," and still another ancestor who was "inspector general of the Inquisition"; he thinks again of Gonzalo de Sandoval as, passing disdainfully by La Niña Chole, he regards her as one of the native women who "felt love at being raped and conquered." He is more envious of Cervantes for his career as a soldier than for having written *Don Quixote.*

But what has the military career of Bradomín been? We never learn how Xavier Bradomín won the reputation which makes him so welcome at the court of the pretender Carlos VII at Estella in *Sonata de invierno,* "known to the world," and a "famous figure." Hints at Bradomín's chronology are sprinkled throughout the *Sonatas.* The Ligurian book takes place "in the fortunate times of the Pope-King's reign," presumably Gregory XVI, on the papal throne from 1831 to 1846, whose conservatism would have won the heart of a Bradomín; when La Niña Chole confesses to Bradomín that she has committed the "most abominable of sins," a forced marriage with her own father, the marquis proposes that they go on a pilgrimage to Rome and throw themselves at the feet of Pope Gregory.

At the beginning of *Sonata de estío,* Bradomín, disappointed in love by the singer Lilí, sails for Mexico aboard the *Dalilah:* has he played Samson to Lilí? He has lived in London since the "act of treachery" at Vergara; the "embrace of Vergara" of August, 1839, between the Carlist general Marotto and the Isabelline commander Espantero, brought an end of the first Carlist war and the flight of the old pretender Carlos V to France. (General Ramón Cabrera, unusual even in this bloody conflict for his cruelties, tried for a while to continue fighting for the Carlist cause; in *Sonata de invierno* he is praised as being "brave as a lion.") In Mexico, Bradomín reaches his family's hereditary hacienda on the plains of Tixul, and is greeted by the majordomo Brión, a Carlist veteran who has migrated after "the betrayal at Vergara"; it is his dream, Brión says, to make Carlos V emperor of Mexico and to return him as king to Spain itself, a Carlist vision Bradomín meets with "a prick of mockery." Another bit of family information: Bradomín tells the mother superior at the convent that his grandfather was in Mexico during the "Hidalgo uprisings" against Spanish rule in 1810–11; it must be assumed that the grandfather fought on the royalist side in the revolt that led to the defeat and execution of the rebel priest Miguel Hidalgo y Costilla. Brión's plan is not mentioned again; Bradomín is absorbed by his chance reunion with La Niña Chole, after her kidnapping by her husband and father, and his return to the "altar of Venus Turbulenta."

Bradomín seems to have returned to Mexico after the events of the *Sonata de estío* or to have stayed on there. In Estella, he is presented to the children of Carlos VII, the new pretender and the instigator of the second (or by some reckonings the third) Carlist war (1873–76). The little infanta asks if he is the one who "made the war" in Mexico and undertook a trip to the Holy Land. The pilgrimage must be placed early in Bradomín's curriculum vitae; he remembers it with pleasure on his way to Mexico aboard the *Dalilah*, in the distasteful company of "Lutheran rabble, English heretics, and merchants." (In the episode's original version, they are Americans.) But the identity of the Mexican war can only be guessed at; the hard facts of Bradomín's exploits are almost never laid out. The infanta has heard the story from María Antonieta Volfani, a sometime lover of Bradomín and a lady-in-waiting to Carlos's pious Queen Margareta. Was it Mexico's disastrous war with the United States (1846–47) or the so-called civil War of Reform (1858–61), or was Bradomín attached to the French force which accompanied Maximilian of Hapsburg during his short-lived empire of 1864–67? Much is left to the reader's historical imagination.

Bradomín can firmly be placed in Estella during the last winter of the last Carlist war, after the fall of Carlos's previous capital at Tolosa and before the surrender of Estella on February 19, 1876, and the conflict's end. In conversation, the loss of Tolosa is blamed on the priest of Hernilde, Manuel Ignacio Santa Cruz Loidi, who broke with the Carlists and carried on a savage guerilla war against both the troops of Carlos and those of the new, legitimist king, Alfonso. Santa Cruz is a central figure in Valle-Inclán's' great *La guerra carlista* (1908–1909). Early in that trilogy's first part, *Los cruzados de la causa* (The Crusaders of the Cause), Bradomín appears briefly as a supporter of the Carlists; he has returned to his castle in Galicia to recover from a wound received in the war. It will not be Bradomín's only appearance in Valle-Inclán's works subsequent to the *Sonatas*.

The attitude of the marquis toward Carlos and his "holy cause," turns out on the one hand to be Jacobite in its sentimental loyalty. On the beach at Veracruz, he has thought first of the wounds he has received in love (the affair with Lilí) and then of the history of Spain, from which, reading it as a child, he "learned that triumphing and making defeat glorious are the same." Now, in Estella, realizing that Carlism is about to be defeated again, he explains his devotion: "Fallen majesty was more beautiful than [majesty] seated on the throne, and I was the defender of tradition for aesthetic reasons. Carlism has for me the solemn enchantment of the great cathedrals." As usual, Bradomín gazes backwards. He admires the regal look of Carlos VII, the "only sovereign prince worthy of the ermine," almost paraphrasing Verlaine's sonnet to Ludwig II of Bavaria, "le seul vrai roi de ce siècle." Yet when asked by Carlos to accompany him to an assignation, even as the Carlist cause is crumbling, Bradomín's remarks have an undercurrent of moral criticism. The Count Volfani—whose wife, María Antonieta, Bradomín has just reseduced—arranges the excursion, and the marquis impudently congratulates his monarch on having done such justice to Volfani's great talents. (About Volfani, the memoirist writes: "We were great friends.") The adventure ends grotesquely; Volfani has a stroke, evidently *in coitu,* and has to be bundled away from the house in which the willing women— never identified—wait for Carlos and his entourage. Carlos sends Bradomín off on another petty expedition and gives him "one of his looks—friendly, noble, serene, sad, the look of a great king." Carlos is as much the actor as Bradomín, who carefully and repeatedly calculates the effects of the looks *he* gives in his arts of seduction, and is as well constantly mindful of *how* he looks, for example, cultivating an air of Byronic sadness. Bradomín sees through Carlos but obeys him. He has said that "Carlos prefers to fast with all his vassals," and a bishop attached to the royal suite chides him for his joking, just as Carlos is annoyed by Bradomín's remark about Volfani's gifts. But Bradomín abets the king in his excursion, while the queen sews bandages for the wounded troops. The seducer is readily seduced.

Bradomín, who holds himself in exceptional esteem, proclaims to La Niña Chole that he is the greatest member of his nation: "We divide the Spaniards into two great groups, one, the marquis de Bradomín, and in the other, all the rest." But he gives surprising and plentiful evidence in his memoirs that he is quite accustomed to fear. He does not possess the icy composure of the dandy; he readily admits his weakness, as does his model, Casanova. In the first novel, he feels afraid, "contemplating the blood on his hands," as he picks up the body of little María de las Nieves, and flees, hearing the repeated cries of María del Rosario: " 'It was Satan!' " In the second, he is assaulted on his way back to the *Dalilah* at San Juan de Tuxtlan by an Indian who means to rob and perhaps kill him. As a weapon he has only a staff bought as a souvenir at the ruins of Tequil. He advances on the assailant as "one would have described a warrior of two centuries ago"; here, the earlier editions have: "Me afirmé los quevedos" (I secured my pince-nez), a superbly or comically dandyistic gesture, later changed into the neutral and logical "Me afirmé en guardia" (I put myself on guard). What happens next is unclear: Bradomín takes a swipe at the Indian which the Indian "avoid[s] with the dexterity of a savage," and Bradomín remembers nothing more, save an "agonizing impression as of a nightmare"—his vision clouds, his arms grow tired, as the Indian crouches with "the fantastic fury of a bewitched cat," throws his knife, and vanishes—not a very glorious encounter for the would-be conquistador. When the father-husband of La Niña Chole, "the fierce Mexican," carries her off, Bradomín does nothing. Crossing Lake Tixul on his way to his ancestral hacienda, he has to ride through a swarm of crocodiles; the horsemen that accompany him, a "troop of black centaurs," have already passed through, but he is seized "by the coldness and the trembling of fear." The best-known scenes in the tetralogy are those when Concha dies in his arms and in his room. "The coldness and the repose of death terrified me," and, "I thought of fleeing"; as in the encounter with the Mexican footpad, his actions are confused: he goes toward Concha's bedroom but, since her cousin Isabel's bedroom is just opposite, he decides to "tell her everything": Isabel believes that he has come to make love to her, which he does. Returning in this macabre bedroom farce to his own room, he at last, terrified again, picks up Concha's body and after a long detour, shaking—Concha's hair becomes entangled in a door—he deposits her in her bed, where she will be found the next morning.

Long ago, criticism deduced that this seminecrophiliac adventure of Bradomín was a reworking of "Le rideau cramoisi" in Barbey d'Aurevilly's *Les Diaboliques* (1876). The "old dandy," the vicomte de Brassard, whose cool bravery is legendary—his deportment during the July Revolution is described at length as proof—recalls an event of his youth for the listener-narrator. Quartered in the house of an old couple, the seventeen-year-old ensign has carried on a secret affair, night after night, with their daughter Alberte, while her parents slept. She dies in his arms—the cause is never revealed—and the boy is seized by a "terrible physical dread," and starts to carry "the horrible burden" back to her room, through the chamber of her parents, but loses his nerve. Leaving the body on his sofa, he flees, aided by his colonel, and never learns how the matter is resolved. The point of the story, the narrator says, is that "this fine flower of dandyism had other sides to his character."

In the memoirs of Bradomín, he is frank about his fear, and the question must return about Valle-Inclán's intention with his creation's behavior in a crisis, here as elsewhere. Does the author humanize him with these confessions ("I confess" is the prelude to his descriptions of his repeated fears)? Casanova himself is often afraid. Or does he indulge in sly mocking of his braggart? The incomparable valor of the marquis, implied both in his declarations about himself and in the opinions of others, is demonstrated only once by his deport-ment in the memoirs; the situation occurs as he tries to perform a small and, as it turns out, meaningless commission for Carlos VII, persuaded by the "true" king's royal glance. A benighted country priest has captured two Russians — one of them the handsome homosexual traveler from some thirty years ago — and threatens to burn them as heretics. Bradomín is dispatched to dissuade the priest. His little troop is ambushed by the *alfonsistas;* his Bourbon lancers, whose bravery is legendary, run away, and the marquis is shot in the left arm, a shot that breaks the bone. Because of the danger of gangrene, the arm is amputated, without anesthetic, by a village doctor. Bradomín's errand to the priest is handily carried out by a nun, Simona, who gets the Russians set free, after learning that the priest had only wanted to convert them. The expedition and the wound have been in vain, like the Carlist cause itself. Autobiography enters literature; in July 1899, Valle-Inclán got into an argument with a friend in a Madrid café, and an impromptu duel with canes followed. The friend's weapon drove a cufflink into Valle-Inclán's wrist, gangrene set in, and the left arm was amputated. According to Valle-Inclán's claim, as he made the am-putation part of his personal legend (he had become one-armed, like Cer-vantes), the operation was performed without chloroform. (In an interview of 1915, Valle-Inclán recalled that the procedure was carried out on two succes-sive days: first to a point above the elbow, then, as infection spread, to the shoulder. He endured the pain "without moving and without uttering a cry or even a moan.")

The operation becomes a peak of the marquis's dandyism. Valle-Inclán had studied Barbey's *Du Dandysme et de George Brummel* (1845); in the *Sonata de estío,* Bradomín makes an aside about "my noble friend Barbey," and in the story *La generala* in *Femeninas* (1892/1895, later included in *Corte de amor,* 1903) the seducer, Sandoval, presents a book he values highly, *Ce qui ne meurt pas* to the general's wife. Its author is identified as "the old dandy" Barbey.

(Barbey had a life after death elsewhere in literature; he becomes the old dandy M. de Bougrelon in Jean Lorrain's novella collection of that name [1897].) The marquis conforms neatly to Barbey's characteristic of the dandy who "lives in a restless search for the approval of others"; during the operation, Bradomín is sustained by pride and vanity and listens carefully to the praise uttered by all those present at the "sacrifice." As in Barbey, pride is "silent as shame," and "vanity remains with one, even [when one is being broken] on the wheel."

Valle-Inclán, in his book built on books, has taken more than a partial plot from Barbey. Like one of Barbey's specimen dandies, Prince Kaunitz, he indulges in a "majestic frivolity." ("Caprice," according to Barbey, is the dandy's weapon against closed aristocracies, "frivolity" that against a people rigidly utilitarian, "imagination" against a morality too narrow to be authentic.) Bradomín demonstrates these qualities in his apostrophe to the "bagatelle," spoken near the end of *Sonata de invierno* to shock a bishop and the queen: "My whole doctrine is a single phrase, 'Long live the bagatelle.'" Yet Barbey concedes about Brummel: "Take away the dandy and what is left?" Valle-Inclán expands the character of Bradomín but contradicts his dandyism both by means of Bradomín's admitted fears, which never assail the true dandy's icy calm, and by the veneration he gives to his loves, whose fates he regrets, although he has helped create them. In a footnote, Barbey attributes to Brummel a motto, *nil admirari* (to be astonished at nothing) taken over by Sperelli in *Il piacere;* Bradomín's motto is more self-serving and is cited by him after the beating and kidnapping of La Niña Chole, when he does nothing: "Despreciar a los demás y no amarse si mismo" (Scorn the others, and do not love yourself), a feeble excuse for his passivity.

Barbey observed that Brummel "attached much less importance than has been supposed to the art of dressing." In the other basic text on dandyism, "Le Dandy" in *Le Peintre de la vie moderne,* about the work of Constantin Guys (1859), Baudelaire states categorically that "the dandy has no interest in clothing." (No direct evidence exists that Valle-Inclán knew the essay; he did know *Les Fleurs du mal.*) Bradomín's dress receives very little attention. He wears the uniform of a captain of the papal guard at Liguria, and, arriving at Estella, he still has it on beneath his cassock. (It must have grown very shabby over the decades.) Also, Baudelaire's statement that the dandy is a representative of the dying aristocracy against the "rising tide of democracy" can be immediately applied to Valle-Inclán's representatives of the prideful Galician gentry, not only Bradomín but his mentor, Don Juan Manuel Montenegro, with his "pale hands which were noble and thin, like those of an ascetic king." (Does Valle-Inclán make fun of the uncle? Don Juan Manuel is no ascetic in his behavior; the "visionary and prodigal gentleman" has one hundred godchildren in the neighborhood of his great house at Lantañon, products of activity spelled out in the character as he reappears, full length, in Valle-Inclán's subsequent dramatic trilogy, *Comedias bárbaras* [1907/1908/1922].) Baudelaire goes on: "Need I say that when M. G[uys] commits one of his dandies to paper, we might also sing his legendary character." Bradomín and Don Juan Manuel are both turned into oversized figures of legend by their creator.

An effort has been made in Catholic scholarship to argue that the marquis is, if not Satan himself, Satan's instrument; the circumstantial evidence is mostly found in *Sonata de primavera*. The marquis prefers the darkness for his movements about the palace of the Princess Gaetani, he spends the daytime sleeping or drowsing; a parallel in Dracula's nyctophiliac routine comes to mind. More convincingly for the argument: before he enters the bedroom of María del Rosario, he hears the "song of the toad" and recalls that, as a child, he read in a devotional book that the Devil could assume a toad's shape. Leaving the room after his failed attempt on the girl's virtue ("I was afraid"), he hears the song of the toad again. María del Rosario thinks that "sometimes" the marquis is the Devil himself, and after the little sister's death, she cries, eight times (the memoirist loves verbal repetition), a cry repeated once more by "the poor withered, fearful shadow," in Bradomín's projection of the madwoman who lingers on in the palace. "Fue Satanás!" is the last line of the *Sonata de primavera*. The claim about the marquis's satanic quality can be supported by other references in the tetralogy: "The breath of Satan passed over my body, kindling every sin," in *Sonata de estío;* the look of Bradomín, "like a contrite Satan," making the sign of the cross, excites poor Concha; about to die, Concha hears Satan's voice in Bradomín's request that she whip him. After Sister Simona has accused him of knowing that plain little Maximina was his daughter when he seduced her, in word if not in accomplished deed, he flees "as if [he] were the Devil himself." But these hints can readily be dismissed as figures of speech or verbal titillations. Valle-Inclán frequently indulges in the practice: in "Mi hermana Antonia"—with the demonic student Maximo Bretal—and in "Beatriz," originally called "Satanás," both in the collection *Jardín umbrío* (1903). The chaplain of the countess of Cela, Fray Angel, the would-be seducer of Beatriz, has his soul exorcised out of a mirror (with "the sad weeping of an injured spirit"); his body is found floating in a river. In two other stories in *Jardín umbrío*, both told from a child's viewpoint, "El miedo" (The Fear) and "Del misterio" (Concerning the Mystery), the supernatural intimation also occurs, but as a bow to the local gift for uncanniness: "In Santiago of Galacia, inasmuch as it has been the sacred place of the world, the souls keep their eyes open by means of miracles."

Bradomín's declarations about decadence are also ornamental or ambiguous, but ultimately telling. In *Sonata de otoño*—the part of the tetralogy written first—the memoirist goes out of his way to say that he is not at all concerned about Concha's invisible husband, the father of her daughters. (In his dramatic version of the Concha novel, *El Marqués de Bradomín: Coloquios románticos* [1906], the husband lies ill, somewhere offstage.) "There are husbands and there are lovers who are not even able to serve as precursors," and, "God knows, perversity, that bloody rose, is a flower that has never opened in my love affairs. I have always preferred to be the marquis de Bradomín rather than the divine marquis de Sade." ("Divine" is one of the extravagant marquis's throwaway words; Petrarch and Raphael are also divine.) In *Sonata de estío,* Bradomín denies holding membership either in the company of the Don Juan-ists ("sin ser un donjuanista") or the decadentists: "I have never felt the decadentisms [*los decadentismos*] of the new generation." The introduction to the memoirs, apparently by another hand, calls him "an admirable Don Juan! Perhaps the most admirable!" but he is quite unlike the typical Don Juan in the concern he gives to his victims after the fact; Casanova is his model, not the Burlador. His denials of "perversity" and "decadentism" are contradicted by his own words. After he has witnessed the death of the giant negro, urged by La Niña Chole to jump into the shark-filled water in the anchorage off Veracruz, his recollection of the events—the tearing to pieces, La Niña Chole's cruel and contemptuous reaction (she tosses the promised reward into the bloody waters), the horror of the other witnesses, the sound of a violin weeping—were "for [him] the object of a depraved and subtle voluptuousness." After La Niña Chole has fallen into his hands again, he puts off their physical union with "the profound, exquisite, and sadistic knowledge of a decadent." Having returned to the body of Concha after the encounter with Isabel, he has "voluptuous, sad memories" awakened in him, and the memory of his lover lying dead on her bed is "for [him] of a sadness depraved and subtle," "tristezza depravada y sutil." Hearing "frightened female voices" after his approach to Maximina, his soul is filled, once more, "with a depraved and subtle sadness, larval lust of a mystic and poet."

A more diffuse decadent sensibility in Bradomín is apparent in his reaction to locations and atmospheres, e.g., the prim garden of the Princess Gaetani, the lush and overwhelming heat of "la Tierra Caliente," or the decaying garden at the Palacio de Brandeso. Bradomín's keen susceptibility to his surroundings extends even to details of occasional music and furnishings. At the Princess Gaetani's he senses, in the song of the youngest daughter to her doll, "the charm of those old-fashioned gallantries that seeem to have vanished with the last sounds of a minuet." At the Palacio de Brandeso, he notices the "decadent lavishness of the eighteenth century" in the silver box where Concha keeps her letters, and in the balcony doors, made with the "artistry of the gallant century that imagined the pavane and the gavotte." These musical inserts, appearing, in their delicacy, only in the gentle ambiance of María de Rosario and Concha (seeing Carmen, the former duchess of Uclés again, he thinks simply of "flamenco cries of 'Olé' "), are imitated from D'Annunzio's use of the "Gavotte of the Yellow Ladies" at Schifanoja, María Ferres's retreat, in *Il piacere*.

Valle-Inclán puts Bradomín's decadent refinement on obvious display in the catalogues of specially chosen loves that make up the tetralogy; in their small number they are altogether unlike the one hundred and thirty-two conquests of the mentor, Casanova, or Da Ponte's "mille e tre." Valle-Inclán's pattern for his selectivity must have been Barbey's *Les Diaboliques*, the cycle of six stories about unusual sexual attachments and their denouements. Following "Le rideau cramoisi," the other five stories in Barbey's collection are "Le plus bel amour de Don Juan," in which a prepubertal girl believes she has become pregnant through the glance of a notorious Don Juan; "Le bonheur dans le crime," the story of how two "pantherlike" fencing partners poison the man's wife, marry, and live happily ever after; "Le dessus des cartes d'une partie de whist," in which a baby's body is buried in a jardinière; "À un dîner d'athées" in which an officer, during the peninsular wars, mutilates the genitals of his unfaithful wife; and "La vengeance d'une femme": the wife of a member of the loftiest Spanish nobility takes revenge on her husband for the murder of her lover (his heart is cut out, in the intention of having it eaten by dogs) by becoming a common prostitute in Paris. After her death from galloping syphilis, her proud station is proclaimed in the inscription on her catafalque.

Less violent, the *Sonatas* are also filled with shocks and blood and thunder, and not only in the main events. In *Sonata de primavera*, it is intimated that the bishop of Betulia's fatal accident has been caused by the ambitious Monsignor Antonelli; in keeping with her "youthful reputation," the Princess Gaetani exerts a pull on Bradomín, "passionate and violent" in the way she reminds him of Rubens's portrait of Maria de' Medici. (He gives his voice "a certain feline sweetness" as he tells her of the attempt on his life she has arranged; shortly she, or her majordomo Polonio, will try to have him rendered impotent by witchcraft. Her eyes are "as round and as vibrant as those of serpents.") In the story "La Niña Chole" in *Femeninas*, and in earlier versions of the tetralogy, Chole is called a Salammbô, the mistress of the serpent, "hieratic and serpentine"; in subsequent editions she is ameliorated into a figure suggesting a "Japanese musmé," a slightly exotic young girl. The memoirist suggests — by references to Myrrha, who in *Metamorphoses* falls passionately in love with her father, and to Salome — that Chole's incestuous marriage to her father was not at all unwilling. Another element in Chole is her piety; the memoirist gives readers a special frisson by having her drink from the penis, "the diminutive pure white manhood," of a statue of the Infant Jesus, a Mexican Manneken-Pis, in the convent courtyard. The passage was omitted in the Broun-Walsh translation.

The sickliness of Concha in *Sonata de otoño,* emphasized again and again, has a source in D'Annunzio: the first coupling of Sperelli and Elena Muti in *Il piacere* takes place when she is ill, lying amidst smells of chloroform with a white bandage on her forehead, like a nun's wimple, a crucifix above her bed. The descriptions of Concha's debilitated physique have both sacred and pro-fane details: "Her neck bloomed from her shoulders like a sickly lily; her breasts were two white roses, perfuming an altar"; her costume is variously the black silk slip in which Bradomín clothes her or a white robe like a nun's habit, sweeping the tiger's skin on the floor beside her. Bradomín has taught her inventive foreplay; she has long black hair with which he once upon a time asked her to whip him; now he asks her to cover him with that mane as he unlaces her robe and "kisses her skin, anointed with love as by a balsam," a suggestion of a cunnilingus counterpart to the implied fellatio in *Il piacere.* On the way to the final coition, Concha lifts her breasts, "roses of snow consumed by fever," and sighs so violently that Bradomín thinks she is dying: "With a sad voluptuousness such as I had never tasted before, my soul grew drunk on that perfume of a sick flower." Just before she dies, Bradomín asks her to whip him with her hair until *he* dies. Still, Concha has the "noble stamina for pleasure of a goddess," a classic *femme fragile,* she is nonetheless preternaturally active to the very end.

Having been Concha's skilled teacher in eroticism, Bradomín momentarily suspects that she has made a lover of the boy Florisel who tames blackbirds for her. She pretends to be shocked but reminds the marquis that he made his first conquest when he was only eleven, Concha's Aunt Augusta. (Casanova, *Mémoires,* Book 1, chap. 2, is initiated into the mysteries of sex at the same age.) Valle-Inclán has a penchant for transferring characters and their names from book to book; one wonders if this Augusta is identical with Augusta the passionate matron in Valle-Inclán's *Epitalamio,* published in the Colección Flirt in 1897 and included as "Augusta" in *Corte de amor: Florilegio de honestas y nobles damas* (1903). Involved in an affair with the Italian diplomat and poet, Attilio Bonaparte, who has just written a "d'aurevillesque" dedication to her in his collection of erotic verses, *Salmas paganas,* she arranges to have her young daughter, Beatriz, with her "pre-Raphaelite looks . . . still almost a child," married off to him, so that Augusta can keep him near her.

Just so, in *Sonata de invierno,* the semiseduction of the novice Maximina is made all the more piquant by its circumstances. Bradomín is old, he repeats, and shores up his one-armed condition with his languishing looks and his voice. He knows that Maximina has a yearning for him, something Valle-Inclán has him spell out much later on in the fantastic comedy, *Luces de Bohemia* (1920, *Bohemian Lights*). There, the marquis, advanced in age, walks through a graveyard with the Nicaraguan poet Ruben Darío; the grave-diggers remind him of Hamlet, whom he calls a simpleton (*babieca*) for not having seen that Ophelia was "in the age of the peacock" ("en el edad del pavo"), the age of sexual awakening, and should have been taken. Like Ophelia, Maximina is led into madness or suicide—a repetition of the fate of María del Rosario. Valle-Inclán was fascinated by the notion of the seduction of young innocence by the old dandy. In "Rosarito" in *Femeninas,* the pre-paratory exercise for the *Sonatas,* the countess of Cela—now grown old since her adventures with the student Aquiles Calderón in the volume's first story (reprinted in *Corte de Amor*)—gives shelter on her estate to the old dandy and libertine Don Juan Manuel Montenegro (not quite identical with Bradomín's uncle, although bearing the same name). Before he recrosses the border into Portugal, he quickly seduces her niece Rosarito, again a tender pre-Raphaelite beauty, in the room where, according to legend, a saint, Fray Diego de Cádiz, died, and where the girl herself is found dead, either a suicide or the victim of murder, stabbed with the golden pin from her braid.

A subsidiary female figure in *Sonata de invierno* should not be overlooked in the memoirist's gallery of erotic decadence. Bradomín is brought to the house of María Antonieta Volfani by the lady-in-waiting's chaplain, Brother Ambrosio, Bradomín's sometime Latin teacher; the chaplain has undertaken to act as pimp to extract money from his former pupil in order to pay his gambling debts. María Antonieta, like Concha, is not well; she suffers from the "mal sagrado," epilepsy, and since she has "the soul of a saint and the blood of a courtesan," she sometimes renounces love in winter but, having been Bradomín's lover in the past, she quickly succumbs to him—her husband will arrive the next day—and in her passion she is "as frank and egoistic as a little girl," "her breasts trembling like two white doves, her eyes clouded, her half-open mouth revealing the cool whiteness of her teeth between the fiery red roses of her lips," a description which outdoes those of Chole and Concha, and we suspect that her epilepsy in Valle-Inclán's nonmedical view contributes to her ecstasy. She is almost too much for Bradomín, no longer the man he was in the days of La Niña Chole. After her husband's stroke, she rejects a second approach from Bradomín, now one-armed, but she still loves him, and their parting is the final scene in the book. "If war did not give me the chance to show my heroism, love gave it to me in sending me away, perhaps forever."

It is not the only rejection Bradomín receives in the winter of his life. Going to the house of the duchess of Uclés for Carlos's and Volfani's assignations, before the mission that costs him his arm, he is rejected by the duchess. However, as a consolation, and in memory of her times past as the dancer Carmen, she throws her sable boa around his neck, like Elena Muti in the carriage scene of *Il piacere*. The doorkeeper at her house has caught Bradomín's attention; he is reputed, sometime in the past, to have replaced Bradomín in the dancer's affections. Once a famous picador, he has lost his leg, it may be guessed, in a bullfight — a prefiguration of what is about to happen to Bradomín. The bullfighter has also grown old, with only a single tuft left on his "head of Caesar," even more out of service than Bradomín, who has kept his hair, albeit white. Although not quite the fetishist, Bradomín surely does not lack a decadent awareness of hair, especially in the case of Concha, whose chevelure has been important in their amatory games and after. He is terrified by the sight of the disheveled Christ hanging in the anteroom, which he cannot force himself to pass on the way to Concha's bedroom with her corpse — a minatory figure like the tormented Christ with "tangled woman's hair" that the poor little visionary, Luís, avoids in Pérez-Galdós's *Miau*.

The tone of the memoirs steadily darkens as Bradomín recuperates from his wound. In the "sweet, sad velvety eyes" of Maximina, he is reminded of the "sentimental language" of his youth and the slow destruction of his romantic dreams over the years; melancholy returns, the "melancholy Don Juanesque perversion that weeps along with the victim it itself creates." In the hospital courtyard, after a bad night, he hears the troops muttering that they have been betrayed; the Carlist commander in chief Cabrera has gone over to Alfonso XII. Bradomín senses then that the war is coming to its end. He has his moments of gloomy clarity and, as a memoirist, can look steadily at them but then employs prevarication to cloak them. When Ambrosio asks him for the truth about his conversion, Bradomín utters his apostrophe to the lie, the device on which Spain itself must live. The cities of Spain, the apostrophe goes on, are "parched *Tebaidas*, historical cities full of solitude and silence," "perishing dead beneath the sound of bells," a dig at a frozen Roman Catholicism. They are enjoined not to let the saving lie slip away through their "crumbling city walls"; they will need it to survive: the protective lie of Ibsen's Dr. Relling and Söderberg's Dr. Glas here occurs in a national context. The climax of the speech is directed to the over-romanticized tourists' Spain, "the land of the sun and the bull." The passage is readily interpreted as an address, mocking and devoted, to Spain herself after the cataclysm of 1898; it should preserve, for all eternity — "even though the free soups of the convents and the Indies themselves are lost and gone" — its "mendacious, hyperbolic, blustering genius," amid the strumming of guitars. Just so, Bradomín must preserve the image of himself he has created, as a descendant of the *miles gloriosus* of Roman comedy and of Francesco Andreini's "Capitano Spavento da Valle Inferno, sopranominato il Diabolico."

Coming to the court at Estella in his monk's garb, bearing his false story of conversion, Bradomín comments on his other symbolic clothing. Feeling the approach of old age and disillusion with vainglory, he still has worn about his shoulder "the cloak of Almaviva, the helmet of Mambrino," i.e., the amorous disguises of the comte d'Almaviva in Beaumarchais and Rossini, and the expensive helmet of the dead Moorish king from Boiardo's mock-heroic *Orlando inamorato,* much chattered about by the cowardly Sancho Panza in *Don Quixote.* His apprehension of the loss of virility and of grand exploits to come is "sadder still than death itself." Waiting in the kitchen of a farmhouse to set out on the king's escapade, he listens to the (historical) Carlist generals Lizarraga and Dorregaray praise the valor of their troops — shortly to receive their ultimate defeat from the Alfonsine general Primo de Rivera at the decisive battle of Montejarra. Dorregaray (who will be put on trial for treason against the Carlist cause) catalogues the bravery of the Castilians, the Catalans, the Navarrese, and a third voice, of the nonhistorical General Aguirre, claims that Navarre is the true Spain.

Always sensitive to others' voices as he is to his own, Bradomín hears "tears" in Aguirre's; Valle-Inclán especially admired the speaking skills of his idol Cortés, a "marvelous orator." (He is also sensitive to languages themselves; in Yucatan he hears the "sweetness and innocence of primitive tongues" in the Mayan spoken by Chole to her servants; Chole also speaks to him, at his request, in Mayan "on their second night of love, like a princess held captive by a conquistador captain." In Estella, uncomprehending, he listens to a sermon in Basque, sounds "as rough, firm, full of notches, as weapons of the stone age.") The passage subsequent to Aguirre's speech is unusually convoluted. Bradomín feels pity for Aguirre and others like him, belonging to another age, ingenuous souls who still place trust in the old-fashioned and austere virtues, blind to the fact that "the people . . . are only happy when they forget what they call historical consciousness," taking refuge in a "blind instinct" for a future that "triumphs over death." They have forgotten the "harsh sentence which condemns those yet unborn," that all things must die. "What a people, who have set a transcendental fool's cap on the yellowing skull that once filled the souls of ancient hermits with somber thoughts," the memento mori. The solemn discourse continues with an attack not on the all-too-human masses but on a specific few: "What a people of elegant cynics . . . breaking all the laws . . . by refusing to create new life and preparing themselves for death at some bright seaside resort." "Would it not be the most

amusing way to end the world, with the coronation of Sappho and Ganymede," the Lesbian poetess and the cupbearer of the gods, a youth beloved of
Zeus. The jeremiads and proposals of Bradomín, in their exceptional absence
of lucidity, can be untangled as follows. Bradomín sets himself apart from the
mass, with its blithe belief that life will always somehow continue; he comes
close, with his ancient hermits and the skulls adorning their cells, to the man of
action's notion of retreat from the world to contemplate eternity, as in Mateo
Alemán's novel, *Guzmán de Alfarache* (1599–1602), and in the ninth book of
the memoirs of an actual swashbuckler, Alonso de Contreras (c. 1630). Then
he turns suddenly to strike out at fashionable contemporary decadence, as in
the homosexual Riviera of Jean Lorrain's *Le Vice errant.* His punitive sermon
out of the way, Bradomín recovers his old self, making love to innocent Maximina, uttering his praise of the bagatelle. For him, "humanity's greatest triumph lies in having learned to smile," a sentiment greeted by the Carlist court,
on the verge of dissolution and exile, with a delighted murmur. The bishop,
annoyed, observes that " 'there must always have been smiling in hell.' " In
Chesterton's *Napoleon of Notting Hill,* the king cries: " 'All men are mad but
the humorist, who cares for nothing and possesses everthing.' "

Do the *Sonatas* belong — Bradomín curling his moustaches, ever on the
prowl, haughty, disdainful, the show-off, the occasional poltroon — to the
category of the spoof-memoir, a precursor of Richard Schaukal's *Leben und
Taten des Herrn Andreas von Balthesser* (1907) or of A. G. Macdonell's minor
masterpiece *The Autobiography of a Cad* (1938)? (There, Edward Percival
Fox-Ingleby is the prideful scion of a family of spurious ancient heritage, an
untiring womanizer, who despises the tenants on his estate, tricks his fellows
at Eton and Oxford, and sits out the First World War in England as a profiteer-
ing and powerful supply officer, later dropping hints about his fictitious deeds
of bravery. He never gets his comeuppance.) The *Sonatas* can indeed be interpreted as just such a spoof, even as they may be a spoof on decadence in their
details. Yet their consistently supple style, their exceptionally strong sense of
place (the little episcopal seat in Italy in springtime, the "Tierra Caliente,"
Valle-Inclán's rainy homeland of Galicia, wintry Estella on the eve of capture), and their not unloving dissection of the heroic Spanish pose give them a
strength that carries them beyond the spoof's narrower intentions.

18

Germany

THOMAS MANN

The comparatist Erwin Koppen has written that the early work of Thomas Mann—that is, from his debut with the novel *Buddenbrooks: Der Verfall einer Familie* (1901, *Buddenbrooks: The Decline of a Family*) through *Der Tod in Venedig* (1912, *Death in Venice*)—is stamped by the European decadence, and its motifs and attitudes, down to small details: "Since [his work], beyond that, also shows high literary quality (a claim that cannot always be made for the products of the few German decadents), we [may] see in it a peak of European literature of the fin de siècle."

Before turning to three specimens of Mann's works composed under the aegis of decadence, it may be useful to conjecture for a moment why (in contrast to France, England, Italy, and Denmark, for example), the literary fad of decadence thrived so ill in Germany—in some contrast, it may be added, to Austria. Speaking very generally, we can point to the strong current of optimism and even of arrogance that ran through German public life in the latter part of the nineteenth century: in three wars, those of 1864, of 1866, and of 1870–71, Bismarck, and Prussian troops and their allies, had defeated one not unimportant and two major European powers, Denmark, the Austro-Hungarian Empire, and the France of Napoleon III. The new Germany, long since a major cultural and philosophical and musical force, had become a dominant European political power, united in January 1871, under Wilhelm I, king of Prussia, who became emperor of Germany. A decadent frame of mind seemed incompatible with the flourishing Germany of those years. Also, speaking very generally again, the strong idealistic mind-set of German Classicism and Romanticism was not conducive to thought about decay, cultural or erotic; it may be significant that a German novel of the early twentieth century, Gerhard Ouckama Knoop's *Die Dekadenten* (1898, The Decadents), is set wholly in France and has Frenchmen as all its characters.

To be sure, Friedrich Nietzsche, recovering from his Wagnerian enthusiasm, had made a trenchant examination of that most German of musical geniuses in *Der Fall Wagner* (1888, *The Wagner Case*), condemning the composer as a decadent — "Wagner's art is sick," "Wagner is a neurosis," and, "Yes, taken large, Wagner seems to have been interested in no other problems than those which, today, fascinate little Parisian decadents. Always five steps away from the madhouse." Borrowing a formula from Paul Bourget, Nietzsche characterized Wagner as a decadent artist in whom the details had rebelled and were leading independent lives, such that there was no longer any sense of the whole. Max Nordau, the author of *Entartung,* the contemporary reckoning with decadence which Mina Harker had read and applied to Dracula, had also seen Wagner as a specimen of extremely harmful and worthless degeneration, "the last little mushroom on the manure pile of Romanticism." However, while ignoring Wagner's fascination with the German and the Germanic past, Nordau himself admired the Nordic strength he perceived in right-thinking, moral Germany; Nordau it will be noted, was a pseudonym, "Northmeadow" — the journalist was Jewish, from Budapest, and his real name was Südfeld, "Southfield," something he wanted to forget as he chose his nom de plume. In other circles, Wagner's music dramas, their sometimes strongly patriotic flavor (see the salute to German art and the German people and Hans Sachs in *Die Meistersinger von Nürnberg*) and their Germanic heroism (*Der Ring des Nibelungen* celebrates the Germanic-Norse gods and the heroic race of the Volsungs) made listeners pay less attention to the illicit eroticism in *Tristan and Isolde,* the incest in *Die Walküre,* and the destruction of the realm of these deities in *Götterdämmerung*. The purity of Lohengrin, the cavalry-battle music of that orchestral chestnut "The Ride of the Valkyries," the blond valor of Siegfried, the emphasis on *Treue,* loyalty, were powerful signs to the German public that Germans were somehow always high-minded, fearless, strong. Essentially, that is what the Wagner enthusiast Adolf Hitler wanted to see in Wagner; the "March to the Cathedral" from *Lohengrin,* the "Pilgrims' Chorus" from *Tannhäuser* (but not, of course, the Venusberg music), "The Ride of the Valkyries" (again) were favorite numbers of German military bands as late as the Second World War. Wagner thus provided two aspects, the one decadent, the other patriotically brave and healthy; his simple-minded admirers—like Diederich Hessling in Heinrich Mann's attack on German superpatriotism *Der Untertan* (1918, *The Subject* or *The Patrioteer*), as it flourished during the reign of Wilhelm I's bombastic and sword-rattling grandson, Wilhelm II, accurately detected the latter side in Wagner's music and texts: In *Lohengrin,* "[Diederich] noticed that one immediately felt at home. Shields and swords, much rattling metal, a spirit true to the emperor, 'Ha' and 'Heil' and banners held high and the German oak: why, one would like to have taken part."

But, to return to Thomas Mann, and his special affinity for the decadence: the fact should not be overlooked that he came from a North German city-republic, Lübeck, once a Hanseatic town of great importance, and a formidable power in Baltic and Scandinavian politics: the Lübeck fleet and Lübeck money could make or break Swedish kings, and Danish kings warred against or sought the favor of Lübeck. A comparison with the power of another mercantile city-republic, Venice, can easily be made; and, like Venice, Lübeck had fallen on less prosperous days and become quite unimportant in the larger German scheme of things—it had decayed. Mann's *Buddenbrooks* is, in its way, a description not just of a declining commercial house and patrician family, but of a moribund city—not as beautiful, to be sure, in its decline as Venice or Bruges, but still attempting to keep up its old forms, to maintain old social strata. Further, Mann's inherent pessimism was nurtured by his favorite philosopher Schopenhauer (whom Thomas Buddenbrook, the last head of the firm, reads avidly before his early death), with special attention to Schopenhauer's teaching that the will must be destroyed in order for one to achieve a happy oblivion; Schopenhauer was also the favorite philosopher of the decadents—remember Des Esseintes's tribute to Schopenhauer in *À rebours,* Gabriel Gram's apostrophe to "Schopenhauer, Schopenhauer" in *Weary Men,* and Jacinto's Schopenhauer craze in *The City and the Mountains.* Finally, Mann was one of those young men, born in the 1870s, for whom decadence was not merely a literary style to tempt the superficial imitator, it was an attitude of spirit which he took very seriously and whose literary products he studied with his customary thoroughness. A well-known passage in *Die Betrachtungen eines Unpolitischen* (1918, *Reflection of a Nonpolitical Man*) recalls—from the days of the First World War—his involvement: "Intellectually, I belong to that generation of writers, spread over the whole of Europe, which, emerging from decadence, destined to be chroniclers and analysts of decadence, simultaneously bore the emancipatory wish to turn away from it (or, let us pessimistically say, bore an inactive awareness of this renunciation), and at least *experimented* with the conquest of decadence and nihilism." In all

Mann's decadent works, there lies a marked awareness of the lure of decadence as well as a criticism or rejection of it — but this statement could be made
about almost all the major "decadent" novelists.

The earliest of the trio is *Tristan,* initially and amazingly rejected by *Neue
Rundschau* (it was written in 1901) and then published in book form together
with five other stories in 1903. Quite apart from its undeniable literary value,
the story has long had — as a kind of *nouvelle à clef* — a certain sensationalism
attached to it because of its portrait, in the unproductive author Detlev Spinell,
of a real German-language author who had the misfortune to be a good friend
of Mann during the latter's early Munich days, after the Manns had left Lübeck for the South German artistic capital. The author in question was Arthur
Holitscher, a member of a well-to-do German-speaking Jewish family from
Budapest who had likewise been attracted by Munich's literary and cultural
nimbus. According to the autobiography of Holitscher, who was six years
Mann's senior, Mann played the violin to his piano accompaniment; once,
leaving Mann's apartment, Holitscher chanced to look back and saw Mann
watching him through an opera glass. Later, Mann visited Holitscher in *his*
"pretty" chambers, which were decorated, Holitscher remembered, with photographs of Pre-Raphaelite paintings by Dante Gabriel Rosetti; on the table
lay the "holy" work of the German superaesthete Stefan George, *Der Teppich
des Lebens* (1899, *The Tapestry of Life*). Holitscher had just published a
decadent novel called *Der vergiftete Brunnen* (1900, The Poisoned Well),
which Mann had recommended to the publisher Albert Langen. (In the novel,
a female decadent named Désirée Wilmoth — female decadents in continental
literature are often English, or have English-sounding surnames — tries to seduce the languid poet Sebastian Sasse and arranges for lascivious performances of *Tannhäuser,* and especially of the Venusberg scene, to be performed
in a giant greenhouse.) Holitscher much admired *Buddenbrooks* and claims to
have recommended it in turn to the publisher S. Fischer; then Mann gave
Holitscher the story collection *Tristan,* and Holitscher's enthusiasm for Mann
suddenly waned: "I immediately recognized myself in one of [the book's]
maliciously distorted figures and directly remembered that opera glass which
an eye, sharp by nature, had polished until it was sharper still." Holitscher
wrote to Mann, complaining bitterly, and got a "hateful and indignant" reply;
Mann's "tender, melancholy irony had suddenly turned as bitter as gall."

Certainly, Spinell is a pathetic and scarcely an admirable figure. We never
learn precisely why he is at Sanatorium Einfried — a name recalling the name
of Wagner's villa at Bayreuth, Wahnfried. He tells Gabriele Klöterjahn: " 'Oh,
I'm having myself electrified a bit. Nothing worth mentioning,' " but then, as
the aesthete he is, he reveals another reason, his " 'feeling for style . . . Einfried

is perfect Empire.'" In the 1960s, analyzing the symptoms the novella gives (Thomas Mann had the decadent author's taste for close detail), a Danish physician, Henry Olsen, diagnosed Spinell's case: his prematurely graying hair, his beardless face, soft and puffy, his large, decaying teeth that seem to get in the way of his tongue, also too large, his unusual height, and his large, soft hands and huge feet point, according to Olsen, to a disease of the glands, acromegalia, and to an accompanying dystrophia adiposo-genitalia: he is impotent. Moreover, the fact that he cannot look directly at the people he approaches but gazes at them "with his head on one side" indicates still another effect of his disease: his field of vision has been radically reduced. The details about his sight are numerous: bright weather seems to bother him, and, on that overcast day when most of the ambulatory patients go on their sleighing excursion, he tells Frau Klöterjahn: "After all these brilliant weeks a little dullness is good for the eyes.'" There is no way of knowing (until someone takes the trouble to write the biography of Holitscher, a by no means uninteresting figure) whether Holitscher suffered from such an ailment; he lived to the age of 72 and became a well-known author of travel and political books; however, his autobiography hints at some problems with his erotic life. If Olsen's hypothesis is correct, Holitscher's physical appearance perhaps suggested the disease to Mann; *Buddenbrooks* had already demonstrated how keenly interested Mann was in medical matters.

The possible ailment of Detlev Spinell aside (and it would help to account for his platonic seduction of Frau Klöterjahn), he has other features that immediately demand notice. The circumstance that Spinell comes from Lemberg (Lvov) in Galicia, a city in the old Austro-Hungarian Empire with an extremely large Jewish population, has led to the probably correct assumption that he, like Holitscher, is Jewish; thus, he would be a representative, too, of that surprising phenomenon, the many Jewish admirers (and financial supporters) of the anti-Semite Wagner. Surely, Spinell is a full-time aesthete; shortly after we are introduced to him, we learn that he can be carried away by "an aesthetic fit" at the sheer sight of beauty; his single book is remarkable for its imitation of the love of handsome objects also demonstrated by Des Esseintes, Dorian Gray, and Sperelli. "Its scenes were laid in fashionable salons, in luxurious boudoirs full of choice objets d'art, old furniture, gobelins, rare porcelains, precious stuffs, and art treasures of all sorts and kinds. On the description of these things was expended the most loving care." (Dr. Leander's ever hopeful head housekeeper, Fräulein von Osterloh, has found the book, in the quarter of an hour she dipped into it, to be "very cultured . . . her curious locution for inhumanly boring.") Spinell's aestheticism pops up again and again; he waxes "almost hysterical" at the experience of the beautiful, as the narrator once puts it, flinging his arms about anyone standing nearby when he has his "moments of ardor," telling Frau Klöterjahn how he has seen "a beautiful woman" on his walk (in the process he gives an aesthetic reason for not looking directly at whomever or whatever he encounters: he is an impressionist, "not avid of actuality"), falling to "his knees, both knees," after the musical experience with Frau Klöterjahn: "His long black coat spread out on the floor. He had his hands clasped over his mouth, and his shoulders heaved" — to Frau Klöterjahn's somewhat dreamy dismay. That he belongs to the tribe of decadents goes almost without saying: he has "an upper lip, swelling and full of pores, like an ancient Roman's"; he expresses the decadent's sense of belonging to a small and select band of sensitivists (as in the young Hofmannsthal's statement about the few unhappily happy, day blind creatures); in the explanation he gives to Frau Klöterjahn about his habit of rising early, he says: "We are feckless creatures and, aside from a few good hours, we go around weighted down, sick and sore with the knowledge of our own futility. We hate the useful; we know it is vulgar and unlovely, and we defend this position as a man defends something that is absolutely necessary to his existence.' " Yet this decadent policy statement is encased within another and somewhat different belief — a typical one for Thomas Mann — about the decadent's bad conscience; elsewhere, it is the artist's bad conscience that Mann depicts. Spinell gets up early because he is in reality a late riser, and such minor self-discipline assuages his niggling worries. However, his conscience, as we learn in the scene of musical seduction, is quiet when it comes to a crucial case of allowing himself the supreme moment of beauty.

In this novella of convincing parodies, Spinell is to be contrasted with Anton Klöterjahn, whose very name, as Spinell thinks, sounds so ugly that he will not use it to address Klöterjahn's wife. Klöterjahn is the vigorous, vulgar, and self-assertive businessman, who likes to pinch chambermaids in dark corners of the sanatorium when he comes to visit his wife. Klöterjahn is a pronounced Anglophile — that is, he tries to be what he regards as the successful English merchant and wears "English side-whiskers and English clothes and it enchanted him to discover at Einfried an entire English family," with whom "he partook of a good English breakfast every morning." His language is full of English phrases, rendered into French by the translator: when he tells his Gabriele not to open her mouth lest the cold air harm her trachea, he says in the English translation: " 'Be careful, Gabriele, doucement, doucement, my angel' " — for which the original has " 'Langsam, Gabriele, take care, mein Engel.' " He is a much simplified version of Gabriel Gram's Anglophile Georg Jonathan in *Weary Men,* altogether without the nuances.

In Mann's nastily funny re-creation of the constellation of emotions in the opera *Tristan and Isolde,* Klöterjahn is the blustering equivalent of the melancholy and noble King Marke of Cornwall, the husband of the fair Isolde, who falls in love with Tristan as he does with her. Tristan is Spinell, and the Isolde of the tale is Gabriele Klöterjahn, *née* Eckhof, who — even as Spinell is an exaggeration of the aesthetic decadent and Klöterjahn of the bluff and robust man — is a representative of a third type from letters of the time, the femme fragile: she is literally ill, she is "pale and weak," her head has "unspeakable sweetness, delicacy, and languor," and she is marked by the "little blue vein" which (as opposed to the femme fatale's undulating gait, hard laughter, and boa) is the hallmark of the fragilely fascinating woman around the turn of the century, "an odd little vein, pale blue and sickly . . . that dominated quite painfully the whole fine oval of the face," the little vein that "stood out alarmingly" when she laughed at Spinell's remark that "anybody who calls you Klöterjahn ought to be thrashed,'" the vein that "came out" as she smiled (in gladness, it must be noted: Gabriele Klöterjahn seems to love her husband), telling Spinell about her first meeting with Klöterjahn in her father's garden. Gabriele Eckhof, though, is a fitting victim for Spinell's, "the decayed baby's" (the German is "der verweste Säugling," literally "the decayed suckling infant") single act of genuine creation, or semicreation, at the sanatorium: his transformation of her birthplace, Bremen (which had a strong commercial tradition, like Lübeck), into a fairy-tale place, and his quick attribution to Gabriele of an old if not ancient family, living in an old house: "'Tell me, madame, your family is old, is it not? Your family has been living for generations in the old gabled house'" — a supposition which turns out to be accurate. (With a hint of advertisement for *Buddenbrooks,* where the same argument is advanced in much more detail, Spinell goes on to assume that Gabriele's family, too, has been mercantile and patrician, but "'it not infrequently happens that a race with sober, practical bourgeois traditions will toward the end of its days flare up in some sort of art'" — which is also what happens to the last Buddenbrooks. It predicts, too, Spinell's decadent argument, repeated in his letter to Klöterjahn, that Gabriele herself is the last of the line.) Onto this Bremen background, Spinell then superimposes Gabriele and her six friends of the sewing circle, transformed as in a fairy tale or a poem of Maurice Maeterlinck or a Pre-Raphaelite painting or a picture by the Bremen artist Heinrich Vogeler, a court composed of a queen and six princesses: "'A little old crown showed in your hair — quite a modest, unostentatious little crown — still, it was there.'"; into this enchanted garden — the magical space of aestheticism, as in a verse play of Hofmannsthal or D'Annunzio — the intruder, Klöterjahn, comes. The story of the crown sticks in Gabriele's mind; she brings it up "abruptly" two weeks after the tale has been told: "'Is it really true, Herr Spinell, . . . that you would have seen the little gold crown?'" She is slipping into Spinell's large, white, spongy hands. And when, a few days later still, another guest inquires after the health of her offspring Anton junior, she gives "a quick glance" at Spinell before she utters her perfunctory reply: "'Thanks, how should he be? He and my husband are quite well, of course.'" This episode in the novel immediately precedes the day of the excursion and the musical performance.

Spinell, it must be granted, is a great improviser or opportunist: he quickly weaves the fairy story into Gabriele's past, he lures Gabriele back into the realm of music, into which she was led, as a child, by her beloved father, "'surely more of an artist than some who call themselves so,'" she recalls. (The theme of the musical father comes from German Romanticism, from E. T. A. Hoffmann, and has a contemporary parallel in George Moore's novel about the Wagnerian singer, *Evelyn Innes* [1898].) Spinell does this with great cleverness, although he knows very well (he has been told about it at least twice) that "'our family physician, as well as Dr. Leander, expressly forbade'" her to play, to which Spinell, again the seducer, replies that what they don't know won't hurt them. "'But they aren't here — either of them. We are free agents.'" Gabriele refuses and refuses; at last, with another ploy, Spinell apparently gives up ("'We shall leave the beauty dead and dumb that might have come alive beneath your fingers'"), then mentions the golden crown which she has already laid aside when — "'not caring about [her] bodily welfare'" — she left the fountain in the garden for the company of the unbearable Klöterjahn. Spinell has already found Chopin's nocturnes (the sensual music that so charmed Henry Wotton when Dorian played for him on their last night together) on top of the piano, and so Gabriele yields: "'But only one'" — and she plays three. Then Spinell (who may well have scouted out the pile of music in advance) pretends to come across the piano reduction of the score of *Tristan and Isolde.*

The re-creation of the Prelude, the Love Music from the second act, and the Love-Death from the third, has become, by means of Thomas Mann's own stylistic magic, and the use of fragmentary quotations from the Wagner libretto, a justly famous bravura passage in Mann's work. (A zealous Swedish scholar has counted sixty-six quotations: Mann, however, avoids using any of Wagner's dreadful rhymes.) The art of quotation is leavened, too, by a single borrowing from the Bible: "The soaring violins following Brangäne's dark notes of warning [go] higher than all reason," a reference — for the purpose of describing the sexual love of Tristan and Isolde — to Philippians 4:7, "the peace of God, which passeth all understanding." One detail of the reaction Gabriele's performance elicits must be mentioned: the Prelude bores Frau Magistrate Spatz so much that she, the insensitive creature, goes up to her room, leaving the two music lovers alone in the growing twilight. After the completion of the passionate music of the second act, Gabriele turns to Spinell, who has become her mentor now, for an explanation of a difficult line in the text ("Even then I am the world") and unwittingly homes in on the artistic barrenness, the decadent's barrenness, of Spinell: " 'How is it you understand it all so well yet cannot play it?' " At the end, melodramatically, the ghostly Frau Höhlenrauch appears (her name is spooky: 'cave smoke') — a woman made utterly witless by the bearing of fourteen children — while deep shadows gather beneath Gabriele's eyes, and "the little pale blue vein . . . showed fearfully plain and prominent." (The ruin wrought by childbearing and the lethal production of music for Spinell's pleasure may be connected.) The performance takes place on February 26; on the 27th, Gabriele, like a lover after a happy encounter, is "in capital health and spirits," but on the 28th she brings up blood, and on the 29th is turned over to Dr. Müller, the caretaker of hopeless cases. (These events occur some two weeks after the anniversary of Wagner's death in Venice, February 13, 1883.) Klöterjahn, having been summoned, arrives with little Anton (whom Spinell regards from his window with "a peculiar gaze, at once veiled and piercing"). Spinell writes his accusatory letter to the husband "with pathetic slowness, considering the man was a writer by trade," as he twists "one of those downy hairs he had on his cheek." (Does Spinell think that the birth of little Anton has weakened Gabriele? It may have. Or does he feel some sexual jealousy of the potent Klöterjahn?).

In the letter, for Klöterjahn's profane eyes, he repeats — even more aesthetically decked out — the tale of the garden and the seven maidens (a scene, Spinell writes, Klöterjahn never saw or could see), and makes his decadent's charge against "this plebeian gourmand, a peasant with taste." And Spinell continues: "It was a peaceful apotheosis and a moving one, bathed in a sunset beauty of decadence, decay, and death. [Mann's words are "Verfall, Auflösung, Verlöschen."] An ancient stock, too exhausted and refined for life and action, stood there at the end of its days; its latest [the text actually says "last"] manifestations were those of art: violin notes, full of that melancholy understanding which is ripeness for death." Spinell has added new elements to the tale, not mentioned to Gabriele: "decadence, decay, and death . . . too exhausted and refined for life and action . . . ripeness for death," as if in justification and celebration of the fact that Gabriele is dying; it is a justification, as well, of his own action in persuading her to play. The letter now turns to insults of a Darwinian nature for Klöterjahn: "You stand upon an extremely low evolutionary level; your own constitution is coarse-fibered." (We remember the passages from Johannes Jørgensen's *Livets Træ* [The Tree of Life] in which the coarse-fibered fir tree triumphs over the delicate Danish beech.)

Unfeelingly, Spinell returns to the apotheosis of Gabriele in death, "passing on, in ecstasy, with the deathly hue of beauty on her brow," for which he takes credit. He fires off two parting shots, one at the future pillar of society, Anton junior (Spinell will have no children and will have nothing to do with society's solid props), and the other at Klöterjahn himself: "You are stronger than I—I have only the Word, the weapon of the weak." (Théophile Gautier described "the Word," in his essay on Baudelaire, as being summoned "to express everything"; words are indeed the decadent's great weapon, and the unproductive Spinell may never have used them so well or so foolishly.)

Klöterjahn's comeback makes amusing reading, and is the practical man's blunt and indignant retort to the decadent, with an inattention to words that is perhaps more upsetting to Spinell than the several insults Klöterjahn heaps on his head; at last, Klöterjahn threatens Spinell (a not unreasonable reaction) with a libel suit for the remarks about his name, coupled with a second suit from Klöterjahn's father-in-law for the remark about the decaying family. In the midst of Klöterjahn's attack, though, on Spinell's squinting, impressionistic way of looking at people, the husband is called to Gabriele's bedside; she is dying or dead, and Frau Spatz blurts out that " 'she was sitting up quite quietly in bed and humming a little snatch of music' " when the final hemorrhage came.

We never find out what she was humming; it may have been the "yearning motif" from *Tristan* which, we know, Spinell hums as he walks through the garden. Spinell's reaction to the death of Gabriele Klöterjahn is vastly egocentric, selfish; his thoughts dwell more on the lambasting from Klöterjahn than on the awful reality of the briefly beloved's passing. "Crude experiences like this were too much—he was not made for them"; the walk—during which he moves through the large garden of the sanatorium in "the splendid colorful afternoon light" (which, however, "coming from a visibly sinking sun," cannot trouble his eyes)—is meant to calm him. Then he spies the figure of Anton Klöterjahn junior, tended by the buxom maid who is a kind of goddess of fruitfulness. As the baby crows and yells (perhaps set off by Spinell's "long black figure"), Spinell turns tail and runs. He ends confronted neither by his physical weakness and the vulgar *siècle*, like Des Esseintes, nor by emptiness and the democratic mud, like Sperelli (although there are strong points of resemblance, not least in their names), but by his cowardice in the face of vitality and what to him appears to be the crass future. As so often in the study of decadent literature, the reader cannot feel wholehearted sympathy for either side. Probably, Anton will grow up to be like his father—not so dreadful a fate, in truth, for Klöterjahn loved his wife, despite his animal appetite for chambermaids and good food; Spinell has shown himself to be the self-centered decadent — a woman's life has been sacrificed to give him a few moments of aesthetic pleasure. (The argument has been presented that Spinell, with his big teeth, is a vampire, who bleeds Gabriele to keep his own artificial life alive; there is something to the proposal.) Yet apologists for Spinell will say that Gabriele, fragile as she is, would have died at any rate, and that Spinell has, indeed, given her a death in beauty. Was it, after all, the yearning motif from *Tristan* that she hummed just before she died?

The story of the publication of *Wälsungenblut* (*The Blood of the Volsungs*) is a complex and painful one. It was intended to appear in S. Fischer's *Neue Rundschau* for 1906. At the last moment, it was abruptly withdrawn; it was printed privately in 1921 in a few copies, a French translation, *Sang réservé*, came out in 1931, and, in 1958, it was included at last in the so-called Stockholm edition of Mann's works and thus became generally available in German. (It could be read in Mrs. Lowe-Porter's English translation after the publication of Mann's *Stories of Three Decades* in 1936.) In the printed versions, however, it lacked a final sentence that had been in the manuscript sent to the *Neue Rundschau*. Instead of Siegmund's remark " 'His [von Beckerath's] existence will be a little less trivial from now on,' " the original text has read, in an ugly and vulgar way: " 'Well, why worry about him anyway. We've tricked him, the gentile.' " (Here, Siegmund uses Hebrew and Yiddish expressions he may have picked up from his mother; apart from her grotesque appearance, the hair piled atop her head, held in place with a jeweled brooch, "adorned in its turn with a bunch of white aigrettes," we learn about Frau Aarenhold that "her speech was interlarded with guttural words and phrases from the dialect of her childhood days." Siegmund says *beganeft*, or "tricked," and *Goi*, or *Gentile*.) Ugly rumors were circulated in Munich that the Pringsheim family, into which Mann had married in February 1905, was portrayed in the story, and that pressure from the family made the author withdraw it at the last minute. Much later, in the 1960s, Klaus Pringsheim, the twin brother of Thomas Mann's wife, Katja, wrote an essay in which he said that Mann had read the story to the Pringsheims in the late autumn of 1905, and that they had found nothing offensive in it. As a matter of fact, the new son-in-law had asked his father-in-law for advice concerning the Yiddish word for "betrayal" or "trick." Klaus Pringsheim added that he had recognized his physical self in Siegmund, but "the twin brother was not me any longer." Awareness of the rumors had made Mann withdraw the story, Pringsheim concluded.

Certainly, there were radical differences (and some dismaying similarities) between the Pringsheims of Munich and the Aarenholds. The Pringsheims were a highly cultured family, whose home was one of the sights of the city, with its collection of Italian majolica, displayed as if in a museum, that had achieved international fame; there was also a painting of the Pringsheim children (three older brothers and the twins), dressed as Pierrots, by the fashionable Bavarian master, Wilhelm von Kaulbach. The twins had made the news when they took their final examination together at the venerable Wilhelmsgymnasium — Katja was the first Munich girl to get a gymnasium degree, there being no feminine educational equivalent in the conservative city. She was a brilliant student, had had private instruction, and continued at the university, studying mathematics with her father, Alfred Pringsheim, and physics with Wilhelm Röntgen of X-ray fame. Professor Pringsheim himself was a passionate Wagnerian, having once fought a duel over an insult to Wagner's reputation; the mother, equally cultured, was the daughter of the satirist Ernst Dohm and his wife Hedwig Dohm, an early battler for women's rights. Katja's twin brother Klaus theorized in his memoir that sheer envy had made tongues wag about the story and about the putative literary "revenge" the son-in-law had taken for bad treatment. (He might have added that Bavarian Catholic anti-Semitism had fueled the gossip as well.) A talkative bookstore employee had let the cat out of the bag about the story's existence when a shipment of books arrived, wrapped in copies of the proof sheets from *Neue Rundschau;* he had them copied and sold a few under the counter.

The location of *The Blood of the Volsungs,* however, is Berlin, in the section of mansions near the Tiergarten belonging to the nouveaux riches. Herr Aarenhold has come "from a remote village in East Prussia, [has] married the daughter of a well-to-do tradesman, and by means of a bold and shrewd enterprise, of large-scale schemings . . . [has] diverted a large and inexhaustible stream of gold into his coffers." He is a self-made man, a little vulgar, and his children mostly despise him "for his origins, for the blood which flowed in his veins and through him in theirs, for the way he had earned his money, for his fads, which in their eyes were unbecoming, for his valetudinarianism, [and] for his weak and whimsical loquacity, which in their eyes traversed the bounds of good taste." Their household has an ostentatious museum quality about it, as is made clear in the opening paragraph, with the gong that sends "its brazen clang, savage and primitive . . . through the warm and even atmosphere, heavy with exotic perfume." Aarenhold is a collector of old books, an ancient church organ stands on the stairs, and the dining room has paneling and tapestry from a French chateau; there are liveried servants, Wendelin and Florian; there are carriages and spanking horses to draw them. The children are immensely spoiled and somehow intent, as far as the male offspring are concerned, upon symbolically blotting out their Jewishness: Kunz is a reserve officer in the hussars, with curling lips and a large dueling scar; Siegmund washes himself constantly and sprinkles himself with perfume: "The blond-haired citizenry of the land might go about in elastic-sided boots and turn-over collars, heedless of the effect. But he — and most explicitly he — must be unassailable and blameless of exterior from head to foot." The older daughter Märit, the law student with "a hooked nose," has sunk into an apparent bitterness, going her own way in life; Sieglinde, the female twin, and Siegmund both have "slightly droopy noses." Sieglinde is engaged to a Gentile.

Von Beckerath is treasured precisely because of his "Germanness"; the jealous Siegmund tells his sister to do him "the favor of not mentioning that Germanic" (not just "German," as it says in the translation) to him on the evening of the opera. Kunz, the reserve lieutenant, has been a zealous supporter of von Beckerath's cause, as has the mother, and Aarenhold has maintained a benevolent neutrality. The circumstance that von Beckerath (is the name supposed to suggest the pedantic Beckmesser of *Die Meistersinger?*) is badgered by the children, with their urge to argue and their brittle negativism, does not mean they are unaware of his value to them; in a way, their treatment of him resembles their treatment of their father. They manage, however, to summon a moment of respect for Aarenhold when he opposes von Beckerath's bumbling defense of artists who have "good intentions"; the self-made man says, in effect, that it is winning that counts, and his children secretly applaud him, although, "with their spoiled and dissatisfied faces," they have never had to win anything. "They sat in splendor and security, but their words rang as sharp as though sharpness, hardness, alertness, and pitiless clarity were demanded of them as survival values." Their conversational brilliance, their united front, and their condescension beat poor von Beckerath down: "He grew smaller and smaller in his chair, pressed his chin into his breast, and in his excitement breathed through his mouth — quite unhorsed by the brisk arrogance of youth. They contradicted everything . . . Toward the end of luncheon von Beckerath's eyes were red, and he looked slightly deranged." (Does von Beckerath put up with all this because he needs Aarenhold's money? Frau Aarenhold says that he will not want to miss a free meal.) Perhaps von Beckerath is not altogether aware of what is being done to him; it would seem he does not understand the implication of the leitmotif from *Die Walküre* whose rhythm Kunz drums on the table linen after Siegmund has asked mocking permission of him to see the opera with his sister once more. (After all, their names have been taken from those of the incestuous lovers in it.) Unsuspecting, von Beckerath says he will be able to go with them, only to be promptly told that he is not wanted — a rebuff he likewise accepts. Perhaps he would not have been so calm were he a Wagnerian, or any more musical person, who had grasped the import of Kunz's pounding. What Kunz raps out is the motif of Hunding, the crude husband of Sieglinde, who will be cuckolded by Siegmund and Sieglinde before the first act of the opera is done. The magical moonlight shines, in the opera, through the open door, stage rear; Siegmund's last words in the act are

> Braut und Schwester
> bist du dem Bruder —
> so blühe denn, Wälsungenblut!
>
> (Bride and sister
> Thou art to the brother —
> So bloom then, blood of the Volsungs!)

The stage direction says: "He pulls her to himself with raging passion; she sinks on his breast with a cry. The curtain falls rapidly."

The twins, whose habit it has been to engage in mildly amorous play before the eyes of their family, set out for the opera in one of the family's carriages: " 'Shall I shut us in?' Siegmund asked. She nodded, and he drew the brown silk curtains across the polished pane. Quite safe and shut away, they sat among the wadded brown cushions, hand in hand" — a passage that recalls the erotic carriage scene in D'Annunzio's *Il piacere*. Having arrived, they pass by the less fortunate mortals before the entrance to the opera house — possibly another D'Annunzian echo, recalling the malaria-stricken idlers, the obese mother, and skeletonlike child whom Sperelli and Elena Muti meet at the inn in the Campagna, or the threatening crowd through which they are driven after the chamber concert, in the streets of Rome. "A little group of gray-faced, shivering folk stood in the brilliance of the arc-lights and followed them with hostile glances as they passed through the lobby." (Are these Munich's poor — which would add an element of social criticism to the story — or are they simply waiting to get tickets in the gallery?) Enclosed within their box, as they have been enclosed within their carriage, the twins watch the opera. In keeping with the malicious yet serious tone of the story, Mann achieves a wonderful balance between showing admiration for Wagner's music and making fun of the singers who execute it. Both Siegmund and Sieglinde, the singers, keep looking carefully at the conductor (the tenor "imploringly"), and both are overweight: he lies on the bearskin rug, "his head cushioned on his plump arms"; she has "an alabaster bosom which rose and fell marvelously . . . she pressed her chin upon her breast until it was double." The twins speak contemptuously of the performance, as we might expect, but they are plainly stirred by it too; after the Magic Fire music and Wotan's farewell are past (the second act of the opera is not mentioned at all, and the third gets short shrift), they return to their carriage, "their warm little silk-lined retreat," and they are aware "of their blessed isolation and their sense of belonging to one another alone."

They sit "as silent and remote as they sat in their box," and "nothing was there which could alienate them from that extravagant and stormily passionate world which worked upon them with its magic power to draw them to itself."

Work upon them it does; after getting home, they have a snack and retire to their rooms. In his, Siegmund—Gigi—surrenders himself to the pleasant atmosphere, and behaves, ever the decadent actor, "like a man [who] will console himself with some delicate pleasure of the senses for the harshness of his lot." He looks "at the marks of his race," and goes "with dragging steps, full of tragic meaning," to his bearskin rug, lies down, and is surprised by Sieglinde, who has slipped into a lighter robe: "Beneath the lace of her chemise Siegmund saw her little breasts, the color of smoked meerschaum." (The reader is supposed to contrast the nineteen-year-olds, "the two dark, slender, exotic creatures," with the hefty Germanics on the stage.) Siegmund embraces her, looks at her just as he has been looking in the mirror at himself (there is a strong element of narcissism in their attraction on one another) and says, " 'You are just like me,' " and they make love. The translation has "caresses, which took the upper hand, passing over into a tumult of passion, dying away into a sobbing." The verbal effects are reminiscent of the re-creation of the opera music of before, and, as before, Thomas Mann introduces an element of burlesque. The translator's "tumult of passion" is in fact "hastiges Getümmel," a "hasty tumbling," mocking their would-be sublime and operatically inspired final passion. It has been argued that, in this episode, Mann was inspired by a novel of Élémir Bourges from 1884, *Le Crépuscule des dieux*. In it, a pair of royal siblings, Christine and Hans-Ulric, are the stars in an (unbelievable) amateur performance of *Die Walküre*. It has been arranged by an Italian Wagnerian soprano and adventuress, Giulia Belcredi, their father's mistress, who wants to gain power in the little principality; she has noted both their unconscious incestuous attachment and their high-mindedness. A reading of the incest scene in John Ford's *'Tis Pity She's a Whore* fails to move them, but the opera succeeds. Their inhibitions vanish, they fall into one another's arms, and, afterward, Hans-Ulric shoots himself, his sister enters a Carmelite nunnery, and the field is clear for Belcredi.

Bourges's novel is less cynical than Mann's novella, and it does not make a point about tricking an outsider: Bourges's lovers themselves are tricked. In betraying von Beckerath, too, the twins have not only shown their familial and racial unity, they have demonstrated their contempt for the orderly, respectable world that von Beckerath represents. The portrait of Siegmund is more complex than that of Sieglinde; we are told of her simply that she has "a gaze as vacant of thought as any animal's," while she holds the hand of her male twin under the table. Both of them, as decadents, are incapable of achieving their sexual union without the stimulus of the stage action and the music, which has supplied for them that passion whose existence they denied at the luncheon, even laughing at it. Siegmund is more self-aware: his amateur painting is worthless, and he knows it, he loves to read but can never "lose himself in a book," he has, in his idleness, "no time for a resolve," he lives for the momentary impression, and he is a product of the superfluity which he enjoys and cannot give up. Mann makes a strong point here about the financial superabundance necessary to produce the decadent: "This affluence never ceased to thrill and occupy him" — he forever gets a new frisson from it. (Actually, in this he is his father's son; he resembles old Aarenhold in practicing the art of never getting used to anything.) Siegmund wants to create, but the act of creation is incomprehensible to him: during the second (and undescribed) act, he looks into the orchestra pit and reflects: "Creation? How did one create? Pain gnawed and burned in Siegmund's breast." Then, to creation, he adds the word *passion.* In the coupling with Sieglinde, he does the best he can in the way of creation and passion, yet it is really at second hand. The twins, Siegmund says, have made von Beckerath's life a little less trivial from now on (how, we wonder: because they have condescended to cuckhold him, and he may someday suspect it?); but their lives will continue trivially too, and Siegmund, if not Sieglinde, will be aware of it.

The third story in Thomas Mann's decadent trilogy is the well-known *Death in Venice.* There the passion of Gustav von Aschenbach for the Polish boy Tadzio is genuine. Unlike Spinell and Siegmund, he gives his life for it, staying in the plague-ridden city until he dies in his chair on the Lido, in the famous autumnal beach scene. Aschenbach, the descendant of Prussian officials, has lived up to the motto of his hero, Frederick the Great, "Durchhalten" — "Hold fast," "Endure." (Mann no doubt expected his more sophisticated readers to know that Frederick himself was homosexual.) But, as a decadent, he has played a role in his lifelong Friderician pose.

The concern of decadence with death is apparent everywhere, laid on, it might seem, with almost too heavy a brush. Reading the story in installments in the *Neue Rundschau,* Rilke told Hedwig Fischer, Samuel's wife, that he was much impressed by the first half, but the second was too much of a good thing; it contained so much of "smells and odors and dismal darkening" that it "overflows and impregnates everything, and one sees it get larger and larger like spilled ink." The death signals are numerous indeed. Aschenbach is fifty and feels his creative powers flagging; he can no longer maintain the discipline necessary for his work. He is anxious, as pre-1914 Europe itself is ("Europe sat upon the anxious seat beneath a menace that hung over its head for months"); to calm himself, he takes a walk to Munich's North Cemetery, where he sees a stranger, red-thatched, obviously not Bavarian, and with an incongruous straw hat and a walking stick or club — the stranger with a "curiously domineering, even a ruthless air," the stranger with "large, glistening white teeth," the first of the tale's *psychopompoi,* its guides to the realm of the dead. (Has a rufous Dracula appeared in Munich, the city where — in the omitted chapter of Stoker's novel — Harker had his initial contact with the vampire?) This stranger, although Aschenbach "had forgotten him the next minute," prompts him by his "pilgrim air" to still greater unrest and thoughts of places far away, to his vision of a "primeval wilderness world," his yearning for "new and distant scenes" and "freedom and forgetfulness," and finally to his decision to go to the south. The unnamed "island in the Adriatic" is swiftly exchanged for Venice — the city in which Wagner died, the city which itself was moribund, the city of D'Annunzio's *Il fuoco,* permeated with "la bellezza autunnale," "autumnal beauty," the city about which Maurice Barrès wrote a whole essay, "La mort de Venise," concerning the deaths that had occurred in it (in *Amori et dolori sacrum,* 1901). The ancient hulk in which Aschenbach sails over to Venice is easily interpreted as Charon's boat; the old man on the boat who pretends to be young is a kind of debased repetition of the stranger at the cemetery, with "his rakish Panama and his red cravat," and he of course foreshadows Aschenbach's own grotesque effort at rejuvenation, in *his* straw hat, his dyed hair, his artificially red lips.

The gondola of Venice is "black as nothing else on earth except a coffin . . . What visions of death itself, the bier and solemn rites and the last soundless voyage" it conjures up! (Young René, or Rainer Maria, Rilke had used the coffin resemblance of the gondola in his Venice suite: "traun: Ich bin ein toter Kaiser, /und sie lenken mich zur Gruft" ["indeed: I am a dead emperor, /and they steer me to the tomb"].) The sinister gondolier, another Charon, has a "shapeless straw hat" (like the straw hat of the stranger and the old dandy) "and a short snub nose" that calls to mind "the little turned-up nose" of the cemetery stranger. The impudent singer in the hotel garden, whom the nervous Aschenbach asks about the plague in Venice, has — again like the stranger — "a great shock of red hair" and "a snub-nosed face" and a tongue which "plays dissolutely in the corner of his mouth" like that of the dandy on the ship. Aschenbach himself drinks pomegranate juice with soda water, dark red: pomegranates are the fruit of Hades whose seeds Persephone swallows in the land of the dead, thus becoming bound to it forever. Black plainly indicates death in these scenes, most directly in "the emaciated, blackened corpses of a bargee and a woman who kept a greengrocer's shop" that are the first overt signs of the coming of the plague to Venice; yet red — traditionally the color of passion — attaches itself to death as well, not just to the stranger, the dandy, and the singer and to Aschenbach (in several ways), but to the red sand in the hourglass that Aschenbach remembers from his childhood. The strawberries that Aschenbach twice eats in the story are red — it is hinted that they are the means by which the plague (if that is what kills him) enters his body. As Aschenbach sits on the beach, pondering Tadzio's name, he devours "a second breakfast of the great, luscious, dead-ripe fruit" (here the translation could lead us into an oversupport of our death argument, the original says "vollreif," "fully ripe"); again, as he follows Tadzio through the "labyrinth of little streets" near the end of the story (and smells the disinfectant carbolic acid he has also detected on the clothes of the street singer), he buys and eats some strawberries: "They were large and soft; he ate them as he went." (Strawberries, red strawberries, are more ominous than we might at first think; in German folklore they are a food of the dead (*Totenspeise*) and Oscar Wilde uses them in a similar sense when, in the penultimate chapter of *The Picture of Dorian Gray,* Dorian and Lord Henry eat them together.)

Aschenbach has been led to "the most improbable of cities," where he will die, conducted by sinister and even satanic guides; he confronts death itself, though, in the form of Tadzio, "the pale and lovely Summoner of the beach." Death has been given the handsome and inviting features of Eros Thanatos, Love-and-Death, and Tadzio's white linen suit also has its red breast-knot, its "red neckcloth." We might be tempted to think of the red that, elsewhere in the literature of decadence, can be so frightening — the scarlet of sin, maybe, as in the verse from Isaiah quoted by Basil Hallward to Dorian before the former's murder. Aschenbach does not consider his love for Tadzio sinful (Christianity plays no apparent role in the story), but he does realize that his trip to the south, and his visual succumbing to Tadzio, are a part of his relaxing the clenched fist of duty, a part of his abandonment of his sustaining attitude, a part of his dissolution. While the passion for Tadzio can be adorned or ennobled with thoughts of Plato's apology for homosexual love, of Socrates and Phaedrus (" 'Thus, great are the heavenly blessings which the friendship of a lover will confer upon you, my youth' "), Aschenbach also senses that he has entered into a chaotic world, a world without rules. Immediately after seeing the stranger in Munich, he has the hallucination of a landscape, a "tropical marshland, beneath a reeking sky, steaming, monstrous, rank," "a primeval wilderness world," where "the eyes of a crouching tiger gleam"; his plans for the trip go in this southerly direction, "although not all the way," he thinks, "to the tigers." Watching Tadzio, Aschenbach makes an association with the primeval world; the sight of the boy is like "a primeval legend, handed down from the beginning of time"; the plague that comes to Venice has been "bred in the mephitic air" of the Ganges swamps, "that primal island jungle, among whose bamboo shoots the tiger crouches," a dangerous and passionate and devouring beast. As Venice falls into the clutches of the plague, an orgiastic disorder prevails; Aschenbach has the "fearful dream" of the sexual orgy around the phallic god (and here the cries of the celebrants have the "soft consonants with a long-drawn *u* sound at the end" of Tadzio's name). The dream leaves Aschenbach "powerless in the demon's grip." Aschenbach possesses the common knowledge that Venice has been built on islands and swamps — as it were, a supreme act of civilization superimposed on wild formlessness. The original swamplike nature of the place is repeatedly borne in upon Aschenbach; as he opens the window in his hotel, he thinks he smells "the stagnant odour of the lagoons," a smell he detects again as he takes the vaporetto over to San Marco "across the foul-smelling lagoon" and "the canals sickened him with their evil exhalations." Returning to the hotel on the Lido, he catches the "faintly rotten scent of swamp and sea," and is "torn" by the thought he will never be strong enough to visit Venice again.

That Tadzio himself may be connected to this decaying world underneath Venice is apparent not only from the jungle-and-tiger images and the sounds in the phallic dream, but from a minor physical detail noted about him, the sign of inherent sickness — his bad teeth, "imperfect, jagged, and bluish, without a healthy glaze, and of that peculiar brittle transparency the teeth of chlorotic people often show." For Aschenbach the lover of form, the effort to cling to the classic shape of Tadzio cannot be sustained forever; the deeper appeal of Tadzio has been not aesthetic but sexual. That Aschenbach maintains his illusion of an ideal affection for Tadzio so long, without allowing its darker meaning to come to the surface of his mind, is the last of his many acts of will. Venice is a proper place for him to die, not only because it is the lovely city of death, but because — as Rilke observed in a sonnet — it is a place created and sustained by the will, which someday must fail. Aschenbach does not wish to be a decadent, on the contrary; but he has gone to the most alluringly decadent of cities and has given way, this refugee from pleasure (he was "not pleasure-loving"), to his most decadent desires — but only in spirit. He never speaks to Tadzio.

How much Aschenbach clearly realizes about the nature of these desires can only be guessed; once, sitting on the beach after his flight from the hotel, he is annoyed with himself for "his ignorance of his own desires." Thomas Mann — who, as his diaries have revealed, had a strong homosexual component beneath his exterior of the pater familias, the highly respectable man — lets his Aschenbach die in beauty, facing the "lovely Summoner." To be sure, it is an "elderly man" whose corpse is found in the deckchair. "And, before nightfall, a shocked and respectful world received the news of his decease."

19

Sweden

OSCAR LEVERTIN

GUSTAF AF GEIJERSTAM

HJALMAR SÖDERBERG

KJELL STRÖMBERG

A year after Strindberg's *I havsbandet*, the short novel *Lifvets fiender* (1891, The Foes of Life) by Oskar Levertin (1862–1906) was published. At the time, it was seen as a criticism of the tendentious literature which had flourished in Sweden, as in the rest of the North, during the previous decade: the forces of reformist radicalism are set against ultraconservatism, the former represented by the journalist Otto Imhoff, the latter by the political leader Bernt Gottfrid Hessler who, as the first member of his peasant family to receive a university education, has come into money and power. Levertin's intention was to show how such widely disparate standpoints were, in both cases, the foes of life, of a truly human development exploring the "richness of existence." Conflicted as he took two years to write his little book, Levertin was—next to Ola Hansson—the Swedish author most keenly aware of the currents of European decadence; these intrude upon his initial plan and turn *Lifvets fiender* into a document of Imhoff's decline and destruction. Plagued by his memory of the hatefulness with which he has pursued Hessler, he himself falls prey to a persecution complex, in which what he perceives as Hessler's brutal face repeatedly appears before him. Learning that Hessler lives on the first floor of the apartment house where, much higher up, he leads a penurious existence, he is tormented by the auditory hallucination of Hessler's footsteps on the stairs (something like the words that Klercken imagines he hears in *I förbund med döden*), and contemplates both the murder of Hessler and his own suicide. One moment he plans (as in his editorials) for a better world from which such obscurantists as Hessler have been eliminated; the next he takes refuge in a "sense of tired destruction, when thought and will seem like wounds [of the spirit] and the senses are filled with a simple longing for the wise man's hidden, simple Thébaïde," Schopenhauer's nirvana.

A good deal of information is given about Imhoffs' lineage: he is a patrician (Hessler, by comparison, has plebeian roots), whose mother is French, and whose father, a kindly collector of objets d'art, lives in reduced circumstances. He has a strange softness (Levertin uses the Italian *morbidezza*) in his pale skin; with his nervous hands and weak wrists, he resembles one of Velázquez's figures from the Escorial. He is an admirer of *Tannhäuser*, "a magic brew of reverence, repentance, and lust," and *Parsifal*. This "overwrought and hopeless dreamer" is not sexually active; he maintains a chaste relationship with his demure fiancée, who resembles an "ingénue of Kate Greenaway." He is also a lover of his native Stockholm, whose parks he observes in all seasons, but particularly in the autumn; he is fascinated by falling leaves. Imhoff is labile in his emotions: directly after he and Annie plan their modest domestic happiness, he sets out by streetcar for his and Hessler's address, perhaps with the intent of killing Hessler. Underway, he has a vision of his execution by Hessler in a scene from the Spanish Inquisition, falls from the car's platform, and is mortally injured. Seeing the accident, the real Hessler has the dying man carried into his rooms. "Imhoff's face hallucinated [*sic*] for him as a pain-crowned image of an Ecce Homo." It is Pentecost afternoon, and the verses from 1 Corinthians about the sounding brass and tinkling cymbal run through Hessler's mind: "In the presence of death, their struggles of opinion seem empty and base to him." Death, the thought of which Imhoff has secretly cherished throughout the novel, is the actual victor, rather than the "life-joy" (Oswald's word from *Ghosts*) halfheartedly sought with Annie. Imhoff has been destroyed not by Hessler but by his own fragility; as an aggressive journalist he took on himself a task he could not bear. (In the novel, Hessler has a victim parallel in some measure to Imhoff, a sensitive and refined wife, again from an old family, deeply loved by Hessler but forever cowed by him. She and Imhoff never meet.) Levertin made a kind of self-portrait in Imhoff; after a brilliant career as a poet and essayist, culminating in his appointment as the chief reviewer at *Svenska Dagbladet*, he died under circumstances never quite cleared up.

Meeting Annie for an excursion shortly before his death, Imhoff feels for a moment "the flood tide of existence flowing through his veins," liberating him briefly from "the petrifaction of his being before the Medusa's head of annihilation," i.e., his fascination with his death, his thanatophilia. The same phrase (as popular in its literary time as Ibsen's *life-joy*) comes back in the title of a novel by Gustaf af Geijerstam (1858–1909), *Medusas hufvud* (Medusa's Head, 1905). In his day, Geijerstam was a much-read and prolific author, whose collected narratives appeared after his death in twenty-five volumes; abroad, he was recruited for Samuel Fischer's stable of Scandinavian authors, and many of his novels came out in German during his lifetime, followed by a five-volume *Gesammelte Romane* (Collected Novels) in 1910. (In Felix Poppenberg's *Nordische Porträts aus vier Reichen* [1904], a volume in Georg Brandes's widely distributed series *Die Literatur,* Geijerstam had been Sweden's representative, alongside Denmark's Herman Bang, Norway's Knut Hamsun and Sigbjørn Obstfelder, and Finland's Juhani Aho.) His *Äktenskapets komedi* (1898; *Komödie der Ehe,* 1902) was favorably reviewed by Rilke; Geijerstam was an author whom "one must follow attentively from book to book." Rilke appears to have taken his own advice and read aloud from Geijerstam's novel about a young girl, *Karin Brandts dröm* (1904; *Karin Brandts Traum,* 1906) to the noble ladies who were his hosts at the Villa Discopoli on Capri in 1907. But his Swedish reputation had begun to decline even before his death, and only two of his novels were translated into English, both about problems of marriage, *Boken om Lille-bror* (1900; *The Book about Little Brother,* 1921) and *Kvinnokraft* (1901; *Woman Power,* 1922). Strindberg, in *Svarta fanor* (Black Banners, completed in 1904, published in 1907), savagely caricatured Geijerstam as the author Lars Peter Zachrisson, or Zachris, together with the feminist Ellen Key, who appears as the lesbian bluestocking Hanna Paj, the "crude and stupid intimate" of Zachris's spouse, Jenny. Zachris himself is a drug addict and toady who, in Strindberg's formulation, "occupied an outstanding place among the men of the decadence of decay." Describing Jenny's unwanted pregnancy, Strindberg says that, for nine full months, Zachris had to gaze at "Medusa's head—his wife's."

In the prologue of *Medusas hufvud,* a "little poet" — who has been identified as the Norwegian impressionist Sigbjørn Obstfelder — addresses a company at a banquet about the "head of Medusa, the many injustices, the many base deeds [of existence] . . . Everyone who looks at it turns to stone." The narrator Sixten Ebeling, a researcher of some indeterminate sort who hears and remembers the poet's words, goes home from the party to his bachelor quarters, and his thoughts turn to his sometime friend, Tore Gam. Uncanny events take place: lost keys, strange cries, the appearance of the ghost or image of Gam himself, at which the terrified Ebeling fires his revolver. (The subtitle of the book was *Ett spöksyn ur lifvet,* A Ghostly Vision from Life.) The next day, Ebeling recalls at length (Book 1) the course of his friendship with Gam, with whom, once upon a time, he shared rooms. The idealist Gam becomes a newspaperman and marries; having left his detested job, he is forced to borrow money from Ebeling. Book 2 consists of Gam's journal, an account of his disappointments and humiliations, his abandonment of his reporter's career, his move to the country with his wife and children, the death of his dog under a train, and his preparation for suicide. He will be crushed like Don, the dog. To his horror, Ebeling reads the newspaper account of Gam's death, which took place on the night of the ghostly apparition in Ebeling's rooms.

The novel is an obvious parallelizing of the two men, the ambitious Ebeling, who has compromised his ideals, and Gam, who has not, yet has been turned to stone by gazing at the head of Medusa, life's essential brutishness, while Ebeling has timidly averted his glance. For the student of decadence, the novel's interest lies in the slow petrifaction of Gam, which takes ten years instead of the half-year of Axel Borg's decay. Ebeling has noticed that Gam is infatuated with a fellow idealist, the quasi-scientist Reinhold: "To say that my friend [Gam] loved him, would not even approximately express what his feelings for this man contained." Reinhold leaves Stockholm for St. Petersburg, where, cutting himself off from human contact altogether, he rejects even Gam and dies in an insane asylum. Gam's wife observes that her husband has loved Reinhold more than her; Gam has grown indifferent to her and to his three children. (Tavaststjerna's Klercken in *I förbund med döden*, married to a devoted wife with whom he cannot discuss the nature of his illness, may have suggested similar elements in the portrait of Gam; it will be remembered that Geijerstam, visiting Finland, devoted a detailed lecture to Tavaststjerna's book.) Claes Ahlund sees a faint echo of Des Esseintes's retreat to Fontenay-aux-Roses in Gam's withdrawal, with his family, to a house outside Stockholm, and connects Des Esseintes's hatred of metropolitan life with Gam's, symbolized by the noisy train that kills first his dog, then himself. But elements of the aesthete are hard to find in Gam; he has no detectable literary interests (apart from his vaguely described attempt to become a free-lance writer), and his only artistic passion is for *La Grande-Duchesse de Gérolstein*, Offenbach's satirization of the falseness of the Second Empire.

The homosexual subtext of the novel cannot be overlooked, as hinted at in Ebeling's jealous aversion to Reinhold and Gam's blind devotion to him. Like Couperus in *Noodlot*, the best-seller Geijerstam may have been afraid to risk the loss of his public by an overemphasis on this still almost taboo trait in Gam — readers may have concluded that Gam simply admired Reinhold as a supreme self-destructive idealist. Elsewhere, in *Nils Tuvesson och hans moder* (1902; Nils Tuvesson and His Mother), Geijerstam gave mother-son incest the central position — the son's wife is murdered by the guilty couple; but the shock was softened by its historical setting and its basis in fact, the sensational "Yngsjö murder." Over against *I havsbandet* and *Lifvets fiender, Medusas hufvud* attaches few of the obvious trappings of decadence to Gam, hypersensitive but aesthetically indifferent, lacking the grand egocentricity of Borg, the refinement of Imhoff, and Imhoff's awareness of Stockholm. Like Imhoff, Gam is appalled by the cheap routines of the journalistic profession, which stand for the whole coarsening of modern life, but here again Geijerstam omits telling detail, although, like Levertin, he knew the calling from the inside. The large newspaper was in vogue as a literary setting at the end of the century, as an accompanying phenomenon to the growth of great metropolitan centers; de Maupassant's *Bel-Ami* (1885) may have served as a model in its cynicism for Bang's *Stuk* (1887, Stucco) and for Knut Hamsun's *Redaktør Lynge* (1893, Editor Lynge) and *Ny jord* (1893, *Shallow Soil*), and, more distantly, for the carefully portrayed *Nationalbladet* (i.e., *Svenska Dagbladet*) in Hjalmar Söderberg's *Den allvarsamma leken* (1912, *The Serious Game*). But *Medusas hufvud,* blurry and hasty as it is, remains the best of Geijerstam's many books, as Claes Ahlund has argued, and a novel tangentially of decadence.

Doktor Glas (1905) is the third of Söderberg's (1869–1941) four novels, coming after *Förvillelser* (1896, Aberrations) and *Martin Bircks ungdom* (1901, *Martin Birck's Youth*). It has been translated twice into English, in 1963 by Paul Britten Austin, and in 1998 by Rochelle Wright. Like *Förvillelser* and *Martin Bircks ungdom,* it was translated fairly early into German (1907) but failed to attract much attention, perhaps because of its extremely local quality — Söderberg is a classic Stockholm novelist, altogether uninterested in the grandeur of Nordic nature or in Nordic peasants, qualities which helped to win readers for his contemporaries Hamsun and Lagerlöf. During the heyday of his career, he became an idol of young Swedish-language writers in Helsinki, who could identify with the dispiritedness of his protagonists, as the Finland-Swedes nervously watched the growth of czarist despotism in the semiautonomous Grand Duchy, and became aware, simultaneously, of the displacement of their minority by the rapid growth in cultural and political strength on the part of the Finnish majority. (It goes almost without saying that Herman Bang, the great portrayer of the defeated, was an important inspiration for Söderberg's work.)

The weak-willed Tomas Weber of *Förvillelser* is an inactive medical student who devotes himself to erotic adventures, impregnates a girl of good family, Märta Brehm, and, in the clutches of a loan shark, makes an ineffectual attempt to shoot himself. Weber is neither decadent nor even decaying; he resembles a "rider who during some all-too-foolhardy ride is thrown from the saddle, and afterwards gets up with aching limbs, to resume his journey again on foot, limping, bloody, and soiled." He will take his examinations and become a respectable member of society. Söderberg's irony becomes apparent in the exculpatory doze Weber experiences after his attempt at suicide and his unexpected financial salvation: he dreams of a counterfeit to Märta Brehm (safely in Norway), who has "yellow teeth and withered skin," and of Ellen, a shopgirl he has seduced — now conveniently married to a hunchback clock-maker — similarly grown "old and withered." Tomas persuades himself that he is well out of his aberrations. *Förvillelser* does contain, however, a semideca-dent, a portrait left undeveloped: Weber's older friend, Johannes Hall, who sports "a large, pale green orchid" as his boutonniere; its strange form almost frightens Weber's sister, Greta, for it seems to resemble a large animal more than a flower, a "photophobic aquatic animal, fished up from the greenest depths of the sea." Hall is not quite Robert Hichens's Esmé Amarinth (*The Green Carnation* had come out a year before *Förvillelser*); he is heterosexual and makes an attempt to seduce Greta in his apartment, lighted by a lamp with an orange-colored lace shade and hung with photographs from his many journeys and a collection of etchings based on "a number of remarkable paint-ings." He shows her reproductions of works by Franz Stuck, not only those with fairy-tale motifs but the shocking *Die Sünde*. "White with terror," Greta flees, knocking over a taboret with a bottle of curaçao. A connoisseur of contemporary literature, Söderberg included in Hall faint reminiscences not only of the interior decorations of Des Esseintes but also of Bernhard Hoff in Bang's *Haabløse Slægter*. He may well have read *Bruges-la-Morte* and *I havs-bandet*, as well, and learned the effectiveness of a suggested soundtrack from them. Wandering through Stockholm in his desperation, Weber hears the "long-drawn howl" of a foghorn being tried out on Kungsholm (Stockholm place names are sprinkled throughout), "as from some enormous and enor-mously hungry animal," "day in and day out, always threatening"; the bells of Stockholm pursue him, as if the very tower of Östermalm Church were ring-ing, "so that the earth shook and the air sang and the houses staggered like drunks, back and forth."

In *Martin Bircks ungdom*, a subsidiary and unimpeachably decadent figure also appears. A bored government clerk and would-be author, Martin Birck, comes across a poet who confides to Martin quite baldly that he is a decadent. He "worship[s] everything that is in process of decay and rottenness and doomed to destruction. He hate[s] the sun and the light . . . He love[s] the night and sin and those alcoholic drinks tinged with green . . . He [has] most known venereal diseases" and agoraphobia to boot, but his illnesses fill him with quite a special joy, for he regards them as the harbinger of general paresis. "And *paralysie générale* was the great sleep — it was nirvana." Söderberg was not a creator of characters out of the whole cloth: the poet-decadent was based on Emil Kleen (1868–98), an imitator of Baudelaire, Swinburne, and Verlaine. Later, Martin sees the poet's picture in a bookshop window — in death, he has suddenly become a great man, his picture standing next to those of the Italian politician Francesco Crispi, the desposed king of Serbia, Milan Obrenović, and Hippolyte Taine. Martin himself is not a decadent; he is devoted to his father and the memory of his late mother, and maintains a hole-in-the-corner affair with a nameless young woman, which must be kept secret for the sake of her reputation — a detail which came in for some ridicule from reviewers, one asking why Martin did not work a little harder, earn a little more, and marry the girl. They attend a performance of *Hamlet,* for which they arrive late, so that they will not be seen. Afterwards, kissing the girl outside her apartment, with a "despairing passion" unusual in him, he hears Hamlet's rueful words, " 'I loved Ophelia,' " as if the anonymous beloved had already been driven into the water by his indecision. Fredrik Böök, the malicious critic, perhaps will-fully overlooked the circumstance that Birck, like Söderberg's other protago-nists, suffered from abulia, a weakness of the will, the literary disease that flourished at the end of the century.

   Doktor Glas has had many admirers and remains today (like Söderberg's other novels) a Swedish classic, but it has also had its critics. Writing about it in 1906, Söderberg's nemesis Böök said that the physician, in his "somewhat indolent unenterprisingness," was the latest version of Tomas Weber and Mar-tin Birck. The difference between Glas and his predecessors lay in the fictional fact that, after a lengthy inward struggle with himself, Glas poisons Pastor Gregorius, whose wife has sought aid from the physician: she wants to be freed from her marital duties on specious grounds of illness; she loathes the pastor who, because of his calling, will not consider divorce, and she is, in effect, repeatedly raped by him. The moral problem was once upon a time roundly debated in the press: Does Glas have the right to take Gregorius's life? Glas finds Gregorius repulsive in his very physical appearance — it comes up in the first entry of the diary novel — and for his sanctimonious hypocrisy. In his distant way, Glas falls in love with Helga Gregorius, although, as he learns, she is involved in an affair with Klas Recke, handsome and athletic, toward whom, as Glas observes him on Stockholm's streets — Glas is a flaneur and scopophile — the physician's feelings are ambiguous. Böök decided that "the great problem in *Doktor Glas* [is] an empty construction." The effort to trans-form "[Söderberg's] only half seriously intended opinions about the justifica-tion for murder" into a novelistic figure is a failure because "an *acting* person, in contrast to a mere *writing* one, must treat such matters as the contemplated

murder with quite a different earnestness, unless he suffers from moral insanity." (Böök employs the then popular term *moral insanity* from James
Cowles Prichard's *Treatise of Insanity*.) Böök does not think that Glas is insane, but rather that he is superficial and opinionated. Still, Böök concludes
that the book provides a causerie about a serious matter, by which the critic
means the predicament of Helga Gregorius.

Writing half a century later, Olle Holmberg confessed that in his youth one
could read the book without worrying too much about the moral problem
"Can one kill pastors because one loves their wives?" Whatever the case may
have been with Glas's private morality, the morality of style is beyond dispute;
it "has never been higher in any Swedish book, and it has to be admitted that
today *Doktor Glas* can still be read for the sheer pleasure of Söderberg's
manner of expression; nothing is left to chance, to bluff, to a passing notion" — an observation that also bears in on the remarkable detail work of
Glas's diaristic references and reactions. Almost simultaneously, though, with
Holmberg's encomium, the censorious Erik Hjalmar Linder, in a standard
history of Swedish literature, argued that *Doktor Glas* was badly flawed and
out of date: "Its quality of being a pertinacious problem-discussion . . .
weakens its effect . . . In its essence it is a sort of pamphlet of the 1880s,
directed against the concept of marriage at the time." Other social problems
that Dr. Glas reflects on in his diary, which covers a summer and part of an
autumn, from June 12 to October 7 — another seasonal novel, ending with
nature's decay — are the authority of the Lutheran (state) church and its representatives, and the justification of abortion and of prostitution. "[*Doktor
Glas*] can give rise to a sense of alienation [in the modern reader], more than
any other of Söderberg's novels."

Doktor Glas will not alienate readers familiar with the patterns and figures
of decadence; it is a treasure trove of debts and contributions to that literature:
the neurasthenic protagonist with his stunted emotional life, the protagonist
as murderer or semimurderer (see Couperus's Frank Westhove, D'Annunzio's
Tullio Hermil, Przybyszewski's Gordon, Rodenbach's Hugues Viane, Valle-
Inclán's marquis de Bradomín, Dorian Gray, and Dracula), and the city or
town as a major character. As in the case of Andrian's Vienna, Barrès's Aigues-
Mortes and Toledo, D'Annunzio's Rome and Venice, George Moore's sinister
Dublin in *A Drama in Muslin,* Henry Handel Richardson's Leipzig in *Maurice
Guest,* and Rodenbach's Bruges, Glas is constantly aware of summertime
Stockholm and its locations (Tom Geddes's commentary volume for the novel,
intended for British university students of Swedish, provides a necessary city
map). There are the meaningful musical allusions (as in Bang, the young
Thomas Mann, and Rodenbach), and allusions to literature: Glas quotes

Baudelaire's "Spleen" in the days after he slips Pastor Gregorius the lethal pill. (As one more important contrastive detail among the many in the novel: directly before the hidden murder, Glas has just seen his friend Martin Birck, "a melancholiac . . . I felt no desire to be with him now." Birck cannot act; Glas will, in the next few minutes.)

At the end of the first diary entry, Glas reveals what has been the main burden of his solitary life, in which he has been sometimes able to help others but never able to help himself. "[H]aving finished thirty-three years of life," he has never been close to a woman. The statement is not altogether true. On Midsummer Eve, he recalls his only erotic experience: as a very young man he and a girl, "in the full bloom of her twenty years," had left the celebration after dancing "a wild and dizzy dance" around the maypole, and, "behind a hedge of lilacs," he kissed her and pressed his hand against her breasts as they stared straight into the rising sun. Glas never sees her again; she is drowned in a swimming accident, a few days later, and Glas has an Ophelian vision: "The white body amidst the water weeds and mud . . . the grapnel hooked its claw in her breast." (In his diary, Glas mentions her twice again, after the murder, dreaming of her and the midsummer kiss and, in passing, remembering her at Gregorius's funeral: "I was in love with a girl.") Yet the shock of her death (and young Glas's vision of the retrieval of the corpse) have not been the start of his coitophobia. As a schoolboy he was disgusted by the dirty words scribbled on walls, "as if God himself had scribbled something ugly on the blue spring sky"; as an adult he wonders, in the same passage, about the circumstances of coition — like Crazy Jane in Yeats's poem, he could ask why "Love has pitched his mansion in/the place of excrement." Recalling his horror at the discovery of sex, he writes that he has still not recovered from his astonishment. As a boy, too, he was repulsed by contact with his father's naked body as the father tried to teach him to swim. His experiences as a physician have further fed his loathing for the physical act and its results: "A pregnant woman is something horrible, a newborn child is disgusting."

Glas is a fanatic of purity: he constantly looks for the pure blue of the sky, which hung, "vast and light and blue," over him and the girl before their brief encounter. But then, as he stroked her hand, "an old song ran through his mind: 'There burns a fire, he [*sic*] burns so clear/he burns like a thousand wreaths./Shall I enter that fire and dance/with my dearest dear?'" (The traditional text is patently sexual, even in its "wreaths," *kransar,* the sign of a girl's virginity: one says, "She has lost her wreath.") The clash between the blue of purity and the red of sexual passion, a commonplace but telling symbolism, has been present in Glas's diary from the start, in a passage about the sultry evening of June 12, followed by "the great blue night." Strolling, Glas has felt a "quiet and peaceful mood," but it is disturbed by a chance sighting of Gregorius, whose very appearance — he recalls an anecdote about Schopenhauer's unreasoning misanthropy — instantly makes hatred well up in Glas, and the thought — long before Glas knows about the intimacies of the Gregoriuses' marital life — that the pastor should die, freeing his pretty young wife for a better husband. The temperature and the horizon change; the heat seems "as oppressive as in the middle of the day," red dust clouds gather over Kungsholm, resembling "slumbering disasters." On June 18, he records his "blue and light" dreams of the night before, in which, one fine summer morning, he rides out toward Haga, and, very un-Glaslike, seizes a "brown-eyed girl," not further identified in the text, swings her around, kisses her hair, and rides off — as far as Glas can presently go in imaginary boldness. His next recorded dream, from July 6, after he has been visited by both Gregoriuses, is violent and under the sign of red. Pastor Gregorius is ill. Glas listens to Gregorius's heart (as he in fact has done in his consulting room, warning him — to protect the pastor's wife from his advances — against sexual activity) and says, while pressing a button in the wall, that he will have to remove it. (The lethal button has appeared before, in the diary entry where Glas first contemplates killing Gregorius.) The pastor dies, and Helga, who has been playing a parlor organ in a corner, hands Glas a bunch of dark flowers. "And only then I saw that she was smiling ambiguously and that she was naked." He stretches out his arms toward her, but she slides away, and Glas is interrupted by Helga's lover, Klas Recke, who places him under arrest. A shine of red fire comes through the window, and a woman twice cries from another room: " 'The world is burning! The world is burning!' " For Glas, sexual passion is dangerous, he is afraid of Helga, and Recke's appearance saves him, perhaps, from destruction. Glas has a set of defenses: Recke, of whom he might well be jealous, seems to him extremely good-looking ("I've scarcely seen a more handsome man"), whereas Glas regards himself as ugly; Recke has a right to the satisfaction of his sexual desire, the problem of desire solves itself directly for Recke, but Recke's solution causes Glas "no envy, only disgust." Glas does not object when Birck, at a sidewalk café, remarks that Helga Gregorius looks like a "blond Delilah." The doctor recalls his "horrible dream"; he has never seen Helga smile that insinuating way in reality, "and never wishes to."

Another detail about the dream of destructive sexuality is filled out in an entry written the day after Glas kills Gregorius; learning that the departed's mother is still alive, he feels a twinge of remorse. His own mother is long since dead, and if she were still alive, her "blue eyes, lighter than everyone else's," would have grown lighter still from age. Glas has been devoted to his gentle mother, even as he has detested his father, who shouted at him — another painful memory — when Glas, twelve years old, sat up in bed and sang "the wonderful melody" from Chopin's twelfth nocturne, the onset, as he was transformed by music, of Glas's adolescence. The day after the sidewalk conversation with Birck, and Glas's other friend, the cynical journalist Markel, Glas corrects his dream of the naked Helga Gregorius; the "dark flowers" may have been red, "perhaps red but very dark." The red flowers come up again in subsidiary mentions of a Miss Mertens, whom he sees "as if in a dream" while out riding; she has "two clear, honest eyes and rich brown hair," like the girl in the pleasant dream whose brown hair Glas brushes with his lips. Glas senses that Miss Mertens is interested in him; not without defensive self-satisfaction, he reasons that it is perhaps fortunate that "the gulf" between her soul and his is too large. At the end of the Mertens passage, Glas, scopophilic as ever, manages by mental implication to debase her: looking out his window at Clara Churchyard, he sees a prostitute; he has "port and brandy and beer and good food and a readied bed." Of course, he does not leave his window; he rounds off his slapped-together precoital dinner fantasy by noting: "Of course, it would be heaven for her."

The second night after the murder, the ragged clouds assume "a dirty brick-red and fire-colored glow," taking the shapes of dirty red devils — "who blew horns and whistled and screeched and whipped the rags off one another's bodies and indulged in all sorts of whoredom." The same evening he finds a bunch of dark flowers on his hall table, "dark red roses, a couple almost black," which makes him imagine that they are the flowers from his dream, from Helga. They are not; they come from Eva Mertens. Glas fears them and will not touch them.

In the next entry, that of August 24, Glas plays solitaire and ponders, again, the possibility of marrying Eva Mertens, who has a good heart: "Suppose I let her love me?" He is lonely and misses his cat, which ran away at the first sign of spring. As the "glow of the first autumn fire dances on the red-striped mat" in his rooms, Glas remembers the tomcat and conjectures, in the Swedish text, that he has "kommit på dekadans," has "gone to pot" in Austin's translation, has "come down in the world" in Wright's. With subtle intention or not, Söderberg uses the word *dekadans* in a then popular financial sense, as in Balzac's novel about business success and failure, *Histoire de la grandeur et de la décadence de César Birotteau* (1837) and in Thomas Mann's story "Der Wille zum Glück": "Der Baron . . . geriet plötzlich in Décadence" ("The Baron suddenly fell on hard times"); but Söderberg may also call attention to the literary mode to which *Doktor Glas* belongs. Murre, the tomcat, has been dragged away by his animal passions from his red-striped mat. Other objects or beings in Glas's apartment are destroyed by flame: a curtain catches fire; a nocturnal moth settles on one of his lamps; at the end of his long argument with himself about the contemplated murder of Gregorius, he has seen the lamps burning with "dirty-red flames" and the moth lying dead with scorched wings.

The climax of *Doktor Glas* comes neither with the poisoning of the pastor nor at his funeral, during which the remorse of Glas subsides, as he decides that he feels no guilt — but a little later. After the funeral, he meets Markel in a Turkish bath, a physical move toward his purification and his recovery from a bad cold. Unaware of Glas's deed, Markel cries out in the bath, " 'It's as warm and nice in here as in a little departmental office of hell.' " The friends decide to have dinner at an outdoor restaurant, Hasselbacken. Taking off his black mourning clothes, Glas has a sudden outburst of dandyism; he unpacks a new suit, "a dark gray frock-coat outfit," which he ordered on the eve of the murder; the box contains, as well, "a blue, white-dotted vest." Glas feels "rejuvenated and free." Attention is further called to Glas's outfit by an equally careful description of Markel's, "a scarf resembling a scaly green snakeskin," suggestive of the Mephistophelean role Markel likes to play in conversation — albeit he has had nothing to do with Glas's plan to kill the pastor or with the physician's rejuvenation. The menu is also worked out with dandyistic care: "Potage à la chasseur, filet of plaice, quail, fruit, Mumm extra dry, Manzanilla." The orchestra — or band, the Swedish *orkester* is ambiguous — begins to play the Boulanger March, in which the Dreyfusard Markel senses an anti-Dreyfus demonstration, "arranged by a coterie of lieutenants." (Boulanger was a French general and politician of the far right; exiled from France, he killed himself, dramatically enough, on the grave of his mistress.) Is the mention of the quickstep, "En revenant de la revue," only a preparatory detail, calling attention to the much clearer meaning of the music to come, or did at least some of Söderberg's contemporary readers remember Boulanger's romantic fate? The same readers could have drawn a comparison between the loyal Boulanger and Klas Recke, at another table in the restaurant, accompanied by a wealthy Miss Levinson, for whom Recke has cast Helga aside.

Music and its implications have an important role in Söderberg's novels. In *Martin Birck,* at the same restaurant, Hasselbacken, the orchestra plays the overture to Arrigo Boito's *Mefistofele* before Birck meets the Mephistophelean Markel for the first time. In the opening scene of *Den allvarsamma leken,* young Lydia Stille can distinguish the voice of Arvid Stjärnblom in her father's group of amateur singers as they perform Heinrich Marschner's "Warum bist du so ferne?" After their respective marriages to others, Lydia and Arvid carry on a long affair, until Lydia betrays Arvid with other men. Stjärnblom, a music critic, has been reunited with Lydia when he goes to the opera to hear the great soprano Klarholm-Fibiger as Senta, devoted unto death, in *Der fliegende Hol-länder.* In the late story "Aprilviolerna" (April Violets), Docent Jerneld has heard a voice singing Emil Sjögren's "Sover du, min själ?" (Do You Sleep, My Soul?) on his way to a party at the house of Professor Grendel; the voice belongs to Grendel's lovely wife, with whom Jerneld begins a flirtation. He almost attends Offenbach's *Tales of Hoffmann* with her; when she feigns a headache, he uses the tickets to take the waitress Lena, with the same first name as Fru Grendel, to the opera. Under the influence of the music, he falls in love with simple Lena and marries her. Later, after Fru Grendel has run away with an Italian sculptor, the Jernelds visit Grendel; Jerneld remembers the former Fru Grendel's performance of Sjögren's song, and Lena, smitten by Grendel's playing of the barcarole from *Hoffmann* on the violin, is captivated by the older man and deserts Jerneld for him. By that time (1929), Söderberg's employment of musical influence and allusion had become heavy-handed.

The Chopin episode in the life of the boy Glas has already been mentioned; when a little older, Glas falls distantly and shyly in love with his beautiful cousin Alice, an amateur singer; he saw "Chopin's moon" when his father interrupted *his* Chopin song, and now, in the diary, seeing the same moon, he remembers Alice: "I loved her." In the diary entries of July 10–11, directly following his description of the potassium cyanide pills he has prepared in the event that he wants to commit suicide (like Hamsun's Nagel in *Mysterier,* Przybyszewski's Gordon in *Satans Kinder,* and Zeyer's Jan Maria Plojhar, he keeps a supply of poison at hand), Glas mentions the "hot although surely passing" sensation of power he feels when — in a corner at the Opera, just as he heard Alice from a corner of the porch at the Glas summer villa — he hears the Coronation March from Meyerbeer's *Le Prophète.* On August 8, looking out his window at Clara Churchyard, while still trying to make up his mind to kill Gregorius, he sees the redness of the church's brick tower, the dark and mighty green of the trees, and the "blue sky beyond . . . so deep." Somewhere a man in shirtsleeves is playing the Intermezzo from *Cavalleria Rusticana* on the flute, "admired and loved by countless people, and awakening boredom and disgust in others . . . often the very ones who had loved it at first." Whether or not the much-played tune catches Glas's ear because of a connection with Glas's much-recited arguments about Gregorius cannot be determined; but surely Glas repeats one of the reflections of the exclusivist Des Esseintes: "Le plus bel air du monde devient vulgaire, insupportable, dès que le public le fredonne, dès que les orgues s'en emparent."

During the Hasselbacken dinner, hearing that Miss Mertens talks con-stantly about him, Glas gives Markel a free field, to which Markel replies that he is "out of the game" and grows "serious and pale." Does he suffer from impotence, like Des Esseintes, or, for that matter, like his dinner companion? The waiter serves champagne "med en tempeltjänares allvar": Austin translates "with the gravity of an acolyte"; Wright, "with the solemnity of a temple attendant." The players begin the Prelude ("förspelet") to *Lohengrin,* translated by Austin as "overture," a rendering of which a Wagnerian would not approve. For a Wagnerian, too, "tempeltjänare" has a precise resonance; in Lohengrin's farewell, he tells of his starting place, "eine Burg, die Monsalvat genannt; /ein lichter *Tempel* stehet dort in Mitten." The clouds have disappeared, and Glas sees the blue of the sky, "up there, space had blued into a deep, infinite blue, blue as this wonderful blue music," the virgin blue the dirty words in the schoolyard had besmirched. "The thoughts and ponderings of the recent past and the action in which they ended seemed to me to flow away into the blue like something already far away and unreal." Listening to the descent and ascent of the Grail in the Prelude's divided strings (or flutes and clarinets, if it is a band), Glas has devised an exculpatory and ennobling legend of his own; he is the savior knight, in his blue vest dotted with white. Markel says, without being aware of Glas's thoughts: "A good Wagnerian erects a whole philosophy of life on a motif from *Parsifal.*"

Glas is not the only literary figure of the time to act like an imaginary Lohengrin. In Ibsen's *When We Dead Awaken* (1899), in the antiphonal retelling by the artist Rubek and his model Irene of what happened at Rubek's retreat on Lake Taunitz, as he resisted sexual temptation in favor of his art, Rubek pretended to be the chaste knight launching water lilies and dock leaves like swans on the lake. (And Irene joined in the game.) Before Ibsen, in the sensational novel *Le Roi vierge* (1887), based on the rumors surrounding Ludwig II of Bavaria, Linderhof, and Neuschwanstein, Catulle Mendès had his king, Frédéric of Thuringia, reject women and sail in his swan-boat on the lake of his artificial paradise. The princess who loves him, Lisi, clambers into the swan-boat with him, it capsizes, and she catches a fatal case of pneumonia. He stabs — but not mortally — the sexually voracious singer Gloriana Gloriani, sent by the king's mother to seduce him. At length, Frédéric castrates himself and orders a special performance of the (mislocated) Oberammergau Passion play to take place in which he is crucified; a spear is thrust into his side by a faithful servant, clad as a Roman soldier, and a Mary Magdalene, Gloriana, kneels at the foot of the cross. Wagner appears in the novel as the king's favorite composer, Hans Hammer. In his youth, Frédéric experienced a shock comparable to those of Glas. Going to an innocent tryst in a bower of lilacs with Lisa (as Glas kissed the girl behind a lilac hedge), he finds a fat girl of the village, "sweating and half undressed," giving herself to a robust boy, who holds her shoulders in his "gross hands." "All swollen with immense disgust,

[Frédéric] had learned the vile mystery of the sexes and the filthy hideousness of copulation": lovers are "pigs from the same trough."

Something odd, though, lies in the description of the wonderful blue music of the Prelude to act 1 of *Lohengrin,* which sounds much like Wagner's own turgid prose from 1853: "The clearest blue heavenly air seems in the beginning, to the enchanted gaze of the highest unworldly yearning for love, to consolidate itself into a wonderful, scarcely perceptible apparition which nonetheless magically captivates the eye." As Glas listens to the music, he notices that the motif of "Thou shalt not ask" breaks through in the orchestra or band. But the *"four* words" of Lohengrin's command about his name and identity, repeated four times by Glas in his diary, fit neither the German text or the melodic line "Nie sollst du mich befragen" nor the standard Swedish translation by Frans Hedberg (1874), the manager of Stockholm's Royal Opera, again five words: "Aldrig du mig skall fråga" ("Never shall you ask me"). The author of a book on *Doktor Glas* from 1987, Lars O. Lundgren, comments that Glas never wants Helga to find out what he has done, and she does not. But how carefully has Glas been listening? The musical phrase, the question motif (*Frageverbotmotif*), does not appear in the score of the Prelude.

Several possibilities exist as reasons for Glas's misremembering. He may have heard, and Söderberg may have remembered, for the purpose of his fiction, one of those numerous "fantasies" or "potpourris" based on *Lohengrin* that were so popular at the time. Or Glas, and Söderberg, may have mixed the ending of the Prelude to act 1, where the strings float away into the blue, with the ending sometimes used in band arrangements of the equally much-played Prelude to act 3, in which, instead of going over into the bridal music as the curtain rises, the brasses intone the imposing question motif. Or finally, making the music fit his own intentions, Glas only imagines that he has heard the motif in question, illuminating a larger message of *Doktor Glas* that intrudes with some insistency as the diary moves toward its end. Glas has kept his thoughts about the "wonderful blue music" to himself: "I listened and concealed myself." The loquacious Markel continues to chatter, proposing that in a statement to the Riksdag requesting an increased subsidy for the Opera, one could say: " 'Music stimulates and strengthens; it enhances and confirms.' "

On August 7, having dreamed again that he kills the pastor (which he will do, two weeks later), Glas lights the lamp at his bedside, then ignites the lights in all his rooms and continues his inner arguments about the necessity of the deed: "One of the basic drives in my nature is not to endure anything half-conscious and half-clear within me, when it is in my power to take it out and hold it up in the light." Yet he quickly retreats from this standpoint on August 10; he looks at the night sky, "the great infinite night," realizes that night is "really only a little pointed cone of darkness in the midst of a sea of light," and remonstrates with himself: "Oh, what kind of plague has seized mankind, to ask about everything what it is?" The sheltering darkness, which he loves, is not an ultimate shelter at all. Too much inquiry after the truth destroys, and, in his case, sexual desire also destroys. In his dream of August 7, he has again seen Fru Gregorius, naked, in a corner half in darkness, trying to cover herself with a black handkerchief. He recalls the voice of the woman crying, in the first dream about the killing of Gregorius and about the naked wife, " 'The world is burning! The world is burning!' "

On the afternoon before the excursion to Hasselbacken, in the heat of the sauna, Markel long-windedly divides humanity into three groups: thinkers, scribblers, and cattle. The thinkers' task is to look for the truth. But if they had their way, they would steer the earth straight into the sun and destroy it. Their activity sometimes causes the cattle to bellow: " 'Put out the sun, in Satan's name, put it out!' " The newspaperman's or scribbler's business is to understand with the thinkers and feel with the cattle, protecting the thinkers from the rage of the cattle and the cattle from too much truth. But, according to Markel, a subdivision of the thinkers exists, one which hides among the cattle, a class in which Markel locates Glas. Then the great Lohengrinian masquerade at Hasselback begins.

In the diary entry of September 7, Glas, still convinced that he has done the right thing, although he has begun to dream of the pastor again, returns to these sauna thoughts of Markel and his own thoughts at Hasselbacken. Mankind blesses the sun because it lies at a safe distance; a little nearer or farther and mankind would burn or freeze to death. He adduces a "Finnish myth": "He who sees God's face must die," an echo of a poem by the poetaster and self-deluder Martin Birck, and thinks of Oedipus, who solved the riddle of the Sphinx and became the unhappiest of men. Lohengrin's Frageverbot comes back — "Don't ask!" — and is extended to "Don't think!" Glas has become a brother to Ibsen's Dr. Relling in *The Wild Duck,* the deviser of the protective life lie. The afternoon before he murders Gregorius, Glas has met Helga Gregorius on the knoll before Karl Johan's Church on Skeppsholm, crouched on the church steps, looking "straight into the sun." It has to be concluded that she has just been told by Recke — whom Glas met on the road to the church, looking at first uncomfortable and then jaunty — that he will take her away to America, a lie she cannot believe. She understands that he will back out of their affair, as he in fact does; she has beheld the truth and, as she says, wants to die. Glas never speaks to her again, only seeing her at a distance at her husband's funeral and once again, on September 20 as, lurking outside her windows, he has a final and incomplete sexual fantasy about her, slowly "undoing her clothes." He rejects a prostitute who passes him, looking at him with "hungry eyes," and he sees "a dark figure" emerge from the house to mail a letter, with a face "pale as wax." Glas does not approach her. On October 7, the last entry, the autumn leaves fall; significantly enough, Glas never sees the sun, snow is in the air, and he has hung "new curtains, pure white" in his study to replace those which burned. The eternal virgin ends his diary in total whiteness: "In my room, the light was just as it is after a first snowfall."

The not always accurate self-observer Glas has lived his life at second hand, through fantasies, musical allusions, literary ones. Aware of the ennui of his solitary life, in a moment of insight he thinks his thirst for action may spring from this ennui, a devaluation of his attempt to save Helga. He comes up with a quotation from Marguerite de Navarre, not unflattering to himself: "L'ennui commun à toute créature bien née," a sentiment to which Des Esseintes and Dorian, growing old in his youthful mask, would have subscribed. Glas looks—once more—out the window of his apartment toward the grave of Carl Michael Bellman, the Rococo poet-singer of sexual passion and life's brevity, lying in Clara Churchyard, under "two little trees, wretched and thin, whereas he should sleep beneath great sighing ones." For the reclusive Glas, Bellman is the poet not of vulgar conviviality but of sexual melancholy and death. Glas quotes four lines from Baudelaire's "Spleen I," about rain falling on Paris and the tedium it causes. The first two, from the end of the sonnet's octet, are: "L'ombre d'un vieux poëte erre dans la gouttière/avec la triste voix d'un fantôme frileux" (The shade of an old poet wanders in the roof's gutter, / With the sad voice of a shivering ghost); Söderberg quotes from the 1851/1857 edition of *Les Fleurs du mal,* with *L'ombre* instead of the later *L'âme.* The lines suggest Bellman, and also, in their context in the poem, Baudelaire's cat, like Glas's restless Murre: "My cat flits without stopping, looking for a place to rest, on the paving tile, skinny and shabby." The second half of Glas's quotation from Baudelaire, from the conclusion of the sonnet's sestet, is about playing cards, "redolent of dirty perfumes, the fatal heritage of an old, dropsical woman": "Le beau valet de coeur et la dame de pique / causent sinistrement de leurs amours défunts" ("The handsome jack of hearts and the queen of spades/Chatter dismally of their dead loves"). Glas is playing solitaire and observes that cards were invented to drive away the melancholy of sick and insane princes; he almost slips for a moment into the role of Charles le Fou and into the role of "le beau valet de coeur." If his love for Helga is debased by turning her into the queen of spades in a soiled deck of cards, it is further degraded by another of his condescending sexual fantasies, that he will go across the cemetery—the scene of outdoor couplings in better weather, the cemetery from which now, in the dampness, the smell of corpses seems to come — to a dirty old hovel, drink with the girls, and play cards with the fat madam; the Swedish is *dra en spader,* draw a spade, and the queen of spades is *Spader Dam.*

The decadent Glas can express himself only through allusions and live only through masquerades ("wearing a mask, always, for everyone"); another of the revelatory remarks Glas makes about himself is that he has no eyes of his own (July 5), that he cannot look at a tablecloth without thinking of Strindberg (an allusion to an episode in *Tjänstekvinnans son*) or see rowers in their striped jerseys without having memories of de Maupassant turn up; he sees the shadows on the wall of his room and thinks of Hans Christian Andersen's story "The Shadow," in which the professor, himself become a shadow, is executed by his shadow, which has taken over his existence. Much as he loves the moon, "Chopin's moon," he realizes that moonshine, after all, is only "sunshine at second hand. Weakened, counterfeit." Glas is "born as an observer."

Fredrik Böök, in a essay from 1926, wrote disdainfully about the morally indifferent fin de siècle mode of Söderberg's novels, which formed like "stagnating fluids" in "this peaceful, thriving social body" of Sweden. Wrong about much, the archconservative Böök was right about Swedish decadence; its literary specimens struggle with their own neuroses or madness but are never aware of the threatened destruction of their healthy nation, in which they — Borg, Imhoff, Gam, Tyko Gabriel Glas — are foreign bodies. Sweden was not troubled by a general sense of decline and fall; a comic-opera war with Norway during the Union Crisis was averted by good sense on both sides.

In 1915, Kjell R. G. Strömberg (1893–1975) published a novel called *Gabriel Nepomuk: En poet i XX. Seklets begyndelse* (Gabriel Nepomuk: A Poet at the Beginning of the Twentieth Century). "Gabriel Nepomuk, count of Parzifal zu Georgenstein," like Strömberg, is an Uppsala student; he fancies that, at his maturity, he will inherit the family castle in Bohemia. He tries very hard to imitate the externals of a decadent lifestyle, dresses as a dandy (with violet stockings), enjoys his *spleen* and reads the necessary literature, *Dorian Gray, À rebours, De profundis,* Barbey, Baudelaire, Poe, Dante Gabriel Rossetti, Verlaine; like Bang's Joán, he decides that he is a "Chosen One of Pain." In fact, Gabriel Nepomuk is an innocent, the virginal admirer of the temptress Izabel Tiger, who is somewhat impressed by his literary plans. When his family — not Central European nobility after all: his father is a Swedish railroad functionary — loses its money, Gabriel Nepomuk decides to set out for Prague and Monte Carlo and perhaps commit suicide: he wants to die, he says, "in a Catholic country." His despairing journey is also hastened by the knowledge that Izabel Tiger has an athletic fiancé, an engineer. Not having broken the bank at Monte Carlo and not having killed himself, he returns home ill, recovers, and is taken into the physical favor of Izabel, on a polar bear skin in his room; but the relationship snaps off during a love scene in which they imagine that they are Eskimos: she has just come back from skiing and, undressed, reveals a sign, a love bite, of her continued affair with the engineer. Gabriel Nepomuk's reasonable friend Walter, in the novel's final sentence, calls him a "new Samson, . . . stranded on the cunning of Delilah." A "Commentary and Epilogue" states that people such as Gabriel Nepomuk have been made superfluous by the outbreak of the Great War, "especially in their capacity as poets of the decadent genre." With the present book, "a specimen of this extinct sort of person, such as could still be found at the century's beginning in most countries, has been preserved." As for Gabriel Nepomuk himself, it is rumored that "a young and eccentric gentleman from the polar regions" has gone to Abyssinia and found his way to the source of the Nile. The reader can well imagine "the Polish-Swedish poet as the victorious chieftain of an unknown Negro tribe with notably gentler customs than those of the European peoples." Gabriel Nepomuk has become a Rimbaud; the book's epigraph is from the conclusion of "Le Bateau ivre": "Mais vrai, j'ai trop pleuré. Les aubes sont navrantes./Toute lune est atroce, et tout soleil amer" (But, true, I have wept too much! The dawns are heart-rending,/Every moon is dreadful, and every sun bitter).

In the text proper, Gabriel Nepomuk fears that his works will fall into the hands of "the stern critic," Fredrik Böök, and they did: on November 3, 1915, in *Svenska Dagbladet,* Böök gave a short but savage review, asking how such a "boring and insignificant book could be written about such a boring and insignificant figure." Böök missed the point; *Gabriel Nepomuk* is an interesting and in its way significant spoof of a dying literary mode. Its equivalents can be found in Robert Hichen's send-up of Wilde as Esmé Amarinth and in Schaukal's extravagant *Leben und Meinungen des Herrn Andreas von Balthesser.* Strömberg's pure fool, rightly having Parzifal among his fictitious names, spends his youth "trying different poses," always the would-be decadent — disguises through which guileless innocence shines. One wonders how much a self-portrait the book may have been. Not shattered by Böök's review, Strömberg had a successful career as an interpreter of France's literature for Sweden, and of Sweden's for France.

20

Denmark

HERMAN BANG

Herman Bang (1857–1912) has long been considered the chief representative of the decadent literary spirit in Denmark. The reasons are not far to seek. In his personal life, Bang lived up fully to the public's notion of the decadent: he was homosexual and made little effort to hide it, he was a drug addict, he posed as a nobleman, "Herman de Bang," he was dandyistic, he liked publicity, and he brought his flamboyant personality to the fore both in highly successful readings from his works and in much less well received stage appearances, particularly on tour in Scandinavia, as the "worm-eaten" Oswald in *Ghosts*. He resembles his contemporaries Oscar Wilde and Louis Couperus in his self-stylization.

Bang has never been well known in the English-speaking world: only five novels have appeared in translation, *De uden Fædreland* (1906, *Denied a Homeland*, 1927), *Ludvigsbakke* (1897, *Ida Brandt*, 1928), *Les Quatre Diables* (1890, *Four Devils*, 1928), *Tine* (1889, *Tina*, 1984) and *Ved Vejen* (1886, *Katinka*, 1990). In the countries where German was spoken, however, Bang quickly won a large following when the major German publisher Samuel Fischer added Bang to his stable; most of his novels appeared quite early in translation, and after his death his collected works in four volumes came out in 1919, expanded to six in 1926.

Thomas Mann was a devoted reader of Bang ("an author to whom I feel deeply related" is what he wrote in 1902, for reasons better understood since the publication of Mann's diaries), and contributed an obituary article on Bang to Fischer's *Neue Rundschau*. Hofmannsthal, in his early diaries, noted that "Bang puts things in a way no one else can, the sense of being weaker," and Rilke wrote enthusiastic reviews of the novelistic memoir *Det hvide Hus* (1898; The White House) and *Tine*. Rilke called Bang "this great artist" but shied away from a personal meeting with the Danish author, describing him to his wife (1904), presumably on the basis of Scandinavian gossip, as "exhausted and a morphine addict." Almost two decades later, Rilke told a Swiss correspondent that, when he thought of Bang, he would "designate a star of the first magnitude, on whose appearance and location I long oriented myself in the darkness of my youth." Bang's enduring German reputation was (and is) built to great extent on his artistry; but the element of the sensational was never missing, surely not during the Weimar Republic: in 1922, the Berlin psychiatrist Max Wasbutzski, who had treated Bang for depression, printed a German-language manuscript Bang had entrusted to him, *Gedanken zum Sexualitätsproblem*.

Bang's semiautobiographical debut novel, *Haabløse Slægter* (1880; Hopeless Generations, or Hopeless Families) transgressed against Denmark's pornography laws because of the eroticism of some of its passages, in particular those about the seduction, degradation (this was the heyday of Sacher-Masoch), and ultimate impotence of the protagonist, William Høg, who falls victim to a middle-aged British femme fatale, the Countess Hatzfeldt. Otherwise, the novel is the story of Høg's devotion to shadowy memories of his ancient family, and of his failed attempt to restore its "honor" through his success as an actor. (Høg's mother, to whom he is devoted, as later Bang protagonists are to theirs, dies of tuberculosis; his father, for whom the youthful William has to care, goes mad.) Twenty years before *Buddenbrooks*, *Haabløse Slægter*—translated into German as *Hoffnungslose Geschlechter* (1900)—is the account of a family's decline: Bang's great-grandfather (1747–1820) had been professor of medicine at Copenhagen, his grandfather was Oluf Lundt Bang (1788–1877), the inventor of "Bang's stethoscope."

The 1880 edition of the novel was immediately confiscated, and the author paid substantial fines for what he called the "life story of the last male member of a physically, spiritually degenerate clan." In a revision and shortening of 1884, Bang put the Hatzfeldt episode into softer focus and removed William's diaristic reflections from this "chaotic book." A third, "final" version of 1905 had mostly stylistic changes. In the initial version—which was not reprinted until 1965—William ends as an obscure actor in the provinces, whereas in the recasting he takes his own life—the last deed of the last member of a heroic line. (Bang liked to toy with the thought that he—and William—were descended from a mighty Danish family of the Middle Ages, the Hvides; in *Haabløse Slægter,* the real medical forebears are ignored, but the doctor-grandfather will turn up in a later novel.) The moral objections to *Haabløse Slægter* did not extend to the novel's other main male character, Bernhard Hoff, the Copenhagen man-about-town who maintains a perfumed apartment, plays the "decadent" composers Schumann and Anton Rubinstein on the piano, and keeps a bust of the Bithynian boy Antinous deified by Hadrian on his mantel. His initials are Bang's in reverse. For safety's sake, Bang implies that Hoff is heterosexual and frequents female prostitutes as he leads young Høg down the primrose path. Also, Høg himself has had his first sexual experience, before Countess Hatzfeldt, with Camilla Falk, the flirtatious and experienced sister of a schoolmate. She has "a sensual, full figure and small, perfect teeth."

Bang's next novel, *Fædra* (1883), was likewise risqué; an unhappily married noblewoman falls in love with her stepson, and ends her life—typically for the time—"sinking deeper and deeper into morphine's lethargy." Meanwhile, Bang had established himself as the up-and-coming man in Copenhagen's journalistic world, and his sense for the capital informed *Stuk* (1887, Stucco), a title alluding to the false building fronts and the corruption of the growing metropolis—a successful offshoot of what Bang had learned from reading novels about the Paris of Napoleon III, Octave Feuillet's *Monsieur de Camors* (1867), Zola's *La Curée* (1872), and Daudet's *Le Nabab* (1877). Bang's literary orientation was toward France, toward Turgenev, and toward "the impressionist" Jonas Lie in Norway.

Humiliated by Georg Brandes's characterization of him as possessing "a woman's mediocre intelligence," Bang set out on a continental trip during which he had to leave Berlin abruptly because of his insulting article (in a Norwegian newspaper) about members of the Hohenzollern family; as abruptly, he departed from Prague after his abandonment by an actor, Max Eisfeld. His account of the Prague stay contains a passage bearing directly on his novel of almost two decades later, *De uden Fædreland:* "You [Prague] have taught a stranger that everyone, even the poorest person, possesses one thing, the dedication of his love to his homeland . . . The proud Hradčany speaks of love for the homeland, the king of stone ruling over the whole of Bohemia's land."

In Vienna (with Austrian detectives watching him, he thought, from his landlady's kitchen) he completed the collection of stories *Stille Eksistenser* (1886, Quiet Existences), of which *Ved Vejen* is the crown, to be followed in 1889 in another little masterpiece, *Tine.* The Danish title of the former literally means "Beside the Way": the frail wife of a coarse stationmaster falls in love, distantly, with a gentlemanly estate manager; when he leaves, she wastes away from tuberculosis. In the latter, the family of a forester, Berg, lives in a Danish country paradise until the Dano-Prussian War of 1864; Berg's wife and son are evacuated, and Berg, a reserve lieutenant, engages in a desperate affair with Tine, a schoolmaster's daughter who is his wife's best friend, before he is mortally wounded during the Prussian cannonade at Dybbøl. Realizing that Berg has never loved her, Tine drowns herself. Reviewing the German translation in 1903, Rilke praised "his wonderful way of drawing female figures." These stories were popular because of their gentle sentimentality and, in the latter case, an implicit patriotism; the public did not know the private background for their theme of abandonment. With *Les Quatre Diables,* Bang returned to a milieu that had interested him early on, the circus. In the *Excentriske Noveller* (Eccentric Novellas) of 1885, the bond between brothers, the "Fratelli Bedini," a lion tamer and a trick rider, has been broken by the equestrian's passion for a trapeze artist, in *Les Quatre Diables* heterosexual passion destroys two of the four members of a troupe of acrobats. Hofmannsthal especially admired the story "Franz Pander" in *Excentriske Noveller:* a room-service waiter realizes that he is only an "object" for a luxury hotel's "sweet-smelling" female guests, to be exploited and cast aside.

The exposure of a homosexual ring in Copenhagen made Bang decide to go abroad again, this time to Paris, where he lived from 1892 to 1894: his activities were almost entirely in the theater, as a producer at Antoine Lugné-Poe's Théâtre de l'Oeuvre, helping to bring the Scandinavian repertoire to the French stage. (Decades later, in his memoirs, Lugné-Poe compared Bang to André Antoine, Max Reinhardt, and Stanislavsky; the actress Gabrielle Réjane said that, without Bang's aid, she could not have created her Nora in *A Doll's House.*) Bang should have been happier than in Copenhagen, where he had contemplated suicide and briefly entered a mental hospital. But Lou Andreas-Salomé—the past friend of Nietzsche, the coming friend of Rilke, and the future friend of Freud—who visited him in Saint-Germain in the summer of 1894, found him "constantly sickly"; he told her how afraid he was to begin a new work, claiming that sometimes he would run to the window of his room, to see if there were not some diversion to keep him from his author's task.

On a stay in the winter of 1894–95 at a Norwegian resort (he had been on a Scandinavian tour with Lugné-Poe's troupe) he made the chance acquaintance of Claude Monet, gone north to get a good look at snow; Monet's refusal to discuss the theory of painting had bolstered Bang in his own "naive" gift as a painter of human nature. *Ludvigsbakke* (1897) is a fruit of this new self-confidence. After the death of her oppressive mother, Ida Brandt, sweet and naive, has moved to Copenhagen, to become a nurse in the asylum where Bang himself had been a patient; she is seduced—for her small inherited fortune—by Karl von Eichbaum (compare Eisfeld), the ne'er-do-well scion of the family which once owned the estate Ludvigsbakke, the manager of which had been Ida's father. (A nouveau riche butter manufacturer has bought it, destroyed the manor house, and chopped down the orchard's trees, six years before *The Cherry Orchard*.) The eye of Bang for detail in the creation of milieu and character—the comfortable Ludvigsbakke of Ida's sheltered childhood, the small town of her girlhood under the thumb of her mother, a veritable Fafnir sleeping on her gold, the mental hospital and its routines, the cramped apartment in Copenhagen where Karl and his mother cling to their social prejudices, the love nest Ida outfits for herself and Karl, and where she lies shattered after learning that Karl will make a profitable marriage in his own class—give the book the air of ineluctable defeat which Hofsmannthal recognized as the special Bangian quality.

Bang's next three novels are on the same level of artistic creation: *Det hvide Hus* (1898) is Bang's fictionalized tribute to his childhood home and his mother, a fragile woman whose husband no longer loves her; the Maman of Rilke's pseudo-Danish *Die Aufzeichnungen des Malte Laurids Brigge* is partly patterned on her. Near the end of the little book, Bang introduces the mother's sexually liberated and cynical friend, Lady Lyton, who has taken a young lover and asks: " 'Is love anything but knowing desire and feeling ashamed that one does?' " Bang had once again begun one of those attachments that inevitably led to despair. The beloved was Fritz Boesen, a naval cadet with theatrical ambitions, whom Bang showered with gifts and money, and whose interest in women made Bang miserable. The sequel, *Det graa Hus* (1901, The Gray House), takes the unhappy parents, Fritz and Stella from *Det Hvide Hus*, to Copenhagen, to visit the husband's father, an aged physician, a close portrait of Oluf Lundt Bang. Quoting Danish literature of the Golden Age (to which Bang was deeply devoted), Stella gives her husband his freedom; the grandfather, too, has spent a life of erotic deprivation, unloved by his wife, whose affection he has had to buy. As in *Haabløse Slægter*, the family declines, the old man remains strong in the presence of death, the father Fritz is good-looking, weak, and ineffectual, and the grandson (i.e., Bang) is in constant financial difficulties. The glance exchanged between the grandson and the old excellency's handsome servant is telltale, as is the grandfather's remark to a hunchbacked patient, whom he long ago aided in her pregnancy: " 'There come after-pains, miss, following the pleasures.' " After these hidden biographies and autobiographies, Bang turned to the tragicomic tour de force of *Sommerglæder* (1902,

Summer Joys), a virtuoso performance in which, over less than a hundred pages, Bang introduces some ninety sharply delineated characters crowded into a Danish country hotel which, like John Cleese's Fawlty Towers a century later, cannot meet the demands placed on it. Bang knew small hotels well; he did much of his writing in them.

The decadent thematology, put on display in *Haabløse Slægter,* makes few patent appearances in the books from *Ved Vejen* to *Sommerglæder,* save in *Det graa Hus,* although much about Bang himself can be read between their lines. During this middle period, Bang's protagonists are surely not the exceptional and egomaniacal figures of the decadence, nor are they overtly afflicted with some unspecified nervous illness; they are for the most part pathetic and often appealing human beings. A possible exception is the excellence of *Det graa Hus,* supremely contemptuous of the human race. But his contempt is mixed with a condescending sympathy. And all these novels take place in a small Danish world; there are no dead cities here, and Copenhagen is simply a town that has lost its coziness as it turns into a metropolis.

Bang's belief that he had become a novelist of international stature may have led him to undertake the last works in his fictional production: *Mikael* (1904) and *De uden Fædreland* (1906). *Mikael* takes place in a glittering Parisian society; Bang was under the spell of de Maupassant's last novels, *Fort comme la mort* (1889) and *Notre Coeur* (1890). The painter Claude Zoret, in late middle age, has imported the Czech youth Eugene Mikael from Prague, made him his principal model, and set him up in an apartment no less splendid than Zoret's own. Zoret corresponds to Bang himself, Mikael to Boesen; but Bang has taken some pains with his disguises: Zoret is a peasant's son, and his affection for Mikael springs ostensibly from his desire to have a son of his own. The novel gives a painful account of the loans to Mikael and even the theft of Zoret's works by the model, who is involved in a passionate love affair, describing in surprising heterosexual detail, with an impoverished Russian princess. Informed by Zoret's Jewish friend, the art dealer Charles Schmidt (Bang was strongly philo-Semitic), that Zoret is on his deathbed, Mikael does not budge from his mistress's side.

After *De uden Fædreland,* Bang left his homeland again, having been attacked by the new white hope of Danish letters, Johannes V. Jensen, in an article called "Society and the Moral Criminal." Mocking Bang's support for a strong military establishment in Denmark, a radical turnaround from his former pacifism, Jensen reminded his readers that Bang was at present involved with a lieutenant. Lighting in Berlin, Bang finished his last fictional work, the collection *Sælsomme Fortællinger* (1907, Strange Tales), about ghosts and lethal psychic influences and death. He was treated by the psychiatrist Wasbutzski, and in the Russian journalist Ossip Melnik found a friend who could help him with literary contacts. Too late for the Balkan setting of the first part of *De uden Fædreland,* he was dispatched once again to Vienna, Budapest, and Bucharest as a foreign correspondent in 1908. Back in Denmark, he continued his other careers as a stage director and reader of his works, first in Danish and then in German, and he published his essays on great actors and actresses he had known, *Menschen und Masken/Masker og Mennesker* (1909/1910).

In the fall of 1911, he set out on a lecture tour to Norway, Sweden, and Finland; Professor Werner Söderhjelm reported to Brandes that Bang was "worn out, sick, impractical, lamentable." He extended the trip to Russia, where two editions of his collected works had already appeared in translation; he read in German in St. Petersburg to large audiences, but in Moscow he appeared before almost empty houses. Retreating, he went west to Berlin for a visit with his psychiatrist, and then, aided in practical matters by Melnik, continued to Cuxhaven, from where he set sail for New York. Despite his ignorance of English, he planned a lecture trip around the world.

His cabin number on the *Moltke* was eight, which he regarded as an evil omen: for him, it meant handcuffs. He made his last public appearance before a Danish audience in New York, then took the train to Chicago, was met by the Danish consul, and got on to the Central Pacific's Overland Express for San Francisco. The consul asked a young German-speaking American named Lowenstein to keep an eye on him. On the second evening of the trip, Lowenstein accompanied Bang, disoriented and weak, to the dining car. The next day the writer was found unconscious in his compartment. At Ogden, Utah, he was taken to a Mormon hospital, where he died the following morning. The sensationalism of his life followed him into death; in Denmark, rumors of foul play by the porter were spread, but the Pullman Company concluded that they were unfounded. As late as 1950, in the posthumous memoirs of an actor friend, Christian Houmark, the claim was made that Bang's neck had shown signs of throttling.

With *De uden Fædreland,* Bang ventured into a more varied world than that of *Mikael.* The book's opening section is set on the central Danube near the Iron Gate. A good many novels of the time had imaginary Balkan locales, e.g., Anthony Hope Hopkins's *Prisoner of Zenda* (1894), the Transylvanian episodes in *Dracula* (1897), the "Kingdom of Liparia" in Couperus's royal novels (1893, 1894), and "the kingdom of Dalmatia" in Heinrich Mann's *Die Göttinnen* (1903–1904). Bang chose an identifiable location and on it superimposed what Jean Améry, in *Bücher aus der Jugend unseres Jahrhunderts* (1981), has called a myth. The place was already well known to readers of

Hans Christian Andersen from *En Digters Bazar* (1842, *A Poet's Bazaar*). Sailing up the Danube from Constantinople to Budapest and Vienna, Andersen and his companions passed the island of New Orsova (Ada Kale), then still in Turkish hands: "Red-painted houses, white minarets, and green gardens . . . the largest building was the [local] Sultan's harem." The little island's fortress fired a salute as they continued to Old Orsova, where they went into quarantine for ten days. Bang gave Ada Kale a much darker tone. In a story published in one of Peter Nansen's Christmas albums, called in Danish "Uden Fædreland" (Without a Fatherland), which is principally about a "Scandinavian" Christmas spent in the home of the German ambassador to Bucharest, whose wife is Danish, Bang has her say that " 'It seems as though we have no fatherland.' " (The story was based on a hasty trip Bang had made to Vienna, Budapest, and Bucharest in the autumn of 1904.) For a German selection of his stories, *Aus der Mappe* (1908), Bang provided this sentimental tale, here called "Der rumänische Weihnachtsbaum" (The Rumanian Christmas Tree), with an introduction, in which he implied that he had first seen the island of Ada Kale sometime in the past (probably in 1886, while he was serving as an underinformed Balkan correspondent for *Politiken*) and had recently seen it again: "Then the island of stone suddenly lay there in the foaming river, gray and somber and bare and icy cold, without trees or bushes, stern and distant as an apparition and now as a threat. Its barrenness is like a curse. And its houses were gray and its church gray and its manor house gray . . . this house of stone, built from the gray stones of the gray island. If Hades were not here, there would be no Hades at all. It was the homeland of all misfortune . . . No, I would never forget the sight . . . And I saw the 'Island of the Damned' again, as I had named it, in my thoughts." He implies that a desire to see the island once more was the true cause of his trip of 1904: "Was . . . my journey to Bucharest not really a pretext?" The journey was a part of the genesis of *De uden Fædreland*, Bang continued, which had appeared as *Die Vaterlandslosen* a year after its Danish original. Perhaps with a thought to winning more German readers, Bang went on to describe the protagonist of his novel, Joán Ujházy. "On this island he was born, and here he lived. After the second sighting of the island, even tighter cords were drawn around me. Soon I could not escape them."

The island had passed from Turkey to Austro-Hungary in the Peace of San Stefano after the Russo-Turkish War of 1877–78. Thus Bang's fictional feint that the island is commanded by Joán's father, earlier an officer in Austro-Hungarian service, has a possible grounding in reality; according to the text, Hungarian gendarmes are present on the island. But Bang builds a whole imaginary edifice. The Ujházys have possessed the island for six hundred years (as ancient a family as Harald Malcorn's in "Die Letzten"), having wrested it from the Turks. An ancestor of little Joán, whose name he bears, hanged the last pasha, a tale the boy likes to hear. (In fact, the Ujházys were a distinguished Hungarian family, as military men and patriots; after the uprising of 1848–49, one of them, Ladislaus, emigrated to Iowa and Texas. Bang may also have taken the name from Ferenz Ujházy, a nineteenth-century Hungarian painter of some reputation.) The island — which Joán's Greek tutor, Mr. Christopulos, says cannot be found on any map — is radically heterogeneous: Hungarians (the gendarmes, the father's groom), Romanians (cooks), Serbians (cowherds, Hana the scullery maid, Carol the village elder), screaming Ruthenian washerwomen, blind Hans from Transylvania, who may be German. There is no common language on the island, and Joán has no firm control of any tongue. Apart from the crumbs of the several local languages he hears around him, he listens to the English of his governess, strangely named Miss Teker, and the Danish of his beloved mother (another of Bang's fragile, early-dead women) and the nurse Ane, who tries, like his mother, to speak Danish with him, but, realizing that he does not understand, showers him "with foreign fragments, mixing Serbian and Hungarian and Romanian and Ruthenian from the scolding language of the laundry cellar." His mother, before her death, sings to him in Danish; one may assume that, on the few occasions they talk, Joán's father addresses him in Hungarian. Joán's blood lines are similarly mixed: he has "a Romanian head" and "Hungarian hair." But the mother-in-law of the pig farmer Iwo (language unidentified) remarks flatteringly to Joán's father that " 'Joán has his father's face; foreign blood never comes out in that family,' " at which the father slightly winces, thinking of his Danish wife.

Joán's awareness of his outsider status becomes acute when, during one of his father's numerous absences, Mademoiselle, his French governess, takes him across the river to visit the wife of the (Austro-Hungarian) commandant; Mademoiselle can speak French with her, and also spend time at Marinka's "little room which had a door on it," a hangout for the garrison's officers. Marinka is the former maid of Joán's mother: the moralizing Hungarian Josef tells Joán that " 'all the tarts and all the sluts who've had to beat it from their own country land here.' " The commandant's wife gives Joán his sobriquet, "le petit Sans-Patrie," and her son translates the name for the other boys of Orsova; Joán incurs the boys' hatred through his attempt to protect David, the son of the peddler Simon, from mobbing. On this occasion, as on others, Joán is saved by the "white officer" (i.e., one in the white dress uniform of the imperial army) — Bang's secret bow to his friend Stellan Rye, a reserve officer and actor. The last of these assaults on the frightened but determined Joán is made when the boy takes the hunchback Peter to a tailor for a suit of clothes.

Peter has decided to leave the island: " 'One goes home . . . Home to one's country.' " On the excursion to Orsova for Peter's clothes, even the family of Simon and David jeers at Joán, who comes to believe that he — like the Jews, according to the Greek tutor — is under the curse of God.

Mr. Christopulos leaves the Ujházy service (he will be killed fighting the Turks); the white lieutenant leaves the Austro-Hungarian army " 'to flee from these animals who call themselves human beings.' " Joán is to be sent off to school in Paris. Just before his departure, while out riding, he witnesses still another scene of hatred: the Serbian Ignaz, pursued by a crowd of Romanians, is saved by Joán's father who, before the ride ends, tells his son that he, the father, will never leave his island again. Joán puts a question which has tormented him for a long time, all the more so because of the episodes in Orsova: " 'Why don't we have a country?' " and the father, bringing up the curse that rests on the family, replies: " 'The Ujházys have none.' " Bang has already become intoxicated with his self-constructed legend of the Ujházys as a family under a curse, just as he has — in the welter of characters so swiftly introduced in this first part — with his ability to populate and overpopulate his stage. He is careless, too, in a small detail left unexplained: at their parting, the white officer says that Joán, in his bravery and pride, reminds him of "the young majesty." Does the white officer mean Archduke Rudolf of Hapsburg, romanticized in popular opinion after his suicide at Mayerling? There are no clues. At the putative time of the novel's first part, circa 1880, the "young majesty" was still alive.

Two briefer sections follow, *textes de liaison* between Joán's childhood and the trip to Denmark which comprises the second half, or more, of the book. Joán is not unhappy in his Paris school; the Babel of tongues he hears in the Jardin de Luxembourg does not seem threatening. He has found friends: a Danish nobleman, Erik Holstein, with whom the violinist Joán plays Danish folksongs, the tune of which — but not the words — he learned from his mother and the servant Ane, and a patriotic Norwegian Harald Nissen: Erik and Harald engage in good-natured teasing about their respective countries. For Harald, a great day comes when he receives a "clean" Norwegian flag from home; the "union flag" of Norway, in effect the merchant flag with the Swedish crown in the corner, was a long-standing source of irritation for Norwegians. The union was dissolved in 1905, while Bang was at work on his novel. The episode in the school dormitory, when Erik and Joán hang the cleansed flag over Harald's bed, again must have taken place sometime in the 1880s; when the Dane and Joán are reunited in the book's finale, they have not seen each other for thirteen years.

Joán is accepted as a fellow by the Scandinavians but, as usual, feels a longing for a homeland he will never have. Otherwise, he is made to feel his rootlessness with a vengeance; he speaks Hungarian to a lady visiting another schoolboy, Josef Aponyi, and identifies himself as a Hungarian "from the southern part"; but Aponyi contradicts him, saying that he is not a Magyar but " 'an Ujházy from the Isle of the Damned.' " Joán punches him and is dismissed from the school. Before Joán goes, Aponyi has a chance to humiliate him again when, in a German conversation class, Joán is struck dumb, still angry at Aponyi, and is reproached by the teacher, a lieutenant in the Prussian reserves, for his inability to speak German, which the teacher assumes is his mother tongue. In what may be a sly linguistic trick on Bang's part, Joán — finally able to speak — says correctly: "Ich habe die Kenntnisse nicht" (I do not have the knowledge), and the lieutenant, miscorrecting him, uses the wrong grammatical form of the noun. Further to humiliate Joán, Aponyi is quick to point out that Joán has no mother tongue at all. The class laughs at him, as even his mother and Ane did when he tried, as a child, to speak Danish. Joán transfers to a music teacher and begins serious study of the violin.

Joán has made a further acquaintance at the boarding school, a mysterious Prince Chira from India, one of Bang's more fantastic creations. Chira has been sent to the West by "the Brotherhood," which recruits its members from every corner of Asia: " 'We are in our thousands and tens of thousands, and we are Asia's apprentices,' " intending some day to destroy the white man and his hegemony. Chira's other acquaintances are two Japanese, who "like all Japanese" wear spectacles: Chira tells Joán that " 'we [Orientals] put your polished glasses before our eyes so that you will not see the slant-eyes' glance, which rests on you.' " The dignified Chira and the Japanese are a nod to current events, for example, the foundation of the Indian National Congress in 1885, the Boxer Rebellion of 1900, and the Russo-Japanese War of 1904–1905, and to the shibboleth of the Yellow Peril. The thought of a general "Oriental" revenge on the West had been in the political air for some time, famously voiced in Kaiser Wilhelm's warning to the peoples of Europe ("Protect your most holy possessions"), and in literature — variously in Kipling's "Recessional" ("lesser breeds without the law"), in Couperus's *De stille kracht,* and, after *De uden Fædreland,* in such adventure novels as John Buchan's *Greenmantle* and Talbot Mundy's *King of the Khyber Rifles* (both 1916), as well as in Sax Rohmer's tales of *Dr. Fu Manchu* (1913). Long since, the notion had appeared in the person of the Japanese ambassador, Cavaliere Sakumi, again faintly comical but menacing, at the marchesa d' Ateleta's banquet in *Il piacere.* The eponymous young Dane of *Einar Elkjær,* by Johannes V. Jensen (1898), predicts that someday the Chinese will come, with "axe and hoe," to find the rusted ruins of Western civilization; the threat would come back, in

the streets of Bely's *Petersburg:* a motorcar, "belching kerosene" and containing "yellow Mongol mugs," races across Senate Square. As the prince, who has
been summoned to India, to be dispatched wherever Asia needs him, bids
farewell, Joán weeps, in his obsessive envy of those who have a country. Chira
asks: " 'Why do you weep, Joán? All this will one day be destroyed,' " the *fin
du monde* of the West to be massively predicted in Spengler's *Untergang des
Abendlandes* (1918–22, *The Decline of the West*). Bang, the journalist, liked
to insert contemporary happenings or currents, sometimes too many, into his
fiction; the finale of *De uden Fædreland* almost founders under the weight of
Danish politics.

The second connecting text offers a measure of amusement, one of those
dining scenes with multiple voices in which Bang excelled. Joán has become a
famous virtuoso and sits in the restaurant car of the Orient Express, on his
way to Bucharest. He is with his Australian accompanist, Henry Collyett, like
Harald Nissen a healthy member of a new nation, unburdened by history. As a
reader and actor, Bang knew the life of traveling artistes and their vanities
well; in "Charlot Dupont," written twenty years earlier, about a child prodigy
grown up, Bang had already given a classic formulation to the emptiness of the
virtuoso's life. Assembled in the dining car, the musicians are lionized by the
blue-blooded nonperformers, a Romanian princess and a Prussian ambassador, with his wife, on their way to Bucharest. Not a little proud of belonging,
as Count Ujházy, to a higher social class than his fellow performers, Joán
manages to conceal himself, save for his shoulders, in a group photograph of
the musical company taken by the princess; his companion, Collyett, takes
care to get his "handsome legs" photographed, since he has a side line as an
athlete. (Bang was especially aware of men's legs — see the groom Josef in the
present novel — as his narratives repeatedly reveal.) The European celebrities
in the car are the French operatic composer Bizot and his adding machine of a
wife (he is the composer of the "Legend of Saint Cecilia," and has grown
wealthy from the whorehouses he owns); the tenor Jean Roy, who has sung
Lohengrin but whose favorite role is Don José in *Carmen,* with his accompanist, Mme de Stein, whose dream is to be buried in Père Lachaise; the Dutch
pianist, Herr Haagemester, who likes to tell of his consorting with royalty and
his contempt for contemporary French music as "the proof of French decadence." (With him, he has a very young man, a North German cellist, "whose
mouth was exactly the size of a cherry.") What elements there are here of a
scène à clef cannot be made out: Bizot's name leads one astray, to the long-
dead Georges Bizet, his money-grubbing wife to gossip about the Massenet
ménage; Jean Roy's skills as a comedian and cartoonist suggest Caruso, but his
interest in the economic possibilities of America and his name suggest Jean

de Reszke and the baritone Anton van Roouy — both singers cultivated profitable transatlantic careers. (Haagemester shares a name with the German-born but Swedish-trained violinist Julius Hagemeister.) The athletic Australian Collyett may have been suggested by Percy Grainger, an exuberant sportsman, who began his international pianistic career early enough to catch Bang's attention. But Bang's knowledge of the musical world and of music was superficial; one of the several weaknesses of *De uden Fædreland* is the shadowy nature of Joán's career and skill. All save Joán and Collyett (who practices ten hours a day) have an overwhelming interest in money; the braggart Germanophile Haagemester sketches "ornaments on his napkin," which turn into numbers and offers of engagement. Joán says little, save to express his aristocrat's indifference to finances and to hint at his fear, very Bangian, of going mad: asked by Mme de Stein when he would prefer to die, he answers that he would like to pass away while still in possession of his senses, thereby making her observe that he speaks as though he were " 'the ghost in a comedy.' " Jean Roy, the jolliest of the musicians, is afraid of madness too: he tells how a Mr. Thomson lost his mind during a performance on a London stage. Leaving the car, the Prussian ambassador's wife expresses her sympathy for both Roy and Joán: " 'I feel sorry for Count Ujházy. In the long run, you'd have to go quite crazy in that company.' "

One figure in the dining car has been silent, Jens Lund, a rival virtuoso to Joán with an empty face and hands like an oarsman's. He has been identified as Johannes V. Jensen (1873–1950), whose historical novel, *Kongens Fald* (1900–1902, *The Fall of the King*), about the reign, defeat, and long imprisonment of the Danish Renaissance monarch Christian II, is directed in part against what Jensen regarded as the indecision and decadence of his own time in Denmark. *Kongens Fald* had put him at the center of the literary stage, and his "American" novels, *Madame d'Ora* (1904) and *Hjulet* (1905, The Wheel), expressed his admiration for the brutal and energetic republic in the West, as did his Whitman-influenced poem "At Memphis Station." Bang knew and feared him: he told Boesen about Jensen's "monstrously large red hands, which he keeps clenched all the time, so that they resemble clubs on sticks," and his white teeth, looking "as if they had a good bite." In his account of the genesis of *De uden Fædreland*, continued in the introduction to another story, "Geschlagen" ("Beaten"), in *Aus der Mappe,* Bang transposes Jensen once again into a musician, a conqueror, "standing erect," and the Bang-Ujházy figure kneels beside him. Confusingly enough, the victor is a Croatian, Joán de Lonja; the conquered rival is called Josef Caiz — which, with a nasal added, is the name of the Austrian actor Josef Kainz (1858–1910), much admired by Bang, who issued a small memorial for him when he died, then incorporated into *Masker og Mennesker*. Bang has woven a few details from the real Josef Kainz into the Joán Ujházy of his novel: Kainz was born, as Bang says, "on the border of gypsy land" (in fact, Moson in Hungary near the Danube) and had "a gypsy face"; in the novel's final part, one of Joán's detractors calls him a "salon gypsy." Also, in the Kainz essay, Bang has the actor say that " 'the gifted personality is homeless in society and on earth.' "

Joán has been aware for some time that Lund is the greater artist; a fit of weeping came on him, he remembers, after he heard Lund play in Brussels. At the station in Vienna, Joán's demotion is rubbed in by the impresario Lecock, who beats the drum for Lund to the press while not giving Joán "so much as half a glance." Visiting Joán in his compartment, not shaking hands, Lund talks endlessly about himself: he has no use for books ("I have myself"), and, altogether unlike Joán, the self-sufficient Lund denies the importance of belonging to any nation: " 'I *have* a country, and that, sir, is called myself.' " His parents were Danish, but he was begotten at Arkhangelsk and born on the equator: " 'The man without a country is a free man.' " And: " 'Country . . . is a tenfold chain forged around our necks and feet by our forefathers . . . a prison and a pit.' " He realizes that Joán will not be able to see his, Jens's, new world, where " 'there are no more laws, crime is not crime, and shame is not shame.' " Suddenly and astonishingly, Jens Lund becomes a spokesman for a world of which Bang could only dream in his brushes with the law. Did the real Jensen, so contemptuous of Bang as a homosexual, fully understand how Bang had used him as a mouthpiece here? However, Lund's most telling thrust at Joán is that the latter is out-of-date, " 'from the last century,' " a " 'Prince of Pain.' " Lund's parting shot is that Joán " 'remembers too well and too much' ": a description that fits, as well, the majority of the other decadent protagonists around 1900, who constantly look backward. By means of Lund's words, Bang has delivered a critique of the mind-set of decadence, from which Ujházy — and Bang — cannot be released.

The novel has opened as Joán sits on a local train, in Denmark, and what follows, on the Isle of the Damned, in Paris, on the Orient Express, is actually a long flashback. At the beginning of the second part, Joán descends from the train somewhere in the south of Jutland. He is on a farewell tour, to find his roots, and his accompanist is now the Sudeten-German Hans Haacke (who thinks constantly of his fiancée in Brüx in Bohemia). This first and only trip Joán makes to Denmark is a sentimental journey, a tribute to his mother's memory; he arrives at his goal, a little border town, on his mother's birthday. The nameless town itself has been identified as Vamdrup, and scholarship has gone further, discovering the originals of some of Bang's characters: a merchant named Jørgensen was the source of the all-powerful Johansen, and his daughter Kaja became the fragile Gerda, a sister to Katinka Bai and Ida Brandt. Bang gave a reading at Vamdrup in March 1904, not long before the trip to Bucharest, and the back-to-back trips apparently spurred him to write *De uden Fædreland.*

Joán has chosen the town for the first stop on his tour because it lies not far from Vejle, his mother's birthplace. Also, it may be a patriotic demonstration on the part of Joán, the would-be Dane, and of Bang, who had entered his new patriotic stage. After the Dano-Prussian War of 1864 and the annexation of the duchies of Lauenburg, Holstein, and Slesvig by Prussia in the Peace of Vienna, the Danish-Prussian border was moved far to the north, leaving a large portion of Danish-speaking South Jutland in German hands, until a plebiscite of 1920 returned most of it to Denmark. (Bang's birthplace on the island of Als had also become Prussian.) Vamdrup was an important border crossing-point on the railroad between Denmark and the German Empire; the audience at Joán's concert is augmented by South Jutlanders who, living on the far side, dare to make the trip north for the evening: their names are noted by the German officials as they pass. A detail in the preparations for the concert is that the electrician in charge of the lighting at Joán's concert is a German from Itzehoe, in Holstein. One of the many undercurrents in the conversation during Joán's long evening in the town is that the German occupation, and German technology, have brought modern prosperity.

The town to which Joán and his entourage, the homesick accompanist and a supercilious valet from Berlin, have come is not an attractive place: barely nineteen years old, its main public building is the already tumbledown Hotel Denmark, where Joán is put up and gives his concert. The gable of the inn slants, and the plaster has already fallen off some of the letters in the hotel's name, in the Danish colors, white and red. A hole is in the hotel's facade instead of a planned portecochere, the hinges on its posts hang empty. Joán's room is damp, and some of its windows are stuffed with paper; the hotel itself, erected in a hurry, is settling, as Jensen, the hotel's waiter, explains. Opposite, the house of the merchant Johansen is much more substantial and better cared-for: Johansen controls the town's and the region's economy. Joán's first informant, the seedy waiter (who has ambitions as an actor and tries on Joán's dress clothes in the latter's absence), claims that the community is the center of " 'a progressive district.' "

Although Joán is aware of the marks of premature decay, he is caught up in a mood of nostalgia and then of tenderness for Gerda with her "little head" — a final member of Bang's long string of femmes fragiles. At the Johansens, he looks at Gerda's picture album, a tiny equivalent to other, full-size picture galleries of the novels of decadence, in which the strength of the past gives way to present weakness: the vigorous great-grandmother who outlived her daughter and her granddaughter, Gerda's early-dead mother, together with Gerda's late sister, in her student's cap. An intimation of Gerda's own frailness comes as her confidante, the local pastor's wife, tells how Gerda backs out of amateur theatricals at the last minute; on an excursion, she has become confused at a railroad station. For Joán, she is reminiscent of his own mother: a copy of Corot's *Le Créspuscule,* his mother's favorite, hangs on the parlor wall; Vejle, his mother's birthplace, is Gerda's favorite spot; the softness of Gerda's Danish, which Joán heard from his mother and Ane, the Danish songs whose melodies he knows but not the words all bring his mother back. Like his mother, Gerda is devoted to her birthplace, in this case the simple cottage in which she was born and of which she also has a photograph, eagerly displayed. The two walk to the station in the long Danish twilight for Joán to send a telegram, on his mother's birthday, to old Ane "in Serbia"; they climb the town's little hill (and Gerda gets out of breath), and fall wordlessly in love. Joán decides to change his program and to play the Mendelssohn concerto, performed the year before — to Gerda's delight — by a local violinist, and praised by her. Joán means to outdo him.

Back at the hotel, Joán reflects on the musty smell of the Johansen house; it comes from old wine casks in the cellar (he will learn that Johansen, who controls the sale of alcohol, like everything else in the community, has the nickname "The Poisoner"), and remembers the eau de cologne with which Gerda has sprayed the parlor. Nonetheless, he is happy because he is at last in Denmark; this happiness is directly noticed by Erik Holstein, his old schoolmate, who, by Bangian coincidence, lives on the nearby estate of Højerup. Erik's appearance has coarsened, Joán notes, while Joán's has not — Joán is not without vanity.

The preconcert dinner at the Johansens' gives Bang the chance for the last of the great set pieces in his oeuvre, the gathering in which a number of voices speak, quickly characterizing their owners. At a dinner in Copenhagen, before setting out for the provinces, Joán was disappointed by the superficiality of the other guests; now he will see "real people," of whose flaws, or worse, Joán, as far as his faulty Danish allows, only slowly becomes aware: Lorentzen, the owner of the burgeoning cloth factory, with one hundred and fifty employees; Dr. Raabel, the physician, the arbiter of culture, who gives discreet care to the factory girls Lorentzen has impregnated; Mrs. Raabel, amateur pianist and painter, carrying on an affair with young Ussing, an assistant teacher at the People's High School (adult education); the school principal, the long-winded spokesman for an empty Danish nationalism; the fat and comical twins the Larsens, gossips; the strange hunchback called Mephisto, who, ridiculed for his idealistic political efforts in Copenhagen, has withdrawn to the border station; two black-clad South Jutlanders, with wives who, it turns out, prosper under German rule and buy up property in the north; Johansen's manager Petersen, to whom, it seems, Gerda has been promised in marriage after he serves Johansen for a biblical seven years. The brightest spot in the company is the pastor's wife, Fru Jespersen, Gerda's special friend, who notices the growing affection between Gerda and the visitor, as does her husband, the pastor, come later after sitting at the deathbed of a music-loving old lady who has sent flowers to the virtuoso before dying — Bang can never resist the sentimental touch. Joán concludes that " 'life and death are good friends here.' " Belatedly, Erik shows up too, and stuffs himself with his thickened hands.

The concert itself goes by swiftly. Joán plays the Mendelssohn as he has never played it before (and asks the phantom of Jens Lund if the rival could have done better); Haacke's portion of the program is mostly Chopin, brilliantly but badly performed, according to Erik, a genuinely accomplished pianist; and Joán makes a surprise addition to his program. Noticing how the South Jutland farmers are bored by the classics, he persuades Erik to join him in a medley of the folk songs and patriotic songs they played together in their youth — they receive tremendous applause, albeit Fru Raabel observes that the songs were served with " 'Hungarian sauce.' " Bang uses a device he found extremely effective in his earlier work: *Ved Vejen* employs song inlays — a song about Sorrento, which Katinka Bai will never see, one about "Poor Marianna," and the hymn at Katinka's funeral; *Tine* has soldiers' songs from 1864. Opening the song floodgates wide for its portrait of Bang's mother, *Det hvide Hus* begins with "Long, Long Ago," goes on to folk and Christmas songs, and then, not leaving well enough alone, ends with made-up songs (of the mother's composition?), one of them to "an Irish melody." In *Ludivgsbakke,* one bond of Ida Brandt to her childhood home is Christian Winther's "Fly, Bird, Fly," and at a nurses' party, song quotations follow one after another. The effect is lost on English or German readers: some thirty song texts are included in *De uden Fædreland,* often quoted at stanzaic length.

Of these, the most important for the novel's development is the ballad "Aage and Else," which was turned into a classic of the Danish Golden Age by Bang's admired Adam Oehlenschläger in the tragedy *Axel og Valborg* (1810); it is sung by the heroine as she kneels by Axel's corpse. The ballad resembles the Scottish air "Sweet William's Ghost"; Sir Aage woos and wins the "fair maiden" Else, dies — in the first stanza — and then, taking his coffin on his back, returns to tell Else that, when she is happy, his coffin is filled with rose petals, and when she is sad, with blood. The cock crows, Aage departs, and Else looks up at the stars. A month to the day afterward, Else herself dies. " 'It's a sad song,'" Gerda has said in the Johansens' parlor as Joán recalls the melody but not the words he never understood as a child. He is especially curious about the term "væn" (fair, lovely), and asks Gerda about it, as part of his shy wooing. It becomes a topic of conversation at dinner, with philological explications by the principal. After the concert, Joán tells Gerda that his middle name is Aage.

Joán and Erik return to the Johansen house for a party; in high spirits, Joán, presumably thinking of Gerda, remarks to Erik, "'We'll go home.'" In the street, Fru Jespersen, doing all she can to encourage the romance between Joán and the girl, observes that the brightest heavenly body is Venus. An idea has taken shape in Joán's mind — he will return to the Island of the Damned and transform it into a sanctuary where, as he repeatedly says, all the refugees will be happy. Having seen the brightness of Venus, he reveals his plan to Gerda, gazing into her face. (During the dinner, questioned by Fru Jespersen about his home, he has told her of a Serbian legend concerning an enchanted island of the damned where no woman lives: salvation will come to its inhabitants only when a woman appears who can love a man who is blind and deaf and dumb.) Joán hopes that he will be able to carry Gerda off to his island; but he is overcome by an uneasy feeling at the Johansens': Fru Jespersen tells Joán the story of the suicide of Gerda's sister, and how Gerda has comforted her father, softening the "'hard side of his nature'" a little.

Here and there throughout *De uden Fædreland,* a habit or tic of Joán's has been mentioned: as a child on his way to Old Orsova, he kept his eyes half closed, as a means of self-protection shutting out the sight of the hateful rabble; he had also been taken to Budapest for an eye operation, an event about which we learn no more. (Bang may have thought of Anna Karenina half closing her eyes; in Thomas Mann's story "Ein Glück" [1904] the ensign, shy and out of place at a military ball, has "eyelids which were much too long, so that he could never really open his eyes.") Reminiscing about school days, Erik tells Gerda that Joán always kept to himself, his eyes shut. During the party at the Johansens, Gerda fetches her *rafraîcheur,* and sprays Joán's hands at his request; then, at Fru Jespersen's suggestion, she sprays his face as well, and his eyes sting. Fru Jespersen adds that "'after a little they'll be so clear,'" in which she is seconded by Erik, who tells Gerda to make Joán open his eyes: "'All the Ujházys have half-closed eyes.'" The intentions of Fru Jespersen and Erik are in fact at odds: Fru Jespersen wants Joán to perceive his growing love for Gerda, Erik wants him to open his eyes to the impossibility of such a love, a subject to which Erik will return later on. At the concert, in his moment of imagined triumph over Jens Lund, Joán is seized by a desire to see clearly — but does not.

Joán does not realize that his plan to take Gerda to his island would bring about a repetition of his mother's isolation. Erik rightly perceives it as a hopeless dream; thinking of his own failed marriage to a German countess from Lauenburg, constantly absent, Erik remarks that " 'love is not an article for export . . . [it is] unsuitable to pass frontiers.' " His suggestion that Joán should have his eyes opened belongs to his admonitory project for Joán, as is the fact that when he, Erik, plays the song of Aage and Else again, the narrator adds — or Erik mouths? — the final line of the song's first stanza again: " 'A month to the day thereafter/He lay in the black earth.' " Gerda is by no means unaware of Joán's affection for her; to Erik she wonders: " 'But if he should stay here now?' " After all, she has been a chief listener to Joán's many expressions of affection for the place which, he thinks, among "such people," has received him so well. Erik makes one of his several thrusts at the country to which he is bound: " 'Do you really think that it's so nice to stay here — for those who are *born* to stay here?' " but then seems briefly to aid Gerda's cause — keeping Joán in Denmark — by telling Joán that Gerda believes he ought to stay. Joán sticks by his plan: " 'But my place is not here.' "

The exchange takes place just before Joán receives a clear sign that his plan for himself and Gerda cannot succeed. More wine is needed, and Erik is sent off by Johansen to fetch it from the cellar. (Insultingly, Johansen, who has the alcoholized Erik in his financial power, tells him that he, Erik, knows where it is.) Erik takes Joán with him and — to get back at the merchant, who is also aware of the threads spun between his daughter and the violinist — suggests that Gerda come along, " 'to light us,' " in which Erik is seconded by Joán. Gerda admits that she never goes into the cellar: " 'Great-grandmother would never allow it' " and has always been frightened of it; she takes a couple of steps down " 'into the underworld' " but cannot continue, an underworld she, a female Orpheus, is afraid to enter to save her male Eurydice. Erik and Joán must descend alone into the heavy air; Erik thinks that the fumes have permeated the house, as they have, and taken away Gerda's willpower: " 'She ought to get out of this house straightaway.' " (Like Joán after he heard Jens Lund in Brussels, Erik breaks down in tears: his willpower is gone.) Upstairs again, Joán — realizing that he is losing the game — tells Gerda that she is always frightened, and that she should get away. Almost as an excuse for her failure to enter the cellar, she tells Joán the cause of her sister's death — she drowned herself, aware that she had " 'taken on herself something she could not carry through,' " university studies and independence from her tyrannical father. The same is said of the philosopher Mephisto, who took up an impossible (and undescribed) political program.

The penultimate section of Book 2 leads Joán and the non-Danish reader into unfamiliar territory, a discussion about a change of course in Danish military policy: from now on, Denmark will be armed, since otherwise its neutrality will not be respected. Uncomprehending, Joán asks Gerda what the others are talking about. He becomes more and more isolated from the company, even as the remarks of the Danes grow more and more hateful or xeno-phobic — particularly those of the envious Raabels and the chauvinistic principal, who " 'spreads more poison through his rhetoric,' " Erik says, " 'than the Poisoner himself.' " The kindly Jespersens persist in encouraging Joán to rescue Gerda, the husband by means of an allusion to Hamlet's hesitation and Ophelia's fate, the wife by remarking that Gerda, who appears to be the victim of a protective narcolepsy (or simply of exhaustion from playing hostess for her father), resembles Sleeping Beauty, to which Joán adds: " 'Behind her thicket of briars.' " In an outburst of defensive talkativeness against the barbs of the Danes, and in a last, lengthy effort to capture Gerda, who has never been abroad, Joán delivers a speech about his life in Paris, about the authors he has known, particularly de Maupassant, about a ring given him by "the last of the dukes of Monthieu, killed in duel." (Bang refers, without further explanation, to a character and an episode in *Mikaël*.) Desperate, seeing Gerda's face, which seems to be fading away before his eyes, Joán falls back into his macaronic tendencies, "mixing the languages without finding the words," the linguistic experience of childhood which made even those who loved him laugh, and he realizes that he is the object of laughter again. Cruelly, Dr. Raabel says: " 'Speak German, Count, it will go better.' " Yet Joán plows on, describing the sanctuary he intends to create on the Isle of the Damned, and how they — he and Gerda — will build a hospital for its outcasts, and " 'the many whom life [has] wounded.' " All in vain: Erik tells him he has been " 'talking too much' " and " 'ought to know the lay of the land before setting out.' " Ussing says: " 'These Hungarians always have plenty of embroidery on their frock coats,' " i.e., are show-offs. Haacke plays a mazurka, of which Fru Jespersen says, " 'The ghosts are dancing!' " Joán, who was called "a ghost in the comedy" in the dining car, walks "straight as a ghost" through the crowd, defeated. He asks Gerda, " 'You too?' " when Mephisto says: " 'We shall long remember you.' "

Outside, Erik condemns the guests and the land itself, " 'a damned theatrical country,' " where " 'baseness sits in the prompter's box.' " Back at the Hotel Denmark, where the staircase shakes, Joán tells Erik that he will cancel his concert tour but will never build his "hospital" on the island, and, on a final walk to the hill where he has been that afternoon with Gerda, he says, "in a voice as pale as his face," that he will die alone: " 'The island has no women,' " and, " 'If I loved, how should I be able to speak? After all, I have no mother tongue.' " " 'We must stay on the island, and die on the island, all of us whose name is Ujházy,' " and Joán is the last of the line. (The real Ada Kale ceased to exist in the 1980s when a dam and hydroelectric station raised the level of the

Danube and submerged the island.) He will not play again, since he has heard "a Greater One," Jens Lund, who has " 'leaped over hedge of thorns,' " playing a " 'new jubilation,' " no Prince of Pain but a man of the future. Erik is also the last of *his* line: his estate is in control of the merchant, or of the merchant's manager, Petersen; Erik's class is done for: " 'We people from the estates only hang on to our main buildings by grace of the peasant merchant.' " After Erik leaves, Joán meets Haacke, who informs him that he has found friends here (the admiring Fru Raabel); fancying himself a great artist, he will depart in the morning for the bigger world of Germany, to which he belongs linguistically. Joán goes to bed; candles placed around him, he lies in cruciform posture — a repeat of the cruciform pose of Ida Brandt in the final scene of *Ludvigsbakke*.

The finale of *De uden Fædreland* is overloaded with allusions, undercurrents, backgrounds: the endless political talk; the emphasis Bang places on the petty-mindedness and maliciousness of the Danes; the shattering of Bang's vanity at the success of Johannes V. Jensen (the prominence of "Aage and Else," may well be a response to Jensen's extensive employment of the same ballad in the third part, "The Great Summer," of *Kongens Fald*); the carefully tended central myth of the Isle of the Damned and of the curse that rests on the Ujházys (we are, as it were, back at *Haabløse Slægter* and the end of the Høgs' line); the fragmented and aborted love story with Gerda; the passing allusions to Orpheus and Eurydice, to Hamlet and Ophelia, to Sleeping Beauty and her prince. Everywhere, the outsiderness status of Joán — a more painful case than that of his contemporary of mixed blood, Thomas Mann's Tonio Kröger — is on almost monotonous display: without a country, without a language, without love. Certainly, too, the novel's jeremiad — and the construction of the Island of the Damned — can be read as Bang's suffering from his homosexuality. A secret signal may be sent, in the novel's last pages, to Bang's beloved Stellan Rye, the model of the white officer in Orsova. The South Jutlanders, setting out for the border, sing the song of Olaf Rye, the general who fell at the defense of Fredericia in the Danish Slesvig War of 1848–50. Fru Jespersen has interpreted it for Joán: "On honor's field Olaf Rye sleeps," and it is the last sound Joán hears as he falls asleep, the palms of his hands turned upward in surrender. (Stellan Rye had followed the Rye military tradition, but he resigned from the army in 1907, upon his imprisonment for homosexuality. After going to Germany in 1912, he became an important director in the pioneer German film industry, and his best-known work is the classic *Der Student von Prag*, with its Dorian Gray theme. Having volunteered for the German army, he was wounded at Ypres and died in French captivity during the first autumn of the war.)

Jens Lund's most telling thrust at Joán is that he is a leftover, as a Prince of Pain from the previous century, and a hopeless spokesman, in his vain search for a lacking homeland, for one of the century's most precious tenets, nationalism. This was the age of Scott's "Breathes there the man, with soul so dead" in *The Lay of the Last Minstrel,* Edward Everett Hale's "Man Without a Country," William S. Gilbert and Sir Arthur Sullivan's "He is an Englishman" from *H.M.S. Pinafore,* and nationalism moved from these innocent expressions to infinitely more savage forms. Bang himself had an "Oriental" or Jewish appearance, of which he was at once proud and ashamed; Chira told Joán that he was "a yellow" among whites. As for Joán's often-mentioned lack of a language, the necessity of having a "language of the heart," as Kierkegaard said, likewise seems less important today than it did in the nineteenth century, when it was a pressing matter—to be sure often urged on by local circumstances. (Glorification of the Czech language was a cardinal factor in the Czech national movement; conversely, the language philosopher *in spe,* Fritz Mauthner, rejoiced when, as a young man, he traveled from Prague to Germany and heard authentic German dialects for the first time. Another German speaker from Prague, the young Rilke, complained of the "gnawed" edges of the German language there.) From another area of latent linguistic tension, the Finland-Swedish author Jac Ahrenberg (1847–1914) published a story "Utan modersmål" ("Without a Mother Tongue") in *Österut* (1890, Eastwards), which gave the question of lack of language a burlesque turn. On a steamer in the Bay of Viipuri, in polyglot Karelia (Finnish, Swedish, Baltic German, Russian), the narrator meets a former schoolmate, a product of mixed nationalities (Finnish, German, Polish, Russian, Swedish) who was the butt of jokes because of his macaronic way of speaking and writing. As an adult he is somehow shapeless: slovenly, fat, and lazy. To pass the time, the unfortunate—Fredrik Nikolaivitsch von Drawershausen Kaporion—recounts the story of a fateful event in his life: he tried to tell a young woman, a Swedish speaker, that he loved her, but he made a glaring grammatical error that ruined his case. Like Joán, he says he has no mother tongue. Later, he married a Russian woman. His children are even uglier mongrels than he, and like him in possession of only the coarse scraps of four languages. Elsewhere, in his novels, Ahrenberg shows traces of the racial thinking of Artur de Gobineau, the author of the *Essai sur l'inégalité des races humaines* (1853–55). As a young man in Stockholm, Ahrenberg had been the art teacher and informant on Finnish affairs to the diplomat Gobineau. Ahrenberg's story is admonitory and Gobinesque, whereas Bang's novel about the Prince of Pain is ultimately tolerant.

A comparison of *De uden Fædreland* with Maurice Barrès's *Les Déracinés* (1897) could be made: spiritual salvation for the survivors among Barrès's uprooted Lothringians comes when they discover a new rootedness in their native earth. Barrès is regarded as a forerunner of Fascism.

21

Australia

HENRY HANDEL RICHARDSON

Ethel Florence Lindesay Richardson, born in Melbourne on January 3, 1870, was a piano student at the Leipzig Conservatory from January 1889 until April 1892, when she left without having completed the prescribed four-year course. A biographer remarks that, still a schoolgirl at Melbourne's Presbyterian Ladies' College, she may have been encouraged in her musical ambitions by the example of Helen Mitchell, an earlier product of the college, who had been renamed Nellie Melba for her sensational debut as Gilda at Brussels in 1887. Ethel Richardson had become engaged to the widely read Scot, John George Robertson, a student of *Germanistik* at Leipzig, and discovered that she did not have the necessary devotion to the piano to become a concert artist. Encouraged by Robertson, she began a translation of J. P. Jacobsen's *Niels Lyhne* from the German version, but aided by the Danish original; Jacobsen was at the height of his posthumous European fame. It was published in William Heinemann's International Series in 1896, together with her translation of Bjørnstjerne Bjørnson's *Fiskerjenten* (*The Fisher Lass*), under the title *Siren Voices*. In the meantime, she married Robertson, and set up household with him first in Munich, where her sister Lilian, or Lil, was studying violin, and then in Strasbourg, where Robertson had obtained a post as lector in English. In Munich she studied composition with Ludwig Thuille (1861–1907), remembered today as the dedicatee of Richard Strauss's *Don Juan*.

She began *Maurice Guest* in the autumn of 1896, worked on it intermittently during the Strasbourg years, and completed it in London in 1907. Meanwhile, Robertson had been appointed as the first professor of German literature at London University in 1903. The manuscript was submitted to Heinemann in July 1907 and was published a year later. Her brother-in-law, Dr. Walter Neustätter, made a German translation, brought out by S. Fischer in 1912, after Robertson had spent some three years correcting it. Robertson's role in the composition of *Maurice Guest* should not be underestimated, and his remarks about it in "The art of Henry Handel Richardson" (the masculine nom de plume under which Ethel published all her books), written in 1928–29 but published only in 1948, fifteen years after his death and two after hers, are an extremely valuable commentary on her œuvre.

Henry Handel Richardson came to be regarded as a central figure of Australian literature because of her school novel *The Getting of Wisdom* (1910) and *Australia Felix* (1917), *The Way Home* (1925), *Ultima Thule*, collectively as *The Fortunes of Richard Mahony* (1930), based on the life and correspondence of her parents during the Victoria gold rush days and "marvelous Melbourne's" meteoric growth. Her father, the physician Walter Lindesay Richardson, born in Dublin, died in 1879 at fifty-three, evidently in the last stages of general paresis, the result of syphilis contracted three decades before; the awful death of Richard Mahony forms the conclusion of the trilogy, although the cause of Mahony's decline is never named. (The nature of Dr. Richardson's disease was probably unknown to his daughter.) Having left Australia at eighteen, Richardson returned only once, for a short stay in 1912. A last novel, *The Young Cosima* (1939), based on the correspondence and memoirs of Cosima Wagner, her father (Liszt), her first husband (Hans von Bülow), and Richard Wagner, did not get the critical attention accorded off and on to *Maurice Guest* and the Australian trilogy, for which she was nominated, in 1932, for the Nobel Prize for Literature. (John Galsworthy got it for the *Forsythe Saga* instead.)

The documentation around *Maurice Guest* is extensive and can be examined in the critical edition of Clive Probyn and Bruce Steele (1998), which includes passages excised from the manuscript as well as Richardson's marginalia. Probyn and Steele also edited and annotated the three-volume collected letters of Richardson and her correspondents (2000). (In the present chapter I gratefully take the work of Probyn and Steele into account but endeavor to make new observations as well.) The correspondence with her French translator, Paul Solanges (1846–1914) is especially revelatory in its responses to Solanges's searching queries. (Solanges's letters in French are quoted below in the English translation of the editors.) Before his sudden death, Solanges had not found a French publisher for his labor of love, and the translation was lost; he never knew that the secretive "Cher Monsieur et ami" in London was in fact a woman; at his request for a photograph, she sent him a postcard of Goethe, claiming "it has always been said that the portrait on it has a certain likeness to me."

When Carl Van Vechten wrote about *Maurice Guest* in 1917 (in *Interpretations*), he, like the shocked reviewers on its initial appearance who found it morally depraved, called it "a sordid story," but approved its "direction and a vivid attention to the matter in hand which is very arresting . . . the maelstrom of student sex life"; he singled out Louise Dufrayer, "one of those young women with a certain amount of money who find food for the gratification of their sexual desires in the atmosphere of a musical school," and the homosexual Heinz Krafft. Van Vechten, though, says nothing direct about other details whic make *Maurice Guest* fit readily into the patterns of the decadent novel.

Maurice Guest is a city novel, like *Il piacere, Il fuoco, Bruges-la-Morte,* Hjalmar Söderberg's Stockholm books, or the Dublin episodes of *A Drama in Muslin.* The players in *Maurice Guest* have street addresses attached to them, and their walking routes are often given. Madeleine Wade, the sensible English girl who discreetly loves Maurice Guest, lives on Mozartstraße, the third and longest-lasting of Richardson's addresses in Leipzig. (She is alone; Richardson was accompanied by her mother and Lil; they were joined by a cello student from Glasgow, Mathilda or Marthe Main, who confessed, years later, that she was devastated when Richardson became engaged.) Louise Dufrayer, from a station (ranch) in Queensland, lives on Brüderstraße, in a room with a special door through which her lovers, the violinist Schilsky and then the pianist Maurice Guest, can come and go. Schilsky stays nearby on Talstraße when he is in Leipzig; he is supported by a Frau Schaefele and by Louise. Maurice, who has gone to Leipzig thanks to the financial sacrifice of his father, a schoolteacher, puts up on Braustraße; Madeleine — seeking him out in an effort to rescue him from Louise — does not like to visit this ugly part of town. The wealthy American Mrs. Cayhill, the sedentary mother intoxicated on sentimental fiction, her elder daughter Johanna, an intellectual destined to be an old maid, and the babyish Ephie reside in a plush pension on Lessingstraße. The conservatory's most talented piano student, Fürst, shares a crowded apartment with his widowed mother and siblings on Brandvorwerkstraße, a lower-middle-class location at some distance from the conservatory and the Gewandhaus. Schwarz, the piano teacher of Madeleine, Maurice, and Louise, lives, appropriately, on Sebastian-Bach-Straße, close by the conservatory. These street names all appear in italics, as if for emphasis.

The parks on the western side of the city contribute to the sense of topography, the expanse of the Rosenwald, the Scheibenholz, the Nonne, reached by Schleußingerweg. In winter, Maurice, an excellent skater, has some of the happiest times of his first Leipzig year with comrades from the conservatory; gliding along the Pleiße, the skaters end up at Wagner's Waldcafé in Connewitz to the south. Almost everyone in this peripatetic novel is a good walker, save Mrs. Cayhill and Louise, who tires easily. Also, as an Australian, she cannot skate.

In 1898, *Roman aus der Décadence* by Kurt Martens appeared, in which Thomas Mann's quondam friend devoted a section to Leipzig's summer heat and "poisonous odors," as experienced by the junior barrister Just. Erotically, Just is caught in a relationship with Alice Fiedler, teasing but chaste; he finds relief with a juvenile prostitute, whom he dresses *à la grecque*. After Alice's marriage to a lieutenant, who is often away drilling his troops, she gladly gives herself to Just, sings naughty French songs for him, accompanied on the parlor piano which he has rented at her command for their love nest, and pretends to throttle him with her hair. Aware of the injustices of the German legal system, Just also makes acquaintances in socialist circles, the reformer Esther Bernheim and her saintly brother, and the Russian Dimitri Teniawsky; the last-named was ordered, in his anarchist days, to blow up the Gewandhaus during a concert but was relieved when the bomb was not delivered. Adding to the decadent picture: Just converts to Catholicism, a process mockingly described, and attends a Black Mass in Prague. As a sedulous observer, he also witnesses "das Fest" held by his friend Erich Lüttwitz at the latter's Leipzig villa. The spectacular orgy begins with a performance by full orchestra of Berlioz's *Symphonie fantastique,* followed by a play, Oskar Panizza's notorious *Das Liebeskonzil,* about papal erotic escapades. Like Dorian Gray, Lüttwitz has unlimited financial resources; he reads Swinburne, Mallarmé, and "Loris" (the young Hofmannsthal) in precious editions and decorates his villa in accordance with the "accumulation prose of Huysmans's Des Esseintes." At the novel's conclusion, Just devotes himself to the serious study of cultural history and responds with a noncommittal smile to Teniawsky's efforts to recruit him for an international political movement. After the orgy, Lüttwitz is too cowardly to carry out his promised suicide and is last espied by Teniawsky in Berlin with "an older, bedizened lady."

No indication can be found in Richardson's papers and notes that she read Martens's sensational picture of decadence in Leipzig of the fin de siècle; the book appeared six years after she left Leipzig, but her husband closely followed contemporary German literature, and Leipzig friends may well have told her about the scandal it caused. (A copy in the Sterling Library at Yale shows that it was eagerly read by members of the German Book Club, includ-

ing the president's wife, Mrs. Arthur Twining Hadley!) News of a second
Leipzig literary scandal must also have come Richardson's way. The premiere
of Frank Wedekind's *Erdgeist,* whose main character is the man-killer Lulu,
was given at Leipzig's Literary Club in February 1898, a happening described
by Martens in his *Schonungslose Lebenschronik* (1921); in its first printing the
play was titled *Lulu.* In *Maurice Guest,* Louise Dufrayer is called Lulu by both
Schilsky and Krafft, although for Maurice she is always Louise.

Like Martens, the narrator of *Maurice Guest* describes the oppressive heat
and the "nauseous and penetrating odors" rising from the drains and the
streams in this "city of the plains." (Visiting Leipzig in December 1883, Richard Strauss told his parents that it was "filthy and rather uninteresting.") Richardson's descriptive phrase is geographically correct. As Baedeker's *Northern
Germany* (1886) says, Leipzig lies on an extensive plain, but Richardson's
phrase inevitably calls to mind the "cities of the plain" in Genesis, Sodom and
Gomorrah. Richardson knew what she was doing; toward the end of August,
Heinz Krafft begins his persistent efforts to seduce Maurice, tugging at his lapel
and telling one of his obscene jokes.

Writing about literary influences on *Maurice Guest,* Robertson did not
agree with critics who thought its seasonal structure was borrowed from the
Russians, Tolstoy in particular; for him, it was an integral part of the novel's
construction: "Spring, summer, autumn, winter . . . are intensely connected
and interwoven with the action." Maurice comes to Leipzig in spring, meets
Madeleine, Krafft, and Louise, and spends the hot summer there. In the autumn Schilsky performs his tone poem *Also sprach Zarathustra* and, after a
raucous farewell party, leaves town; Louise falls ill and is nursed by first
Madeleine, then Maurice; when winter comes, Maurice bows out of a Christmas party to take Louise on a ride over the ice to the Connewitz Waldcafé; she
tells him, " 'You are my friend.' " In what must be February, Maurice is persuaded to accompany Louise to a ball and is desperately unhappy at her
sensuous dancing to the strains of "Wiener Blut" and her pleasure in the
company of a British medical student, Herries. In the springtime, Louise goes
away to Dresden, and on her return she shocks Maurice with the readiness
with which she has considered a proposal of marriage from a wealthy American. On a warm evening, Maurice and Louise make love for the first time, to
the smell of lilacs; in July and August they spend some weeks in the village of
Rochlitz; in Indian summer they make another excursion to Grimma and walk
to the ruined cloister of Nimbschen. Their relationship rapidly declines as the
autumn progresses; by November, after a second ball, which Maurice does not
attend, she appears to have taken the "cad" Herries as a lover; Maurice spends
his time in her room to hinder her in this and other adventures, about which

anonymous letters have informed him. On a "radiant April day" he tells her that Schilsky has returned, and she orders the "poor crazy fool" to drown himself. Drunk, he spends the night with a prostitute, Luise, then goes to a park and shoots himself. It has been just two years since he came to Leipzig, full of hopes for his musical career.

The routines of the conservatory and the music played in its official "evening entertainments" and its test recitals are not very meaningful for the furtherance of the plot. (Probyn and Steele detect irony in the lines the chorus sings in the finale of Beethoven's Ninth at the closing Gewandhaus concert, before Maurice's final humiliation and suicide: "Wer ein holdes Weib errungen,/ Mische seinen Jubel ein.") But the opera performances at the Neues Theater send a number of signals. Richardson became an ardent but not uncritical Wagnerian during her Leipzig days, guided by Robertson, who knew his Wagner well. The Wagnerian allusions occur mostly in the first of the novel's three books, and some are heavily ironic. Fürst's father, an oboist, has caught a chill and died after a performance of *Die Meistersinger,* Wagner's longest work. Trying to get rid of Louise, who wants sex when Schilsky is composing, he explains to her the properties of the Wagner tubas, invented by the master for the *Ring;* in his treatise on musical instruments, Cecil Forsyth termed Wagner's notation for them "an unholy muddle." Having just heard his first orchestral concert (Beethoven's triumphant Fifth and "the great phrase in C Major" of the last movement), Maurice is confronted by a placard on a pillar announcing a performance of *Siegfried.* Inspired to study piano in Leipzig by the tales of an old music teacher, he has come, an innocent Siegfried, from the English provinces; the members of the Anglo-American colony notice his youth and naivety immediately: Madeleine Wade thinks him "a very young man" who tosses his head with "the impetuous movements of a young horse," and the careerist Edward Dove summons him by whistling Siegfried's horn call beneath his window. From the same window, Maurice hears the "mournful notes of a French horn, which some unskillful player had gone out to practice."

Dove leads Maurice to the conservatory; Maurice tries out for the teacher Schwarz, who informs him that he has " 'talent, great talent . . . and [is] not wanting in intelligence.' " A girl enters and asks to perform; she lets her eyes run "absently" over Maurice, and "they seek their eyes in each other's." For Louise — who here plays the piano for the only time in the book — the contact means nothing, but Maurice's life is changed. The author of a weighty study of Richardson's fiction, Dorothy M. Green (1973, 1986), suggests that the glance is equivalent to the famous "Blick," the glance whose motif is played in the Prelude to the first act of *Tristan und Isolde* and mentioned by Isolde in her narration to Brangaene about the wounded Tantris. Green comments that

"Maurice is a Tristan without Isolde"; further, Maurice, according to Green, will suffer a conflict between his musical duty, outlined by Schwarz, and his passion for Louise, even as Tristan suffers conflict between his duty to King Marke and his overwhelming love for Isolde.

Maurice's first opera, *Die Walküre,* to which he is taken by Madeleine and Dove, makes little impression on him, on the lookout for Louise in the audience; Madeleine, who can be maddeningly superior, chides him for his inattention: " 'this is the only act you're going to make anything of.' " He is not the only bored listener; the Cayhill sisters are present, at the insistence of Ephie, who hopes to see Schilsky; she complains to Maurice at the first pause: " 'I think it's stupid. And they're all so fat.' " Louise and Schilsky also attend, but Schilsky too is bored: "He yawned . . . [and] showed all his defective teeth." At the next intermission, Schilsky and Louise squabble. Schilsky looks sulky, Louise "suddenly older and very tired." An hour later, "after a tedious colloquy between Brünnhilde and Wotan," the "more human strains of the *Feuerzauber*" come as a relief for Maurice. (One must imagine that Maurice, like the Cayhill sisters, has almost stopped listening; Wotan's farewell expresses the god's quite genuine humanity.) On the walk home — Louise, now alone, has joined Madeleine and Maurice — he gets his first glimpse of Louise's apartment and sees "three large photographs of Schilsky, one more dandified than the rest." As for poor Ephie Cayhill, she has spotted Schilsky and "the woman in white" after all. In a flashback in the next chapter, she remembers her wretchedness as the performance wore on: " 'How long would the fat, ugly Brünnhilde stand talking to Siegmund and the woman [Sieglinde] who lay so ungracefully between his knees?' "

Preparatory to *Walküre,* Dove and Madeleine try to initiate Maurice into the "leading motifs" of the opera; Dove, a fluent talker ("by no means a fool," is Madeleine's tart estimate), goes on to mention "the idée fixe of Berlioz." According to the program of the *Symphonie fantastique,* for the young musician "la femme aimée, elle-même, est devenue . . . une mélodie et comme une idée fixe qu'il retrouve et qu'il entend partout." In the last movement, the Witches' Sabbath, the melody turns into "un air de danse ignoble, trivial et grotesque." As in a fate tragedy, Louise knocks at the door. Maurice, who has watched her from afar for two months, is finally introduced to her; she starts to shake hands with him but withdraws, claiming that first handshakes on Friday are bad luck " 'to you, if not to me.' "

Before Maurice's affair with Louise has been consummated, although he is now her "constant companion," he takes her to *Carmen,* her favorite opera; sitting in his dark corner, he murmurs, " 'I love you, Louise — I love you.' " [Is he prompted by Don José's desperately repeated "Carmen, je t'adore"?) She is so absorbed in Carmen's "gaudy fate" that she would not have heard him "if he had called the words aloud." Longing for the absent Schilsky, Louise decides to accept Maurice as her lover ("after all, it meant so little"), and goes to the opera house again, this time to hear, by chance, the "showy music" of *Aïda*'s last two acts. The reader does not become privy to what the opera may tell her; is the tomb scene an ironic prolepsis of Louise's semicaptivity with Maurice in her room? Like Louise and Carmen, Aïda is a dark southerner.

Schilsky, "the genial [i.e., highly gifted] Pole," is a violin virtuoso, player of a number of instruments, and the composer of *Also sprach Zarathustra,* performed at the Fürsts' apartment. The new term at the conservatory is just beginning, and Louise is in England — inexplicably — but, according to Madeleine, "all her cry is to be back in Leipzig." Madeleine and Maurice attend, with Schilsky's admirers, largely women. Richardson may have met Richard Strauss in passing (for example, in Munich in 1903), and she surely saw him conduct in Leipzig; his *Also sprach Zarathustra* had its debut at Frankfurt in November 1896. To Solanges she wrote, in 1912, that she had heard a "superb performance" of *Der Rosenkavalier* in Dresden; "I hold [Strauss] for out and away the greatest genius alive at the present time." Schilsky's *Zarathustra* is somewhat shorter that the original, six parts based on Nietzsche's text to Strauss's eight, and the parts are not identical. (Richardson would take epigraphs for several chapters of *The Getting of Wisdom* from the same source.) Schilsky's climax is "Das trunkene Lied," sung by Krafft. "Schilsky himself was barely able to cope with the difficulties of the score." Once more, Maurice does not listen, but surreptitiously watches Schilsky; "the composer was a slippery, loose-jointed, caddish fellow, who could never be proved to be worthy of Louise." Richardson brings her knowledge of music to bear in her reconstruction of "Das trunkene Lied"; however, she was unaware, evidently, of the setting Mahler included in his Third Symphony, which likewise had its premiere in 1896 — her extant letters contain no mention of Mahler. A passage omitted from the printed *Maurice Guest* makes it clear why Schilsky abruptly deserts Louise during the *Walküre* performance. He stays until the middle of the second act, "when Wotan was confiding in Brünnhilde." Louise feels a "shiver" run through him; he has solved a problem in the composition of the *Taranteln* section of his *Zarathustra* and must hurry home to note it down. "When Brünnhilde groped at Wotan's feet," he leaves, "despite . . . [Louise's] look of passionate anger."

Schilsky, tall and gangly, supremely gifted, is a quasiportrait of Strauss. But Schilsky's erotic power is beyond anything known of Strauss, although his putative affair with the older (and married) Dora Wihan and his stormy marriage with the capricious Pauline de Ahna provided the stuff of gossip. The

Strauss-Schilsky trail is covered over by the "fact" that Schilsky is the son of a Warsaw blacksmith, discovered by a teacher from the Leipzig conservatory, whereas Strauss was the dutiful son of Franz Strauss, Richard Wagner's favorite hornist and most obstreperous opponent. As Richardson told her Australian friend Mary Kernot in 1929, Schilsky's red hair and behavior were drawn from the violinist Felix Berber, at Leipzig during Richardson's time there, who was reported to have had an affair with the wife of the professor of composition Gustav Schreck (thus "Frau Schaefele") and with an "English girl." The name Schilsky was borrowed from a composer, a neighbor in Munich. But Schilsky's appearance came mainly from Strauss, "of whom at this time I thought the world."

Robertson wrote that *Maurice Guest* was a "web of literary influences," "a kind of mosaic of influences . . . while *Richard Mahony* is almost startlingly free of them"; he predicted that *Maurice Guest* would be a "hunting ground for the industrious searcher." He directed attention to the "conspicuous debt" owed to Flaubert's objectivity, and to a resemblance between the novel's opening — Maurice before the Gewandhaus — and the opening of Turgenev's *Smoke,* before the Kurhaus in Baden-Baden, and he added that without "books such as *Crime and Punishment* and *The Brothers Karamazov*," Richardson's novel would not have been written: she whetted her psychological acuity on them. Just the same, reproduction of the impressions of the outer world on her characters "was Danish rather than Russian": Robertson had his eye on Jacobsen's *Niels Lyhne.* He also saw in its "passionate note" something of D'Annunzio's *Il fuoco.* Richardson's entries in her diary and elsewhere are frank about her enthusiasms and sources. She had read Turgenev's *Smoke* in German translation, and a connection may exist between the trio Maurice, Louise, and Madeleine, and Turgenev's Litvinov, Irina, and Tatiana — Litvinov's passion for Irina almost wrecks his life before he is saved by Tatiana. As for Jacobsen, her admiration fills her notes, as it does her essay on the "Danish Poet" of 1896, "unapproached in modern Scandinavian literature." Niels suffers from a weakness like Maurice's for constructing ideal images of the several women who cross his path — his aunt Edele, the worldly Tema Boye, Fennimore, the wife of his friend Refstrup, the childlike Gerda — and in all these instances save the last (and even Gerda, dying, rejects the atheist Niels for a consolatory Christianity), the women send him away with brutal words, the leitmotif, "Go, Niels, go!" A plain verbal borrowing from *Niels Lyhne* lies in Niels's "Vinland in the wide world of books" and "the Wineland of our dreams" used to describe Maurice's reaction on first seeing Louise; the yellow and red roses in the preamble to Jacobsen's story "Der burde have været Roser" come back in the yellow and red roses which play a role in the affair between Maurice and Louise. Richardson's love for *Niels Lyhne* did not abate: for her story "Death" (1911), later retitled "Mary Christina" (1931), she originally took the last words in *Niels Lyhne,* "den vanskelige Død," "difficult death," as an epigraph. Richardson had also praised *Fru Marie Grubbe* in her Jacobsen essay and singled out Marie's "desire to drink life in large draughts . . . her keen and ill repressed vitality"; but this "Interior from the Seventeenth Century" apparently did not interest the author of *Maurice Guest:* she was aware of the yawning difference between Marie's vitality and the lazy sensuality of Louise.

Richardson had another model for her Louise (as Robertson was aware), the great Italian actress Eleanora Duse, at the turn of the century as much the object of cultlike adoration as Jacobsen. (Rilke was devoted to them both.) The Robertsons traveled by bicycle and train from Strasbourg to Frankfurt to see the Duse in *Hedda Gabler* and *La Dame aux camélias* in 1900, and they saw her again in London in 1905. Richardson took the trouble to make her way through the Italian text of Luigi Rasi's *La Duse* (1901) and kept a picture of Duse in her London study; after Maurice has met Louise, he goes to Zeitzerstraße, near his room, to gaze at a "large photograph" of her in a shop window, "a source of great pleasure for him." It has been argued that the dedication of *Maurice Guest,* "To Louise," is in fact to the actress; in Richardson's hand-annotated printed copy of her novel, she wrote "In Memoriam May 1894," the time when she had first seen the Duse at Daly's Theatre in London, beside the passage describing Maurice's initial sighting of Louise: "And then her eyes! So profound was their darkness that when they threw off their covering of heavy lid, it seemed to his excited fancy as if they must scorch what they rested on; they looked out from the depths of their setting like those of a wild beast crouched within a cavern." A little later, Maurice has a vision of Louise's "Medusa-face, opaquely white, with deep unfathomable eyes"; beside it, Richardson wrote, in the margin of her copy, "The D."

A. P. Riemer has commented in some detail on the features of Eleonora Duse taken by Richardson for Louise from D'Annunzio's *Il fuoco:* " 'the eyelids like violets,' " the lethargy, the fear of aging, the jealousy of a younger woman, and her outbursts of uncontrollable laughter and weeping, after Maurice has brought Ephie to her for her inspection. On the excursion to Murano in *Il fuoco,* having questioned Stelio Effrena about Donatella Arvale, her young rival, La Foscarina bursts into a "frenzied convulsion of laughter that sounded like a peal of heartrending sobs." But striking discrepancies exist between Foscarina-Duse, magnificently talented (" 'I have been Juliette!' "), and Louise Dufrayer. The piano in Louise's room remains untouched; except for *Carmen,* she has no musical interests, and when Schilsky performs his *Zarathustra,* she is absent in England. On the empty days when Maurice has to practice, he tries to find ways of distraction for her: "He took her his favorite books, but — with the exception of an occasional novel — Louise was no reader. In those he brought her, she seldom advanced further than the first few pages; and she could sit for hours without turning a leaf." He never sees her sew — by Maurice's middle-class lights, something she might well do — and at home, she is a slattern.

Another literary source existed for Louise's magical eyes; while still in Australia, giving "so-called music lessons," she found Longfellow's *Hyperion* in the room where she taught; when Longfellow's Flemming sees Mary Ashburton, he thinks: "And O, those eyes — those deep, unalterable eyes . . . with falling-down eyelids." Not all Richardson's sources were so high-toned. The sexual badinage of Rodolfo, Marcello, Colline, and Schaunard with their landlord Benoit in the first act of *La Bohème* (1896, German premiere 1897) bears a resemblance to Fuerst's and Krafft's teasing of Schilsky about Louise's demands. Krafft quotes Luther's instruction in the *Tischgespräche,* "In der Woche zwier" (Twice a week), but Richardson in fact found it in Paolo Mantegazza's manual, *Hygiène de l'amour,* as Probyn and Steele have discovered. In this magpie's nest of borrowings and resemblances, the editors mention in passing George Moore's *Evelyn Innes* (1900), about the making of a Wagnerian singer, which Richardson read shortly after its publication. But Knut Hamsun's *Pan,* published in German in 1895 and very popular, is conspicuously missing from their commentary, as it is in Richardson's *paralipomena;* had Robertson, much interested in Nordic literature, and his wife not read it? In it Lieutenant Thomas Glahn becomes fixated on the mysterious Edvarda Mack, is tempted and tormented by her, and causes himself to be shot by a fellow hunter in India.

Maurice Guest is unusual among the novels of decadence because of its large cast of subsidiary characters. Fascinating as they are, Wade, Krafft, Dufrayer, Guest, do not suck out all the novel's air, as do Des Esseintes, Dorian, Borg, Hugues Viane, Bradomín, Przybyszewski's narrative voices, and Machen's Lucian. A determinedly realistic novel, *Maurice Guest* is a picture of a little society, like *A Drama in Muslin* and *The Real Charlotte;* all its members are attached, in one way or another, to the conservatory: the Americans, the soprano Philadelphia Jensen, studying the role of Sieglinde, as good-hearted as she is large, Miss Martin, gossipy but again kindly, speaking her American lingo (to which M. D. Herter Norton would object). Edward Dove, the ambitious seeker after a career in England and a bride in Leipzig, is a contrastive figure to Maurice. The musically incompetent and credulous Ephie Cayhill, believing Schilsky's yarn of a wedding in New York, is almost destroyed by the jealous contempt of Louise, who sees a rival in her: Maurice Guest, breaking his gentlemanly code, has led her to Louise at the latter's command. When Maurice, having neglected the piano for Louise, visits Schwarz on Sebastian-Bach-Straße, he overhears a terrible row between Schwarz and his wife, who accuses him, the father of four children, of hugging a pupil; Madeleine Wade, all-observant, has let slip to Maurice that Schwarz has a weakness for pretty girls and is indulgent toward Louise. The interview between Maurice and Schwarz, in a parlor cluttered with furniture and decorated with a faded laurel wreath bearing the inscription "To the great artist, Johannes Schwarz," takes place while Schwarz devours a large plate of *Pfannkuchen,* and laments the twenty and more years he has spent as a teacher. His clientele is slipping away to a modish competitor, the Lisztian Schrievers.

Madeleine Wade has a sharp eye and sees through not only Dove and Schwarz, but Louise. She nurses Louise after the latter's breakdown and is driven away because she confronts Louise with the Australian's passion for Schilsky, and the pleasure she takes in being looked at by strange men, " 'in a way no decent woman allows.' " Louise rejoins that Madeleine is " 'trying to make someone here like [her], without any thoughts of pride or self-respect' " (the pot calling the suspected kettle black). Among the taunts Louise hurls at Maurice near the novel's end is that Madeleine, " 'that ineffable creature, [is] no better than she ought to be,' " and, " 'You were never man enough to see what it was she wanted.' " A thrifty and no longer very young woman (she is twenty-seven, and being paid court by an elderly, corpulent German, Lohse), Madeleine proposes to Maurice that they start a music school in " 'America, or Australia, or Canada,' " for which she would supply the capital. Bumping into Madeleine after he has become Louise's lover (Madeleine has spent the summer at Baden-Baden as the companion of "an invalid lady" with a distinguished name, Frau von Kleist), Maurice reminds her, out of the blue, of the conservatory they were going to found in America. His unspoken plan is to marry Louise, and he needs money. Madeleine believes he is laughing at her, but then is recaptivated by his boyishness, and is "on the point of uttering that personal word they had not yet exchanged." The whole passage is omitted, perhaps because Richardson thought it made the possibility of a reciprocal love between Maurice and Madeleine too strong. As Maurice's decay progresses, Madeleine tries to talk to him in his shabby room on Braustraße, but he is distracted by one of the anonymous letters he receives about Louise; suddenly, he realizes that Madeleine has returned to her old plan in new form, a brother-and-sister trip to Italy. He does not rise to the bait (she is "all that is good and kind" but is "talking nonsense"), and she has no more to say to him, save that she will " 'come over for the funeral.' " Once upon a time, Maurice repaid Madeleine for her kindnesses by calling her "a brick." In reading Schiller's *Jungfrau von Orleans* together, they came upon the lines spoken by Dunois to his friend La Haie: "Wir waren Herzensbrüder, Waffenfreunde./Für eine Sache hoben wir den Arm." Maurice is inattentive; he wants to be introduced to Louise.

With her acid tongue and intelligence, Madeleine has a limited double in Johanna Cayhill, another reader of German literature. Maurice's tutelage by Madeleine has prepared him for his jousts with Johanna about Lessing, Goethe, and Heine ("a miserable Jew" in Johanna's opinion). To Maurice, Johanna is condescending, but she softens toward him because of his recently won knowledge; however, her chilly favor is withdrawn as Maurice is forced to confess to her that he has taken Ephie to Louise for display, and to tell the story of Ephie's involvement with Schilsky. (Not without some satisfaction: he has the chance to call Schilsky rotten.) The Cayhills leave for America; Johanna will, she says, go to Harvard. (Herter-Norton informed Richardson that Johanna would have had to attend Radcliffe instead, which *did* admit women.) Johanna forswears her overwhelming love for her sister and, looking at Maurice with her "short-sighted eyes," thinks "how little . . . one mortal knew and could know of another." After *Die Walküre,* Johanna has objected, inwardly, to the treatment in the "so-called opera" of "relations so infamous that, by common consent, they are considered non-existent." The spelling out of an incestuous, lesbian affection for Ephie would have been more than the reading public could bear. In the posthumously published *Myself When Young* Richardson admitted that she had "weakened" the central, autobiographical story of Laura's passion for Evelyn in her schoolgirl novel, *The Getting of Wisdom.*

Heinz Krafft, the "full-blooded Wagnerite," does not attend the *Walküre* performance, but he is present at its preamble, an afternoon in Madeleine's apartment on which Maurice waits in vain to be introduced to Louise. As is his custom, Krafft appears unexpectedly, with "a short, thickset girl, in a man's felt hat and a closely buttoned Ulster," Avery Hill; he has come to borrow a volume of De Quincey. Maurice reminds Krafft of a previous meeting at Seyffert's Café: there, without introduction, Krafft asked Maurice if he could recall the opening bars of the Prelude to *Tristan und Isolde* (the so-called Grief and Desire motifs in the cellos and oboes). At Madeleine's, Krafft plays the chords that precede Siegfried's awakening of Brünnhilde ("Wie wach ich die Maid/daß sie ihr Auge mir öffne"); Avery Hill pushes him aside at the piano, and continues the music "with a firm masculine touch" until she suddenly breaks off. The meaning of the fragmentary performance is two-fold. Krafft, having learned from Madeleine that Louise is coming, ironizes musically about Maurice's —

Siegfried's — awakening of Louise, whose erotic past he knows well; Avery, Krafft's devoted companion, hopes that he — small chance — will awaken *her.* Laughing as always, Krafft calls Madeleine a *Kupplerin,* a procuress. Leaving and coming back again, he wishes Maurice " 'success . . . from the bottom of my heart' "; Maurice is annoyed at this by-play, which he does not understand. Accompanying Krafft to his room, in the hot summer in the city of the plains, after Krafft has saved a half-blinded cat from children who are tormenting it, the innocent Maurice listens to more of Krafft's Wagnerian allusions. Avery Hill is annoyed at Krafft for adopting another pet but, ever protective (as Madeleine is toward Maurice), she goes to set matters right with the landlady; as she returns, Krafft sings: "O Lene! Lene! Magdalene!" from *Die Meistersinger,* the apprentice David's words to Magdalene, Eva's duenna (David sings "Sie ist so gut, so sanft für mich"). Maurice resents Krafft's abuse of Avery's patience, but Krafft rejoins, " 'It's all she wants' " and quotes the dictum from *Also sprach Zarathustra* about not forgetting the whip when going to women. After Krafft's playing and singing of *Tristan* for Maurice, and Maurice's rejection of Krafft's offer that he can "sleep on the sofa," Krafft tells Maurice that he never wants to see him again and demonstratively devotes all his attention to Avery: "He called her by a pet name, was anxious for her comfort, and hung affectionately on her arm." "Evchen" in the manuscript is omitted after "pet name" in the book; Avery has been briefly promoted to the heroine of *Die Meistersinger.*

The true passion of Krafft's life is Schilsky. Leaving the *Zarathustra* performance, Madeleine, warning Maurice against Krafft's friendship, asks Maurice if he does not realize that Krafft is the " 'attendant spirit of the heaven-born genius.' " Maurice also learns from Madeleine that Schilsky is going away; he meets Krafft and Avery and lets the cat out of the bag (the real cat, called Wotan because he is one-eyed, is present at the conversation). Krafft is shocked, Avery drops a plate (she is overjoyed at Schilsky's departure), and Krafft blurts out, " 'No one has loved him as I have.' " At Schilsky's farewell party, Krafft makes cutting remarks to the guest of honor about the money his Frau Schaefele has given him, and Schilsky calls him " 'you bitch.' " Maurice takes Krafft, drunk, to the latter's room and has to spend the night with him, caught in the uncomfortable embrace that ends Book 1.

For readers as slow to comprehend as Maurice, the evidence of Krafft's homosexuality is piled up. In his first Leipzig November (Book 2), Maurice visits Madeleine, as he often does, and Krafft, long absent from the conservatory, suddenly pops in. As Madeleine asks with "a certain asperity": " 'What news from St. Petersburg?' " Maurice and Krafft leave together, Krafft calls Maurice "Liebster" and wants to know why Maurice has changed. In oblique language, Maurice replies that he has heard "something from Fuerst." Maurice's tone is so harsh that "a beautiful flush [spreads] over Krafft's face." At Maurice's demand that Krafft pledge his word that the "something" is not true, Krafft wants to know what telling the truth means — " 'there is no such thing as absolute truth,' " surely not in Krafft's world.

In a deleted passage that explains Madeleine's remark about St. Petersburg, Maurice meets Krafft again at the opening of his second year at the conservatory, never to be completed. Krafft introduces him to his new friend, a "bullet-headed Russian," "a sallow-headed boy of unclear skin and hair, [who] adopted a greasy, familiar way of speaking which made Maurice long to kick him." The Russian and Krafft go inside Seyffert's Café, but Krafft — another of his sudden reappearances — returns, asking Maurice if he remembers a promise from "last summer," i.e., the summer before last, when Maurice and Krafft, at the latter's proposal, agreed to say "du" to each other, a time when Maurice, Krafft's hand in his, sensed a "hitherto unknown feeling of kindliness coming over him." Maurice interrupts this reminiscence of the promise, made as a "result of too much music and moonshine," by informing Krafft that they will be better friends when Krafft became " 'more considerate of that girl,' " Avery Hill. " 'Until then, keep your soft talk for your Alexis or Boris or whatever it is you call him.' " Krafft makes another promise: " 'Say the word, and I'll never see him again.' " Maurice pulls his arm away; Krafft insults him for his lack of talent (which he claims the Russian possesses in great measure) and leaves with a snide greeting to Louise, " 'Aspasia,' " the hetaera.

It is too bad that Richardson dropped this last set of clues about Maurice's ambivalent feelings toward Krafft, and her not so subtle depiction of Krafft's activities. At the *Hauskonzert*, Madeleine says of Krafft, with his pink cheeks and his curly hair, that he ought to have been a girl and, walking home, she warns Maurice that Krafft belongs to a " 'bad set here — and Schilsky too.' " A member of the bad set turns up at the farewell party for Schilsky, "a slender youth of fantastic appearance . . . [his] overcoat was molded to a shapely waist . . . his fingers wore numerous rings, his bushy hair scented and thickly combed, his face painted and penciled like a woman's"; he makes fun of Schilsky's complaints about taking care of three women at once (Frau Schaefele, Ephie, and Louise, or Lulu), and Schilsky calls him "a pap-sodden suckling." (As in the case of Schilsky's " 'bitch," Richardson strives hard to create double entendres.) Slyly, Solanges approached Richardson on the question of "our friend Krafft" and sex; Krafft makes him think of Oscar Wilde. Richardson agreed that Solanges was right: "This is a particular detail in my book to which I never draw attention: for those who can see, it is there, for the rest it is not . . . On the other hand, my picture of the *Tun und Treiben* in Leipzig would not have been complete without some indication of this failing, which was fairly common there."

The Krafft case is not exhausted by the proofs of his homosexuality. (Did Richardson put the extra *f* in his name as a bow to Krafft-Ebing?) A relationship between Krafft and Louise has existed since before either Schilsky's or Maurice's arrival in Leipzig. At the vie de Bohème scene in his room on Talstraße, Schilsky boastingly complains about the demands of Louise and gives Krafft and Fuerst her love letters to read; he calls Krafft a "Joseph" — one who has refused the demands of Potiphar's wife. Krafft tells Schilsky that *his* letters from Louise were burned when Schilsky came to town. In her account of Louise to Maurice, Madeleine mentions that Louise has always had " 'an admirer of some kind in tow. This [Schilsky] is her last particular friend.' " Following Krafft's joke that Madeleine has been a procuress for Maurice, and when both he and Maurice have left, Louise arrives. Learning that Krafft has been there, she flushes, asking with an effort at playfulness, " 'Does he still exist?' " Pondering Louise's attraction for men, Madeleine remembers "the afternoon on which Heinz had burst in to rave to her of his discovery," Louise; he was "infatuated, mad." As Maurice's decay progresses, Madeleine reminds Krafft that "three years behind," he visited her, crying that he had just met "the most beautiful woman in the world, and was drunk with her: " 'If I remember aright, your admiration was by no means the platonic, artistic . . . hm! . . . affair that it is now.' " In her book on Richardson (1985), Karen McLeod contends that Louise — enflamed by Krafft's admiration — had "written him love letters and had been unsatisfied." He has been a perverse Joseph, enjoying her "humiliation" by his refusal to take her. McLeod hypothesizes a meeting with Krafft in Louise's room after her falling in love with Schilsky, at which she begs Krafft to burn her letters to him and offers herself to him in return; Krafft rejects her again, pointing out that he, too, is in love with Schilsky. This hypothesized scene might serve to explain Krafft's remarks after Madeleine has asked him to interfere with Louise and "save" Maurice from her; he says to Louise that it is only her "extremely bad conscience" that makes her afraid of him, and he agrees that Louise's "great affair" with " 'the poor fool who was once my friend' " has gone far enough. What follows is a demonstration of Krafft's manipulative powers. Krafft goes to Louise, who believes that Krafft knows where Schilsky is, and asks her to let down her hair before he does it for her; she falls to her knees, her cheek on his knee, and he looks "with approval on the broad, slender shoulders, the lithe neck — all the sure grace of the crouching body." She continues to beg him for information about Schilsky, and he whispers "a few words" in her ear; what he says is unknown — probably a request for sexual intercourse, from which he will then turn away at the last moment — and Louise becomes enraged. He leaves: " 'A word at any time will bring me if you change your mind.' "

Another scene at Seyffert's Café ensues; Krafft gives Maurice "the quick and witty narration of an episode in which he and Louise had played the chief parts . . . the story, grossly told, of a woman's unsatisfied fancy." Maurice slaps him. Worse follows: Maurice asks Louise about the "gross words" of Krafft, and she asks him if he did not know " 'from the first there had been . . . something between Heinz and me.' " As she sits up in bed with her hair undone, he reflects that he has "never seemed to know before how brutally black it was"; she gives Maurice "a reason" which shocks him so badly that he breaks the bedpost, as she goes on to reveal her jealousy of Krafft because of Schilsky's affection.

Understandably, Solanges was puzzled by this conclusion of Book 3, chapter 9. "It seems to contain something hidden which I don't quite understand . . . have you not made the mystery a little too deep?" Richardson replied: "Do not ask me to explain Chapter IX. It does not, I admit, say enough — it was my intention that it should not. I willfully chose to leave unexplained Louise's relations to Krafft as not being of vital importance to the story." Solanges did not pursue a further mystery in the text: Maurice receives a letter with an Austrian stamp (thus from Krafft), which drives him to drink; he shows it to Louise, who cries, " 'The scoundrel,' " and when Maurice asks her forgiveness for believing its contents, she tells him that what it says (whatever it may be) is true. He knocks her down; "the knowledge that, under her dressing-gown, she had nothing on but a thin nightgown, gave him pleasure; he felt each of the blows fall full and hard on her firm flesh." What else has Krafft reported? Has he told Maurice about other contemporaneous affairs of Louise? Or about the charged scene in which he let down her hair?

On May 19, 1911, Richardson wrote to Solanges that a friend had congratulated her "on the way in which [she] had caught and expressed in [Krafft] the fluidity of artistic temperament . . . the only firm point in his character is his art — his devotion to it . . . He is limpid as a child and exaggeratedly affected by the happenings of the moment. Which is to say that he is blown about by every impulse." Part of the attraction of *Maurice Guest* is the way in which Richardson avoids pinning her characters down, Krafft chief among them. Does Krafft mean to "save" Maurice by telling him about Louise's promiscuity? Does he intend, enriching him " 'for the rest of his life,' " as he says to Madeleine, to make a superior being of Maurice, the greater artist for having endured the pain of losing Louise? Maurice must become " 'a gourmand, a connoisseur in beauty,' " although here Krafft entertains " 'doubts of our friend.' " Or does he intend to drive Maurice to suicide? After Maurice strikes him, Krafft gives him a scrap of paper — with his "customary indolence of movement" — bearing the address of a gunsmith's shop, Klostergasse 12. Like her husband, Richardson was an Ibsenite and wrote an attack (1897) on William Archer's translation of *John Gabriel Borkman.* Certainly, she remembered the dueling pistol Hedda Gabler gives Ejlert Løvborg so that, she hopes, he will die "in beauty."

Krafft himself has talked much about death to Maurice during their walk through the August night, after having played Chopin to his guest until the landlady Frau Schulze puts a stop to it at Avery Hill's jealous behest. He tells Maurice about "gay, melancholy Vienna," his home, and rattles off a catalogue not only of composers ("from Beethoven and Chopin to Berlioz and Wagner, to Liszt and Richard Strauss") but of authors and works, Nietzsche, Dehmel, Schnitzler in his *Anatol,* "the gentle 'Loris' " of the early verses, Holz and Schlaf with their *Papa Hamlet,* and so on; the artist Max Klinger is not forgotten. Abruptly, he asks the nonplussed Maurice if he ever thinks about death — his own life is a "perpetual struggle against suicide." In Krafft's penultimate conversation with Madeleine, "a battered volume of Reclam's Universal Library" falls out of his pocket, *Niels Lyhne* (in Mathilde von Borch's German translation), his "death book," in which " 'one can study death . . . in all its forms.' " As he flirts with Madeleine, knowing she will not respond, except with flattered indignation, he develops his theory of Maurice's possible ennoblement through suffering and defends "Lulu" on the grounds of her "genius for living." To Madeleine's interjections about " 'contamination' " and " 'the soul,' " he declares that " 'such a woman has no soul, and doesn't need one' "; men " 'leave her something — a turn of thought — it may be only an intuition — which she has not had before.' " Krafft paraphrases Otto Weininger's *Geschlecht und Charakter* (1903), in which Weininger, in presenting his denial of spiritual or intellectual qualities in W(oman), attributes all of these to M(an). To woman he allotted a kind of secondary thought process. Weininger's coinage is *henid,* a single, inferior element: "[Woman] thinks more or less in *henids;* [Man] thinks in clear, distinct ideas." Both Weininger and Krafft are Wagnerians, both Weininger and Krafft are Viennese, both are anti-Semitic — Weininger was born Jewish but converted to Protestantism — and both contemplate suicide. Weininger killed himself at twenty-three.

Krafft is twenty-seven at the time of the August walk with Maurice but "much younger than he looks." After his study of medicine he worked in his uncle's commercial house and as a journalist; he was a companion to Hans von Bülow on the conductor's tours. He is devoted to Schilsky as von Bülow was to Wagner; in *The Young Cosima,* Richardson would adumbrate a homosexual component in von Bülow's behavior. Although Krafft could have made a career as a performer of Chopin, he has a dream of withdrawing to a cloister near Vienna, where he has already stayed after a breakdown, reading Novalis "day to day." The record of Krafft's compositions is small; he makes settings of melancholy texts—Lenau's "Einsamkeit," which Madeleine and Maurice have trouble playing, and "Genügen," by Ferdinand von Saar, another Austrian and a suicide. ("The slow, melancholy ditty" can be identified only by the quotation of its key words, "ein wenig Sonne.") The Saar song is performed as a preamble to Schilsky's portentous *Zarathustra,* together with a setting of Krafft's own verses, quoted only in English, "I am weary of everything under the sun," in which Probyn and Steele see Nietzsche's "Der Herbst," a text Richardson set to music in her composing days.

The telling exception to Krafft's mournful production is "The Rose of Sharon," his signature text and tune. The song is heard by Maurice after his first student party, sung at a distance by Krafft in a "clear, sweet voice," with the refrain taken up in chorus: "Give me the Rose of Sharon,/And a bottle of Cyprian wine." It echoes through the "glorious tangle" of Maurice's dream that night, in which he sees the "Medusa-face of opaque white, with deep unfathomable eyes" that fascinated him at the tryout for Schwarz; its owner had worn a yellow rose at her belt. The repertoire of the students, male and female, skating in line toward Connewitz, begins with "The Rose of Sharon," "Jingle Bells," and "There is a Tavern in the Town" and continues with solo numbers, among which an aria from *Le Prophète* that Philadelphia Jensen sings, no doubt because of the once famous "skating ballet" in that opera's third act, "Allerseelen" of Richard Strauss, sung by Miss Martin; all join in the refrain "Wie einst im Mai" of Hermann von Gilm's poem. (Is the surprising intrusion of the Strauss *Lied* another of Richardson's prolepses? Maurice gains Louis's affection "once upon a time in May" and loses it in the autumn.) On leaving Madeleine's room after the conversation about men and women, and again after his final visit, Krafft—flirting as usual (" 'Remember I was sorry when you wouldn't have me' ") whistles his number.

Enigmatically, Richardson recalled she got "the two lines" of Krafft's song on the balcony of the Robertsons' Strasbourg apartment. Its source is chapter 2 of the Song of Solomon, the black but comely daughter of Jerusalem's description of herself: "I am the rose of Sharon, and the lily of the valleys." Christian tradition took it as a prefiguration of Jesus; three hymns from the seventies and eighties sprang from it, W. H. Doane's "I am the Rose of Sharon," John Horn's "The Rose of Sharon," and D. F. Blakey's, whose chorus ends: "He's the Rose of Sharon, O glory! O glory!" Krafft is not alone in his blasphemous usage inspired by Louise and her rose. At the first student party, Schilsky, the star, has not yet appeared, and Dove is interrupted as he says

" 'perhaps, by now, he is safe in the arms of——'." A cockney cellist calls out " 'Jesus or Morpheus?' " and a tipsy pianist sings Frances Jane Van Astyne and W. H. Doane's hymn for drowned seamen "Safe in the Arms of Jesus" but is silenced by Krafft's "O sink' hernieder,/Nacht der Liebe" from Tristan's second act. "Much laughter" bursts out—everyone except Maurice knows about Schilsky and Louise.

The opinions offered by Madeleine in quick succession after Krafft's final disappearance contradict one another; "she had never expected Heinz to behave like a normal mortal . . . there was something indecent about his behavior." She sizes him up as the master manipulator: "Only a person who thoroughly despised others would treat them in this way, playing with them up to the last minute, as one plays with dolls or fools." But she defends him after the suicide of Avery Hill, a few days later. Philadelphia Jensen claims that she has known many men, " 'but Mr. Krafft is the only one I've met who didn't appear to me to have a single good impulse.' " Madeleine's reply is not far removed from Richardson's to Solanges about Krafft. " 'He was never happier than when he had succeeded in giving a totally false impression of himself . . . He never showed a good impulse; but that is as much as saying that he swarmed with them.' " Mysteries attach to Krafft from every side. When he makes his first entrance at Seyffert's Café, "His face was one of those which, as by a mystery, preserve the innocent beauty of childhood, long after childhood is a thing of the past . . . Girlish too were the limpid eyes . . . the small, frail body existed only for the sake of the hands, narrow hands, with long fleshless fingers, nervous hands, that were never still." (Their fragility is noticed by Maurice as he presses them.) Krafft's prenatural youth and beauty easily summon up thoughts of Dorian Gray, as do his sudden absences; his dishevelment at Schilsky's farewell party resembles Bertie's after his London excursions in Couperus's *Noodlot*. The scraps of food he has with him, unexplained, are perhaps intended for strays; he will save the cat Wotan. In his comings and goings again, as in his capacity of an agent provocateur of the emotions (to Madeleine, to Maurice, to Louise), he suggests Loge in the *Das Rheingold*. "He disappeared from Madeleine's apartment, leaving his elfin laughter behind him like smoke." Solanges noticed the phrase and made wordplay out of it, calling Krafft *ce fumiste,* "this chimney sweep," this prankster. In Max Dauthendey's *Maja: Eine skandinavische Bohème-Komödie* (1911), the character patterned on Stanisław Przybyszewski is named Loge, and is elusive, manipulative, destructive.

Captivated by Krafft ("he is alive, I seem to have known him"), Solanges makes little comment on Schilsky, who must have seemed almost a stock figure to him. Indeed, Schilsky has a predecessor in recent German literature; in the

best-seller by Ernst von Wolzogen, *Der Kraft-Mayr* (1897), the Polish composer Antonin Przewalski, gifted but lecherous and dishonest, is set up against
wholesome Florian Mayer of Bayreuth. Richardson came back to the type in
the story "Succedaneum" (1930): the composer Jerome Moçs loses his talent
and regains it by seducing a simple girl, whom he then abandons. (*Moc* means
strength or power in Polish, i.e., *Kraft*.)

On the other hand, Solanges had a measured and unfriendly interest in
Louise Dufrayer. Compared with Krafft, "Louise . . . is simpler. It's enough to
have rubbed shoulders with women a little in order to understand her, with
her failings, her whims, her harshness, her feeble heart and her outbursts of
nerves, not to mention that instinct for demanding total attention for herself,
which makes her an enemy of all higher occupation or work. She is one of
those women who inevitably render powerless the man who associates his life
with hers, unless the man is of the nature of a Schilsky" (May 31–June 1,
1911). Solanges had no inkling that Richardson had partly portrayed Eleonora Duse in Louise. But in a letter immediately preceding, Solanges attacked
D'Annunzio: "You see all the noise that buffoon [*polichinelle*] D'Annunzio is
making in Paris!" Richardson informed him in turn that she had fallen under
the spell of *Il trionfo della morte* and *Il fuoco* "in their day," although she
could now no longer endure "the repetition of this Superman's descriptions of
his own relations to one or another woman." She went on to ask Solanges,
who lived in Italy, if he knew Eleonora Duse "personally, or by repute . . . She
has interested me extraordinarily, both as artist and as woman." Solanges had
indeed met her socially, twice, and recounted a "little story" about a friend of
his, a "great artist," who was besieged by Duse. "One day he received . . . the
entire contents of a violet-seller's little barrow." Solanges had caught sight of
her across from his friend's door, "patiently eating a bun in a most graceful
pose." The anecdote no doubt confirmed Richardson in her suspicions about
the actress's sexual appetites, long since incorporated into Louise Dufrayer.

Maurice Guest, of course, contains numerous bedazzled portraits of Louise
by Maurice; when he suggests marriage, she looks at him with eyes "that
reminded him of an untamed animal or a startled child." On the other hand,
Madeleine is catty: "Beautiful she had never thought Louise; she was not even
pretty, in an honest way — at best, a strange foreign-looking creature, dark-
skinned, black of eyes and hair, with flashing eyes and a wonderfully mobile
mouth . . . At this moment" — Louise has belatedly arrived — "she was looking
her worst . . . There was nothing young or fresh about her, she looked her
twenty-eight years, every day of them — and more." To Krafft she calls Louise
a vampire. At their introduction, Louise's "strong white teeth" directly catch
Maurice's attention, and she bites Maurice's lip when he tells her he must

practice. (Elsewhere in her dental characterizations, Richardson resembles Thomas Mann; Spinell's teeth in *Tristan* are large but carious, whereas Tadzio's are "rather notched and pale." At Schilsky's farewell party, an Italian violinist — and thus a southerner like Louise — has "huge white teeth," Schilsky has defective teeth, childish Ephie has an "even line of teeth, with slightly notched edges." The victim of Jerome Moçs in "Succedaneum" has "a line of strong little notched teeth.")

The affection of Richardson for Eleonora Duse shines through in her defense of Louise to Solanges. "I had some difficulty in making my German translator understand that Louise, with all her goings on, remained a *lady* and was not the ordinary fast woman of fiction." In reply to Solanges's query about "how much sincerity, how much comedy" lay in Louise's offstage behavior, her readiness to marry the American in Dresden, Richardson answered: "Louise is *always sincere*. Where she fails, and makes the impression of being insincere, it is only because she does not understand herself what she wants." Returning to the matter a month and a half later (January 1912), Richardson slammed the door on Solanges, not having the time to go into the question of Louise's sincerity once more: "She *was* sincere, no one stood for her portrait." The latter clause, a nonsequitur, was not true any more than was her claim, in the same letter, that she was called Mr. Richardson in conversation.

Louise's sincerity, staunchly maintained by Richardson, is present in painful transformation in the last book. Arguing her cause to Solanges, Richardson added that in one section, at the end of Part 3, chapter 1 (the return from Rochlitz), "I had given her a couple of pages to herself. After her return to her room, she realizes the limitations of her tie to Maurice." The passage itself says: "She knew it all now — knew him and what he could give her — like a page learned by heart," but still she longed for him "as never before." The couple of pages were deleted, perhaps because her change is portrayed on the trip to Grimma and Nimbschen: she sees some bulrushes and idly asks for them; ever obedient, Maurice takes off his shoes and stockings — his "movements were of an impossible circumstantiality" — and she instantly knows she does not desire him any longer. She keeps him at a distance for "three whole days," but then "asked, in returning to him, neither affection nor comradeship, only the blind gratification of sense." Richardson is frank about Louise's revulsion and her concomitant clinging to sexual satisfaction: "She shut her eyes and went forward, determined to extract every particle of pleasure or, at least, oblivion, that the present offered . . . she brought to bear on their intercourse all her own hard-won knowledge, and all her arts." Louise gradually lets her nymphomaniacal strain run free. With Maurice, she still has "insatiable lips," yet she goes on evening walks alone, afterward reporting to Maurice, with her "fitful, somewhat unreal laugh," that a man has approached her; she carries on her affair with Herries, she hints in her hateful conversations with Maurice that there are others. Nevertheless, she continues her physical relations with Maurice; a passage at the end of Book 3, chapter 9, when she gives Maurice the reason for her semiaffair with Krafft, Maurice kneels down and takes her, "warm with sleep, into his arms . . . their lips met in a long kiss." Following the bout of insult in which Maurice beats her, she collapses sobbing, and Maurice embraces her: "The beloved body was in his grasp." The subsequent "when he had finished" is ambiguous. Knowing that "she [has] given herself to another" (Herries?), he has also recognized that "despite the ungovernable aversion she felt for him, she could still tolerate his endearments. Not once, as long as they had been together, had she refused to be caressed."

Solanges wrote to Richardson that he could not understand "how some among your readers could have taken Louise for the principal character"; she is a "creature of destiny, made for the ruin of unhealthy impressionable imaginations like Maurice. I consider her a *femme fatale,* not a conventional one, but one who is inevitably destined to do evil, even involuntarily, by virtue of a certain charm . . . She is an agent of disintegration that is instinctive," the closest he comes to exculpating Louise. Richardson has Louise pity Maurice ("poor Maurice") one night, when she comes home: "For once no cruel words passed her lips, her eyes filled with tears"; she weeps as they sit on the sofa before their last night together, on which "Louise let him do what he would," another deleted sentence. Yet at the same time Louise — "always a lady" in Richardson's statement to Solanges — has become a vicious termagant, hurling insult after insult ("wretched scoundrel," "worse than furniture," "never man enough to know what it was that [Madeleine] wanted," "a man who is content with other men's leavings"). The culmination comes as Louise, surmising that Schilsky has returned, goes out "refreshed and rejuvenated" in a light spring dress, and Maurice, who has sighted Schilsky, "the insolent short-sighted eyes and the loose, easy walk," insists on going with her along Schleußingerweg. He confirms that Schilsky has indeed come back, and she calls Maurice a "mean-souled, despicable dummy of a man," tells him to throw himself into the river, and spits on the ground at his feet, a gesture far more vulgar than Carmen's throwing the ring at Don José outside the bullring as she waits for Escamillo. The germ cell of this unpleasant page may lie in the *Carmen* libretto of Meilhac-Halévy, or in Fennimore's assult on Niels Lyhne, as he ludicrously teeters on skates: " 'You came with your poesy and your filth and pulled me down with lies into the mud with you.' " (In their final conversation Maurice threatens to kill Louise, who retorts: " "Such as you don't kill,' " making her counterproposal of his suicide; in *Thérèse Raquin,* Thérèse and Laurent exchange invective and think to kill one another; the novel ends with their double death.) Richardson had a gift for cutting conversation — for example, the exchange between Mary Mahony and her husband, once so deeply loved, in the trilogy, as Mahony is going mad, and the fight scene between the sisters in the story "Sister Anne."

Solanges complained about the epilogue: "After the tragic and moving — very moving — death of Maurice, [the reader] has not the least desire to learn, nor the least surprise in learning, that Louise has married Schilsky and that the latter has a fine career." She cut him off: "I say that life is a monstrous, cruel, and delightful piece of irony, and that, no matter what happens, it goes on, just the same." A couple of years after Maurice's death, Schilsky, now Kapellmeister in a large south German city (Munich?), emerges from the Gewandhaus after a concert. He has composed a new symphonic poem, *Über die letzten Dinge,* its title taken from the collected essays of Weininger. An American bystander tells a friend to take a good look at Schilsky's wife, " 'who is said to have been very handsome . . . An English chap killed himself on her account.' " Maurice has been reduced to an anonymous figure in an old story, Schilsky is successful, and Louise has gotten her wish to marry him. (Probyn and Steele suggest a possible Straussian allusion in a detail, "a Jewish-looking stranger in a fur-lined coat is with Schilsky"; Strauss had begun his collaboration with Hofmannsthal with *Elektra* in 1906.) Louise is accompanied by a pianist, "a shabbily dressed young man with a world of enthusiasm in his candid blue eyes." Her cloak catches in a door, their hands meet, and the young man blushes. Dorothy Green thinks the young man may be Krafft, ever youthful. Rather, it may be a replacement for Maurice, helping Louise pass the time as Schilsky goes his triumphant way.

An episode during the last January of Maurice's life has not received as much attention as it might. Avery Hill drowns herself after Krafft's disappearance; she had loved and served him, but she had also found his egomania hard to bear, calling him to his face " 'the most self-conscious person alive.' " Krafft admitted to Maurice that she was right, " 'And it's only the naïve natures that count,' " thus making a distinction between Schilsky and himself, the natural and the analytical, Schiller's naive and sentimental. Rummaging through Avery's effects, Philadelphia Jensen expressing sympathy and regret, assumes that "the poor young thing" has killed herself out of despair at Krafft's "falsity" and her own poverty. Madeleine, who not long ago had ordered Krafft to " 'take pity on the poor thing's constancy,' " has hardened: Avery could have waited until her friends had taken their test recitals. And: " 'Could anyone help her ever having set eyes on that attractive scoundrel?' " Hill and Krafft are a parallel to Maurice and Louise. Louise is still more dismissive of Avery: " '[Krafft] was never her lover.' " Even at this stage of the game, Maurice is shocked at her having discussed sexual matters with Krafft. Nor is Maurice concerned about Avery's death, he has never liked her, because of the secret language, verbal and musical, she spoke with Krafft, and her jealous aversion to the interloper, Maurice.

Louise insists on going to the morgue to view Avery's body; Louise looks almost ugly to Maurice, a dangerous ugliness, "more seductive than her beauty had ever been." With some justification, Maurice calls her perverse, but he accompanies her all the same. Avery's corpse, in the opinion of the attendant, the *Leichenfrau,* is a pretty one, she was in the water no more than half an hour. Louise stares intently at the corpse "without a spark of feeling." Then her attention is drawn to the "hairy breast" of another suicide, a man who has taken poison. She lingers; Maurice wonders how she can bear the smell in the chamber. The morgue scene, done in naturalistic detail, was doubtless suggested to HHR by the thirteenth chapter of *Thérèse Raquin* in which Laurent haunts the Paris mortuary to see if Camille's body has been fished up. The Paris morgue provides erotic titillation for its visitors: one of them in particular catches Laurent's eye, delicate and elegantly dressed, "Autour d'elle traînait une senteur douce de violette." She gazes at a large, strong man, with a big chest and bulging muscles; she turns him over, as it were, with her gaze. Louise purchases a bunch of violets, which she presses to her nose and mouth. Not gratuitously, the morgue scene reveals a necrophiliac Louise.

Robertson wrote that readers of *Maurice Guest* "have always been divided into ardent partisans of Maurice and even more ardent partisans of Louise." "In spite of the opaque veil" of objectivity, his wife had "a certain sympathy with Louise," a statement supported by her letters to Solanges. Conversely, Richardson's remarks about Maurice in the letters to Solanges and in the marginalia are condescending. Explaining Maurice's hesitation to go to the room of Louise, whom he scarcely knows, together with Madeleine (Book 1, chap. 9), she wrote to Solanges that "young men in his walk of life do not visit young women in their bed-sitting rooms at eleven o'clock at night . . . You see, you must always think of Maurice as of a young man who, brought up in the narrowest circumstances, has known no women and still has an exaggerated respect for them." In a manuscript note, having deleted her single reference to Louise's smoking (her idol Carmen smokes), Richardson added that Louise does not "paint" either, but she uses powder, "which horrifies that Simple Simon Maurice." At the beginning of Book 2, Maurice is concerned for the physical and mental health of Louise and is putting her unpaid bills in order: "A deep sense of responsibility filled him. In obedience, however, to a puritanic streak in his nature, he hedged himself about with restrictions, lest he should believe he was setting out on an all too primrose path."

To Robertson, as to Solanges, Maurice, compared with Louise, was "the more finely conceived and executed figure, which . . . stands alone in the literature of his time, in our English literature, at least, and in Richardson's own work only Richard Mahony is endowed with a deeper spiritual life." Thus Robertson put himself squarely in the camp of the Maurice partisans. From a narrow Glasgow home, Robertson, who defied his parents in order to study literature in Germany, had good reason to make at least a limited identification with Maurice; we have Richardson's word for it that he was shy and a poor dancer, but an excellent skater. (Like Louise, Richardson was no skater.) Maurice has considerable to be said for him as he starts out on his *Lehrjahre.* Although Robertson undercuts him as he introduces him in his essay (he "falls through lack of talent and temperament"), Maurice, despite his poor pianistic preparation and the dulling four years of schoolteaching, gets a surprising vote of confidence from Schwarz. On his first Leipzig evening, his German is fragmentary; shortly, thanks to Madeleine's tutelage and his own industry, he reads and speaks well. Madeleine tells him that he absorbs like a sponge; he ventures into Jean Paul, Schiller, and Heine, he accepts the loan of the first volume of a Friedrich Spielhagen novel about a poor young man's development, *Hammer und Amboß,* from Johanna Cayhill and reads it "deep into two nights," carries off the second, then goes on to Spielhagen's *Problematische Naturen.* (Spielhagen's *In Reih und Glied,* cited in the manuscript, was omitted; Richardson no doubt felt she had laid it on a little too thick. Gustav Freytag's historical cycle, *Die Ahnen,* also discussed with Johanna, was likewise dropped from the printed version.)

As Maurice practices his scales, he has a volume of Goethe's poems, lent by Johanna, propped on the piano. "At a particular favorite, he stopped playing and held the book in both hands." The Cayhills leave Leipzig in the aftermath of Ephie's misadventures with Schilsky and Louise, Madeleine is at work on Beethoven's Third Piano Concerto, and Maurice, believing Fürst's gossip, avoids Krafft, and Krafft him: he is left alone with his piano, and applies the words of the harpist in *Wilhelm Meisters Lehrjahre* to himself: "Wer sich der Einsamkeit ergibt, ach, der ist bald allein." But as he takes Goethe's *Dichtung und Wahrheit* along to Rochlitz, to read while Louise sleeps and oversleeps, his thoughts wander; "the writing seemed stiff and strained, the work of a very old man," while Maurice, on his Venusberg with Louise, is at the peak of his youth and happiness. In consideration of what awaits him, it might be expected that Richardson would have Maurice read *Die Leiden des jungen Werthers,* but he does not. The classic novel of suicide for love's sake is mentioned only at the *Walküre* performance, by Madeleine. Disappointed by Ephie's failure to pay attention to him, Dove has a gloomy air: " 'He might sit for Werther tonight.' " To be sure, Dove will never kill himself for love, and after Avery's suicide, "bearing the whole brunt of Saxon officialdom," he efficiently makes arrangements for the funeral.

Germaine Greer proposed that Maurice's last name came from Stephen Guest in *The Mill on the Floss,* seized by passion for Maggie Tulliver; Probyn and Steele note that in *Die Walküre,* Siegmund is introduced as "Gast." J. G. Robertson, a Goethe scholar of distinction, hovered on the brink of still another source. Describing Richard Mahony, Robertson wrote that Mahony always felt himself to be in a world "as uncongenial and fatal to his well-being as the musical bohèmes had been to Maurice Guest . . . he had been a stranger and a wanderer on the earth." Robertson's language calls to mind Goethe's "Selige Sehnsucht" in *West-Östlicher Divan.* Man must be prepared to be consumed like a moth in the flames: "Und wenn du aber dies nicht hast,/Dieses stirb und werde!/Bist du nur ein trüber Gast/Auf der dunklen Erde." Unable to put Louise behind him and begin a new life, Maurice dies a melancholy guest in the park where he shoots himself. Or he is "ein Gast auf Erden," the "stranger on the earth" of Psalms 119:19. He leaves the world in its strangeness: his vision of Louise is "disfigured by [her] hatred of him, horribly vindictive"; he was "on his back, without knowing how he had got there." Music, which drew him to Leipzig, comes to his ears a last time, as he hears "the familiar melody," to which a detachment of soldiers marches off to exercise. In one more of the deleted passages (Maurice has knelt down to kiss Louise after one of their terrible battles), he ponders the reason for his longing to be reconciled with her: "It was more than mere desire. It was that feeling of homesickness for the sight of her and the touch of her — a vital nostalgia which had its roots deep down in his being, and he realized anew, in this midnight hour, that he would never overcome it." Maurice, of whom his landlady says "there wasn't a decenter young man anywhere," is a nympholept, a brother to Hugues Viane, the quiet widower.

On his way to the conservatory (and the first sight of Louise) with Dove, Maurice has "already, in dress and being, taken on a touch of musicianly disorder." Dove, aiming for success in England, dresses as he used to "in the provincial English town to which he belonged." Maurice and Dove come from more or less the same beginnings, but Maurice bears a germ of excessiveness which will lead to his disorder, suffering, and death. The excessiveness within Maurice gives him a warning, even before he has seen Louise. His first night in Leipzig, he writes a dutiful letter to his parents, pledging that not a day of his time will be wasted; he has been driven to embark on his German venture: " 'Something stronger than myself drove me to it.' " That night he awakes in a cold sweat from a strange dream. He bumps into a crowd gathered around an object in the road, from which "horror" everyone runs away, as he does.

Proposals have been made that the dream is a prefiguration of the minor street accident Maurice comes across in Zeitzerstraße before sighting Schilsky, who has returned, or that a connection may be made between Raskolnikov's dream of the peasant beating a horse to death in *Crime and Punishment* (Book 1, chapter 5), or with the street suicide which opens D'Annunzio's *Il trionfo della morte,* an event witnessed by the eventual murderer and suicide Giorgio Aurispa. These comments do not take into account the cry of the crowd in Maurice's dream, "Moloch, Moloch." While studying Flaubert carefully in her Strasbourg years, HHR must have read *Salammbô*. In its gruesome finale, Mathô, the priestess's devoted lover, running the gauntlet, is tortured by the people of Carthage, worshipers of Moloch; he dies, horribly mutilated, at her feet. The dream of Maurice is left a puzzle; sitting up in bed, "clammy with fear," he thinks no more about it.

Maurice's second dream comes after first seeing Louise with a yellow rose at her belt, and hearing Krafft's "Rose of Sharon": he dreams of "her," the yellow rose "she" wore, and the Rose of Sharon, which is transformed into "a giant flower, with monstrous crimson petals." In *À rebours,* female genitals turn into a huge and dangerous flower. Flowers come back in the third dream of Maurice, at the opening of Book 1, chapter 8. He has spent much time with Madeleine and has succumbed to the flirtatiousness of Ephie Cayhill, who puts a sprig of lilac behind his ear. He kisses her, at which she bursts into tears and agrees with Maurice's self-condemnation that he has acted like a "horrid brute." (In the pendant to the scene, alone, Ephie curtsies to herself in the mirror and says, " 'Him too' " — she is not as innocent as she seems. The vignette grows out of an incident in *Niels Lyhne,* in which Tema Boye, who has an "opened little mouth" like Ephie, "with milk-white teeth," flirts with Niels as he pushes her in a rocking chair. She sends him away, aroused, and looks at herself in the mirror, "with a discreet smile, as at an accomplice . . . She liked scenes.") Maurice's "vivid dream" starts in a garden filled with lilacs; he steps toward the nearest bush but finds it has been stripped bare. Her arms filled with lilacs, Ephie appears, telling him he is too late, and then changes into Louise, coming toward Maurice, her "laden arms" outstretched; but he can neither move nor speak. Louise becomes Madeleine, "who laugh[s] at his disappointment"; his "revulsion of feeling" is too great: he turns away "without taking the flowers held out to him," and wakes up. The dream, an easily interpreted variation on the judgment of Paris, is the last view into Maurice's subconscious world.

As the novel goes along, the disorder in Maurice comes to the surface repeatedly: his drunkenness, his would-be assault on Schilsky ("a primitive hatred grip[s] him" as he mumbles in the language of a Victorian gentleman, "the sneak—the cur—the filthy cad," in response to which Schilsky calls him, along with other vilifications, " 'you drunken hog' "), the trick played on Ephie to please Louise (Maurice realizes that it is ungentlemanly but cannot help himself), his threat to beat up the man who has accosted Louise on the first of her night walks alone (" 'Let me catch him here, and I'll make it impossible to him to insult a woman again' "), his altercation with Herries, the slap in Krafft's face, the beating of Louise, and the drunken night with the prostitute Luise. In a last act of orderliness, he loosens his collar before shooting himself, fearing he may do the deed "clumsily."

Not long after arriving in Leipzig, walking with Madeleine in the Nonne, Maurice sees Louise with Schilsky, a "mere boy," Maurice thinks, "with a disagreeable, dissipated face," and learns the couple's names from his well-informed companion. Saying good-bye to Madeleine, who has given him an "Open Sesame," Louise's name, he goes home but immediately leaves again: "Guiltily, with a stealthy look around him, though wood and night were black as ink, he knelt down and kissed the gravel where he thought she had stood." An evening in early summer, taking a "quick solitary walk along one of the paths of the wood," he hears Louise say to Schilsky: " 'You have never given me a moment's happiness,' " a "torture and a joy" for the eavesdropper. Near the novel's end, going along Schleußingerweg with Louise, Maurice demands the yellow rose she wears in her belt and throws it into the muddy Pleiße; the place Maurice speaks with Louise for the last time is once more in the vicinity of Schleußingerweg: Louise's "gaudy dress" trails in the mud of the path, and they cross the suspension bridge into the Nonne. Learning that Schilsky has returned, as she has suspected, she heaps her last insults on Maurice and spits at his feet. The site of Maurice's suicide is near "the well-known seat with the bosky background." At his "favorite seat," on a melancholy autumn day a year and six months ago, Maurice had fallen into despair when he thought he had learned from Madeleine that Schilsky was to leave Leipzig and that Louise would go with him; here, Madeleine was wrong for once. In the winter woods after Krafft's story of "a woman's unsatisfied fancy," Maurice, face down on a park bench, meets "a smell of rotting and decay."

22

The United States

JAMES GIBBONS HUNEKER

The only novel by James Gibbons Huneker (1857–1921), *Painted Veils* (1920), was a potboiler, written from July 9 to August 25, 1919, "seven breathless weeks." An immediate cause for the author's haste was the cost of the medical treatments both he and his (third) wife, Josephine, were receiving. Behind the practical need, however, lay Huneker's long-held ambition to write a full-length novel. In his short fiction, collected in *Melomaniacs* (1902), *Visionaries* (1905), and the concluding section of *Bedouins* (1920), he had demonstrated a narrative urge which somehow never panned out. The protagonist of "The Corridor of Time" in *Melomaniacs,* an occasional musician and music critic who has been disappointed in love, at his death leaves behind a single sentence of a novel: " 'And the insistent clamor of her name at my heart is like the sonorous roll of the sea on a savage shore.' "

Until the sensation created by *Painted Veils,* Huneker's reputation had been that of a superior cultural journalist. In *Mezzotints in Modern Music* (1899), essays on Brahms, Tchaikovsky, Chopin, Richard Strauss, Liszt, and Wagner, Huneker, at forty-two, at last ventured to write in book form, after a decade or more of diurnal journalism. Immediately, he showed himself to be an extremely well-informed, technically competent, and stylistically fluent expert on what was then modern music; that the book was dedicated to Henry Edward Krehbiel, the conservative dean of New York music critics, was as much a challenge as a compliment. It was followed by *Chopin: The Man and His*

Music (1900). Chopin was a composer to whom Huneker — a gifted but non-public pianist and teacher of piano — gave all his genuine affection; *Overtones* (1909) offered a further tribute to Richard Strauss. (It also contained, among other pieces, "Literary Men Who Loved Music," devoted in part to George Moore, who would have a part in the conception of *Painted Veils*.) *Iconoclasts* (1905) was on drama, especially Ibsen; *Egoists: A Book of Supermen* (1909), dedicated to George Brandes, has essays, again among many others, on authors who figure in *Painted Veils*, Huysmans and Maurice Barrès. *Promenades of an Impressionist* (1910) was on painting, *Franz Liszt* (1911) returned to the "startling splendor" in the piano works of a composer already admired in *Mezzotints*. *The Pathos of Distance* (1913) has another essay on George Moore, with a telling section on Moore's "astonishingly fresh" *Memoirs of My Dead Life* (1906), recollections of the Irishman's activities in Paris a quarter of a century before, not unimportant for the memories of Ulick in *Painted Veils*. (With "The Celtic Awakening" in the same volume, Huneker called attention to his own half-Irish heritage.) *Old Fogy* (1913) was a reprint of feuilletons written for Theodore Presser's *Étude* magazine, reflections of a musical curmudgeon resident at the Mozartean "Dussek Villa on Wissahickon," near "dear, dirty Philadelphia," Huneker's birthplace, and includes "Old Fogy's" account of his first experience of *Die Walküre*, later subsumed, in *Painted Veils*, into the ecstatic reconstruction of a *Tristan* rehearsal under Anton Seidl at the Metropolitan Opera. *New Cosmopolis* (1915) is Huneker's tribute to New York City, the main scene of *Painted Veils*; *Ivory, Apes, and Peacocks* (also 1915) has the acrobatic Huneker on display again: literature (Joseph Conrad, Lafcadio Hearn, de Maupassant, Schnitzler), music (Mussorgsky, Schoenberg with "Pierrot Lunaire," Strauss), graphic artists (Alfred Kubin, Puvis de Chavannes, "the Italian Futurist Painters"). *Unicorns* (1917) is another mixed bag, containing among other figures the James Joyce of *Dubliners*, as well as, once more, Huysmans and "the sad, bad, mad George Moore, who, regrettably, has reformed." The commissioned works on *The Development of Piano Music* (1915–16) and the *Philharmonic Society of New York* (1917) betray, in the former instance, Huneker's professional expertness on his chosen instrument and, in the second, his lack of interest in orchestral playing. (However, once upon a time in *Mezzotints*, he proved that he knew his way through the details of Tchaikovsky's symphonic scores.) He wrote about the Met during the glory years of Toscanini but said little about the conductor, just as the *Tristan* rehearsal in *Painted Veils* makes only vague remarks about the great Seidl; to the novel's heroine, Seidl was "a magician whose wand evoked magic spells, but soon she forgot Time and Space" and the conductor himself. The heroine, to be sure, is a supreme egoist.

In 1920, the year of *Painted Veils*, Huneker published the two volumes of his autobiography, *Steeplejack*, again very swiftly written; the title alludes both to Ibsen's Master Builder Solness and to a jack-of-all-trades. Volume 1 falls into two parts; the first, "In Old Philadelphia," is about his childhood, boyhood, and "music madness"; the second, "Paris Forty Years Ago," describes with more imagination than fact his youthful trip to Paris to study piano. Volume 2, "New York (1877–1917)," expatiates on these forty years almost without chronology. H. L. Mencken, Huneker's great and good friend, was so disappointed that he called it "a feeble stream of inconsequential reminiscences." Perhaps Mencken was exasperated by Huneker's keeping mum about his love life, on which otherwise — in correspondence and in reminiscences — he was so voluble, and saying little about his musical experiences. However, in the fifth chapter, a comparison is made between the sopranos Lillian Nordica (1857–1914), who "toward the end of her career looked like a large, hastily upholstered couch," and the Swedish-Norwegian-American Olive Fremstad (1871–1951). Fremstad's "Brangaene and Sieglinde were the most satisfying to the eye and ear I ever experienced." *Variations* (1921) is posthumous; the publisher's note says that it shows Huneker's "wide-reading discovery of aesthetic material for the consideration, the illumination, and — preeminently — the entertainment of the cultivated." Supported by Charles Scribner's Sons, Huneker had played — and would play for a couple of decades after his death — the role of a disseminator of European (and New York) culture to a country that still had too little contact with larger worlds. But by the 1940s much of Huneker's cultural writing was regarded as overblown, superficial, undependable, old hat.

Painted Veils, which Huneker claimed was a sequel to *Steeplejack,* is a roman à clef and an autobiographical wish-dream. The male lead, Ulick Invern — whose Irish name Huneker lifted from the mentor of the eponymous heroine in George Moore's *Evelyn Innes,* which is about a Wagnerian soprano — is the younger son of a dissolute Irish nobleman ("the family is an ancient one in Kerry") who married American money and became a naturalized citizen. (The older son is named Oswald, probably after Ibsen's Oswald Alving.) The family moved to Paris before Ulick's birth, since France "offered [the father] an escape from what he called the Puritanism of New York"; he dies an "aristocrat drunkard." Like the painter Oswald, Ulick became "a Frenchman in externals and by culture, [knowing] the men and women of the early nineties who made Paris a center of artistic and intellectual life." An acquaintance of Edmond de Goncourt, Henry James, Rémy de Gourmont, Maurice Barrès, and especially Huysmans, Ulick can be readily contrasted with the out-of-pocket Huneker, hampered by the ball and chain of a wife and baby during the Philadelphian's nine early months in Paris. Back home, Huneker had set out on a program of self-education and, after his move to New York, turned himself into a man-about-town. Here, the portrait of Ulick converges, somewhat, with the reality of Huneker: having returned to the States to find his American roots, Ulick — like Huneker — is a music teacher and reviewer, but also, decidedly unlike his creator, a teetotaler, because of his father's bad example.

On a central point, Invern and Huneker are pretty well identical; as a hobby, Ulick lectures on music at the Conservatoire Cosmopolitaine, directed by Antonín Dvořák during his New York years, and Huneker taught piano from 1888 to 1898 at the National Conservatory: Dvořák appears briefly in *Painted Veils,* as he does in *Steeplejack.* The "Mme Meyerbeer" of the conservatoire is the conservatory's patroness Jeanette Thurber, to whom Huneker paid court, and the "Maison Felicé," the artists' boardinghouse where Ulick and the singer-heroine live when she first comes to New York, is a small hotel, Maison Félix, Huneker's New York residence between his divorce from his long-suffering first wife and his marriage (1892) to the sculptress Clio Hinton. (The Mona Milton of the novel, a "maternal nymphomaniac" whom Ulick almost marries, is assumed by Huneker's biographer, Arnold Schwab (1963), to bear some resemblance to Clio.)

Schwab also notices that, in the self-portrait via Ulick, Huneker makes himself younger than he was: Ulick is in his twenties, if we take 1895 as the terminus a quo of the action, and Huneker in his late thirties; Ulick is quick to action and athletic, Huneker, the constant barfly, had already grown portly. Huneker had a kind of decayed handsomeness; looking at Ulick, Mona saw "the long, nervous fingers with their suggestion of fineness, of power, saw the oval face and the clear-cut features, — his profile made her dream of the profiles of decadent emperors of the Lower Empire, saw that his nose and brow modulated in the Napoleonic way, . . . saw his sensual lips," and so on. Huneker's self-encomium by means of the carefully composed picture of the multi-talented Ulick is reminiscent of D'Annunzio's efforts to turn his unprepossessing self, short and bandy-legged, into the vastly gifted and handsome Sperelli of *Il piacere* and Sperelli's later brethren. Nonetheless, Ulick and Ulick's acquaintances reveal a good deal of Huneker's doubts about himself. Ulick thinks that he can be good at his "avocation of critic," because he has a "smattering of the Seven Arts — Jack of all, master of none." The professional critic Alfred Stone tells Mona that: " 'Generosity of spirit [Ulick] abounds in. It is his strong point but also his weakest. He is too receptive.' " To Ulick's face, Aldred grows crueler: " 'Ulick, my lad, you write your novels in the air. You will never publish one.' " Finally, after Ulick is dead, Alfred goes on with his analysis: " 'Poor Ulick never had the staying power. Brilliant? Yes — after a fashion. His mind was a crazy-quilt. Mince pie and Chopin.' "

Ulick's consuming passion is for the singer Esther Brandès, nicknamed

Easter, from Richmond, Virginia, who arrives in New York in chapter 1, determined to become a great dramatic soprano. Alfred Stone takes her under his wing, tells her that her voice is " 'big, fruity, lots of color, velvety,' " and tells others that she possesses "presence, intelligence, ambition." To himself, Stone reflects that Esther is "hard as steel," "crude but not coarse," "the victim of the normal unintelligent education of small towns." On Stone's advice, she takes lessons from Frida Ash (Frida Ashforth, a longtime friend of Huneker), hears her first Wagner at the *Tristan* rehearsal under Seidl's direction, and auditions for Lilli Lehmann, the somewhat overaged Isolde. Lehmann finds her "very effective," with a "cold temperament . . . brilliant but hard." From her side, Easter calls Lehmann "a nice but condescending old lady" but follows Lehmann's advice to "sing at Bayreuth if only the humblest of roles." Despite her Southern birth, Easter has vague European connections; according to her father's story, her grandfather was a Dane, a statement meant to suggest a relationship to George Brandes, another of Huneker's trails leading nowhere.

For her initial trip to Europe, Easter procures the financial support of Allie Wentworth, the daughter of Wentworth the Olive Oil King; in Allie, Huneker introduces a lesbian theme, already brought up in the quotation from the poet Steeplejack, one of the novel's epigraphs ("Lo! the Lesbians, their sterile sex advancing"), and an element in the denouement of the novel. But when Easter's steamer leaves Hoboken in May (chapter 3), Paul Godard, a wealthy playboy, is also in her entourage. (Godard has already appeared as a dilettantish young man, "that brightwinged butterfly of aestheticism," in two stories of *Melomaniacs*. In "The Rim of Finer Issues," he runs off with a married woman, Ellenora Bishop-Vibert, in the other, "An Ibsen Girl," Ellenora, now married to and deserted by Paul, feels that she may have been misled by the example of Ibsen's Nora Helmer. An author, her prose poem "Frustrate," is quoted at length in the former story; in *Painted Veils,* it is read by the sexually frustrated Mona, who has been given a copy of *Melomaniacs* by Ulick.) During a postdeparture party at the Terrace Garden on East 58th Street — Huneker is very careful about accurate references to actual New York locales — Ulick is concerned not about Allie but rather about Godard, from whose attempt at rape he saved Easter at the Maison Felicé; Stone points to the other sexual danger by reciting Byron, "The Isles of Greece, the Isles of Greece, where burning Sappho loved and sung." (An patient listener to the Terrace Garden conversation is Milt, or Milton, Mona's brother, a candidate for the priesthood whose real and unused name is Melchizedek. He will become one of Easter's many victims.)

Easter is offstage for chapter 4, the longest in the book, which is given over to Ulick's background and life before coming to America, his budding love affair with Mona Milton, and a bachelor's orgy at the apartment of the millionaire Ned Haldane; Huneker adds to the verisimilitude of his New York scene by having Ulick introduced to Haldane's circle by the quasi-decadent author Edgar Saltus (1855–1921), whose erotica included *Imperial Purple* (1892) and *The Pomps of Satan* (1904). At the banquet, Ulick rescues Dora, one of the girls hired for a private "ballet infernal" by the host, and carries her off. (Huneker loosely imitates the "black dinner" in *À rebours* and depicts, somewhat more directly, the notorious "Pie-Girl dinner" given by the multimillionaire Henry M. Poor in May, 1898.) Ulick becomes a favored customer of Dora, a dumb Dora who is financially astute, but he learns that, here too, Paul Goddard is his rival.

Easter is also absent from chapter 5, which is mostly about Milt's friendship with Ulick, Mona's passion for him, and his break with Dora. Nonetheless, Huneker must have realized, however rapidly he wrote, that the novel's most interesting character had too long been missing. The author has Alfred Stone, on vacation in Atlantic City, present a long report to the inquisitive Mona about Ulick and Easter. Easter has been away for a year now. " 'She possesses what Ulick lacks; a singleness of purpose. In ten years [she] may be treading in the august footsteps of Lilli Lehmann.' " Stone also mentions a duel, already described at the end of chapter 4, fought in the Bois de Boulogne between Easter and her coming operatic rival, Mary Garden (1874–1967). To Alfred the duel, in which the "lithe, elastic and younger" Mary gets the better of Easter, was simply a publicity stunt on Easter's part: " 'Mary is canny, Easter is cannier.' " (Later on, Easter will demonstrate exceptional athleticism.) At the chapter's end, Ulick reads an account of Easter's debut as Isolde in Munich and her invitation to Bayreuth, to appear as Isolde, Brünnhilde, and Kundry. " 'Easter has changed her name to Istar . . . Istar the daughter of sin,' chuckled Alfred Stone."

In chapter 6, in which the story of Mona's pregnancy by Ulick, her miscarriage, and her peritonitis is played out, Ulick's thoughts, as he attempts to be loyal to his "bride," drift repeatedly toward Easter, from whose rapid European career reports come thick and fast; she elopes briefly with a Bavarian princeling and horsewhips the princeling's dowdy wife. Contemplating Easter-Istar's imminent New York debut, Ulick makes a mental review of contemporary divas: Lehmann and Milka Ternina have retired, Geraldine Farrar and Mary Garden are still in Berlin and Paris respectively. "Fremstad would provide a serious rival to Easter" on the latter's homecoming, but Fremstad is no longer a novelty at the Met. Easter's *succès fou* as Isolde is "like the debut of the pre-elected, coming, singing, conquering." Much more is reported about her private return. A "tall woman" arrives in a "red touring car, latest model," at Frida Ash's house, and shakes the maid's hand "in manlike fashion"; her appearance in Ulick's music room at the Maison Felicé makes Ulick's legs tremble, and she seizes his wrists with "the grasp of a giantess" to make him stop his advances. She still has Paul Godard and Allie Wentworth in tow; they wait in the limousine. As she leaves, she tells Ulick about her dislike for Debussy ("not a virile bar in him"), her admiration for "the big passionate style" of Rodin and D'Annunzio, and, lest the reader has missed the point about her mixed sexuality, her love for those "sumptuous" literary characters, Gautier's Mlle de Maupin and the perverse Satin in Zola's *Nana*.

Easter's House of Life (so-called after Dante Gabriel Rossetti's sonnet sequence) is an apartment near 72nd Street on Central Park West, where she takes long walks; her robust physique (like Fremstad's) requires many cubic feet of fresh air. Still, as befits her station, she keeps two cars, the red limousine and an electric brougham. (An automobile enthusiast, Huneker presages Fitzgerald in *The Great Gatsby*.) Paul is her premier public companion, and she readily brings Mona, who at first is frightened by her attention, into her circle: " 'You sweet duckling.' " Treated as a eunuch by Easter, Ulick returns to Dora, who lives in an apartment house called The Sappho on upper Lexington Avenue. Her interest piqued, Easter decides to discover where Ulick spends his nights; she wants fidelity from him as she does from Paul, mere "pawns" to be subject to her will. "With me it's Either-Or, as they say in some Ibsen play," is dictum of Easter, who also thinks that Walt Whitman was a medical student. For all her imperiousness and sophistication, she still suffers from the poor education Alfred Stone notices once upon a time. Mona, in contrast, reads her "beloved Frenchmen," Huysmans in particular.

In a furious and carefully laid-out chase by automobile, Easter tracks Ulick and Dora, who have escaped her by taking refuge in Jack's Restaurant at Manhattan Beach on Coney Island. On their return to Dora's apartment at The Sappho, they find Easter waiting. The "big woman" (as a chauffeur describes her) has arrived before the couple, gone to the top floor, rung the bell of Dora's neighbor, and taken a detour into Dora's apartments, leaping from the neighbor's window ledge to Dora's balcony. She becomes a superwoman, or, as Ulick says, "she has muscles of steel." Alfred Stone, always perceptive, has remarked on Ulick's weakness for women like Rider Haggard's She-Who-Must-Be-Obeyed. Now Huneker, rushing to finish the manuscript, piles the details of a lurid or vulgar decadence one on top of another. Easter and Dora sexually tease Ulick and begin their own coupling after Easter dismisses him. "Jeering laughter followed him to the lift."

Just before the chase, at the "old Vienna Café next to Grace Church," Easter has invited Ulick, Milt, and Mona to a party at her apartment. Again,

Huneker was confident that the shock effect of lesbianism had not worn out. Three or four girls, among them Allie Wentworth, are "sprawled on luxurious divans." "A huge woman, with a face that recalls the evil eyes and parrot-beak of an octopus" holds a long black cigar between her puffy lips. " 'We call her Anactoria,' " the queenly one, Allie says; Swinburne's "Anactoria" is a poem addressed by Sappho to a love object of that name. In this company, Easter sings gloriously, Schubert's "Almighty," and the song of child abduction "Der Erlkönig" — perhaps telling choices, since, all-mighty as she is, she plans to seduce the naive and childlike Milt, as she does the day after her lesbian tea. Calling on Easter, Ulick finds Milt babbling that "your Else-Istar" has coaxed his secret out of him — his priestly name, Melchizedek — after making him drunk, as Delilah did Samson. (Opera fans directly caught the reference to Elsa's attempt to get Lohengrin's — the virginal knight's — name out of him.) Feeling poorly since the night with Easter and Dora at the Sappho ("a mild stroke perhaps, yet something that threatened worse"), Ulick confronts Easter and receives the unkindest cut of all.

Years ago, in chapter 2, Ulick spent a vacation at Franconia in New Hampshire, to escape hay fever, from which he suffered, like Huneker. At an inn, he chances on the leaders of a "prohibitionist organization," the "Holy Yowlers" — Brother Rainbow, a "gigantic noseless Negro" and his consort, Roaring Nell, a "mere deluded creature under the control of the monstrous African." All three are offered bourbon by "a tall beautiful girl in white," who identifies herself as Miss Richmond, " 'a southerner, born and bred down there,' " and Ulick calls himself Mr. Paris. Going off together to a "Rotunda" for the Yowlers' festival, Miss Richmond and Mr. Paris observe the congregation behaving as if possessed by devils, "an orgy of sound and motion." The Southern girl seems frightened, Ulick moves to protect her, Brother Rainbow, "a sinister grin on his noseless face," commands "Lights out!" and promiscuous fornication begins; dragged down "amidst the rutilant groaning" by the "importunate, lascivious embrace" of a woman, Ulick concludes, when the lights go up, that it must have been his companion — who now, Brother Rainbow says, has experienced " 'true religion' " and is "one of de Holy Yowlers." Ever the gentleman, Ulick apologizes to "Miss Richmond" for his behavior and even tells her that he loves her, but is slapped in the face by the girl, who is transformed: "Her olive skin was drawn and yellow, . . . [her] great eyes . . . narrowed to slits and their hazel fire was like a cat's eyes in the dark." Understandably bemused, Ulick walks home across "the low-lying Franconian hills." After Mona's almost fatal illness, Ulick longs for "New Hampshire, the Franconian landscape"; in "Eili, eili, lomo asovtoni?" in *Variations*, largely a brief history of his own witty philo-Semitism ("Wagner looks like a Jew"),

Huneker tells how, at Bayreuth in 1896, he tramped the "Franconian hills" between performances. The association between New Hampshire's Franconia Notch and Germany's Franconia indicates that the "horrid mess" (as Easter dismissively calls it to Ulick) at the American Franconia was a first self-liberating stage on the mysterious Miss Richmond's journey to Bayreuth; in the autumn of the same year, the ambitious soprano first turns up in New York.

Throughout the novel, Ulick has maintained his love for Easter, whom he recognizes as "Miss Richmond, down east in New Hampshire," on their initial meeting at the Maison Felicé. Easter, refusing to listen to his hints and pleas " 'to begin again,' " says " '[If] we ever really began.' " In Easter's apartment, reproaching her for Milt's debauchment, Ulick calls her a beast, in revenge for her having called him a beast at the camp meeting. Easter sets him straight: he fornicated with Roarin' Nell and she with Brother Rainbow. Shattered, Ulick drinks for the first time in his life; at Dora's he suffers a paralytic stroke. The revelation, near the novel's end, of the coition between "Miss Richmond" and Brother Rainbow administered a shock, for the 1920s, perhaps difficult to imagine today. In Thomas Dixon's *Leopard's Spots* (1902), little Flora is apparently raped and murdered by the Negro Dick (who is burnt alive by a lynch mob); in Dixon's *The Clansman* (1905) Gus, the black captain of the "African Guards," rapes a girl in her mother's presence, and mother and daughter commit suicide together. The episode, somewhat changed, is included in D. W. Griffith's *Birth of a Nation* (1915). Still worse than her bisexuality, the clenching example of Easter's depravity is her remark about Brother Rainbow: " 'I consented — physiologically.' " The "monstrous black man" was an ultimate villain of turn-of-the-century narrative: in Bram Stoker's last novel, *The Lair of the White Worm* (1911), the black servant Oolanga, lusting for Lady Arabella March, is thrown to the White Worm by the lady, another superwoman with the mythical trappings Huneker would attach to Easter.

Commentators — Huneker's friends and the biographer Arnold Schwab — have tried to find the real-life Easter. According to Schwab, Huneker told both Frida Ashforth and Robert Mackay in 1905 that he was at work on a book whose heroine would be a mixture of Olive Fremstad and Emma Calvé. Huneker knew Fremstad both from Bayreuth in the summer of 1896 and from her career at the Met (1903–14); Calvé had starred at the Met from 1893 to 1904 and was notorious for the sensuality of her interpretations. (For Huneker in 1907, Fremstad's Salomé — which caused the opera to be removed from the Met after a single performance — was "not nearly as offensive, lewd and suggestive" as Calvé's Carmen.) Like Easter, Fremstad had come to New York as an unknown, both were protégées of Lilli Lehmann, both had a breakthrough at Bayreuth and specialized in the same Wagnerian repertoire, and both were great dramatic singers and extraordinarily strong, Fremstad a Brünnhilde who bounded about the stage. (Mona Milton makes a comparison between Fremstad and Easter that is to the latter's advantage.) As for the lesbianism Huneker repeatedly attaches to Easter, it may have been sour grapes from the past; Fremstad seems to have broken off their Bayreuth affair in 1896 when she discovered that Huneker had a wife and child in Philadelphia. Fremstad's two marriages to well-to-do husbands were terminated in short order by the diva, there was persistent gossip about Fremstad's relationship to her "buffer," the young Vermont pastor's daughter Mary Fitch Watkins, who lived with Fremstad from 1911 until 1918, two years after Fremstad's last performance at the Met. *The Rainbow Bridge* (1954) by the former Miss Watkins, now Mrs. Cushing, gives no hint of aberrant sexual behavior on Fremstad's part, but the memoirist was writing in a more discreet age: much of Mrs. Cushing's book is about Fremstad's moodiness and perfectionism. One wonders whether Huneker had read Willa Cather's *Song of the Lark* (1915), based on the earlier life of Fremstad, and if in some measure the sexual extravagances of *Painted Veils* were a reaction against Cather's sober and sometimes eulogistic tone. Less likely candidates for Easter's original were Mary Garden, Aberdeen-born but reared in Chicago, and Sibyl Sanderson (1865–1905) from California, for whom Massenet, one of her reputed lovers, wrote *Esclarmonde* and *Thaïs*. Huneker pretended to have had affairs with both these singers, and H. L. Mencken believed that Sanderson was the true original for Easter, but "with traces of Olive Fremstad." Two details about Fremstad do not jibe with the description of Easter. Fremstad possessed an iron artistic discipline, but Easter is indifferent to her art as art: after the *Tristan* rehearsal, "like the egoist she was, [her] personal impressions were intrinsically of more importance to her than the music or the singing." Further, Fremstad was born in Stockholm and reared in the Middle West, whereas Easter boasts of her Southern birth. But both differences helped Huneker slightly to cover up the Fremstad trail, and the second instance afforded him the chance at an implied naughty joke about the true sexual predilections of Southern belles.

In another character portrayal from a model, Huneker blackened the memory of a male friend. Alfred Stone is Albert Steinberg (?–1901) of the *New York Herald,* Huneker's closest companion among the city's music critics. He was deeply moved when Steinberg died prematurely of cancer; he wrote to Frida Ashforth that Steinberg's funeral was "the saddest thing I ever went through." In *Painted Veils,* Alfred Stone is Ulick's sidekick and an invaluable source of information — to Easter, freshly arrived in New York, about Ulick and the operatic world, to Ulick about Allie Wentworth, to Mona about Easter and Ulick. (For the not wholly skillful novelist Huneker, Stone does much to keep the action moving.) But in the novel, Steinberg-Stone lives on, becoming the wretched "fetch and carry" of Easter. At Lüchow's, the German restaurant near Washington Square, the "much-married, much-harried, much-divorced" newspaperman Bell, a subsidiary Huneker self-portrait, says that " 'Alfred must be fifty but he's a wiry old rum hound, . . . he is a parasite on Easter. He does her dirty jobs.' " At Lüchow's, before Bell's summing up, Stone reveals that Ulick, after his stroke, has been sent back to Paris, and has died within a few months of his brother Oswald. Stone conjectures that both sons received the Spirochaeta Pallida from their father — Ibsen's *Ghosts* again. Before his collapse, Ulick tells Milt about his " 'bad blood' " and not having received " 'a clean bill of health from [his] father's side of the house.' "

Huneker also uses Stone and Bell in the Lüchow scene to tie up other loose ends. According to Stone, Mona has become " 'self-righteous' " and a " 'blooming matron' " with a " 'houseful of children' " from her marriage to Paul Godard, " 'who now wears slippers and goes to bed early.' " Bell adds that " 'Dainty Dora, fair, fat, and forty, is a fashionable modiste — a Madame. All her customers are men.' " Simultaneously with *Painted Veils*, Huneker included two stories in *Bedouins* which complement the novel. "Venus or Walkyr?" (first printed as "The Last of the Valkyries" in the *Musical Courier* of 1896) is the disguised story of Huneker's Bayreuth affair with Fremstad. Paul Godard, with "Irish blue eyes," plays Huneker's part; he is rejected by Rue Towne, "a contralto, an Eastern girl from Maine," who sings the roles of a Rhine Maiden and a Valkyr, and turns against Godard when she learns he is also paying court to a beautiful and perverse Romanian. In the "odd name," Towne, the second component of *Fremstad*, "town," is evident. As for "Rue," Huneker may allude to Perdita's bouquet of "rosemary and rue" in *The Winter's Tale* (for "grace and remembrance"), or, hopefully, to Rue's regret at her harsh decision. Also, in "The Supreme Sin" of *Bedouins,* Ulick's brother Oswald falls in love with a devil worshiper but refuses to obey Satan, goes to Asia Minor, and perhaps enters a monastery. In *Painted Veils,* Oswald becomes an absinthe drinker and a "Manichean, a devil worshipper," decadent trappings that Huneker throws in for good measure.

Huneker provided what he thought a sophisticated audience wanted, "a riot of obscene wit," as Mencken called it, put together from his own embellished life of two decades before, and from European decadent literature as it had flowered at roughly the same time. One of the features of this determinedly decadent novel after the fact is the persistence with which Ulick remembers his French literary friends of the past; visiting Ulick in his music room, Mona finds him reading *Le Jardin de Bérénice,* taking refuge in the "subtle Barrès" of the "culte du moi." Ulick's friend Gourmont has used the example of Barrès's *Les Déracinés* to persuade his "dear young friend" to go home to America. From Huysmans, Ulick acquires his taste for Latinity, Petronius' *Satyricon* on the one hand, Thomas à Kempis's *De imitatione Christi* on the other, as well as for the occasional "epithète rare" (*coprolitic, parsiphallic, rutilant*). In the mixture of name-dropping and literary criticism which makes the fourth chapter swell to such an exceptional length, Huneker had as his model *À rebours* and its literary-historical and literary-critical chapters; but he does not follow Huysmans in the latter's re-creation of works of art (by Gustave Moreau, Jan Luyken, Odilon Redon), although Huneker had the expertness to do so. Another source is George Moore's *Confessions of a Young Man* with *its* manifold literary tributes, the account of the young Moore's own self-education in Paris. However, Ulick mentions Pater's *Marius the Epicurean* as his special icon, albeit Pater's refinement of style surely did not rub off on the improviser. When the candidate for priestly orders, Milt, calls on Ulick in the latter's chambers at the Maison Felicé, he runs his eyes over the library, Stendhal, Baudelaire, Flaubert, France, Huysmans, Barrès, Nietzsche ("unfortunate madman"), Ibsen, Max Stirner, William Blake ("another lunatic"), calling them "a nice gang of mind poisoners," save Huysmans, as he reads Des Esseintes's prayer, the last lines of *À rebours:* "Take pity, O Lord, on the Christian who doubts, on the skeptic who seeks to believe." (In *Steeplejack,* Volume 2, Huneker writes about a "reform" he almost went through in 1895: "If I had gone down on my shin bones and echoed Durtal's despairing prayer in *À rebours* . . . it would have been better for the health of my soul." As often, Huneker misremembers: it was Des Esseintes.) Milt's ambition, encouraged by finding Thomas à Kempis among Ulick's authors (alongside Petronius), is to return Ulick to his Roman Catholic faith — the conversion theme so frequent in the careers and works of the literary decadents, from Huysmans and Johannes Jørgensen on; but this aspect of the decadent novel is, again, window dressing, never developed. As a part of his admonitory program, Milt lists the dreadful fates of the "most depraved of degenerates": de Maupassant's coprophagy, the syphilis of Stendhal and Heine and Nietzsche and Baudelaire, "wallowing in nastiness," Huysmans's cancer of the throat, Ibsen's madness, Tolstoy's religious degeneracy. At Oscar Wilde, the catalogue breaks off. Milt-Melchizedek loses his proselytizer's validity by succumbing to Easter, after which, according to Stone, he is "sent away to some monastery out West" before finally being ordained and going to China as a missionary.

The literary catalogues are scarcely the only imitative features of *Painted Veils.* Another element in the decadent construct is the heavy use of epigraphs and textes de liaison as specimens of the author's colorful and variegated learning. *À rebours* has a quotation from the Flemish mystic Jan van Ruysdael as its epigraph, *Il trionfo della morte* has an epigraph from *Jenseits von Gut und Böse,* about books which have a contradictory value for soul and health, dependent on the baseness or lofty-mindedness of the reader, *Il fuoco* has a line from Dante, "Fa come natura face in foco," and *The Picture of Dorian Gray* a set of paradoxes, containing Wilde's apologia. *Painted Veils* goes these predecessors several better, first mockingly, with the "Seven Deadly Virtues" (such as Humility), and sincerely, with "The Seven Deadly Arts" (from Poetry and Music to Dancing), then with a translation of the "Épopée d'Izdubar" about the stripping of Istar, then a dedication of "This Parable" to the "charming morganatic ladies, les belles impures, who make pleasanter this vale of tears for virile men" (Mencken made fun of Huneker's own impotence in late life), and four quotations — from Mme d'Èpinay, a protectress of Rousseau, about modesty, "qu'on attache sur soi avec des épingles"; from Catulle Mendès about love, "cette forme meilleure de la charité"; the antilesbian tag from *Steeplejack;* and lines from *King Lear* (act 4, scene 6), the mad king's attack on his false daughters: "Down from the waist they are Centaurs,/Though women all above." Huneker's aversion to lesbianism is surprising in so broad-minded a man: in a letter, he arrived at a bizarre judgment about Cleland's *Fanny Hill:* "A conversion! Nothing more nor less than the conversion of a Lesbian lady to the strait and narrow patch [sic] of normal fornication."

Out of this preliminary apparatus, the *Épopée d'Izdubar* is put to extensive and repetitive use; a verse from the *Épopée* precedes each of the novel's seven chapters, from "At the first gate the warder stripped her, he took the high tiara from her head," to "He took off the last veil that covers her body." After publication, Huneker called *Painted Veils* "a damnably jejune book," in which he had been "sinfully crumpled [sic] by the use of the Istar device of the Seven Gates." In Germany, Istar had become Easter's stage name (as Olive Fremstad sometimes used as hers the more exotic Olga); in New York, attending a concert with Ulick, she reveals that she has gotten the idea from Vincent d'Indy's "masterpiece," *Istar: Variations symphoniques,* Opus 42, in which the theme on which the variations are based is revealed only at the end of the number, each variation representing a stage of Istar's disrobing. (The novel's seven chapters are called Gates, after the seven stations of Istar's way into the abode of the dead.) Still believing that he has fornicated with Easter during the New Hampshire orgy, Ulick remarks: " 'You reversed the order of disrobing with me, didn't you, Easter?' " to which Easter answers from her "tallest tower of disdain": " 'Don't be too sure, Jewel.' " (Jewel is the pet name given Ulick by Dora, Mona, and Easter.) At one time, Huneker considered "Istar" as his novel's possible title and rendered a name in the Babylonian text, as translated in D'Indy's score "Istar, fille de Sin" (i.e., the moon god), as English "sin," the way he also described the goddess in a letter to his Irish-American friend, John Quinn, "daughter of sin, you recall the old Babylonian epic." (Huneker liked such intentional linguistic misapprehensions: "Tempus fugit" turns into "Time fugued" several times in his writing, including *Painted Veils*. Mona resides, she likes to think, in an "Ebony Tower," a mistranslation of the Vulgate's "turris eburnia," the ivory tower in the Song of Songs.) Other possibilities for a title, according to Huneker's correspondence, were "Istar: Daughter of Sin" and "The Seven Deadly Sins." He rejected "The Seven Veils" because it would have too strongly suggested Strauss's opera. The *Épopée* and the chapter headings were finally reduced by Huneker, for the Lüchow finale, to Stone's description of Easter as " 'the great singing harlot of modern Babylon, a vocal Scarlet Woman' " and the toast offered by the whole Lüchow crowd to " 'Esther Brandès, the unvanquished Istar, the Great Singing Whore of Modern Babylon.' " The capital letters were a kind of fortissimo in type. But the end was not yet; Stein's epitaph for the (now late) Istar follows as the very brief chapter 7. "She had renounced the Seven Deadly Virtues for the Seven Deadly Arts, and was given the boon of the Seven Capital Sins" (the standard deadly sins, from Pride to Sloth) plus, inscrutably, the Eight Deadly Sin, Perfume (a stray allusion to chapter 10 in *À rebours?*), the Sin Against the Holy Ghost, "the sweet sin of Sappho," and "the Supreme Sin, denial of the Devil." Huneker never knows when to stop: "Istar, Daughter of Sin, was happy and her days were long in the land and she passed away, in the odor of sanctity." Does Huneker hint at the veneration Fremstad received from the Metropolitan audience during the unique demonstrations at her retirement performance in 1914? The coda also bids goodbye to Ulick and "the tragic-comedy of his existence." Two books had formed Ulick's "reverse aspirations": "Petronius, his thirst for an Absolute in evil; Thomas à Kempis, his God-intoxicated craving for the Infinite."

How aware Huneker was of the popularity of Istar (or Astarte and Ashtaroth) in the literature of his time is impossible to guess. The goddess hovered for a long time in the literary penumbra: in Eduard Stucken's "ballad" "Die Höllenfahrt der Ischtar" (1898); in the "vision délirante" of Jean Lorrain's diary novel, *Monsieur de Phocas: Astarte* (1899), in Pierre Louÿs's sonnet "Astarte" ("Elle tient dans ses doigts extatiques et bleus/Au pli vierge du sexe un lotus fabuleux"); in Przybyszewski's *Pentateuch* (1893); in the "great goddess" of Paul's erotic dream in Richard Beer-Hofmann's *Der Tod Georgs* (1900); in Heinrich Mann's erethic trilogy, *Die Göttinnen* (1901); in the Presbyterian John Buchan's "Grove of Ashtaroth" (1911): the Jewish engineer

Lawson, in a remote part of southern Africa, is bewitched by the goddess's spirit dwelling in a temple ruin on his property and is about to castrate himself in her service when he is saved, in the nick of time, by his manager, "a big, gruff Scot from Roxburgshire," and the narrator, who together blow up the sacred grove. Two years before *Painted Veils*, Édouard Dujardin's "mimodrame" "La Légende de Sainte Istar et des sept démons" was published, "a Christianization of the old Babylonian drama" inspired by D'Indy's tone poem. Huneker was in fast company.

The removal of Istar's veils may have helped Huneker, forever associating, to choose his final title, which appears not to have been the one most favored by him. But *Painted Veils* has a — bogus — biblical air about it, suggesting the "whited sepulchers" of Matthew 23:27, the concealers of corruption. After his seduction, Milt cries: " 'Painted Veils; — Oh Jewel, Jewel, she is irresistable!' " The words are taken from Shelley's admonitory sonnet: "Lift not the painted veil which those who live/Call life," and "I knew one who had lifted it — he sought/For his lost heart was tender, things to love,/But found them not, alas! Nor was there aught/The world contains, the which he could approve." The words of the sonnet apply better to Ulick than to Milt; the rending of her Painted Veil by Easter's confession about Brother Rainbow will destroy the nympholept Ulick in his hopeless passion, but not Milt who, recovering from his contact with her, regains his sacerdotal state. To be sure, before his fall, Milt has paraphrased the question hurled at the world by Des Esseintes: " 'The whole world is morally out of joint. It has become godless; and were it not for the saving remnant, God in his just wrath would destroy the earth as he destroyed Sodom and Gomorrah.' " Huysmans's Des Esseintes asks if "the terrible God of Genesis and the pale martyr of Golgotha would not prove their existence once for all by rekindling the rain of fire that once consumed . . . the cities of the plain." Milt's rhetoric does not reach Huysmans's level.

Mencken generously judged *Painted Veils* a masterpiece and, before all else, the story of Ulick's destruction. Ulick is destroyed like other heroes of decadent narratives: Dorian, D'Annunzio's Aurispa, Harald Malcorn, Andrian's Prince, Mann's Aschenbach. Yet *Painted Veils* also employs another pattern of decadence: the city, a specific city, plays as major a role in it as, e.g., Rome in *Il piacere*, Bruges in *Bruges-la-Morte*, Stockholm in *Doktor Glas*, Venice in Mann's novella, Russia's western capital in *Petersburg*. Still, New York is not a dead city (no Bruges, no Venice) but bustling and vital. Huneker's *New Cosmopolis* of 1915 is one of his best books, a paean to New York, "Intimate New York," with subjoined essays on certain European cities which not quite measure up — Vienna, Prague, Rotterdam, Brussels (and Bruges), Madrid, "dear dirty Dublin," and a resort, Marienbad, where the traveler has gone to fight fat. A coda is about "sand and sentiment," Atlantic City and Newport. Huneker then plundered and paraphrased the former of these for the Atlantic City episode of *Painted Veils,* describing the town — in its glory days — at night: "Miles of electric lamps up the boardwalk . . . a carnival of flame."

In *Painted Veils,* there are four major apostrophes to New York. The first, an isolated stab at the dead-city trope, is about the view Mona has from her "attic of dreams," her "Tower of Ebony": "a petrified Venice, a Venice overtaken by a drought eternal. Venice aerial, with cliff-dwellers in lieu of harmonious gondolas." The passage is lifted from *New Cosmopolis,* Huneker's own view of a nocturnal Madison Avenue. The next apostrophe is to the crepuscular New York seen from the balcony of Dora's apartment, "up on Lexington Avenue, somewhere in the nineties." The magic of New York begins to operate, and Ulick sees — unbelievably — the West Side Circle, "theatre-land," the bridges, the Avenues, "the moonlight mansions of Fifth Avenue," the synagogue opposite the park, the park itself, "a lake of velvety foliage," the Brooklyn side, Battery Place and the bay. The panorama, "the fantasy of an Oriental sorcerer," evoking "the long lost Atlantis," is taken from "Night Hath a Thousand Eyes" in *New Cosmopolis.* Before Easter's debut, Alfred, his eyes glistening with malice at the thought of the "rocky road" ahead of her, looks out at "the great White Way, more cosmopolitan than Piccadilly Circus, the Friedrichstraße, the Grand Boulevard." Moralizing, Alfred condemns "this City of Dis, this place where is worshipped the Goddess of Lubricity," and proceeds to the Met, to witness Easter's triumph. During the scene at the Vienna Café, where Broadway debouches into Union Square, Alfred is again ambiguous toward New York, "alternately hypnotic and repellent . . . Its specific beauty savors of the monstrous." Like Alfred, Huneker had his moments of fearing New York, and in a letter written on October 10, 1920, just before the publication of *Painted Veils,* he called it "vulgar and sinister." Yet, as noted, he favored it over European cities (only Toledo and Prague were "more dramatic"), and, once more through Alfred's thought, claimed it was "a picture of titanic energy, cyclopean ambition."

Huneker's affection for the city is attested to throughout the novel by references to real cafés, restaurants, hotels — from "the old Vienna Café next to Grace Church" (where Easter issues her fateful tea invitation to Mona, Ulick, and Milt) to Valkenberg's and to the Everett House; Moretti's is a favorite hangout and Delmonico's is not. The list of the places for food, drink, and entertainment is quite as detailed as de Maupassant's in *Bel-Ami* or *Fort comme la mort,* and Huneker, the admirer of energy, has the advantage over de Maupassant that the motorcar has been invented. After reading the manuscript for Huneker's publisher, the editor Burton Roscoe objected that the author had first said

Ulick was a nonsmoker and then had him smoking, decadently enough, Turk-ish cigarettes, and that high-powered automobiles were an anachronism for circa 1895. A little later in fictive time, the Dane Johannes V. Jensen, likewise energy-possessed, presents a New York filled with fast cars in *Madame D'Ora* (1904). (Jensen's Leontine D'Ora is a man-devouring opera singer. Did Hune-ker know about the novel? A German translation appeared in 1907.) In the finales of Otto Julius Bierbaum's *Prinz Kuckuck* (1907) and D'Annunzio's *Forse che sí, forse che no* (1910), Henry Felix Hauart and Paolo Tarsis, both lovers of machines and women, crash — the one dies smashing his racer into a wall, the other survives the landing of his burning monoplane, *L'Ardea,* the Heron, after a dawn flight over the Tyrrhenian Sea to Sardinia.

Huneker's own attitude toward his book was mixed. He boasted of the speed with which he had written, and was proud of the apparent obscenities, which were "but the final ejaculation of the verbal sperm"; a working title was "Painted Tails." All the same, he was nervous about the contents, deleting some six hundred words before publication. The "sex side was dealt with," he claimed, as by "a medical expert," and "the lascivious frills" were "merely frill." He doubted that he had accomplished his intention: "I started to write a psychological study of character. I did not succeed." Attempting to explain what he thought — or pretended to think — was the basic structure, he called it "music or nothing," a three-voice fugue with an elaborate coda; the three heroines, Easter, Mona, and Dora, were all "hot and hollow." The estimate is not quite correct; despite her absence for long stretches, Easter outshines the other two women through the energy (and evil) she shares with New York. Nonetheless, Huneker's strongest interest lies with Ulick, his exaggerated counterfeit, who is the novel's actual tie to an "elevated" decadent tradition; Easter is the spokeswoman of a more extravagant or vulgar decadence, as in the novels of Jean Lorrain and Heinrich Mann.

Painted Veils was preceded in the belated American outburst of an imitative decadence by James Branch Cabell's *Jurgen* (which Huneker thought "cold") and followed directly by George Jean Nathan's *Heliogabalus* (1920) and Ben Hecht's *Fantazius Mallare* (1922) and its sequel, *The Kingdom of Evil* (1924). At a more disciplined level of accomplishment, Carl Van Vechten's *Peter Whif-fle* (1922) was a refined spin-off of *Painted Veils;* Whiffle is the aimless and cultivated eponymous hero — like Ulick, living in New York and dying sud-denly at the novel's end; he has the job of distributing the obligatory Parisian and Huysmanian references. Of all these books, only *Painted Veils,* slapped together, remains alive in all its grotesqueness, a roman à clef less obsessive and more expansive than its hateful near-contemporary in the genre, Strind-berg's *Svarta fanor.*

23

Iceland

HALLDÓR KILJAN LAXNESS

Halldór Guðjónsson was born in Reykjavík on April 23, 1902; his father, Guðjón Helgi Helgason, had worked his way up from obscure beginnings to a position as road-building foreman. In 1903, the little family — Halldór was the first child and only son of Guðjón and Sigríður Halldórsdóttir — moved to a farm, Laxnes, outside the town; from it, Halldór eventually took Laxness as his pen and legal name. His childhood was extraordinarily happy, as he described it in *Í túninu heima* (1975, On the Home Meadow); his father, self-taught, was unusually cultured, and his mother and maternal grandmother, Guðný Klængsdóttir (whom he treasured because of the "pure" — i.e., un-Danicized — Icelandic she spoke and her store of folktales) were loving company during his father's long summer absences. He could be called a special or even pampered child, who managed to avoid farmwork in order to devote himself to his passions for nature, reading, and home music, his father's hobby, so that, for a while, his parents thought of a musical career for him. In the winter of 1915–16 he took lessons from an organist in Reykjavík; remarkably, he also wrote his first novel, *Afturelding* (Dawn), which has been lost. In the fragment *Heiman eg fór* (written 1924, I Left Home), the anonymous narrator tells how in the "not much less than a thousand pages" of *Afturelding* he attempted to imitate the style and the edifying message of Bjørnstjerne Bjørnson. The novel's intention was "to proclaim love as the most powerful force in the world." He was going on fifteen.

After some tutoring, Halldór took an entrance examination for the Menntaskólinn (gymnasium) in Reykjavík, attending in 1918–19, but discovered he was unsuited for formal education; in *Sjömeistarasagan* (1978, The Tale of Seven Masters), one of his autobiographical volumes, he gives unflattering portraits of some of his teachers. He led a much more profitable intellectual life in the town's cafés and literary circles. After his father's death, in June 1919, he traveled to continental Europe for the first time, leaving behind another novel, *Barn náttúrunnar* (Child of Nature) — the author called himself Halldór frá Laxnesi — which was published in October of the same year, while Halldór was in Copenhagen; he lodged there with an Icelandic businessman, an experience brought up with some irony in another autobiographical volume, *Úngur eg var* (1976, I Was Young), then went on to Sweden in the autumn, and in the city library of Hälsingborg discovered *Inferno,* August Strindberg's account of his mental and religious crisis in Paris in 1897. In the "Inferno" chapter of *Úngur eg var* he wrote: "Twenty-two years later, the book fell into my hands . . . Strange that five more years should pass before I found myself in the same situation . . . I actually wrote the same story as Strindberg . . . save that it was called *Vefarinn mikli frá Kasmír*" (The Great Weaver of Kashmir). Halldór returned to Denmark, to an estate in South Sjælland, "wandering in fields and forests," then, after spending Pentecost in Jämtland in Sweden, at last went back to Iceland by way of Norway in the summer of 1920. (How was this itinerary arranged and financed?) For a short time he worked unhappily as a teacher in eastern Iceland and composed another lost novel, *Salt jarðar* (Salt of the Earth); writing easily, he was careless with his manuscripts. By the spring of 1921 he was back in Reykjavík and spent the summer on the family farm; he produced a number of stories, collected and published in 1923 as *Nokkrar sögur* (Some Tales), of which four had first been written in Danish for the leading Copenhagen paper, *Berlingske Tidende;* a couple, "Kvæði" (Poem) and "Àsa," because of their sexual boldness, might be regarded as pale predecessors to scenes in *Vefarinn mikli frá Kasmír;* also, the occasional overstrained religious tone offers an inkling of what was to come in Halldór's life and in the main action of *Vefarinn.*

A second trip to the Continent was undertaken in 1921–22, to Germany — he was shocked by what he saw in inflation-ridden Berlin — and Austria; he was now at work on a large pamphlet, *Rauða kverið* (The Red Booklet), preserved but never published, in which, according to Peter Hallberg, the author of a basic study of *Vefarinn* (1954), he employs the ejaculatory style of Strindberg's *Inferno,* wallows in a pessimism influenced by the Norwegian impressionist Sigbjørn Obstfelder (1866–1900), absorbs the aggressive misogyny of Otto Weininger's (1880–1903) *Geschlecht und Charakter,* and is obsessed by a fear of death. In the second chapter of *Heiman eg fór*, the narrator says he gave the manuscript the German name, "Das rote Büchlein," "because it seemed to me unfitting to write about such important matters in anything but red ink, which stands for blood." From his Luxemburg cloister, to be described later, he told the Icelandic Jesuit Jón Sveinsson that the booklet's central figure at last "discovers prayer and its power." Yet seven years later, he confessed to his friend Stefán Einarsson that the booklet was just "the head-shakings of a fragile-nerved boy about the world's transitoriness and suchlike."

An embarrassing episode took place in April 1922: Halldór set sail from Hamburg (or Holland) for New York but, lacking American references and sufficient funds, was turned back at Ellis Island; he had intended to support himself by writing movie scenarios. (Undertaking the American adventure in 1927–29, he settling in Los Angeles, with the aid of Upton Sinclair.) His eye had been in America for some time; one of the twelve tales in *Nokkrar sögur,* "Júdith Lhoff," takes place partly amidst New York high society, with which the young author had had no contact at all. The summer was spent on the Danish island of Bornholm, where he again supported himself by writing for Danish newspapers.

According to the "Inferno" chapter in *Úngur eg var,* Laxness had been impressed by Strindberg's reading of the "youthful memoirs" of Johannes Jørgensen (1866–1956), the Danish impressionist poet and prosaist who had become a Roman Catholic in 1896: Jørgensen had stayed at a Benedictine monastery in Bavaria and written an apostrophe to the order's founder, Benedict of Nursia, in *Beuron* (1896). Never shy, Laxness wrote to Jørgensen, "a lighthouse shining in the darkness," and through him wangled an invitation to visit another Benedictine establishment, Saint Maurice de Clervaux, in Luxemburg; he arrived in December 1922. His diary from his stay, *Dagar hjá múnkum* (Days with the Monks) was published in 1987, with an introduction by Laxness, then eighty-five, which revealed that, while living on Bornholm as the guest of a Danish-Icelandic Catholic couple, the sculptor Julius Schou and his wife, he had fathered a child with an Icelandic woman "between twenty and thirty," employed in the Schou household. The introduction also contained a glowing tribute to Jørgensen, "the pioneer of neo-Catholic literature" in the North.

Halldór officially became Halldór Kiljan Laxness on the occasion of his Roman Catholic baptism and confirmation on January 6, 1923. The middle name was taken from Saint Kilian, an Irish missionary and the patron saint of Würzburg, who was martyred in 689; Laxness liked the sound of the name. To judge by the diary, which goes from February 14 to June 26, 1923, Laxness was quite happy in the monastery; he admired the superiors, the abbot Dom Alardo, to whom he looked up with "filial enthusiasm," his confessor, the German Beda Hessen (with whom Laxness could easily converse, the cloister being mostly Francophone), and the prior, Alexander Ely, who would appear as a major character in *Vefarinn*. He did a great deal of reading, was captivated by the Latin of Thomas à Kempis's *De imitatione Christi,* and very quickly mastered French, so that he was able to cope with Francis de Sales's *Introduction à la vie dévote*. "I gabble French and German one after the other, but am sad because I never have the chance to speak Icelandic." But he could speak Danish with a few members of the community. He was deeply moved by the sudden death of Bengt Ballin, the son of Jørgensen's great friend, the Danish Jewish convert Mogens Ballin. (Because of Laxness's passion for languages, the cloister was a linguistic playground for him.) All the while, he was at work on his new novel, which appeared in 1924 with the title *Undir Helgahnúk* (Beneath Holy Mountain), as well as on the never completed *Heiman eg fór*. Throughout his stay, he was attracted — fancying they had also cast an eye on him — to the young women he saw in church and in the streets of the village.

In October 1923, Laxness was made a Benedictine *oblatus secularis,* like Huysmans before him, and left the cloister for Paris, as the guest of Jón Sveinsson, who wrote children's books under the pseudonym of "Nonni"; Laxness saluted him first in an essay, "Við Nonni" in *Reisubókarkorn* (1950, Travel-Book Grist) and then in *Úngur eg var,* where he boasted that he seldom had to go hungry during his many travels. As an illustration, he gave the circumstances of his trip to Lourdes, paid for by a rich old lady in Paris, whose life he was supposed to save, "with the help of Ave Marias, alms, and candles lit at the exit of the grotto where the Mother of God had revealed herself . . . Although the fee for my efforts was paid in cash, the miracle unfortunately failed. The woman died. Instead, I used the money to attend the private school of the Jesuits at Osterly near London." His next station was St. Hugh's Charterhouse in Sussex, a stern Cistercian establishment, to which he went in would-be imitation of Alexander Ely, who had left Clervaux and its Benedictine comforts to become a novice in the Carthusian order. The rigors of St. Hugh's were too much for Laxness, and, "emaciated, sleepless, nervous, and morbid," he went home to Iceland by way of London and Bergen in the spring of 1924. The Icelandic stay turned out to be longer than he had planned; he intended to take an examination which would close off the gymnasium studies interrupted in 1919, but he failed to pass, and a second try was not made. Nothing if not aggressive, Laxness, undertaking to spread his new-found religion, debated with Þórbergur Þórðarson (1889–1974), who had attacked Catholicism in *Bréf til Láru* (1924, A Letter to Laura), a collection of autobiographical sketches and feigned epistles which became an Icelandic classic; in the brilliance of his style and the abrasiveness of his personality, Þórbergur was clearly a rival to Laxness, whose *Undir Helgahnúk* had received only mixed reviews, thereby causing Laxness to defend his "living thought" in the press. Laxness's pro-Catholic polemics were published in 1925 as *KaÞólsk viðhorf: Svar gegn árásum* (Catholic Point of View: Answer against Attacks).

Although Laxness's application for a travel grant was turned down by the First Chamber of the Icelandic AlÞing—only one vote was in his favor—he embarked on a third continental trip in May 1925, his supporters declaring that he had a great future but might well be lost for Icelandic letters. However, Laxness was now determined to write entirely in his native tongue, unlike predecessors who had used, and would use, more widely accessible languages, mostly Danish—the dramatist Jóhann Sigurjónsson (1880–1918), the dramatist and novelist Guðmundur Kamban (1888–1945), and the novelist Gunnar Gunnarsson (1889–1975); Laxness's Jesuit friend "Nonni" found his public in German. Laxness's first major stop was in Rome, to which he was drawn because 1925 was a Holy Year of Jubilee, when the pope granted a special indulgence to pious visitors. Also, the apostolic prefect for Iceland was in the Holy City at the same time, and through him the prize specimen of Icelandic Catholicism made contacts with "some of the leading men of the church." Laxness drew on his memories of the Holy Year in Book 2, chapter 9, of the historical novel *Íslandsklukkan* (1943–46, Iceland's Bell): the antiquarian Arne Arnaeus (Árni Magnússon) visits Rome in the Holy Year of 1700 on his search for codices from the Icelandic past. Back home in Iceland, Arne remembers: "We stopped before the basilica of St. Peter, and Rome's bells rang and the pope came out on his balcony with mitre and scepter as we sang the Te Deum. I had been looking for Icelandic books and been saddened for not having found them. I had found something else instead. The next day I left Rome." Arne Arnaeus's ambiguous words may be a comment on what Laxness experienced.

After Rome, Laxness went on to Taormina in Sicily, and stayed until the end of September, working on *Vefarinn mikli frá Kasmír*. A passage in the afterword to the second edition (1948) tells, comically, about how, "in one of the hottest spots in Europe," he turned night into day and "let [his] pen go," as, wearing nothing but a monocle, he held a cane in one hand as a protection against insects. (Monocle and cane are not unimportant: young Laxness, as photographs show, had a good deal of the dandy about him.) On the way north from Sicily he visited Rome again, apparently without much enthusiasm, arriving at Clervaux on October 21 and staying there until the beginning of April 1926. The great event of the second cloister stay was the taking of supplementary vows as *oblatus secularis*. In Los Angeles, on January 30,

1929, he wrote an essay, "Trú" (Belief), which he included in *Alþýðubókin* (The People's Book) the same year. "After two and a half years' absence, I stood once again at the cloister gate of Clervaux, like a deranged woman looking for her child. Of course, the gate was forever shut for my soul. But although I knew that henceforth 'the sounds were closed,' Father Beda's embrace would be open for me." (Laxness quotes, melodramatically, a famous line from Snorri Sturluson's *Heimskringla*, repeated in Adam Oehlenschläger's Romantic tragedy, *Hakon Jarl* and in Ibsen's *Lady from the Sea*.) Father Beda showed great understanding for Laxness's loss of his new faith; they talked about "the heavenly light which shines on Christians and heathens alike." Beda's last words to the failed Catholic were: " 'Wir sehen uns später anderswo, wenn nicht hier.' " Laxness never lost the admiration he felt for the monks he had met in the cloister, "truly a place for seeking souls. But when I told [Beda] farewell, I said farewell to myself to begin a new life. Perhaps this departure was the greatest event of my life." Before April was over, Laxness was home, seeking a publisher for his manuscript; he gave a public reading from it that attracted a good-sized audience, considering that he had to compete with the Whitsuntide horse races.

In Laxness's oeuvre, *Vefarinn mikli frá Kasmír* has been overshadowed by the major novels of the next decades, all set in Iceland: *Salka Valka*, about a fisher girl (1931–32), the international success *Sjálfstætt fólk* (1934–35), the tetralogy on the peasant poet Ólafur Kárason (1937–40), whose collective title was *Heimsljós*, and *Íslandsklukkan*, inspired in part by Iceland's achievement of complete independence from Denmark in 1944. In 1955, Laxness was awarded the Nobel Prize for Literature; the Swedish Academy's citation read: "For his pictorial epics, which renewed the great Icelandic art of narration." The majority of Laxness's novels has appeared in Danish and German; in English, *Salka Valka* came out in 1936, *Independent People* in 1945–46, and *World Light* in 1964, as well as *Atómstöðin* (1948), as *The Atom Station*, in 1961, about an Iceland threatened by Americanization after the Second World War, *Gerpla* (1952, *The Happy Warriors*, 1958), a burlesque reconstruction of the saga world, *Brekkukotsannáll* (1957, *The Fish Can Sing*, 1966), about singers, the search for perfection, and personal vanity, *Paradísarheimt* (1960, *Paradise Reclaimed*, 1962), much of which is set in Mormon Utah, and *Kristnihald undir jökli* (1968, *Christianity at Glacier*, 1972), a Christian picaresque with elements of Jules Verne's *Voyage au centre de la terre*, among others. *Vefarinn mikli frá Kasmír* was translated into Danish in 1975 and German in 1988, but an English translation has never appeared; according to the biography by Halldór Guðmundsson (2002), a translation, on deposit in Iceland's National Library, was made by Laxness with the aid of an anonymous friend, during the author's stay in California. Largely set in Europe, full of references to European literature of the twenties, as well as the fin de siècle, the novel does not fit the Laxness picture the Anglophone world has long since formed.

Laxness's two extant novels from before *Vefarinn* have some bearing on what was to come. *Barn náttúrunnar* is a short, sentimental tale of love lost and abruptly regained; its subtitle is *Ástarsaga* (Love Story). Randver Ólafsson has made money in America, but he remains dissatisfied; to the wise old peasant, Stefán í Hólum, he paraphrases Matthew 16:26: " 'Somewhere it is asked in what way it profits a man, although he possesses all the world, if he suffers harm to his soul.' " Also, he has become a woman-hater, because of some cruel disappointment, but he is smitten again, with Hulda, the child of nature of the title, who has been allowed by her father to grow up in total freedom. Randver decides to lead the simple life of a farmer, Hulda wants to see the great world of "the South," and they break up; Randver falls prey to alcohol, and Hulda, quickly finding another man, is about to leave Iceland, but she chances to see Randver: "His features were in some part the same, despite the deformities caused by drink and suffering." Miraculously, she returns to Randver, and the novel—the work of an adolescent—ends with an exchange of prayers, Randver crying: " 'Heavenly Father! Give us our daily bread!' " and Hulda, in tears as she looks skyward: " 'And forgive us our trespasses!' "

Undir Helgahnúk was a marked improvement yet likewise had a spiritual finale; it was written in the cloister. The prelude—printed in smaller type than the body of the novel—concerns two Icelandic friends who study for the Lutheran clergy in Copenhagen. Out of a sense of obligation, Snjólfur Ásgrímsson marries a Danish-American widow with whom he has had sexual relations and leaves for America with his bride. Kjartan Einarsson undertakes half-hearted sculptural studies in Rome, falls into bad company, returns to Copenhagen as a tramp, and is saved by his devoted mother, who makes him finish his theological training and finds a wife for him. All this is told with great speed; in an introduction to the first edition of 1924, Laxness wrote that the book about Snjólfur and Kjartan had "stopped at a preliminary stage, and would not be presented to the public in its entirety . . . If this preparatory work is ever completed, at any event [it will not happen] during the next seven years." (Laxness alludes to his plans to study for the Roman Catholic priesthood.) However, in the novel's second and much longer part, some essential details about the characters of the first part are added. Kjartan becomes the pastor of a church at the foot of Holy Mountain in northern Iceland. There he is joined by Snjólfur who, widowed, has returned from the United States to become the overseer of the lonely church's farm. The fragile bride of the rough and undependable Kjartan, Johanne, eventually goes mad and hangs herself.

Johanne's only surviving child is Atli Kjartansson; encouraged by his mother while she lives, young Atli is greatly gifted: "a tireless reader of books he understood and did not understand," gulping down "Brandes and Ibsen, Strindberg and Kierkegaard, Bjørnson, Jacobsen, and the big book about the origin of the species." His principal comrade is Áslaug, the daughter of Snjól-fur and his late wife. The chaste and pious Áslaug is contrasted with Anna, a buxom seamstress who awakens Atli's sexual desires and causes a nightmare in which he is saved from the forces of evil. In another dream, the king of the elves offers Atli "the stone of power" in exchange for his own heart, and he accepts; when he awakes, he finds a red, heart-shaped stone in his pocket, a sign of his election, and a sign that Laxness has read Wilhelm Hauff's "Das kalte Herz." The evening before Atli leaves for study in Reykjavík, he meets Áslaug, riding on a white horse, and to her proclaims what the future has in store for him, as he showed her the little heart of stone. " 'Áslaug, imagine — if generation after generation had to kneel in reverence at my name, as men today kneel at the memory of Napoleon.' " Áslaug seizes the stone and, with the silver cross hanging from her neck, scratches the word 'Jesus' on it. Atli tries to scrape the name away with his pocket knife, but cuts himself badly and grows frightened; Áslaug staunches the flow of blood, and asks him to sing the folksong, "Ólafur reið med björgum fram" (Olaf rode along the rocks), in which Ólafur resists the forces of evil. She joins in: " 'I will not dwell with the elves . . . rather I place my trust in Christ." and " 'If I turn my song to the cross/ . . . Blessed Mary be with us,' " a grand finale, to which something operatic attaches. *Vefarinn* will semiquote from *Der fliegende Holländer,* and Laxness must have known *Tannhäuser.*

The novel or novella begun in the autumn of 1924 in Iceland, but never finished, *Heiman eg fór,* was first printed in 1952. According to Laxness's introduction, his friend Stefán Einarsson, from Johns Hopkins, had found it "long ago," "somewhere southward in Europe," among "some trash [Lax-ness] had left behind with French monks when [he] was young," thus during his second visit to Clervaux. He finished twenty-five chapters but abandoned the project on realizing that the presence of two protagonists in the work, the anonymous narrator and Steinn Elliði, the superior being the narrator first meets in chapter 11, was a fatal flaw. It was a "self-portrait from youth, a young man's *Dichtung und Wahrheit,* about the puppy years up to the age of seventeen." The title is taken from the second of Blind Gestr's riddle-poems in *Hervarar saga og Heiðreks:* "I left home, from home I made a journey." In the first chapter, the narrator — read Laxness — remembers how, "at Christmas three years ago," he was in a drafty summer hotel in the Alps, working on *Das rote Büchlein;* now, soon to be twenty-two, he calls himself a pilgrim. There are many autobiographical details in the first ten chapters: the narrator, twelve years old, decides that his father's faith, "the one true Lutheran faith," is non-sense (at which his patient father smiles sadly); his attitudes toward women are complex, in that he has learned from "some book" that they stand lower than men on the scale of humanity, but the nearness of feminine beings is disturbing. Like Faust, he finds the opening of Genesis difficult to understand (does he imply that he has already read Goethe's dramatic poem?); he has an intimate relation to nature ("The world is like a maiden's bed"); he has a dog he loved as much as any human.

Chapters 11 to 25 take place in Reykjavík and environs. The country boy meets Steinn Elliði and is immediately impressed by the latter's gifts, his so-phistication, and not least, his very appearance, repeatedly described: tall, slender, broad-shouldered, glasses in one hand and hat in the other, "as the air blew through his reddish-brown wavy hair, [he had] a slightly arched fore-head, a slightly bent nose and a mouth more beautiful than any I had ever seen." "I scarcely reached up to his shoulder; he ruled the conversation and talked about a great many things." Steinn is a dandy: his cane is of ebony, ending in a silver tip, his coat is belted, his boots shine, and his trousers have sharp creases. Elliði invites the dazzled boy to give a lecture to a literary club, the Milky Way, which he does in chapter 14; the narrator's appearance is quite unlike the magnificent Steinn's: "Can one imagine a more comical sight than a sixteen-year-old whelp who knows everything? Tall and thin, his face white, his blond hair combed back, he was wearing a striped suit and new shoes, his navy blue hands sticking out of his stiffly starched cuffs." His lecture is an attack on the cult of the sagas and the stultifying effect it has had on modern Icelandic literature and life. "Everywhere the old folks lay their hand on our national life"; "What greater evidence of our national decay than seeking [our] special qualities hundreds of years in the past?"; "The principal virtues of the golden age were courage and bellicosity"; "As far as I'm concerned, there is no more tiresome piece of writing than the Heimskringla of Snorri"; "*Marie Grubbe* of J. P. Jacobsen is a far better book than *Njáls saga,* [for] here a far deeper and more intelligent spirit is at work." Laxness has the farmboy ex-press the author's own opinion at the time; he disliked the saga tradition and meant, by means of the gestating *Vefarinn,* to bring Icelandic literature into the twentieth century.

The shy narrator and Steinn blend briefly into one; Steinn has already told him that " 'the turn has come to our people and they must recognize the hour of their calling; for this country, the major works of the century can be awaited in literature and art, as truly as I live'." Another figure may be in the mix as well. At a dinner in Book 7 of *Vefarinn,* Steinn, asked by a guest to name his favorite poet, says "David," whom the shocked lady directly identifies as

David frá Fagraskógi, David Stefánsson (1895–1964), a poet whom Halldór met during his year at the gymnasium. An essay by Laxness on David described him as he looked during their schooldays: "our great and elegant man, recently come home from abroad, tall and broad-shouldered, . . . and, if memory serves, with a cane and a bowler, with glasses, which were necessary in those days" — in other words, Steinn in *Heiman eg fór.*

A striking woman has been present in the audience at the Milky Way lecture, "in the best years, with a wise and friendly child's face, dark hair, a soft, round form, and shining eyes." Her name is Svala, and the narrator is introduced to her through Steinn at a soirée in her home (her husband is invisible), as well as to the equally wise and mysterious Master Ásgrímur, a veritable magus, according to Steinn. (Ásgrímur is patterned on Erlundur Guðmundsson í Unuhúsi [1892–1947], a legendary figure in Reykavík intellectual life, a nonproductive inspirer and mentor of the young Laxness, who gave portraits of him in *Reisubókarkorn* and in *Sjömestarasagan;* Fru Svala may be a portrait of Erlundur's mother, shown much younger. The narrator falls in platonic love with Svala and directs a Catholicizing eulogy to her: "I'll never forget you, the mother, the maiden, the angel image in your eyes," the sacred woman "who has given the world nothing and everything to God." On an excursion to the hills, they commune with nature together; at dawn they return to her house: "A little after sunrise, everyone was still asleep, save that a few roosters began to crow. And we looked silently at our shadows in the street, like fairy forms in the morning light." Here, *Heiman eg fór* breaks off. Svala does not appear in the misogynistic *Vefarinn,* and the narrator disappears as well. As for Steinn, in chapter 19 Ásgrímur and the narrator seek him out as his rooms. The Master enters first, and two girls emerge; the kindly Master attempts to get Steinn, intoxicated, to bed, and is cursed for his pains. The disillusioned narrator sees no more of Steinn.

The title of *Vefarinn mikli frá Kasmír* remains something of a puzzle. In response to an inquiry by Hallberg, Laxness answered that he had in mind the old tale of "the great weaver with the wisdom of twelve kings" and that, wanting to choose some exotic place instead of mundane Reykjavík, he picked Kashmir because of the fame of its weavings. There may have been other sources: in 1914, Rabindranath Tagore's translations of one hundred poems of Kabir (ca. 1440–1518) appeared, a mystic whose name means "great" in Arabic. Tagore, who had won the Nobel Prize for Literature in 1913, was much admired by Laxness; in the Clervaux diary for February 15, 1923, he reported that he was "enchanted by Tagore," and he praised Tagore's *Gitanjali* in the first edition of *Vefarinn.* Kabir was actually from Benares (Varanasi), called by its ancient name of Kasi, which may have suggested the more poetic and better-known Kashmir to Laxness. In the novel, "the great weaver of Kashmir" functions as a source of inspiration and object of identification for Steinn Elliði. Boasting to the girl Diljá (Book 1, chap. 7), he claims: "My bread and wine are God's splendor in the countenance of things, the Lord's image and God's coin. I am the son of Tao in China, the perfect yogi in India, the great weaver from Kashmir, the snake charmer in the valley of the Himalayas, the saint of Christ in Rome." Haranguing the monk Alban during their chance meeting on the train in Book 3, chapter 33, he boasts: "'My soul is like Kashmir, the vale of roses, I have been provided with a splendid gift and, what's more, the urge to use it.'" But he loses confidence in his weaving: writing to Alban from London at New Year's of 1925 (Book 3, chap. 43), he reports on the failure of his efforts and mankind's to achieve greatness as he quotes a chorus from Swinburne's *Atalanta in Calydon:* "He weaves and is clothed with derision,/sows, but he will not reap." (In the first edition "Swinburne" is Icelandicized into "Sveinbjörn," whereas in subsequent editions he is not named at all.) In Taormina (Book 5, chap. 58), contemplating suicide, Steinn thinks about himself that "he had been born in Kashmir, in the vale of roses, with a harp in his hand like the gods"; now the connection with the great weaver of Kashmir is used by Steinn for self-abasement: one day he awoke from his playing of the harp and saw himself. Beneath his feet the roses had withered and dried. When in Book 6 he arrives, dirty and disheveled, at Alban's cloister in Belgium, "the rain washed the dye out of his cap and ran brown over his face. The great weaver of Kashmir." Steinn has hardly lived up to his wonderful vision.

Like H. H. Richardson, who opens the last book of *Maurice Guest* with a despairing tag from the *Inferno,* Laxness chose an epigraph from Canto XVIII of the *Paradiso,* the words of Cacciaguida to Dante: "Ma nondimen, rimossa ogni menzogna, tutta tua vision fa manifesta," and so forth (11.127–132): "But nonetheless, every lie put aside,/let your whole vision be made plain/and let the salt sting where it scratches!/For if our voice will be unfriendly/at the first taste, it will give/true nourishment when digested," which can be taken as a recantation of the ascetic Catholicism of the novel's cruel ending. (Laxness does not bother to translate for his Icelandic readers.) For the rest, Laxness gives his novel, almost mechanically, somewhat the same structure as the *Divine Comedy* in dividing it into one hundred chapters of widely disparate lengths, distributed over eight books.

Chapters 1 to 10 of Book 1 are set at the summer villa (outside Reykjavík and near Þingvellir, the historical meeting place of the Icelandic Alþing) of the rich and powerful Ylfing family, the owners of a great shipping firm. (Betraying more knowledge of Old Norse literature than his hostility would lead one to expect, Laxness took the name from a family of kings, the Ylfingur, in the Hyndla Song of the Poetic Edda.) The members assembling at the Ylfingabúd, the House of Ylfing, are the widowed maternal grandmother Valgerður, of an old family and a conservative turn of mind; her ward Diljá, whose mother died in childbirth and her father during the influenza epidemic of 1918; her sons Grímúlfur Ellidason, an obsessive businessman, and Örnólfur, who runs the concern during Grímúlfur's many trips abroad; Grímúlfur's consumptive and neglected wife, Jófríður, and their son Steinn Ellidi, "something over eighteen," described in an expansion of what Laxness had set down in *Heiman eg fór*—in his face were "cold ruthlessness, impudence, even shamelessness." (The significance of his first name, Steinn, "Rock," becomes clear in the finale at St. Peter's basilica. "Ellidi" is altogether appropriate for the shipping family, a word for 'ship' in Old Norse, come into popular parlance in the nineteenth century as the almost human ship feminized into Ellida in Esaias Tegnér's international success *Frithiofs saga* (1825), and as the name of Ellida Wangel in *The Lady from the Sea*.) The date of the opening, 1920, is easily calculated, and Steinn shares his birth year with Laxness. Diljá recalls that Steinn was twelve and she ten when they first met; Steinn and his mother had been abroad (as they often were) when they were forced to return home by the outbreak of the First World War. Now Steinn is eighteen, and Grímúlfur, Jófríður and he are about to go abroad again. During chapters 5 through 10, Steinn and Diljá, whose admiration for Steinn is boundless, go for a walk, starting at one in the morning, over Þingvellir.

About his imminent departure Steinn says, "in his old, peremptory, ruthless voice," that he is " 'happy as an American boxer' " (Jack Dempsey?) or " 'as Douglas Fairbanks, who from sheer ecstasy jumps over fences and grins like a horse,' " as Diljá listens patiently to the first of Steinn's many self-explanatory tirades in the novel. He informs her that he will never marry, quoting John Tanner ("Marriage is an ignominious capitulation") in Shaw's *Man and Superman*. Women are a lower order; making a neat reduction of thoughts from Otto Weininger, he grants that " 'women may have a soul,' " but no man cares whether they have souls or not. He himself has suffered from *cupiditas carnis* (already, Steinn likes to sprinkle his conversation with ecclesiastical Latin) but has chosen the spiritual way, *spiritus adversus carnem*. He lost his virginity at twelve, to a "disgusting woman" in the laundry room. (Not at all shy, he asks Diljá if she has heard rumors of his subsequent sexual excesses, known to his friends but not his mother, for whom he has always been the good child.) To impress Diljá, he goes on to the climax of his erotic adventures; the past spring, while his parents were away in the north, he systematically debauched the housemaid Helga, having found the keys to the liquor cabinet. After eight days, God spoke to him in his exhaustion through the beauty of Iceland's nature. As the sun rises, he now declaims to Diljá—a replay of the claims of Atli in *Undir Helgahnúk*—that he is "mighty" and believes he can achieve world power; he has found Christianity, his life will be a song of praise to Christ, and God has told him that, if he is chaste, he can introduce a new phase in world literature, like Dante Alighieri. At great length, he exacts a corresponding vow of chastity from Diljá, albeit he may not see her again. (She has been lying prone before him, burying her face in the spring grass, "itself bursting with fruitfulness, . . . already a woman made to be the mother of generations.") God is called on to witness their mutual vows.

Book 2 consists, in chapters 11–19, of letters by Diljá, never sent; much information can be gleaned from them about the adolescent Steinn—his studied cruelty to cats and birds (of which Diljá, despite her admiration, cannot approve), his musical talent as a pianist, composer, and singer (he sings like Caruso), his phenomenal gift for languages (he can read Unamuno and Pirandello in the original), and his knowledge of poetry: he attempted to give her a sense of the invalidity of existence by having her read Shelley's sonnet about painted veils. The family has evidently made an immediate postwar trip to the Continent after the armistice, when Steinn was seventeen, Diljá fifteen. On his return, he was a full-fledged dandy (he wore a checked summer suit and a green necktie, and his collar had a shape Diljá had never seen before), the waves in his hair looked as if they had been painted, and he smoked perfumed cigarettes. Also, after his days in Madrid and Barcelona, Paris and London, he brought back literary news, recited whole pages of Max Jacob, Mayakovsky, and Marinetti, talked about André Breton, Philippe Soupault, and Ilya Ehrenburg, and was attracted by the redemptive power of the Russian Revolution. The catalogue is intended to impress Diljá, who has never heard the names, even as Laxness means to impress his public. Samples of Steinn's (and Laxness's) own modernist poetry are presented (chap. 18), which Laxness then recycled in *Kvæðakver* (1931, Song Book). In her innocence, Diljá sets down (chap. 19) six *Märchen*, with fairy-tale themes of her own, which Steinn will never see.

The epistolary narrative form is continued in chapters 20–27, Jófríður's giant letter to Diljá from Naples in 1922; she reports on Steinn's activities during the previous year, as far as she knows them. Mother and son have gone to Brighton, and Steinn has fallen under the spell of Carrington, "a little old man with a white linen suit and a bright red face"; they continue to Naples, but Steinn directly abandons his mother to return to England and his mentor Carrington. Jófríður gives Diljá the story of her icy marriage to Grímúlfur ("a businessman and no lover"), Steinn's birth, her tuberculosis—she is sent away from her beloved baby to Nice and begins her flirtations with diplomats and artists. On a trip to Spain when Steinn is seven (thus 1909), she and Grímúlfur separate, although he supports her in style. She hovers on the brink of an affair with the South American José ("'Cuando?'" is his question) but sends him away, aware of little Steinn's presence in the next room: she continues to seek for a "mèta profetata fuori del mondo," "a prophecied goal beyond the world," one of Laxness's quotations from the modernist Massimo Bontempelli. Like mother, like son, as far as quotations are concerned; but she or Laxness misremembers the content of Baudelaire's "Invitation au voyage." Reunited with Grímúlfur, who takes her back to Iceland's lukewarm diurnal life, vague piety, lies, and hypocrisy, she regrets "having cast away the chalice of pleasure, which only sin can offer." Appalled, Diljá can read no more of Jófríður's confession, written on rose-red stationery, and goes out to look for mementos of Steinn, who alone, in Diljá's eyes, knows "what was true and what was false." The caretaker admits her to Grímúlfur's town house, and she remembers the days when Steinn and she sang and played together, Grieg's setting of an Ibsen poem ("Jeg kaldte dig mit lykkebud,/jeg kaldte dig min stjerne"), Schubert ("Leise flehen meine Lieder" is quoted in German, "Der Doppelgänger" in Icelandic), and Massenet's "Élégie" and its refrain: "Ô, doux printemps d'autrefois, vertes saisons,/Vous avez fui pour toujours!" Laxness's art of the quotation becomes effectively sentimental.

The third book goes back a little in time, to the fall of 1921; having left his mother in Naples, Steinn is en route on the Rome-Paris express to England (chaps. 30–32). At Modena, the border station, a new traveler enters Steinn's compartment, whom Steinn recognizes by his dress as a member of a Catholic order, a deduction confirmed when the traveler begins to read his breviary — he is an imposing figure, "the form of whose hand and features leaves no doubt about the outstanding characteristics of his personality." Steinn has never before sat in the presence of a man sustained by Christian asceticism, he cannot restrain himself and begins an extended declaration in which he informs the monk concerning his own enormous Catholic reading — Newman's *Loss and Gain,* about a conversion at Oxford, the three volumes of apologetics by the theologian Weiss, which he says are "mediocre enough to be regarded as logical and noble," Bossuet (" 'of whom I must regrettably say that he is only a clever fool' "), and Pascal, who arouses his abhorrence. Of "aesthetic writers" Steinn has read Huysmans, Henri Bordeaux, Paul Bourget, "all unimportant petits bourgeois with the exception of Huysmans," René Bazin, Léon Blois, Ambroise Marsis, Robert Hugh Benson, Hilaire Belloc, G. K. Chesterton, Johannes Jørgensen. By means of his customary showing-off, Steinn attempts to bait the monk; Laxness was in fact an admirer of Bordeaux and Bourget. " 'Recently I finished the new book of Papini's *Storia di Cristo,* which of course is nothing but flowery babbling and chatter, and stylistically a step backward from *Un uomo finito,* ' " i.e., the *Story of Christ,* which became an international best-seller on its appearance in 1921, and the autobiographical *The Failure* of 1912. Again, Laxness in reality admired both books. The monk responds to Steinn's provocations with diplomacy: " 'It is a pleasure to converse with such a well-read man.' " Steinn continues his lecture: the New Testament is the most important book he has ever read, the ironist and unbeliever Renan's *Vie de Jésus* the most unimportant. The monk's "charming, embarrassed smile" is taken by Steinn as an encouragement to forge ahead, with a discourse about the church's reaction to political and social radicalism, in which he inquires whether Catholicism, in its acceptance of social injustice, has not " 'played the fiddle for two thousand years while Rome burned.' " Deftly ironizing Steinn's bumptiousness, the narrator observes that Steinn was accustomed, at home, to convince his audience within five minutes, and "he would not have been surprised if the monk had thrown off his soutane and cried, 'Eviva la bandiera rossa.' " The monk goes on smiling, not thinking it worth his trouble to defend Christian culture against the "hothead from the North."

Steinn shifts direction: he is not a Communist, he is on his way to England to visit a friend, Carrington, professor of classics at an Indian university, currently spending three years in his homeland, just as Steinn means to spend three years working on his personal perfection. Slowly, Steinn runs down, and the monk defines for him the nature of *his* faith, which demands not works of literature (Steinn plans to write fifty poems in English about God) but the soul itself for God. " 'Your gifts are of no value to me,' says the Lord," and the monk — as handy with a quotation as Steinn — cites St. Bonaventura's "quantum unusquisque est in oculis tuis, domine, tantum est et non amplius" (however much a being is in your eyes, oh Lord, thus much is he worth and not more), and, in Icelandic, Francis of Assisi: "You are what you are in God's eyes, and not a jot more." Steinn realizes at last that the monk is "not a lamb but an eagle"; he has met his match, and a tone of desperate pleading for grace enters his voice. He falls silent as the monk informs him that "one thing is worth more than all else, *la vie spirituelle,* the labor for grace in the heart of man." To Steinn, the monk seems a mighty maple, planted thousands of years ago, Steinn is but a stick that a tramp has plunged into the ground. Steinn also takes comfort in a story from Hinduism — learned from Carrington? — to the effect that the monk is a "two-thousand-year-old master, speaking on behalf of the highest spirit," and he, Steinn, is King Arjuna. Thus Laxness expects his readership to know that the conversation on the train has re-created the dialogue between the divine charioteer and the monarch in the *Bhagavad-Gita,* about the necessity of following spiritual duty, without regard for the result. The monk gets off the train as Steinn is asleep, leaving his card in Steinn's pocket: "Fr. Alban, moine bénédictin, Sept Fontaines, Belgique."

From Sussex in the summer of 1924, Steinn writes a long letter to Frater Alban (chapters 33–42). The chronology is not consecutive; the giant letter is preceded by events — of which Steinn is unaware — in Iceland, recounted in Book 4. Carrington, "this English bulldog," "this colonial hyena," "has gone to hell to preach to the captive spirits, the Indians in the British empire's rat traps," and has left his house in Hounslow at Steinn's disposal. Steinn now attempts to find a "fixed point" in his life; he compares himself to the Flying Dutchman or Ahasuerus, and quotes a whole stanza from the seamen's chorus in *Der fliegende Holländer* — or rather re-creates one; as given by Laxness, the stanza does not appear in the libretto. He has abandoned the great project of the fifty poems about God at number twenty-eight; Carrington has purloined them and had them printed, and reviewers call them masterpieces. Steinn wishes to be a poet no longer; artists are erotomaniacs, and the introduction to *Dorian Gray* claims no moral standards (Wilde said, "No artist has ethical sympathies"). Instead, Steinn has seen the vanity of human life, and quotes from the Psalms (Vulgate, 143:4) to prove it: "Homo vanitati similis factus est . . . Dies ejus sicut umbra praetereunt," "Man is like to vanity, his days pass away as a shadow." Yet man still has a task to do on earth — Steinn quotes from the "Vorspiel auf dem Theater" in *Faust,* the clown's words, "Greif [nur] hinein ins volle Menschenleben," and from 1 Corinthians, 6:15: "Know ye not that your bodies are the members of Christ?" After demonstrating the falseness of the patriotic goals of the Great War, Steinn proclaims that he is "one of these great, strong men the world needs to carry on a battle against the foes of humanity," a reprise and extension of what Atli Kjartansson said about himself. He is ready to have every tenth person in the world beheaded if circumstances demand it, he will be deceitful, he will appear as a man of God with a dagger concealed in his crucifix — an allusion to the crafty Jesuit Hieronymus in the Finlander Zachris Topelius's historical cycle, *Fältskärns berättelser* (Tales of a Field Surgeon).

But the great man must be chaste, as Steinn told poor Diljá on Þingvellir: "The chaste man is married to his ideal." Correspondingly, Steinn indulges in a lengthy denigration of women (chaps. 38–41), listing with examples — such as dancers beheld in Paris and in Rome, in *pose orridamente oscene* — the temptations presented by the sex, which appeal to the evil in man's nature, a passage again inspired by Strindberg and Weininger — a misogynistic carpet into which, along with much else, Steinn manages to weave an example from Nordic home ground, Jóhann Sigurjónsson's Dano-Icelandic stage hit of 1911, *Bjærg-Eyvind og hans hustru (Eyvindur of the Mountains,* 1961), which had been turned into a Swedish silent film by Victor Sjöström (1918): a man and his mistress come to hate one another as they starve in the wintry mountains. In Steinn's interpretation: "Man loves woman and will love woman only because of her sexual organs, as Dr. Weininger puts it, so frankly and brutally that I don't wish to quote it directly," sparing the monk's blushes.

In the letter's London continuation at New Year's 1925 (chaps. 43–46), Steinn excoriates humanity as a whole: "It is madness to want to struggle for the future or the happiness of humanity," thereby coming up with a statement that aroused much horror or prurient excitement when the book appeared. "I have tried all winter long to develop three urges in myself, namely homosexuality, drug addiction, the drive to suicide. In these three passions I see the highest ideals of humanity. Humanity can have no higher ideal than dying out." And: "I despise human beings as I do myself. I amuse myself by catching infants on my bayonet and, like European soldiers in Africa, by smashing the teeth of raped Negresses with the heel of my boot." After inserting the strophe from Swinburne's *Atalanta,* Steinn asks: "What other goal should mankind have than satisfying its passions and dying. *Il piacere è la sola virtù,*" Steinn's citation of a D'Annunzian-sounding maxim, taken, according to the first edition, from Bontempelli. Worse comes. At seventeen (thus on the first postwar trip of 1919) he took part in Spanish and French "nocturnal orgies," at which naked women, painted from top to toe, "performed lesbian dances for show [and] leaped on gigantic Negroes, who lay tied on the divan, and the whole company lay embracing on the floor." "Homosexuality is the most innocent of all means of sexual satisfaction, since it does not lead to the catastrophe of a new human being's birth." (The marquis de Bradomín, in one of his rare dark hours, posited a similar praise of homosexuality.) Laxness's own attitude toward homosexuality was mixed. At Clervaux, he met the Danish cultural philosopher and world traveler Konrad Simonsen (1875–1945) and talked with Simonsen about the latter's forthcoming monograph, *Dostojevsky* (1924); he already knw Simonsen's *Den moderne Mennesketype* (1917), which demanded a new idealism from corrupt mankind. "Simonsen was one of the most entertaining men I have known. He did not hide his homosexuality and on that account gave the new monks a cartload of chocolates the day he was baptized," an example of the lightheartedness with which Laxness treated his cloister experience in *Skáldatími* (1963, Poet's Hour).

Those who would help mankind are "foolish martyrs" and come to ludicrous ends: old Tolstoy wandered off from Yasnaya Polyana to die in a railroad station, Nietzsche went mad in Turin and believed he was Christ on the cross, Strindberg went insane on his deathbed, crying, "O ave, crux, spes unica." As usual, Steinn depends on a battery of quotations to shore up his arguments — the Italian modernist Fausto Martini's "Chi siete voi [due] che uscite dall' eterno silenzio" (Who are you [two] who issue forth from the eternal silence?), from the novel *Il cuore che m'hai dato* (1925), Nietzsche's cry to death, "Gieb, ja ergieb, grausamster Feind, mir — dich," and a strophe from Philippe Soupault: "And so the sun will disappear,/and earth's dust will pass away./And all will turn to nothing,/and world will be no more" in Icelandic. The first edition attributes the translation to Þórbergur Þórðarsson. At the start of chapter 46, Steinn utters his own cry to the monk: "Where shall I refresh my soul?" No refuge can be found: "I prefer a jazz band to angelic harps, Tivoli and Luna Park to Paradise . . . I could vomit thinking about the chosen [in Heaven], nothing but simple folk, *bonhommes,* peasants who have never heard of Anatole France, Gabriele D'Annunzio, or Marcel Proust." Nevertheless, with an unexpected turn, Steinn claims that no paradise exists, here or yonder, as wondrous as an Icelandic valley — a yearning for the long forgotten homeland which will return *in extenso.* The great letter ends with an apostrophe, in Icelandic, to nature in Iceland, "the mountains shining and adorned."

Book 4 takes place in Iceland, in the winter before Steinn's tormented Sussex and London letter. On a clear, cold February day, Örnólfur, the director of the Ylfing firm, returns from a trip abroad and is met by the matriarch Valgerður and Diljá. He has seen Steinn in London and Grímúlfur in Le Havre, but he has forgotten to ask about Jófríður. Steinn, he reports with satisfaction, is busy as a poet, "with dirty cuffs," "stuck up to his ears in Marxism." The brief Book 4 is the tale, without quotations or other learned apparatus, of Örnólfur's love for the much younger Diljá, now twenty; when she was six and he was attending the last year of gymnasium, he taught her to read. Following his engineer's examination in 1915, he became the effective, energetic, and hard-handed director of Ylfing's shipping activities but, in doing so, sacrificed any emotional life. Örnólfur cannot deny that he detests Steinn as a "lying monster," "the poet who has put himself in the service of lies." Diljá admits that she thinks of Örnólfur as a great man within the Icelandic sphere; the Ylfing blood is active within him, as in his nephew; both are ruthless and desire to rule. But Örnólfur has carried out his plans for Iceland's economy in order to win Diljá's love. Diljá herself, to keep up with distant Steinn, has become a modern girl, reading Rolland's *Jean-Christophe* and wearing her blond hair shingled, in a boy's haircut.

In London (Book 5), Steinn receives the last of many letters sent him by his mother, from a luxury hotel in Taormina, on April 15, 1925, and left unread; a telegram informs him that she had died, and Steinn fishes the letter out of the wastebasket. She has yearned to see "the blue, pure eyes of the boy" who once saved her from a dreadful step; Steinn know nothing of the interrupted affair with José, which condemned her, by her own volition, to a sexually unfulfilled and restless life. Steinn decides to ignore the telegram, and Nietzsche helps out: "An seinem Mitleiden mit den Menschen ist Gott gestorben," but a dream of his mother, in a blood shroud, stained with earth, makes him change his mind, a switch he supports by remembering Raskolnikov, who killed an old woman "and walked in a circle around himself in a hundred thousand rings," and he sets out for Taormina, putting up at the hotel where his mother expired. The manager lets him knows the circumstances: after dinner and a walk with her companion, Bambara Salvatore, she danced the Charleston and died of a hemorrhage in Salvatore's arms. Salvatore is slender and pale with black circles beneath his eyes, a monocle in the left, and dressed in a black Fascist shirt of silk; he speaks faultless English with a Boston accent, probably acquired from the many American clients who buy his objets d'art. He is a world traveler, in England consorting with lords, in Paris with artists, in Berlin with homosexuals, in New York with millionaires, in California with film actors, in India with yogis, and in Moscow with chess players. Steinn is much impressed by this new mentor, as he has been by Professor Carrington and by the monk on the train; he is a child, "a greenhorn," compared to Salvatore, and *Vefarinn* is clearly a *Bildungsroman* of sorts. Salvatore — based on an acquaintance of Laxness in Taormina — has his roots in the world of decadence; he seems to have lost his potency, like Des Esseintes, by indulging in excessive sexual pleasure and consoles himself by means of the best poppy (i.e., opium) the earth produces ("Chinese") and through his hobby of iconography. A nihilist, he is under way to becoming the ultimate criminal, for an American biologist has offered, on his behalf, "to let loose a germ which will wipe out all humanity within two weeks," but Salvatore has demurred, preferring to let "cocaine, syphilis, and psychoanalysis" do the job gradually. His motto, by "our incomparable Signor D'Annunzio," is given full length in Italian, with Icelandic translation: "La vita . . . c'insegna che il piacere è il più certo mezzo di conoscimento offertoci dalla Natura, e colui il quale molto ha sofferto è men sapiente di colui il quale molto ha gioito" (Life teaches us that pleasure is the single source of knowledge which nature offers, and he who has suffered much is less wise than he who has known much pleasure).

Steinn looks for his mother's tomb and learns that she lies in an out-of-the-way cemetery, "for Turks, Jews, and heretics, where they are buried like dogs." (He speaks perfect Italian, and lets the cemetery keeper's wife think that he comes from the North of Italy.) When she leaves, he breaks down weeping; the epigraph of the chapter is from the Vulgate, Psalms, 22:6: "Ego autem sum vermis et non homo; opprobrium hominum et abjectio plebis" (Moreover I am a worm and not a man, a reproach of men and despised of the people). He meets Leonardo Peppino, a crippled beggar who plays the flute; Peppino learned his art from a murderer in prison, to which Peppino had been sentenced for fourteen years for molesting a twelve-year-old girl. Having found this comrade in debasement, Steinn decides to commit suicide, but "not for fear of becoming a criminal, like the suicide Dr. Weininger"; he persuades himself of the beauty of death, writes a letter to the Danish consul at Palermo to the effect that he will take cyanide at two the next morning, and regrets that he will die without having raped a woman or, like Egil Skallagrímsson, having bitten through a man's neck. Meaning to make an impression on Salvatore, he plans a second letter, not written, to show the art dealer that the "son of Mrs. Elliða" had not lacked "a piercing spirit's fresh courage." Having watched the moon over Etna, a moon seeming to make fun of him (he is no Empedocles), he jumps off his balcony and turns twelve somersaults, like an acrobat, before landing. His will to live has been too strong; before his leap, he recalls the "idiotic aphorism" closing de Maupassant's *Une Vie:* "La vie, ça n'est jamais si bon ni si mauvais qu'on croit."

The remainder of Book 5 is a surreal comedy, a dream like the Hall of the Mountain King episode in *Peer Gynt,* after Peer has knocked himself unconscious. Stein pursues a little girl tending geese, as he sings an Icelandic parody on "La donna è mobile," but is himself pursued by the gander; he sees that he, like Peppino, has only one leg, sits down, and plays on Peppino's flute, as the little girl sings an Icelandic variation on "Ach, du lieber Augustin." The flute turns into a water pistol, with which Steinn shoots the little girl. The sixtieth chapter bears the superscript "The Situation in Cairo." Odalisques in the sultan's harem have castrated their master and invited the country's important men to an orgy; the carpets on the floor are from the great weaving lands (Kashmir?), the eunuchs serve wine, the girls wear silken wraps, easily torn from top to bottom, the male guests have "white teeth, long mustaches, and fezzes but otherwise resemble dandies from London to Paris." The girls and their guests sit down primly in foursomes, and exchange multilingual toasts: "Steinn has never seen a less intelligent or more insipid company." A song is sung in Icelandic: in it, drunken hippopotami stand on their hind legs, and "snort/whinny/rear/hiss/grunt/piss," an example of Laxness's freshly minted Surrealist verse. Cries ring out, "Il piacere, il piacere," "Ave Dionysus," "Om mane padmi hum"; "the eunuchs sprinkle wine and perfumes" on the supine and lustfully groaning company, "entwined like seaweed," and then "strew roses on the corpses." (Had Laxness seen a reproduction of Alma-Tadema's

Roses of Heliogabalus?) At a summons from a minaret, "Allah is Allah," the men hurry away to midnight prayers, the girls lie topsy-turvy on the floor and the ottomans, hopelessly drunk and naked. The scene shifts to London, Steinn meets the Benedictine from the train, and they go to Leicester Square. Jesus, dressed fashionably like a young academic or dandy, is crucified; in the crowd, Steinn sees nothing but whores of both sexes, and Steinn himself is one. "The day of wrath has come" — it appears to Steinn that the "veil of the temple has been rent from top to bottom," "ofanfrá og niðrúr," the same phrase used to describe the odalisques' garments. The phantasmagoria is shot through with sexual and religious anxiety.

In Book 6, despairing after what he has experienced and imagined in Taormina, Steinn makes his way to the prior Alban, at Sept Fontaines. (In the cloister, Alban is called Father, not Brother as on his visiting card.) Steinn is well received by his old acquaintance, quickly falls into the cloister's routine, and after a series of prayers, twelve in all, he is converted to Roman Catholicism, under the guidance of Father Alban, and is impressed by the other monks, "the most cultivated men he had ever known." (Alban's story is told in chapter 69: a violin virtuoso of world rank, he has smashed his instrument, become a novice in Rome, won a doctorate in Thomistic theology, been consecrated as a priest, been sent to the Benedictines at Solesmes, and, in 1921, been transferred to Sept Fontaines as *père maître* and prior. His life is based on that of the Alexander Ely whom Laxness knew and admired at Clervaux; in a letter, Laxness claimed that a character in Huysmans's *L'Oblat* had been patterned on Ely — a chronological impossibility, but Laxness, as always, wanted a literary confirmation. Steinn's general confession to Father Alban is fairly detailed, although he says, ameliorating, that he lost his virginity at fourteen, whereas he told Diljá it had happened when he was twelve. Even after the conversion, enjoying *la douceur bénédictine,* Steinn is keenly aware of the women attending high mass in the cloister church on Sundays: "The whole church was filled with the odor of woman . . . an unbelievable torment"; as in the diary, the sight of a beautiful girl in the village street becomes "his greatest suffering." In the spring, nostalgia for Iceland fills him, and memories of the young girl he left almost five years before at Þingvellir. Before he goes, he is made an *oblatus secularis,* wedding him to the church; Father Alban tells him to keep his prayers alive when he returns to Iceland. Steinn replies: "Credo in unam sanctam apostolicam ecclesiam," the last of the many quotations from liturgy, the Church Fathers, and *De imitatio Christi* that litter the sixth book.

Back in Reykjavík (Book 7), Steinn is shocked to learn that Diljá has been married to Örnólfur for two years; their child, a boy, died the past February. Örnólfur having gone to Spain on company business, Steinn and Diljá grow close to one another again, although the approaches come from Diljá. Avoiding temptation, Steinn lives in a hotel. When he falls ill after climbing Mount Esja in the rain, Diljá brings him candy in his room. He shakes off her hand, but when she leaves, lines from Heine's *Buch der Lieder*—the necessary literary reference—run repeatedly through Steinn's mind: "Mein Herz pocht wild beweglich,/es pocht beweglich wild/Ich liebe dich so unsäglich,/Du schönes Menschenbild," and to protect himself he recites a passage, carefully identified, from the third book of *De imitatione Christi:* "It is often a small thing which leads me into great temptation" (not quite what Thomas à Kempis says: "Saepe parva res est, quae me deicit et contristat"). Then, radically switching fields of reference, he quotes Eve's temptation of the devil Bululu in Bontempelli's *Eva Ultima* in *Due favole metafisiche* (1921–22): "Qui, qui, in mezzo, sotto questi alberi così spessi, tu potresti." (Laxness does not translate the Italian: "Here, here, in the midst, under these dense trees, you could."), before reciting the *De profundis* (Psalm 124 in the Vulgate) at full length.

For the summer months, Valgerður and Diljá move out to the villa near Þingvellir where the novel began; Steinn, who has gone to Iceland's wild east with some English tourists (and abandoned them), suddenly turns up and charms Valgerður's conservative guests with stories of honest and forthright Icelandic peasants. Living at the villa, he ransacks *De imitatione* for aid; in his room he finds Diljá arranging Icelandic flowers in a vase. He embraces her, then throws the flowers on the floor and tramples them; he slaps her face and tells her that he loves her, but that he is a servant of the Lord, and intends to be a monk at Solesmes, the great Benedictine monastery praised by Huysmans in *De tout.* In his room, next, he finds a bottle of champagne with two glasses, and a message from Örnólfur to Diljá: he is on his way home. Steinn prays with his rosary. Diljá enters in her kimono, and he rejects her again; she calls him a wretch and slaps *him;* the seduction is nothing if not protracted.

The following day Steinn, speaking in parables like a seminarian, tells her the story of his experiences in Hounslow, Sicily, and the cloister. That evening they go for a ride across the lava fields; their horses run away, they seek shelter in a peasant's cottage, and there, at long last, come together; put in the same room, Steinn is given the only bed, and Diljá creeps in beside him: She is the only being he loves, he says, with the love of a man for a woman. When he wakes up, she is gone; Steinn is in high spirits and, outside, thinks of a strophe from the *Völuspá* (number 42): "She [the prophetess] sees arise,/a second time,/the earth forever green/from the sea;/the cataract falls/the eagle soars on high/hunting the fish/on the mountains." Steinn mocks the life of a monk: "Don Quixotism. I have wasted my time fighting with windmills for Dulcinea from Toboso"; he has decided to cast aside the monstrous supernatural sham for earthly love. As usual, quotations are needed. One is: "Fais le testament de ta pensée et de ton coeur, c'est ce que tu peux faire de plus utile," another an Icelandic poem, "And what I choose for myself is woman's love/and [the] empire of a simple man." The author of the former is unidentified from the edition of 1948 on; in the first edition it turns out to be Henri Amiel, and there it is placed in Book 1, chapter 8, in Steinn's harangue to Diljá at Þingvellir. Laxness probably did not take it directly from Amiel's *Journal intime;* it is the epigraph of Fausto Martini's *Il cuore che m'hai dato,* and Martini, in his turn, may have taken it from the citation in Paul Bourget's Amiel essay in *Nouvelles Essais de psychologie contemporaine* (1885). Also, in the first edition but not later, the author of the poem is identified as Vilhjálmur Stefánsson, the Icelandic-Canadian arctic explorer. Finally, in the first edition, Laxness quotes the wedding speech by Erling Skjálsson in the saga of Óláfr Tryggvason, chapter 58, in Snorri. King Óláfr offers Erling a jarldom, and he proudly declares: " 'This I will take from you, oh king, if you will let me be the greatest of that name in this land.' " By 1948, Laxness decided that he had been too learned in emphasizing Steinn's newfound Icelandic enthusiasms.

The finale, Book 8, opens with a letter to Father Alban, from Ostende, dated September 10, 1926 — later than Laxness's return to Clervaux but in the same year. Steinn is on his way to Sept Fontaines; disingenuously, he reports to Father Alban that his stay in Iceland has been "a true source of glory and self-cognition." He has become a new man, quoting, in English, "There is no such thing as history"; it would never occur to him to cite writings from the time before 1914. Does Steinn know that the statement is from Ralph Waldo Emerson's *Essays,* First Series of 1841? In a second part of the letter he assures Father Alban of the firmness of his faith: "Jesus Christ is the redeemer of humanity because it is absurd to believe that mankind can redeem itself." Despite his impatience with those monks "who have not gotten past the breviary" and with points of doctrine, ("the whole nonsense of the virgin birth" seems to him to be "both obscene and blasphemous"), he claims that he is an arch-Catholic, now as before, believing in one holy Catholic Church. He does not mention the insight to which he has come in the peasant's hut with Diljá; "If I did not believe in Jesus Christ, I should die." At Sept Fontaines, he quickly succumbs to the magic of the place and the *cantilena romana* sung by the monks, the sounds of which are like beautiful landscapes. To his disappointment, he learns that Father Alban has left the cloister to become a novice with the Carthusians at Valle Sainte — precisely what Father Ely did during Laxness's first stay at Clervaux; on June 18, 1923, according to the diary, "a great event [has taken place], which has had a violent effect on my soul." Steinn's reaction is strange: thinking of Father Alban, Steinn concludes: "He is free," and quotes Goethe's drinking song, "Ich hab mein Sach auf nichts gestellt/und mir gehört die ganze Welt," but Alban is not at all free: the new order will allow him far less liberty than did the Benedictines. Presumably, Steinn believes that Alban's decision, after his life as "nobleman, virtuoso, scientist," will off him an ultimate spiritual freedom from all earthly things. (In his brief stay at La Trappe, Huysmans's Durtal in *En route* decides he cannot bear Trappist austerity after Benedictine luxury.) Steinn finds Father Alban, now Brother Elias, at a cloister which resembles a mountain monastery in Tibet; Brother Elias has not been allowed to read Steinn's letter, and he may speak with him only for an hour. Steinn confesses to Elias "his single sins in thought, word, and deed," and declares he is not worthy of receiving absolution — which, of course, he gets. The affair with Diljá is not expressly mentioned.

Diljá tries to find Steinn, and one of her letters from Copenhagen on February 2 is presented in chapter 92 ("Have all my letters been lost?"): she has written to the cloister in Belgium, and finding out that he is in Rome, asked the Danish legation to forward the present letter to him. She informs Steinn that she has conceived a child by him and has aborted it "during a long illness"; on recovering, she has learned that Örnólfur had shot himself; as soon as he returned from abroad, she told him what had happened in the peasant's hut. "But what does that which I have suffered matter, if you stay true to me." She receives a note from Steinn, staying at the Convento Salesiani in Rome, in which, still (or again) the disciple of Weininger, he informs her that "woman does not love man but only the animal in man . . . You hate my perfection." Steinn shows the same ruthlessness she experienced when they were children.

On a cold morning in March 1927, Diljá arrives in Rome and falls asleep in her hotel room. Her nightmare, chapters 96–97, is harrowing, like Steinn's vision after his attempted suicide. A man with a donkey, "his hat pulled down over his eyes to make himself interesting," offers her a ride. At the entrance to St. Peter's, he takes off his hat, to scratch his head, which is pierced by a bullet like Örnólfur's. In the packed basilica, Peter himself consecrates "some youths, who have run away from their fiancées," to the true faith. The fiancées will be gravel for new roads. One of the youths is dressed in a gorgeous chasuble, and he has a mane like a lion's and a piercing glance; Peter urges him not to become involved in "foolish pranks," and the dreamer, nearing the altar, shouts that Peter may not take him from her. Steinn throws off the chasuble and leads her from the basilica. A herold announces from the balcony that the last Judgment will take place tomorrow, at eight — children under sixteen enter free.

That evening, Diljá goes to the Salesian convent and insists on waiting for Steinn, who with the priests is engaged in the *completorium*. The spiritual exercise ends an hour before midnight; Steinn, dressed in a black soutane, his eyes cold behind steel-rimmed glasses, arrives and speaks with his old hostility. Diljá makes a last effort to reach him, slipping her naked arms beneath the silk sash around his waist. He staggers like a drunken man, lifts his hands, and faces the crucifix on the wall, and his last words to Diljá are: " 'Go and search for God, your creator, for without him all is delusion.' "

In the coda (chapter 100), Diljá wanders through the streets "like a drunken whore" and, at dawn, realizes that she is in the portico of St. Peter's. She sits on the steps of the colonnade, "looks Catholicism in the face," and reads the inscription: "Tu es Petrus, et super hanc petram aedificabo ecclesiam meam." The Icelandic translation follows: "Þú ert *Steinn*, og á Þessum *Steini* mun ég reisa kirkju mína." Two nuns, on their way to market, stop before the basilica, and recite the Angelus, not in Latin but in Icelandic, beginning: "The angel of the Lord greets the maid Maria, and the maid became fruitful of the Holy Spirit," lines that, blasphemously, could be applied to what has happened between Steinn and Diljá.

Laxness quickly explained the intention of *Vefarinn;* in Los Angeles, at Christmas and New Year's of 1923–29, he wrote — in the essay "Trú" — what amounted to an apologia for his Catholic excursus and the triumph of the church at the book's end: "The solution of *Vefarinn* offers no hope. The basic thought of Christianity is altogether irreconcilable with the basic thought of human life — that is the start and finish of *Vefarinn*." Stopping at Rome on his way north (the Holy Year was still going on), he had avoided the prelates to whom he had been presented as a prize in the spring; in the crowds at St. Peter's, he met "ghosts of his previous being." He did not accept an invitation to visit Johannes Jørgensen in Assisi, in the fear that it would be too difficult to see the home of "God's little fool," who "hereafter could not interest [him] from any other standpoint than that of Freud and Adler." The repudiation of his Catholicism continues with his respectful account of the second visit to Clervaux and his departure from Father Beda, once more described with great personal affection. In the afterword to the second edition of *Vefarinn* the apologia is briefer and has a slightly malicious tone: two and a half years before the book was written he had quite unexpectedly been drawn by "a youthful desire for adventure into the embrace of the church itself, the Jewish heaven–Zion on earth, which the sinking Roman imperium had gloomily willed to medieval Europe." An "instructive combat took place between two opposed principles of life, the creative and the uncreative, between the human being and the god, love for creation on the one hand and hatred for it on the other — in short, between existing and not existing."

In the opening essays of *Skáldatími,* he bantered about his cloister stays and the writing of *Vefarinn*. Later still, in his afterword to Erik Sønderholm's Danish translation (1975), he avoided the content of the book altogether and the experience behind it, save to point out that he had excised some of the sources given for the many quotations, as not being appropriate for a belletristic work. Otherwise, he turned to jocularly told facts: he had tried to interest a number of publishers in his manuscript, but it was thrown away at one of the presses; he enlisted the aid of a friend in the Reykjavík police department to recover it, now in tatters. At his own expense, he had it printed and hawked in fascicles by street urchins, the unemployed, and the town eccentrics; with the help of the same police official a subscription was taken up for a book edition of five hundred copies, which sold "like hotcakes," word having gotten out about the risqué passages. With the money earned, Laxness went to California. In the last paragraph, Laxness complains that, until Sønderholm, the book remained untranslated and had been forgotten in Iceland as well. The unstated message of the complaint is that Laxness had meant this most un-Icelandic of his books to be European, nonparochial. Of the eight books, only Book 1 and portions of 3, 4, and 7 are set in Iceland; of the novel's dizzying wealth of quotations and literary allusions, only a few have Icelandic provenance. But Laxness's extensive use of meaningful dreams and visions, as in the sagas, should not be forgotten.

Vefarinn is one more example of a book built on books; the evidence lies not just in the excess of quotations but in the circumstance that other books, mentioned in passing in the text (or in some cases deleted after the first edition), contributed to its formation. Laxness knew Wilde's preface to *Dorian Gray* and surely cannot have stopped there in his reading, and he knew Shaw's *Man and Superman*. One wonders whether Laxness made his way through Shaw's "Epistle Dedicatory" to Arthur Bingham Walkley in the play, in which Shaw informed Walkley that his Don Juan, Tanner, is the quarry instead of the hunter. Shaw added that he "should make formal acknowledgement to the authors whom [he had] plundered in the following pages; if he could recall them all"; Laxness sometimes makes an acknowledgment, sometimes not. Boasting to Diljá, in Book 1 of the first edition, Steinn lists three works high in his estimation. The first is Tom Kristensen's (1893–1974) *Livets Arabesk* (1921); it contain the orgiastic scenes for which Laxness plainly had a weakness, as well as a spiritually tormented protagonist, the gifted and dictatorial society surgeon Baumann. (Baumann is killed during the street battles between Allied forces and a Communist army from Germany which almost captures Copenhagen in Kristensen's concluding arabesque.) The second is Stephen McKenna's *Vindication* (1924), about the postwar corruption of England's upper classes and their hangers-on. The third is Victor Margueritte's *La Garçonne* (1922).

At some point, Laxness found his way to Huysmans's semiautobiographical novels of conversion, probably *En route* and *La Cathédrale,* certainly *L'Oblat;* he had some knowledge of Maurice Barrès, and in his Sussex letter Steinn paraphrases Barrès's explication of his *manières de voir* (from *Le Culte de moi*). According to the cloister diary of February 24, 1923, Laxness was lent a copy of Henri Bordeaux's *La Peur de vivre* (1902) by the chaplain on March 3, stayed indoors all day with Bordeaux, and read the page where Mme Guibert asks her daughter Paule whether her eldest son, a captain in the French army, is dead. (He is, having died while fighting off a Tuareg attack in the Sahara.) "I pray to God to give me the power to write something which would grip me the way this narrative gripped me." The new reader of French was equally gripped by Paul Bourget's *Le Disciple* (1889), lent to him in June: "a mighty work," "a gigantic masterwork," he wrote to an Icelandic friend. It is safe to say that Robert Greslou, the young man of superior intelligence and the calculating seducer of poor Charlotte, whose death he causes (found not guilty, he is shot by her brother), has contributed something to Steinn.

These were psychologically quite acute works from the fin de siècle and could be considered edifying cloister reading. But Laxness also looked with considerable zeal at two sensational novels about postwar Paris. In Margueritte's *La Garçonne,* Monique Lerbier, the proper daughter of a respectable if hypocritical family, discovers on the eve of her wedding that her fiancé has a mistress. After an hour's chance affair, in revenge, with an anonymous stranger, Monique becomes a successful modiste and, the bachelor girl of the title, an imperious lover of both sexes, her couplings described in close physiological detail. The sign of Monique's liberation is her shingled hair; in his catalogue of woman's depravity to Father Alban (Book 3, chaps. 38–39), Steinn adduces the *garçonnes* who are forbidden to enter the Florence cathedral without a head covering; in Book 8, on returning to Iceland, Steinn notices that Diljá has her hair cut *à la garçonne,* and "her eyes had a dangerous shine." Also, Laxness pillaged Georges-Anquetil's *Satan conduit le Bal . . . Roman pamphlétaire et philosophique des mœurs du temps* (1925). Anquetil's huge book pictures "the new Babylon" of Paris during the postwar presidency of Poincaré, as observed by the innocent Hermès, who is unjustly imprisoned and starves himself to death. The descriptions of the bestiality of French colonial troops, and of pederasty, flagellation, and lesbian and gay balls, are lengthy and shocking — see in particular "Le Laboratoire des illusions" and "La Bacchanale macabre."

Laxness began the study of Italian in July 1923 at Clervaux, in order to read Papini's *Storia di Cristo* in the original. He was so overcome by Papini's Christ, the restless traveler, "il Viandante senza riposo" (the wayfarer without rest) "il più grande Rovesciatore," (the greatest upsetter), that he praised the book in a Reykjavík newspaper, recommending translation into Icelandic. (He was quite in sympathy with the socialist spirit in Papini.) Probably after the outburst of enthusiasm for *Storia di Cristi,* Laxness read the autobiographical *Un uomo finito;* Peter Hallberg noted that, like Laxness in *Vefarinn,* Papini took his epigraph from the *Divine Comedy.* It would have not been at all difficult for Laxness to find in *Un uomo finito* sentiments quite like those of Steinn about himself: "I was born with the disease of greatness in my veins," and, "I want to become a great soul, a great man, pure, noble, perfect," but also statements of disappointment or revulsion like Steinn's: "Here a man is buried who was not able to become God," and, "Men . . . I cannot love you. You enrage me. You disgust me." Three decades afterward, to Hallberg, Laxness confessed that he could not remember in which language he had read *Un uomo finito,* but he agreed that the book "had about the same effect on me as Strindberg," and one sees traces of it in *Vefarinn.*

In *Un uomo finito,* Papini looked askance at Gabriele D'Annunzio and "the spirit which was beginning," in Papini's early days, "to swell the heads and rot the brains of Italian youth." The spirit of D'Annunzio, easily the best-known Italian author of the time, glides through *Vefarinn:* the ambiguous figure of Bambara Salvatore offers his lengthy quotation in favor of "il piacere," the principle ruling his life, which tempts Steinn. The text of *Vefarinn* contains two other citations of the word which was the motto of Andrea Sperelli and the title of the book about him, *Il piacere.* In the London section of the letter to Father Alban — before he has met Salvatore — he quotes Bontempelli's "Il piacere è la sola virtù," in the Cairo orgy Steinn hears, amidst "a chaos of glowing glances, glittering diamonds, swelling bosoms, and glistening lips," a voice cry: " '*Il piacere, il piacere,* gentlemen!' " How could Laxness not have known D'Annunzio's trademark novel, either in George Hérelle's French translation (1892), Gagliardi's German of 1898, the Danish and Swedish of 1902, or, late in the game, the Italian original? Steinn Elliði is a full-blown Icelandic Sperelli, self-centered in the extreme, dandyistic, gifted at a multitude of arts and languages, handsome and strong, and as destructive of the adoring Diljá as Sperelli is of Maria Ferres. Even Rome, *Il piacere*'s backdrop, is summoned up in the concluding chapters.

Writing *Vefarinn,* Laxness set out to depict the decadence of postwar Europe; "decadence" is a key word for Antequil, and is constantly implicit in Kristensen, McKenna, and Margueritte, whose "corruption de ce milieu" is the second decadence of the Jazz Age, portrayed in various ways by Michael Arlen, Aldous Huxley, Raymond Radiguet, and Evelyn Waugh. But it is a decadence superimposed on the litarary decadence of the turn of the century; like Huysmans's Durtal after the Black Mass of *Là-bas,* Steinn gets religion and does not abandon it, however, dehumanizing its effect.

Bibliography

Decadence

Andersen, Per Thomas. *Dekadense i nordisk litteratur 1880–1900* Oslo, 1994.

Banuls, André. "La Décadence — existe-t-elle?" *Études Germaniques* (1979): 404–417.

Bauer, Roger. "'Décadence': Histoire d'un mot et d'une idée." *Cahiers roumains d'études littéraires* 1 (1979): 55–71.

——. "'Dekadenz' bei Nietzsche: Versuch einer Bestandsaufnahme." In Joseph P. Strelka, ed., *Literary Theory and Criticism: Festschrift for René Wellek*. Bern, 1984, 35–68.

——. "Gänsefüßchendekadence." *Literatur und Kritik* 191/192 (1985): 21–29.

——. "Das Treibhaus oder der Garten des Bösen: Ursprung und Wandlung eines Motivs der Dekadenzliteratur." *Akademie der Wissenschaften und der Literatur: Abhandlungen der geistes-und sozialwissenschaftlichen Klasse* 12 (1974): 1–22.

——, ed. *Fin de siècle*. Frankfurt, 1977.

Bernheimer, Charles. *Decadent Subjects: The Idea of Decadence in Art, Literature, Philosophy, and Culture of the Fin de Siècle in Europe*. Baltimore, 2002.

Binni, Walther. *La poetica del decadentismo italiano*. Florence, 1949.

Birkett, Jennifer. *The Sins of the Fathers: Decadence in France, 1870–1914*. London, 1986.

Buvik, Per. *Dekadense*. Oslo, 2001.

Calinescu, Mattei. "The Idea of Decadence." In Calinescu, *Faces of Modernity: Avant-Garde, Decadence, Kitsch*. Bloomington, 1977, 151–221.

Carter, A. E. *The Idea of Decadence in French Literature, 1830–1900*. Toronto, 1958.

Cazamian, Madeleine T. *Le Roman et les idées en Angleterre: L'Anti-Intellectualisme et l'esthétisme, 1880–1900.* Paris, 1935.

Charlesworth, Barbara. *Dark Passages: The Decadent Consciousness in Victorian Literature.* Madison, 1965.

Colloques de Nantes: L'Esprit de décadence I–II. Paris, 1980.

Corbineau-Hoffmann, Angelika, and Albert Gier, eds. *Aspekte der Literatur des Fin de siècle in der Romania.* Tübingen, 1983.

Curtius, Ernst Robert. "Entstehung und Wandlungen des Dekadenzproblems in Frankreich." *Internationale Monatsschrift* 15 (1920–21): 35–52, 147–166.

Daiches, David. *Some Late Victorian Attitudes.* New York, 1969.

Daviau, Donald. "Hermann Bahr and Decadence." *Modern Austrian Literature* 10 (1977): 53–100.

Davis, Lisa E. "Oscar Wilde in Spain." *Comparative Literature* 25 (1973): 136–152.

De Deugd, C. "Towards a Comparatist's Definition of 'Decadence.'" In D. W. Fokkema et al., eds., *Comparative Poetics in Honor of Jan Kamerbeek, Jr.* Amsterdam, [1976], 33–50.

Dijkstra, Bram. *Idols of Perversity: Fantasies of Feminine Evil in Fin-de-Siècle Culture.* New York, 1986.

Dowling, Linda C. *Aestheticism and Decadence: A Selective Annotated Bibliography.* New York, 1977.

———. *Language and Decadence in the Victorian Fin de Siècle.* Princeton, 1986.

Eickhorst, William. *Decadence in German Fiction.* Denver, 1953.

———. *Dekadenz in der neueren deutschen Dichtung.* Delmenhorst, Germany, 1953.

Farmer, Albert L. *Le Mouvement esthétique et "décadent" en Angleterre, 1873–1900.* Paris, 1931.

Fischer, Ernst. "Zum Problem der Dekadenz." In Ernst Fischer, *Kunst und Koexistenz: Beitrag zu einer modernen marxistischen Ästhetik.* Reinbek, 1966, 155–179.

Fischer, Jens Malte. *Fin de siècle: Kommentar zu einer Epoche.* Munich, 1975.

Fletcher, Ian., ed. *Decadence and the 1890s.* London, 1979; New York, 1980.

Furness, Raymond. *Wagner and Literature.* Manchester, 1982.

Gilman, Richard. *Decadence: The Strange Life of an Epithet.* New York, 1975.

Goedegebuure, Jaan. *Decadentie en literatuur.* Amsterdam, 1987.

Hanson, Ellis. *Decadence and Catholicism.* Cambridge, Mass., 1997.

Hinterhäuser, Hans. *Fin de Siècle: Gestalten und Mythen.* Munich, 1977.

Hough, Graham. "Fin-de-siècle". In Graham Hough, *The Last Romantics.* London, 1949, 175–215.

Jullian, Philippe. *Dreamers of Decadence: Symbolist Painters of the 1890s.* New York, 1971.

———. *Jean Lorrain ou Le Satiricon, 1900.* Paris, 1974.

Kafitz, Dieter, ed. *Dekadenz in Deutschland: Beiträge zur Erforschung der Romanliteratur um die Jahrhundertwende.* Frankfurt, 1987.

Kamerbeek, J. "Style de décadence: Généalogie d'une formule." *Revue de Littérature Comparée* 39 (1965): 268–285.

Koppen, Erwin. *Dekadenter Wagnerismus: Studien zur europäischen Literatur des Fin de Siècle.* Berlin, 1973.

Koskimies, Rafael. *Der nordische Dekadent*. Helsinki, 1968.

Kreutzer, Helmut. *Die Boheme: Beiträge zu ihrer Beschreibung*. Stuttgart, 1968.

Lester, John A. *Journey through Despair, 1880–1914*. Princeton, 1968.

Lethève, Jacques. "Le Thème de la décadence dans les letters françaises à la fin du 19e siècle." *Revue d'Histoire Littéraire de la France* 63 (1963): 46–61.

———. "Un Mot témoin de l'époque 'Fin de siècle': Esthète." *Revue d'Histoire Littéraire de la France* 64 (1964): 436–446.

Litvak, Lily. "La idea de la decadencia en la crítica antimodernista en España (1888–1910)." *Hispanic Review* 45 (1977): 397–412.

———. "Temática de la decadencia en la literatura española de fines del siglo 19, 1880–1913." *Romance Quarterly* 33/2 (May 1986): 201–210.

Livi, J. *Huysmans: À rebours et l'esprit décadent*. Paris, 1972.

Lloyd, Christopher. *J.-K. Huysmans and the Fin-de-Siècle Novel*. Edinburgh, 1990.

Lyytikäinen, Pirjo. *Narkissos ja sfinksi: Minä ja Toinen vuosisadanvaihteen kirjallisuudessa*. Helsinki, 1997.

———, ed. *Dekadenssi: Vuosisadanvaihteen taiteessa ja kirjallisuudessa*. Helsinki, 1998.

Marquèze-Pouey, Louis. *Le Mouvement décadent en France*. Paris, 1986.

Martini, Fritz. "Dekadenzdichtung." In vol. 1, *Reallexikon der deutschen Literaturgeschichte* Berlin, 1958, 223–229.

Marzot, Giulio. *Il decadentismo italiano*. Bologna, 1970.

Müller, K. J. *Das Dekadenzproblem in der österreichischen Literatur um die Jahrhundertwende: Bahr, Schaukal, Hofmannsthal, Andrian*. Stuttgart, 1977.

Obenauer, K. T. *Die Problematik des aesthetischen Menschen*. Munich, 1933.

Palacio, Jean de. *Figures et formes de la décadence*. Paris, 1994.

Pereira, José Carlos Seabra. *Decadentismo e simbolismo na poesia portuguesa*. Coimbra, 1975.

Petriconi, Helmut H. *Das Reich des Untergangs: Bemerkungen über ein mythologisches Thema*. Hamburg, 1958.

Pick, Daniel. *Faces of Degeneration: A European Disorder, c. 1848–c.1918*. Cambridge, 1989.

Pierrot, Jean. *The Decadent Imagination, 1880–1900*. Chicago, 1981.

Pittock, Murray G. H. *Spectrum of Decadence: The Literature of the 1890s*. London, 1993.

Poggioli, Renato. "Decadenza in miniatura." *Inventario* 18 (1963): 7–31.

Pouilliart, Raymond. "Paul Bourget et l'esprit de décadence." *Les Lettres Romanes* 5 (1951): 199–229.

Praz, Mario. *La carne, la morte, e il diavolo nella letteratura romantica*. Florence, 1948.

———. "Il decadentismo italiano." *Cultura e scuola* 1 (1961): 20–26.

———. *Il patto col serpente: Paralipomeni de la carne, la morte, e il diavolo nella letteratura romantica*. Milano, 1970.

———. *The Romantic Agony*. Cleveland, 1933. [Translation of *La carne*.]

Pujol, Carlos. *1900: El fin de siglo*. Barcelona, 1987.

Rasch, Wolfdietrich. "Die Darstellung des Untergangs: Zur literarischen Dekadenz." *Jarhbuch der Deutschen Schillergesellschaft* 25 (1983): 415–434.

———. *Die literarische Dekadenz um 1900*. Munich, 1986.

———. *Zur deutschen Literatur seit der Jahrhundertwende.* Stuttgart, 1967.

Reed, John R. *Decadent Style.* Athens, Ohio, 1984.

Rehm, Walther. *Der Untergang Roms im abendländischen Denken: Ein Beitrag zur Geschichtsschreibung und zum Dekadenzproblem,* vol. 18 of *Das Erbe der Alten.* Leipzig, 1930.

Richard, Noel. *À l'aube du symbolisme: Hydropathes, Fumistes et décadents.* Paris, 1961.

———. *Le Mouvement décadent.* Paris, 1968.

Ridge, George Ross. *The Hero in French Decadent Literature.* Athens, Ga., 1961.

Rodriguez, Pedro Sainz. *Evolución de las ideas sobre la decadencia española y otros estudios.* Madrid, 1962.

Roosbroeck, G. L. van. *The Legend of the Decadents.* New York, 1927.

Rose, Marilyn Gaddis. "Decadence in Villiers de l'Isle-Adam and His Followers." *Orbis Litterarum* 36 (1981): 141–154.

Rössner, Michael, and Wegner, Brigitte, eds. *Aufstieg und Krise der Vernunft: Komparatistische Studien zur Literatur der Aufklärung und des Fin de Siècle. Festschrift für Hans Hinterhäuser.* Vienna, 1984.

Salinari, Carlo. *Miti e coscienza del decadentismo italiano.* Milan, 1960.

Seroni, Adriano. *Il decadentismo.* Palermo, 1964.

Smith, J. M. "Concepts of Decadence in Nineteenth-Century French Literature." *Studies in Philology* 1 (1953): 640–651.

Spackman, Barbara. *Decadent Genealogies: The Rhetoric of Sickness from Baudelaire to D'Annunzio.* Ithaca, N.Y., 1989.

Steinhausen, Georg. "Verfallsstimmung im kaiserlichen Deutschland." *Preußische Jahrbücher* 194 (1923): 153–185.

Stephan, Philip. *Paul Verlaine and the Decadence, 1882–90.* Manchester, 1974.

Stokes, John, ed. *Fin de siècle/Fin du globe: Fears and Fantasies of the Late Nineteenth Century.* London, 1992.

Swaart, Koenraad W. *The Sense of Decadence in Nineteenth-Century France.* The Hague, 1964.

Sydow, Eckart von. *Die Kultur der Dekadenz.* Dresden, 1922.

Temple, Ruth. "Truth in Labeling: Pre-Raphaelistism, Aestheticism, Decadence, Fin de Siècle." *English Literature in Transition* 17 (1974): 201–222.

Thomalla, Arianna. *Die 'Femme fragile': Ein literarischer Frauentypus der Jahrhundertwende.* Düsseldorf, 1972.

Thornton, R. K. R. *The Decadent Dilemma.* London, 1983.

Weber, Eugen. *France: Fin de Siècle.* Cambridge, Mass., 1986.

———, ed. *Journal of Contemporary History* 17 (January 1982). (Special issue on decadence)

Weinhold, Ulrike. *Künstlichkeit und Kunst in der deutschsprachigen Dekadenz-Literatur.* Frankfurt, 1977.

Weir, David. *Decadence and the Making of Modernism.* Amherst, Mass., 1995.

Whissen, Thomas Reed. *The Devil's Advocates: Decadence in Modern Literature.* New York, 1989.

Wille, Werner. *Studien zur Dekadenz in Romanen um die Jahrhundertwende.* Greifswald, 1930.

Wuthenow, Ralph-Rainer. *Muse, Maske, Meduse: Europäischer Ästhetizismus.* Frankfurt, 1978.

Dandyism

Adams, James Eli. *Dandies and Desert Saints: Styles of Victorian Manhood.* Ithaca, N.Y., 1995.

Carassus, Émilien. *Le Mythe du dandy.* Paris, 1971.

Chehabi, H. E. "The Imam as Dandy: The Case of Musa Sadr." *Harvard Middle Eastern and Islamic Review* 3 (1996): 20–41.

Coblence, Françoise. *Le Dandysme, obligation d'incertitude.* Paris, 1988.

Delbourg-Delphis, Marylène. *Masculin singulier: Le Dandysme et son histoire.* Paris, 1985.

Feldman, Jennifer, R. *Gender on the Divide: The Dandy in Modernist Literature.* Ithaca, N.Y., 1993.

Gnüg, Hildtrud. *Kult der Kälte: Der klassische Dandy im Spiegel der Weltliteratur.* Stuttgart, 1988.

Gruenter, Rainer. "Formen des Dandyismus." *Euphorion* 45–46 (1950–52): 170–201.

Hinterhäuser, Hans. "Der Dandy in der europäischen Literatur des 19. Jahrhunderts." In Albrecht Schäfer, ed., *Weltliteratur und Volksliteratur: Probleme und Gestalten.* Munich, 1972, 168–193.

Kempf, Roger. *Dandies, Baudelaire et Cie.* Paris, 1977.

Jullian, Philippe. *Prince of Aesthetes: Count Robert de Montesquiou, 1855–1921.* New York, 1968.

Lemaire, Michel. *Le Dandysme de Baudelaire à Mallarmé.* Montreal, 1978.

Mann, Otto. *Der Dandy: Ein Kulturproblem der Moderne.* Heidelberg, 1962. (Revised version of the *Der moderne Dandy.*)

——. *Der moderne Dandy: Ein Kulturproblem des 19. Jahrhunderts.* Berlin, 1925.

Moers, Ellen. *The Dandy: Brummel to Beerbohm.* Lincoln, Neb., 1960.

Natta, Marie Christine. *Le Grandeur sans convictions: Essai sur le dandysme.* Paris, 1991.

Reinders, Karel. "Brummel in boekvorm en zijn invloed op de teorie van het dandysme," and "Dandies als schrijvers, schrijvers als dandies." In Karel Reinders, *Onder dekmantel van etiket.* Amsterdam, 1972, 1–39.

Editions and Translations

1. Huysmans, Joris-Karl. *À rebours/Le Drageoir aux épices.* Preface by Hubert Juin. "Fins de Siècles," series. Paris: Union Générale d'Éditions, 1975.

——. *Against the Grain.* Trans. John Howard (pseud.), with an introduction by Havelock Ellis. New York: Three Sirens, 1931; Dover, 1969.

——. *Against Nature.* Trans., with an introduction, Robert Baldick. Harmondsworth: Penguin, 1959.

——. *Against Nature.* Trans. Margaret Mauldon, introduction by Nicholas White, Oxford: Oxford University Press, 1998.

2. Moore, George. *A Drama in Muslin.* Introduction by Norman Jeffares. Gerards Cross: Colin Smythe, 1981.

3. D'Annunzio, Gabriele. *Il piacere.* Ed. Giansiro Ferrata. Milan: Mondadori, 1979.
———. *The Child of Pleasure.* Trans. Georgina Harding. London: William Heineman, and Boston: Page, 1898; reprint, Sawtry: Dedalus, 1991.
4. Strindberg, August. *I havsbandet,* vol. 24 in *Samlade skrifter.* Stockholm: Bonniers, 1912. Vol. 31 in *Samlade verk.* Stockholm: Bonniers, 1982.
———. *On the Seaboard.* Trans. Elizabeth Clarke Westergren. Cincinnati: Stewart & Kidd, 1913.
———. *By the Open Sea.* Trans. Ellie Schleussner. New York, Huebsch, 1913.
———. *By the Open Sea.* Trans., with an introduction, Mary Sandbach. Athens: University of Georgia Press, 1985.
5. Wilde, Oscar. *The Picture of Dorian Gray.* Introduction by Peter Ackroyd. Harmondsworth: Penguin, 1987.
6. Couperus, Louis. *Noodlot,* in vol. 2 of *Verzamelde werk.* Amsterdam: De Samenwerkende Uitgevers, 1953, 7–140.
———. *Footsteps of Fate.* Trans. Clara Bell, with an introduction by Edmund Gosse. Holland Fiction Series. New York: Appleton, 1892.
7. Garborg, Arne. *Trætte Mænd.* Kristiania: Aschehoug, 1890.
———. *Weary Men.* Trans. Sverre Lyngstad, with an introduction by Per Buvik. Evanston, Ill.: Northwestern University Press, 1999.
8. Rodenbach, Georges. *Bruges-la-Morte.* Brussels: Éditions Labor, 1986.
———. *Bruges-la-Morte.* Trans., with an introduction, Philip Mosley. Paisley: Wilfion and Chester Springs: Dufour Editions, 1987.
———. *Bruges-la-Morte.* Trans. Thomas Duncan. London: Swan, Sonnenschein, 1903; rev. ed., introduction by Terry Hale, London: Atlas Press, 1993.
9. Przybyszewski, Stanisław. *Pentateuch: Totenmesse.* Berlin: Fontane, 1893.
———. *De profundis.* Berlin: Rosenbaum & Hart, 1900.
———. *Epipsychidion.* Berlin: Fontane, 1900.
———. *In diesem Erdenthal der Thränen.* Berlin: Rosenbaum & Hart, 1901.
———. *Vigilien.* Berlin: Fontane, 1901.
[No translations.]
———. *Androgyne.* Berlin: Fontane, 1906.
———. *Androgyne.* Trans. Ray Furness. In Ray Furness, ed., *The Dedalus Book of German Decadence: Voices of the Abyss.* Sawtry: Dedalus-Hippocrene, 1994, 142–194.
10. Tavaststjerna, Karl August. *I förbund med döden.* Stockholm: Bonniers, 1893, vol. 8 in *Samlade skrifter.* Helsingfors: Holger Schildt, 1924, 7–175.
[No translation.]
11. Somerville, Edith Oenone and Violet Martin Ross. *The Real Charlotte.* Rickford, R.I.: North Books, 1995.
12. Andrian, Leopold von. *Der Garten der Erkenntnis.* Frankfurt: Fischer, 1970.
Rilke, Rainer Maria. "Die Letzten," vol. 4 in *Sämtliche Werke.* Frankfurt: Insel-Verlag, 1961, 247–282.
[No translations.]
13. Przybyszewski, Stanisław. *Satans Kinder.* Leipzig: Albert Langen, 1897.
[No translation.]
14. Machen, Arthur. *The Hill of Dreams.* New York: Dover, 1986.

15. Stoker, Bram. *Dracula.* Harmondsworth: Penguin, 1979.

16. Eça de Queirós, José Maria. *A cidade e as serras,* vol. 3 in *Obras* (Edição de Centenário), 7–281. Porto, 1946.

——. *The City and the Mountains.* Trans. Roy Campbell. Athens: Ohio University Press, 1965.

17. Valle-Inclán, Ramón María del. *Sonatas: Memorias del Marqués de Bradomín — Sonata de primavera/Sonata de estío.* Madrid: Colección Austral, Espas Calpe, n.d.

——. *Sonatas: Memorias del Marqués de Bradomín — Sonata de otoño/Sonata de invierno.* Madrid: Colección Austral, Espas-Calpe, n.d..

——. *The Pleasant Memories of the Marquis de Bradomín: Four Sonatas.* Trans. May Heywood Broun and Thomas Walsh. New York: Harcourt, Brace, 1924.

——. *Spring and Summer Sonatas.* Trans. Margaret Jull Costa. Sawtry: Dedalus, 1997.

——. *Autumn and Winter Sonatas.* Trans. Margaret Jull Costa. Sawtry: Dedalus, 1998.

18. Mann, Thomas. *Tristan, Wälsungenblut, Der Tod in Venedig,* vol. 1 in *Erzählungen.* Frankfurt: Fischer, 1966, 163–198, 289–312, 338–399.

Death in Venice and Seven Other Stories. Trans. H. T. Lowe-Porter. New York: Knopf, 1930.

19. Levertin, Oskar. *Lifvets fiender,* vol. 4 in *Samlade skrifter.* Stockholm: Bonniers, 1909, 7–152.

Geijerstam, Gustaf af. *Medusas hufvud: Ett spöksyn ur lifvet.* Stockholm: Bonniers, 1895.

[No translations.]

Söderberg, Hjalmar. *Doktor Glas,* vol. 5 in *Samlade verk.* Stockholm, Bonniers, 1949, 7–181.

——. *Doctor Glas.* Trans. Paul Britten Austin. Boston: Little, Brown, 1965.

——. *Doctor Glas.* Trans. with an introduction, Rochelle Wright. Scandinavian Department, Madison: Wisconsin Introductions to Scandinavia, 1998.

Strömberg, Kjell. *Gabriel Nepomuk: En poet i 20. Seklets begynnelse.* Stockholm: Bonniers, 1915.

[No translation.]

20. Bang, Herman. *De uden Fædreland,* vol. 5 in *Værker i Mindeudgave.* Copenhagen: Gyldendalske Boghandel/Nordisk Forlag, 1912, 221–511.

——. *Denied a Country.* Trans. Marie Busch and A. G. Chater. New York: Knopf, 1926.

Richardson, Henry Handel. (Ethel Florence Lindesay Richardson). *Maurice Guest.* Introduction by Karen McLeod. New York: Virago, 1981.

——. *Maurice Guest.* Clive Probyn and Bruce Steele, eds. Brisbane: University of Queensland Press, 1998.

22. Huneker, James Gibbons. *Painted Veils.* New York: Modern Library, n.d..

23. Laxness, Halldór Kiljan. *Vefarinn mikli frá Kasmír.* Reykjavík: Prentsmiðjan Acta, 1927; Helgafell, 1948.

[No translation.]

Index